D1359689

AMERICAN CIVICS

Fourth Edition

PRODUCTIVITY

EGISTER
TO

AMERICAN CIVICS

Fourth Edition

WILLIAM H. HARTLEY
WILLIAM S. VINCENT

Harcourt Brace Jovanovich, Publishers
Orlando New York Chicago Atlanta Dallas

Authors

WILLIAM H. HARTLEY, a former classroom teacher, is Professor of Education, Emeritus, at the Towson State University, Baltimore, Maryland. He is well known to teachers of the social studies as a past president of the National Council for Social Studies. His monthly article "Sight and Sound" was for many years a highlight of *Social Education.* Dr. Hartley has written several textbooks, a number of motion pictures and filmstrip scripts, and many articles in the field of audio-visual education and techniques for learning.

WILLIAM S. VINCENT, a former teacher of junior high school social studies, is Professor of Education, Emeritus, at Teachers College, Columbia University, where he organized and directed the Citizenship Education Project. Dr. Vincent has written several books on citizenship and has produced a number of educational films. He is the author of *Indicators of Quality,* a method of training teachers to measure the educational quality of schools and school systems.

Editorial Consultants

Larry L. Bybee
Social Studies Department Coordinator
Anson Jones Middle School
Northside Independent School District
San Antonio, Texas

Bernice Craig
Social Studies Teacher
Woodrow Wilson Junior High School
Tampa, Florida

George G. Dawson
Professor of Economics
Empire State College
State University of New York
Old Westbury, New York

Roy Erickson
Coordinator of Social Studies and Multicultural Education
San Juan Unified School District
Carmichael, California

Annette Foster
Social Studies Teacher
Peabody High School
Pittsburgh, Pennsylvania

Marcus Shannon
Social Studies Coordinator
Metropolitan Nashville/Davidson County Schools
Nashville, Tennessee

George B. Sherman
Chairman of Social Studies
Montville High School
Oakdale, Connecticut

Irving J. Sloan
Social Studies Teacher
Scarsdale Junior High School
Scarsdale, New York

Elizabeth Zuniga
Social Studies Teacher
Roosevelt High School
East Chicago, Indiana

For permission to reprint copyrighted material, grateful acknowledgment is made to Doubleday & Company, Inc., for "Ten Shopping Tips for Consumers" condensed and excerpted from *Sylvia Porter's Money Book for the 80's* by Sylvia Porter. Copyright © 1975, 1979 by Sylvia Porter.

Printed in the United States of America

ISBN 0-15-371455-7

Contents

Reference Section

Civics Skills

Charts and Maps

Citizenship in Action

UNIT ONE

Citizenship in Our Democracy

CHAPTER

1

We the People

The United States is built on a dream—the hope of a better life for everyone. This dream has been shared by millions of people who believed that in this nation all men and women could be truly free. The dream began in colonial times, and its power is still so great that it draws thousands of people to our shores each year.

What does freedom mean to Americans? For many people, it has meant religious freedom. For those who fled from poverty, it has meant the chance for a new start and a better life. For still others, it has meant safety from political persecution and wars.

Throughout our history, America has held the promise of excitement, adventure, and a better life. It seemed a good place to invest energy, time, and money. Who could tell how far an ambitious, hard-working person could go in a growing land? This idea is still part of the American Dream.

The American Dream, with all its hopes, promises, and possibilities, can have meaning only in a free nation. Each one of us must help protect our precious heritage of freedom so that the American Dream can come true. We accept this responsibility as **citizens**—as members of our nation.

What does it mean to be a citizen? In a way, this whole textbook is the answer to that question. You will begin to explore what being a citizen of the United States means in this chapter as you study the following topics:

1. **Civics in Our Lives**
2. **Who Are American Citizens?**
3. **The American People Today**

1

Civics in Our Lives

What is civics? Why do we study this subject in school? What does civics have to do with my life? These are some of the questions you may be asking as you begin your civics course.

Many of the subjects you take in school teach you about the American way of life and the priceless rights you enjoy as an American. The civics course you are about to begin will explain how you, as a citizen of the United States, can help to keep this precious heritage alive.

The Meaning of Civics

Civics is the study of what it means to be an American citizen. The word "civics" comes from the Latin *civitas,* meaning citizen. The meaning of this word has changed greatly since the ancient Romans first used it many hundreds of years ago. At that time, only a small group of wealthy people who owned property could be Roman citizens. Today almost everyone is a citizen of a nation.

The rights and responsibilities of being a citizen also have changed over time. Moreover, they differ from nation to nation. They depend upon the kind of government a nation has. **Government** is the authority, or power, that rules on behalf of a group of people. Under the American system of government, citizens have many rights and many kinds of responsibilities. Your civics course will teach you the most important ones.

You will discover that American citizenship means more than being a responsible member of the nation. It includes being a useful and sharing member of society. Almost all Americans belong to a family, go to school for a number of years, and work with others. Americans also are members of their local communities—villages, towns, or cities—and of states. Being an effective citizen of the United States means fulfilling your duties and responsibilities as a member of each of these groups.

American Ideals

The importance of being a responsible citizen cannot be stressed too much. As a citizen of the United States, there are many different reasons you can take pride in your nation. It is a land of great natural beauty and has many wonders built by its people as well. Even more important are the **ideals,** or beliefs, of our great nation.

The government of the United States and the American way of life are based on the ideals of freedom and equality. As a citizen of this nation, each one of us is guaranteed the same rights and freedoms. These rights and freedoms are protected by our laws and cannot be taken from any citizen. As a citizen of the United States, you must be willing to do your share to protect this great heritage of freedom, or liberty. It has been handed down to us from one generation to another for over 200 years.

Learning and being aware—these are two keys to becoming and remaining an effective citizen. These students are studying to achieve both these goals.

Our Heritage of Freedom

One important American freedom concerns you directly as you read this. It is the freedom to learn. Americans believe that every young citizen should have the opportunity to learn and become a worthwhile member of our nation. Therefore, our states and communities spend billions of dollars each year to provide free public schools for all young citizens. Each state also has public and private universities for those who wish to continue their education.

Another important freedom is the freedom to choose a job or career. Americans believe that all persons qualified for a job should have an equal opportunity to try for it.

As Americans, we also are proud of many other freedoms. Consider how important they are in our lives. We may live as we wish as long as we respect the rights of others. We are free to own a house, marry the person of our choice, and raise a family. We may start our own business and travel or live anywhere in the nation. We are free to speak and write what we wish as long as our words do not harm another person. We may not be arrested or imprisoned without just cause.

Government by the People

The leaders who planned our government created a system that would guarantee our freedom. The form of government they established continues strong today. Under our American form of government, the people rule through the officials they elect.

These elected officials are responsible to the people. Citizens are free to vote for new officials at election time if those in office do not do their jobs properly. Officials also can be removed from office before the end of their terms if necessary. By making our officials answerable to the people they represent, the founders of our system of government made sure that it would continue to serve the American people.

The Role of the Citizen

As an American citizen, you have many freedoms. Being a citizen also involves many responsibilities. Voting in elections is one of the most important of these responsibilities. However, you can help choose the men and women who will govern us in other ways as well. You can work for a political party, for example. Anyone who answers telephones, stuffs envelopes, or helps prepare for meetings of a political party is playing a part in the American system of government.

It is also your responsibility as a thoughtful citizen to inform officials of your needs or disagreements with government actions. You can do this by taking direct action. You can write or call public officials or write to newspapers.

Knowing how your government works will help you carry out your duties and responsibilities as a citizen. The study of civics will teach you how the powers of government are divided between the nation, the states, and the local communities. As you study the functions of these governments, you will learn what an important part each of them plays in your life.

Qualities of a Good Citizen

As an American citizen and a future voter, you will play a vital role in determining the future of our nation. Your participation in American government is necessary for our form of government to continue to work. Therefore, each of you must study and train to become an effective citizen.

How can you become an effective citizen? What qualities will you need? Here is a list of ten characteristics of a good citizen. You probably can think of several you would like to add.

1. Good citizens are responsible family members.

2. Good citizens respect and obey the laws.

3. Good citizens respect the rights and property of others.

4. Good citizens are loyal to their nation and proud of its accomplishments.

5. Good citizens take part in and improve life in their communities.

6. Good citizens take an active part in their government.

7. Good citizens use our natural resources wisely.

8. Good citizens try to be well informed on important issues.

9. Good citizens believe in equality of opportunity for all people.

10. Good citizens respect individual differences and ways of life that differ from their own.

Like these baseball players, citizens in a free nation must act as members of a team. For our government to work, everyone must obey the rules and cooperate.

The Importance of Civics

It is important for every American citizen to understand how our system of government operates. It is equally important for every American to understand why she or he must take part in it. Participation in government has always been a basic principle of our American form of government.

In your study of civics, you will learn a great deal about American government. Your study also will include many other topics that concern all American citizens. You will study how American communities serve their people and some of the problems our communities face today. Your study of civics will deal with citizenship in the family.

You will also read about our nation's free economic system and how it provides opportunities for all people. You will learn why citizens must pay taxes. You will study jobs and careers and learn what training and abilities they require. You will discover how America's schools are run and how you can get the most from your school years. You will read about America's relations with other nations and learn how over the years our nation has taken a position as a world leader.

Being an American citizen is something we often take for granted. To become a responsible and effective citizen requires effort and training, just as becoming a good athlete or musician does. Our nation needs citizens who are well informed and who are willing to take part in determining how our nation acts. Meeting the obligations of American citizenship is an important challenge. This textbook was written to help you meet that challenge.

Our training as members of a family is our first lesson in civics. With other members of our family, we learn to work together toward shared goals.

CHECK-UP

Vocabulary

citizens
civics
government
ideals

Review

1. What are some of the freedoms that all American citizens have?
2. In what ways can American citizens influence government?

Discuss

What do you think are the most important qualities of a good citizen? Why?

2 Who Are American Citizens?

America's heritage of freedom and equality was formed bit by bit as groups from different parts of the world settled here. These people brought with them their hopes and dreams. Today all Americans can be proud of the interesting and wonderful background they share. For we are all **immigrants**—people who came here from other lands—or descendants of immigrants. From their countries of origin, the immigrants brought different languages, ideas, and customs. These many different ways of life mixed with the ideas already developed in America. This unique blend has given a special energy and richness to our nation.

Early Americans

As you know from your study of American history, the first people to settle in America were the Indians, or Native Americans. Many scientists believe that the ancestors of the Indians came here from Asia at least 25,000 years ago. Gradually, over thousands of years, they moved into many parts of North and South America.

The Vikings came next, but did not stay very long. The Spaniards were the first Europeans to build lasting settlements in the Americas. They settled in Mexico, South America, and what are now Florida, California, and the Southwest in the United States.

The original 13 colonies were settled mostly by people from England. Colonists from other countries included German settlers in Pennsylvania, the Dutch along the Hudson River, and the Swedes in New Jersey and Delaware. Many black people also came to America from Africa. Unlike other immigrants, most of them were brought to America as slaves. They and their children were forced to live in bondage for many years.

DID YOU KNOW THAT . . .

all the people of the Western Hemisphere really could be called Americans? After all, the two continents that make up this hemisphere are North *America* and South *America*. Why aren't the people of Canada, or Mexico, or Brazil called Americans too?

The answer is that the United States was the first *independent* nation in the hemisphere. By the time Mexico and the other nations won their independence in the 1800's, the "American" label already had a specific meaning. It meant a citizen of the United States.

America's Immigration Policy

Over the years, the United States has been settled and populated by people from all over the world. During our early history, the new American nation had to struggle hard to survive. Therefore, most immigrants were welcomed to the United States. Farm and factory workers were needed as our nation expanded from the Atlantic Ocean to the Pacific Ocean. During the first half of the 1800's, our government adopted an "open shore" policy, allowing unlimited immigration. The only persons who were not admitted were criminals and those with certain diseases.

However, as America began to fill up and land became less available, some Americans wanted to change our immigration policies. Slowly the United States began to limit the number of people who were allowed to immigrate to this country. In the 1880's the government began to place restrictions on immigration. It was not until the 1920's, however, that a **quota,** or definite limit, was established on the number of immigrants who could be admitted each year.

The faces of America show the many lands from which our citizens have come. Though our backgrounds may be very different, we are all Americans.

Today the number of immigrants allowed to enter the United States is still limited, as it is in most nations. In 1965 the quota was set at 290,000 immigrants a year. The quota is not used for **refugees,** or homeless people fleeing their nations. These people are admitted under special laws.

In recent years over 400,000 immigrants (including refugees) have been admitted to the United States each year. Almost 40 percent of these new arrivals come from Latin America, with large numbers from Mexico. Many immigrants still come from Europe. Other large groups of immigrants come from Asia.

Citizenship by Birth

Millions of immigrants have become American citizens. Some American citizens belong to families who have lived here for many generations. Other Americans were born in foreign countries. American citizens are of many different races and religions. All citizens, regardless of their background, have the same legal rights and responsibilities.

Americans gain their citizenship either by birth or by a special legal process called naturalization. Since citizenship by birth is the way most of us became citizens of the United States, let us review it first.

If you were born in any one of the 50 states or in any American territory, you automatically became a **native-born citizen.** If your parents were United States citizens, you were a citizen by birth even if they were living in a foreign land when you were born. Citizenship, then, can be acquired by the place of birth or through one's parents.

What about children born in this country whose parents are citizens of a foreign country? Are they citizens of the United States? In most cases they are, if their parents were under the authority of the United States at the time the children were born.

What about children born here whose parents are officials representing a foreign country? They are not United States citizens, because their parents are under the authority of another country. All cases involving claims to American citizenship are handled by the United States Department of Justice.

Aliens in America

Several million people living in the United States are citizens of other countries. These people are called **aliens.** Some are here on a visit. Others live and work here or attend school here but expect someday to return to their homelands. Many aliens in the United States expect to live here permanently.

While in the United States, all aliens must obey the laws of this country. They are also entitled to be protected by its laws. Aliens enjoy most of the benefits of American citizenship. They cannot, however, vote or hold public office. Moreover, various state laws prohibit aliens from working at certain jobs, such as teaching in public schools.

In January of each year, aliens are required to register with the United States Immigration and Naturalization Service. At this time, they must report where they live and where they work or attend school.

Illegal Aliens

In addition to the aliens who register, several million people from other countries live in the United States illegally. It is impossible to know exactly how many illegal aliens there are. Some estimates list as many as 8 to 10 million illegal aliens in the United States.

More than half the illegal aliens come from Mexico. Most come to the United States to find work and a better life. However, life is often difficult for illegal aliens. Many become migrant workers, moving from farm to farm picking crops. Illegal aliens often have to work for very low wages and under poor working conditions. Some United States citizens resent these aliens, who they feel are taking jobs away from them. Moreover, illegal aliens always face the danger of being caught and forced to leave the United States.

How an Alien Becomes a Citizen

Under certain circumstances, citizens of other countries may become citizens of the United States. The legal process by which an alien may become a citizen is called **naturalization.** The first part of this process is entering the United States legally.

These aliens are taking an early step toward becoming American citizens. They are learning about the history and laws of their adopted country.

To be eligible to enter the country, foreigners must prove that they can support themselves and that they can read and write. They must prove they do not have certain diseases and are not mentally ill, drug addicts, or criminals. There are a number of other restrictions that bar people from entering the United States. One of them bars persons who favor violent revolution, that is, the overthrow of the government by force.

When foreigners enter the United States, they are immediately eligible to begin the process of naturalization. They may file a declaration of intention with the immigration authorities. This paper simply states that the person plans to become a citizen. Such a declaration is not required. Some employers, however, ask for it as evidence that the employee plans to stay in this country.

Aliens may apply for citizenship after they have lived in this country for five years. This period is reduced to three years for an alien married to a citizen. Aliens must be at least 18 years old to apply for citizenship.

The first step is to fill out an application called a petition for naturalization. When immigration authorities receive this application, they set a date for the person to appear in a naturalization court.

When the alien goes to court, two witnesses must come along to testify to his or her good moral character. The person applying for citizenship must prove that he or she can read, write, and speak English acceptably. The judge may ask the person questions about the history and government of the United States.

After this preliminary hearing, there is a 30-day wait. During this period, applicants may be investigated to check their qualifications. If they prove to have the background needed to become good citizens, they are called to court for a final hearing. There they take an oath of allegiance, or loyalty, to the United States and are granted a certificate of naturalization. Children automatically become citizens when their parents' naturalization is completed.

Naturalized citizens have the same rights and duties as native-born Americans. There is only one exception. They are not eligible to become President or Vice President of the United States.

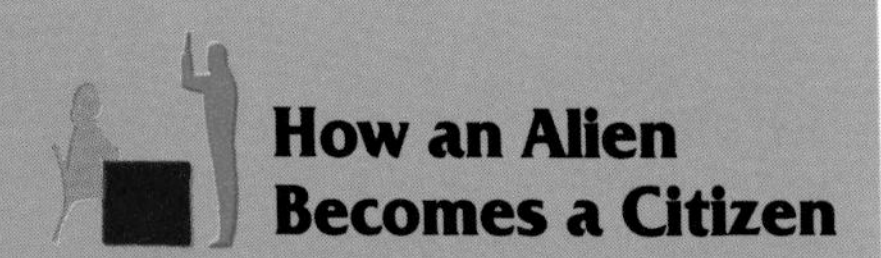

How an Alien Becomes a Citizen

DECLARATION OF INTENTION (Optional)

An alien may file this declaration in any federal court. This written statement declares that the alien plans to seek American citizenship.

PETITION FOR NATURALIZATION

After an alien has lived in the United States at least 5 years (or 3 years if married to an American citizen), he or she files a petition. This petition requests American citizenship.

PETITION WITNESSED

Two American citizens appear as witnesses to declare that the petitioner has lived in the United States for 5 years, has good moral character, and believes in the principles of the Constitution.

EXAMINATION

An examiner, or judge, examines the alien to see that he or she can read and write English and knows American history and government.

CITIZENSHIP GRANTED

The alien becomes an American citizen. The alien swears an oath of allegiance and signs a certificate of naturalization.

CHECK-UP

Vocabulary

immigrants
quota
refugees
native-born citizens
aliens
naturalization

Review

1. In what way did the United States begin to change its immigration policies in the late 1800's?
2. What are the two ways a person can be an American citizen by birth?
3. Describe the main steps in the naturalization process.

Discuss

Would you change the requirements for becoming a naturalized citizen? Explain your answer.

3

The American People Today

The leaders who planned the American government knew that they would need to know how many people—citizens as well as non-citizens—lived in the nation. They decided that every ten years the national government would make an official count of the number of people living in the United States. This count is called a **census.** The most recent census was taken in 1980.

What the Census Tells Us

The main purpose of the census is to find out the size of each state's population. This information is used to determine how many people from each state will be elected to the national government.

The census also tells us a great deal about the United States and the people who live here. For example, it tells us how many children there are in each family, how many people have moved and where, and something about the standard of living of Americans. In addition, the census indicates the rate of population growth in the United States. This and other information gathered by census takers helps the government, business, and individuals to plan for the future. It also helps us learn something about ourselves.

Population Growth

When the first census takers counted our nation's population in 1790, they reported fewer than 4 million people living in the original 13 states. Since that time, our nation has grown greatly in both size and population. Instead of 13 states, there are now 50. According to the 1980 census, more than 226 million people live in our nation. How did the United States grow to its present size and population?

All nations grow in three ways. One way is by natural increase in population. A natural population increase occurs when the birth rate is greater than the death rate. The **birth rate** is the number of births per 1,000 members of the population over a period of one year. The **death rate** is the number of deaths per 1,000 persons over a period of one year.

The second way a nation grows is by adding new territory. The United States has gained new territory from time to time through war, purchase, and annexation. The people living in these new lands have added to the size of our population.

The third source of population growth has been immigration, or the arrival of people from other lands. Since 1820 over 45 million immigrants from all over the world have come to the United States to live.

How America's Population Grew

As the United States expanded from the Atlantic coast to the Pacific coast, it needed a rapidly growing population. However, in the early years of our nation, the population grew slowly.

Life was very difficult in those pioneer days. Many infants died and the death rate of

(continued on page 14)

Learning About "The Good Old Days"

What was life like for teenagers in Springfield, Massachusetts, during the city's "golden years" in the early 1900's? That's what a group of students in Springfield wanted to know, and they set out to discover the facts in an interesting way.

Interviewing Takes Patience

Teenagers from two high school clubs formed an interviewing team. Over a six-week period they taped the comments of senior citizens who had lived through the city's golden years. At first the students were nervous about the oral history project. Many of them had never spent much time talking to older people. The students also had to learn how to use tape recorders and how to conduct an interview. They discovered that interviewing takes a lot of patience.

Learning from Each Other

The major purpose of the oral history project was to help teenagers learn about the past by talking to those who had lived through it. Yet the program had another important result. Young and old realized that each group had something to offer the other. The students and older people became friends during the taping sessions. They called each other by first names and looked forward to their Wednesday afternoons together.

What did the teenagers learn? One elderly man told them that Springfield in the 1920's was alive with baseball teams—just as it is today. There was a difference, however. In those days the teams built their own baseball diamonds. "We'd go to a big field with shovels and rakes," the man recalled. "We'd make our own ballfield."

The idea of having to work to have fun was new to many of the students. Now they say they are more understanding when their older relatives tell them, "We didn't have it easy, as people have it today." Questioning the senior citizens about their

Then, as now, people enjoyed canoeing on nearby lakes and rivers.

schools, work, and recreation taught the teenagers that, indeed, people worked very hard in the 1920's—even at play.

The teenagers also learned that some traditional events were the same, yet different. One example is the celebration of Independence Day on July Fourth. This was as important a holiday in the 1920's as it is today. People in Springfield lit up the sky then too. Instead of using fireworks, however, they used lanterns, which were strung on the streets and in the park.

When the older people were asked what they thought about the oral history project, they were very enthusiastic. It meant a lot to them to share their memories of the past with people who were really interested.

Thinking It Over

1. How do you think students can benefit from an oral history project? How can the people they interview benefit?
2. Besides conducting interviews, what else might the students have done to learn about Springfield's past?

Americans was high. Disease was common, and there were few doctors. Moreover, little was known about diseases and how to cure them. Of course, some Americans lived to a very old age. Nevertheless, disease, poor diet, and the hazards of pioneer living made the average life span short.

Between 1790 and 1830, the population of the nation more than tripled, reaching nearly 13 million. Almost all of this growth was the result of births in the United States. It was common for families to have as many as 10 to 12 children. Large families were a necessity at this time. Most people lived on farms, and large families could help get all the work done. Thus, even though many children died young and the death rate was high, the population grew.

Beginning in the 1830's, great numbers of immigrants started to arrive in the United States. Between 1830 and 1840, more than 500,000 immigrants came, mainly from Ireland. Over the next ten years, a million and a half new immigrants arrived. The population had reached 23 million by 1850.

By 1920 our nation's population had risen to 106 million. Immigrants from many lands, particularly the nations of southern and eastern Europe, accounted for a large part of this huge increase in our total population. However, after 1920, as you have read, the United States began to limit the number of immigrants admitted into our country each year. Most of the population growth after this time was due to natural increase.

Today's Smaller Population Growth

Today the population of the United States continues to grow, though not as rapidly as in the past. In 1970, for example, 205 million people lived in the United States. The population of our nation had increased by more than 25 million people since the previous census in 1960.

By 1980, however, a new trend had appeared. The population increased by only 17 million people between 1970 and 1980. This was the second smallest increase in any ten-year period since 1790. The main reason the population is growing at a slower rate than before is that many people are having smaller families.

A People on the Move

Where do the people of the United States live? The first census found most Americans living on farms, with a smaller number living in villages and in a few medium-sized cities. Over the years this changed. The farm population has gotten smaller every year. In 1980 only a little more than 6 million people lived on farms.

Beginning in the 1800's, Americans began to move away from **rural areas,** or regions of farms and small towns. Most of them went to live in **urban areas,** or cities, in order to work in factories and offices. As early as 1820, the census showed that urban areas were growing faster than rural areas. With each new census, the proportion of Americans living in or near cities continued to grow. By 1920 the census showed that more Americans lived in urban areas than in rural areas.

As the population continued to grow rapidly and people moved to the cities, urban areas became overcrowded. Many Americans could afford to buy automobiles, which made it possible to travel longer distances to work. Therefore, beginning in the mid-1900's, the people of the cities started to move out into the surrounding areas—the **suburbs.**

They moved to the suburbs in search of better homes, schools, and communities. Thirteen of the nation's 25 largest cities lost population between 1960 and 1970. Only one, Los Angeles, showed a gain. Today the people who live in the suburbs outnumber those who live in the cities.

The 1980 census showed a new trend. For the first time since 1820, rural areas and small towns were growing faster than the nation's **metropolitan areas,** or cities and

Rising above the surrounding plain is Dallas, Texas, one of the many fast-growing Sunbelt cities. The region's mild winters and many job opportunities are major attractions.

their suburbs. This did not mean that Americans were moving back to farms. It meant they were shifting businesses, industries, and schools to once-remote rural areas.

Another Population Shift

Throughout our nation's history, Americans have been on the move. This movement continues today, with many Americans moving to different parts of the nation. Such movement of people from region to region is called **migration.** The migration pattern in the United States in recent years has been from the middle of the country and the Northeast to the South and West.

The older industrial areas of the North and East have been losing population. Americans from these areas are moving to states in the South and West. These states are known as the **Sunbelt.** People are moving to the Sunbelt because of the region's warmer climate. Also, they are looking for better jobs and a better life.

California is now the state with the largest population. Nevada is the fastest growing state. Its population increased by almost 64 percent between 1970 and 1980. During this same period the northern states barely grew. For example, New Jersey's population increased by less than 1 percent.

Because of the population shift to the Sunbelt, cities in the South and West are growing. San Diego, California, and Phoenix, Arizona, are now among the nation's ten largest cities. San Jose, in California, is the nation's fastest growing city. Cities in the North and East, however, are losing population. For example, New York City lost 1 million people between 1970 and 1980. Nevertheless, it remained the city with the most people.

Smaller Families

The 1980 census also showed that other changes are taking place in the United States. The size of American households has decreased since 1970. Many couples are having fewer children. Many people, too, now live alone. Therefore, today there are more households with fewer people living in them. The total number of households increased from 63.4 million to 80.4 million. However, the average number of persons living in a household declined from more than 3 people to fewer than 3.

Another change in American families is the increase in the number of one-parent families. Between 1970 and 1980, the number of one-parent families increased by 50 percent. As more couples divorce, more women are becoming heads of households. Generally, women remain responsible for taking care of the children. Today less than a third of the nation's households include the traditional family of mother, father, and one or more children.

As the nation's older population increases, so does the desire of older Americans to stay active. Here a retired teacher helps other older citizens.

Changing Life Styles for Women

Along with changes in the family have come changes in the lives of women. There are 6 million more women than men in the United States. Many of these women are senior citizens, because women generally live longer than men.

Women are also more educated today than ever before. They are staying in school longer, and many more are attending colleges and universities. For the first time, there are about an equal number of women and men in college. Some of these women are older and have grown children. Some are retired and looking for new interests.

Women also are entering the work force in ever-increasing numbers. Today more than half the married women in the United States hold jobs outside the home. Some women must work because the family needs the money. However, a large number of women work because their children are grown and they wish to continue their careers. Many women are now entering professions that once were open only to men. These and other trends are bringing about many changes in American life.

An Older Population

The 1980 census also showed that our nation is "growing older" every year. In the early years of our nation, when both birth and death rates were high, ours was a young population. In 1820, for example, half the population was under the age of 16. By 1900 half the population was under 23. Until the 1970's, the largest age group in our population was under 25.

Today Americans between the ages of 25 and 65 make up the largest group in the population. In this group of about 104 million people are most of our nation's wage earners and heads of families. They hold most of the responsible positions in our nation. They control business, government, and courts.

They greatly influence America's standards of living and conduct.

An increasing part of our population consists of Americans who are 65 or older. This changing population trend results from a drop in both the birth rate and the death rate. Fewer babies are born each year. Also, Americans are generally living longer. In 1900 the average American lived 49 years. In 1980 the average life expectancy for Americans was 73.

According to the 1980 census, about 25.5 million Americans are 65 or older. This means that a large number of Americans are retired. However, many older Americans are eager to remain in the work force. Some work part-time, and others have started new careers or returned to school.

Most older citizens continue to be active and productive. Yet, many are troubled by the problems of low income and poor health. Using the experience and talents of senior citizens offers both a challenge and an opportunity for our nation.

CHECK-UP

Vocabulary

census
birth rate
death rate
rural areas
urban areas
suburbs
metropolitan areas
migration
Sunbelt

Review

1. List some of the information you can learn about the United States and its people from the census.
2. Name the three ways our population has grown.
3. Describe the changes in the makeup of the American population that were revealed by the 1980 census.

Discuss

How do you think the changing trends in American life might affect your life in the years ahead?

CHAPTER SUMMARY

Civics is the study of what it means to be an American citizen. It teaches us our responsibilities and rights as members of our nation. As citizens, we must help keep alive the ideals of freedom on which our nation was built. We also have important citizenship responsibilities as members of our local community and state. In fact, citizenship is important in every group to which we belong, including our family and school.

Citizenship in our nation is gained by birth or by naturalization. Naturalized citizens enjoy the same rights as native-born citizens. The one exception is that they are not eligible to become President or Vice President.

The national government has taken a census every ten years since 1790 to determine how many people live in the United States. The information gathered by census takers has told us how our nation has grown and changed over the years. A nation of farms has become a nation of cities and suburbs.

Recent censuses have revealed that Americans are living longer, having smaller families, and moving to the South and West. Americans are also becoming more educated, and women are entering the work force in ever-increasing numbers.

CHAPTER

2

Foundations of Our Government

What do we mean by the word "government"? You probably have a fairly good idea of what government is. The chances are, however, that you have never before tried to describe it in a few words.

When you think of government, perhaps you think of the Capitol Building in Washington, D.C., or your state capital, or the city hall in your own community. Perhaps you think of the President of the United States, the governor of your state, or the mayor of the town in which you live. Perhaps you think of laws you must obey or the rules of the student council in your school. If you do think of government in this way, you are on the right track.

Yet government is not only buildings and leaders and laws. It includes all of these—and much more. **Government** is the entire system of authority, or power, that acts on behalf of a group of people.

Our American government is a government "of the people, by the people, and for the people." Its main purpose is to serve the people. It provides such services as good schools, modern highways, police and fire protection, and mail delivery. It protects our rights as individuals and safeguards our freedom. The American government is you; it is all of us.

We are fortunate to have a government such as ours. In this chapter you will read about why and how our government was created as you study these topics:

1. **Why Americans Have Governments**
2. **Our First American Government**
3. **Writing and Approving the Constitution**

1

Why Americans Have Governments

To govern means to rule. A government is any organization set up to make and enforce rules. You actually live under three different governments. The city or town where you live has a government. It makes and enforces rules for the people in your community. Your state government makes and enforces rules for the people in your state. Our national government makes and enforces rules for all the people in the United States.

Governments Differ

Every nation in the world has a government. These governments, however, are not all alike. There are many important differences in the way they govern. They differ in the way their rulers are chosen and in the amount of power held by their people. Each nation's government has been shaped by the beliefs of the people and by their history.

In times past, the governments of many nations were controlled by kings or queens. They often held all the power in their nation's governments, and they were able to rule by force. For this reason, they were called **absolute monarchs.** Today there are few absolute monarchs left. Most nations that have monarchs greatly limit their power.

In some nations, one person or a small group of people holds all the power. The government has total control over the lives of the people. It rules the nation by force. We call this type of government a **dictatorship** or a **totalitarian government.**

Other nations have a democratic form of government. In a **democracy,** the people rule directly or they elect officials who will act for them. The word "democracy" comes from an ancient Greek term meaning "rule of the people."

There are different forms of democracy. In a **direct democracy,** all the voters in a community meet together at one place to make laws and decide what actions to take. This works only in small communities.

In a **representative democracy,** the people elect representatives to carry on the work of government for them. This system of government is also called a **republic.** It is the form of government we have in the United States.

Americans are fortunate to live in a republic. We believe that the people should rule themselves. We have a form of government in which the leaders are responsible to the people. The term **American government** refers to the authority that Americans have set up to help them rule their own affairs.

Why Do We Need Government?

Wouldn't it be possible for all of us to live as we chose? Couldn't we manage our own affairs without a government? Do we really need rules for getting along with one another? In order to answer these questions, it is important to understand the purposes of government.

Government Makes It Possible for People to Live Together

Whenever large groups of people have lived together, they have found it necessary to have a government. Under early forms of government, the strongest person was often made the leader of the people. This person could best help the people defend themselves against their enemies. When food was scarce, the best hunter might be the leader, because a hunter could help get a good food supply. In other matters, such as whether the people should move to better land, a group of the oldest and wisest leaders might make the decision.

One of the earliest lessons people learned was that cooperation was useful. It was easier to hunt and kill a large animal for food if the group worked together. The people could be better protected against enemies if they were united. Even the simplest form of government helped to make life safer, easier, and more pleasant.

Government Performs Many Services

Over the years, government has grown more and more complex. Yet its basic purposes have remained the same. It provides ways for people to live and work together. It also enables a large group of people to get things done. It might be possible for each person in the group to do some of these things alone. However, it usually would be more difficult and expensive for each person to do so.

For example, what would happen if each family in your community had to educate its own children? Even if parents had time enough to teach, would they be able to teach well? How would they teach subjects they had forgotten or perhaps had never studied when they went to school? By establishing schools, our government makes it possible for all children to receive a good education.

Government also performs other services that would be difficult or impossible for individual citizens to provide for themselves. Government protects the people from enemy nations. It also provides police to protect our lives and property. Our homes are protected by fire departments.

Because of government, American citizens can travel over highways that stretch from sea to sea and from border to border. A system of money makes it easy for Americans to buy and sell things and to know their value. Trash is collected, and health laws are enforced. Libraries are built and operated. These and many more services are provided by government.

Government Provides Rules, or Laws

Large groups of people need rules to help them live together in peace. When there are rules, all people know what they may and may not do. Without rules, any disagreement would probably end with the strongest members of the group settling things their way.

Providing rules of conduct for the group is therefore one of the most important reasons for establishing governments. These rules are known as **laws.** They are written down so that people can know them and obey them. Laws are written by our government to guide, as well as to protect, all of us.

For example, if you own a house on a city or village street, a law may require you to keep your sidewalk in good repair. If you allow cracks to form, someone may fall and be injured. This law also protects you and your family, since you must depend on your neighbors to keep their sidewalks in good condition if you are to walk safely.

Many of the laws under which we live are contained in **constitutions,** or written plans of government. Americans have used constitutions to establish their national and state governments. A constitution states the purposes of the government. It describes how the government is to be organized, or set up. It also contains the most important laws the government is to uphold.

Vaccinations for young Americans and the trimming of community-owned trees are just two of the hundreds of services provided by our government.

Government Enables a Nation to Put Its Ideals into Practice

A nation's government helps put into practice the ideals of the people, the things in which they believe. Americans believe that the people should rule themselves. We also believe that each person is important and that no one should be denied his or her rights.

What are these rights? In the Declaration of Independence (which you will read about later in this chapter), they are described as "life, liberty, and the pursuit of happiness." This means that all Americans have the right to live their own lives in liberty, or freedom, and to seek happiness for themselves.

To safeguard a citizen's liberty, our government guarantees certain freedoms, such as freedom of speech, freedom of the press, and freedom of religion. These freedoms can never be taken away from any American citizen by the government. Nor can they ever be restricted, except to keep people from using these freedoms to violate the rights of others.

For example, free speech and a free press do not mean freedom to tell lies or write false statements about another person. Each citizen has the right to have her or his reputation protected from efforts to hurt or destroy it with untruths.

Americans believe that if any citizen is denied his or her rights, the liberty of all is endangered. Our government has helped its people put their ideals into practice by passing and enforcing laws that guarantee equal rights for all citizens. For example, we have laws requiring that all Americans be given equal opportunities to get an education, to vote, and to find jobs.

CHECK-UP

Vocabulary

government
absolute monarchs
dictatorship
totalitarian government
democracy
direct democracy
representative democracy
republic
American government
laws
constitutions

Review

1. What are some of the governments you live under?
2. How does a direct democracy differ from a representative democracy?
3. What are three services that governments provide for us?

Discuss

Which of the reasons for establishing governments do you think is the most important one? Tell why.

2

Our First American Government

As you may remember from your study of American history, our nation was once ruled by Great Britain. However, Great Britain was far away on the other side of the Atlantic Ocean. This great distance made it easy for the American colonists to make their own rules and regulations without interference.

When the British government under King George III began to enforce its rules and regulations in the colonies, the Americans were angry. They had become used to doing things their own way. They resented being told what they could and could not do. They especially resented being forced to obey laws they considered unjust. Americans wanted to be free to govern themselves. They fought the Revolutionary War to gain their independence as a nation and to be free.

The Declaration of Independence

When fighting broke out between the American colonies and Great Britain in 1775, the Americans were not yet officially seeking independence. The next year, however, leaders from all 13 colonies met in Philadelphia. At this meeting, called the Second Continental Congress, they named a committee to draw up a **Declaration of Independence.** Most of the Declaration of Independence was written by Thomas Jefferson. It was approved by members of the Continental Congress on July 4, 1776.

The Declaration listed the reasons the 13 colonies had decided to separate from Great Britain and form a free nation. Yet the Declaration of Independence is much more than a document to justify independence. It is also a statement of the ideals of the American people. It explained to the world, in clear and inspiring language, that the purpose of government is to protect the basic human rights of citizens.

The artist John Trumbull painted this version of the signing of the Declaration of Independence. The tallest figure in the center is its author, Thomas Jefferson.

The Ideals of American Government

These rights are clearly defined in the Declaration of Independence:

> We hold these truths to be self-evident: That all men are created equal; that they are endowed by their Creator with certain unalienable rights; that among these are life, liberty, and the pursuit of happiness.

There is no more famous phrase in American writing than "all men are created equal." In this phrase, the word "men" is used to include both men and women. The statement does not mean that we are all born with the same mental and physical abilities. It means that we all have an equal claim to certain rights.

For example, the right of each individual to life, liberty, and happiness must be equal to that of every other individual. In other words, no person has the right to consider her or his own life and liberties more important than those of others.

The leaders who signed the Declaration of Independence realized that these ideals would be difficult to achieve. Yet they believed these ideals were worth—in their own words—"our lives, our fortunes, and our sacred honor."

The Declaration of Independence is one of the greatest documents in the history of our nation. Although written more than 200 years ago, it has remained a lasting symbol of American freedom. (You will find the complete text of this important document on pages 35–37.)

DID YOU KNOW THAT . . .

there was no official ceremony for the signing of the Declaration of Independence? Although paintings show delegates to the Second Continental Congress signing the document as a group, such a ceremony did not actually take place.

The Congress did adopt the Declaration on July 4, 1776—the occasion we celebrate as Independence Day. But only John Hancock, president of the Congress, signed the Declaration on that day. Other signers added their names between then and November 4. The last signature on the Declaration was not added until 1781!

Maybe you have seen a copy of Hancock's signature on the Declaration. He wrote it with such a flourish that we still use the expression "John Hancock" to mean a person's signature.

A Government for the New Nation

The Declaration of Independence did not provide a government for the new American nation. In 1777, while the Revolutionary War was still being fought, the Continental Congress drew up a new plan of government. It was approved by the 13 states and began to operate in 1781. The plan of government was called the **Articles of Confederation.**

The Articles of Confederation

A **confederation** is a loose association rather than a firm union of states. The Articles of Confederation, the young nation's first plan of government, set up a "firm league of friendship" among the 13 states. Each state

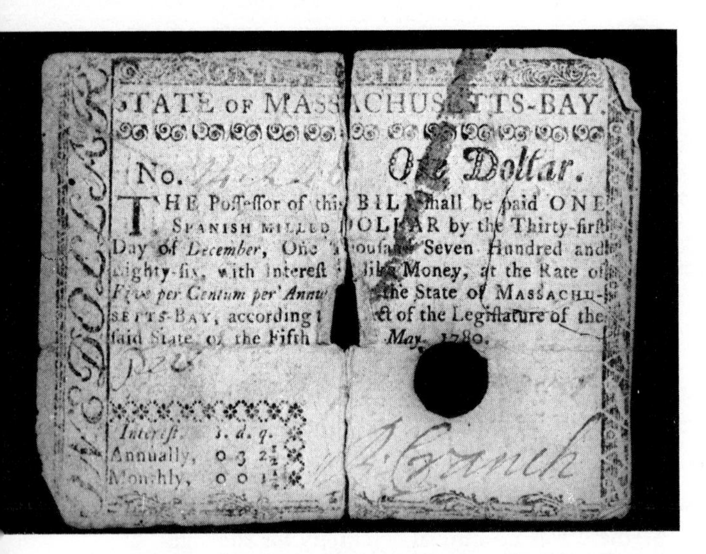

Can you imagine what would happen if each state issued its own money today? That is what the states did under the Articles of Confederation.

was to have equal powers and in most ways was independent of the other states. The central, or national, government was given very limited powers. The people of the 13 states did not want a strong central government. They feared such a government might use its power to limit the freedom of the separate states.

Under the Articles of Confederation, the national government consisted of a lawmaking body of one house, called Congress. The states sent representatives to Congress. Each state had one vote in Congress, regardless of the number of people living in the state.

There was no provision in the Articles for a President or any other strong leader to head the nation's government and to carry out the nation's laws. This was because the people were suspicious of strong leaders after their experience with King George III of Great Britain. The Articles also did not establish national courts to judge the nation's laws and punish lawbreakers. The states kept the power to enforce the laws passed by Congress.

During the Revolutionary War, the 13 states were willing to work together and make sacrifices to achieve victory. Things were different in the years following the Revolution. Many Americans suffered hard times after the war. Property had been destroyed. Trade with other nations had been cut off. American business was badly hurt. Moreover, the war left the young nation deeply in debt. The new government tried its best to handle these difficult problems. But it was too weak to solve them.

The Weaknesses of the Confederation

There were many reasons for the weakness of our nation's government under the Articles of Confederation. Without a President to head the national government, the nation had no strong leadership. Congress had trouble passing laws, because a vote of 9 of the 13 states was needed to pass a law. There were no officials to see that the laws were carried out. Moreover, there were no national courts to judge those who broke the laws.

In addition, it was very difficult to change the Articles of Confederation in order to make the national government stronger. Any changes in the Articles required the unanimous vote of all 13 states.

One of the main weaknesses of the new national government was that Congress lacked the power to collect taxes. Congress could ask the states to contribute money to help the national government meet its expenses. But Congress had no power to force states to make these contributions.

Without money, Congress could not pay its debts or carry on any government programs that might be needed. Congress could not pay the soldiers who had fought in the Revolutionary War or repay its debts to foreign nations.

Under the Articles of Confederation, the national government also lacked other important powers. It could not regulate, or control, trade between the states or with foreign nations. Each state regulated its own trade. This caused many disputes among the states and with other nations. Most of the states issued their own money.

The states were acting more like small separate nations than states in a confederation. The states often refused to obey the laws of Congress. As a result, relations between the states and Congress grew steadily worse.

Why the Confederation Failed

The Articles of Confederation succeeded in establishing a new nation. This was a major achievement. Yet the national government set up by the Articles failed in a number of important ways.

The real trouble with the government set up by the Articles of Confederation was that the states refused to give the national government enough power to operate effectively. The states feared a strong central government and kept most of the real power in their own hands.

The people of each state continued to think of themselves as belonging to their particular state rather than to the nation as a whole. This was natural because the states were separated by great distances and transportation was poor. Also, there was little contact between many of the states. It took years before the states began to think of themselves as parts of a single nation.

The weaknesses of the national government became clear as new problems faced the American nation. The states began to quarrel over the location of boundary lines. They got into disputes over trade. The national government was powerless to end these disagreements. It seemed as if the new American nation was about to break up into several small nations.

A growing number of leaders began to favor strengthening the national government. As a result, in 1787 Congress called upon the states to send representatives to a meeting to consider what could be done to improve the American government.

CHECK-UP

Vocabulary

Declaration of Independence
confederation
Articles of Confederation

Review

1. According to the Declaration of Independence, what is the purpose of government?
2. Why did the Articles of Confederation not set up a strong central government?
3. What were five weaknesses of the government under the Articles?

Discuss

The ideals set forth in the Declaration of Independence have influenced people all over the world for more than 200 years. Why do you think this is so?

3 Writing and Approving the Constitution

On May 25, 1787, a group of the nation's most outstanding leaders met in Independence Hall in Philadelphia. They had been sent as **delegates,** or representatives, of their states to find ways to improve the national government. The delegates soon became convinced that simply changing the Articles of Confederation was not enough. They decided instead to draw up a completely new plan of government, a new constitution.

The meeting became known as the **Constitutional Convention.** The leaders who attended wrote a constitution that established a government for the United States that has lasted for almost 200 years. The new plan of government the delegates drafted is the **Constitution of the United States.** It is the world's oldest written constitution still in effect.

The Delegates

The 55 delegates who attended the Constitutional Convention included some of the most famous leaders in the nation. George Washington had led the American army to victory over the British in the Revolutionary War. Respected by all, he was chosen to preside over the convention. He called on speakers and kept the meetings moving smoothly. Benjamin Franklin—diplomat, inventor, writer—was world famous. Then 81 years old, he was the oldest delegate.

Among the other delegates to the Constitutional Convention were James Madison, Alexander Hamilton, James Wilson, Roger Sherman, William Paterson, and Edmund Randolph. They had all been involved in the nation's struggle for independence.

The English Background

These leaders knew history well, and they had learned many important lessons from the past. The delegates wanted the American people to enjoy the rights the English had fought for and won during past centuries.

This heritage from England included the rights mentioned in the **Magna Carta** (the Great Charter), which the English people had won from King John in 1215. This important document guaranteed that free people could not be arrested, put in prison, or forced to leave their nation unless they were given a trial by other free people who were their equals. It also guaranteed that citizens of England were to be judged only according to English law.

The members of the Constitutional Convention also wished the new American nation to have the rights contained in the English Bill of Rights of 1689. One of these rights was the right to petition, or request, the government to improve or to change laws. Another was the right to a fair punishment if a citizen were found guilty of a crime.

The Convention delegates in Philadelphia also studied carefully the example of the English Parliament. **Parliament** is the lawmaking body of the English government. It is **bicameral.** That is, it consists of two parts, or houses. It is made up of the House of Lords, appointed by the king, and the House of Commons, elected by the people. This has the advantage of each house checking upon and improving the work of the other. The leaders in Philadelphia wanted no part of lords or kings. However, they could see the advantages of a two-house lawmaking body.

Meeting in Secrecy

The delegates to the Constitutional Convention held their meetings in secret. They were forbidden to discuss any of the business of the Convention with outsiders. This rule was put into effect so that the delegates could speak freely. Many delegates feared that if a delegate spoke publicly on a particular issue, he might be subjected to pressure from outsiders. Taking a public stand would also make it harder for a delegate to change his mind after debate and discussion. Some delegates criticized the secrecy rule. Without it, however, agreement on difficult issues might have been impossible.

If the meetings were held in secret, how do we know today what took place at the Convention? We know because of James Madison of Virginia. Madison kept a journal, or record, of the happenings at each meeting. His journal, which was kept secret until after his death, is our chief source of information about the Convention.

Writing the Constitution

The delegates agreed that the national government had to be given greater power. At the same time, most of the members agreed that the states should keep the powers needed to govern their own affairs. In order to achieve

The Constitutional Convention owed much of its success to the wisdom and work of these two delegates—Benjamin Franklin (left) and James Madison (right).

this, the delegates established a system of government known as a federal union, or a **federal system.** In a federal system, the powers of government are divided between the national government, which governs the whole nation, and state governments, which govern the people of each state.

The delegates worked out the new plan of a federal system at their meetings during the hot summer months of 1787. They discussed many ideas and proposals. They had to resolve many disputes as they worked on the Constitution. The delegates settled these differences of opinion by a series of compromises. A **compromise** is an agreement in which each side gives up part of its demands.

The most serious disagreement arose over the question of representation in the new national **legislature,** or lawmaking body. The larger states favored a legislature in which representation would be based on the size of a state's population. The smaller states wanted each state to have an equal number of representatives in the legislature.

For weeks the delegates argued over this issue. Finally both sides agreed to a compromise. Their agreement provided for a lawmaking body of two houses, called Congress. In one house, the Senate, the states were to have equal representation. In the other house, the House of Representatives, each state was to be represented according to the size of its population. This agreement is known as the **Great Compromise.**

A Strong New Nation Is Created

Many other compromises and agreements were reached as the Convention delegates worked on the Constitution. The states agreed to give up some of their powers and to increase the powers of the new national government. The national government was given

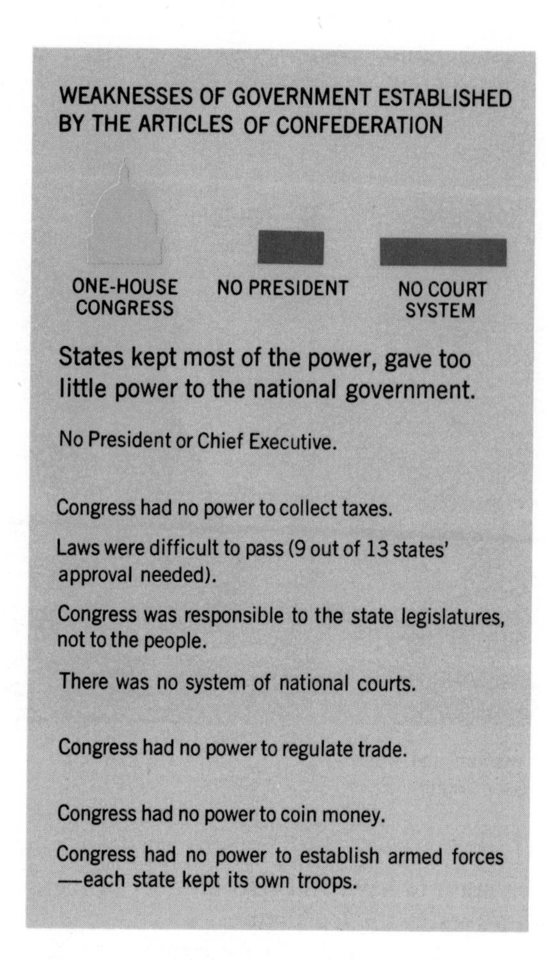

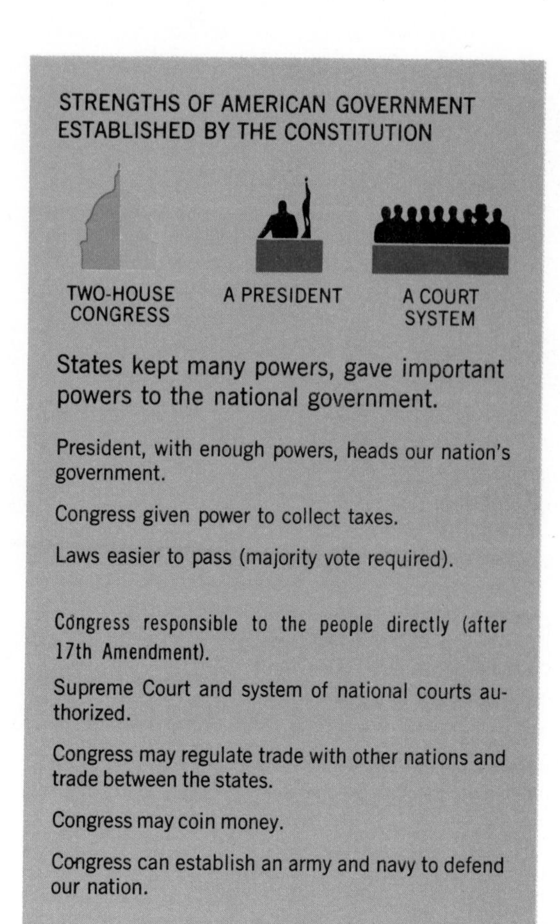

the power to tax, to regulate trade among the states and with foreign nations, to raise armed forces, and to coin and print money. Provision was made for a President to carry out the nation's laws. A Supreme Court and other national courts would enforce these laws. The chart on this page shows the major differences between the Articles of Confederation and the new Constitution.

By September 1787 the delegates had completed their work. Probably no delegate was satisfied with every part of the document. Benjamin Franklin, for example, did not approve of parts of the Constitution. Yet he believed that the delegates had written the best Constitution possible. For this reason, he urged the delegates to sign the Constitution.

Most of the members shared Franklin's feeling. Of the 42 delegates present that day, 39 signed the Constitution. After a farewell dinner, the delegates left for home.

Approving the Constitution

The work of the members of the Constitutional Convention was not over even after they left Philadelphia. The Constitution now had to be sent to the states and the people for their approval, or **ratification.** Before the Constitution could go into effect, it had to be approved, or ratified, by 9 of the 13 states. Each state set up a special convention of delegates to vote on the Constitution.

People quickly divided into two groups over the Constitution. Some supported it. Others were opposed. The public was swamped with pamphlets, letters to newspapers, and speeches by both groups.

Federalists and Anti-Federalists

Supporters of the Constitution were called **Federalists.** They favored a strong central, or national, government. The Federalists argued that the government under the Articles of Confederation was too weak to keep the country united. Unless the Constitution was adopted, they feared the United States would break up into 13 separate nations.

People who opposed the new Constitution were called **Anti-Federalists.** They feared that a Constitution which established a strong central government defeated the purpose of the recent war against Great Britain. The Anti-Federalists did not believe the new Constitution would protect the power of the states and the freedom of the people.

The Constitution Is Ratified

Gradually those who favored the Constitution gained support. However, many citizens were upset that the Constitution did not contain a list of the rights of the people. Finally it was agreed that such a list, or bill, of rights

George Washington was inaugurated as the first President of the United States in New York City on April 30, 1789.

would be added if the new Constitution was ratified.

Most of the states ratified the Constitution in 1787 and 1788. The new government of the United States began to operate in March 1789. Two states, North Carolina and Rhode Island, did not approve the Constitution until after it went into effect.

New York City was chosen as the nation's temporary capital. There, on April 30, 1789, George Washington was sworn in as the first President of the United States. Members of the new Senate and House of Representatives arrived to begin their work. The nation's new government was under way.

The Constitution of the United States is such a remarkable and important document that every American should read and study it carefully. (The complete text of the Constitution is on pages 55–75.) You will learn more about the government established by the Constitution in the next chapter.

CHECK-UP

Vocabulary

delegates
Constitutional Convention
Constitution of the United States
Magna Carta
Parliament
bicameral
federal system
compromise
legislature
Great Compromise
ratification
Federalists
Anti-Federalists

Review

1. What ideas of government did the delegates borrow from England?
2. Why were the meetings of the Constitutional Convention held in secret?
3. How did the delegates settle their disagreement over the question of representation in the legislature?

Discuss

Do you think compromise is a necessary part of government? Explain.

CHAPTER SUMMARY

Government serves many important purposes. Above all, government makes it possible for people to live and work together. Government provides many services that citizens acting alone could not perform.

Americans believe that our people should rule themselves. We also believe that no person should be denied her or his rights. These ideals of the American people are clearly set forth in the Declaration of Independence, one of the greatest documents in the history of our nation.

The Articles of Confederation established the first government of the 13 states. Under this plan, the weak national government could not operate effectively.

In 1787 delegates to the Constitutional Convention wrote a new plan of government for the nation. This plan, the Constitution of the United States, has lasted for almost 200 years. It created a stronger national government. It established a lawmaking body of two houses, called Congress. It also provided for a President to carry out the laws and for national courts to enforce the laws. The Constitution was approved by the states in 1789.

CIVICS SKILLS: Learning from Pictures

According to an old saying, "One picture is worth a thousand words." A picture, however, doesn't speak for itself. You have to know how to read it before you can fully grasp its meaning. Luckily, learning how to read the language of pictures is easy. As you will discover, many of the basic skills you use to read a paragraph can be used to read a picture.

Focusing on the Details

Whenever you read a paragraph in your textbook, one of the first things you do is identify the facts. You do the same thing with a photograph or a painting. You look for the important details in the scene. These are the picture's visual facts. If you study the painting on this page, for example, you will probably immediately notice the hairdos and clothing worn by the men. What other details in the painting do you think are important?

After you have collected this information, your next step is to interpret the facts. You can do this by asking questions about the details. In the case of this painting, you might ask such questions as the following: When did this scene take place? Who are the main figures? What are they doing?

The waistcoats and ruffled shirts shown in the painting give you a partial answer to the first question. They tell you that the scene took place in the past. Your own knowledge of American history might provide you with an even more precise answer—the late 1700's. What details help you answer the other questions?

Finding the Message

Many people think a picture presents only facts. But this is not the case. Any photograph or painting also expresses the artist's own ideas and feelings about a subject. Certain details are emphasized over the rest. Others are left out. Therefore, another important step in reading a picture is discovering what the artist wanted the picture to say.

To find this message, you must once again look at the facts. The way in which the artist used them makes a difference. For example, a certain person or object has a central position in the picture. A serious expression appears on everyone's face. These choices by the artist influence you. If they are dramatic enough, they might even affect the way you interpret an event.

Practicing What You've Learned

You have already studied the details in the painting below and drawn some conclusions about them. As you may have guessed, the painting shows George Washington addressing the Constitutional Convention. Now reexamine the picture, this time trying to determine the artist's message.

1. Which details did the artist emphasize?
2. How did the artist want you to feel about George Washington? What details support your answer?
3. Why do you think the artist made Washington the center of attention?

CHAPTER REVIEW

Vocabulary

On a separate piece of paper or in your notebook, write the terms that appear below. Then read the eight definitions that follow. Choose the definition that best fits each term. Write the definition beside the proper term.

constitution	republic
federal system	compromise
ratification	delegates
confederation	laws

1. Representatives sent by the states to attend the Constitutional Convention.
2. An organization in which powers are divided between the national government and the state governments.
3. A league of states loosely bound together.
4. An agreement in which each side gives up part of its demands.
5. A form of government in which the people elect representatives to carry on the work of government for them.
6. A written plan of government.
7. The approval of the Constitution by the states.
8. Rules of conduct for a group of people to follow.

Check-Up

1. What are some of the important reasons we need government?
2. How do governments help groups of people to run their own affairs?
3. What were the main purposes of the Declaration of Independence?
4. Why did Americans in 1781 fear a strong central government?
5. What were some of the principal weaknesses of the American government that was established under the Articles of Confederation?
6. What were some of the rights guaranteed to English subjects by the Magna Carta and the English Bill of Rights?
7. How did the Great Compromise settle differences between the large states and the smaller states at the Constitutional Convention?
8. Why did the delegates establish a federal system of government?
9. What were some of the powers granted to the national government under the United States Constitution?

Civics Skills

1. Look at the painting on page 31 of your textbook. What event does the painting show? What details does the artist emphasize? How would you describe the expression on most people's faces? Who seem to be the main figures? Based on these facts, what do you think the artist wanted the picture to "say"?
2. Now turn to the painting on page 24. What event does the painting show? What feeling or mood has the artist tried to capture? What details in the painting support your answer?

Citizenship and You

1. A bulletin board committee might prepare a display on "The Great Ideals of American Government."
2. Read a biography of Thomas Jefferson. Then write a report describing Jefferson's role in the writing of the Declaration of Independence.
3. Groups may be set up to report on special topics. Some topics could be: "Why We Need Governments," "How Governments Began," and "How George Washington Contributed to the Success of the Constitutional Convention."

The Declaration of Independence

In Congress, July 4, 1776

The Unanimous Declaration of the Thirteen United States of America

Why the Declaration Was Written

When, in the course of human events, it becomes necessary for one people to dissolve the political bands which have connected them with another, and to assume, among the powers of the earth, the separate and equal station to which the laws of nature and of nature's God entitle them, a decent respect to the opinions of mankind requires that they should declare the causes which impel them to the separation.

Statement of Basic Human Rights

We hold these truths to be self-evident: That all men are created equal; that they are endowed by their Creator with certain unalienable rights; that among these are life, liberty, and the pursuit of happiness.

Government Must Safeguard Human Rights

That to secure these rights, governments are instituted among men, deriving their just powers from the consent of the governed;

That whenever any form of government becomes destructive of these ends, it is the right of the people to alter or to abolish it, and to institute a new government, laying its foundation on such principles, and organizing its powers in such form, as to them shall seem most likely to effect their safety and happiness. Prudence, indeed, will dictate that governments long established should not be changed for light and transient causes; and accordingly all experience hath shown that mankind are more disposed to suffer while evils are sufferable, than to right themselves by abolishing the forms to which they are accustomed. But when a long train of abuses and usurpations, pursuing invariably the same object, evinces a design to reduce them under absolute despotism, it is their right, it is their duty, to throw off such government, and to provide new guards for their future security.

Abuses of Human Rights by the King

Such has been the patient sufferance of these colonies; and such is now the necessity which constrains them to alter their former systems of government. The history of the present King of Great Britain is a history of repeated injuries and usurpations, all having in direct object the establishment of an absolute tyranny over these states. To prove this, let facts be submitted to a candid world.

He has refused his assent to laws the most wholesome and necessary for the public good.

He has forbidden his governors to pass laws of immediate and pressing importance, unless suspended in their operation till his assent should be obtained; and, when so suspended, he has utterly neglected to attend to them.

He has refused to pass other laws for the accommodation of large districts of people, unless those people would relinquish the right of representation in the legislature, a right inestimable to them, and formidable to tyrants only.

He has called together legislative bodies at places unusual, uncomfortable, and distant from the depository of their public records, for the sole purpose of fatiguing them into compliance with his measures.

He has dissolved representative houses repeatedly, for opposing, with manly firmness, his invasions on the rights of the people.

He has refused, for a long time after such dissolutions, to cause others to be elected, whereby the legislative powers, incapable of annihilation, have returned to the people at large for their exercise; the state remaining, in the mean time, exposed to all the dangers of invasions from without and convulsions within.

He has endeavored to prevent the population of these states; for that purpose obstructing the laws for the naturalization of foreigners, refusing to pass others to encourage their migration hither, and raising the conditions of new appropriations of lands.

He has obstructed the administration of justice, by refusing his assent to laws for establishing judiciary powers.

He has made judges dependent on his will alone for the tenure of their offices, and the amount and payment of their salaries.

He has erected a multitude of new offices, and sent hither swarms of officers to harass our people and eat out their substance.

He has kept among us, in times of peace, standing armies, without the consent of our legislatures.

He has affected to render the military independent of, and superior to, the civil power.

He has combined with others to subject us to a jurisdiction foreign to our constitutions and unacknowledged by our laws, giving his assent to their acts of pretended legislation:

For quartering large bodies of armed troops among us;

For protecting them, by a mock trial, from punishment for any murders which they should commit on the inhabitants of these states;

For cutting off our trade with all parts of the world;

For imposing taxes on us without our consent;

For depriving us, in many cases, of the benefits of trial by jury;

For transporting us beyond seas, to be tried for pretended offenses;

For abolishing the free system of English laws in a neighboring province, establishing therein an arbitrary government, and enlarging its boundaries, so as to render it at once an example and fit instrument for introducing the same absolute rule into these colonies;

For taking away our charters, abolishing our most valuable laws, and altering, fundamentally, the forms of our governments;

For suspending our own legislatures, and declaring themselves invested with power to legislate for us in all cases whatsoever.

He has abdicated government here, by declaring us out of his protection and waging war against us.

He has plundered our seas, ravaged our coasts, burned our towns, and destroyed the lives of our people.

He is at this time transporting large armies of foreign mercenaries to complete the works of death, desolation, and tyranny already begun with circumstances of cruelty and perfidy scarcely paralleled in the most barbarous ages, and totally unworthy the head of a civilized nation.

He has constrained our fellow-citizens, taken captive on the high seas, to bear arms against their country, to become the executioners of their friends and brethren, or to fall themselves by their hands.

He has excited domestic insurrection among us, and has endeavored to bring on the inhabitants of our frontiers the merciless Indian savages, whose known rule of warfare is an undistinguished destruction of all ages, sexes, and conditions.

Colonial Efforts to Avoid Separation

In every stage of these oppressions we have petitioned for redress in the most humble terms; our repeated petitions have been answered only by repeated injury.

A prince whose character is thus marked by every act which may define a tyrant is unfit to be the ruler of a free people.

Nor have we been wanting in our attentions to our British brethren. We have warned them, from time to time, of attempts by their legislature to extend an unwarrantable jurisdiction over us. We have reminded them of the circumstances of our emigration and settlement here. We have appealed to their native justice and magnanimity; and we have conjured them, by the ties of our common kindred, to disavow these usurpations, which would inevitably interrupt our connections and correspondence. They, too, have been deaf to the voice of justice and consanguinity. We must, therefore, acquiesce in the necessity which denounces our separation, and hold them, as we hold the rest of mankind, enemies in war, in peace friends.

The Colonies Declare Independence

We, therefore, the representatives of the United States of America, in General Congress assembled, appealing to the Supreme Judge of the world for the rectitude of our intentions, do, in the name and by the authority of the good people of these colonies, solemnly publish and declare, That these united colonies are, and at right ought to be, free and independent states; that they are absolved from all allegiance to the British crown, and that all political connection between them and the state of Great Britain is, and ought to be, totally dissolved; and that, as free and independent states, they have full power to levy war, conclude peace, contract alliances, establish commerce, and do all other acts and things which independent states may of right do. And, for the support of this declaration, with a firm reliance on the protection of Divine Providence, we mutually pledge to each other our lives, our fortunes, and our sacred honor.

President John Hancock

New Hampshire
Josiah Bartlett
William Whipple
Matthew Thornton

Massachusetts
Samuel Adams
John Adams
Robert Treat Paine
Elbridge Gerry

Rhode Island
Stephen Hopkins
William Ellery

Connecticut
Roger Sherman
Samuel Huntington
William Williams
Oliver Wolcott

New York
William Floyd
Philip Livingston
Francis Lewis
Lewis Morris

New Jersey
Richard Stockton
John Witherspoon
Francis Hopkinson
John Hart
Abraham Clark

Pennsylvania
Robert Morris
Benjamin Rush
Benjamin Franklin
John Morton
George Clymer
James Smith
George Taylor
James Wilson
George Ross

Delaware
Caesar Rodney
George Read
Thomas McKean

Maryland
Samuel Chase
William Paca
Thomas Stone
Charles Carroll
of Carrollton

Virginia
George Wythe
Richard Henry Lee
Thomas Jefferson
Benjamin Harrison
Thomas Nelson, Jr.
Francis Lightfoot Lee
Carter Braxton

North Carolina
William Hooper
Joseph Hewes
John Penn

South Carolina
Edward Rutledge
Thomas Heyward,
Jr.
Thomas Lynch, Jr.
Arthur Middleton

Georgia
Button Gwinnett
Lyman Hall
George Walton

CHAPTER

3

The American Constitution

The United States has a **constitutional** form of government. This means that we are governed according to the provisions of our Constitution. Our rights are written into the Constitution and must be respected by the government. The Constitution is the highest law of the land. Everyone, even the President of the United States, is required to obey the Constitution.

A famous English leader, William Pitt, said many years ago that the Constitution of the United States "will be a pattern for all future constitutions and will receive the admiration of all future ages." Time has proved the truth of these words. The Constitution is now the world's oldest written plan of government still working successfully. The constitutions of many other nations have been patterned on it.

The Constitution of the United States has been successful because it is based upon many great ideals concerning government. At the same time, it provides a system of government that enables us to put these ideals into action.

Learning about our Constitution will help you understand the goals and ideals of the American people. It will also help you understand the workings of our nation's government. In the three parts of this chapter, you will study these important topics:

1. **Great Ideals in the Constitution**
2. **The Three Branches of Government**
3. **A Flexible Constitution**

1

Great Ideals in the Constitution

The Declaration of Independence states that governments should receive their powers from "the consent [approval] of the [people] governed." This is one of the basic ideals upon which our nation is founded.

The writers of the Constitution, too, believed that a government must receive all its powers from the people it governs. They believed government must not use any powers that the people do not grant it. Above all, they believed that the people must give their consent before the system of government goes into effect.

Government by Consent of the Governed

The idea of government by **consent of the governed** is one of our most cherished ideals. It is stated in the opening sentence of the Constitution. This part of the Constitution is known as the **Preamble.** It is an introduction that explains why the Constitution was written.

The Preamble begins with the words "We the people." They are very meaningful words. The writers of the Constitution wanted to emphasize the importance of the people. These words stress that our government was established by the people. As the Preamble clearly states, "We the people of the United States, . . . do ordain [order] and establish this Constitution. . . ."

Six Goals of the Constitution

The Preamble itself is not law. Rather, it is a statement of goals. (You can read the Preamble on page 55.)

The Preamble lists these six goals for the government of the United States:

1. "To form a more perfect union." The new government should be a better union of states than the one the people had under the Articles of Confederation.

2. "To establish justice." The government should make laws and establish a system of courts that are fair to all.

3. "To insure domestic tranquillity." The government should preserve peace within the country.

4. "To provide for the common defense." The government should be able to protect the nation from its enemies.

5. "To promote the general welfare." The government should help ensure the well-being of all the people.

6. "To secure the blessings of liberty." The freedom of the people should be carefully safeguarded now and in the future.

These goals reflect the belief that the government should serve its citizens. They remain the goals of our nation today.

Our Representative Democracy

The representative democracy, or republic, that was set up by our Constitution is based upon the consent of the people who are governed. What happens, though, if the people become dissatisfied with the way their representatives are governing them? In that case, the people can let their representatives know what they think should be done. If people do not approve of their representatives' actions, at the next election they can elect new representatives who they hope will do a better job.

Our republic works successfully because Americans believe in **majority rule.** The majority is more than half of the people. When disagreements occur, the decision of the majority is accepted by all. However, under our system of government, the majority must always respect the rights of the minority—the smaller group of people. Moreover, the minority must be free to express its views and try to convince the majority to accept its ideas.

Government Based on a Federal System

As you read in the last chapter, the delegates at the Constitutional Convention decided to establish a **federal system** of government for the United States. In a federal system, the powers of government are divided between a national government, which governs the whole nation, and state governments, which govern the people of each state.

The national government is usually called the **federal government.** It is important to

How the Powers of Government Are Divided

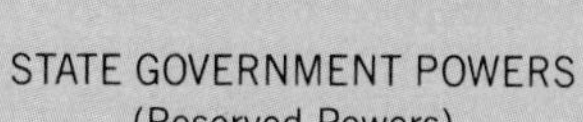

FEDERAL GOVERNMENT POWERS	POWERS SHARED by Federal and State Governments (Concurrent Powers)	STATE GOVERNMENT POWERS (Reserved Powers)
To regulate foreign trade and commerce between the states	To collect taxes	To regulate trade within the state
To coin and print money	To borrow money	To establish local governments
To conduct foreign relations with other nations	To establish courts	To conduct elections
To establish post offices and roads	To enforce laws and punish lawbreakers	To determine qualifications of voters
To raise and support armed forces	To provide for the health and welfare of the people	To establish and support public schools
To declare war and make peace		To incorporate business firms
To govern American territories and admit new states		To license professional workers
To pass naturalization laws and regulate immigration		To keep all the "reserved powers" not granted to the federal government nor prohibited to the states
To make all laws "necessary and proper" to carry out its powers		

remember that the term "federal government" refers to the national government, which is centered in Washington, D.C. The term "federal system" is used to refer to our entire system of government and includes both the federal government and the 50 state governments.

Under our federal system, the federal government is given certain important powers. All powers that are not given to the federal government remain with the states.

Powers of the Federal Government. The federal government's powers are meant to apply to matters concerning all the people. For example, only the federal government can coin money. Only the federal government has the power to control trade among the states and with foreign nations. The federal government alone has the power to provide for the common defense, because an attack on the United States would threaten all Americans.

You recall that under the Articles of Confederation, the federal government did not have these important powers. It was hoped that our new government would now be strengthened.

Powers of the State Governments. The Constitution leaves to the states many important powers to manage their own affairs. Under our federal system, the states or the people have all the powers not specifically given to the federal government by the Constitution. These are known as **reserved powers** because they are reserved, or set aside, for the states or the people. The state governments, for example, conduct elections, regulate trade within the state, and help provide schools.

Shared Powers. The federal and state governments also share many powers. These are known as **concurrent powers.** Both the federal and state governments, for example, can raise funds through taxation. Both also have the power to borrow money. Moreover, they share the power to establish courts, to enforce laws and punish lawbreakers, and to provide for the health and welfare of the American people.

Responsibility for running the nation's Postal Service is one of the powers given to the federal government. Why do you suppose that this is so?

Whenever a state law disagrees with the Constitution or with a federal law, the state must give way to the federal government. The writers of the Constitution made this clear by saying that the Constitution and the laws of the federal government shall be "the supreme law of the land."

Government in Which Powers Are Limited

By establishing the American federal system, the writers of the Constitution set up the stronger national government that our new nation needed. They were determined, how-

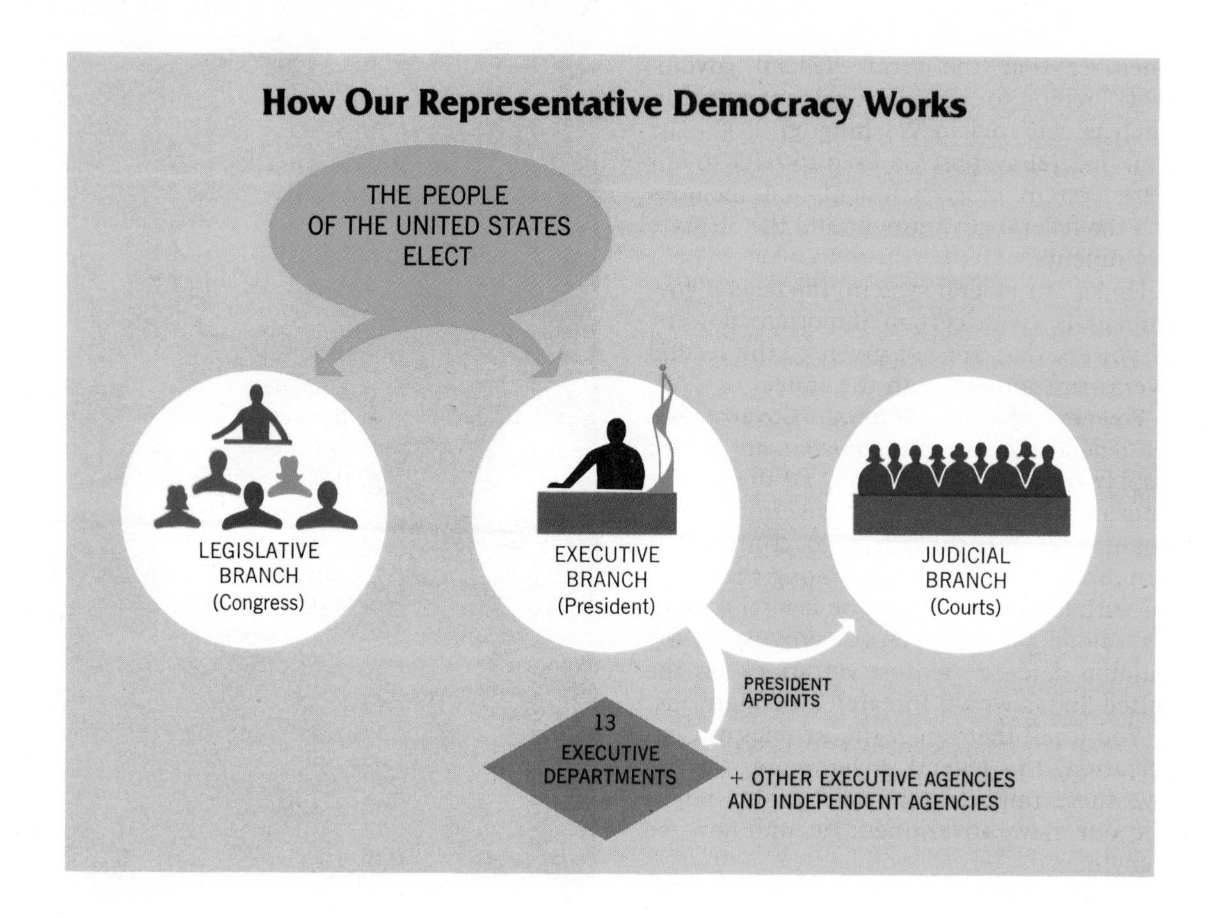

ever, to keep this new federal government from becoming too powerful. Therefore, they spelled out very carefully the various powers of the federal government. In this way, all Americans know exactly what the powers of the federal government are.

The Constitution also provides that all powers not mentioned are reserved for the states or the people. Furthermore, the Bill of Rights (which will be discussed in the next chapter) specifies certain powers that are forbidden to both the federal government and the states. It describes the many freedoms that belong to every American citizen.

As you have read, the writers of the Constitution believed that all governments should have the consent, or approval, of the people. They made sure the new government could have only as much power as the people wanted to give it. The American people clearly wanted to limit, or to check, the powers that their federal government would have. But why?

Nearly all Americans at the time of the Constitutional Convention were against strong governments. They feared that a strong national government might limit their freedom, as the British king had attempted to do. They wanted to be sure that their new government would be responsible to the American people.

CHECK-UP

Vocabulary

constitutional
consent of the governed
Preamble
majority rule
federal system
federal government
reserved powers
concurrent powers

Review

1. What are six goals of the American government?
2. How does the principle of majority rule operate?
3. Why does the Constitution limit the powers granted to the federal government?

Discuss

What do you think is the most important goal of the American government? Explain why.

2

The Three Branches of Government

There are several provisions in the Constitution designed to prevent any person or group of people, or any part of the government, from taking too much power. In the last section you read how our federal system divides powers between the national and state governments. Another provision of the Constitution set up three separate branches, or divisions, in the federal government.

This three-way division of power is known as the **separation of powers.** It ensures that no branch of the federal government can become too powerful. The three branches of government are the legislative branch, the executive branch, and the judicial branch. They were created by the first three articles of the United States Constitution.

Legislative Branch

Article 1 of the Constitution established Congress as the **legislative branch,** or lawmaking branch, of the government. Congress is made up of two houses—the Senate and the House of Representatives.

The writers of the Constitution placed great emphasis on Congress. It is the first branch of government mentioned in the Constitution. The workings of Congress are described in greater detail than either of the other two branches of the federal government. In addition, the other branches must depend on Congress for the money they need to carry out their responsibilities. You will read more about Congress in Chapter 5.

Executive Branch

The **executive branch,** described by Article 2 of the Constitution, is responsible for seeing that the nation's laws are carried out. It is headed by the President, who is the nation's Chief Executive. The executive branch also

The Separation of Powers

Makes the laws.

Carries out and enforces the laws.

Judges laws and punishes lawbreakers.

Checks and Balances in the Federal Government

POWERS		CHECKS ON POWERS
Passes laws. Can pass laws over the President's veto if two thirds of the Congress approves the law. Approves appointments of federal court judges.	 THE CONGRESS	President can veto laws. The Supreme Court can rule that a law is unconstitutional.
Can approve or veto laws. Carries out the laws. Appoints federal court judges.	 THE PRESIDENT	Congress can pass laws over the President's veto by a two-thirds vote. Congress may impeach and remove the President for high crimes or for misdemeanors. Senate approves the President's appointments to the federal courts.
Judges the meaning of laws. May rule that laws passed by Congress and actions taken by the executive branch are unconstitutional.	 THE SUPREME COURT	Congress (or the states) may propose an amendment to the Constitution if the Supreme Court rules that a law is unconstitutional. Senate may refuse to approve the appointments to the federal courts. Congress may impeach and remove a federal judge from office.

includes the Vice President and many other people who help the President carry out the executive duties.

As our nation's Chief Executive, the President represents all the American people. You will read more about the executive branch in Chapter 6.

Judicial Branch

Article 3 established the **judicial branch,** or federal court system, to judge the laws and punish lawbreakers. The Constitution makes the Supreme Court the head of the judicial branch. The Constitution also gives Congress the power to establish lower federal courts to help carry out the work of the judicial branch.

The Supreme Court can declare a law invalid if it is in conflict with the Constitution. You will read more about the judicial branch in Chapter 7.

Government with Checks and Balances

To make sure that no branch of the federal government becomes too powerful, a system of **checks and balances** was included in the Constitution. Each branch of the government has powers that check, or limit, the powers of the two other branches. Each branch has its own powers, which no other branch can assume. In this way, the powers of government are balanced by being divided three ways.

How does this system of checks and balances work? Let's consider lawmaking as an example. Congress is the legislative branch of the federal government. However, the President has the power to **veto,** or turn down, a proposed law. With this power to approve or disapprove laws passed by Congress, the President can check the lawmaking power of Congress.

Does this mean that the President can prevent any law passed by Congress from taking effect? That would give the President too much power. Therefore, the Constitution balances the President's power. It does so by giving Congress the power to pass laws over the President's veto. A two-thirds vote of both houses is required before Congress can pass any law that the President has vetoed. In this way, Congress can check the lawmaking power of the President.

The Supreme Court can also become involved in lawmaking. It has the power to interpret, or decide the meaning of, laws. In addition, the Court can declare that a law is in conflict with the Constitution and must not be enforced.

There are many other checks and balances in the working of our federal government. You will learn more about how the three branches check and balance each other as you study our American government in the chapters that follow.

CHECK-UP

Vocabulary

separation of powers
legislative branch
executive branch
judicial branch
checks and balances
veto

Review

1. Why did the Constitution provide for the separation of powers?
2. Name the three branches of the federal government. What is the purpose of each?
3. How does the system of checks and balances work in our federal government?

Discuss

The writers of the Constitution gave Congress the greatest amount of power. Today some people believe that the President has become more powerful than Congress. Tell why you agree or disagree.

3
A Flexible Constitution

Changing times may call for changes in our government. In 1787, when our Constitution was written, the United States was a nation of 13 states with fewer than 4 million people. Today our 50 states are home to nearly 230 million people. Our nation has changed in many other ways as well. How can the Constitution, which was written in the age of sailing ships, meet the needs of the nation in our jet age? The answer is that the writers of the Constitution were wise enough to plan a government that could be changed to meet new conditions.

The Constitution Provides for Change

One of the most important features of the American Constitution is that it is flexible. The writers of the Constitution knew that the plan of government they were creating would have to meet the changing needs of a growing nation. They could not possibly foresee all the changes the United States would

(continued on page 50)

CITIZENSHIP IN ACTION

The Senate Watergate Committee was created in 1973 in order to investigate the charges in the Watergate break-in.

Watergate—A Test of the Constitution

A few pieces of tape were the first clue. They had been placed over the door latches so that the doors would not lock shut. While on his rounds, a guard named Frank Wills found the pieces of tape and removed them. He thought they had been left there by building workers. However, when Wills returned, he found the doors taped again. He called the police—and set off a chain of events that eventually led to the resignation of the President of the United States.

The Watergate Break-in

In June 1972 the Watergate Building in Washington, D.C., where the taped doors were found, housed the headquarters of the national committee of the Democratic Party. Before dawn on June 16, five burglars broke into these offices. One of them taped the doors so that the others could get in.

When the burglars were arrested, the police found that they were carrying large sums of money, listening equipment, two-way radios, and cameras. It soon became clear that this was not just a routine burglary case. Reporters immediately began asking questions. Why would anyone want to break into the offices of the Democratic Party? What did they hope to find? Slowly the evidence grew. It seemed to point to some assistants to the President in the White House.

The White House Is Involved

The year 1972 was a Presidential election year. Some people wondered if the burglars had been looking for something that might help defeat Democratic candidates and reelect President Richard M. Nixon, a Republican. However, most people did not believe that anyone in the White House would take part in such actions. President Nixon was reelected by a huge margin.

After the election, though, reporters and others continued to ask if there was a link between the Watergate break-in, the Committee for the Reelection of the President, and the White House. Early in 1973 the Watergate burglars were tried and found guilty. It was expected that they would go to jail and that would be the end of the case. But Judge John Sirica, who had tried the case, did not believe the whole truth had come out during the trial. He told the burglars that they would be sent to prison for as long as 40 years unless they told what they knew. One of the burglars broke his silence. He described conversations with top aides in the White House.

Executive Privilege

The Senate formed a special committee—the Senate Watergate Committee—to investigate the charges against President Nixon's aides. At first the President refused to allow his aides to appear before the committee. He claimed executive privilege—the right and need of the President and his aides to keep silent about official conversations. This was the first step in a conflict between the President and Congress.

Some Americans worried that the President was trying to cover up illegal activities in the White House. Members of Congress grew increasingly angry and, as a result, President Nixon changed his mind. He announced that he would permit his aides to testify. Before the hearings began, reports in the news media made it clear that some people in the White House had been involved in the Watergate break-in. Moreover, they had tried to cover up their actions. In April 1973 the President's top aides resigned.

Senate Watergate Committee leaders Sam Ervin (center) and Howard Baker (far left) examine evidence with their aides.

The Senate Watergate Committee began public hearings in May. One Presidential aide, John Dean, testified that President Nixon knew about the cover-up. The President denied the charge.

But the question remained. Was President Nixon involved in the cover-up? Then it appeared there was a way to find out who was telling the truth. The public learned that every conversation between the President and his aides had been recorded on tape. Hidden recording machines had been placed in the White House by order of the President himself. He had hoped that the tapes would serve as a record for future historians of his time in office.

Conflict Over the Tapes

The Senate committee and Archibald Cox, the special prosecutor who had been appointed to investigate Watergate, immediately requested a number of the tapes dealing with that subject. The President refused to turn them over, again claiming executive privilege. In October 1973 a federal court of appeals denied this claim of executive privilege. The court ruled that the President must turn over the tapes so that a criminal investigation could go forward. "The President," the court said, ". . . is not above the law's command."

In response President Nixon offered to release a written summary of the tapes and ordered Cox not to request any additional tapes. When Cox refused to obey the President's orders, he was fired. These actions led to great protests from the public and Congress. The President then agreed to release the tapes and appointed a new special prosecutor, Leon Jaworski.

Then came another shock. The White House announced that some of the requested tapes were missing. Criticism of President Nixon grew, and many Americans began to demand that he be impeached. Under the Constitution, impeachment is the responsibility of the House of Representatives. An official who is impeached, or formally accused of misconduct, by the House must then be tried by the Senate.

President Nixon announced on television that he was releasing written transcripts of the Watergate tapes.

The House Judiciary Committee began its investigation into the possible impeachment of the President—the first such investigation in more than 100 years. The committee asked for additional tapes. Finally, in April 1974, President Nixon released written transcripts, or copies, of the tapes. Many people were angered by the contents and the President's seeming lack of respect for the law. On one tape the President discussed paying "hush" money to the Watergate burglars to keep them from talking about what they knew.

The House committee and the special prosecutor continued to demand the tapes themselves. Finally the question of the tapes was put before the Supreme Court. On July 24, 1974, the Court ruled that President Nixon had to release the tapes.

President Nixon Leaves Office

On the day of the Supreme Court decision, the House Judiciary Committee began a televised debate on impeachment. The committee voted to recommend impeachment of President Nixon on three counts: obstruction of justice, abuse of power, and contempt of Congress and the courts. It was now up to the full House to vote.

Before the House of Representatives could act, the newly released tapes proved that President Nixon had been involved in the cover-up of the Watergate break-in. It quickly became certain that the President would be impeached by the House and tried by the Senate. He was under great pressure from both Republicans and Democrats to resign.

In an emotion-filled speech on television, President Nixon announced that he would resign the next day. On August 9, 1974, he left the nation's capital—the only American President ever to resign from the Presidency.

Vice President Gerald R. Ford became President and declared that "our long national nightmare is over." He went on to say that "our Constitution works; our great Republic is a government of laws and not of men. . . ."

The Watergate case proved that the system of checks and balances set up by the Constitution works. Together the courts and Congress had restrained a President engaged in wrongdoing. Moreover, they reminded the world that even a President is not above the law in the United States.

Richard Nixon waved goodbye to onlookers as he prepared to leave Washington, D.C., and the Presidency on August 9, 1974.

Thinking It Over

1. No one ever proved that President Nixon had anything to do with the Watergate burglary. Why then was he thought to be guilty of crimes in the Watergate case?
2. What are the steps by which a President is impeached?
3. How did the Watergate case prove that the system of checks and balances set up by the Constitution works?

DID YOU KNOW THAT . . .

the Declaration of Independence, the Constitution, and the Bill of Rights all are on display at the National Archives Building in Washington, D.C.? These valued safeguards of American liberties are displayed in a special glass case that prevents air and moisture from seeping in.

Every evening, at the touch of a button, special machinery lowers the documents through the floor. They remain in a vault made of steel and reinforced concrete until morning, when the documents go back on display.

undergo. Yet the government established by our Constitution has been able to change and adapt to new circumstances and challenges.

There are three ways in which the Constitution and the government can adapt to the changing needs and conditions of the nation. They are amendment, interpretation, and custom.

The Amendment Process

An **amendment** is a written change made in the Constitution. The process for amending, or changing, the Constitution is set forth in Article 5 of the Constitution (see page 65). It is not easy to amend our Constitution.

All proposed amendments require the approval of three fourths of the states. Also, amendments may take a long time to pass. This makes it more likely that long, careful thought will be given to any proposed amendment before it is passed. Since the Constitution went into effect in 1789, only 26 amendments have been added to it. (These amendments to the Constitution will be discussed in Chapter 4.)

Proposing an Amendment. Both Congress and the states must be involved in the amending process. An amendment may be proposed in two ways. The first way is to have Congress propose an amendment by a two-thirds vote in both houses. Since a two-thirds vote in Congress is difficult to obtain, members must be sure the change is really needed.

The second way of proposing an amendment to the Constitution begins with the states. With this method, the legislatures of two thirds of the states—34 out of 50—can ask Congress to call a national convention to propose an amendment. This method has never been used successfully. However, it could be used if Congress should refuse to propose an amendment that the American people believed was necessary.

Ratifying an Amendment. After an amendment has been proposed, it then must be approved by three fourths, or 38, of the states. There are two ways an amendment may be approved, or ratified. The method of ratification must be described in each proposed amendment.

The proposed amendment may be sent to the state legislatures for approval. All but one of the 26 amendments have been approved in this way. Or the proposed amendment may be sent to state conventions elected by the people of each state to consider the amendment. This method has been used only once.

After an amendment has been approved by the required number of states, it becomes part of the written Constitution. What happens if the people decide they do not like the way an amendment is working? In that case, the amendment in question can be canceled, or **repealed,** by another amendment. Only one of the amendments to the Constitution has been repealed.

Interpreting the Constitution

Our government also changes when some part of the Constitution is interpreted in a new way. Congress may interpret a certain clause in the Constitution as giving it the right to pass a particular law.

For example, Congress has passed laws setting the minimum wage that workers must be paid. A minimum wage is not mentioned anywhere in the Constitution. However, the Constitution does give Congress the right to control trade among the states. The goods made by workers usually travel from one state to another. Therefore, Congress interpreted the Constitution to mean that it could pass laws affecting working conditions, including wages.

The Supreme Court has the power to decide if Congress has interpreted the Constitution correctly. The Court's ruling is final.

Custom and the Constitution

A number of changes in our government also have come about through custom and tradition. For example, the Constitution did not provide for regular meetings of the leaders in the executive branch of our federal government. However, President George Washing-

Congress used its power over interstate trade to outlaw child labor, which once was common in American factories and mines.

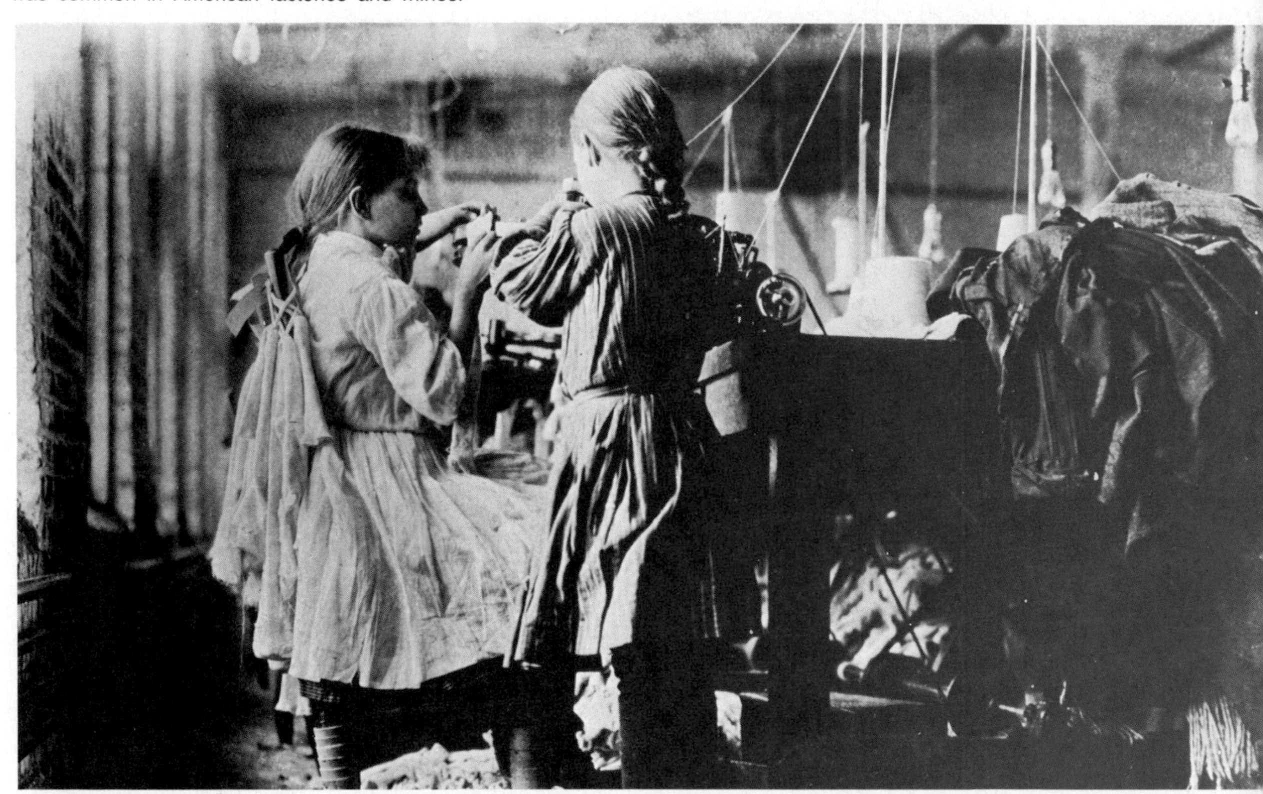

CAN YOU GUESS?

How many people come to see the Declaration of Independence and the Constitution in Washington, D.C., each year?

Answer is on page 562.

ton brought these leaders together regularly to serve as his advisers, or **Cabinet.** Since that time, regular meetings between a President and the Cabinet have become an accepted part of the tradition of our government.

Many other important traditions have developed in our nation's government. These traditions are followed regularly. Yet they have seldom been written down or made into laws. For this reason, they are sometimes called our **unwritten Constitution.**

CHECK-UP

Vocabulary

amendment
repealed
Cabinet
unwritten Constitution

Review

1. Why did the writers of the Constitution make it flexible?
2. Explain the ways an amendment can be added to the Constitution.
3. How does interpretation of the Constitution help change the government to meet changing times?
4. How does custom help to change American government?

Discuss

Our Constitution is a complex document that is open to different interpretations. Do you think this is one of the reasons it has lasted for so long? Explain.

CHAPTER SUMMARY

Our nation's government is based on the Constitution of the United States. This Constitution, together with its amendments, provides us with a workable plan of government.

The government is based upon the approval, or consent, of the people who are governed. It is a federal system in which certain powers are given to the federal government and other powers are left to the states and the people. Certain powers are shared by both the federal and state governments.

The Constitution set up three separate branches of government—the legislative branch, the executive branch, and the judicial branch. This separation of powers is designed to prevent any person or group of people from taking too much power. Each branch of government has powers that check, or limit, the powers of the other two branches.

Our Constitution and government have been able to meet the needs of a growing and changing nation. The Constitution can be amended, and it can be interpreted in a new way. Changes can also come about through custom and tradition.

CIVICS SKILLS: Reading a Flow Chart

"The government that we mean to erect [build]," declared James Madison in 1787, "is meant to last for ages." True to his promise, the plan of government that Madison helped write—the Constitution of the United States—has guided the country for almost 200 years. It has grown along with the nation largely because of the special provisions in Article 5. This is the article that makes it possible to amend, or change, the Constitution. You can see how the amendment process works by studying a flow chart such as the one below.

Identifying the Stages

The main purpose of a **flow chart** is to show the various stages in a process. The first step in making such a chart is to determine the beginning and the end points—the start and the finish. The last stage in the amendment process, for example, is the addition of the amendment to the Constitution. What are the two possible starting points?

After you have determined this information, your next step is to think of all the stages in between. Study the flow chart on this page. Which parts show the middle stages?

Unlike many other kinds of charts, flow charts show movement through time. Arrows trace this flow by connecting all the stages in the order that they occur. If you run your finger from one arrow to another on the chart below, you can easily see the directions in which the amendment process moves. You can also discover where it might get stalled. If, for instance, only 32 state legislatures ratify an amendment, it will not be passed. How else could an amendment be blocked?

Practicing What You've Learned

To practice using a flow chart, answer the following questions:

1. What happens if two thirds of the state legislatures request a constitutional convention?
2. "A majority of the people have to favor an amendment before it can be added to the Constitution." What evidence in the flow chart supports this statement?

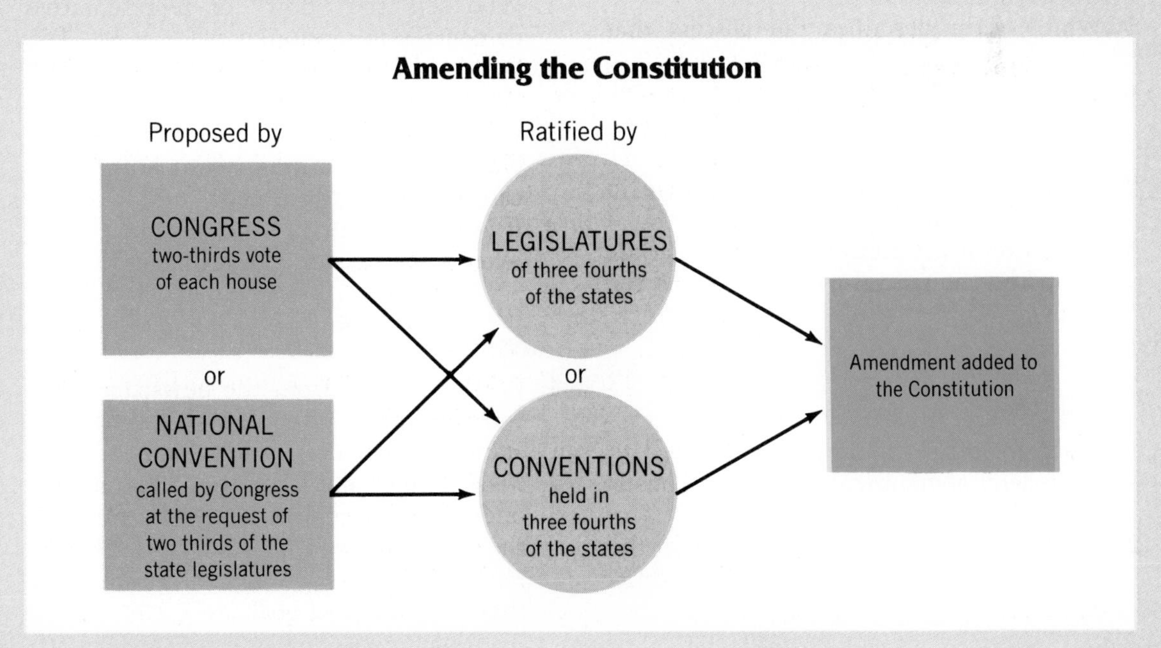

CHAPTER REVIEW

Vocabulary

Each of the terms in the vocabulary list below can be used to answer one of the eight questions that follow. For each term, choose the number of the question it answers.

Preamble	concurrent powers
reserved powers	separation of powers
federal system	veto
checks and balances	amendment

1. In which form of government are the powers of government divided between a national government and state governments?
2. What is the opening part of the United States Constitution that explains why the Constitution was written?
3. What term applies to the power of the President to turn down a law passed by Congress?
4. Which term applies to the power of each branch of the federal government to limit the powers of the other two branches of the government?
5. Which term describes the powers that were set aside for the states?
6. Which term is used to describe the three-way division of the powers of the federal government?
7. Which term means a written change in the Constitution?
8. Which term describes the powers that are shared by the federal government and the state governments?

Check-Up

1. What are some of the powers granted to the federal government under the Constitution?
2. Name some of the powers set aside for the states under the Constitution of the United States?
3. What are some of the powers shared by the federal government and the state governments?
4. List the main responsibility of each branch of the federal government.
5. Why was a system of checks and balances included in the Constitution?
6. In what two ways may an amendment be proposed? In what two ways may an amendment be ratified?
7. Name three ways the Constitution and the government can adapt to the changing needs and conditions of the nation. Give an example of each type of change.
8. In what ways are the powers of the federal government limited? Do you think our government would work better without some of these limitations? Explain.

Civics Skills

Study the flow chart on page 42 of your textbook, and answer the following questions.

1. Who sets the "flow" of representative democracy in motion?
2. Which government officials are elected? Which are appointed?
3. On the basis of this flow chart, what conclusions can you draw about our American system of government?
4. If you were drawing a similar flow chart, what other steps might you include?

Citizenship and You

1. Collect articles from the newspaper that show examples of powers shared by your state and the federal government.
2. Make a chart and label each column with one of the six goals from the Preamble of the Constitution. Under each goal list current activities of the federal government that carry out that goal.

The Constitution of the United States

The parts of the text crossed out in blue have been changed by the passing of time or by later amendments. Explanations and comments are also in blue.

Preamble

We the people of the United States, in order to form a more perfect union, establish justice, insure domestic tranquillity, provide for the common defense, promote the general welfare, and secure the blessings of liberty to ourselves and our posterity, do ordain and establish this CONSTITUTION for the United States of America.

The **Preamble,** or introduction, to the Constitution states the purposes of the Constitution. It also makes clear that the government is established by consent of the governed. "We the people, . . . ordain and establish" the government.

By separating the functions of government among branches concerned with making laws (Article 1), executing laws (Article 2), and interpreting laws (Article 3), the writers of the Constitution were applying the principle of **separation of powers.** They were also developing a system of **checks and balances.** They hoped it would prevent any part of the federal government from becoming too powerful.

ARTICLE 1. Legislative Department

SECTION 1. Congress

All legislative powers herein granted shall be vested in a Congress of the United States, which shall consist of a Senate and a House of Representatives.

The power to make laws is given to Congress. Congress is made up of two houses—the Senate and the House of Representatives.

SECTION 2. House of Representatives

1. Election of Members and Term of Office. The House of Representatives shall be composed of members chosen every second year by the people of the several States, and the electors in each State shall have the qualifications requisite for electors of the most numerous branch of the State Legislature.

Members of the House of Representatives are chosen every two years. They are elected directly by the voters who are qualified to vote for members of their state legislatures.

2. Qualifications. No person shall be a Representative who shall not have attained to the age of twenty-five years, and been seven years a citizen of the United States, and who shall not, when elected, be an inhabitant of that State in which he shall be chosen.

Members of the House of Representatives must be at least 25 years old, United States citizens for at least 7 years, and residents of the states that they represent.

3. Division of Representatives and Direct Taxes Among the States. Representatives and direct taxes shall be apportioned among the several States which may be included within this Union, according to their respective numbers, which shall be determined by adding to the whole number of free persons, including those bound to service for a

The number of representatives for each state is based on its population.

A **census**, or count of the population, must be taken by the federal government every ten years.

term of years, and excluding Indians not taxed, three fifths of all other persons. The actual enumeration shall be made within three years after the first meeting of the Congress of the United States, and within every subsequent term of ten years, in such manner as they shall by law direct. The number of Representatives shall not exceed 1 for every 30,000, but each State shall have at least one Representative; and until such enumeration shall be made, the state of New Hampshire shall be entitled to choose three; Massachusetts, eight; Rhode Island and Providence Plantations, one; Connecticut, five; New York, six; New Jersey, four; Pennsylvania, eight; Delaware, one; Maryland, six; Virginia, ten; North Carolina, five; South Carolina, five; and Georgia, three.

Vacancies in the House of Representatives are filled by special elections called by the governor of the state.

4. Filling Vacancies. When vacancies happen in the representation from any State, the Executive authority thereof shall issue writs of election to fill such vacancies.

The House of Representatives has the power to choose its **Speaker**, or presiding officer, and other officers. It also has the power to **impeach**, or accuse, an official in the executive branch or a federal judge. The trial of the impeached official takes place in the Senate. (See Section 3, Clause 6.)

5. Officers; Impeachment. The House of Representatives shall choose their Speaker and other officers; and shall have the sole power of impeachment.

SECTION 3. Senate

In the Senate, each state is represented equally by two senators. [Amendment 17 provides for the direct election of senators.]

1. Number of Members and Term of Office. The Senate of the United States shall be composed of two Senators from each State, chosen by the Legislature thereof, for six years; and each Senator shall have one vote.

One third of the senators are elected every two years for a six-year term. As a result, the terms of senators overlap, making the Senate a "continuing" body.

Under Amendment 17, Senate vacancies are filled by new senators appointed by the governor of the state.

2. Classification; Filling Vacancies. Immediately after they shall be assembled in consequence of the first election, they shall be divided as equally as may be into three classes. The seats of the Senators of the first class shall be vacated at the expiration of the second year, of the second class at the expiration of the fourth year, and of the third class at the expiration of the sixth year, so that one third may be chosen every second year; and if vacancies happen by resignation, or otherwise, during the recess of the Legislature of any State, the executive thereof may make temporary appointments until the next meeting of the Legislature, which shall then fill such vacancies.

Senators must be at least 30 years old, United States citizens for at least 9 years, and residents of the states that they represent.

3. Qualifications of Members. No person shall be a Senator who shall not have attained to the age of thirty years, and been nine years a citizen of the United States, and who shall not, when elected, be an inhabitant of that State for which he shall be chosen.

The Vice President is the presiding officer of the Senate but may vote only in the case of a tie.

4. President of the Senate. The Vice President of the United States shall be President of the Senate, but shall have no vote, unless they be equally divided.

The Senate elects a temporary presiding officer from among its members. The **president *pro tempore*** serves when the Vice President is absent or becomes President.

5. Other Senate Officers. The Senate shall choose their other officers, and also a President *pro tempore,* in the absence of the Vice President, or when he shall exercise the office of President of the United States.

6. Trial of Impeachments. The Senate shall have the sole power to try all impeachments. When sitting for that purpose, they shall be on oath or affirmation. When the President of the United States is tried, the Chief Justice shall preside; and no person shall be convicted without the concurrence of two thirds of the members present.

The Senate has power to try impeachment cases. A two-thirds vote is needed to convict an impeached official.

7. Penalty for Conviction in Impeachment Cases. Judgment in cases of impeachment shall not extend further than to removal from office, and disqualification to hold and enjoy any office of honor, trust, or profit under the United States; but the party convicted shall nevertheless be liable and subject to indictment, trial, judgment, and punishment, according to law.

If the Senate convicts an impeached official, it can only punish the official so far as to remove him or her from office and disqualify him or her from holding office again. An official who has been impeached and convicted may also be tried in a court of law if he or she has broken the law.

SECTION 4. Both Houses

1. Holding Elections. The times, places, and manner of holding elections for Senators and Representatives shall be prescribed in each State by the Legislature thereof; but the Congress may at any time by law make or alter such regulations, except as to the place of choosing Senators.

Election regulations are set by the states. But Congress may pass laws overruling the state regulations.

2. Meetings. The Congress shall assemble at least once in every year, and such meeting shall be on the first Monday in December, unless they shall by law appoint a different day.

Congress must meet at least once a year. The meeting time of Congress was set by Amendment 20 at January 3.

SECTION 5. The Houses Separately

1. Organization. Each house shall be the judge of the elections, returns, and qualifications of its own members, and a majority of each shall constitute a quorum to do business; but a smaller number may adjourn from day to day, and may be authorized to compel the attendance of absent members, in such manner, and under such penalities, as each house may provide.

Each house of Congress decides whether its members are qualified and have been elected fairly. A **quorum,** or a majority of the members, must be present to carry on the work of each house. Members of either house of Congress may be compelled to attend in order that business may be carried on.

2. Proceedings. Each house may determine the rules of its proceedings, punish its members for disorderly behavior, and, with the concurrence of two thirds, expel a member.

Each house may establish rules for carrying on its business and may punish members who break these rules. In either house, a two-thirds vote is required to expel a member of that house.

3. Journal. Each house shall keep a journal of its proceedings, and from time to time publish the same, excepting such parts as may in their judgment require secrecy; and the yeas and nays of the members of either house on any question shall, at the desire of one fifth of those present, be entered on the journal.

Each house of Congress must keep and publish an official record of its activities. *The Congressional Record* is published every day that Congress is in session. It furnishes a daily account of what the members of Congress do and say.

4. Adjournment. Neither house, during the session of Congress, shall, without the consent of the other, adjourn for more than three days, nor to any other place than that in which the two houses shall be sitting.

The two houses of Congress must remain in session for the same period of time and in the same place.

SECTION 6. Privileges and Restrictions

1. Pay and Privileges. The Senators and Representatives shall receive a compensation for their services, to be ascertained by law, and paid out of the treasury of the United States. They shall in all cases, except

Members of Congress are paid salaries and receive additional sums of money for certain expenses.

Members of Congress cannot be sued or arrested for anything they say in Congress. But they can be arrested for major crimes while Congress is in session.

treason, felony, and breach of the peace, be privileged from arrest during their attendance at the session of their respective houses, and in going to and returning from the same; and for any speech or debate in either house they shall not be questioned in any other place.

Members of Congress cannot hold any other federal office while serving in Congress. Nor can members resign and then accept federal jobs that were created during their term in Congress.

2. Members Cannot Hold Other Offices. No Senator or Representative shall, during the time for which he was elected, be appointed to any civil office under the authority of the United States, which shall have been created, or the emoluments whereof shall have been increased, during such time; and no person holding any office under the United States shall be a member of either house during his continuance in office.

SECTION 7. Method of Passing Laws

Revenue, or money-raising, bills must begin in the House of Representatives. But the Senate can suggest changes in these bills.

1. Revenue Bills. All bills for raising revenue shall originate in the House of Representatives; but the Senate may propose or concur with amendments as on other bills.

A bill passed by Congress must be sent to the President. If the President approves and signs the bill, it becomes a law. If the President **vetoes**, or refuses to sign, the bill, it is returned to the house in which it started.

The President's veto may be overruled by a two-thirds vote of each house of Congress. The President can let a bill become a law without signing it by holding it for ten days (excluding Sundays) while Congress is in session. But a bill sent to the President during the last ten days of a session of Congress is rejected by a "pocket veto" if the President does not sign it.

2. How a Bill Becomes a Law. Every bill which shall have passed the House of Representatives and the Senate shall, before it becomes a law, be presented to the President of the United States; if he approve he shall sign it, but if not he shall return it with his objections to that house in which it shall have originated, who shall enter the objections at large on their journal, and proceed to reconsider it. If after such reconsideration two thirds of that house shall agree to pass the bill, it shall be sent together with the objections, to the other house, by which it shall likewise be reconsidered, and, if approved by two thirds of that house, it shall become a law. But in all such cases the votes of both houses shall be determined by yeas and nays, and the names of the persons voting for and against the bill shall be entered on the journal of each house respectively. If any bill shall not be returned by the President within ten days (Sundays excepted) after it shall have been presented to him, the same shall be a law, in like manner as if he had signed it, unless the Congress by their adjournment prevent its return, in which case it shall not be a law.

The President must sign or veto every resolution, except those on adjournment, passed by both houses.

3. Presidential Approval or Veto. Every order, resolution, or vote to which the concurrence of the Senate and House of Representatives may be necessary (except on a question of adjournment) shall be presented to the President of the United States; and, before the same shall take effect, shall be approved by him, or, being disapproved by him, shall be repassed by two thirds of the Senate and House of Representatives, according to the rules and limitations prescribed in the case of a bill.

SECTION 8. Powers Granted to Congress

The Congress shall have power,

The specific powers delegated, or granted, to Congress are:
to levy and collect uniform taxes in order to pay government debts and provide for the defense and general welfare of the nation.

1. To lay and collect taxes, duties, imposts, and excises, to pay the debts and provide for the common defense and general welfare of the United States; but all duties, imposts, and excises shall be uniform throughout the United States;

to borrow money

2. To borrow money on the credit of the United States;

3. To regulate commerce with foreign nations, and among the several states, and with the Indian tribes;

to regulate interstate and foreign commerce, or trade

4. To establish a uniform rule of naturalization, and uniform laws on the subject of bankruptcies throughout the United States;

to set up uniform laws concerning **naturalization**, or becoming a citizen, and concerning bankruptcy

5. To coin money, regulate the value thereof, and of foreign coin, and fix the standard of weights and measures;

to coin money and set standards of weights and measures

6. To provide for the punishment of counterfeiting the securities and current coin of the United States;

to provide for the punishment of counterfeiting

7. To establish post offices and post roads;

to establish post offices and post roads

8. To promote the progress of science and useful arts, by securing for limited times to authors and inventors the exclusive right to their respective writings and discoveries;

to issue patents and copyrights

9. To constitute tribunals inferior to the Supreme Court;

to set up a system of federal courts

10. To define and punish piracies and felonies committed on the high seas, and offences against the law of nations;

to define and punish piracy

11. To declare war, grant letters of marque and reprisal, and make rules concerning captures on land and water;

to declare war

12. To raise and support armies, but no appropriation of money to that use shall be for a longer term than two years;

to raise and support armies

13. To provide and maintain a navy;

to provide and maintain a navy

14. To make rules for the government and regulation of the land and naval forces;

to make rules and regulations for the armed forces

15. To provide for calling forth the militia to execute the laws of the Union, suppress insurrections, repel invasions;

to provide for calling out the **militia** (National Guard)

16. To provide for organizing, arming, and disciplining the militia, and for governing such part of them as may be employed in the service of the United States, reserving to the States respectively, the appointment of the officers, and the authority of training the militia according to the discipline prescribed by Congress.

to help states maintain their militias

17. To exercise exclusive legislation, in all cases whatsoever, over such district (not exceeding ten miles square) as may, by cession of particular States, and the acceptance of Congress, become the seat of the government of the United States; and to exercise like authority over all places purchased by the consent of the Legislature of the State in which the same shall be, for the erection of forts, magazines, arsenals, dock-yards, and other needful buildings; and

to establish and govern the nation's capital, the District of Columbia, and govern other federal property

18. To make all laws which shall be necessary and proper for carrying into execution the foregoing powers, and all other powers vested by this Constitution in the government of the United States, or in any department or officer therof.

to make all "necessary and proper" laws for carrying out the powers of the federal government. This clause is the **elastic clause** which allows Congress to take many actions not named in the Constitution.

SECTION 9. Powers Forbidden to the Federal Government

[Amendments 1 to 10 also directly or indirectly limit the powers of the federal government.]

The powers forbidden to Congress are:

[to interfere with the foreign slave trade before 1808]

1. The migration or importation of such persons as any of the States now existing shall think proper to admit, shall not be prohibited by the Congress prior to the year one thousand eight hundred and eight, but a tax or duty may be imposed on such importation, not exceeding ten dollars for each person.

to suspend the **writ of *habeas corpus*** except during emergencies. The guarantee of the writ of *habeas corpus* means that people may not be held in jail on little or no evidence.

2. The privilege of the writ of *habeas corpus* shall not be suspended, unless when in cases of rebellion or invasion the public safety may require it.

to pass **bills of attainder** or ***ex post facto*** laws. A bill of attainder is a law, passed by the legislature, that condemns and punishes a person without a jury trial. An *ex post facto* law is a law that punishes a person for doing something that was not illegal at the time it was done.

3. No bill of attainder or *ex post facto* law shall be passed.

to levy direct taxes except in proportion to population [See Amendment 16.]

4. No capitation or other direct tax shall be laid, unless in proportion to the census or enumeration herein before directed to be taken.

to tax exports

5. No tax or duty shall be laid on articles exported from any State.

to pass any laws that would favor the trade of a particular state

6. No preference shall be given by any regulation of commerce or revenue to the ports of one State over those of another; nor shall vessels bound to, or from, one State, be obliged to enter, clear, or pay duties in another.

to spend money without appropriating it by law. This clause is perhaps the single most important curb on the President's power. It prevents the President from using federal funds without the consent of Congress.

7. No money shall be drawn from the treasury, but in consequence of appropriations made by law; and a regular statement and account of the receipts and expenditures of all public money shall be published from time to time.

to grant or accept any title of nobility

8. No title of nobility shall be granted by the United States; and no person holding any office of profit or trust under them shall, without the consent of the Congress, accept of any present, emolument, office, or title, of any kind whatever, from any king, prince, or foreign state.

The powers forbidden to the states are:

SECTION 10. Powers Forbidden to the States

[Supplemented by Amendments 14 and 15]

to make treaties or alliances
to coin money
to pass a bill of attainder
to pass an *ex post facto* law
to pass a law excusing people from carrying out lawful obligations
to grant titles of nobility

1. No State shall enter into any treaty, alliance,or confederation; grant letters of marque and reprisal; coin money; emit bills of credit; make anything but gold and silver coin a tender in payment of debts; pass any bill of attainder, *ex post facto* law, or law impairing the obligation of contracts; or grant any title of nobility.

to levy taxes or tariffs on goods sent into or out of the state without permission of Congress

2. No State shall, without the consent of the Congress, lay any imposts or duties on imports or exports, except what may be absolutely necessary for executing its inspection laws; and the net produce of all duties and imposts, laid by any State on imports and exports, shall be for the use of the treasury of the United States; and all such laws shall be subject to the revision and control of the Congress.

3. No State shall, without the consent of Congress, lay any duty of tonnage, keep troops or ships of war in time of peace, enter into any agreement or compact with another State, or with a foreign power, or engage in war, unless actually invaded, or in such imminent danger as will not admit of delay.

to keep troops or warships in peacetime or deal with another state or a foreign nation without consent of Congress or engage in war unless invaded

ARTICLE 2. Executive Department

SECTION 1. President; Vice President

1. Term of Office. The executive power shall be vested in a President of the United States of America. He shall hold his office during the term of four years, and, together with the Vice President, chosen for the same term, be elected as follows:

Executive power is given to the President, who holds office for a four-year term.

2. The Electoral System. Each State shall appoint, in such manner as the Legislature thereof may direct, a number of Electors equal to the whole number of Senators and Representatives to which the State may be entitled in the Congress; but no Senator or Representative, or person holding an office of trust or profit under the United States shall be appointed an Elector.

The President and Vice President are elected by **electors,** or members of the **Electoral College,** chosen by the voters. Each state is entitled to the number of electors equal to the number of its senators and representatives.

3. A Discarded Way of Using the Electoral System. The Electors shall meet in their respective States, and vote by ballot for two persons, of whom one at least shall not be an inhabitant of the same State with themselves. And they shall make a list of all the persons voted for, and of the number of votes for each; which list they shall sign and certify, and transmit sealed to the seat of the government of the United States, directed to the President of the Senate. The President of the Senate shall, in the presence of the Senate and House of Representatives, open all the certificates, and the votes shall then be counted. The person having the greatest number of votes shall be the President, if such number be a majority of the whole number of Electors appointed; and if there be more than one who have such majority, and have an equal number of votes, then the House of Representatives shall immediately choose by ballot one of them for President; and if no person have a majority, then from the five highest on the list the said house shall in like manner choose the President. But in choosing the President, the votes shall be taken by States, the representation from each State having one vote; a quorum for this purpose shall consist of a member or members from two thirds of the States, and a majority of all the States shall be necessary to a choice. In every case, after the choice of the President, the person having the greatest number of votes of the Electors shall be the Vice President. But if there should remain two or more who have equal votes, the Senate shall choose from them by ballot the Vice President.

This procedure for electing the President and Vice President was changed by Amendment 12.

4. Time of Elections. Congress may determine the time of choosing the Electors, and the day on which they shall give their votes; which day shall be the same throughout the United States.

Today, Presidential elections are held on the first Tuesday after the first Monday in November. Electoral votes are cast on the first Monday after the second Wednesday in December.

The President must be a natural-born citizen of the United States, at least 35 years old, and a resident of the United States for at least 14 years.

5. Qualifications for the President. No person except a natural-born citizen, or a citizen of the United States at the time of the adoption of this Constitution, shall be eligible to the office of President; neither shall any person be eligible to that office who shall not have attained to the age of thirty-five years, and been fourteen years a resident within the United States.

If the President dies, or for any reason cannot carry out the duties of office, the Vice President will act as President. In the event that both officials are unable to serve, Congress has declared that the order of succession is as follows: (1) Speaker of the House, (2) President *pro tempore* of the Senate, and (3) the Cabinet members in the order in which their offices were created. [See Amendment 25 also.]

6. Filling Vacancies. In case of the removal of the President from office, or of his death, resignation, or inability to discharge the power and duties of the said office, the same shall devolve on the Vice President, and the Congress may by law provide for the case of removal, death, resignation, or inability, both of the President and Vice President, declaring what officer shall then act as President, and such officer shall act accordingly, until the disability be removed, or a President shall be elected.

The President receives a salary, the amount of which may not be changed during the term of office.

7. Salary. The President shall, at stated times, receive for his services a compensation, which shall neither be increased nor diminished during the period for which he shall have been elected, and he shall not receive within that period any other emolument from the United States, or any of them.

The President takes an oath of office, or is sworn in, before beginning the duties as **Chief Executive**.

8. Oath of Office. Before he enter on the execution of his office, he shall take the following oath or affirmation:—"I do solemnly swear (or affirm) that I will faithfully execute the office of President of the United States, and will, to the best of my ability, preserve, protect, and defend the Constitution of the United States."

SECTION 2. Powers of the President

The President is **Commander in Chief** of the armed forces.

The head of each executive department is, in practice, a member of the President's **Cabinet**.

The President may grant pardons for offenses against the United States, except in cases of impeachment.

1. Military Powers. The President shall be Commander in Chief of the army and navy of the United States, and of the militia of the several States, when called into the actual service of the United States; he may require the opinion, in writing, of the principal officer in each of the executive departments, upon any subject relating to the duties of their respective offices, and he shall have power to grant reprieves and pardons for offences against the United States, except in cases of impeachment.

The President has the power to make treaties and to appoint such officers as ambassadors, federal judges, and Presidential advisers provided that the Senate approves them.

2. Treaty-making Power; Power of Appointment. He shall have power, by and with the advice and consent of the Senate, to make treaties, provided two thirds of the Senators present concur; and he shall nominate, and, by and with the advice and consent of the Senate, shall appoint ambassadors, other public ministers, and consuls, judges of the Supreme Court, and all other officers of the United States, whose appointments are not herein otherwise provided for, and which shall be established by law; but the Congress may by law vest the appointment of such inferior officers, as they think proper, in the President alone, in the courts of law, or in the heads of departments.

The President may appoint officials to fill vacancies temporarily without the consent of the Senate if Congress is not in session.

3. Filling Vacancies. The President shall have power to fill up all vacancies that may happen during the recess of the Senate, by granting commissions which shall expire at the end of their next session.

SECTION 3. Duties of the President

He shall from time to time give to the Congress information of the state of the Union, and recommend to their consideration such measures as he shall judge necessary and expedient; he may, on extraordinary occasions, convene both houses, or either of them, and in case of disagreement between them, with respect to the time of adjournment, he may adjourn them to such time as he shall think proper; he shall receive ambassadors and other public ministers; he shall take care that the laws be faithfully executed, and shall commission all the officers of the United States.

The President is required to send or to read a report on the state of the Union—the condition of the nation—at the opening of each session of Congress. The President also sends special messages to Congress.

The President may call special sessions of Congress.

The President is required to receive ambassadors, to make sure that the laws of the nation are carried out, and to sign papers that give officers in the armed forces the right to hold their positions.

SECTION 4. Impeachment

The President, Vice President, and all civil officers of the United States, shall be removed from office on impeachment for, and conviction of, treason, bribery, or other high crimes and misdemeanors.

The President and all civil officers may be removed from office if impeached and convicted of treason, bribery, or other high crimes. [See Article 1, Section 3, clauses 6 and 7 also.]

ARTICLE 3. Judicial Department

SECTION 1. Federal Courts

The Supreme Court and Lower Federal Courts. The judicial power of the United States shall be vested in one Supreme Court, and in such inferior courts as the Congress may from time to time ordain and establish. The judges, both of the Supreme and inferior courts, shall hold their offices during good behavior, and shall, at stated times, receive for their services a compensation, which shall not be diminished during their continuance in office.

Judicial power is given to a Supreme Court and lower federal courts established by Congress.

Federal judges hold office for life. But they may be removed by impeachment.

SECTION 2. Jurisdiction of the Federal Courts

1. General Jurisdiction. The judicial power shall extend to all cases, in law and equity, arising under this Constitution, the laws of the United States, and treaties made, or which shall be made, under their authority; to all cases affecting ambassadors, other public ministers and consuls; to all cases of admiralty and maritime jurisdiction; to controversies to which the United States shall be a party; to controversies between two or more States, between a State and citizens of another State [see Amendment 11], between citizens of different States, between citizens of the same State claiming lands under grants of different States, and between a State, or the citizens thereof, and foreign states, citizens, or subjects.

Federal courts may try cases involving the Constitution, federal laws, treaties, and laws relating to ships on the high seas and navigable waters. They may also try cases involving the United States government itself, foreign diplomatic officials, two or more state governments, citizens of different states, and a state or its citizens versus foreign countries or citizens of foreign countries.

2. The Supreme Court. In all cases affecting ambassadors, other public ministers, and consuls, and those in which a State shall be party, the Supreme Court shall have original jurisdiction. In all the other cases before mentioned, the Supreme Court shall have appellate jurisdiction, both as to law and fact, with such exceptions, and under such regulations, as the Congress shall make.

Cases involving ambassadors or officials of foreign nations and cases involving states are tried in the Supreme Court. Other cases begin in lower courts but may be appealed to the Supreme Court.

3. Conduct of Trials. The trial of all crimes, except in cases of impeachment, shall be by jury; and such trial shall be held in the

Every person accused of a federal crime, except someone undergoing impeachment, is guaranteed a jury trial in the state where the crime took place.

State where the said crimes shall have been committed, but when not committed within any State, the trial shall be at such place or places as the Congress may by law have directed. [Expanded by Amendments 5, 6, and 7.]

SECTION 3. Treason

Treason is carefully defined as waging war against our nation or helping its enemies. A person cannot be convicted of treason without the testimony of two witnesses to the same act, unless the person confesses in court.

1. Definition. Treason against the United States shall consist only in levying war against them, or in adhering to their enemies, giving them aid and comfort. No person shall be convicted of treason unless on the testimony of two witnesses to the same overt act, or on confession in open court.

Punishment for treason is determined by Congress and may not extend to the family of the convicted person.

2. Punishment. The Congress shall have power to declare the punishment of treason, but no attainder of treason shall work corruption of blood, or forfeiture, except during the life of the person attainted.

ARTICLE 4. Relation of the States to Each Other

SECTION 1. Official Acts

All states are required to honor each other's laws, records, and legal decisions.

Full faith and credit shall be given in each State to the public acts, records, and judicial proceedings of every other State. And the Congress may by general laws prescribe the manner in which such acts, records, and proceedings shall be proved, and the effect thereof.

SECTION 2. Privileges of Citizens

Each state must treat citizens of other states as it treats its own citizens.

1. Privileges. The citizens of each State shall be entitled to all privileges and immunities of citizens in the several States.

An accused person who flees to another state must be **extradited,** or returned, to the state in which the crime was committed. However, the governor of a state cannot be forced to extradite a prisoner if the governor feels that such action will result in injustice to the accused person.

2. Fugitive Criminals. A person charged in any State with treason, felony, or other crime, who shall flee from justice, and be found in another State, shall, on demand of the executive authority of the State from which he fled, be delivered up, to be removed to the State having jurisdiction of the crime.

This provision for fugitive slaves was in effect until 1865, when Amendment 13 abolished the institution of slavery.

3. Fugitive Slaves. No person held to service or labor in one State, under the laws thereof, escaping into another, shall in consequence of any law or regulation therein, be discharged from such service or labor, but shall be delivered up on claim of the party to whom such service or labor may be due.

SECTION 3. New States and Territories

New states may not be formed by dividing or joining existing states without the consent of the state legislatures and Congress. New states may be admitted into the Union by Congress.

1. Admission of New States. New States may be admitted by the Congress into this Union; but no new State shall be formed or erected within the jurisdiction of any other State; nor any State be formed by the junction of two or more States, or parts of States, without the consent of the Legislatures of the States concerned, as well as of the Congress.

Congress has power to make laws for the territories and for federal property.

2. Powers of Congress Over Territories and Other Property. The Congress shall have power to dispose of and make all needful rules and regulations respecting the territory or other property belonging to the United States; and nothing in this Constitution shall be so construed as to prejudice any claims of the United States, or of any particular State.

SECTION 4. Guarantees and Protection for the States

The United States shall guarantee to every State in this Union a republican form of government, and shall protect each of them against invasion; and on application of the Legislature, or of the Executive (when the Legislature can not be convened), against domestic violence.

Each state is guaranteed a republican form of government; that is, government by representatives of the people. The federal government must protect the states against foreign attack or violence within their borders.

ARTICLE 5. How Amendments Are Made

The Congress, whenever two thirds of both houses shall deem it necessary, shall propose amendments to this Constitution, or, on the application of the Legislature of two thirds of the several States, shall call a convention for proposing amendments, which, in either case, shall be valid to all intents and purposes, as part of this Constitution, when ratified by the Legislatures of three fourths of the several States, or by conventions in three fourths thereof, as the one or the other mode of ratification may be proposed by the Congress; provided that no amendment which may be made prior to the year one thousand eight hundred and eight shall in any manner affect the first and fourth clauses in the ninth section of the first article; and that no State, without its consent, shall be deprived of its equal suffrage in the Senate.

Amendments may be proposed by a two-thirds vote of each house of Congress or by a national convention at the request of two thirds of the states. Amendments may be **ratified,** or approved, by the legislatures of three fourths of the states, or by conventions in three fourths of the states.

No amendment may deprive a state of its equal vote in the Senate.

ARTICLE 6. General Provisions

1. Public Debt. All debts contracted and engagements entered into, before the adoption of this Constitution, shall be as valid against the United States under this Constitution as under the Confederation.

The federal government will honor all debts and contracts of the United States made before the adoption of this Constitution.

2. The Supreme Law. This Constitution, and the laws of the United States which shall be made in pursuance thereof, and all treaties made, or which shall be made, under the authority of the United States, shall be the supreme law of the land; and the judges in every State shall be bound thereby, anything in the constitution or laws of any State to the contrary notwithstanding.

The Constitution, federal laws, and treaties of the United States are the supreme law of the nation. No state or local laws may conflict with them.

3. Oaths of Office. The Senators and Representatives before mentioned, and the members of the several State Legislatures, and all executive and judicial officers, both of the United States and of the several States, shall be bound by oath or affirmation to support this Constitution; but no religious test shall ever be required as a qualification to any office or public trust under the United States.

All federal and state officials must promise to support the Constitution.

Religion may not be a qualification for federal office.

ARTICLE 7. Ratification

The Constitution was to become the law of the nation when it was ratified, or approved, by nine states.

The ratification of the conventions of nine States shall be sufficient for the establishment of this Constitution between the States so ratifying the same.

DONE in Convention, by the unanimous consent of the States present, the seventeenth day of September, in the year of our Lord one thousand seven hundred and eighty-seven, and of the Independence of the United States of America the twelfth. *In Witness* whereof we have hereunto subscribed our names.

(Signed by) *G. Washington,*
PRESIDENT AND DEPUTY FROM VIRGINIA

NEW HAMPSHIRE

John Langdon
Nicholas Gilman

NEW YORK

Alexander Hamilton

NEW JERSEY

William Livingston
David Brearley
William Paterson
Jonathan Dayton

MARYLAND

James McHenry
Daniel of St. Thomas Jenifer
Daniel Carroll

VIRGINIA

John Blair
James Madison

MASSACHUSETTS

Nathaniel Gorham
Rufus King

DELAWARE

George Read
Gunning Bedford
John Dickinson
Richard Bassett
Jacob Broom

SOUTH CAROLINA

John Rutledge
Charles Cotesworth Pinckney
Charles Pinckney
Pierce Butler

CONNECTICUT

William Samuel Johnson
Roger Sherman

PENNSYLVANIA

Benjamin Franklin
Thomas Mifflin
Robert Morris
George Clymer
Thomas FitzSimons
Jared Ingersoll
James Wilson
Gouverneur Morris

NORTH CAROLINA

William Blount
Richard Dobbs Spaight
Hugh Williamson

GEORGIA

William Few
Abraham Baldwin

Attest: William Jackson,
SECRETARY

Amendments to the Constitution

The first ten amendments to the Constitution are called the **Bill of Rights.** The Bill of Rights limits the powers of the federal government and protects the rights of the people.
The date in parentheses is the year in which ratification of each amendment was completed and in which the amendment was therefore adopted.

AMENDMENT 1. Freedom of Religion, Speech, Press, Assembly, and Petition (1791)

Congress shall make no law respecting an establishment of religion, or prohibiting the free exercise thereof; or abridging the freedom of speech, or of the press, or the right of the people peaceably to assemble, and to petition the government for a redress of grievances.

Congress may not set up an official church nor pass laws that limit freedom of religion, speech, the press, assembly, and the right to petition.

AMENDMENT 2. Right to Keep Arms (1791)

A well regulated militia being necessary to the security of a free state, the right of the people to keep and bear arms shall not be infringed.

The right of states to have a militia (National Guard) is guaranteed. The right of citizens to keep weapons to resist a tyrannical government is also protected.

AMENDMENT 3. Quartering of Soldiers (1791)

No soldier shall, in time of peace, be quartered in any house, without the consent of the owner, nor in time of war, but in a manner to be prescribed by law.

In peacetime, troops may not take over private houses.

AMENDMENT 4. Search and Seizure; Warrants (1791)

The right of the people to be secure in their persons, houses, papers, and effects, against unreasonable searches and seizures, shall not be violated, and no warrant shall issue but upon probable cause, supported by oath or affirmation, and particularly describing the place to be searched, and the persons or things to be seized.

The government is limited in its right to search and take custody of persons and property. A **search warrant** can only be issued by a judge if there is a good reason for its use and if it describes the place to be searched and the persons or property to be seized.

AMENDMENT 5. Rights of Persons Accused of Crime (1791)

No person shall be held to answer for a capital, or otherwise infamous crime, unless on a presentment or indictment of a grand jury, except in cases arising in the land or naval forces, or in the militia, when in actual service in time of war or public danger; nor shall any person be subject for the same offense to be twice put in jeopardy of life or limb; nor shall be compelled in any criminal case to be a witness against himself, nor be deprived of life, liberty, or property, without due process of law; nor shall private property be taken for public use without just compensation.

A person cannot be tried for an important crime unless first **indicted,** or accused, by a grand jury. An accused person cannot be tried twice for the same crime nor forced to testify against himself or herself. No person can be deprived of life, liberty, or property except by lawful means. The government cannot take private property for public use without paying a fair price for it.

AMENDMENT 6. Right to Speedy Trial (1791)

An accused person is entitled to a speedy, public trial by a jury in the state where the crime was committed. The accused person must be told of the charge against him or her and is entitled to have a defense lawyer. The accused person has the right to question anyone who gives testimony against him or her and to call defense witnesses.

In all criminal prosecutions, the accused shall enjoy the right to a speedy and public trial, by an impartial jury of the State and district wherein the crime shall have been committed, which district shall have been previously ascertained by law, and to be informed of the nature and cause of the accusation; to be confronted with the witnesses against him; to have compulsory process for obtaining witnesses in his favor, and to have the assistance of counsel for his defense.

AMENDMENT 7. Jury Trial in Civil Cases (1791)

A jury trial in civil cases is guaranteed when the matter amounts to more than $20.

In suits at common law, where the value in controversy shall exceed twenty dollars, the right of trial by jury shall be preserved, and no fact tried by a jury shall be otherwise reexamined in any court of the United States, than according to the rules of the common law.

AMENDMENT 8. Excessive Bail or Punishment (1791)

Bails, fines, and punishments must not be unreasonable.

Excessive bail shall not be required, nor excessive fines imposed, nor cruel and unusual punishments inflicted.

AMENDMENT 9. Powers Reserved to the People (1791)

The listing of these rights guaranteed in the Constitution does not mean that these are the only basic rights. Nor does it mean that other basic rights may be restricted.

The enumeration in the Constitution of certain rights shall not be construed to deny or disparage others retained by the people.

AMENDMENT 10. Powers Reserved to the States (1791)

All powers not given to the federal government nor denied to the states are left to the states and to the people.

The powers not delegated to the United States by the Constitution, nor prohibited by it to the States, are reserved to the States respectively, or to the people.

AMENDMENT 11. Suits Against States (1798)

Any suit brought against a state by a citizen of another state or of a foreign country must be tried in the courts of the state that is being sued and not in a federal court.

The judicial power of the United States shall not be construed to extend to any suit in law or equity, commenced or prosecuted against one of the United States by citizens of another State, or by citizens or subjects of any foreign state.

AMENDMENT 12. Election of President and Vice President (1804)

This amendment changes Article 2, Section 1, Clause 3. Before this amendment, the electors (members of the Electoral College) voted for two persons without specifying which person was to be President and which Vice President.

The Electors shall meet in their respective States, and vote by ballot for President and Vice President, one of whom, at least, shall not be an inhabitant of the same State with themselves; they shall name in their ballots the person voted for as President, and in distinct ballots the person voted for as Vice President; and they shall make distinct lists of all persons voted for as President, and of all persons voted for as Vice President, and of the number of votes for each, which lists they shall sign and certify, and transmit sealed to the seat of the government of the United States, directed to the President of the Senate;—the President of the Senate shall, in the presence of the Senate and House of Representatives, open all the certificates, and the votes shall then be counted;—the person having the greatest number of votes for President shall be the President, if such number be a majority of the whole number of Electors appointed; and if no person have such majority, then from the persons having the highest numbers not exceeding three on the list of those voted for as President, the House of Representatives shall choose immediately, by ballot, the President. But in choosing the President, the votes shall be taken by States, the representation from each State having one vote; a quorum for this purpose shall consist of a member or members from two thirds of the States, and a majority of all the States shall be necessary to a choice. ~~And if the House of Representatives shall not choose a President, whenever the right of choice shall devolve upon them, before the fourth day of March next following, then the Vice President shall act as President, as in the case of the death or other constitutional disability of the President.~~ [See Amendment 20.] The person having the greatest number of votes as Vice President shall be the Vice President, if such number be a majority of the whole number of Electors appointed, and if no person have a majority, then from the two highest numbers on the list the Senate shall choose the Vice President; a quorum for the purpose shall consist of two thirds of the whole number of Senators, and a majority of the whole number shall be necessary to a choice. But no person constitutionally ineligible to the office of President shall be eligible to that of Vice President of the United States.

The candidate receiving the majority of electoral votes became President; the person with the next largest number became Vice President. In the election of 1800, there was a tie. Amendment 12 was established to prevent such situations. It instructs electors to cast separate ballots for President and for Vice President.

AMENDMENT 13. Slavery Abolished (1865)

SECTION 1.

Neither slavery nor involuntary servitude, except as a punishment for crime whereof the party shall have been duly convicted, shall exist within the United States, or any place subject to their jurisdiction.

Slavery is abolished.

SECTION 2.

Congress shall have power to enforce this article by appropriate legislation.

AMENDMENT 14. Rights of Citizens (1868)

SECTION 1. Citizenship Defined

All persons born or naturalized in the United States, and subject to the jurisdiction thereof, are citizens of the United States and of the State wherein they reside. No State shall make or enforce any law which shall abridge the privileges or immunities of citizens of the United States; nor shall any State deprive any person of life, liberty, or property, without due process of law; nor deny to any person within its jurisdiction the equal protection of the laws.

Citizenship is given to black Americans. The states are forbidden to deny equal privileges and protection by law to any citizen. In effect, the basic protections of the Bill of Rights apply to state governments as well as to the federal government.

SECTION 2. Apportionment of Representatives

A state's representation in Congress may be reduced if the state denies the right to vote to any eligible [adult male] citizen.

Representatives shall be apportioned among the several States according to their respective numbers, counting the whole number of persons in each State, excluding Indians not taxed. But when the right to vote at any election for the choice of electors for President and Vice President of the United States, Representatives in Congress, the executive and judicial officers of a State, or the members of the Legislature thereof, is denied to any of the male inhabitants of such State, being twenty-one years of age and citizens of the United States, or in any way abridged, except for participation in rebellion or other crime, the basis of representation therein shall be reduced in the proportion which the number of such male citizens shall bear to the whole number of male citizens twenty-one years of age in such State.

SECTION 3. Disability for Engaging in Insurrection

Certain former officials of the Confederate states were barred from holding public office.

No person shall be a Senator or Representative in Congress, or Elector of President and Vice President, or hold any office, civil or military, under the United States, or under any State, who, having previously taken an oath, as a member of Congress, or as an officer of the United States, or as a member of any State Legislature, or as an executive or judicial officer of any State, to support the Constitution of the United States, shall have engaged in insurrection or rebellion against the same, or given aid or comfort to the enemies thereof. But Congress may, by a vote of two thirds of each house, remove such disability.

SECTION 4. Public Debt

All debts of the federal government connected with the Civil War are to be paid. All debts of the Confederate states are declared illegal and will not be paid by the federal government. No payment will be made for the loss of former slaves.

The validity of the public debt of the United States, authorized by law, including debts incurred for payment of pensions and bounties for services in suppressing insurrection or rebellion, shall not be questioned. But neither the United States, nor any State shall assume or pay any debt or obligation incurred in aid of insurrection or rebellion against the United States, or any claim for the loss or emancipation of any slave; but all such debts, obligations, and claims shall be held illegal and void.

SECTION 5. Enforcement

The Congress shall have power to enforce, by appropriate legislation, the provisions of this article.

AMENDMENT 15. Right of Suffrage (1870)

SECTION 1.

Citizens cannot be denied the right to vote because of their race or color, or because they were formerly slaves.

The right of citizens of the United States to vote shall not be denied or abridged by the United States, or by any State, on account of race, color, or previous condition of servitude.

SECTION 2.

The Congress shall have power to enforce this article by appropriate legislation.

AMENDMENT 16. Taxes on Income (1913)

The Congress shall have power to lay and collect taxes on incomes, from whatever source derived, without apportionment among the several States, and without regard to any census or enumeration.

Congress is given the power to pass a law taxing personal incomes. [This amendment changes Article 1, Section 9, Clause 4.]

AMENDMENT 17. Election of Senators (1913)

SECTION 1.

The Senate of the United States shall be composed of two Senators from each State, elected by the people thereof, for six years; and each Senator shall have one vote. The electors in each State shall have the qualifications requisite for electors of the most numerous branch of the State legislatures.

Senators are to be elected by the voters of each state. [This amendment changes Article 1, Section 3, Clause 1, under which senators were elected by state legislatures.]

SECTION 2.

When vacancies happen in the representation of any State in the Senate, the executive authority of such State shall issue writs of election to fill such vacancies. Provided, that the Legislature of any State may empower the executive thereof to make temporary appointment until the people fill the vacancies by election as the Legislature may direct.

A vacancy in the Senate may be filled by a special election. Or the governor of the state may be given the power by the state legislature to appoint someone temporarily to fill the vacancy.

SECTION 3.

This amendment shall not be so construed as to affect the election or term of any Senator chosen before it becomes valid as part of the Constitution.

AMENDMENT 18. National Prohibition (1919)

SECTION 1.

After one year from the ratification of this article the manufacture, sale, or transportation of intoxicating liquors within, the importation thereof into, or the exportation thereof from the United States and all territory subject to the jurisdiction thereof, for beverage purposes is hereby prohibited.

The making, sale, and transportation of alcoholic beverages in the United States are prohibited. [This amendment was repealed by Amendment 21.]

SECTION 2.

The Congress and the several States shall have concurrent power to enforce this article by appropriate legislation.

SECTION 3.

This article shall be inoperative unless it shall have been ratified as an amendment to the Constitution by the Legislatures of the several States as provided in the Constitution within seven years from the date of the submission hereof to the States by the Congress.

AMENDMENT 19. Woman's Suffrage (1920)

SECTION 1.

The right of women to vote is guaranteed.

The right of citizens of the United States to vote shall not be denied or abridged by the United States or by any State on account of sex.

SECTION 2.

Congress shall have power to enforce this article by appropriate legislation.

AMENDMENT 20. "Lame Duck" Amendment (1933)

SECTION 1. Beginning of Terms of Office

A defeated candidate who holds office after his or her replacement has been elected has little influence and therefore is called a "lame duck." This amendment shortens the time in office of "lame ducks." The President and Vice President are to take office on January 20 (instead of March 4). Members of Congress are to take office January 3. (Previously, new members of Congress had to wait 13 months before taking their seats.)

The terms of the President and Vice President shall end at noon on the 20th day of January, and the terms of Senators and Representatives at noon on the 3d day of January, of the years in which such terms would have ended if this article had not been ratified; and the terms of their successors shall then begin.

SECTION 2. Beginning of Congressional Sessions

Congress is to meet at least once a year.

The Congress shall assemble at least once in every year, and such meeting shall begin at noon on the 3d day of January, unless they shall by law appoint a different day.

SECTION 3. Presidential Succession

If the President-elect should die before January 20 or fail to qualify, the office of President is to be filled temporarily by the Vice President.

If, at the time fixed for the beginning of the term of the President, the President-elect shall have died, the Vice President-elect shall become President. If a President shall not have been chosen before the time fixed for the beginning of his term, or if the President-elect shall have failed to qualify, then the Vice President-elect shall act as President until a President shall have qualified; and the Congress may by law provide for the case wherein neither a President-elect nor a Vice President-elect shall have qualified, declaring who shall then act as President, or the manner in which one who is to act shall be selected, and such person shall act accordingly until a President or Vice President shall have qualified.

SECTION 4. Filling Presidential Vacancy

This amendment gives Congress the power to decide what to do in the event a Presidential candidate dies when the election must be decided by the House. Congress may also make a determination in similar cases when a candidate dies and the Senate must elect a Vice President.

The Congress may by law provide for the case of the death of any of the persons from whom the House of Representatives may choose a President whenever the right of choice shall have devolved upon them, and for the case of the death of any of the persons from whom the Senate may choose a Vice President whenever the right of choice shall have devolved upon them.

SECTION 5. Effective Date

Sections 1 and 2 shall take effect on the 15th day of October following the ratification of this article.

SECTION 6. Limit on Time for Ratification

This article shall be inoperative unless it shall have been ratified as an amendment to the Constitution by the Legislatures of three fourths of the several States within seven years from the date of its submission.

AMENDMENT 21. National Prohibition Repealed (1933)

SECTION 1.

The eighteenth article of amendment to the Constitution of the United States is hereby repealed.

Amendment 18 is repealed.

SECTION 2.

The transportation or importation into any State, Territory, or possession of the United States for delivery or use therein of intoxicating liquors, in violation of the laws thereof, is hereby prohibited.

States may prohibit the sale of alcoholic beverages.

SECTION 3.

This article shall be inoperative unless it shall have been ratified as an amendment to the Constitution by conventions in the several States, as provided in the Constitution, within seven years from the date of the submission hereof to the States by Congress.

AMENDMENT 22. Two-Term Limit for Presidents (1951)

SECTION 1.

No person shall be elected to the office of the President more than twice, and no person who has held the office of President, or acted as President, for more than two years of a term to which some other person was elected President, shall be elected to the office of the President more than once. But this article shall not apply to any person holding the office of President when this article was proposed by the Congress, and shall not prevent any person who may be holding the office of President, or acting as President, during the term within which this article becomes operative from holding the office of President, or acting as President, during the remainder of such term.

A President is limited to two full terms in office. If a Vice President has already served more than two years as President, this person may be elected President only once.

This amendment did not apply to Harry Truman, who was President when the amendment was proposed.

SECTION 2.

This article shall be inoperative unless it shall have been ratified as an amendment to the Constitution by the Legislatures of three fourths of the several States within seven years from the date of its submission to the States by the Congress.

AMENDMENT 23. Presidential Electors for District of Columbia (1961)

SECTION 1.

The District constituting the seat of Government of the United States shall appoint in such manner as Congress may direct: A num-

Residents of Washington, D.C., are given the right to vote for President and

Vice President. In effect, this amendment gives the District of Columbia three electoral votes.

ber of Electors of President and Vice President equal to the whole number of Senators and Representatives in Congress to which the District would be entitled if it were a State, but in no event more than the least populous State; they shall be in addition to those appointed by the States, but they shall be considered, for the purposes of the election of President and Vice President, to be Electors appointed by a State; and they shall meet in the District and perform such duties as provided by the twelfth article of amendment.

SECTION 2.

The Congress shall have power to enforce this article by appropriate legislation.

AMENDMENT 24. Prohibition of Poll Taxes for National Elections (1964)

SECTION 1.

A poll tax may not be a requirement for voting for federal officials. In 1966 the Supreme Court ruled that poll taxes were also illegal as a requirement for voting in state and local elections.

The right of citizens of the United States to vote in any primary or other election for President or Vice President, for Electors for President or Vice President, or for Senator or Representative in Congress, shall not be denied or abridged by the United States or any State by reason of failure to pay any poll tax or other tax.

SECTION 2.

The Congress shall have power to enforce this article by appropriate legislation.

AMENDMENT 25. Presidential Disability and Succession (1967)

SECTION 1. Filling the Empty Office of President

If a President dies or resigns from office, the Vice President becomes President.

In case of the removal of the President from office by his death or resignation, the Vice President shall become President.

SECTION 2. Filling the Empty Office of Vice President

If the office of Vice President becomes empty, the President may appoint someone to fill this office. The appointment must be approved by a majority vote in both houses of Congress.

Whenever there is a vacancy in the office of the Vice President, the President shall nominate a Vice President who shall take the office upon confirmation by a majority vote of both houses of Congress.

SECTION 3. When the Vice President Acts as President

If the President feels unable to carry out the duties of office, the President is to notify Congress in a written message. The Vice President takes over as Acting President until the President is again able to carry out the duties of office.

Whenever the President transmits to the President *pro tempore* of the Senate and the Speaker of the House of Representatives his written declaration that he is unable to discharge the powers and duties of his office, and until he transmits them a written declaration to the contrary, such powers and duties shall be discharged by the Vice President as Acting President.

SECTION 4. When Congress Decides Who Shall Be President

If the Vice President and a majority of the Cabinet members feel the President

Whenever the Vice President and a majority of either the principal officers of the executive departments, or of such other body as Congress may by law provide, transmit to the President *pro tempore* of the Senate and the Speaker of the House of Representatives their written declaration that the President is unable to discharge the powers and duties of his office, the Vice President shall immediately assume the powers and duties of the office as Acting President.

is unable to carry out the duties of office, they are to notify Congress in a written message. The Vice President then takes over as Acting President.

Thereafter, when the President transmits to the President *pro tempore* of the Senate and the Speaker of the House of Representatives his written declaration that no inability exists, he shall resume the powers and duties of his office unless the Vice President and a majority of either the principal officers of the executive departments, or of such other body as Congress may by law provide, transmit within four days to the President *pro tempore* of the Senate and the Speaker of the House of Representatives their written declaration that the President is unable to discharge the powers and duties of his office. Thereupon Congress shall decide the issue, assembling within 48 hours for that purpose if not in session. If the Congress, within 21 days after receipt of the latter written declaration, or, if Congress is not in session, within 21 days after Congress is required to assemble, determines by two-thirds vote of both houses that the President is unable to discharge the powers and duties of his office, the Vice President shall continue to discharge the same as Acting President; otherwise, the President shall assume the powers and duties of his office.

When the President feels ready to carry out the duties again, the President may notify Congress. But if the Vice President and a majority of the Cabinet members do not agree, then Congress must decide who is President by a two-thirds vote within 21 days.

AMENDMENT 26. Voting Age Lowered to 18 (1971)

SECTION 1.

The right of citizens of the United States, who are 18 years of age or older, to vote shall not be denied or abridged by the United States or any state on account of age.

The minimum voting age is lowered to 18 in all federal, state, and local elections.

SECTION 2.

The Congress shall have the power to enforce this article by appropriate legislation.

CHAPTER

4

Duties and Rights of Citizenship

Birthdays are very special days in our lives. We may celebrate with candles on a cake. We may receive presents. Our 18th birthday, though, is particularly special. On that day we receive the right to vote. Why is this such an important event? From that day on, we can help to elect our leaders and vote on important issues. Above all, we can fully take part in our government.

Many of us take voting for granted. Yet voting was not always a right of all Americans. In fact, if you had turned 18 in the 1960's, you would not have been able to cast your ballot. Why? Eighteen-year-olds were not granted the right to vote until 1971. Before then only citizens at least 21 years old could vote.

Voting is only one of the many rights we have as American citizens. We have the right to express our ideas both in speech and in writing. We have the right to live in any town, city, or state in our country. We have the right to own property. Each of these rights has been guaranteed to all Americans by the Constitution.

We can add many other rights to this list. However, we must also realize that rights are accompanied by responsibilities. In exchange for our rights, we must fulfill certain duties. For example, in exchange for the right to a free education, we must try to learn as much as we can and to do our best. In exchange for our right to a trial by jury, we must serve on a jury when asked. Both duties and rights enable us to be good citizens.

This chapter is about the rights as well as the duties and responsibilities of citizenship in the United States. You will study the following topics:

1. **The Bill of Rights**
2. **Guaranteeing Other Rights**
3. **Duties and Responsibilities of Citizenship**

1 The Bill of Rights

Most of the writers of the Constitution believed that the safeguards written into that document would protect the rights of Americans. However, when the Constitution was sent to the states in 1787 for ratification, or approval, many Americans were not happy with it. As you have read, they demanded that a bill, or list, of rights be added to the Constitution. A number of states ratified the Constitution only on condition that a bill of rights would be added.

The new American government went into effect in 1789. Two years later the **Bill of Rights** was added as the first ten amendments to the Constitution. Congress discussed nearly 200 proposals for amendments before it presented these ten to the states for approval. The states ratified these amendments, and they became part of the Constitution of the United States in 1791. (The complete text of the Bill of Rights is on pages 67–68.)

The First Amendment

The rights described in the First Amendment of the Constitution are probably the most familiar to us because they are so close to our daily lives. First Amendment rights are basic rights that are essential to a free people.

Freedom of Religion. The first right, or freedom, guaranteed in the Bill of Rights is freedom of religion. This freedom guarantees to all Americans the right to practice any religion they choose, or to practice no religion at all.

Congress is forbidden to establish any religion as our nation's official religion. Congress cannot favor any one religion over others or tax American citizens in order to support any one religion.

Like all rights in the Bill of Rights, freedom of religion had its origins in colonial times. As you know, several colonies were established mainly by settlers who were seeking the freedom to practice their religion in their own way. However, some of these colonies denied this freedom to people with different beliefs.

Gradually the ideal of religious freedom developed in America. This right eventually was guaranteed to all Americans by the First Amendment.

Freedom of Speech. The right to express your ideas and opinions when you speak is called freedom of speech. Freedom of speech also means the right to listen to the thoughts and opinions of others. This freedom guarantees that Americans are free to express their thoughts and ideas about anything. We may talk freely to our friends and neighbors or deliver a speech in public to a group of people.

The First Amendment guarantees Americans the right to express opinions about our government and to criticize the actions of

A ride down any country road gives evidence of the freedom of the press guaranteed by the First Amendment. How does this picture show that freedom?

government officials. Under a totalitarian government, on the other hand, the people have no right to speak freely. They do not dare to criticize the actions of the government. If they do, they may be punished.

Of course, you are not permitted to use your freedom of speech to injure others. You do not have the right to say things about others that you know are false. If you do, you may be sued in court by those who believe they have been harmed by what you said.

Furthermore, the right of free speech cannot be exercised in a way that might cause physical harm to others. A person does not have the right to call out "Fire!" in a crowded room just to see what might happen. Such an action could cause panic, and many people could be injured in the rush to get out.

In other words, like all our freedoms, the right of free speech is not an absolute freedom. There are limits based on the rights of others and on what is good for all.

Freedom of the Press. The freedom to express your ideas in writing is known as freedom of the press. This freedom is closely related to freedom of speech and is also guaranteed by the First Amendment.

Americans struggled in colonial times for this important right. At that time newspapers were not allowed to criticize the government or public officials. An important court case, however, led to more freedom of the press.

A printer named John Peter Zenger was arrested and jailed in 1734 for publishing newspaper articles that criticized the royal governor of New York. According to the law, Zenger was guilty even if what he had written was true. However, the jury found Zenger not guilty. The jury agreed with his lawyer that writing the truth was not a crime.

Freedom of the press gives all Americans the right to express their thoughts freely in writing, provided they do not state falsehoods that might cause harm. This writing may be in newspapers, books, magazines, or any other printed or written form.

Americans are also free to read what others write. Because they are free to read a variety of facts and ideas, Americans can become better informed citizens.

Freedom of Assembly. Another priceless freedom guaranteed by the First Amendment is freedom of assembly, or freedom to hold meetings. Americans are free to meet to discuss their problems and plan their actions. They can gather together to express their views about government decisions. Of course, such meetings must be peaceful.

Freedom of Petition. The right to ask your government to do something or stop doing something is freedom of petition. The First Amendment also contains this guarantee. Freedom of petition gives you the right to write to your representatives in Congress and ask them to work for the passage of laws you favor. You are free to ask your representatives to change laws you do not like. The right of petition also helps government officials know what Americans think and what actions they want the government to take.

The Second Amendment

The Second Amendment to the Constitution guarantees Americans the **right to bear arms.** The government cannot forbid Americans to own weapons, such as handguns and rifles.

During the colonial period, Americans organized militias, or volunteer armies, to defend their communities. The militias played an important part in the American Revolution. Later, in the early years of our nation, Americans needed weapons in order to serve in the militias that were established to defend the states. The militias provided protection during emergencies, too. Many Americans also believed that without weapons they would be powerless if the government tried to overstep its powers and rule by force.

Today, because of the increase of crime in the United States, gun control is widely debated. Some people have demanded that guns be regulated. They say that gun control laws would lower the crime rate. Other people argue that the Second Amendment gives them the right to own weapons. They say that this amendment prevents the government from passing laws limiting that right.

The Third Amendment

The Third Amendment states that the government cannot force Americans to quarter, or give housing to, soldiers in peacetime. Under British rule, the colonists sometimes had to house and feed British soldiers against their will. As a result, Americans wanted a "no quartering" right in the Bill of Rights.

The Fourth Amendment

The Fourth Amendment protects Americans from unreasonable searches and seizures. This means that in most cases our homes cannot be searched and our property cannot be taken from us.

However, a search is considered reasonable if a judge has issued a **search warrant.** This is a legal document that describes the place to be searched and the persons or things to be seized. A search warrant can be issued only if there is good reason to believe that evidence about a crime will be found.

The Fifth Amendment

The Fifth Amendment contains several provisions protecting the rights of a person accused of a crime. Before a person can be brought to trial, he or she must be **indicted,** or formally accused of a crime, by a group of citizens known as a grand jury. This protects an accused person from hasty action on the part of the government.

The Fifth Amendment also protects an accused person's right to be silent. People cannot be forced to give evidence against themselves. Also, a person who has been found not guilty cannot be tried again for the same crime.

These Americans are attending a public meeting to give their views and to listen to the views of others. What two important freedoms are they exercising?

Freedoms Guaranteed by the Bill of Rights

	FREEDOM OF RELIGION  Freedom of worship. Freedom to belong to any religion, or to none. No official religion may be established.	FREEDOM OF THE PRESS  Freedom to print books, newspapers, and magazines. No one may print falsehoods or writings that harm our citizens.	FREEDOM OF PETITION  Freedom to urge our governments to pass laws. Freedom to ask our governments to take certain actions.
RIGHTS TO EQUAL JUSTICE  All persons accused of a crime must receive fair and equal treatment in a court of law.	FREEDOM OF SPEECH  Freedom to express ideas and opinions. No one may use this freedom to speak falsely in order to harm or to injure other citizens.	FREEDOM OF ASSEMBLY  Freedom to hold meetings. Meetings must be peaceful and obey local laws.	FREEDOM AND SECURITY OF CITIZENS  No unlawful search may be made of our homes. Right to bear arms to protect ourselves. No troops may be stationed in our homes.

Another Fifth Amendment protection says that no person can be denied life, liberty, or property without **due process of law.** This means that a person can be punished for a crime only after receiving a fair trial.

The last clause of the Fifth Amendment guarantees all Americans the **right to own private property.** It states that the government cannot take private property for public use without paying a fair price for it. For example, if the government needs to build a road or a school, property owners may have to give up their property to make way for a public need. However, the government must pay a fair price for the property.

The government's power to take private property for public use is known as **eminent domain.** Property may be taken only for the public good and with just compensation.

The right to own private property is one of our nation's basic freedoms. Our free economic system is based upon this right.

The Sixth and Seventh Amendments

The Sixth Amendment guarantees a person accused of a crime the right to a prompt, public trial by a jury. Accused people must be informed of the crimes they are charged with committing. They also are guaranteed the right to hear and question all witnesses against them and to call witnesses to appear in court.

The Sixth Amendment also guarantees a person accused of a crime the right to have the help of a lawyer. In recent years, the Supreme Court has ruled that if the accused person cannot afford a lawyer, the judge will assign one. The government will pay the lawyer's fee.

The Seventh Amendment provides for a trial by jury in certain kinds of cases that involve conflicts over money or property.

The Eighth Amendment

The Eighth Amendment says that the court cannot set bail that is excessive, or too high. **Bail** is the money or property an accused person gives the court to hold as a guarantee that she or he will appear for trial. After the bail is paid, the accused person is allowed to leave jail. The bail is returned after the trial.

Furthermore, the Eighth Amendment forbids "cruel and unusual punishments." The exact meaning of these words has been debated for a long time.

The Ninth Amendment

The writers of the Bill of Rights did not want to give the idea that the people had only those rights guaranteed in the first eight amendments. To make doubly sure that Americans would enjoy every right and freedom possible, the Ninth Amendment was added to the Constitution. This amendment states that the list of rights contained in the Bill of Rights is not complete. There are many other rights that all Americans have and will continue to have even though they are not mentioned in the Bill of Rights. Among these rights are:

1. Freedom to live or travel anywhere in our nation.

2. Freedom to work at any job for which we can qualify.

3. Freedom to marry and raise a family.

4. Freedom to receive a free education in public schools.

5. Freedom to join a political party, a union, and other legal groups.

The Tenth Amendment

As a final guarantee of our rights, the Tenth Amendment set aside, or reserved, many powers of government for the states or for the people. This amendment says that all powers not expressly given to the federal government or forbidden to the states by the Constitution are reserved for the states or for the people. This provision leaves with the states the power to act in many ways to guarantee the rights of their citizens.

CHECK-UP

Vocabulary

Bill of Rights
freedom of religion
freedom of speech
freedom of the press
freedom of assembly
freedom of petition
right to bear arms
search warrant
indicted
due process of law
right to own private property
eminent domain
bail

Review

1. Why was the Bill of Rights added to the Constitution?
2. What five rights are included in the First Amendment? Give an example of each.
3. What rights are guaranteed to a person accused of a crime?
4. What is the purpose of the Ninth Amendment to the Constitution?

Discuss

Which of the freedoms in the Bill of Rights do you think is most important to Americans today? Why?

2
Guaranteeing Other Rights

Since the passage of the Bill of Rights, other amendments have been added to the Constitution. These amendments were passed as changing conditions in our nation and changing beliefs brought about new needs. Today our Constitution has 26 amendments in all. Some amendments changed the way the government works. (You will read about these in later chapters.) In this section we will look at the amendments that increased the rights of the American people.

Extending Civil Rights

Rights guaranteed to all American citizens are called **civil rights.** Our Constitution, especially the Bill of Rights, is the foundation for civil rights in this nation. However, until after the Civil War, the protection of civil rights was left largely to the individual states. The Thirteenth and Fourteenth Amendments were added after the Civil War to protect the rights of newly freed black Americans.

The Thirteenth Amendment. The Thirteenth Amendment, ratified in 1865, outlawed slavery in the United States. President Abraham Lincoln had ordered an end to slavery in the Confederate States during the Civil War. But his order, the Emancipation Proclamation, had actually led to the freedom of very few slaves. The Thirteenth Amendment officially ended slavery in all the states and in all lands ruled by the United States.

The Fourteenth Amendment. The Fourteenth Amendment, added in 1868, was intended mainly to protect the rights of black Americans. However, it contains important rights for all the American people.

The first part of the amendment grants full citizenship to blacks. Next the amend-

Women held marches and demonstrations for years before finally gaining the right to vote with the ratification of the Nineteenth Amendment in 1920.

ment says that no state can take away a citizen's "life, liberty, or property without due process of law." Also, no state can deny citizens the equal protection of the laws. Thus the Fourteenth Amendment protects citizens against unfair actions by state governments, just as the Fifth Amendment protects American citizens against unfair actions by the federal government.

Voting Rights

One of our most important civil rights is the right to vote, or **suffrage.** The struggle to gain the right to vote for all Americans was not won easily. Voting rights are the subject of six amendments to the Constitution.

The Constitution at first made no mention of voting rights. It was left to the states to decide who could vote. Most states limited the vote to white males over the age of 21 who owned a certain amount of property. Furthermore, some states only allowed those who held certain religious beliefs to vote.

Gradually the states did away with property and religious qualifications for voting. Between the late 1800's and the 1970's, amendments to the Constitution extended the right to vote to all American citizens.

The Fifteenth Amendment. Black Americans were guaranteed the right to vote by the Fifteenth Amendment, approved in 1870. It says that no person can be denied the right to vote because of race or color. However, in the late 1800's and early 1900's many states, especially in the South, passed laws that kept blacks from voting. Finally, in the 1960's, Congress passed a number of civil rights laws that truly brought about equal voting rights for black Americans.

The Seventeenth Amendment. The right of eligible voters in a state to elect the state's United States senators was granted by the Seventeenth Amendment. Before this amendment was approved in 1913, United States senators were chosen by members of the state legislatures.

DID YOU KNOW THAT . . .

early in our history women won (and lost) the right to vote in New Jersey? That state's first constitution said that "any person" with property worth a certain amount of money could vote. At first not many women voted. Soon, however, their votes began to decide some close elections. The state's all-male legislature took away women's right to vote in 1807. Female suffrage was an idea whose time had not yet come.

The Nineteenth Amendment. Women were granted the right to vote by the Nineteenth Amendment. Women won this right only after a long, hard struggle. It was led by such courageous women as Lucretia Mott, Elizabeth Cady Stanton, Susan B. Anthony, and Carrie Catt. They argued that the women of our nation should not be treated as second-class citizens.

In 1869 Wyoming became the first state in the nation to give women the right to vote. Gradually other states began to grant the vote to women. The suffragists, those who fought for the right of women to vote, finally won in 1920, when the Nineteenth Amendment was ratified. Because women make up about half of our population, the amendment doubled the eligible voting population of the United States.

The young people here show their eagerness to take advantage of the Twenty-sixth Amendment. They are registering to cast their first votes in an election.

The Twenty-third Amendment. The Twenty-third Amendment, ratified in 1961, further extended voting rights. It gave people living in the District of Columbia (Washington, D.C.), the nation's capital, the right to vote for President and Vice President. Before this amendment, they could not vote in national elections.

The Twenty-fourth Amendment. Beginning in the 1890's, some states established a requirement that all persons must pay a special tax, called a **poll tax,** in order to vote. Many Americans believed this tax was aimed at the poor, and especially at black Americans, to discourage them from voting. In 1964 the Twenty-fourth Amendment forbade the use of a poll tax as a qualification for voting in national elections. In 1966 the Supreme Court ruled that the poll tax is also unlawful in state elections.

The Twenty-sixth Amendment. The right to vote was extended to another large group of Americans in 1971. In that year the Twenty-sixth Amendment lowered the voting age in national, state, and local elections to 18. Previously, most states had set 21 as the age at which people could vote for the first time. With the adoption of this amendment, young Americans were given a greater voice in our government.

CHECK-UP

Vocabulary

civil rights
suffrage
poll tax

Review

1. What was the purpose of the Thirteenth and Fourteenth Amendments?
2. What four groups of Americans were given the right to vote by amendments to the Constitution?

Discuss

How have the amendments to the Constitution put into practice the American ideals of freedom and equality?

3

Duties and Responsibilities of Citizenship

So far in this chapter, you have been learning about the rights that are guaranteed to all American citizens. Along with their rights, the citizens of our nation also have important duties and responsibilities.

Duties of Citizenship

Certain actions are the duty of all American citizens. These duties are the "musts" of citizenship. That is, all American citizens are required by law to perform these actions. The duties required of all citizens are described in the Constitution of the United States and in the laws of our nation and states.

Most Americans are familiar with these duties of citizenship, but sometimes we forget how important they really are. The success of our system of government depends upon all citizens fulfilling these duties.

Obeying the Law. One of the most important duties of citizenship is to obey the laws. Our American government can work in an orderly way only if citizens respect and obey its laws. Of course, it is important to know what the laws are. For example, when you learn to drive a car, you must also learn the traffic laws. "Ignorance of the law excuses no one," is an old saying that continues to hold true today.

Attending School. One of the first duties of all Americans is to attend school. Our nation places a very high value on educating its citizens. Free public schools guarantee all young Americans the opportunity to study and learn in order to develop their talents and abilities. Education also gives us the skills and knowledge needed to fulfill the duties and responsibilities of good citizenship. In order to ensure our freedoms and the future of our nation, our citizens must be educated.

Paying Taxes. Another important duty of citizenship is to pay taxes. Our taxes pay for the many different services that government provides. In paying taxes, we are paying for police and fire protection, good streets, schools, and countless other services. Tax money also pays for the costs of maintaining our nation's military defenses. The United States must be able to defend itself in order to protect the rights and freedoms of American citizens.

Serving in the Armed Forces. As an American citizen you have a duty to help your nation if it is threatened. You may be called upon to help defend the nation by serving in the armed forces.

During several periods in our history, the United States has used the **draft.** That is, men were required to serve in the military. Since 1975 the United States has used only volunteers in the armed forces. In 1980, however, 18-year-old men again had to **register,** or sign up, for military service. This lets the government know the names and addresses of all men of draft age. Registration ensures that if a war or other crisis required that the nation quickly expand its armed forces, the draft could be used again.

Appearing in Court. American citizens must, if called, serve as members of a jury. Citizens must also testify in court if called as witnesses. Appearing in court sometimes is seen as an inconvenience. Often we must take time out from our regular work to attend court. However, our right to a trial by jury depends on citizens fulfilling their duty to serve on juries and appear as witnesses.

These young Americans are aware that our recreational areas are more enjoyable for all people when everyone who uses them respects and obeys the rules.

Responsibilities of Citizenship

American citizens should vote in elections.

American citizens should be interested in their government and study its activities.

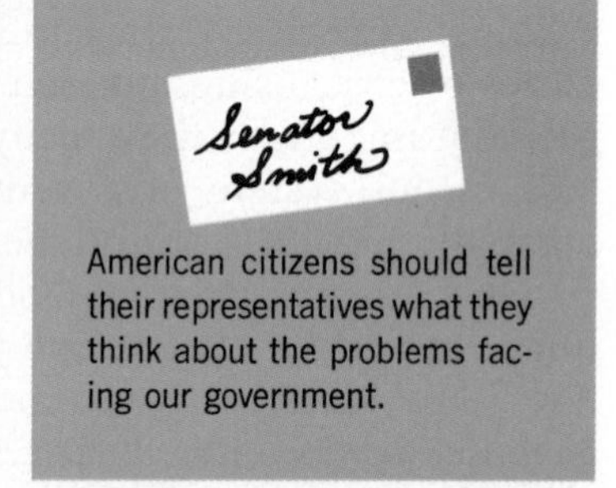

American citizens should tell their representatives what they think about the problems facing our government.

American citizens should be willing to serve as officials of government if elected or appointed to these jobs.

American citizens should be willing to help in their communities.

American citizens should help their government to enforce the laws by cooperating with the police.

Responsibilities of Citizenship

In addition to the duties of citizenship, Americans have many responsibilities of citizenship. These responsibilities are the "shoulds" of citizenship. That is, American citizens are not required by law to carry out these actions. Most Americans, though, accept these responsibilities because they are so important to the successful operation of our system of government.

Voting in Elections. As you read earlier in this chapter, voting is one of the most important rights of American citizens. However, voting is also one of our most important responsibilities. By voting on election day, each citizen plays a part in deciding who will be the leaders of our government. Each voter also helps to determine what actions our government will take. It is the people we elect who, when they are in office, plan our government's actions.

The vote of every citizen counts. Only by exercising the right to vote can citizens carry out our great constitutional ideal of government by consent of the governed.

Being Informed. In order to cast their votes wisely, American citizens have a responsibility to be informed. Of course, education helps prepare citizens for this important responsibility.

Americans should take an active interest in the programs and activities of the government. They also should learn what policies are favored by each candidate running for office. Furthermore, Americans have a responsibility to tell their representatives what they think about public issues.

Taking Part in Government. Citizens should be concerned with their government either as members of a political party or as independent voters. In addition, American citizens should be willing to serve as officials of government if they are asked to serve by election or appointment to public office. The quality of any government depends upon the quality of the people who serve in that government.

Helping Your Community. One of the most important ways to be a responsible citizen is to take pride in your community and make sure that your community can take pride in you. For example, it is essential that all members of the community respect the property of others. Being careful not to litter, and even picking up after those who do, is an important part of citizenship.

It is also important to take an active part in the affairs of your community. Citizens should be willing to give their time to help improve their neighborhood, town, or city. Local groups can help clean up a park or assist in the library.

Fulfilling Our Responsibilities

As you can see, the responsibilities of American citizenship are not easy. To fulfill them requires time and effort on the part of every citizen. Carrying them out, however, gives all Americans a chance to take part in our representative democracy. All Americans must take part if our nation is truly to have a "government of the people, by the people, for the people."

CHECK-UP

Vocabulary
draft
register

Review
1. Name some of the duties of all American citizens.
2. Name some of the responsibilities of all American citizens.

Discuss
Why do you think getting an education is one of the most important duties and responsibilities of American citizens?

CHAPTER SUMMARY

Our Constitution has 26 amendments. The first ten amendments, known as the Bill of Rights, clearly define the rights of all Americans. These amendments guarantee such priceless rights as freedom of speech and press, freedom of assembly, freedom of religion, and the right to a speedy and fair trial by a jury. Moreover, the Ninth Amendment says that the rights mentioned in the Constitution are not the only rights held by the American people. The Tenth Amendment set aside, or reserved, to the states and to the people all powers not specifically given to the federal government by the Constitution.

Later amendments to the Constitution further increased the rights of all Americans. The Thirteenth and Fourteenth Amendments protected the rights of the newly freed black Americans after the Civil War. Six other amendments to the Constitution enlarged the voting rights of the American people.

Along with the rights and freedoms of American citizenship go important duties and responsibilities. Our nation can remain free and strong only if its citizens respect and obey its laws and carry out the duties and responsibilities of citizenship.

CIVICS SKILLS: Reading a Bar Graph

On November 4, 1980, a whopping 85 million Americans turned out to cast their votes for President. Although this figure was a record, it represented less than 53 percent of the voting-age population—the lowest percentage since 1948.

How often have you heard or read fact-filled statements such as the one above? If you are like most Americans, probably just about every day. You see them in newspapers. You study them in textbooks. You listen to them on the evening news. But how can you find your way through all this information, or **data?** One way is by using graphs.

Graphs are important tools for helping us learn and remember numerical facts. A single graph can condense large amounts of written and statistical data into one, easy-to-read diagram. From this diagram, you can answer such questions as "how much," "how many," or "how long." You can also make comparisons or draw relationships, often with only a quick glance at a graph.

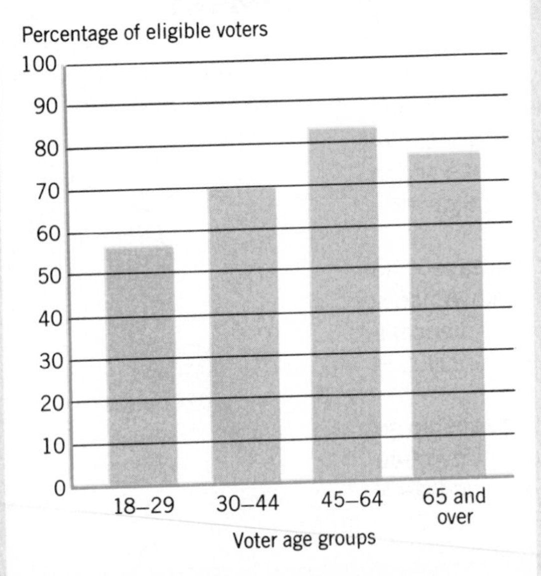

The graph on this page is called a **bar graph,** because it uses bars to show amounts. Other graphs use different symbols, such as lines, pictures, or parts of circles. Many of the steps you follow in reading a bar graph also can be used to read these other types of graphs.

Identifying the Facts

The first step in reading any graph is to identify the information on it. What does the title of the graph on this page tell you? Now look at the line that runs sideways across the bottom of the graph. This is the **horizontal axis.** What information is recorded on this part of the graph? Ask yourself the same question about the line that runs up and down, or **vertical axis.** Based on your answers to these questions, what do you expect to learn from the graph?

Bar graphs are especially useful for comparing two or more sets of information at definite points in time. This graph, for example, compares the turnout of eligible voters in four different age groups in the 1980 election. Study the four bars that represent these groups. Which bar is the shortest? Your answer to this question tells you which group had the lowest turnout—people aged 18–29. Which group had the highest turnout?

To get more precise information, draw an imaginary line from the top of each bar to the vertical axis at the left. If you do this for the 18–29 group, you'll discover that about 56 percent voted. What percentage of each of the other groups voted?

Practicing What You've Learned

1. Based on evidence in the bar graph on this page, what conclusions can you draw about the relationship between age and voter participation?
2. If you were running for office, how might this information influence your campaign?

CHAPTER REVIEW

Vocabulary

Can you find the right word or phrase in Chapter 4 to answer each of the following questions? Copy the questions in your notebook and write the correct answer after each.

1. What are the first ten amendments to the Constitution called?
2. What legal document describes the place to be searched and the persons or things to be seized?
3. What term means that a person can be punished for a crime only after receiving a fair trial?
4. What word refers to the money or property an accused person gives to a court to hold as a guarantee that he or she will appear for trial?
5. What term refers to the right of Americans to hold peaceful meetings to discuss their views?
6. What is the term used to describe the right to vote?
7. In the past, what special tax did people in some states have to pay in order to vote?
8. What word is used to describe the system that requires men to serve in our nation's military?

Check-Up

1. What are some of the rights and freedoms you possess as an American citizen?
2. What role did the Zenger case play in the establishment of freedom of the press?
3. What amendments deal with the rights of persons accused of a crime? What rights do these amendments guarantee?
4. Which amendments deal with the voting rights of Americans? How did these amendments extend voting rights?
5. What is a poll tax? How was it used to prevent black Americans from voting in some states?
6. What are some of your duties and responsibilities as an American citizen? Which do you think are most important?
7. In what ways have the amendments that deal with voting rights made the United States more democratic?
8. Make a list of what you think are the characteristics of a good citizen.

Civics Skills

The following facts tell you about the percentage of voters who participated in Presidential elections from 1964–1980.

Year	Percentage
1964	61.9
1968	60.9
1972	55.5
1976	54.3
1980	52.9

On a separate piece of paper, show this same information in the form of a bar graph. Be sure to give your graph a title. Also label clearly both the horizontal and the vertical axes. When you have finished your graph, study its facts carefully. What general statements can you make about voter participation on the basis of this bar graph?

Citizenship and You

1. In your notebook, make a list of Amendments 1–10 of the Constitution. Next to each amendment list the rights it guarantees to each citizen. Write a short description of how each of these rights affects you in your daily life.
2. A bulletin board committee may prepare a display on "Good Citizenship." Students can draw posters and cut out articles from newspapers and magazines.
3. Collect newspaper or magazine articles that deal with the Bill of Rights today.

UNIT ONE REVIEW

Reviewing the Facts

Write your answers to the items below on a separate piece of paper.

1. The Bill of Rights guarantees all of the following *except*
   a. freedom of the press.
   b. right to equal justice.
   c. freedom from military service.
   d. freedom and security for all citizens of the United States.
2. Civics can best be defined as
   a. the study of laws.
   b. the study of what it means to be a citizen.
   c. the study of elections.
   d. the study of government agencies.
3. When a state law and the United States Constitution conflict with each other, which one must give way?
4. The 1980 census showed that
   a. the average household in the United States is getting smaller.
   b. the population of the United States is moving to the northern states.
   c. the population of the United States is getting smaller.
   d. the population of the United States is getting younger.
5. Complete this sentence: The United States Constitution set up a ________ system in which power is divided between the state governments and the national government.
6. One group of Americans who directly benefited from an amendment to the Constitution was ________.
7. Correct the underlined part of this sentence: One reason for setting up a government is to give a few people the power to rule over all the other people.
8. Correct the underlined part of this sentence: The executive branch of the American government is made up of the House of Representatives and the Senate.
9. The Articles of Confederation were replaced because
   a. they did not include a Bill of Rights.
   b. George Washington had not been elected President.
   c. the Supreme Court had been given too much power.
   d. the national government had not been given enough power.
10. The Constitution established a system of checks and balances so that
    a. no branch of government would become too strong.
    b. the Senate would not be stronger than the House of Representatives.
    c. Congress would have the right to establish lower courts.
    d. the President would have the help of a Vice President.

Applying What You Know

1. Make a flow chart that illustrates the steps a person must take to become a naturalized citizen.
2. Consider the findings of the 1980 census about recent changes in the American population. Then write a paragraph that explains how these changes might affect life in your community.

Expanding Your Knowledge

Bates, Elizabeth B., *The Making of the Constitution,* Viking. An overview of the process by which the Constitution was created and ratified.

Padover, Saul K., *The Living Constitution,* New American Library. A guide to the Constitution, including important Supreme Court cases and their meaning.

Riis, Jacob, *The Making of an American,* Macmillan. The autobiography of this famous immigrant, expressing his faith in his adopted land.

UNIT TWO

The Federal Government

CHAPTER

5

Congress Makes Our Nation's Laws

The third day of January is always a busy and exciting day in Washington, D. C. In the Capitol Building, where the Congress of the United States holds its meetings, doorkeepers take their places. Clerks prepare to keep careful records of the proceedings. Members of the Senate and the House of Representatives take their seats. A new session of Congress is about to begin.

What is the job of these members of Congress? According to the Constitution, their main job is to make our nation's laws. As lawmakers they make important decisions that affect the lives and welfare of the American people.

Members of Congress may have to decide such important questions as how large our armed forces should be or how high federal taxes should be. Only Congress holds "the power of the purse." This means that only Congress has the right to tax, to regulate interstate and foreign commerce, and to coin and borrow money for the federal government. Members of Congress may declare war. They may propose amendments to the Constitution. Also, of course, they must keep in touch with the people of their home states and take care of their problems.

In this chapter you will learn more about Congress, its organization, and the way in which laws are passed. You will study these topics:

1. **The Senate and the House of Representatives**
2. **How Congress Is Organized**
3. **The Powers of Congress**
4. **How a Bill Becomes a Law**

1

The Senate and the House of Representatives

As you know, the work of our national government is divided among three separate branches—the legislative branch, the executive branch, and the judicial branch. The writers of the Constitution believed the legislative branch was so important that they discussed it first, in Article 1 of the Constitution (pages 55–61).

The Two Houses of Congress

The work of the legislative branch is carried out by the **Congress** of the United States. Congress is the lawmaking body of our national government. The Constitution provides that Congress shall be composed of two houses—the Senate and the House of Representatives.

The leaders who drew up our plan of government in 1787 had two main reasons for creating a lawmaking body of two houses, or a **bicameral legislature.** First, they believed a lawmaking body of two houses would help to "check and balance" the work of this branch of the government. Having two houses to share the responsibility of making the nation's laws allows each house to check the actions of the other. As a result, there is less danger that Congress will pass laws in haste or pass laws that are not needed or wanted by the people.

Second, the writers of the Constitution established a bicameral Congress in order to settle a dispute between the large and the small states. As you read in Chapter 2, the smaller states feared they would be dominated by the larger ones. The dispute was settled by the Great Compromise. It provided that the states should be represented equally in the Senate, and according to the size of their population in the House of Representatives.

The House of Representatives

The **House of Representatives,** or the House, as it is sometimes called, has 435 members. It is the larger of the two houses of Congress. Members of the House are referred to as **representatives.** According to the Constitution, the number of representatives each state may elect to the House is based on the size of the state's population. Each state, regardless of population, is entitled to at least one representative.

Originally each state elected one representative for every 30,000 persons living in the state. In the first Congress, which met in 1789, there were 59 representatives in the House. Then, as new states joined the union and the nation's population increased, the House steadily grew in size. To prevent the membership from growing too large, Congress finally limited the size of the House of Representatives. In 1929 Congress set the limit at 435 members. Today each member of the House represents about 500,000 people.

How Membership Is Divided. Every ten years, after the census is taken, Congress determines how the 435 seats in the House of Representatives are to be distributed. Congress itself divides these seats among the states according to population.

If a state's population decreases from one census to the next, the number of its representatives may be reduced. On the other hand, states whose populations grow may be entitled to more representatives. But the total size of the House of Representatives can never be more than 435 members. The map on this page shows the number of representatives each state sends to the House as a result of the 1980 census.

Congressional Districts. Each of our representatives is elected from a **congressional district.** Each state legislature is responsible for dividing the state into as many congressional districts as it has members in the House. The boundaries must be drawn so that each district in a state is nearly equal in population. After every census, the state legislature must redivide the state's congressional districts if the number of people has changed.

Electing Representatives. Elections for members of the House of Representatives are held in November of each even-numbered year. All representatives are elected for two-year terms. They may be reelected, and there is no limit on the number of terms they may serve. Because representatives often are reelected, there are always many experienced lawmakers in the House. If a representative dies or resigns before the end of a term, the governor of her or his home state must call a special election to fill the vacancy.

The Senate

The **Senate** is the smaller of the two houses of Congress. The Constitution provides that each state, regardless of size, be represented in the Senate by two members. These members are known as **senators.**

The first Senate consisted of 22 senators, representing 11 states. (Two of the 13 states, North Carolina and Rhode Island, had not yet approved the Constitution.) Today the Senate has 100 members—two senators elected from each of the 50 states. Each senator represents his or her whole state.

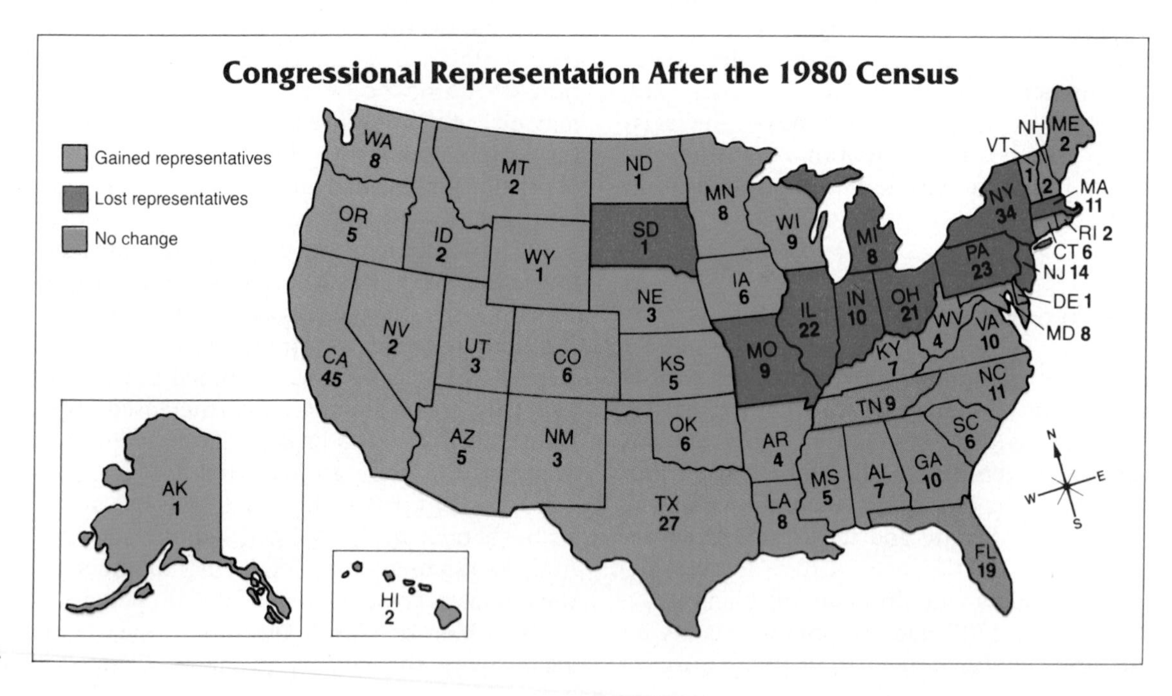

Senators are elected for six-year terms and may be reelected any number of times. Elections for senators, like those for representatives, are held in November of each even-numbered year. Only one third of the Senate's membership comes up for election every two years. Therefore, a new Senate begins its work with at least two thirds of the members having had experience in the Senate.

The senator from each state who has served the longest period of time is called the state's **senior senator.** If a senator dies or resigns before the end of his or her term of office, the governor of the state may appoint someone to fill the vacancy until the next regular election or until a special state election is held.

CAN YOU GUESS?

What is a person called who holds office after his or her replacement has been elected?

Answer is on page 562.

Qualifications of Members of Congress

The Constitution lists the qualifications that members of Congress must meet. These are the qualifications for members of the House of Representatives:

1. A representative must be at least 25 years old.

2. A representative must have been a United States citizen for at least seven years.

3. A representative must be a legal resident of the state he or she represents. Usually a representative lives in the district from which he or she is elected. However, the Constitution does not make this a requirement for office.

The qualifications for members of the Senate differ slightly from those for representatives. The Constitution lists these qualifications for senators:

1. A senator must be at least 30 years old.

2. A senator must have been a citizen of the United States for at least nine years.

3. A senator must be a legal resident of the state he or she represents.

In addition to these qualifications, members of Congress traditionally have shared a number of other characteristics. Most have attended college. A majority are lawyers. Many others are business people or bankers. Their average age is about 50.

Throughout our history most members of Congress have been men. Only a small percentage of representatives today are women, and only a few women have served in the Senate. However, the number of women is slowly increasing.

Members of Congress usually have had previous political experience, often in their state legislature. Most members of Congress also have been active members of community and voluntary organizations.

Salary and Benefits of Members of Congress

Senators and representatives each receive a yearly salary of almost $61,000. In addition, they receive many benefits free or at greatly reduced cost. All members of Congress have offices in one of the office buildings on Capitol Hill. To help run their offices, they receive an allowance to pay a staff of assistants, clerks, and secretaries.

All members get free trips to their home states, an allowance for local district offices, and a stationery allowance. They also have the **franking privilege**—the right to mail official letters free of charge. In addition, senators and representatives frequently have the opportunity to make free trips abroad on congressional business.

Members of Congress cannot be arrested when they are attending Congress or are on

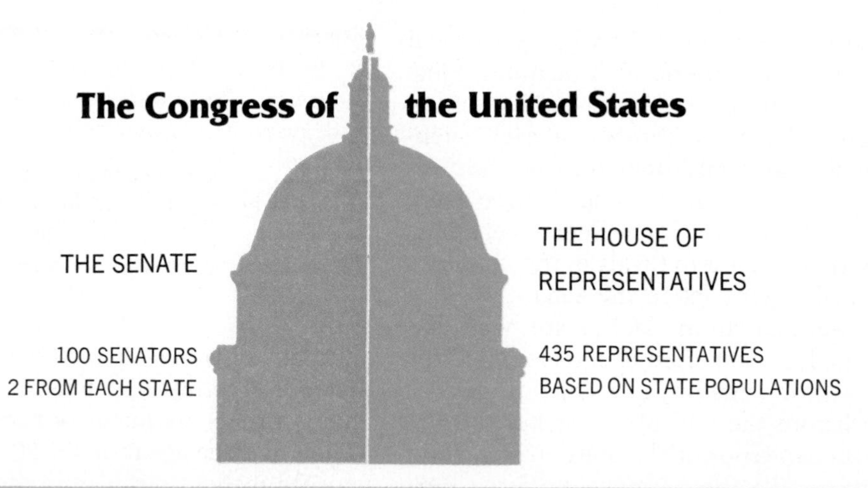

	LENGTH OF TERM	WHEN ELECTED	REQUIRED AGE	CITIZENSHIP	LEGAL RESIDENCE	SALARY
SENATORS	6 years	One third of Senate elected every 2 years	At least 30 years old	American citizen at least 9 years	Resident of state where elected	$60,662.50 + expenses
REPRESENTATIVES	2 years	Entire House elected every 2 years	At least 25 years old	American citizen at least 7 years	Resident of state where elected	$60,662.50 + expenses

their way to or from a meeting of Congress, unless they have committed a serious crime. This ensures that no one can interfere needlessly with federal lawmakers as they perform their duties.

Members of Congress cannot be sued for anything they may say while they are speaking in Congress. This provision in the Constitution is intended to protect their freedom to debate. On the other hand, members of Congress are not free to behave just as they wish. Both the Senate and the House have rules of conduct that members must follow.

Rules of Conduct

Both houses of Congress have the right to decide who shall be seated as members. This means that if the Senate or House questions the methods by which any member was elected, the member may not be seated until an investigation is made. If either house finds that dishonest or questionable methods were used, it can refuse to seat this member. The Senate or the House can also require the state to hold a new election. Fortunately, Congress seldom has to refuse to seat a member.

The House and Senate have passed strict codes of conduct for their members. For example, members may not use campaign funds for personal expenses. There is a limit on the amount of outside income they may earn. In addition, members of Congress are required to disclose any financial holdings worth $1,000 or more.

Serious misconduct by a member of the Senate or House may result in **expulsion** from office by a vote of two thirds of the senators or representatives. Expulsion of a member means that the member must give up his or her seat in Congress. Grounds for expulsion are limited to the most serious offenses, such as treason or the accepting of bribes.

Less serious offenses may bring a vote of **censure,** or formal disapproval of a member's actions. A censured member must stand alone at the front of the House or Senate and listen as the charges are read.

CHECK-UP

Vocabulary

Congress
bicameral legislature
House of Representatives
representatives
congressional district
Senate
senators
senior senator
franking privilege
expulsion
censure

Review

1. For what two reasons did the writers of the Constitution decide to create a bicameral legislature?
2. How many members are there in Congress? in the House? in the Senate?
3. What are the qualifications for representatives and senators? How do they differ?

Discuss

Do you think members of Congress should vote on issues according to what they believe are the best interests of the nation? Or should they vote the way the people of their state or district want them to vote? Explain.

2 How Congress Is Organized

Beginning with the first Congress in 1789, each Congress has been identified by number. Thus the Congress that began its term in 1789 was known as the First Congress. The Congress that will begin its term in 1987 will be the 100th Congress.

Terms and Sessions of Congress

In each term of Congress, there are two regular **sessions,** or meetings. The first session begins on January 3 in the odd-numbered year following the congressional election in November. The second session begins on January 3 of the next year.

Each session may last as long as Congress wishes. In the past, sessions usually lasted from January 3 until August or September. In recent years, the growing workload has led to longer sessions. Both houses of Congress must agree upon the date to adjourn, or end, the session.

Sometimes serious problems come up after Congress has adjourned its regular session. In such cases, the President of the United States may recall Congress for a **special session.** Usually the President calls both houses into special session. However, the President may decide to call only one of the two houses.

Under certain circumstances, the House of Representatives and the Senate will meet together. This is known as a **joint session** of Congress. For example, a joint session will be called if the President wants to address the Congress.

The Organization of Congress

The Constitution provides for only three congressional officers. First it directs the House of Representatives to select a presiding officer. Second it names the Vice President of the United States as president of the Senate. Third it calls for the selection of a senator to preside in the Vice President's absence. These are the only directions given by the Constitution about the organization of Congress.

Over the years, Congress has developed procedures to organize itself. Shortly after the opening day of each term, the Republican and Democratic members in each house gather separately in private meetings. These private meetings are called **party caucuses.** At these caucuses, the Republican members of each house choose their own leaders, and the Democratic members choose theirs.

The political party that has more members in each house is known as the **majority party.** The political party that has fewer members is called the **minority party.**

Leaders of the House

According to the Constitution, the presiding officer of the House of Representatives is the **Speaker** of the House. The Speaker is the most powerful officer in Congress. No representative may speak until called upon, or recognized, by the Speaker. The Speaker also has great influence in deciding the order of business in the House.

The Speaker, because of these important responsibilities, is paid $79,125 a year. The Speaker is always a member of the majority party. Like other leaders in the House and Senate, the Speaker is usually a longtime member of Congress.

House members also choose a number of other leaders. At their private caucuses, House Democrats and Republicans each choose a floor leader and a party whip. The **floor leader** of each political party guides the party's proposed laws through Congress. The floor leader of the majority party is called the majority leader. The floor leader of the minority party is the minority leader. Each floor leader is assisted by a **party whip,** who tries to persuade party members to vote for party-sponsored legislation.

Leaders of the Senate

The Constitution provides for the Vice President of the United States to serve as the presiding officer of the Senate. However, the Vice President is not a senator and therefore cannot take part in Senate debates. The Vice President may vote only in the case of a tie.

In recent years, the Vice President has had many other responsibilities and has spent little time in the Senate. During the Vice President's absence, the Senate is presided over by the **president *pro tempore*** (pro TEM·pa·ree)—a president "for the time being." This leader is elected by the members of the Senate. The president *pro tempore* is by custom the long-

The Senate and the House of Representatives meet together in a joint session when the President wants to address Congress.

est serving member of the majority party.

The most powerful officers of the Senate are the majority leader and the minority leader. Like the floor leaders of the House, they are elected in party caucuses. They too are assisted by party whips.

Congress Works Through Committees

Every year Congress has to consider thousands of **bills,** or proposed laws. Members of the First Congress could have read every one of the 268 bills they considered. Today Congress handles as many as 20,000 bills in a two-year term. It would be impossible for all the members of each house to consider every bill that is proposed. Therefore, the members divide their work among many smaller groups, or **committees.**

Most of the work of Congress is done in committees. The congressional committees study all bills before they are considered by Congress. To get information needed to do their work, committees hold meetings and conduct investigations.

Standing Committees. Each house of Congress has a number of permanent committees, or **standing committees.** As you can see in the chart on page 100, the Senate has 15 standing committees. The House has 22. Each committee is responsible for a special area. In the House, for example, the Ways and Means Committee handles all matters concerning taxes. In the Senate, bills related to taxes go to the Finance Committee.

Before any bill is considered by Congress, it is carefully studied by a standing committee. The committee holds special meetings called hearings to gain information on the good and bad points of a bill. Committee members may revise a bill. It is then sent to the entire membership for consideration, with the committee's recommendation for or against it. This recommendation usually determines whether the members will or will not approve the bill.

The teenagers shown here are Congressional pages, who carry messages for members of Congress. Each morning they receive their assignments for the day.

Subcommittees. Each standing committee is divided into **subcommittees.** These subcommittees deal with specific issues in the area handled by the committee as a whole. For example, the subcommittees of the Senate Foreign Relations Committee include those on Africa, Asia, Europe, and the Western Hemisphere.

Select Committees. From time to time, each house of Congress will appoint **select committees** to deal with issues that are not handled by the standing committees. Select committees have investigated government scandals, for example. After holding hearings on a problem area, a select committee recommends solutions that may lead to new laws. Select committees are disbanded when they have finished their work.

Joint Committees. Congress also has committees made up of an equal number of representatives and senators. These **joint committees** are set up when the two houses of Congress decide they can take care of certain matters better by working together. One example of a joint congressional committee is the Taxation Committee.

Conference Committees. Another kind of House-Senate committee is known as a **conference committee.** This is formed to work out a compromise when the House and Senate pass different versions of the same bill. Each conference committee is temporary and considers only one bill.

Standing Committees of Congress

HOUSE COMMITTEES

- Agriculture
- Appropriations
- Armed Services
- Banking, Finance, and Urban Affairs
- Budget
- District of Columbia
- Education and Labor
- Foreign Affairs
- Government Operations
- House Administration
- Interior and Insular Affairs
- Interstate and Foreign Commerce
- Judiciary
- Merchant Marine and Fisheries
- Post Office and Civil Service
- Public Works and Transportation
- Rules
- Science and Technology
- Small Business
- Standards of Official Conduct
- Veterans' Affairs
- Ways and Means

SENATE COMMITTEES

- Agriculture, Nutrition, and Forestry
- Appropriations
- Armed Services
- Banking, Housing, and Urban Affairs
- Budget
- Commerce, Science, and Transportation
- Energy and Natural Resources
- Environment and Public Works
- Finance
- Foreign Relations
- Governmental Affairs
- Judiciary
- Labor and Human Resources
- Rules and Administration
- Veterans' Affairs

Membership on Committees

Each member of the House usually serves on only one major standing committee. This enables each representative to specialize in one subject area. In the Senate, each senator serves on at least two major standing committees. Members of Congress eagerly seek assignment to the most important standing committees.

The membership of the standing committees is divided in proportion to the number of members each party has in each house. If the Senate contains 60 Republicans and 40 Democrats, a ten-member committee would include six Republicans and four Democrats. Thus the majority party has a great advantage. It is able to control much of a committee's work.

Each party in each house of Congress has its own **committee on committees.** This group nominates, or names, members of the party to serve on the various standing committees. Then a party caucus reviews the nominations. Loyal party members and longtime members of Congress usually are rewarded with the best committee assignments.

Committee Chairpersons

Since congressional committees are so important, their chairpersons are very powerful. They decide when a committee will meet and when it will hold hearings. Chairpersons create subcommittees and hire and fire committee staff. Their importance gives them great influence in Congress.

How does someone get this position? For many years, the post of committee chairperson automatically went to the member of the majority party who had the most years of service on the committee. This **seniority system** was a long-established custom.

Some people believe the seniority system works well. They say it assures experienced leadership. In recent years, some people have questioned the use of seniority in choosing committee chairpersons. Critics believe that younger members with fewer years of service might provide more vigorous committee leadership.

As a result of such criticism, Congress has changed its method of selecting chairpersons. The majority party in each house now chooses the heads of committees by secret vote in a party caucus. However, the person with the longest service is almost always chosen.

Congressional Staffs

Congressional staffs include special assistants, clerks, and secretaries. Members of Congress need large staffs to run their offices in Washington and in their home districts or states. Their staffs also provide information on bills being considered by Congress. In addition, staff members help keep senators and representatives informed on important issues. Furthermore, they keep members of Congress informed on how the people they represent feel about issues being considered.

CHECK-UP

Vocabulary

sessions
special session
joint session
party caucuses
majority party
minority party
Speaker
floor leader
party whip
president *pro tempore*
bills
committees
standing committees
subcommittees
select committees
joint committees
conference committee
committee on committees
seniority system

Review

1. When does each session of Congress begin? How long does each regular session last?
2. Why is the Speaker of the House an important official?
3. Why does Congress work through committees?
4. How are committee assignments made? Who usually gets the best committee assignments?

Discuss

Although the seniority system has been revised, the person with the longest service is almost always chosen as the committee chairperson. Do you think this is a good idea? Why or why not?

3 The Powers of Congress

The Congress of the United States is very powerful. Under the Constitution, Congress' most important job is to make laws. These laws do not simply tell us what we can and cannot do. They affect us in many other ways as well. For example, laws passed by Congress determine how high our taxes are. They provide for the building of highways and dams. They decide what military equipment we will sell to other nations. Thus Congress' actions affect the lives of millions of people in the United States and throughout the world.

The Powers Given to Congress

Article 1, Section 8, of the Constitution lists the powers granted to Congress. These specific powers are known as **delegated powers** because they are granted, or delegated, to Congress by the Constitution. They give Congress the right to make laws in the following five important areas:

1. Financing our government. Congress can raise and collect taxes, borrow money, and print and coin money. It can use the

DID YOU KNOW THAT . . .

a member of Congress once declared his horse to be a "public document"? As you recall, every member of Congress has the franking privilege—the right to send official mail without paying postage. Instead of a stamp, a copy of the congressperson's signature appears on the envelope. In the past, the franking privilege was sometimes abused. The most extreme example involved a senator in the 1800's. He put his signature on his horse's bridle and had him shipped home—for free!

funds it collects to pay the debts of the United States and to provide for the country's defense and for the general welfare of the people.

2. Regulating and encouraging trade and industry. Congress can regulate trade with foreign countries and among the states. It can also help American businesses by setting a uniform standard of weights and measures and by passing laws that protect the rights of inventors. Congress also establishes post offices and builds roads that help business and industry in our nation. In addition, Congress can set punishments for piracy and other crimes committed against American ships on the seas.

3. Defending the nation. Congress has the power to declare war and to maintain an army and a navy. It also can provide for a citizen army that can be called to duty during wartime or national emergencies.

4. Enforcing the nation's laws. Congress can pass laws concerning such crimes as counterfeiting and treason. To see that these and other federal laws are upheld, Congress can establish a system of national courts.

5. Providing for the nation's continuing growth. Congress has the power to govern the nation's territories and to provide for the admission of new states. Congress also has the power to pass naturalization laws. Naturalization laws make it possible for people born in foreign nations to become American citizens.

The "Elastic Clause"

The last power listed in Section 8 of Article 1 is among the most important. It says that Congress has the power "to make all laws which shall be necessary and proper for carrying into execution [carrying out] the foregoing powers."

This is the famous **elastic clause.** It is called the elastic clause because it has allowed Congress to stretch the powers listed in the Constitution in order to cover many other subjects. The clause has permitted Congress to pass laws covering situations that developed long after the Constitution was written.

For example, Congress has set up national military academies to train army, navy, and air force officers. The Constitution does not specifically give Congress this power. But Congress says that the academies are "necessary and proper" in order for it to carry out its constitutional right to establish an army and a navy. Congress claims that this part of the Constitution implies, or suggests, that Congress has the right to establish military academies to train military officers. For this reason, the powers that Congress claims under the elastic clause are sometimes called **implied powers.**

The Power to Impeach

The Constitution gives Congress other important powers in addition to lawmaking. One of Congress' most serious responsibilities is its power to accuse high federal officials of serious crimes against the nation and to bring them to trial. The highest officials in our government—including the President, Vice President, and federal judges—may be removed from office if they are found guilty of treason or some other serious crime.

The charges against the accused official must be drawn up in the House of Representatives. The list of charges is read before the entire House. Then the representatives vote. If a majority of them vote in favor of the list of charges, the official is formally accused, or impeached, and will be put on trial. The procedure of drawing up and passing the list of charges in the House is called **impeachment.**

The trial on the impeachment charges is held in the Senate. During this trial, the Senate becomes a court. The Vice President usually acts as the judge. If the President is impeached, however, the Chief Justice of the Supreme Court presides instead. That is because the Vice President would become President if the President were found guilty.

The members of the Senate act as the jury. They hear the evidence and examine all witnesses. Then they vote on whether the official is innocent or guilty. Two thirds of the Senate must find the official guilty before he or she can be dismissed from office.

The impeachment process has been used rarely. Altogether, 12 federal officials have been impeached. Only four of them, all judges, were found guilty and dismissed from office. Only one President, Andrew Johnson, has ever been impeached. In his impeachment trial in the Senate in 1868, President Johnson was found not guilty by one vote. In 1974 the threat of impeachment caused President Richard M. Nixon to resign.

Special Powers of Each House

The Constitution gives each house of Congress a number of special powers. The House of Representatives has three special powers:

1. The House alone can start impeachment proceedings.

2. All bills for raising money must start in the House.

3. If no candidate for President receives the number of votes needed to be elected, the members of the House of Representatives choose the President.

The Senate has four special powers:

1. The impeachment trial must be held in the Senate.

Powers of Congress

THE SENATE

THE HOUSE OF REPRESENTATIVES

DELEGATED POWERS

- Collect taxes to pay for the cost of the federal government
- Regulate trade with foreign nations
- Regulate trade and industry among the states
- Declare war and make peace
- Raise armed forces to defend our nation
- Establish post offices and roads
- Print and coin money
- Make rules about naturalization and immigration
- Govern the District of Columbia
- Admit new states to the Union
- Borrow money
- Establish a system of courts

IMPLIED POWERS

- To make all laws "necessary and proper" to carry out the delegated powers
- To "provide for the general welfare" of the United States

An important part of the job of members of Congress is to meet with the people they represent. In this way, they learn the views of the voters.

2. If no candidate for Vice President receives the number of votes needed to be elected, the members of the Senate choose the Vice President.

3. All treaties, or written agreements, with foreign nations must be approved by the Senate by a two-thirds vote.

4. Certain high officials appointed by the President must be approved by the Senate by a majority vote.

Limits on the Powers of Congress

The powers of Congress are limited in several important ways. The Supreme Court has the power to decide when Congress has gone beyond the powers granted to it by the Constitution. (You will read more about this in Chapter 7.) When the Court rules that Congress has passed a law that exceeds Congress' constitutional powers, this law has no force.

Another limit of Congress' powers is the Tenth Amendment to the Constitution. It declares that the states shall keep all the powers not actually granted to the national government. These powers, as you recall, are the reserved powers. They include the states' authority with regard to elections, education, and marriage.

In addition, Article 1, Section 9, of the Constitution denies certain powers to Congress. The Constitution specifically forbids the following powers to Congress:

1. Congress cannot pass *ex post facto* laws. A law that applies to an action that took place before the law was passed is called an ***ex post facto* law.** For example, it is not against the law today to buy and sell foreign automobiles. If tomorrow Congress forbids the buying and selling of foreign cars, a person cannot be arrested for having bought one of these cars in the past.

2. Congress cannot pass bills of attainder. A law that sentences a person to jail without granting the person a trial is called a **bill of attainder.** The Constitution provides that anyone accused of a crime must be given a trial in a court of law.

3. Congress cannot set aside, or suspend, the writ of *habeas corpus*. A person accused of a crime has the right to a **writ of *habeas corpus*.** This is a court order requiring that the accused person be brought to court to determine if there is enough evidence to hold the person for a trial. If Congress had the right to set aside the writ of *habeas corpus*, a person might be kept in jail indefinitely with no formal charges being brought. The only exception to this rule is in times of rebellion or invasion.

4. Congress cannot tax exports. Goods that are sent to other countries are called exports. A tax on exports would harm our foreign and domestic trade. Congress can, however, tax imports—goods that are brought into the country from abroad.

5. Congress cannot pass any law that violates the Bill of Rights. The first ten amendments to the Constitution, as you recall, spell out the rights and freedoms of all American citizens. (See pages 67–68.) Congress is forbidden to pass any law that violates these rights.

6. Congress cannot favor the trade of one state over that of other states. Congress cannot pass a law giving any state or group of states an unfair advantage in trade. Of course, Congress can pass laws regulating trade. But these laws must apply equally to all states.

7. Congress cannot grant titles of nobility to any American citizen. Americans believe that all people are created equal. Therefore, they are opposed to establishing a noble class, or small group of persons with rights superior to those of other citizens.

8. Congress cannot withdraw money from the Treasury without a law. Congress must pass a law telling how money shall be spent and the exact amount to be spent before the public funds are made available. This means that Congress must pass money laws to provide the money for carrying out the other laws it passes.

Other Roles of Congress

Over the years, the job of members of Congress has expanded greatly. Their responsibilities have grown to include roles that were not anticipated in the Constitution.

Aiding Constituents. One of the most important jobs of members of Congress is to serve the interests of the people who live in their home districts or states. These people are called their **constituents.**

Members of Congress receive thousands of letters from their constituents every week. Some of this mail gives opinions on issues. Other letters ask a representative or senator to vote for or against a certain bill.

Most of the mail is from people asking for help. For example, a disabled veteran may complain that the Veterans Administration has lost his claim. The owner of a small company may ask how to apply for a government contract.

Conducting Investigations. Another important responsibility of Congress is its power to conduct investigations. Either house of Congress may investigate national issues. The purpose of these investigations usually is to determine whether a new law is needed or if an existing law is being carried out as Congress intended.

CHECK-UP

Vocabulary

delegated powers
elastic clause
implied powers
impeachment
ex post facto law
bill of attainder
writ of *habeas corpus*
constituents

Review

1. Name the five powers that are delegated to Congress by the Constitution.
2. What special powers does the House of Representatives have? the Senate?
3. Name four ways in which the powers of Congress are limited.

Discuss

Besides writing laws, members of Congress have many other tasks. As one member of Congress said: "It is true that we just don't have much time to legislate around here." Do you think so many demands should be made on members of Congress? Can anything be done to help make their jobs easier?

4 How a Bill Becomes a Law

Each day that Congress is in session, an interesting scene takes place. As the members of the House enter their legislative hall, some of them approach the front of the chamber. Then they drop papers into a box on the clerk's desk. The box is called the hopper. The papers dropped into it are bills, or written proposals for laws.

Of course, not all these proposals become laws. The process of getting a law passed is long and difficult. This sometimes makes us think that government is not responsive enough. In the long run, however, the process helps to ensure that our nation's laws will be good laws.

How the Idea for a Bill Begins

Each year the Senate and the House of Representatives consider thousands of bills. These bills may be introduced in either house. The only exception to this rule is an **appropriation bill,** or bill approving the spending of money. An appropriation bill must originate in the House of Representatives. Every bill must be passed by both houses of Congress before it may be signed by the President and becomes a law. A law is also known as an **act.**

Where do the ideas for all these bills begin?

1. Ideas for bills may come from any American citizen. The people are a powerful force in influencing laws. When a large number of constituents request a law, a representative or senator usually introduces a bill containing their ideas.

2. Ideas for bills may come from organized groups. Members of Congress sometimes introduce bills because they are requested to do so by certain groups. For example, business people may want to limit competition from industries in other countries. Labor groups often call for laws establishing improved working conditions or higher hourly wages.

How Ideas for Bills Begin

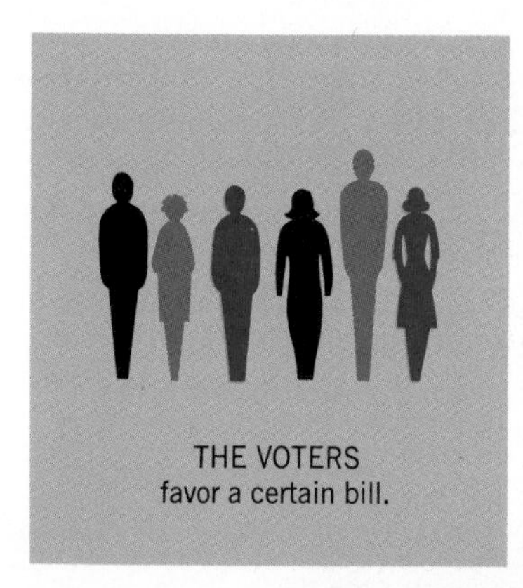
THE VOTERS
favor a certain bill.

INDIVIDUAL
MEMBERS OF CONGRESS
may introduce a bill they favor.

LARGE GROUPS OF AMERICANS
ask for a certain bill.

CONGRESSIONAL
INVESTIGATING COMMITTEES
may recommend a bill.

THE PRESIDENT
urges certain laws in
speeches to Congress.

3. Ideas for bills may come from committees of Congress. Many bills begin in Congress itself. Suppose that a congressional investigating committee conducts a study of certain kinds of crime. Suppose that its findings convince the committee that the federal government needs a new law for crime control. The committee can then draw up a bill and introduce it in Congress.

4. Ideas for bills may come from members of Congress. Members of Congress often become experts in certain fields. A senator or representative who has had long experience with farm problems, for example, may introduce a bill to aid agriculture.

5. Ideas for bills may come from the President of the United States. The President has great influence on bills introduced into Congress. Early in each session of Congress, the President appears before a joint session of the two houses to deliver a State of the Union Message. In this speech, the President recommends laws that the President feels are needed to improve our nation's well-being. Many of these ideas are soon introduced as bills by members of Congress.

How an Idea Becomes a Bill

Although anyone can suggest an idea for a bill, only members of Congress can introduce the bill itself. Suppose, for example, that a group of citizens favors creating a new national park. They write to their senators or representatives and explain their idea. The leader of the group arranges for a personal meeting with a senator or representative.

At this meeting, the leader provides facts and figures on the subject and urges that a bill be introduced. If the senator or representative is convinced that the group's idea is a good one, she or he may agree to introduce the bill.

To see how a bill becomes a law, let us study the progress of this bill as it is considered first by the House of Representatives and then by the Senate.

The Bill Is Introduced in the House

How does the representative introduce this bill in the House? First the proposed bill is carefully written out. Bills are not always written by representatives. In fact, many bills are written by a committee, by the group who suggested the bill, or by an assistant to the representative.

After the bill is dropped into the hopper, it is given letters and a number. Let us suppose that the bill to create a new national park is marked HR 1215. The letters *HR* show that the bill is being considered by the House of Representatives. The number *1215* shows its place among all the bills presented in this particular session of Congress.

What happens to the bill after it is introduced? First it is sent to one of the standing committees for study. Usually the subject of the bill determines which committee will study it. In some cases, two committees may be interested in studying the bill. The Speaker of the House then decides to which committee it will be sent.

The Bill Is Sent to a Committee

In the case of HR 1215, the Speaker sends the bill to the House Interior and Insular Affairs Committee. This committee deals with all bills concerning the national park system.

Each bill is given careful attention by the committee to which it is sent. Many of the bills are found to be unnecessary. These are set aside and are never sent back to the House for further action. In this way the committees cut down on the amount of legislation Congress must consider.

The Committee Holds Hearings

HR 1215 is not set aside. Instead, the House Interior and Insular Affairs Committee holds special meetings, called **hearings,** to consider the bill. Most committee hearings are open to

Congressional committees hold hearings to get information on bills they are considering. Here witnesses testify before a Senate committee.

the public. Some important hearings are shown on television. At the hearings, the committee calls witnesses to testify for and against the bill. These witnesses help give the committee members the information they need in order to recommend that the bill be accepted, rejected, or changed.

Some of the witnesses who testify may be lobbyists. A **lobbyist** is a person who is paid to represent a certain group's point of view, or interests, at committee hearings. Lobbyists and expert witnesses, letters and telegrams from citizens, and evidence that committee members gather from many sources—all these help the committee reach a decision on the bill.

The Committee Studies the Bill

In the case of HR 1215, the Interior and Insular Affairs Committee decides to change the bill in certain ways. Members reword lines and add new sections to parts of the bill. When they are finished, the bill is very different from the one they originally received. The majority of committee members decide to recommend that the House pass the bill as amended, or changed, by the committee.

The House Considers the Bill

When HR 1215 is reported out of committee and sent back to the House of Representatives, it is placed on the House calendar. The **calendar** is the schedule that lists the order in which bills are to be considered. In a real emergency, a bill can be moved up on the calendar so that action may be taken quickly.

HR 1215 must be given three readings in the House of Representatives. By the time its turn comes on the calendar, the first reading really has already occurred. It took place when the Speaker first read the title of the bill to the House before sending it to the appropriate committee. The second reading will occur while the bill is debated.

The Rules Committee decides how much time will be given to debate on this bill. The time to be spent in debate, or discussion, is divided evenly between those members in favor of the bill and those against the bill.

For the debate, the House usually acts as a

How a Bill Becomes a Law

This chart shows a bill that begins in the House of Representatives.

The same procedure is followed when a bill begins in the Senate.

HOUSE OF REPRESENTATIVES

A representative introduces the bill.

Clerk of the House

The clerk reads the bill's title to the House, gives the bill a number, and has it printed.

Speaker of the House

The Speaker of the House sends the bill to the proper committee.

House Committee

The committee or one of its subcommittees holds hearings on the bill, and may amend, rewrite, or approve the bill. If the committee approves the bill it is placed on the House calendar.

Floor of the House

The bill is read and debated. The House amends it, returns it to the House committee for revision, or approves it and sends it to the Senate.

Passed by the House

Sent to the Senate

SENATE

Clerk of the Senate

The bill is given a number, its title is read, and it is printed.

Presiding Officer of the Senate

The presiding officer of the Senate sends the bill to the proper committee.

Senate Committee

The committee or one of its subcommittees holds hearings on the bill, and may amend, rewrite, kill, or approve the bill. If the full committee approves the bill, it is placed on the Senate calendar.

Senate Floor

The bill is read and debated. The Senate amends it, returns it to the Senate committee for revision, or approves it. If the Senate approves a version different from the House version, the bill is sent to a conference committee of the House and Senate.

Conference Committee

The conference committee irons out differences between the House and Senate versions of the bill. It returns the revised bill to both houses for approval.

President

The President signs or vetoes the bill or allows it to become law without signing it. Congress can overrule a veto by a two-thirds vote of both houses.

Committee of the Whole. As one big committee, the House can act less formally and really turn the meeting into a work session. The bill now is given its second reading. A clerk reads a paragraph, and then amendments may be offered. Debate on each amendment to the bill is usually limited to five minutes for each member who wishes to speak. A vote is then taken on the amendment. It is usually a voice vote with all in favor saying aye and those opposed, no.

Each paragraph of the bill is read and amended in similar fashion until the entire bill has been considered. When the House meets again in formal session, a member may demand a "quorum call." A **quorum,** or majority, of the members must be present in order to do business.

The House Votes on the Bill

When a quorum is present, the House is ready for the third reading. This reading is usually by title only. However, any member may demand that the bill be read in its entirety. The vote is then taken. A majority of the members present is required to pass a bill.

On important bills, a **roll-call vote** is usually taken. Each member's name is called and a record is made of his or her vote. Our bill to create a new national park, as amended, passes the House. But it is not yet a law. Like all bills, it must now be considered by the other house of Congress, the Senate.

The Senate Acts on the Bill

In the Senate, the bill is called S 2019. The way in which a bill is handled in the Senate is similar to the process followed in the House. Bill S 2019 is read by title, for its first reading. It is then sent to the Senate Energy and Natural Resources Committee for consideration.

After holding hearings, the committee revises S 2019. The committee then recommends that the bill be passed by the Senate.

The senators usually are not limited in their debate as are members of the House of Representatives. In the Senate, speeches may go on and on. Some senators have talked for many hours in order to prevent the Senate from taking a vote on a bill. This method of delay by making lengthy speeches is called a **filibuster.** Senators have sometimes tried to "talk a bill to death." Debate in the Senate can be limited only if three fifths of the full Senate votes to limit it. Limit on debate in the Senate is called **cloture.** It has seldom been voted.

After the members of the Senate finish their debate on S 2019, a roll call is taken. Bill S 2019 passes. What happens next?

The House and the Senate Must Agree on the Final Bill

When a bill passes the House and Senate in identical form, it is ready to be sent to the President. Usually, however, the two houses pass different versions of the same bill. If a bill is changed in any way, it must be sent back to the house in which it originated. In our example, the House of Representatives does not agree to the Senate changes. When this happens, a conference committee must be called.

A conference committee meets to try to reach an agreement on the bill. The committee is made up of an equal number of senators and representatives. The committee members from each house may have to give up something in order to reach a compromise.

Finally a compromise bill is sent back to both houses. Usually both houses approve the work of their conference committee.

The President Approves the Bill

The bill as passed by both houses is sent to the President of the United States. The President may take one of three possible actions on a bill:

1. The President may sign the bill and declare it to be a law.

2. The President may refuse to sign the bill and send it back to Congress with a message giving the reasons for rejecting it. This action, as you have read, is called a **veto.**

3. The President may keep the bill for ten days without signing it. If Congress is in session during this ten-day period, the bill becomes a law without the President's signature. However, if Congress is not in session and the President does not sign the bill within ten days, the bill does not become a law. When this happens, we say the bill has been killed by a **pocket veto.**

The President does not use the veto often. Even then, Congress can pass a bill over the President's veto by a two-thirds vote of both houses. In the case of our national park bill, it becomes a law and goes into effect after the President signs it.

The long and involved process of making laws may be slow. However, it prevents hasty legislation while providing a way for the national government to pass needed laws.

CHECK-UP

Vocabulary

appropriation bill
act
hearings
lobbyist
calendar
Committee of the Whole
quorum
roll-call vote
filibuster
cloture
veto
pocket veto

Review

1. Where do the ideas for bills introduced into Congress originate?
2. Trace the steps by which a bill becomes a law.
3. What three possible actions can the President take on a bill that has been passed by Congress?

Discuss

Congress is the lawmaking branch. In recent years, however, most bills have been suggested by the executive branch. Why do you think this has happened? Do you think this is a good idea? Why or why not?

CHAPTER SUMMARY

The legislative, or lawmaking, branch of our federal government is called Congress. It consists of two houses, the House of Representatives and the Senate. Each state is represented in the Senate by two senators. The number of representatives each state elects to the House of Representatives is based on the size of the state's population.

Congress meets for a two-year term. The two houses organize their work and operate in similar ways. Much of the actual work of Congress is done by committees.

Congress has been given many important powers by the Constitution. The delegated powers set forth specific functions of Congress. The "elastic clause" has permitted Congress to exercise powers not specifically granted to it. The Constitution also limits the powers of Congress. It reserves certain powers for the states and specifically forbids some powers to Congress.

Congress considers thousands of bills, or proposed laws, each year. To become a law, each bill must be passed by both houses of Congress before being signed by the President.

CIVICS SKILLS: Interpreting Political Cartoons

Most Americans recognize him at a glance. If his white beard doesn't give him away, his clothes surely will. He has been wearing the same outfit for more than 100 years: striped pants, a cutaway coat, and a stovepipe hat decorated with stars. His name is Uncle Sam—the figure who has come to represent the United States.

You see Uncle Sam and many other equally famous characters all the time. They appear regularly in a special form of art called the **political cartoon.** This is a cartoon that uses pictures to express a point of view. Because these pictures are often funny, your first reaction might be to laugh. It is important, however, to look beyond the humor. Every political cartoon has a serious message.

Reading the Cartoon

You begin reading a cartoon the same way you read any picture. You look at the details. As you do this, keep in mind that a cartoonist often works with **symbols,** or drawings with special meanings. Some symbols, such as Uncle Sam, represent groups of people or places. Other symbols represent ideas. You probably have seen drawings of a blindfolded woman holding a set of scales. This is a symbol for justice. What other symbols represent ideas?

Sometimes cartoonists help you find the meaning of their symbols by using words. For example, labels can identify the main symbols. Captions can sum up the cartoon's message. Or characters can speak for the artist. How are words used in the cartoon on this page?

Recognizing the Opinion

After you have identified the important symbols in a political cartoon, your next step is to find out how they are used. Some figures, for example, might be **caricatures.** These are sketches that exaggerate, or distort, a person's features. Caricatures can be positive or negative, depending on the artist's point of view.

You should also think carefully about the effect symbols might have on you. Suppose an artist showed high oil prices in the form of a shark. This would give you an idea of how the artist viewed the problem.

The final step in reading any political cartoon is to consider your own opinion. Has the cartoon changed your point of view? Do you agree with the cartoonist? Or had you never really thought about the issue before reading the cartoon?

Practicing What You've Learned

Use the following questions to interpret the cartoon below.

1. What is the subject of the cartoon?
2. Why do you think the cartoonist chose to show the seniority system as an old king?
3. What is the cartoonist's opinion of the seniority system? Do you agree with this opinion? Why or why not?

CHAPTER REVIEW

Vocabulary

On a separate piece of paper or in the vocabulary section of your notebook, copy the following paragraph. Then, choosing from the list of words below, fill in the blanks in the paragraph.

Speaker of the House	committees
lobbyists	Senate
bills	bicameral
President	House of Representatives
president *pro tempore*	filibuster

A civics class, visiting Washington, D.C., learned that Congress is a two-house, or (1) ______, legislature. Its two houses are the (2) ______ and the (3) ______. In a representative's office they saw people called (4) ______ try to persuade the representative to vote a certain way. Then, in the Senate, they watched several senators conducting a (5) ______, or making long speeches to delay a vote. They saw the (6) ______, the presiding officer who takes over when the Vice President is absent. In the House of Representatives, the presiding officer is the (7) ______. The members of Congress were discussing (8) ______ that might become laws if they passed both houses and were signed by the (9) ______. To manage all their work, both houses divide their work among small groups called (10) ______.

Check-Up

1. Why is our national legislature divided into two houses?
2. How are the 435 seats in the House of Representatives distributed?
3. What is the difference between a conference committee and a joint committee?
4. Who has the power to call a special session of Congress? Why might such a session be called?
5. Who are some of the main officers of each political party in Congress? What do these officials do?
6. What are some of the powers shared by both houses of Congress?
7. What are some of the things Congress cannot do?
8. What are the main steps by which a bill becomes a law?
9. Some Americans think that our process of lawmaking is too slow. What do you think?

Civics Skills

In either a newspaper or newsmagazine, find a political cartoon that deals with the subject of Congress. Mount this cartoon on a piece of paper. Then study it and answer the following questions.

1. What are the symbols in the cartoon?
2. How has the cartoonist used words to help you interpret these symbols?
3. What is the cartoon's main point?

Citizenship and You

1. Pretend that you have been elected to Congress. List what you think are the most important tasks of a member of Congress in order of their importance.
2. Learn about the members of Congress from your state. Who represents your congressional district? Who are the senators from your state? Who is the senior senator? How many representatives does your state have? Did the 1980 census change your state's representation in Congress? If so, how?
3. How long has the representative from your district and each senator from your state been in Congress? On which committees do they sit?

CHAPTER

6

The President Carries Out Our Nation's Laws

"The terms of the President and Vice President shall end at noon on the 20th day of January . . . and the terms of their successors shall then begin."

—Amendment 20,
Constitution of the United States

The day on which the new President takes office is called Inauguration Day. It is an exciting day in Washington, D.C., and indeed throughout the nation. Visitors pour into the nation's capital from our 50 states and from foreign lands.

The inaugural ceremony is held on a large, flag-draped platform set up at the Capitol Building. The highlight of the ceremony is the swearing in of the President. The President-elect places one hand on the Bible and repeats the oath of office. The Chief Justice of the Supreme Court administers the oath, reading these words from the Constitution:

"I do solemnly swear (or affirm) that I will faithfully execute [carry out] the office of the President of the United States, and will, to the best of my ability, preserve, protect, and defend the Constitution of the United States."

After the oath of office, the President delivers an Inaugural Address. Americans throughout the nation, as well as people in other lands, listen carefully to the President's words. They know they are listening to the person who will lead the United States for the next four years.

In this chapter, you will study these important topics:

1. **The President of the United States**
2. **The Powers and Roles of the President**
3. **The Executive Departments and the Cabinet**
4. **The President and the Independent Agencies**

1 The President of the United States

The executive branch of the federal government, described in Article 2 of the Constitution, is headed by the **President** of the United States. In 1789 George Washington became the nation's first President. Since then only 38 other men have served as President. Hundreds of people, however, have sought the office. The President is the nation's most powerful elected official.

Qualifications

The Constitution sets forth certain qualifications that the President of the United States must meet:

1. The President must be a native-born American citizen.

2. The President must be at least 35 years of age.

3. The President must have been a resident of the United States for at least 14 years.

These are the only qualifications for President mentioned in the Constitution. However, there also have been a number of unwritten rules about who could be elected President. For example, all American Presidents have been men. All have been white. All have been Christian. Most Presidents have attended college. Many have been lawyers. Most have held other political offices before becoming President.

This does not mean, however, that these unwritten rules cannot change. Throughout most of American history, only Protestants were elected President. John F. Kennedy, who was a Roman Catholic, broke that unwritten rule when he was elected President in 1960. In recent years, more women and minority group members have become involved in politics. Therefore, in the future, more and more of the unwritten rules about who can be elected President most likely will be broken.

Term of Office

The President is elected to a four-year term and may be reelected for a second term of office. The original Constitution did not state how many terms a President could serve.

CAN YOU GUESS?

- **How young was the youngest person ever elected President? Who was he?**
- **How old was the oldest person ever elected President? Who was he?**

Answers are on page 562.

The President of the United States conducts much of the nation's business in the Oval Office of the White House.

George Washington set the tradition of a limit of two terms. He refused to run for the Presidency a third time when he was urged to do so. This two-term tradition was not broken until Franklin D. Roosevelt was elected to a third term as President in 1940. In 1944 he won a fourth term.

In 1951 the length of time a President could serve was limited by passage of the Twenty-second Amendment (see page 73). This amendment set a two-term limit to the Presidency.

Salary and Benefits

The salary the President receives is fixed by Congress. However, Congress cannot change the salary during a President's term of office. This restriction was included in the Constitution to prevent Congress from punishing or rewarding a President.

Today the President is paid a salary of $200,000 a year plus $50,000 for official expenses. Since the President must travel frequently, there is also an annual allowance for travel costs.

The President is provided with many additional benefits. The President's family lives in the White House. This beautiful building has been the home of all American Presidents since John Adams. The White House is also the site of the President's office and the offices of the President's closest assistants. Parts of the White House are open to visitors.

For special meetings and for relaxation on weekends or holidays, the President can use Camp David, in the mountains of Maryland. When the President travels, there is a large fleet of cars, helicopters, and planes, including a special jet plane called Air Force One.

The Vice President

The Constitution provides that if the President dies, resigns, or is removed from office, the **Vice President** becomes President. The Constitution gives the Vice President only one other job—to preside over the Senate.

John Adams, the country's first Vice President, called the office the most insignificant ever invented.

The first Vice President to succeed to the Presidency was John Tyler. He became President in 1841 when President William Harrison died. Since then eight other Vice Presidents have succeeded to the Presidency. In fact, five Vice Presidents have succeeded to the Presidency since 1900.

The Vice President thus holds a very important position. Moreover, in recent years Presidents have given their Vice Presidents more responsibilities. Vice Presidents must be fully informed and prepared to take over the important job that could become theirs.

The Vice President must meet the same constitutional qualifications as the President. The Vice President also serves a four-year term and receives a salary of $79,125 a year plus $10,000 for official expenses.

Vice Presidential candidates often are chosen for their ability to help the Presidential candidates win election. Increasingly, political parties have also chosen Vice Presidential nominees who are fully qualified by experience to succeed to the Presidency.

Presidential Succession

Eight Presidents of the United States have died while in office. One President resigned. In each case, the Vice President took the oath of office and became President as provided by the Constitution.

What would happen if both the President and the Vice President should die while in office? The Constitution gave Congress the right to decide who should then fill the office of President. This is known as the order of **Presidential succession.**

According to a law passed by Congress in 1947, the Speaker of the House of Representatives becomes President if both the regularly elected President and Vice President die or are removed from office. If the Speaker dies or is removed from office, then the president *pro tempore* of the Senate succeeds to the Presidency. Following them in succession to the Presidency are the members of the Cabinet, in the order in which their departments were created.

The Twenty-Fifth Amendment

If the President dies or resigns and is succeeded by the Vice President, who then becomes Vice President? Until 1967 the answer to this question was, no one. The office of the Vice President remained empty when the Vice President moved up to the Presidency. Under the Twenty-fifth Amendment (see page 74), the new President nominates a new Vice President. The nomination must then be approved by a majority vote of both houses of Congress.

The first test of the Twenty-fifth Amendment came in 1973. Vice President Spiro

Chief Justice Warren Burger swore in Gerald Ford as the 38th President of the United States on August 9, 1974, the day that President Richard Nixon resigned.

Agnew resigned after he was charged with income tax evasion. President Richard M. Nixon nominated Gerald R. Ford as the new Vice President. The nomination was confirmed by Congress.

This amendment was used again in 1974. When President Nixon resigned because of the Watergate scandal, Vice President Ford became President. Ford then nominated Nelson A. Rockefeller as Vice President, and Congress approved the nomination. Thus, for the first time in our history, the nation had a President and a Vice President who had not been elected by the vote of the people.

The Twenty-fifth Amendment also provides that if the President is too ill to serve, the Vice President will serve as Acting President until the President is well again. Suppose, however, that the President wants to serve again, but the Vice President and the Cabinet do not think the President is fit to do so. Then Congress must decide by a two-thirds vote whether the President will return to office or whether the Vice President will continue as Acting President.

CHECK-UP

Vocabulary

President
Vice President
Presidential succession

Review

1. What qualifications does the Constitution set forth for the President of the United States?
2. How many terms may a President of the United States serve in office? Where is this stated in the Constitution?
3. Describe the order of Presidential succession in this country.
4. How may the office of Vice President be filled if the Vice President succeeds to the Presidency or leaves office?

Discuss

Do you think the Vice President should be given more responsibilities? Explain.

2 The Powers and Roles of the President

Article 2, Section 1, of the Constitution provides that "the executive power shall be vested in [given to] a President of the United States of America." This means that the President is responsible for executing, or carrying out, the laws passed by Congress. Because the President has the job of executing the nation's laws, the President is often called the nation's **Chief Executive.** As Chief Executive, the President must take an active role in all phases of government.

The President Influences Legislation

The President plays a large role in shaping the laws of the United States by recommending, or suggesting, needed laws to Congress. In fact, the Constitution requires that the President "shall from time to time give to the Congress information of [about] the state of the Union, and recommend to their [Congress'] consideration such measures as he shall judge necessary. . . ."

To carry out this constitutional provision, the President delivers several messages to Congress each year. These messages may be delivered as speeches before Congress or in writing.

Every year, usually in late January, the President delivers to Congress a **State of the Union Message**. As you read in Chapter 5, this speech sets forth the programs and policies that the President wants Congress to put into effect as laws.

The President also sends Congress a budget message, recommending how the federal government should raise and spend its money. In an economic message to Congress, the President reviews the nation's economic condition and recommends various laws to aid the economy.

The President's Veto Power

The President also influences legislation by the power to veto, or reject, laws. Sometimes the threat of a Presidential veto discourages Congress from passing a bill. Congress knows how difficult it is to pass a bill after it has been vetoed by the President. For this reason, Congress considers carefully before passing a bill it knows the President does not approve.

Commander in Chief

As head of the armed forces of the United States, or **Commander in Chief,** the President has important powers. All military officers, in time of war or in peacetime, take their orders from the President. The President does not actually lead American forces into battle. However, the President is in constant touch with our nation's military leaders. The President also has the final word in planning how a war is to be fought. This is a serious responsibility in our age of modern weapons.

Under the Constitution, only Congress can declare war. As Commander in Chief of the armed forces, however, the President may send American forces into any part of the world where danger threatens. Presidents have sent troops into action in foreign countries many times in our nation's history.

Sending American troops into certain situations sometimes involves the risk of war. Therefore, Congress passed the War Powers Act in 1973 to try to limit the President's war-making power. This act requires that troops sent abroad by the President be recalled within 60 days unless Congress approves the action.

Foreign Policy Leader

The President, as Chief Executive of one of the most powerful nations of the world, must give constant attention to our **foreign policy.** It is the President who is responsible for the way the United States conducts its relations with other nations of the world. The President seeks to secure friendly relations with foreign governments while preserving the security of our nation.

As foreign policy leader, President Jimmy Carter helped Anwar Sadat (left) of Egypt and Menachem Begin (right) of Israel work out a peace agreement.

To conduct our relations with other governments, the President appoints officials to represent the United States in foreign nations. The President also meets with leaders of other nations and with their representatives in the United States. In addition, the President often travels abroad to meet with foreign leaders.

Treaty-Making Power. The government of the United States makes written agreements, called **treaties,** with other nations. The President is responsible for making these treaties with foreign governments. Other officials do most of the actual work in reaching agreements with other nations. The President, however, assumes the final responsibility for all treaties.

All treaties must be made with the advice and consent of the Senate. The Senate must approve a treaty by a two-thirds vote before it becomes effective. If the treaty is approved, it is the President's job to see that its provisions are carried out.

Chief Diplomat

Great skill and tact are required in dealing with friendly and unfriendly nations. The art of dealing with foreign governments is called **diplomacy,** and the President is our chief diplomat. The President often visits foreign nations to build up international friendship and security.

Powers of the President

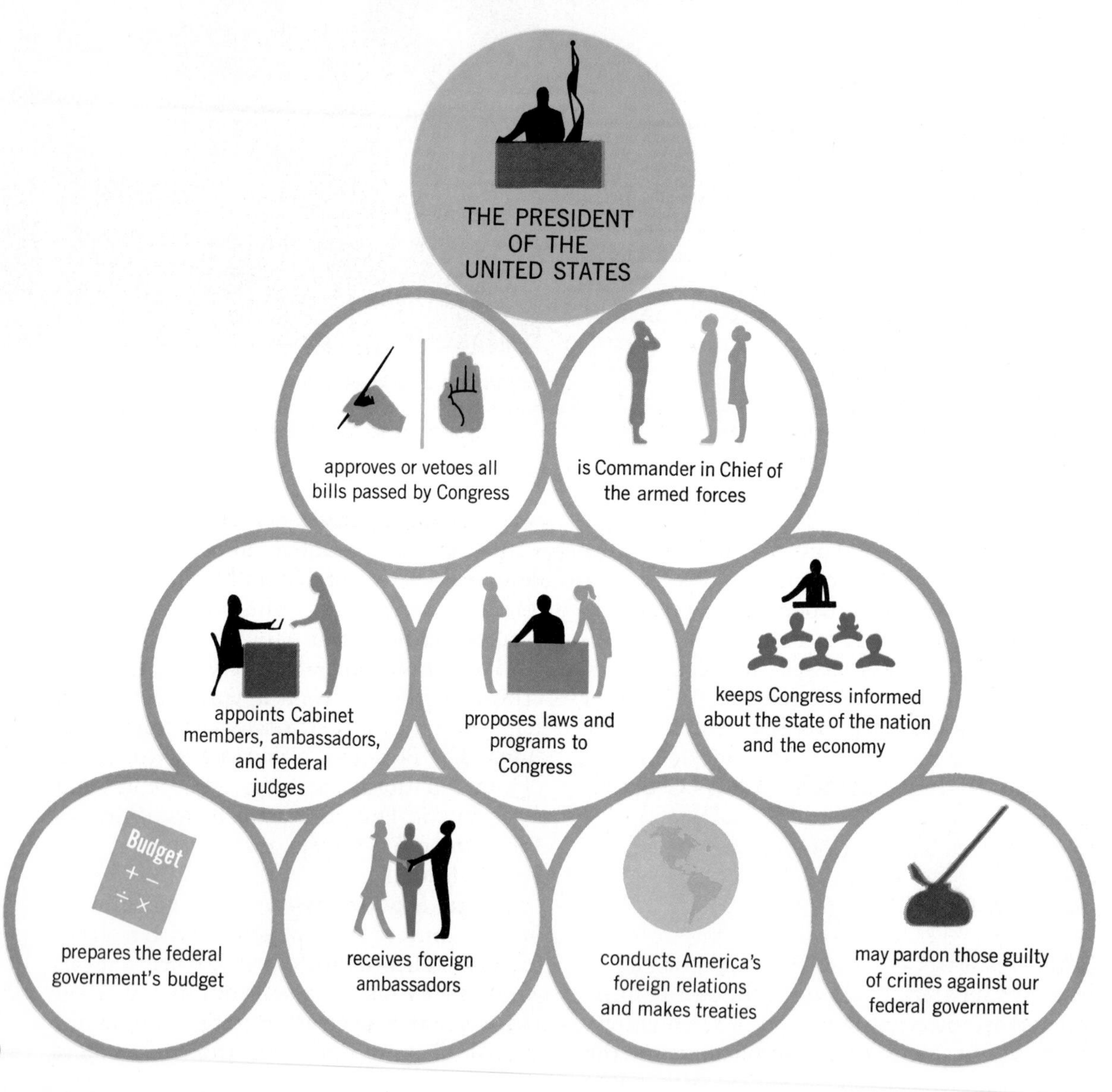

As the nation's chief diplomat, the President often corresponds with the heads of foreign governments. These written communications are called **diplomatic notes.** In addition, the President can telephone other world leaders. For example, on the President's desk is a special phone that enables the President to make direct connection with the government of the Soviet Union in an emergency. Such an exchange of views between world leaders is very helpful. It often prevents governments from taking actions that might have dangerous consequences.

Judicial Powers

The Constitution gives the President the power to appoint Supreme Court Justices and other federal judges. These appointments must be approved by the Senate by a majority vote.

The President also has the power to grant reprieves and pardons to those who have committed certain federal crimes. A **reprieve** postpones the carrying out of a sentence. It gives a convicted person the opportunity to gather more evidence to support his or her case or to appeal for a new trial. A **pardon** forgives a person convicted of a crime and frees her or him from serving out the sentence. The President also has the judicial power of **commutation,** or making a convicted person's sentence less severe.

Other Presidential Roles

Over the years, the President has also taken on other roles that are not mentioned in the Constitution. These roles include Chief of State and leader of a political party.

As **Chief of State,** the President is the symbol of the United States and its people. It is the President who greets visiting foreign leaders and travels to other countries to strengthen ties and improve relations. The President performs many ceremonial duties.

Answering reporter's questions is an important Presidential duty in our free society, as President Ronald Reagan shows in this press conference.

These include awarding medals to honor worthy citizens, lighting the nation's Christmas tree, and throwing the first baseball to open the baseball season.

The President is also the leader of a political party. Members of the President's party worked hard to help elect the President. In return the President makes speeches to help other party members who are running for office. The President helps the party raise money for its political campaigns.

The President's Day

In addition to making many important decisions, the President must find time to carry on a wide range of other activities from day to day. At all times, the President's office must be in touch with other high officials of the nation's government. Thus the President can never be far away from the telephone.

The activities that occupy the President's time are varied. Many hours of the day are spent in meetings with Presidential advisers. When Congress is in session, the President may have a breakfast or luncheon meeting with congressional leaders. Meetings are also held with members of the President's political party to talk over the bills before Congress, appointments of officials, or political plans important to the party. In addition, the President meets regularly with members of the Cabinet.

The President delivers speeches by the dozen. President Franklin D. Roosevelt established the custom of reporting directly to the American people. He did so by radio talks, which he called "fireside chats." Today the President appears on television to speak directly to the people, to inform them of proposed new programs and ask for their support. The President also holds press conferences to explain government decisions and answer questions from reporters.

In addition, the President must find time to attend to many other important duties. The President must sign (or veto) bills, write speeches, appoint officials, and examine budget figures. The President must also deal with matters of foreign policy and reach decisions on national defense problems. Furthermore, the President must find time to read newspapers and magazines and to study reports received from government officials at home and abroad.

CHECK-UP

Vocabulary

Chief Executive	diplomacy
State of the Union Message	diplomatic notes
Commander in Chief	reprieve
foreign policy	pardon
treaties	commutation
	Chief of State

Review

1. How can the President influence the lawmaking process?
2. What powers does the President have as Commander in Chief of the armed forces? How are these powers limited?
3. In what ways does the President carry out the responsibility of conducting the nation's foreign policy?
4. What judicial powers does the President have?

Discuss

In your opinion, what are the President's most important powers and responsibilities? Why?

3 The Executive Departments and the Cabinet

The duties of the executive branch of the federal government have grown greatly since George Washington served as the nation's first Chief Executive. During the early years of our nation, Presidents could carry out their duties with the help of a few assistants. Today there are more than 5,000 people assisting the President.

The Executive Office of the President

The President's closest advisers and assistants are part of the **Executive Office of the President.** The Executive Office was established in 1939. It has been reorganized by every President since then. The agencies and offices that make up the Executive Office advise the President on important domestic and international matters.

The **Council of Economic Advisers,** for example, furnishes the President with facts and figures about the nation's economy. It recommends programs to aid economic growth and stability.

Another agency of the Executive Office is the **Office of Management and Budget.** It assists in the preparation of the federal budget, which the President must present to Congress.

A number of agencies provide the President with the accurate information necessary to strengthen our national security. The **National Security Council,** for instance, is the top-ranking group of advisers on all matters concerning the nation's defense and security. The **Central Intelligence Agency (CIA)** gathers and studies information about other nations.

The **White House Office** includes the President's closest personal and political advisers. Also part of this office are researchers, clerical staff, social secretaries, and the President's doctor. Members of the White House staff perform many important jobs for the President. They schedule appointments and write speeches. They help maintain relations with Congress and with other departments and agencies of the government. The **press secretary** represents the President to the news media and the public.

★ ★ ★ ★ ★ ★ ★ ★ ★ ★ ★ ★

DID YOU KNOW THAT . . .

when George Washington became the nation's first President, no one knew what to call him? Vice President John Adams wanted to call him "His Highness, The President of the United States and Protector of the Rights of the Same." The Senate called him "His Highness." This was the title used for the British king.

It was the House of Representatives that began to refer to the nation's Chief Executive as "the President of the United States." This simple title soon won everyone's approval.

The Executive Departments

The people who wrote the Constitution drew up a plan of government with plenty of room for growth. They did not try to work out every detail of government. For example, they did not try to plan for each person who would help the President carry out the laws. The Constitution made no mention of the President's assistants except to state that "he may require the opinion, in writing, of the principal officer in each of the executive departments. . . ."

Today there are 13 **executive departments** in the federal government. Each has specific areas of responsibility. The chart on page 127 shows you the main duties of each executive department.

Congress has the power to establish executive departments, combine several under one head, or even drop a department. The President must then direct these departments, working within the structure set up by Congress.

The Cabinet

George Washington had the help of only three executive departments: the Departments of State, Treasury, and War. He met frequently with the heads of these departments to discuss policy and get their advice on important matters. The heads of these executive departments, as you recall, became known as the President's **Cabinet.** Every President since Washington has followed his custom of holding Cabinet meetings.

The present Cabinet consists of the heads of the 13 executive departments plus the United States representative to the United Nations. The President often invites the Vice President and other key government officials to attend Cabinet meetings.

Members of the Cabinet are appointed by the President. However, these appointments must be approved by a majority vote of the Senate. The title of most Cabinet members is **Secretary.** For example, the head of the Department of State is the Secretary of State. The head of the Treasury Department is the Secretary of the Treasury. The head of the Justice Department, however, is known as the **Attorney General.**

What kind of work is done by the 13 executive departments represented in the President's Cabinet?

Department of State

The conduct of our nation's relations with other countries is the special responsibility of the Department of State. The Secretary of State heads a large staff of officials in Washington, D.C., who direct the worldwide work of the department. In addition, the officials who are sent to other countries to represent our nation report to the Department of State.

Ambassadors are the highest-ranking American representatives in foreign countries. The official residence of an ambassador in a foreign country is called an **embassy.** In a few smaller countries, the United States is represented by officials called **ministers.**

There is also another kind of representative called a **consul.** An American consul's office, or consulate, can be found in most large foreign cities. The consuls and the members of their staffs work hard to build up our foreign trade and commerce. They also help to protect citizens of the United States who do business and own property in foreign lands. Citizens of the United States traveling in foreign lands may go to the consulate if they need help.

At home the Department of State is the keeper of the Great Seal of the United States. The Great Seal is put on all laws and treaties. In addition, the Department of State issues documents known as passports and visas. **Passports** allow our citizens to travel abroad. **Visas** allow people from other nations to come to the United States.

These pictures show the steady growth of the size of the Cabinet from President Washington's time (left) to President Reagan's time (right).

Department of the Treasury

The Department of the Treasury manages the nation's money. It collects taxes from our citizens and pays out the money owed by our national government. When necessary, the Department of the Treasury borrows money for our government. It also supervises the coining and printing of money, and it keeps the President informed about the financial condition of our country.

There are several important divisions within the Department of the Treasury. The Internal Revenue Service collects personal and corporate income taxes. The Customs Service collects taxes on goods brought into the country. The Secret Service protects the President and helps prevent counterfeiting—the making or distributing of fake money.

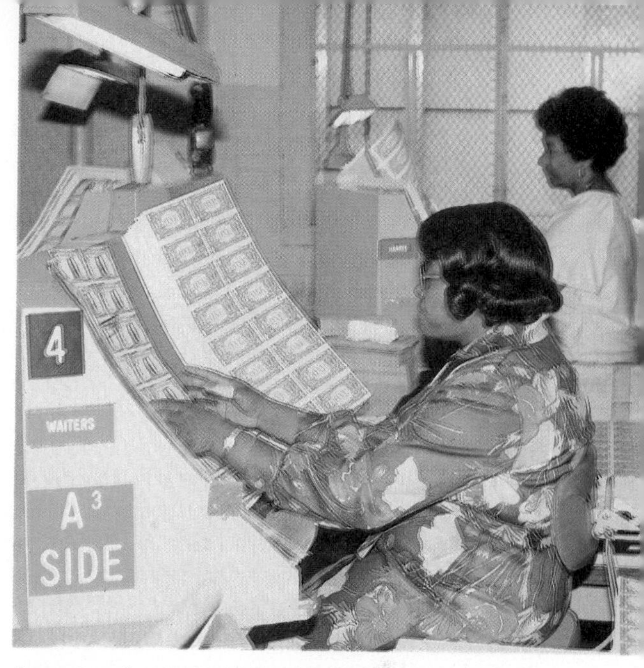

Inspectors for the Department of the Treasury study sheets of bills to see that they are properly printed. Each printing press can turn out 6,000 bills an hour.

Department of Defense

Until 1947 the nation's armed forces were administered, or directed, by two separate departments—the Department of War and the Department of the Navy. Then in 1947 Congress placed all the armed forces—the Army, Navy, Air Force, and Marine Corps—under one department, the Department of Defense. Its head, the Secretary of Defense, is always a civilian. However, the Secretary has many military officers as assistants. These officers help the Secretary plan the military defense of our nation and provide for the training and equipping of the armed forces.

There are three major divisions within the Department of Defense. The Department of the Army commands our land forces. The Department of the Navy has charge of our seagoing forces and includes the Marine Corps. The Department of the Air Force is responsible for our air defenses. Each of these divisions of the Defense Department is headed by a civilian Secretary.

The highest-ranking military officers of the Army, Navy, and Air Force are members of the **Joint Chiefs of Staff.** The head of the Marine Corps attends all meetings of the Joint Chiefs and takes part as an equal member when matters concerning the Marines are discussed. Members of the Joint Chiefs of Staff have the duty of advising the President on military matters.

Training Our Military Leaders. The Department of Defense is also responsible for our four officer-training schools. These are the Military Academy at West Point, New York, the Naval Academy at Annapolis, Maryland, the Air Force Academy at Colorado Springs, Colorado, and the Coast Guard Academy at New London, Connecticut.

Candidates for the various academies are nominated by the representative from their district or by one of the senators from their state. Usually four candidates are named for each vacancy, or opening. All candidates must have good high school records. They must also pass a series of scholastic and physical tests.

The successful candidate receives a free four-year college education and upon graduation becomes an officer in one of the military services. Since 1976 women have been admitted into all the service academies on an equal basis with men.

Department of Justice

The Department of Justice, under the Attorney General, enforces federal laws. It also defends the United States in court when a lawsuit is brought against the federal government for any reason.

The Federal Bureau of Investigation (FBI) is an important agency of the Justice Department. The FBI investigates crimes that break federal laws and arrests those accused of crimes against the United States. The Immigration and Naturalization Service and the Bureau of Prisons are also within the Justice Department.

Department of the Interior

The Department of the Interior manages our nation's natural resources. Its duties are to encourage the wise use of America's land, minerals, water, fish, and wildlife. The department also manages our national parks and federal dams.

There are several important divisions within the Department of the Interior. The Bureau of Indian Affairs deals with matters involving our Indian population. The Bureau of Reclamation sponsors water irrigation projects. The Office of Territories supervises American overseas territories. Other divisions within the department are the National Park Service, the Bureau of Mines, and the Fish and Wildlife Service.

Department of Agriculture

The Department of Agriculture aids American farmers in the important task of raising and marketing crops. Special agencies in the department, such as the Agricultural Research Service and the Soil Conservation Service, encourage better methods of farming. The department also prepares reports on market conditions for crops and livestock to aid farmers in their planning and planting.

Other divisions within this department include the Farmers Home Administration, which provides loans for buying and operating farms, and the Forest Service, which helps to protect our nation's woodlands. The Food and Nutrition Service manages the food stamp and school lunch programs.

Department of Commerce

American trade and business are encouraged by the Department of Commerce. There are many important agencies within this department. For example, the Bureau of Economic Analysis studies business conditions in the United States. The Industry and Trade Administration promotes the nation's foreign trade. The Patent and Trademark Office protects the rights of inventors. The National Bureau of Standards establishes official weights and measures.

Also under this department are the Census Bureau, which counts the population every ten years, and the Maritime Administration, which aids American ocean shipping and commerce. The National Weather Service is part of the department's National Oceanic and Atmospheric Administration.

Department of Labor

The American worker receives important services from the Department of Labor. It gathers information on working conditions in various businesses and industries. The Wage and Hour Division is responsible for carrying out federal laws that regulate the wages and hours of workers in businesses engaged in interstate commerce.

Another division of the Department of Labor is the Bureau of Labor Statistics, which collects information about employment and

Principal Duties of the Executive Departments

EXECUTIVE DEPARTMENT (YEAR ESTABLISHED)		PRINCIPAL DUTIES
DEPARTMENT OF STATE (1789)		Conducts our foreign relations Protects our citizens abroad Issues passports
DEPARTMENT OF THE TREASURY (1789)		Prints, coins, and issues money Collects taxes and pays bills Manages government funds
DEPARTMENT OF JUSTICE (1789)		Investigates violations of laws Prosecutes cases before courts Administers naturalization laws Enforces immigration laws
DEPARTMENT OF THE INTERIOR (1849)		Controls our public lands Maintains our public parks Supervises Indian reservations Controls our water resources
DEPARTMENT OF AGRICULTURE (1862)		Conducts studies to help farmers Manages food stamp and school lunch programs Aids farmers to raise and market crops Directs soil conservation programs
DEPARTMENT OF COMMERCE (1903)		Fixes standards of weights and measures Encourages and regulates foreign trade Publishes reports on business and trade
DEPARTMENT OF LABOR (1913)		Determines standards of labor Publishes employment information Directs public employment services
DEPARTMENT OF DEFENSE (1949)		Maintains our armed forces Carries on military studies Operates military bases
DEPARTMENT OF HEALTH AND HUMAN SERVICES (1953)		Directs our public health services Operates our Social Security program Sees that our foods and medicines are safe
DEPARTMENT OF HOUSING AND URBAN DEVELOPMENT (1965)		Aids urban housing programs Helps cities plan traffic control Helps cities plan mass transportation Cooperates with metropolitan area planners
DEPARTMENT OF TRANSPORTATION (1966)		Helps develop our nation's transportation policy Supervises federal-aid highway program Promotes air, highway, and railroad safety
DEPARTMENT OF ENERGY (1977)		Helps develop our nation's energy policy Promotes conservation of energy Controls use of nuclear energy Regulates hydroelectric power
DEPARTMENT OF EDUCATION (1979)		Sets guidelines for granting financial aid to schools Does research on educational subjects Administers federally sponsored education programs

labor-management relations. The Unemployment Insurance Service aids workers looking for jobs.

Department of Health and Human Services

The Department of Health and Human Services gathers information, does research, and conducts programs to promote the health and well-being of all citizens. It was known as the Department of Health, Education, and Welfare (HEW) until 1979. In that year the Education Division became a separate executive department.

The largest division of the Department of Health and Human Services is the Social Security Administration. It assists the aged, the unemployed, and other persons in need. The Public Health Service, another important division of the department, has several agencies that promote the health of all Americans. For example, the Food and Drug Administration sees that our food and medicines are safe and pure.

Department of Housing and Urban Development

The Department of Housing and Urban Development is sometimes referred to by the initials HUD. It offers aid to city and state governments in working out programs for such local problems as housing, mass transportation, and traffic. HUD helps cities to solve such regional problems as those concerning water conservation and air pollution.

Department of Transportation

The Department of Transportation helps to coordinate and develop our nation's rail, highway, and air transportation. It also promotes safety and deals with problems of mass transportation.

Among the important agencies of the Department of Transportation are the Federal Aviation Administration and the Urban Mass Transportation Administration. The Coast Guard is part of the Transportation Department in peacetime. In wartime it becomes part of the Navy.

Department of Energy

The Department of Energy was created in 1977 to help plan and manage the nation's energy policy. One of the department's main goals is to lessen the amount of energy that is wasted in our nation. It also provides money for research to find new sources of energy. In addition, it is responsible for carrying out our energy laws. Furthermore, the Department of Energy regulates the development and use of our hydroelectric power, gas and oil pipelines, nuclear power, and energy deposits.

Department of Education

The Department of Education, the newest executive department, was created in 1979. It provides advice and information to the nation's school systems. It also is responsible for distributing federal funds to schools throughout the United States.

CHECK-UP

Vocabulary

Executive Office of the President
Council of Economic Advisers
Office of Management and Budget
National Security Council
Central Intelligence Agency
White House Office
press secretary
executive departments
Cabinet
Secretary
Attorney General
ambassador
embassy
minister
consul
passport
visa
Joint Chiefs of Staff

Review

1. What are the chief responsibilities of the various agencies and offices of the Executive Office of the President?
2. How are members of the President's Cabinet selected?
3. Describe the work of each of the executive departments.

Discuss

Which of the executive departments affects your life most? Why?

4

The President and the Independent Agencies

In addition to the executive departments, Congress has set up a number of **independent agencies.** These agencies help the President carry out the duties of office. The independent agencies are separate from the executive departments because they perform specialized duties that often do not fit into any regular department. In addition, some of these agencies serve all the departments. Therefore, they function best as separate and independent organizations.

NASA designed the space shuttle *Columbia* to be the first reusable spacecraft. The *Columbia* blasted off for the first time in 1980.

The Independent Agencies

There are about 50 independent agencies. Each was created by Congress to perform a specific job. For example, the **Veterans Administration** assists the men and women who have served in the armed forces. The **Farm Credit Administration** helps farmers obtain loans. The **National Labor Relations Board** helps settle disputes between workers and their employers. The **National Aeronautics and Space Administration (NASA)** runs the nation's space program.

Several independent agencies assist the work of the entire government. For example, the **Civil Service Commission** gives tests to persons who apply for jobs with the federal government. The **General Services Administration** buys supplies for the federal government. It also builds and maintains federal government buildings.

Regulatory Agencies

A number of independent agencies have the power to make rules and bring violators into court. These are called **regulatory agencies.** Their decisions often have the force of law.

courtesy of Historical Pictures Service, Inc.

This cartoon is more than 30 years old, yet it illustrates a complaint still common today.

The **Interstate Commerce Commission (ICC),** for example, regulates railroad, bus, and truck transportation that crosses state lines. The commission has the power to regulate rates and services. Established by Congress in 1887, it is the nation's oldest independent regulatory agency.

The **Civil Aeronautics Board (CAB)** is responsible for regulating all airlines flying in the United States. Like the ICC, it can regulate rates and services.

The **Securities and Exchange Commission (SEC)** helps enforce laws regulating the buying and selling of stocks and bonds. This helps protect Americans when they invest their money in stocks and bonds.

The **Environmental Protection Agency (EPA)** works to end water and air pollution in all parts of the country. It also regulates the disposal of solid wastes.

Who Runs the Regulatory Agencies?

The regulatory agencies were given independence so that they could have the freedom they needed to do their jobs. The heads of these agencies are appointed by the President, with the approval of the Senate. However, they have long terms, often as long as 14 years. This means that no President can appoint more than a few agency leaders.

The independence of the regulatory agencies has often been criticized on the grounds that it makes them too powerful. Some people say that these agencies regulate too much and interfere too much in our lives. Other people defend the regulatory agencies. They say that their regulations are needed to protect the public.

The Bureaucracy

The many departments and agencies in the executive branch of the government form the federal **bureaucracy.** About 3 million people work in the bureaucracy. They include administrators, lawyers, scientists, doctors, engineers, secretaries, and clerks. People in the bureaucracy do the day-to-day work of the executive branch. They work in Washington, D.C., in other cities throughout the United States, and in other nations.

The bureaucracy has many rules and regulations for carrying out a wide range of activities. Often these rules and regulations lead to bureaucratic delay, or "red tape." People dealing with a government agency often must spend a lot of time filling out forms. They must stand in seemingly endless lines. Sometimes they must go from department to department before getting the help they need. Yet in spite of these problems, the people in the bureaucracy keep the executive branch functioning under every President.

CHECK-UP

Vocabulary

independent agencies
regulatory agencies
bureaucracy

Review

1. Why are the independent agencies separate from the executive departments?
2. Name three independent agencies and describe what they do.
3. Name three regulatory agencies and describe what they do.

Discuss

Do you think the executive branch of the federal government has grown too large? Why or why not? Can you think of any departments or agencies that could be eliminated?

CHAPTER SUMMARY

As the head of the executive branch, the President is responsible for seeing that our nation's laws are carried out. The President is elected for a four-year term.

The President has a difficult and demanding job. The President must provide leadership in such vital areas as foreign policy, planning our nation's defense needs, and promoting our nation's prosperity. As Chief Executive of one of the world's most powerful nations, the President plays a large part in shaping the history of our nation and the world.

For aid in these tasks, the President turns to the members of the Cabinet—the heads of the executive departments. These departments carry on much of the work of the executive branch of the federal government. A number of independent agencies also assist in the day-to-day work of the executive branch. These agencies deal with such matters as interstate commerce, protection of the environment, veterans' affairs, national defense, and many other important activities of government.

CIVICS SKILLS: Reading an Organization Chart

Wanted: Native-born American over the age of 35 to fill top executive position. Must be willing to work long hours for at least four years. Combination lawyer, diplomat, and financial wizard preferred. Excellent salary and benefits.

Ever since this position was opened in 1789, many people have competed for it. Over the years, the responsibilities have grown. Still, there never seems to be a shortage of applicants for the job of President of the United States.

As you learned in this chapter, a President has many different roles. President Harry S. Truman once called these roles "hats." A President, he said, has to wear at least six hats, sometimes more. What hats do you think President Truman was talking about?

Wearing a lot of hats also means a lot of work. A President cannot do the job alone. Today, for example, the executive branch employs more than 3 million people. How does the President receive advice from such a large staff? How are orders given? An **organization chart** helps you answer these questions.

Identifying Relationships

An organization chart has two basic functions. First, it provides a framework, or outline, for taking notes on an organization. Second, it shows relationships between the parts or people within that organization.

The organization chart below uses a series of boxes to show the order of the major positions in the Department of Defense. The lines that connect these boxes identify the channels of communication and authority. Suppose, for instance, an officer in an air force command wants a new jet fighter. How is this request relayed to the President? To find out, simply slide your finger along the lines that connect the two boxes. Whom does the officer contact first? Who finally speaks to the President?

Practicing What You've Learned

1. What is the role of the Joint Chiefs of Staff? To whom do they report?
2. What role is played by civilians?
3. Why do you think civilians hold the top positions in the Department of Defense?

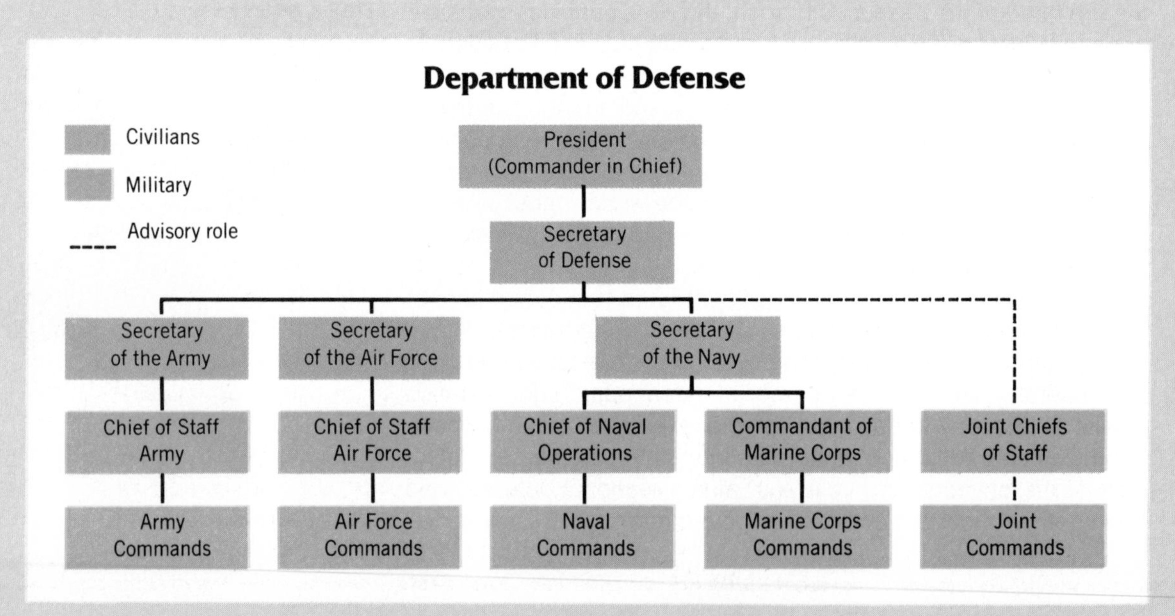

CHAPTER REVIEW

Vocabulary

Tell how each of the following terms is related to the powers and duties of the President of the United States.

Presidential succession
Chief Executive
veto
executive departments
ambassadors
independent agencies
Chief of State
regulatory agencies
Commander in Chief
foreign policy
treaties
State of the Union Message
Cabinet
diplomacy
Office of Management and Budget

Check-Up

1. What qualifications does a person have to meet to be elected President of the United States?
2. What purpose does the Twenty-second Amendment serve?
3. If the President becomes unable to serve, what official takes the President's place? Who is next in succession?
4. In what three ways is the President able to influence the lawmaking power of Congress?
5. How is the President's war-making power limited?
6. How can the President check the power of the Supreme Court?
7. Which department of the federal government aids farmers?
8. To which department would the President turn for advice on foreign affairs? Why?
9. Name the executive departments whose heads are in the President's Cabinet.
10. In what ways has the increased size of the federal government and the position of the United States as a world power changed the role of the President?
11. Do you think the President of the United States has too much power? Why or why not?

Civics Skills

There are three main levels of authority in our federal government. At the top is the Constitution of the United States. The next level consists of the legislative, executive, and judicial branches of government. Below the executive branch are the 13 executive departments that are identified on page 127 of this chapter.

Draw an organization chart that shows the relationship among these different levels. If you need help in drawing your chart, check the organization charts in references such as the *U.S. Government Manual* or the *Statistical Abstract.*

Citizenship and You

1. A group may research and prepare a chart showing the executive branch of the federal government.
2. Keep a record of news reports of the President's daily activities. Explain how each of these reported activities is related to the President's responsibilities. To which responsibility has the President been giving the most attention during this period of time? Report your findings to the class.
3. Practice your discussion skills by taking part in a class debate on one of the following topics: "Will a Woman Ever Become President of the United States?" "Should a President Be Limited to Two Terms in Office?" "How Can We Better Protect the Lives of Our Presidents?"
4. Find newspaper or magazine articles on the activities of the executive departments. Make a scrapbook using these articles.

CHAPTER

7

The Federal Courts Judge Our Nation's Laws

Whenever a group of players get together in a game, they must be governed by a set of rules. When a player breaks the rules, penalties are handed out. If the players disagree about the meaning of the rules, there are always officials who have the authority to make the final decision. In a football game, for example, the referees interpret the rules and set penalties if the rules are broken.

Government, too, needs officials to interpret its rules, or laws, and to decide how those who disobey them should be punished. That is the purpose of our court system, which is headed by the Supreme Court.

The goal of our courts is to provide equality under the law. They also protect every citizen from the tyranny of bad government. In accordance with the American ideal of justice, our courts should protect, defend, and uphold the rights guaranteed by the Constitution of the United States.

No function of government is more important to study than the way in which the enforcement and interpretation of laws help improve the lives of free people. The idea of justice for all is one of democracy's great achievements. Without equal justice for all, our republican form of government cannot exist. In this chapter you will learn how our court system works. You will study these topics:

1. **Providing Equal Justice Under Law**
2. **Our Federal Court System**
3. **The Supreme Court**

1 Providing Equal Justice Under Law

Carved in marble over the entrance of the Supreme Court Building in Washington, D.C., is the motto "Equal Justice Under Law." It proclaims that in the United States all citizens are considered equal and are guaranteed equal protection by our laws.

Laws for the Good of All

We enjoy freedom in the United States because we have laws to protect our rights. Of course, some laws limit our freedom. A law against robbery, for example, denies the robber's freedom to steal. However, it gives the rest of us freedom to use and enjoy our own property.

Laws usually represent the feelings of the majority as to what is right and what is wrong. When most of the American people feel strongly that something should or should not be done, a law is passed on the subject. Or, if they change their mind about an issue, a law can be replaced. In this way, our laws grow and change with the times.

Every American citizen is responsible for knowing and obeying the laws. It is our responsibility to get to know the laws that concern any activity we expect to undertake. A person who rides a bicycle, for example, must know about road signs and traffic regulations. The law-abiding citizen realizes that laws are passed for the good of all. By learning and obeying the nation's laws, you are practicing good citizenship.

Kinds of Laws

There are four different kinds of laws in the United States. All these laws must follow the principles set forth in the Constitution, which is the supreme law of the land.

Statutory Law. Laws that are passed by lawmaking bodies are known as **statutory laws.** They are passed by Congress and by state and local governments. For example, a state law that requires fire exits in all public buildings is a statutory law.

Common Law. What happens if there is no statutory law covering a specific situation? Then we follow certain rules that have been accepted by Americans as the proper ways in which to act. Some of these rules are based on both common sense and common practice.

For example, before automobiles became a major form of transportation, there were no laws about driving them. Suppose at that time someone was driving an automobile at its top speed and ran into a horse-drawn wagon, crushing the wagon. The driver might argue that his case should be dismissed because there was no law regulating the speed of automobiles.

The judge might reply that there is an established principle that people cannot use their property to injure others. Thus the judge would apply the rule of common sense and common practice in such a case.

The judge's decision might be remembered by another judge hearing a similar case. Eventually most judges might follow the same **precedent,** or earlier decision, in such cases. In time, those guilty of recklessly driving their automobiles would be punished according to this customary rule. This rule would become a part of our customary, or common, law. **Common law,** therefore, is law that comes from judges' decisions.

In time, most common law is passed as statutory law by the nation's lawmaking bodies. In this way, it is written down so that all of the nation's citizens may know it.

Administrative Law. Many of the laws that affect our daily lives are made by government agencies. These laws are known as **administrative laws.** For example, the Consumer Product Safety Commission is making an administrative law when it rules that a toy is unsafe and must immediately be taken off the market.

Constitutional Law. The Constitution of the United States, as you know, is supreme above all other types of laws. If any law comes into conflict with the Constitution, the Constitution prevails. **Constitutional law** is law based on the Constitution and on Supreme Court decisions interpreting the Constitution.

The Idea of Courts

These different kinds of laws are used by courts to help settle disputes. Disputes between people, between people and the government, and between governments are brought before a court. The court applies the law and reaches a decision in favor of one side or the other.

To be just, a law must be enforced fairly. For example, it is against the law for workers in an atomic energy plant to give or sell secrets about their work to a foreign government. What would happen if an FBI agent found an engineer who worked in an atomic energy plant talking to a foreign spy? Could the federal government arrest the engineer on suspicion of treason and put the engineer in jail for 10 years? The answer is no! Under our American system of justice, the engineer must be given a fair public trial.

To guarantee justice in the United States, we have accepted the important idea that a person is innocent until proven guilty. The proper way to determine whether or not a person is guilty is to hold a trial in a court of law. Our courts are made up of persons who have been given the authority to administer justice. We believe that only a system of courts can assure equal justice to all people.

The Right to a Fair Trial

The Constitution guarantees every American the right to a fair public trial. It is important that you understand this guarantee as you study our federal court system and learn how equal justice under the law works in the United States. What does the right to a fair trial mean? Consider our example of the atomic engineer who is accused of giving secret information to a foreign government.

1. The right to have a lawyer. All persons accused of a crime are entitled to the services of a lawyer. The lawyer will represent them in court and help protect their rights. If the atomic engineer cannot afford a lawyer, the court will appoint one and pay the lawyer's fees out of public funds.

2. The right to be released on bail. A person accused of a crime does not ordinarily have to spend months in prison waiting for the case to come to trial. Usually the accused person may be released if he or she can put up bail. **Bail,** as you have read, is a sum of money deposited with the court as a pledge that the accused will appear in court at the time of trial. The amount of bail is set by a judge. However, a person accused of a serious crime, such as murder or treason, may be denied bail and have to remain in jail until the trial is held.

3. Indictment by a grand jury. Just because a person is arrested on suspicion of a crime does not mean that this person must come to trial. There must be enough evidence against someone to justify bringing that person into court for trial. The group that decides whether there is enough evidence to bring the accused person to trial is called the **grand jury.** In federal courts, the grand jury is made up of 16 to 23 citizens who live in the district in which the trial is to be held.

The grand jury examines the evidence against the accused person. It questions witnesses and investigates the facts in the case. If a majority of the grand jury decides that the evidence against the accused is strong enough, the person is **indicted,** or formally accused of a crime. In the case of the atomic engineer, the grand jury found the evidence strong enough. As a result, the engineer was indicted and held for trial.

4. The right to a jury trial. Individuals who go on trial must be judged on the basis of the evidence for and against them. But who shall judge the evidence? The Sixth Amendment to the Constitution guarantees an accused person the right to be tried before a **trial jury.** A trial jury is also called a **petit jury.** It is made up of from 6 to 12 persons who live in the community. The men and women of the trial jury who judge the evidence are called **jurors.**

Jurors on trial juries and grand juries are selected from a list of people in the community. A court official draws the names and sends notices ordering the people to report for **jury duty.** From this group, or panel of jurors, the required number of jurors are chosen for the trial.

The trial jury must determine the true answer, or **verdict,** in the case. Usually the jury's verdict must be a unanimous vote. This means that all the members must agree on whether the accused person is guilty or innocent.

5. Innocent until proven guilty. The burden of proof in a jury trial rests with those who bring charges against the person on trial. They must prove their case "beyond a reasonable doubt." Accused persons cannot be forced to testify against themselves. Their lawyers have the right to question all witnesses to make sure their testimony is accurate and honest. Accused persons have the

The right to a jury trial is a cornerstone of the American system of justice. Why is it important for all citizens to be willing to serve on a jury?

The Right to a Fair Trial

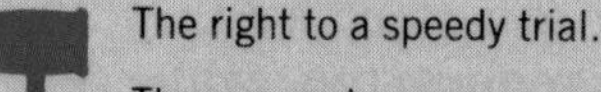

The right to have a lawyer.	The right to a speedy trial.
The right to be released on reasonable bail before the trial is held.	The accused person cannot be forced to testify against himself or herself.
The accused person is innocent until proven guilty.	The right to hear and question all witnesses.
The grand jury must find there is enough evidence to indict, or to officially accuse, the person of the crime.	The right to appeal the verdict if there is reason to believe that the person did not receive a fair trial.

right to present their own witnesses to help them defend themselves.

The atomic engineer accused by the federal government of selling secrets to a foreign country was found not guilty by the trial jury. The jury found the engineer innocent because the government lawyers could not prove guilt. The American system of justice is carefully designed to protect the innocent and punish the guilty.

6. The right of appeal. Since courts are made up of human beings, it is only natural that courts sometimes make mistakes. To make sure that justice is done, our nation's court system provides the right to **appeal,** or ask for a review of a case. If there is reason to doubt that justice was done in the court trial, the convicted person can appeal to a higher court.

CHECK-UP

Vocabulary

statutory laws	indicted
precedent	trial jury
common law	petit jury
administrative laws	jurors
constitutional law	jury duty
bail	verdict
grand jury	appeal

Review

1. What are the four different kinds of laws in the United States?
2. Why do we have courts?
3. What rights to a fair trial are guaranteed by the Constitution?
4. Why is it important that citizens have the right to appeal?

Discuss

In what ways does our American court system protect the rights and freedoms of American citizens?

2
Our Federal Court System

Under our federal system of government, the United States has two court systems. One is the federal court system. The other is the system of state courts. (You will read about the state court system in Chapter 8.)

Article 3 of the Constitution of the United States provides that "the judicial power of the United States shall be vested in one Supreme Court, and in such inferior [lower] courts as the Congress may from time to time . . . establish." The First Congress used this constitutional power to set up a system of federal courts.

In 1789 Congress passed the Judiciary Act, which established what has grown into one of the great court systems of the world. This system of federal courts makes up the judicial branch—the third branch—of our federal government.

Cases Tried in Federal Courts

The Constitution grants the federal courts jurisdiction in several different kinds of cases. **Jurisdiction** means the authority to judge and administer the law. Listed below are the kinds of cases that are brought to trial in federal courts:

1. Any person accused of disobeying any part of the Constitution, including the amendments, is tried in a federal court.

2. Anyone accused of violating a treaty of the United States is tried in a federal court.

3. Anyone accused of breaking laws passed by Congress is brought before a federal court.

4. Federal courts have jurisdiction when a foreign nation sues the government of the United States or a citizen of the United States.

5. American ambassadors and consuls are tried in federal courts if they are accused of breaking the laws of the nation in which they are stationed.

6. Crimes committed on American ships at sea are tried in federal courts.

7. Crimes committed on certain federal property are tried in federal courts.

8. Any disagreement between states is tried in a federal court. Lawsuits between citizens of different states also come under federal jurisdiction. However, the Eleventh Amendment provides that any lawsuit against a state brought by a citizen of another state or of a foreign country shall be tried in a state court.

How Our Federal Courts Are Organized

Federal courts are organized in several levels. They are also classified according to their jurisdiction. The lowest courts are trial courts, which have **original jurisdiction.** This means they are the first courts in which most federal cases are heard.

Above these trial courts are courts that have **appellate jurisdiction.** That is, they review decisions made by lower courts. "Appellate" means "dealing with appeals." Every convicted person has the right to appeal his or her case to an appellate court. An appeal is usually made when lawyers believe the law was not applied correctly in the lower court. A case can also be appealed if new evidence is found.

United States District Courts

There are three main levels of federal courts. The chart on page 140 shows the relationship of courts in the federal system.

At the base of our federal court system are the **district courts.** There is at least one district court in each of the 50 states and the District of Columbia. Some of the larger states are divided into as many as four federal court districts, each with its own district court. Today there are 90 federal district courts in the United States.

The district court is the only federal court in which jury trials are held. District courts have original jurisdiction in most federal cases. They cannot hear appeals from other courts.

The Constitution is definite about where federal cases shall be tried. Article 3, Section 3, states in part that "such trial shall be held in the state where the said crimes shall have been committed. . . ."

The reason for this provision is to make sure that the accused person receives a fair and convenient trial. The witnesses who will testify are usually close at hand. No one has to travel long distances to be heard. Furthermore, the jury will be familiar with the location of the crime, and it can judge the truth of the evidence more intelligently.

District Court Officials

Most district courts are presided over by a single district court judge. In very busy districts, there may be a number of judges. All district court judges are appointed for life. District court judges decide matters of court procedure and explain the law involved in the case to the jury. They decide the sentence if the accused person is found guilty.

A number of other officials are needed to help the district courts work smoothly. Each district court has a United States **marshal.** Marshals arrest persons accused of breaking federal laws. They also deliver official court orders called **subpoenas,** which require persons to appear in court. The United States marshal also sees that the court's verdict is carried out.

Each district court also has a United States **magistrate.** This official hears the evidence against an accused person and decides

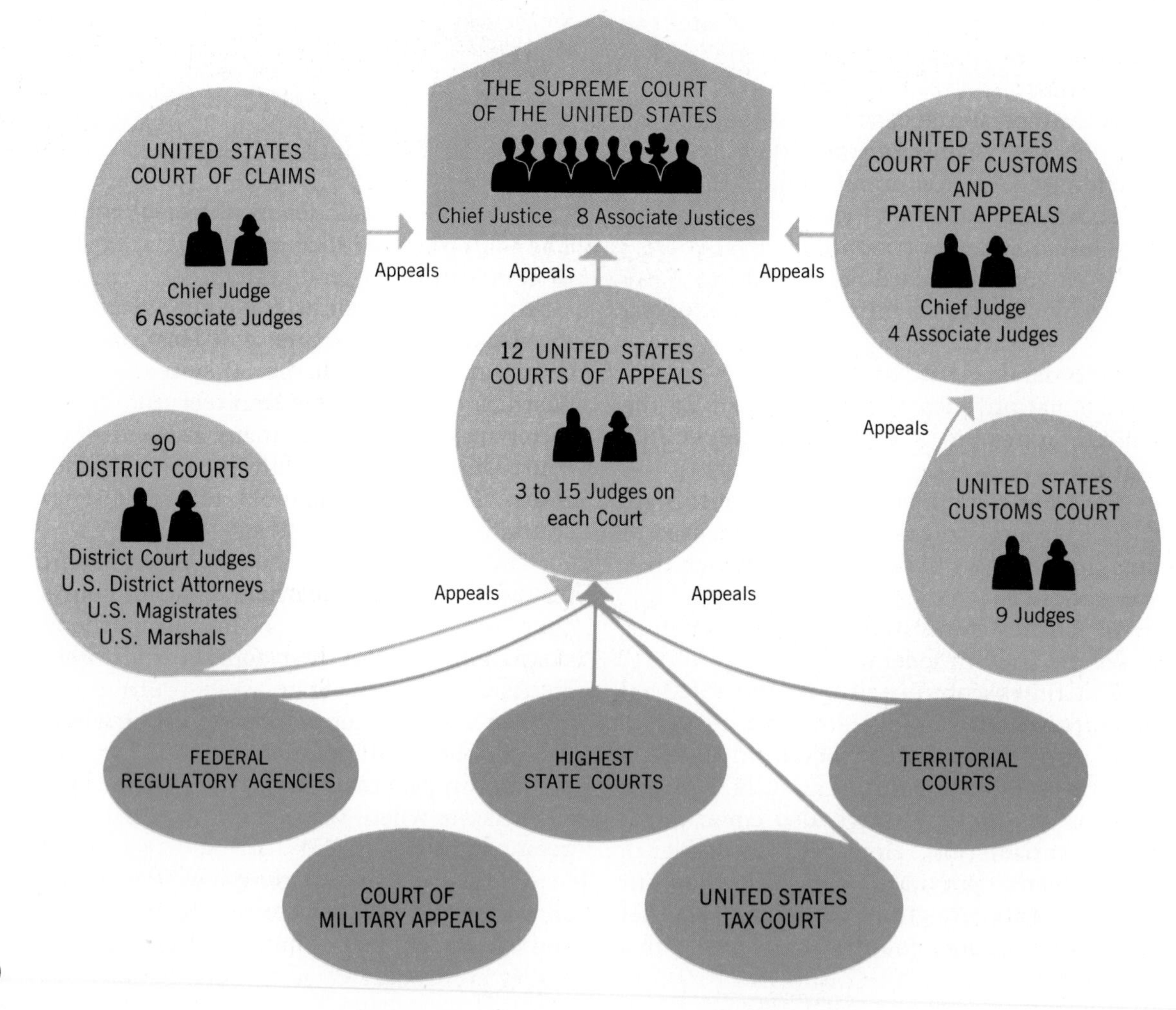

whether the case should be brought before a grand jury. Magistrates also try certain minor cases themselves.

Another district court official is the **United States attorney.** This official is a lawyer for the federal government. It is the job of the United States attorney to try to prove to a jury that the accused person is guilty of the crime he or she is charged with committing.

United States Courts of Appeals

The next level of the federal court system consists of **courts of appeals.** These courts review cases that are appealed from the district courts. Courts of appeals also hear appeals from decisions of federal regulatory agencies. For instance, a railroad company might believe that the fare rates set by the Interstate Commerce Commission are unfair. If so, it can ask a court of appeals to review the commission's decision.

There are 12 United States courts of appeals. Each covers a large judicial district known as a **circuit.** The 50 states are divided into 11 circuits. The twelfth circuit is the District of Columbia. Each court of appeals has from 3 to 15 judges. The senior judge of each circuit serves as the chief judge. The judges of the courts of appeals are appointed for life.

Jury trials do not take place in the courts of appeals. Instead, a panel of at least three judges reviews the evidence and makes the decision. The judges examine the records of the district court trial and hear arguments by the lawyers for both sides. The judges do not determine whether the accused person is guilty or innocent. They are not holding another trial of the case. That is not their job. Their job is to determine if the person who appealed the case was granted full legal rights during the trial.

The judges reach their decision by majority vote. If the court of appeals finds that justice was not done, it sends the case back to the district court for a new trial. If the court

In the American court system, judges are sworn to act "without fear or favor" in making their decisions. They must listen carefully and weigh all evidence fairly.

of appeals finds that justice was done, it upholds, or accepts, the decision of the district court. In most cases the decision of the court of appeals is final. Sometimes, however, another appeal is made. This appeal is made to the United States Supreme Court.

United States Supreme Court

The highest court in the land is the **Supreme Court** of the United States, which meets in Washington, D.C. It works chiefly as an appeals court. It reviews cases that have been tried in lower federal courts and in state courts.

In addition, the Constitution gives the Supreme Court original jurisdiction in the following three types of cases:

1. Cases involving diplomatic representatives of other nations.

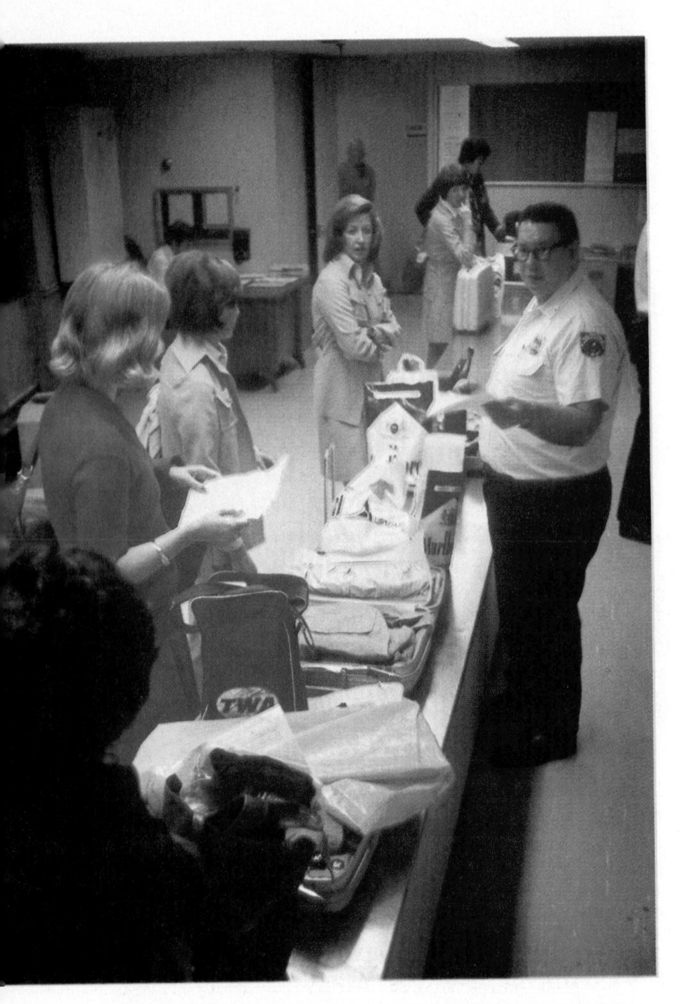

These people are going through customs on entering the United States. They can appeal to the Customs Court if they feel they are being taxed unfairly.

2. Cases involving disputes between states. For example, in 1963 the Supreme Court settled a dispute between Arizona and California over use of waters from the Colorado River basin.

3. Cases involving a state and the federal government. The ownership of public lands has often been a source of conflict between states and the federal government.

Decisions of the Supreme Court are final. Its decisions cannot be appealed. (You will read more about the Supreme Court later in this chapter.)

Other Federal Courts

Congress also set up a number of special courts to handle specific types of cases. You will see each of these courts listed on the chart on page 140.

The **Court of Claims** hears cases involving money claims against the federal government. If the court rules against the government, the person bringing the suit is usually granted a sum of money. Congress must then authorize the payment of the claim.

The **Customs Court** hears cases involving import taxes, or tariffs. An individual or a business firm importing certain goods into the United States from another country must pay taxes on them. People who feel the tax required is too high may take their cases to the Customs Court. Its headquarters are in New York City, but it also hears cases in other port cities.

The **Court of Customs and Patent Appeals** is an appeals court. It reviews decisions of the Customs Court. Decisions of the Patent Office concerning inventions also are appealed to this court.

Territorial courts were established by Congress to bring justice to the people living in the territorial possessions of the United States. There is one each in the Panama Canal Zone, Guam, the Virgin Islands, and Puerto Rico. These courts handle the same kinds of cases as district courts. In addition, they hear cases that would go to a state court.

The **Tax Court** hears appeals from taxpayers who disagree with a ruling of the Internal Revenue Service concerning their payment of federal taxes. The Tax Court is an independent agency, but it has powers like those of a court.

The **Court of Military Appeals** is the appeals court for the nation's armed services. People in the armed services who are accused of breaking a military law are tried at a **court-martial.** This is a trial conducted by military officers. The Court of Military Appeals consists of three civilian judges. Their decisions cannot be appealed.

Federal Court Judges

All the federal courts are presided over by judges. Federal court judges are appointed by the President. Their appointment must be approved by the Senate by majority vote.

Federal judges are appointed for life. The job is theirs for as long as they want it. They can be removed from office only by impeachment. Congress may not lower a judge's salary during her or his time in office. These guarantees were written into the Constitution to ensure that judges could not be punished or rewarded for their decisions. Judges are aided in their work by many other people, including clerks, secretaries, and court reporters.

CHECK-UP

Vocabulary

jurisdiction
original jurisdiction
appellate jurisdiction
district courts
marshal
subpoenas
magistrate
United States attorney
courts of appeals
circuit
Supreme Court
Court of Claims
Customs Court
Court of Customs and Patent Appeals
territorial courts
Tax Court
Court of Military Appeals
court-martial

Review

1. What are four kinds of cases that are brought to trial in federal courts? Which federal courts have original jurisdiction in most federal cases?
2. What is the purpose of the United States courts of appeals?
3. In what types of cases does the Supreme Court have original jurisdiction?

Discuss

When the President appoints judges to the federal courts, they are appointed for life. There is no way that they can be removed by the President. Do you think this is a good idea? Why or why not?

3
The Supreme Court

The Supreme Court is the head of the judicial branch of the federal government. It is the only court actually established by the Constitution. Decisions of the Supreme Court affect the lives of all Americans.

Justices of the Supreme Court

The size of the Supreme Court is determined by Congress. The number of **Justices,** or judges, of the Supreme Court has been fixed at nine since 1869. The Court has a Chief Justice and eight Associate Justices.

Supreme Court Justices, like other federal judges, are appointed by the President. Their appointments must be approved by a majority of the Senate. Justices are appointed for life and can be removed from office only by the impeachment process. The salary of the Chief Justice is $84,675. Associate Justices are paid $81,288.

The Constitution did not set any requirements for Supreme Court Justices. However, all have been lawyers. Many have served as judges on lower courts. Others have taught law or held public office. Until 1981 all Justices were men. In that year, Sandra Day O'Connor became the first woman to serve on the Supreme Court.

Presidents generally try to appoint Justices who share their political beliefs. Once appointed, however, a Justice may make decisions with which the President disagrees.

Power of Judicial Review

The Supreme Court has the power to study and review any law passed by Congress. Before it may do so, however, someone must challenge the law and bring a case to court.

(continued on page 146)

The Tinkers Take a Stand

Mary Beth Tinker, her brother John, and Christopher Eckhart did not set out to get their names in American law books. All they wanted to do was take a stand on an important national issue. That's why they wore black armbands to school in December 1965. Little did they realize that their actions would lead to a Supreme Court case.

Protesting the War

In 1965 the United States was deeply involved in a war between North Vietnam and South Vietnam in Southeast Asia. Many Americans were in favor of American support for South Vietnam. However, others thought that the United States should stay out of the war.

A group of students in Des Moines, Iowa, where the Tinkers and Chris Eckhart lived, decided to wear black armbands to school to protest the war. The armbands were meant to be a symbol of mourning for the American soldiers who were dying in Vietnam.

Members of the Des Moines school board heard about the armbands and became worried. They thought the armbands might cause trouble and banned them from the schools. When several students wore the armbands, they were suspended from school.

The Supreme Court Hears the Case

The Tinker family took the school board to court on behalf of Mary Beth, John, and Chris Eckhart. Their lawyers argued that the school board had denied them their constitutional right of free speech.

The case went all the way to the Supreme Court of the United States. The Justices agreed to hear the case because they thought it raised two important questions. First, was wearing an armband really a form of free speech? Second, how far did the right of free speech apply to students? Schools must keep discipline in order to allow students to learn.

The Supreme Court announced its decision in the case of *Tinker v. Des Moines Independent Community School District* in 1969. The Court ruled that wearing a symbol, such as an armband, is a form of "speech." It is therefore protected by the Constitution. The second question, however, was more difficult to decide. All the Justices stressed that schools must be protected against disturbances. What the Justices could not agree upon was whether or not wearing armbands had caused trouble in school.

Two Justices sided with the school board. They thought that wearing armbands had taken the students' minds off their studies. Therefore, the schools had acted properly in banning the armbands.

The majority of the Justices supported the students. They thought there was no evidence that the armbands had caused any disturbances in class. The Court's opinion ruled that the ban on armbands was unfair. The Justices pointed out that schools had allowed students to wear campaign buttons for political candidates. Wearing buttons is also a form of "speech."

The Supreme Court Justices did not say that schools could never limit the expression of opinions by students. What they said was that in this case the students had acted within their rights.

The Court's ruling is now part of United States law. As a result, students and school officials have a clearer idea of the rights of free speech for students and teachers.

Thinking It Over

1. What were the two main questions that the Supreme Court had to decide in the Tinker case?
2. What reasons can you think of for allowing students to express their political opinions in school? for not allowing them to do so?

The most unique feature of the Supreme Court is its power of **judicial review.** This means that the Court can determine whether a law passed by Congress or a Presidential action is in accord with the Constitution. If the Supreme Court decides that a law is in conflict with the Constitution, that law is declared **unconstitutional.** That is, the law is no longer in force.

The Constitution does not say that the Supreme Court has the power of judicial review. This power was established for the Court by John Marshall. As Chief Justice from 1801 to 1835, Marshall laid the foundations for the Supreme Court's great power.

The Influence of John Marshall

During his 34 years as Chief Justice, John Marshall established three basic principles of American law. Marshall stated the idea of judicial review for the first time in 1803, in the case of ***Marbury v. Madison.*** The case involved William Marbury, who had been promised appointment as a justice of the peace, and Secretary of State James Madison.

Marbury claimed that the Judiciary Act of 1789 gave the Supreme Court the power to order Secretary of State Madison to give him the promised appointment. In his now-famous opinion, Chief Justice Marshall found that the Judiciary Act was in conflict with the Constitution. The act gave the Supreme Court powers not granted by the Constitution. Since the Constitution is the "supreme law of the land," the act passed by Congress was unconstitutional.

Under Chief Justice Marshall, the Supreme Court also established the principle that laws passed by state legislatures could be set aside if they were in conflict with the Constitution. The third important principle established by Marshall was that the Supreme Court had the power to reverse the decisions of state courts. Over the years, the Supreme Court came to have the final power to decide what the Constitution meant.

John Marshall was one of our nation's most influential Chief Justices. Under his leadership, the Supreme Court made some of its most important decisions.

The Supreme Court Decides What Cases to Hear

As you have read, the Supreme Court cannot begin a case itself. It must wait until a person files an appeal or a lawsuit. All cases heard by the Court involve real legal disputes. A person cannot simply ask the Supreme Court for an opinion about whether or not a law is constitutional.

The Supreme Court itself decides what cases it will hear. Several thousand cases are appealed to the Court each year. However, the Court turns down about 80 percent of the applications it receives for review. If the Court had to review all cases that were appealed to it, it would still be deciding cases that originated in the 1950's!

How, then, does the Supreme Court decide what cases it will hear? The Justices accept only those cases that involve issues of significant public interest. Cases heard by the

The nine Justices of the Supreme Court act as the final court of appeals in American law. They are the final judges in interpreting the Constitution.

Supreme Court generally deal with important constitutional or national questions. At least four of the nine Justices must vote to hear a case. If the Supreme Court refuses to review a case, the decision of the lower court remains in effect.

The Supreme Court in Action

The Supreme Court begins its session each year on the first Monday in October. It usually adjourns in late June. The Justices spend much of their time reading written arguments, hearing oral arguments, and holding private meetings.

After the Supreme Court has agreed to hear a case, the lawyers for each side prepare a **brief.** This is a written statement explaining the main points of one side's arguments about the case. Each Justice then studies the briefs.

The next step takes place in a public session. The lawyers for each side appear before the Court to present an oral argument. Each side is limited to a half hour, and the time limit is strictly enforced. The Justices often question the lawyers about the case. The entire procedure is designed to bring out the facts and issues in each case as quickly as possible.

On most Fridays, the Justices meet in private to discuss and vote on the cases they have heard. Each Justice has one vote. Decision is by majority vote. If there is a tie vote, the decision of the lower court remains in effect.

Supreme Court Opinions

One of the Justices who supported the majority decision is assigned to write the **opinion** of the Court. This explains the reasoning that led to the decision. The Court's opinion is binding on all lower courts.

Sometimes a Justice agrees with the decision of the majority, but for different reasons. In that case the Justice may decide to write a **concurring opinion.**

DID YOU KNOW THAT . . .

the words "Oyez, oyez, oyez!" are called out as the Supreme Court Justices file into the courtroom? "Oyez" sounds like "Oh, yes." An odd way to open a court? Actually, the word means "Hear ye," and it comes from the French language. It is one of many French words that are used in conducting government business.

Justices who disagree with the decision of the Court may explain their reasoning in a **dissenting opinion.** Although dissenting opinions have no effect on the law, they can still be important. Many dissenting opinions eventually have become the law of the land when the beliefs of society and the Justices change.

Checking the Power of the Supreme Court

The Supreme Court has gained great power over the years. What can the other branches of government do to check the powers of the Supreme Court?

Let us take a closer look at what happens if the Supreme Court rules that a law passed by Congress is unconstitutional. As you know, this means that the law has no force. However, Congress may pass a new law that follows the Constitution and that the Supreme Court may uphold. In this way, laws may be improved while the rights of people under the Constitution remain protected.

Another way to make a desired law constitutional is to change the Constitution. Let us see how this happens. In 1895 the Supreme Court declared that an income tax law passed by Congress was unconstitutional. The Court pointed out that the Constitution (Article 1, Section 9, Clause 4) states that direct taxes must be apportioned according to the population of each state. In other words, such taxes must fall evenly on all people.

The income tax did not meet this constitutional requirement and thus was unconstitutional. However, in 1913 the states ratified the Sixteenth Amendment, which gave Congress the power to tax incomes. The income tax then became legal and constitutional.

The Supreme Court Can Change Its Mind

The Supreme Court has helped to make the Constitution a long-lived document by interpreting it differently at different times. In this way, the Court has helped the Constitution meet the demands of changing times. Supreme Court Justices are aware of changing social, political, and economic conditions. In reaching decisions, they take into account the beliefs of the people and the advancing ideas of justice for all.

Let us consider one example of the Court's changing attitude to meet new ideas. In the late 1800's, many of the states passed **segregation laws.** These laws segregated, or separated, black Americans. They meant that black people and white people could not share the use of such public services as trains, schools, hotels, and hospitals.

A Decision for Segregation. In 1896 an important case about segregation was brought before the Supreme Court. The case, ***Plessy v. Ferguson,*** challenged a Louisiana law that required blacks and whites to ride in separate railroad cars. Homer Plessy, who was part black, had taken a seat in a passenger car that had a sign reading "For Whites Only." When he refused to move to a car for blacks, he was arrested.

Plessy was found guilty of breaking the Louisiana law and appealed the decision to the Supreme Court. He argued that the segregation laws of Louisiana denied him the "equal protection of the law" guaranteed by the Fourteenth Amendment of the United States Constitution.

The Supreme Court did not accept Plessy's argument. It ruled that segregation laws did not go against the Fourteenth Amendment if the separate facilities provided for blacks were equal to those for whites. This decision established the "separate but equal" principle. That is, the decision made legal "separate but equal" facilities for blacks in all areas of life.

A Decision Against Segregation. In most places, however, facilities for blacks clearly were not equal to those for whites. For example, schools for blacks often were overcrowded and lacked much of the equipment provided for white students.

After World War II, conditions in the nation began to change. Many Americans began to realize that the nation's black citizens were not being treated fairly under the system of segregation.

In 1954 the Supreme Court decided another important segregation case. The case of ***Brown v. Board of Education of Topeka*** concerned eight-year-old Linda Brown, a black girl living in Topeka, Kansas. The school only five blocks from Linda's home was for whites only. So Linda had to travel 21 blocks to a school for blacks. Her father sued the school district. He claimed segregated schools were unconstitutional.

In a unanimous decision, the Supreme Court agreed. It ruled that segregated schools were not equal and therefore violated the Fourteenth Amendment. Segregated schools, said the Court, denied students equal protec-

One of these pictures was taken in the 1930's and the other was taken fairly recently. What evidence tells you which one came earlier and which later?

tion under the law. Therefore, the Court ruled that public schools should be desegregated "with all deliberate speed." Thus the Supreme Court had reversed its earlier decision.

Strengthening Our Constitutional Rights

In recent years, decisions of the Supreme Court have made far-reaching changes in three areas of American life—the rights of accused persons, voting, and civil rights.

The Rights of Accused Persons. A number of Supreme Court decisions in the 1960's greatly strengthened the rights of accused persons. For the most part, these decisions applied to the time immediately following a person's arrest.

In the famous 1966 case of ***Miranda v. Arizona,*** the Supreme Court declared that the police must inform suspects of their rights before they may question them. They must inform suspects that they have the right to remain silent, that anything they say may be used against them, and that they have the right to have a lawyer present when they are questioned. If they are too poor to afford a lawyer, a lawyer will be appointed.

There have been differences of opinion over the Supreme Court decisions involving the rights of accused persons. Some Americans have felt that the Court's decisions protected criminals. Others have said that they guaranteed justice to all Americans. What is the proper balance between the rights of the individual and the rights of society as a whole? This is an important question in a democratic nation.

"One Person, One Vote." The Supreme Court also made several important decisions in the 1960's in the area of voting and representation in state legislatures and the House of Representatives. The "one person, one vote" decision was the most far-reaching of these rulings. According to this decision, election districts for choosing representatives to Congress and the state legislatures must be divided by population as equally as possible. This means that every citizen's vote must be equal in value and will result in genuinely representative government at both state and federal levels.

Civil Rights and Civil Liberties. The third area in which the Supreme Court's rulings have had important results is in civil rights and civil liberties. The 1954 *Brown* decision against segregated schools has not completely ended segregation in American schools or American life. The Court's decision, however, struck a blow against segregation in our nation by suggesting that all segregation laws were unconstitutional.

The civil rights movement and civil rights legislation followed. Laws providing for segregation were removed one by one. Laws were passed guaranteeing black Americans the precious right to vote. By its decisions, the Court has provided leadership in showing that the rights guaranteed in the Constitution apply to all Americans.

The Prestige of the Supreme Court

Throughout its history, the prestige and dignity of the Supreme Court have grown. The Supreme Court Justices, for the most part, have not become involved in politics and have not been influenced by favors or bribes. Most Americans believe the Court is an important part of our democratic system.

The decisions of the Supreme Court have not, however, been free of controversy. Some Courts have seemed too liberal and others too conservative. In the late 1930's, President Franklin D. Roosevelt attempted to change the nature of the Supreme Court by adding more Justices to the Court. But public outcry caused Roosevelt to drop his plan. Americans did not want to change the balance of power among the executive, legislative, and judicial branches. They wanted the Court to remain free of political influence.

The debate over the Supreme Court's

power has continued throughout our history. Nevertheless, it must be remembered that the Court's power is limited. The Court makes important decisions that affect American policy and American life. It cannot, however, enforce these decisions. The Court must depend on the executive branch to carry out its decisions. Finally, the cooperation of the public is necessary if Supreme Court decisions are to be effective.

CHECK-UP

Vocabulary

Justices
judicial review
unconstitutional
Marbury v. Madison
brief
opinion
concurring opinion
dissenting opinion
segregation laws
Plessy v. Ferguson
Brown v. Board of Education of Topeka
Miranda v. Arizona

Review

1. What three basic principles of American law were established by the decisions of John Marshall?
2. How does the Supreme Court decide what cases it will hear?
3. In what two ways can Congress make a law constitutional after the Supreme Court has ruled that the law is unconstitutional?
4. How has the Supreme Court helped the Constitution of the United States meet the demands of changing times and conditions? Give an example.

Discuss

Which of the recent decisions made by the United States Supreme Court do you think will have the most impact on American life? Do you agree with the Court's decision? Why or why not?

CHAPTER SUMMARY

The federal courts make up the judicial branch of our federal government. The job of these courts is to judge laws and to bring to trial those accused of breaking laws. In the United States, we believe in the idea of government by law. These laws, however, must be enforced fairly. Thus the federal courts also make sure that every accused person enjoys the Constitution's guarantee of a fair trial.

There are four different kinds of laws in the United States. These are statutory law, common law, administrative law, and constitutional law.

The Constitution gives the federal courts jurisdiction, or authority, to hold trials in a wide variety of cases and to judge these cases. District courts are the only federal courts in which juries are used. Under certain conditions, convicted persons may take their cases next to a court of appeals and then perhaps even to the Supreme Court.

The United States Supreme Court is the highest court in the land. It hears appeals from lower federal courts and from state courts. Its decisions are final. A unique feature of the Supreme Court is the power of judicial review. That is, it hears cases to decide if the laws involved are constitutional. Decisions of the Supreme Court affect the lives of all Americans.

CIVICS SKILLS: Making Decisions

You look at the menu and order chicken rather than fish. You try on three pairs of jeans, but you don't buy any of them. Nothing on television interests you, so you read a book.

These are only three kinds of decisions that you make every day. You probably don't think such decisions have much in common with those made in a courtroom. Yet all decisions share certain basic features. Even if you have never served on a jury, you act as a judge all the time.

No matter how big or how small, every decision involves alternatives, or choices. A juror reaches a verdict. You select an item from a menu. In each case, at least one alternative was rejected and another was chosen. To make these decisions, both you and the juror had to go through a series of steps called the decision-making process.

Setting the Process in Motion

You begin the decision-making process by defining the problem. In other words, you clearly state the decision facing you. Next you examine all the facts, or evidence, surrounding that decision. In the case study on this page, José has to decide if he should accept a part-time job. One fact that might affect this decision is José's desire for good grades. What are some of the other important facts?

After you have gathered this information, your next step is to identify all the alternatives. José, for example, has two clear-cut choices. He can accept the job, or he can turn it down. If José gave some more thought to the situation, he could probably identify another alternative. For example, he might be able to split the job with one of his friends. Can you suggest other choices?

Evaluating the Alternatives

Once you know your alternatives, you must think about them carefully. Every choice has many possible outcomes, or results. To help you compare these, it is useful to write each alternative at the top of a sheet of paper. On one side of the paper, list all the advantages that an alternative might have. On the other side, list all the disadvantages.

Using this information, you can begin to evaluate, or judge, the alternatives. Consider, for example, the short-term and long-term effects of each choice. An alternative might seem attractive to you today, but what about tomorrow? Also, keep in mind your personal goals. Will any of the alternatives make it easier for you to achieve them?

Your answers to such questions will help you arrange alternatives in their order of importance. You will reject some and study others more closely. Then you're ready to complete the final step in the decision-making process—choosing an alternative.

Practicing What You've Learned

Use the following questions to evaluate José's two main alternatives.

1. What are the advantages and disadvantages of José's taking a part-time job?
2. What are the advantages and disadvantages of his not working at this time?
3. If you were in José's position, what choice would you make? Why?

JOSÉ'S PROBLEM: Should I take the part-time job at the ice cream shop? I need to save at least $500 a year for college, and I might not find work this summer. The hours could be a problem—three hours every day after school and all day Saturday. There goes basketball practice. And suppose my grades drop. I won't even get into college then. Still, I could study after dinner—that is, if I'm not too tired. What should I do?

CHAPTER REVIEW

Vocabulary

In the eight sentences below, the words in *italics* are used incorrectly. On a separate piece of paper, correct the sentences by putting in the words that make each statement true.

1. When a law is passed by a legislature, it is called *common law.*
2. The *grand jury* sits at the court trial of a case and hands down the verdict.
3. The *court of appeals* has original jurisdiction in cases involving foreign ambassadors, ministers, or consuls.
4. The *Supreme Court* is the only federal court in which jury trials are held.
5. Cases involving financial claims against the government of the United States are tried in the *Customs Court.*
6. *Federal courts* have jurisdiction when a citizen of a foreign nation sues a state of the United States.
7. The power of the Supreme Court to decide whether a law passed by Congress is unconstitutional is called the power of *original jurisdiction.*
8. A sum of money deposited with the court as a pledge that the accused will appear in court is called *appeal.*

Check-Up

1. What is the difference between statutory law and common law?
2. What are six rights that guarantee a person a fair trial?
3. What are the responsibilities of a grand jury?
4. What is meant by the term "appellate jurisdiction"?
5. How does each of the following officials serve the district court: United States marshal, United States magistrate, and United States attorney?
6. In what court would you appeal a decision about your federal income tax?
7. What actions can Congress take to make constitutional a law declared unconstitutional by the Supreme Court?
8. What was the significance of the case of *Miranda v. Arizona*?
9. The nine Justices of the Supreme Court are appointed for life and are not elected by the people. Do you think they should have the power to declare unconstitutional laws passed by legislatures elected by the people? Why or why not?

Civics Skills

In the Tinker case (see pages 144–45), the Supreme Court faced a difficult decision: Did students have the right to wear black armbands to school in protest against the Vietnam War? Analyze the Tinker decision by answering the following questions:

1. What alternatives, or choices, did the Supreme Court have?
2. What were some of the possible outcomes of each of these alternatives?
3. Which alternative did the majority of the Justices choose? Why?

Citizenship and You

1. You may want to visit a federal court in your district. Arrangements for such visits are usually made by writing to the presiding judge. If this is not possible, perhaps you can visit a local or state court. Prepare a report on your visit.
2. Invite a local lawyer or judge to visit your class and answer questions about court procedure.
3. Read a biography of a well-known Supreme Court Justice. Prepare a report on that Justice's ideas and attitudes toward law and justice.

UNIT TWO REVIEW

Reviewing the Facts

Write your answers to the items below on a separate piece of paper.

1. Which branch of the federal government holds each of the following powers?
   a. arranging a treaty with the leader of a foreign nation
   b. approving a treaty
   c. planning the federal budget
   d. raising the funds needed to pay for federal programs
   e. deciding if a law is constitutional
2. There are many steps in the process by which a bill becomes a law. Listed below are a few of them. Arrange the steps in the correct order.
   a. A member of Congress drops a bill in the hopper.
   b. The bill is sent to the President.
   c. The Speaker of the House sends the bill to the proper committee.
   d. A majority of the House approves the bill.
   e. The House committee votes to support the bill.
3. According to the Constitution, the President has all of the following powers *except* the power to
   a. make treaties with other countries.
   b. veto bills passed by Congress.
   c. impeach the Vice President.
   d. appoint Supreme Court Justices.
4. Complete this sentence: A law that is declared ________ by the Supreme Court can not be enforced.
5. Complete this sentence: The right to declare war rests solely with ________.
6. The executive department in charge of handling American relations with foreign nations is the
   a. Department of Commerce.
   b. Department of Defense.
   c. Department of State.
   d. Department of the Interior.

Applying What You Know

1. In recent years, some people have proposed that the length of time a President can serve should be changed from two full four-year terms to one term of six years. Do you think this change would be a good idea? Explain your answer.
2. The following situation could never have happened in the United States. Under our Constitution, the rights of all citizens are protected. In what specific ways were George Sanalic's rights violated?

   George Sanalic was a newspaper editor. Five years ago he wrote an article criticizing the ruler of his country. The day after the article appeared in the newspaper, the police came to George's home. They arrested him and took him to jail. George was held in jail for eight months without being allowed to speak to anyone. He was not even told the charge against him. Finally he was brought to trial. The government lawyer presented the case to a judge. George was not allowed to tell his side of the story. He was found guilty by the judge. George Sanalic was sentenced to life in prison.

Expanding Your Knowledge

Johnson, Gerald, *The Presidency,* Morrow. A history of the Presidency and the Chief Executive's role in government.

Johnson, Gerald, *The Supreme Court,* Morrow. A history of the Supreme Court and its place in our nation.

Kane, Joseph, *Facts About the Presidents,* Wilson. Biographical and historical information on our nation's Presidents.

Weiss, Ann E., *The American Congress,* Messner. How the Congress and President work together.

UNIT 

UNIT THREE

State and Local Government

CHAPTER

8

How State Governments Serve Their Citizens

The United States is made up of 50 states. They differ in many ways. For example, Texas covers a much greater area than Rhode Island. California has a larger population than Delaware. Colorado's climate is colder than Florida's. When people in Colorado are ice skating or skiing, people in Florida are sunbathing and swimming.

The governments of the states also differ from one another. Yet they have important similarities. Like the federal government, every state has three branches of government—legislative, executive, and judicial.

The actions of your state government directly affect your daily life. For instance, the state government decides how many days you must attend school each year. It helps pay the costs of all the public schools and colleges in the state. It often decides what should be taught in the schools and what textbooks will be used.

States provide other basic services as well. State governments build and maintain highways and bridges. They run hospitals. They help care for the needy.

How else do state governments serve their citizens? How do state governments govern their citizens? How do state governments and the federal government work together? You can find the answers to these and other questions as you read this chapter and study these topics:

1. **The States of the United States**
2. **State Lawmakers**
3. **The State Executive Branch**
4. **State Courts**

1

The States of the United States

When the American colonies won their independence, the original 13 states acted like small nations. Under the Articles of Confederation, you may recall, each state issued its own money. Each state regulated trade crossing its borders and often treated neighboring states as though they were foreign nations. Moreover, there was no President or system of national courts and the Congress had little power. For a while it looked as though the United States would break up into 13 small, weak nations.

In 1787 the delegates to the Constitutional Convention worked long hours to establish a better form of government. The Constitution that they wrote created a stronger national government. The 13 states agreed to give up some of their powers in order to form "a more perfect union." However, the states also kept certain powers for themselves. The resulting form of government, as you read earlier, is known as a federal system, or federal union.

The Division of Powers

In our federal system, the powers of government are divided between the 50 states and the federal government. What powers were given to the federal government, and which ones were retained by the states?

The states gave to the federal government those powers that affected all the people of the nation. For example, only the federal government can regulate trade between the states, coin money, and conduct foreign affairs. The federal government alone can set up a postal service and maintain an army and a navy.

The states still have many powers. Furthermore, the states and the federal government share some important powers. Although the powers of government have been divided between the states and the federal government, the states have remained strong. The states have considerable power to govern the people who live within their borders. State governments are close to the people and provide them with many needed services.

The Reserved Powers of the States

When the states approved the Constitution, they wanted to make certain that the rights of the state governments would always be protected. Therefore, the Tenth Amendment was added to the Constitution. As you have read, it provided that "the powers not delegated [given] to the United States by the Constitution, nor prohibited by it to the states, are reserved to [set aside for] the states respectively, or to the people." These reserved powers make it possible for states to govern their inhabitants effectively.

State governments are responsible for conducting elections. States decide most of the qualifications for voting. Of course, states must respect the federal Constitution's provisions about voting. States also set up procedures for holding all local, state, and national elections. Our federal system of government depends on the states to see that Americans are given the opportunity to elect their own representatives.

Another important function of state governments is education. The power to establish and maintain schools belongs to the state governments. The states have the power to decide what kinds of schools they will have. However, state school regulations cannot conflict with the United States Constitution or with the rulings of the Supreme Court.

The states make laws concerning marriage and divorce. They regulate traffic on the highways. State laws deal with health, safety, welfare, and the regulation of business within their borders. In addition, state governments have control over all local governments within their boundaries—cities, towns, townships, and counties. Local governments get their powers from the states.

Concurrent Powers

The states also share many powers with the federal government. These shared powers, as you recall, are called concurrent powers. Just because the federal government was granted certain powers in the Constitution does not mean that state governments do not also have these powers. Unless a power is forbidden to the states by the United States Constitution, state governments may exercise that power.

A good example of a shared, or concurrent, power is the power of taxation. Both the federal government and the state governments have the power to tax. They both collect various kinds of taxes to carry on their activities. State governments may raise money by taxing such items as gasoline, liquor, cigarettes, real estate, income, and personal

The American Federal System

THE NATION

THE FEDERAL GOVERNMENT
has authority over the whole nation.

MAJOR POWERS

Foreign Relations
Foreign Trade
National Defense
Money System
Trade Among the States

EACH STATE

EACH STATE GOVERNMENT
has authority over most affairs within the state's borders.

MAJOR POWERS

Elections
Public Building Programs
Education
Health and Safety
Police
Highways

EACH COMMUNITY OR LOCAL AREA

EACH LOCAL GOVERNMENT
has authority over the affairs of a town or city or county or township.

MAJOR POWERS

Schools
Parks and Playgrounds
Police
Libraries
Fire Protection
Public Utilities
Sewage Systems
Streets and Traffic
Zoning and Building Codes

Each American is a citizen of the nation, of a state, and of a local community.

property. The money raised through state taxes is used to pay for education, highways, health and safety programs, welfare, and other activities of the states.

From 13 States to 50 States

The 13 original states became part of the United States when they approved the Constitution. Most of the other states that were added later, however, were once territories of the United States. A **territory** is an area, governed by the United States, that is eligible to become a state.

In 1787, under the Articles of Confederation, Congress passed an important law called the **Northwest Ordinance.** It provided a way for territories to join our nation as new and equal states.

Under the Northwest Ordinance, a territory was eligible to become a state once it had a population of 60,000 or more voters. Then the territory lawmakers sent a petition to Congress asking to be organized as a state. If Congress agreed, it asked the lawmakers of the territory to write a state constitution. This constitution had to be approved by the people of the territory and by Congress. After these steps were completed, Congress voted to admit the territory as a new state.

The United States has admitted 37 states since it became an independent nation. In 1959 Hawaii became our 50th state. In the future, the United States could grow still larger.

Do you recognize this scene? A state police officer is enforcing the law in an area over which each state has control—safety along the state's highways.

State Constitutions

Each of our 50 states has its own constitution. Your own state constitution probably interests you most of all, and it is worth careful study. This written plan of government for your state contains the rules that direct how your state government is to be organized and how it is to carry on its work. Most state constitutions contain the following parts.

1. A preamble, or beginning, which states the basic ideas and ideals on which the state government is founded.

2. A bill of rights, sometimes called a declaration of rights, listing the freedoms guaranteed to all citizens of the state.

3. An outline of the organization of the state's government, with the duties of the legislative, executive, and judicial branches carefully spelled out.

4. Provisions for elections, including qualifications for voting that must be met by the citizens of the state, as well as rules for conducting elections.

5. Provisions for managing state affairs, including education, keeping law and order, building highways, regulating business, and raising money by means of taxes.

6. Methods of amending, or changing, the state constitution, and a list of the amendments passed.

Most state constitutions have been amended many times. This has been necessary because the powers and duties of state governments have changed greatly since their constitutions were first written. The Texas constitution, for instance, has been amended more than 200 times. During recent years, a number of states have drawn up new constitutions. Several states have had more than six. A new constitution usually is drawn up at a state constitutional convention by delegates who are elected by the people.

The States as Good Neighbors

In joining the Union, the states agreed to work together in harmony. One way they promised to cooperate is stated in Article 4, Section 1, of the Constitution of the United States. It states that "Full faith [belief] and credit [acceptance] shall be given in each state to the public acts, records, and judicial proceedings [court decisions] of every other state."

The **"full faith and credit" clause** makes certain that each state will accept the decisions of courts in other states. If a court in Texas, for instance, decides that one of its citizens owns a certain piece of land, the other states will accept this legal decision. Another example of the "full faith and credit" clause is the acceptance of the official records of other states. A marriage certificate or a birth certificate issued by any state is accepted by all other states.

States work together in other ways, too. For example, a person convicted of a crime cannot escape justice by fleeing to another state. If a prisoner escapes from jail in Utah and flees to Arizona, the governor of Utah can ask the governor of Arizona to return the prisoner. This method of returning escaped prisoners is called **extradition.**

States cooperate on many projects. A bridge that crosses a river bordering two states is built and maintained by the governments of both. States also work together to reduce water and air pollution.

The States and the Federal Government

In our federal system, it is important that the 50 states and the federal government cooperate. What are some of the ways in which the federal and state governments join to provide services for Americans?

The Constitution of the United States, in Article 4, Section 4, promises that "The United States shall guarantee to every state in this Union, a republican form of government. . . ." As you have read, in a republican form of government the people elect representatives to carry out the work of government. Every state, as it joined the Union, has been required to provide for a republican form of government in its state constitution.

The Constitution of the United States also promises that the federal government will "protect each of them [the states] against invasion." Therefore, it is the responsibility of the federal government to provide strong military forces to defend the states and the nation against attack.

In addition, the Constitution says that the federal government must stand ready to help any state put down "domestic violence" within its borders. An example of domestic violence might be rioting in a town when a mob has gotten out of control. The governor may call on the National Guard of the state if local police cannot control the disorder. In extreme cases, the state legislature or the governor may ask the federal government for assistance.

The federal and state governments share the costs of furnishing a number of services to the American people. Federal and state governments work together to build highways, aid jobless workers, help the needy, and conserve natural resources. Together the federal and state governments provide low-cost lunches for schoolchildren and offer job training for the handicapped. These are some of the important ways in which state governments and the federal government cooperate to serve the American people.

CHECK-UP

Vocabulary

territory
Northwest Ordinance
"full faith and credit" clause
extradition

Review

1. What are some of the powers reserved to the states?
2. How may a territory become a state?
3. What are the six parts of most state constitutions?
4. Give examples of federal and state cooperation in your state.

Discuss

Do you think state governments should be given more power? Why or why not?

2 State Lawmakers

Each state has a lawmaking body elected by the people of the state. In 26 states, this lawmaking body is called the Legislature. The term General Assembly is used in 19 states. In Montana, North Dakota, and Oregon, the lawmaking body is the Legislative Assembly. In Massachusetts and New Hampshire, it is the General Court. In this chapter we shall use the general term **state legislature.**

State Lawmaking Bodies

All but one of the states have a bicameral, or two-house, legislature. The larger of the two houses usually is called the House of Representatives. The smaller house is known as the Senate. Only Nebraska has a one-house legislature, or **unicameral legislature,** called the Senate.

State legislatures vary greatly in size. Alaska and Nevada have the smallest legislatures, with 40 representatives and 20 senators. The nation's largest legislature is in New Hampshire, which has 400 representatives and 24 senators.

The members of each state legislature are elected by the people of the state. Each member represents the people who live in a particular district of that state. The state legislature divides the state into election districts.

Originally, the upper house (Senate) of the state legislature usually had one senator from each county, or from each election district into which the state was divided. The counties or districts, however, often were unequal in population. Therefore, sparsely populated areas of the state often had as many senators as heavily populated areas.

In 1964 the United States Supreme Court ruled that all state election districts must be equal in population—or as nearly equal as possible. As you read in Chapter 7, this was the famous "one person, one vote" ruling. Since this decision, most states have set up election districts of nearly equal population.

Qualifications and Terms of State Lawmakers

Members of a state legislature must be American citizens. They must live in the state and district that they represent. In most states, a state senator must be at least 25 years of age. A representative must be at least 21 years old. Some states have lowered the age to 21 for senators and 18 for representatives. In Texas, senators must be at least 26.

Our State Governments

THE VOTERS ELECT

GOVERNOR AND LIEUTENANT GOVERNOR

STATE LEGISLATURE
House of Representatives
Senate

STATE COURTS*

STATE EXECUTIVE DEPARTMENTS

TREASURER

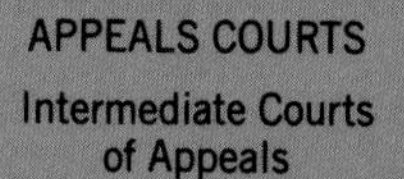

SECRETARY OF STATE

AUDITOR

ATTORNEY GENERAL

SUPERINTENDENT OF EDUCATION

DIRECTOR OF PUBLIC HEALTH

+

OTHER STATE AGENCIES

STATE SUPREME COURT

APPEALS COURTS
Intermediate Courts of Appeals

GENERAL TRIAL COURTS
County Courts
District Courts
Circuit Courts
Superior Courts
Courts of Common Pleas

LOWER COURTS
Justice Courts
Magistrate or Police Courts
Traffic Courts
Domestic Relations Courts
Juvenile Courts

*In most states the judges of most state courts are elected by the voters, but in some states some of the judges are appointed by the governor or the legislature.

In most states, senators are elected for four-year terms and representatives for two years. In a few states, however, both senators and representatives are elected for four-year terms. In some states, they both serve two years. The senators who serve in Nebraska's one-house legislature are elected for four-year terms. In all states, members of the legislature may run for reelection and serve any number of terms.

★ ★ ★ ★ ★ ★ ★ ★ ★ ★ ★ ★

CAN YOU GUESS?

Four of our state capitals have been named after Presidents. The capitals are listed at the left below. Can you match them with the correct states at the right?

Jefferson City	**Nebraska**
Madison	**Mississippi**
Jackson	**Missouri**
Lincoln	**Wisconsin**

Answers are on page 562.

How State Legislatures Are Organized

The legislatures in more than half the states meet in regular sessions every year. Other state legislatures meet once every two years. California has a two-year session that meets for that entire period. In other states, a session can last from 20 days to six months or more. The governor, or sometimes the state legislature, may call special sessions to meet emergencies.

At the beginning of the session, the presiding officer and other leaders are chosen. Committees are appointed. In most states, there is a lieutenant governor who presides over the Senate. In the other states, the Senate chooses its own presiding officer. Members of the lower house in all states choose their own presiding officer, who is usually called the Speaker.

As in the United States Congress, most of the work of the state legislatures is done in committees. In the upper house, committee members are chosen by the presiding officer or by all the members of the house. In the lower house, the Speaker usually appoints the committee members.

How State Legislatures Pass Laws

The lawmaking process in state legislatures is similar to the procedure followed in Congress. Almost every step you studied in the making of federal laws (Chapter 5) is followed by state legislatures. Here is a brief summary of the way in which a bill becomes law in a state legislature.

1. A bill is introduced. Any member of either house may introduce a bill, or proposed law. It is first handed to the clerk and given a number. The presiding officer reads the title of the bill aloud and sends it to the appropriate committee.

2. The bill goes to a committee. The committee listens to various witnesses for and against the bill and then questions them to obtain necessary information. The members may discuss the bill for many hours. The committee may vote to pass the bill, to change it, or to kill it.

3. The bill reaches the floor. If the committee approves the bill, it is sent back to a full meeting of the house. The bill is read aloud, line by line. The members of the house now begin to debate the bill. Each part of the bill is discussed. Amendments may be offered, and if passed they become a part of the bill.

Then the members vote on the bill. Bills that are passed are signed by the presiding officer and sent to the other house.

4. The bill goes to the second house. When the bill is introduced in the second house of Congress, it is sent to a committee. If the bill survives the hearings, debates, and changes in this committee, it is sent back to

The state legislature is the lawmaking branch of state government. Here members of the Texas Senate debate a bill under consideration.

the floor of the second house. Here it is debated, perhaps changed again, and then voted upon.

Bills that pass one house and fail in the second house are dead. If both houses of the legislature pass a bill in the same form, it is then sent to the governor to be signed. Frequently, however, both houses pass the bill, but in different forms. In this case, it is sent to a conference committee.

5. The bill goes to a joint conference committee. This committee is made up of members selected from both houses. They must try to reach a compromise, or agreement, that will be acceptable to both houses. The compromise bill worked out by the joint conference committee is then voted on by the two houses. Usually each house accepts this final version of the bill.

6. The bill is sent to the governor. The final step in making a state law is to send the bill to the governor. If the governor signs the bill, it becomes a law. In all states except North Carolina, the governor may veto a bill he or she does not support. In most states, the governor also has the power to veto only one part, or item, of a money bill. This is known as an **item veto.** The legislature can pass a bill over the governor's veto by a two-thirds vote in each house.

Direct Action and Legislation

Some state constitutions allow the people to take a direct part in making laws. Citizens are able to initiate, or start, new legislation through a process called the **initiative.**

First they must draw up a petition that describes the law they propose. Then they must get a required number of voters to sign the petition. If they succeed, the proposed law will appear on the ballot at the next general election. If enough people vote for the bill, it becomes a law. In this way, people who feel strongly about an issue can take an active part in getting laws passed.

In many states, certain bills that are passed by the legislature must be approved by the voters before they can become law. This method of referring questions directly to the people is called a **referendum.** For example, a state constitution may require that a law which would increase the state's debt be voted upon in a referendum.

CHECK-UP

Vocabulary

state legislature
unicameral legislature
item veto
initiative
referendum

Review

1. What are the qualifications for members of state legislatures?
2. How does a bill become a state law?
3. How do some state constitutions allow the people to take a direct part in making laws?

Discuss

Do you think the referendum should be used more often in your state? Explain your answer.

3

The State Executive Branch

The state's legislative branch makes the laws for the people of the state. These laws are executed, or carried out, by the state's executive branch. The executive branch is headed by the **governor.** It also includes other officials, as well as numerous agencies, who assist the governor.

Qualifications and Terms of the Governor

The governor is the chief executive in each state. He or she is elected by the people of the state in a statewide election. The qualifications for governor are set forth in each state constitution. In general a candidate for governor must be a citizen of the United States and must have lived in the state for a certain number of years. Most states require a governor to be at least 30 years old. A few, however, allow persons 25 years of age to run for governor.

Most governors serve four-year terms. In other states, they are elected for two years. In a number of states, governors cannot serve two terms in a row.

The salaries of the governors vary greatly from state to state. For example, the governor of New York receives $85,000 a year and the Texas governor $71,400. The governor of North Dakota receives $27,500. In addition to a salary, governors usually receive an allowance for expenses. In most states, governors and their families live in an official residence in the state capital.

The Governor's Powers and Duties

The main job of the governor, as chief executive of the state, is to carry out the laws. Like the President of the United States, however, many governors also have legislative and judicial responsibilities.

Chief Legislator. Only the state legislature can pass laws. The governor, though, plays an important part in proposing new laws. The governor usually appears before the state legislature at one of the early meetings. At this meeting, the governor outlines laws he or she thinks should be passed. From time to time, the governor talks to leaders of the legislature, urging them to pass specific bills. State legislators know that if they pass a bill the governor opposes, it may be vetoed.

After the legislature has passed a law, it is the responsibility of the governor to put it into force. If the legislature passes a new tax law, for example, it is the duty of the governor to issue orders that will determine how these taxes are to be collected. The orders that set up methods of enforcing laws are called **executive orders.** Almost every law passed by the legislature requires such executive orders.

Chief Executive. In most states, one of the governor's most important responsibilities is to draw up a budget for the state. The **budget** is a plan of income and spending. A budget director or a budget bureau aids the governor. Long hours are spent in figuring out the amount of money the state will need during the next one- or two-year period, and the taxes that will be required to meet this need. The completed budget is sent to the legislature for approval.

As chief executive of the state, the governor also may appoint a number of officials with the approval of the state Senate. The governor works with these officials to carry out state laws.

Political Party Leader. The governor is the head of his or her political party in the state. State senators and representatives pay close attention to what the governor says. They know the governor can aid them during their next election campaigns.

Other Powers. The governor has many other powers. The heads of the state police force and militia report to the governor. In times of emergency, such as floods or hurricanes, the governor may call out the National Guard to help keep order. The governor also has the power to pardon, or free, certain prisoners. In such cases, the governor gets advice from a state pardon board.

Other State Executive Officials

The voters of each state elect a number of officials in addition to the governor to help run the state government. The following officials are the more important members of

The Powers and Duties of the Governor

each state's executive branch. In most states, these officials are elected by the voters. In some states, however, they are appointed by the governor. Most of these officials are in charge of the executive departments of the state government.

Lieutenant Governor. All but seven states have lieutenant governors. The lieutenant governor becomes head of the state executive branch if the governor dies, resigns, or is removed from office. In some states, it is possible for the lieutenant governor and the governor to belong to different political parties. The lieutenant governor often serves as presiding officer of the state Senate.

Secretary of State. This official keeps the state's records, carries out the election laws, and fulfills other duties described in the state constitution. Only Alaska and Hawaii do not have secretaries of state. In states that do not have a lieutenant governor, the secretary of state serves as governor if the governor dies, resigns, or is removed from office.

Attorney General. This official takes care of the state's legal business, or matters concerning the law. If any state official wants advice about the meaning of a certain law, the attorney general gives it. The attorney general or an assistant represents the state in court when the state is involved in a lawsuit. The attorney general may also assist local officials in the prosecution of criminals.

State Treasurer. This official is in charge of handling all state funds. The state treasurer supervises the collection of taxes and pays the state's bills.

State Auditor. This official makes sure no public funds are paid out of the state treasury unless payment is authorized by law. Usually the treasurer cannot pay any bills without a written order that is signed by the auditor. This order to pay out money is called a **warrant.** The auditor also examines the state's financial records from time to time to make sure they are correct. The auditor is sometimes called the **comptroller.**

Superintendent of Public Instruction. The chief duty of this official is to carry out the policies of the state Board of Education (which in some states is known by other titles). The state board makes regulations, under state law, that govern the various local school districts of the state. The superintendent is in charge of the distribution of state funds to the local school systems according to the law. This official is sometimes called the superintendent of public schools or the state commissioner of education.

The Governor's Cabinet

In some states the officials you have just read about are a part of the governor's Cabinet. In other states they are not considered members of the Cabinet unless they are appointed by the governor. Like the President's Cabinet, the governor's official advisers head the executive departments of the state government.

Most states have a Department of Justice (headed by the attorney general), a Department of Labor, a Department of Agriculture, and a Department of Highways. In addition, there is a Department of Safety, which includes the state police. The Department of Public Works is responsible for all public construction projects in the state except work done on highways.

State Executive Agencies

A number of state agencies exist to help the governor carry out the laws. These agencies are also part of the executive branch of our state governments. They are sometimes called boards, commissions, or departments.

Most state agencies are headed by officials appointed by and responsible to the governor. In some states, the heads of the agencies are appointed by the state legislature. They are responsible directly to the legislature.

Each state agency has a specific area of responsibility. For example, the state Board of Health enforces health laws and recommends measures to improve the health of state citi-

CAN YOU GUESS?

- **Which state was an independent republic before being admitted to the Union?**
- **Only one of our 50 states contains a former royal palace. Which state is it?**

Answers are on page 562.

zens. The Board of State Welfare supervises programs that aid the poor, unemployed, and handicapped. The state Civil Service Commission is in charge of hiring most of the people who work for the state. Other state agencies administer state laws on agriculture, highways, and conservation. Other agencies regulate banks and public utilities.

State Government Employees

Our state governments employ a great many people. Most state employees get their positions through the state Civil Service Commission. State examinations are given as a means of choosing the most qualified workers. Other state jobs are not under civil service. These jobs are filled through recommendations of political party leaders and office holders. Such jobs often go to those in the party who have helped in some way during the election campaign. However, most state government jobs are under civil service. They are open to any qualified citizen.

CHECK-UP

Vocabulary

governor	state treasurer
executive orders	state auditor
budget	warrant
lieutenant governor	comptroller
secretary of state	superintendent of
attorney general	public instruction

Review

1. What are the qualifications for governor in most states?
2. Name three important duties performed by the governor.
3. What services do state agencies perform for the citizens of the state?

Discuss

Does the governor of your state play an important part in the lawmaking process of the state? Explain your answer.

4

State Courts

Each state government has the power to keep peace and order within its boundaries. It exercises this power through all three branches of state government. The legislature passes laws to provide for the welfare and safety of the people of the state. The executive branch sees that these laws are put into effect. The judicial branch—the state court system—has the job of judging, or interpreting, these state laws and punishing those who break them.

The Work of the State Courts

Federal and state courts handle both criminal and civil cases. **Criminal cases** deal with violations of the law. They involve acts that harm individuals or the community as a whole. A criminal act is considered an offense against society. In such a case, a lawyer for the state presents the evidence against the accused. She or he represents the people of the state, because breaking a state law is a crime committed against the people of the state. Serious crimes such as burglary, kidnapping, or murder are **felonies.** Less serious offenses, such as traffic violations, disorderly conduct, or violation of health laws, are **misdemeanors.**

Civil cases deal with disputes between individuals or businesses. They may also involve disputes between a business and the government or an individual and the government. These disputes are usually over property or money. For example, if one person claims that another owes him or her money and asks a state court for help in collecting the money, the case would be a civil case. Another example of a civil case might be a company's lawsuit against another firm for not carrying out its part of a business contract. In a civil case, the state court must judge who is right and must award damages in the case.

How Our State Courts Are Organized

Each state has its own system of courts to interpret the law and punish lawbreakers. The organization of state courts varies from state to state. Four types of courts are found in most states: lower courts, general trial courts, appeals courts, and a state supreme court. The chart on page 162 shows the organization of most state court systems.

1. Lower Courts. The lower, or local, courts generally hear minor cases. These include misdemeanors and civil cases involving small amounts of money. In most rural areas and small towns, these cases are heard by a **justice of the peace.** This elected official presides over a justice court and tries misdemeanors and civil cases involving small sums. For misdemeanors this official can hand down fines or short jail sentences.

In larger towns and small cities, such cases are handled by a magistrate's court or police court. These courts usually are presided over by an elected judge. All cases are heard by the judge and not by a trial jury.

Many large cities have set up **municipal courts.** These are often divided into smaller courts that handle special matters. Traffic courts, for example, hear cases involving traffic violations. Domestic relations courts hear cases involving family disputes. Juvenile courts hear cases involving young persons under 18 years of age.

In these special lower courts, judges with special legal training are usually in charge. These judges conduct hearings without a jury. They are usually more interested in getting at the cause of the trouble and preventing further difficulty than in handing out fines or jail sentences. Judges in juvenile and domestic relations courts work closely with social workers to help families who are in trouble. The decisions of the judges in serious cases may be appealed to a trial court.

2. General Trial Courts. Major criminal and civil cases are handled in general trial courts. Most cases are heard by a jury, and a judge presides. In about three fourths of the states, the judges are elected by the people of the county or district in which they serve.

Larger cities usually have several general trial courts. Sometimes one of these courts hears only civil cases, and another hears only criminal cases.

About one third of our states have trial courts called county courts. The county court

Many cities have set up a number of special lower courts. In this domestic relations court, a judge tries to help a family that is in trouble.

The right to sue in a law court and the right to appeal a lower court's decision are protected in our nation. These rights, however, have a price. What is it?

is located at the county seat, which is the center of county government in most states. In other states, trial courts are called district courts. There are also circuit courts, in which the judge travels a circuit (complete route) from one county to another to hold court. Other names for trial courts in some states are superior courts or courts of common pleas.

3. Appeals Courts. Sometimes a person believes his or her case was not handled fairly in a trial court. That person may appeal the decision to an appeals court. These courts are often called intermediate courts of appeals. The usual basis for appeal is that the trial judge violated one of the rights to a fair trial guaranteed to all citizens by the Constitution.

There is no jury trial in an appeals court. Instead, a group of judges study the trial record of the lower court and hear the arguments of lawyers. They decide the case by majority vote. The judges must decide whether the trial in the lower court gave the person on trial all the rights guaranteed under the Constitution. If the person is still not satisfied with the decision, he or she can appeal to the State Supreme Court.

4. State Supreme Court. This is the highest court in most states. The judges who sit on the state supreme court hear cases on appeal in much the same way as does the Supreme Court of the United States. In some states, the state supreme court is called the court of appeals.

State supreme court judges are elected in most states. In others they are appointed by the governor with the consent of the state Senate. The decision of the state supreme court is final unless a federal law or a question about the United States Constitution is involved. Then the case may be appealed to the Supreme Court of the United States.

Small Claims Courts

Most states have established special courts that hear civil cases involving small amounts of money. These are called **small claims courts.** They usually handle cases involving $1,000 or less. No lawyers are needed. The people in the dispute explain their side of the argument to the judge. The judge questions each side to try to get all the facts. Then the judge makes a decision in the case.

Our Overcrowded State Courts

There have been many proposals in recent years for the reform of our state court system. The state courts are overburdened with work. So many cases come before them that the court calendar is often a year or more behind schedule. It is not unusual to find automobile accident cases that have waited two or three years for a court settlement.

In many of our largest cities, the jails are crowded with accused persons who are awaiting trial. Some have waited for more than a year. They may or may not be guilty. They have remained in jail because they do not have the money to post bail. They have not been brought to trial because there are so many cases ahead of them.

This backlog of cases makes it impossible to fulfill the constitutional guarantee of a speedy public trial. Critics point to three reasons for this situation. First, there are more cases than ever before and not enough judges to handle the increasing caseload. Second, trials are long and slow. The very guarantees that protect us often cause trials to take a long time. Third, some courts are not conducted in an efficient manner. Judges call frequent recesses, or breaks, in a trial. Lawyers sometimes use delaying tactics.

Many people say that courts have not kept up-to-date. They suggest the courts use modern business tools, such as computers, to make court work more efficient.

The conditions in our courts are serious. Their improvement is an issue well worth the concern and attention of every American.

CHECK-UP

Vocabulary

criminal cases
felonies
misdemeanors
civil cases
lower courts
justice of the peace
municipal courts
general trial courts
appeals courts
state supreme court
small claims courts

Review

1. What are the four types of courts found in most states?
2. Why do states have appeals courts?
3. How do small claims courts differ from other courts?

Discuss

Do you think judges in the state court system should be appointed or elected? Why? How are judges chosen in your state?

CHAPTER SUMMARY

Each of our 50 states has its own state government. The state government manages the internal affairs of the state. Like the federal government, every state government is based on a written constitution.

In the Constitution of the United States, many powers are left to the states. The states have power over such areas as public education, elections, highways, and the establishment of local governments. The states share with the federal government such powers as taxation, law enforcement, and the protection of the health, safety, and welfare of the people.

Each state government has a legislative branch, executive branch, and judicial branch. Most states have a two-house legislative body similar to Congress. The process of passing state laws is similar to that of putting federal laws through Congress.

The governors of the states are the chief executive officers of the state governments. They see that state laws are carried out. Governors are aided in their work by other executive officials and state executive agencies.

State courts judge state laws and bring to trial those accused of breaking state laws. The court system in the states includes lower courts, general trial courts, appeals courts, and a state supreme court.

CIVICS SKILLS: Writing to Your Legislator

You think your state legislature should make it easier to obtain a driver's license. You support the new highway bill. You want to attend one of the nation's four military academies, but a legislator must recommend you.

How do you communicate such information to the people who represent you in local, state, or federal government? One of the most effective ways to let your legislator know what you are thinking is to write him or her a letter.

Letter-Writing Tips

Well-written letters receive more attention than poorly written ones. Luckily, you only have to follow a few basic rules to make sure yours is the kind of letter that gets an answer.

- Include your return address on the letter, so that your legislator can get back to you.
- Always address a legislator as "The Honorable *(name)*." This applies to both the inside address and the address on the envelope.
- In the salutation, or greeting, use the person's correct title. For members of the United States House of Representatives, "Dear Representative *(name)*," "Dear Congresswoman *(name)*," or "Dear Congressman *(name)*" are all acceptable. For members of the Senate, "Dear Senator *(name)*" is the usual style.

  Titles of state officials vary. You should find out the exact title of an official before writing. Call the League of Women Voters to obtain this information.
- Keep the body, or main part, of the letter as brief as possible. Clearly state your position or request in the first paragraph. Point out any facts that will help your legislator understand why you are concerned.
- Put yourself in your legislator's place. Be polite—even if you are angry.
- Neatly type or copy your letter onto a piece of your own stationery. Be sure to check your spelling.
- End your letter with the proper closing, such as "Respectfully yours," or "Sincerely yours." Then add your signature.

Practicing What You've Learned

Use the letter on this page to answer the following questions.

1. What issue concerns Peter Gill?
2. Why might a letter to Representative Downing be more convincing than a telephone call?

32 Wadel Avenue
Elkhart, IN 46516
January 15, 1983

The Honorable Ann Downing
The State House
Indianapolis, IN 46204

Dear Representative Downing:

As you know, there is a bill currently before the legislature that would create 3,000 summer jobs for teenagers in our state. I strongly urge you to support this bill.

Passage of Bill HR 1026 will give many teenagers the chance to earn money for school. It will also provide them with experience for future jobs. Finally, the state stands to benefit from all the work these teenagers will be doing in our parks, hospitals, and civic centers.

I would appreciate knowing your position on this important issue.

Sincerely yours,

Peter Gill

Peter Gill

CHAPTER REVIEW

Vocabulary

Listed below are a number of terms having to do with state government. Copy the terms in your notebook and after each term explain how it applies to your state government.

territory
item veto
initiative
referendum
executive orders
civil cases
governor
extradition
criminal cases
felonies
misdemeanors
justice of the peace
lieutenant governor

Check-Up

1. Why was the Tenth Amendment added to the Constitution?
2. What are concurrent powers? Give several examples.
3. In what ways are state constitutions like the Constitution of the United States?
4. How do the states show "full faith and credit" to other states?
5. Trace the process by which state laws are passed.
6. What is the role of each of the following officials in the state government: governor, lieutenant governor, secretary of state, state treasurer, state auditor, attorney general?
7. What is the main responsibility of the State Civil Service Commission?
8. What kinds of cases are heard in general trial courts?
9. What are some of the problems facing our state courts today? How do you think they can be corrected?
10. In what ways are the state governments similar to the federal government? How are they different?
11. Do you think all state employees should get their jobs through the state civil service? Why or why not?

Civics Skills

Write a letter to one of the state legislators representing your election district. Request information about some aspect of your state government or express your thoughts on an issue currently in the news. Review the letter-writing tips on the opposite page before beginning. If you don't know the names or exact titles of your state legislators, check *The Book of States* or call the League of Women Voters.

Citizenship and You

1. Make a chart of your state government. Include the executive, legislative, and judicial branches.
2. Draw a map showing your state's congressional districts. Outline in red the district in which your community is located.
3. On a bulletin board, display articles, drawings, pictures, and cartoons about the government of your state.
4. A committee may interview a state legislator and report back to the class on what was learned.
5. A group of students may visit a state court and report to the class on their experiences.
6. Prepare a report on your state's constitution. Include the following information: when and how the constitution was adopted, the number of revisions and amendments that have been made, and any outstanding or unusual features that are included.
7. Prepare a report on the legislature of your state. Include the following topics: name of each house, number of members in each house, length of terms for members of each house, number and length of sessions, and important bills passed in the most recent session of the legislature.

CHAPTER

9

How Local Governments Serve Their Citizens

Local governments were our first governments. The primitive tribe that chose the strongest person to be its chief and the oldest leaders to form a council was establishing local government. It was seeking a better, safer life for all.

In the same way, the first English settlers who landed in Jamestown, Virginia, in 1607 soon realized they needed rules and leaders. At first the settlers had to look out for themselves. They had to find their own food and build their own shelter. As food supplies began to run low and the colonists faced hunger and disease, they saw that they needed to work together if they were to survive.

The colonists formed a council to make laws for the colony. They chose Captain John Smith as president of the council. His job was to see that the laws were carried out. This Jamestown government was the first local government in colonial America.

Today local government is still the first and most important government in our lives. It protects our safety and our homes, and it helps keep our environment clean. Local government provides us with schools, libraries, parks, and other important services. We can see the work of our local government every day, and if it fails to do a good job it affects each of us directly.

In this chapter, you will read about local governments and the work they do. You will study these topics:

1. **The Many Units of Local Government**
2. **Town, Township, and Village Governments**
3. **City Government**
4. **How Our Governments Work Together**

1 The Many Units of Local Government

Local government has grown as our nation has grown. As the American people settled in rural communities, towns, cities, and suburbs, they set up local governments. Americans have found that good local governments make their lives easier, safer, healthier, and more pleasant.

How Local Governments Are Established

All local governments are established by and receive their powers from the state governments. State constitutions direct the state legislatures to set up a government for each village, town, county, and city within the state borders. The people of a town or city can change the way their local government is organized, or operates, only with the approval of the state legislature. State governments, however, give local units of government considerable power to manage their own affairs.

Most local governments are incorporated by the state. That is, they are organized by the state. They receive **charters,** or plans of government, from the state legislatures. A charter, like a constitution, describes the kind of government a community will have. The charter also gives the local government authority over its own affairs.

Local governments have the authority to tax their own citizens and to keep law and order. Local governments may own property and may sue and be sued. They have the same rights in courts as individuals have.

Why We Need Local Government

The people who live in each local area or community depend upon local government to serve them in many ways. We take for granted such conveniences as running water in our homes, sidewalks, trash collection, roads, and sewage systems. A great deal of planning by local officials is necessary to make such conveniences possible. Usually only when something goes wrong with local services do we appreciate them.

All these services depend upon a well-run local government. Some services, such as electricity and public transportation, may be provided by privately owned companies. Local government, however, is very much concerned that these services be kept economical and well regulated.

It might be possible for individuals working alone to perform all the services local governments provide. Each person might bury trash in the back yard or hire someone to haul it away. Each person might be able to guard against fire by keeping a fire extinguisher in the home. However, life would be more difficult if every citizen had to do all these things alone. The people in American communities find that by working together they can secure better and more efficient services than by working alone.

Local and State Cooperation

Local governments work closely with state governments to make our communities better, safer places in which to live. Many laws that govern local communities are passed by state legislatures. These laws, along with regulations passed by local lawmaking bodies, are called **ordinances.** They are usually enforced by local government.

What are some state laws that are enforced by local governments? One is the election law. Elections are carried out according to state rules. However, the polling places, where citizens go to vote, and the officials who supervise them are provided by local governments. Another example concerns weights and measures. In most states, the scales on which a butcher weighs meat must meet certain standards required by state law. Yet these controls are often enforced by local inspectors. The police departments of local governments enforce both state laws and local ordinances.

Kinds of Local Governments

There are many kinds of local governments in the United States. These include counties, towns, townships, villages, boroughs, and cities. The chart on this page shows the number of different kinds of local governments in the nation.

Although these governments differ, they also have much in common. The main job of any local government is to provide services for citizens. The first type of local government that we will examine is the county government.

County Governments

Most of our states are divided into parts called **counties.** The number and size of these counties vary from state to state. The state of Texas has 254 counties, while Delaware has only 3. Alaska has no counties. Altogether there are more than 3,000 counties in the United States. In Louisiana these local units are called **parishes.**

In many states, the county government is the largest unit of local government. Counties help carry out state laws. They also serve as court districts and conduct elections.

Connecticut and Rhode Island have counties, but these are geographical areas only, without county governments. In the New England states, most counties are judicial districts. There, the functions of county governments usually are performed by towns.

The county form of government began in the Southern colonies. In this region, agriculture was the main industry and the population was scattered. Tobacco, rice, indigo, and cotton plantations were often located long distances from each other. The county form of government, borrowed from England, seemed well suited to the settlers' needs.

Each Southern colony was divided into a number of counties. The plantation owners in each county met regularly in a central, easy-to-reach town, which became known as

County Government

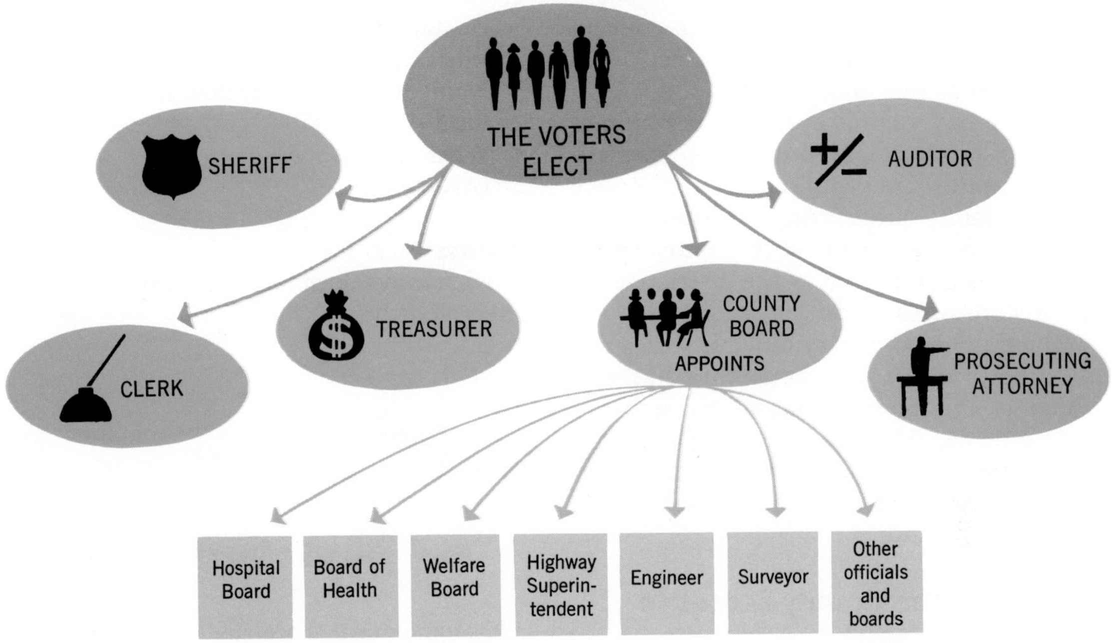

THE VOTERS ELECT
SHERIFF
AUDITOR
TREASURER
COUNTY BOARD APPOINTS
CLERK
PROSECUTING ATTORNEY
Hospital Board
Board of Health
Welfare Board
Highway Superintendent
Engineer
Surveyor
Other officials and boards

the **county seat.** At these meetings, the plantation owners passed the laws of the county government. The chief official in this early form of government was a sheriff, the title of a similar official in England. The sheriff's job was to see that the laws of the county were enforced.

Today, in states where counties are important, county governments serve two main purposes. First, they help the state government collect various state taxes, supervise elections, and enforce state laws. Second, they serve the people by providing them with roads, schools, libraries, health and welfare services, and law enforcement.

County Officials

At the head of a strong county government is a group of officials elected by the voters. This governing body is often called the **county board.** Other names for this group are county commissioners, county council, fiscal court, county court, or board of county supervisers.

The county board is the legislative body of the county. It may pass local laws regulating health and safety. It may collect taxes on real estate or personal property in the county. The county board also supervises such county buildings as the courthouse, jail, and library.

Many counties have no leader for the executive branch of their government. Instead they have several county officials, each with separate responsibilities. These officials are elected by the people of the county.

The **sheriff** enforces the law. He or she selects deputies to help in law enforcement. The sheriff arrests lawbreakers and carries out the orders of the courts. In many places, the sheriff has charge of the county jail.

The **county clerk** keeps a record of the actions and decisions of the county board. The clerk also keeps records of births, deaths, marriages, and election results. Usually she or he informs the public of all laws and regulations passed by the county board.

The **county treasurer** takes care of the

county's money. The treasurer sees that no money is spent unless the county board approves. Sometimes the treasurer collects taxes. Often, however, counties elect a **tax collector** to do this job.

The **county auditor** examines the official records of taxes received and money spent to make sure they are kept properly.

The **county prosecuting attorney** represents the state government in county trials. He or she is also known as the district attorney or state's attorney.

The number of county officials varies not only from state to state but from county to county as well. Some counties have as many as 70 officials. They include a veterinarian, purchasing agent, public defender, park commissioner, and public health nurses.

The Rise of the County Executive

As the population of areas outside the cities has grown, there has been a demand for better county government. With the approval of the voters and the state legislature, a number of counties have reorganized their governments. Many have established the position of **county executive,** or county manager.

This official is usually hired by the county board but in some places is elected by the voters. The county executive's duties are to supervise the work of the county government and put it on a businesslike basis. This type of county government places responsibility in the hands of a single executive.

CHECK-UP

Vocabulary

charters
ordinances
counties
parishes
county seat
county board
sheriff
county clerk
county treasurer
tax collector
county auditor
county prosecuting attorney
county executive

Review

1. How are local governments in our states established?
2. What powers do local governments have?
3. Name four services that are provided by local governments.
4. What are two main purposes of county government?

Discuss

In what ways does local government directly affect your life?

2

Town, Township, and Village Governments

Although counties are the largest of all units of local government, they are not always the most important. In a number of states, counties serve only as election districts, with the real work of local government carried on by other units. In all states, counties must share the job of local government with other units of government.

The Development of Towns and Villages

The **town** form of government began in the New England colonies. Each colony received a grant of land from the English king. The colonists established small towns, where they built their homes and churches.

At the edges of the towns, the settlers established their farms. Every day they left their homes and worked on the farms. The colonists considered these outlying farms to be part of their towns. Later some of the settlers moved to the farms. As long as these farms were located within the town limits, the people who lived on them were counted as members of that town. New England towns stretched out into the countryside, as did counties in other settlements.

In New Amsterdam (now called New York), the settlers set up a **village** government. Only the village itself, which included the homes of the settlers as well as other buildings, belonged to the village government. The outlying parts of the settlement were not considered part of the village, and they later came under the rule of the county government.

As other people pushed farther west, they established new settlements. Some of them called their settlements towns. In Pennsylvania, settlements were often called **boroughs.** Thus many different names were used for these small settlements.

This town meeting is taking place in Lancaster, Massachusetts. Here the tradition of town meeting government, begun in colonial times, continues today.

Early Town Government in New England

The people of the early New England towns worked out a simple yet effective form of local government—the **town meeting.** All the people who lived in a town, as well as those from the surrounding farms, met together regularly in the town hall. At these public meetings, citizens discussed their problems and decided how they should be handled.

Every citizen had a chance to speak on any question. After all opinions were heard, the people at the meeting voted on the question. Thus, each citizen had a direct vote in the government. A New England town meeting was a form of direct democracy. Some small New England towns still carry on their business in this way. Town meetings are also held in several states in the Middle West.

The Town Meeting Today

In New England towns today, the regular town meeting is usually held in the spring. A **warrant,** or notice of the town meeting, is posted in various parts of town well before the meeting. It is the official notice of the time of the meeting, and it lists the town business to be discussed.

On meeting day, the voters gather in the town hall. Before the meeting gets under way, the town elections are held. Some towns, however, wait until after the meeting to hold elections. The voters elect several (usually three or five) officials, called **selectmen.** These men and women manage the town's affairs during the period between regular town meetings. The voters also elect the other town officials. These include a town clerk, members of the school committee, a tax collector, a tax assessor, and fish and game wardens. Some towns elect these officials on a separate election day rather than at the town meeting.

Before or after the elections, the voters discuss the town's business. They elect a **moderator** to preside over this part of the meeting. The selectmen who have been in office for the past year report on their activities. The treasurer gives the financial report, explains the debts the town has incurred, and asks the meeting to vote to pay these debts.

Then comes a discussion of town business for the coming year. The voters may be asked to give their opinions on such matters as street lighting, the building of a new school, the purchase of more snow removal equipment, the improvement of a town road, or a proposed increase in the tax rate. After the discussion ends, a vote is taken on each item. Voting is usually by voice vote. On important issues, the townspeople stand up to cast their vote.

The Representative Town Meeting

The town meeting form of government works well in areas with a small population. There it is easy for all the voters to gather at one central place. As the population of many towns has grown in recent years, some New England towns have had to make changes in the form of their town meetings.

One change that has worked well is the **representative town meeting.** In this type of town government, the voters elect representatives to attend the town meeting and make decisions for them. This system is also known as the **limited town meeting.**

Early Township Governments

In the Middle Atlantic states (New York, Pennsylvania, New Jersey, and Delaware), counties were divided into smaller units of local government called **townships.** These served many of the same purposes as the towns in New England. Townships were responsible for maintaining local roads and rural schools and for looking after the poor.

As county governments grew in the Middle Atlantic states, township governments became less important. In time these states developed a form of local government called **county-township government.** In this mixed form of local government, county and township officials work side by side to help the people govern their local affairs.

A stronger type of township developed in those Midwestern states that were carved out of the old Northwest Territory between the Ohio and the Mississippi rivers. In 1785 Congress worked out a system of surveying, or measuring, this vast area. According to the system, the Northwest Territory was divided into areas 6 miles square (9.6 kilometers square) called **congressional townships.**

Early congressional townships were not units of government. They were only divisions of land. As settlers from New England moved into this territory, they set up governments similar to the town governments in the states from which they came. The new units of government became known as **civil townships.** Sometimes a civil township occupied the same area as a congressional township, but usually it included more territory.

Township Government Today

Today townships exist in 21 states—mostly in the Middle Atlantic and Midwestern states. They provide government for rural areas. Towns or villages within the boundaries of a township have been granted their own forms of government by the legislature.

Township governments vary from state to state. Usually the township is headed by a chairperson, or **township supervisor.** This official is elected by the voters. The voters also elect a **township board of commissioners,** or **board of trustees,** who make the laws or regulations for the township. Laws are enforced by **constables,** and minor cases are tried by a justice of the peace. Most townships also elect an assessor, a treasurer, a tax collector, and school board members.

Special Districts

Often people living in a certain area within their local unit of government have a special need not shared by others living within the area. In such cases, the people may go directly to the state legislature and ask for a charter setting up a **special district.**

For example, in a farming area in a large Western county, the farmers may wish to have irrigation water for their crops. To pay for the pipes, ditches, and other equipment to supply this need, the state legislature may set up an irrigation district. This special district has no purpose other than to supply water and tax land at a rate sufficient to pay the costs. All other local government services remain in the hands of the county.

As you can see from the chart on page 176, special districts are the most numerous of the nation's local governments. They have been formed to meet many different special needs. Some of these, in addition to supplying water, are sewage disposal, fire and police protection, parks and recreation centers, libraries, public transportation, and gas and electric systems. The legislature usually provides for an elected or appointed commission to handle the details of the special district.

The most common special districts are those set up by each state to provide local schools. There are more than 15,000 **school districts** in the United States. Each district has its own governing body called a **board of education.** An executive, usually called a **superintendent of schools,** is employed to manage the day-to-day operation of the schools.

Village and Borough Governments

Village government, as you have read, is another unit of local government. When rural communities grow to a population of 200 to 300 people, their inhabitants often have problems that require them to work and plan together. They may then decide to organize their community as a village or borough and set up their own local government.

Is this a familiar sight to you? Libraries are an important service that local governments provide, whether they are public libraries or libraries in public schools.

The request to establish a village or borough government must be sent to the state legislature. If the legislature approves, it permits the village or borough to establish its own government. The village government may be given the power to collect its own taxes, pave its streets, set up fire and police departments, and provide other services.

The village or borough is often governed by a three- to nine-member council, or board of trustees. The voters also elect an executive called the **chief burgess,** or president of the board of trustees, to carry out the laws. This person is also sometimes called the mayor of the village.

In small boroughs or villages, most of the local officials serve on a part-time basis. There is usually not enough village business to occupy them full time. However, there may be a full-time clerk, constable, street commissioner, and engineer.

If the population of a village or borough becomes large enough, the people may ask the legislature to grant the community a city charter. The number of people needed to qualify as a city varies from state to state. Many states require a population of 2,500 people before a city charter is granted. You will learn more about city governments in the next section of this chapter.

CHECK-UP

Vocabulary

town
village
borough
town meeting
warrant
selectmen
moderator
representative town meeting
limited town meeting
township
county-township government
congressional township
civil township
township supervisor
township board of commissioners
board of trustees
constable
special district
school district
board of education
superintendent of schools
chief burgess

Review

1. Why is the New England town meeting called a form of direct democracy?
2. What are the main purposes served by township government?
3. What advantages might a rural community gain by becoming a village?

Discuss

Today there are almost 80,000 local governments in the United States. Do you think this makes it easier or more difficult to have good government? Explain.

3 City Government

More Americans live under city government than under any other unit of local government. As you recall, a **city** usually has at least 2,500 people. Some cities have over 1 million people. Often a large population is crowded into a small area. Therefore, a city sometimes has more difficult problems than other units of local government.

The city government has to handle a variety of problems dealing with health, education, and safety. It must keep traffic flowing smoothly through neighborhood streets. Police patrols and squad cars must be on the alert to prevent crime. Trash collections must operate efficiently. Street lighting, transportation, water supply, traffic signals, sewage systems—all these and hundreds of other services are the daily business of city governments.

Besides providing such services, city government helps provide cultural activities that are an important part of city life. Cities help support libraries, museums, and parks. City government often contributes to universities, hospitals, and musical groups. Many city governments encourage architects to design buildings that make the city more attractive.

The Organization of City Government

City governments, like all other local governments, are established by state legislatures. That is, they receive charters from the state legislatures. They have only those powers that are granted by the state. As you have read, a city charter is like a constitution. It contains a plan of government, and it sets forth provisions for the city government and outlines the powers granted to it.

City governments differ in the way they are organized. There are three main kinds of city government: the mayor-council government, the commission government, and the council-manager government. The diagrams on page 184 show the organization of these forms of government.

Mayor-Council Government

The oldest and most common form of city government is the **mayor-council plan.** In this kind of government, the lawmaking body is called the **city council.** The chief executive of the city government is the **mayor,** who sees that city laws, or ordinances, are enforced. The mayor and members of the city council are elected by the voters of the city. Their term of office varies, but in most cases it is either two years or four years.

Under the mayor-council government, the city is divided into districts called **wards.** Each ward elects one member of the council. In some cities, though, the people elect several **council members-at-large.** That is, they are chosen by all the voters in the city. Almost all city councils have just one house.

City voters also elect other officials, including a treasurer, judges of the municipal courts, a city attorney, or solicitor, and tax assessors. Other officials, either elected or appointed, are the heads of departments for police, firefighting, traffic, water, welfare, parks and playgrounds, civil defense, housing, licenses, and purchasing.

★ ★ ★ ★ ★ ★ ★ ★ ★ ★ ★ ★

CAN YOU GUESS?

- **What is the oldest city in the United States?**
- **What city has the tallest building in the United States?**
- **What city in the United States has the most people?**
- **In what city is the NASA Space Center located?**

Answers are on page 562.

Weak-Mayor Plan. During the early years of our nation's growth, the American people were slow to grant power to their mayors. The experience of colonists with English governors who did not listen to the people's wishes made Americans fear officials who might have too much power. For this reason, some cities developed the weak-mayor plan.

Under the weak-mayor plan of city government, the city council holds more power than the mayor. For example, the council appoints the heads of city departments. These heads report directly to the city council. In addition, the mayor must obtain the consent of the council in order to spend money or take other actions. The weak-mayor plan often results in conflicts between the mayor and the council.

Strong-Mayor Plan. In recent years, most mayor-council cities have tried to make their governments more efficient by following the strong-mayor plan of city government. Under the strong-mayor plan, the mayor has chief responsibility for running the city's government.

The mayor appoints most of the city officials and can also dismiss them if they do not do a good job. The mayor can also veto bills passed by the council. It is the mayor's responsibility to draw up the city budget. When the council has approved a budget, the mayor must see that the city's money is spent properly. Under this strong-mayor plan,

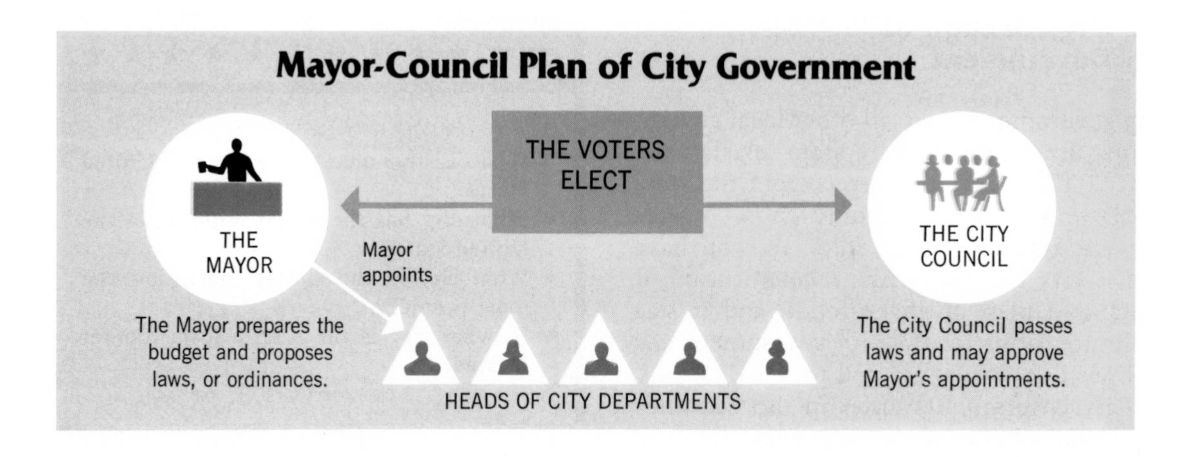
Mayor-Council Plan of City Government
THE VOTERS ELECT
THE MAYOR
Mayor appoints
THE CITY COUNCIL
The Mayor prepares the budget and proposes laws, or ordinances.
HEADS OF CITY DEPARTMENTS
The City Council passes laws and may approve Mayor's appointments.

Commission Plan of City Government
THE VOTERS ELECT
THE BOARD OF COMMISSIONERS
ROAD WORK
COMMISSIONER OF FINANCES
COMMISSIONER OF PUBLIC SAFETY
COMMISSIONER OF WELFARE
COMMISSIONER OF PUBLIC WORKS
COMMISSIONER OF HEALTH
The Commission passes laws and carries on city government.

Council-Manager Plan of City Government
THE VOTERS ELECT
THE CITY COUNCIL
passes laws
Council hires
THE CITY MANAGER
proposes laws
Manager appoints
HEADS OF CITY DEPARTMENTS

the mayor takes the lead in carrying on the city's business.

Commission Government

A new form of government grew out of a hurricane that struck Galveston, Texas, in 1900. A huge tidal wave swept across the city, flooding homes and businesses and causing millions of dollars in damages. Nearly 7,000 of the city's 37,000 residents lost their lives. The city's mayor and council were unable to handle the disaster. Yet something had to be done at once.

Leading citizens in Galveston asked the state legislature for permission to set up a new form of city government. It was called the **commission plan.** Within a few years, this plan of government had been adopted by several hundred other cities.

Under the commission plan, a city is governed by a **commission,** usually consisting of five elected officials. The commission is the city's lawmaking body as well as its executive body. The commission passes the city's ordinances. Each commissioner heads an important department of city government.

One commissioner usually is the head of the department of public safety, which includes the police and firefighters. Another commissioner, in charge of public works, must see that the city has an adequate supply of pure water and that the streets are kept clean and in good repair. A third commissioner oversees the city's finances, including tax collections. Another runs the welfare department, which aids the poor, the aged, and the unemployed. The health department is managed by a commissioner who supervises city hospitals, clinics, and health inspectors.

The commissioners meet as a group to make the city laws. However, they enforce the laws individually. Each commissioner carries out the laws that apply to his or her department. Either the voters or the commissioners choose one of the commissioners to be mayor. The mayor under this plan has no special powers. Except for presiding over meetings of the commission, the mayor has the same powers as other commissioners.

In some cases, the commission form of city government has had certain disadvantages. The voters sometimes have found it impossible to elect officials who know how to run a department of the city's government. Then, too, there are activities of city government that can come under the jurisdiction of several departments. Sometimes commissioners disagree about who should handle these activities. Therefore, the commission plan is now used by fewer than 10 percent of American cities.

Council-Manager Government

In 1908 Staunton, Virginia, was the first city to set up a **council-manager plan** of government. Today this plan of government is used by a growing number of cities.

Under the council-manager plan, voters elect a city council to act as the city's law-

Heavy traffic can choke a city if it is not kept moving. Police officers help local government to keep the traffic—and the city—moving smoothly.

making body. The council then hires a **city manager.** The city manager, as the city's chief executive, appoints the heads of the departments. They report directly to the city manager. Under this plan, the city is run much like any big business firm by specially trained people.

City managers are appointed, not elected, so that they will not take part in party politics or be under any political pressure. They are given a free hand to run city governments efficiently and economically. If a city manager does not do a good job, the council may dismiss him or her and appoint a new manager.

The council-manager plan of government has certain disadvantages. Some smaller cities cannot afford the salary required to hire a good manager. Other cities believe they are better governed when the voters themselves elect the officials who are to run the city's government.

CHECK-UP

Vocabulary

city
mayor-council plan
city council
mayor
wards
council members-at-large
weak-mayor plan
strong-mayor plan
commission plan
commission
council-manager plan
city manager

Review

1. How are city governments established?
2. What are the advantages and disadvantages of the mayor-council plan of city government?
3. What are the advantages and disadvantages of the commission plan?
4. What are the advantages and disadvantages of the council-manager plan?

Discuss

Which plan of city government do you think is most effective? Which could best deal with serious city problems? Why?

4
How Our Governments Work Together

You live under three levels of government—local, state, and national. If each level of government paid no attention to the work of the others, life would become difficult and confusing. City governments might pass city laws that conflicted with state laws. State governments might ignore federal laws and do whatever they wished. No citizen could be sure which set of laws to obey.

How Powers Are Divided Among Our Governments

Fortunately, under our federal system of government, the powers of each level of government are clearly defined and understood. The Constitution of the United States is the "supreme law of the land." All levels of government must obey it.

Our state constitutions, in turn, set up rules that govern the people of each state. These state constitutions must not, of course, take away from the people any of the rights guaranteed in the federal Constitution.

Local units of government, as you have read, have their powers defined for them by the state legislatures. These powers are explained in their charters. In this way, each level of government has its own work. Each is given the powers needed to do its job.

Why Our Governments Work Together

Many of our nation's problems call for cooperation among local, state, and national governments. Consider, for example, the way our modern highway system was built.

Back in colonial days, the building of a road was considered a local project. If the peo-

Sources of Laws and Powers of Our Three Levels of Government

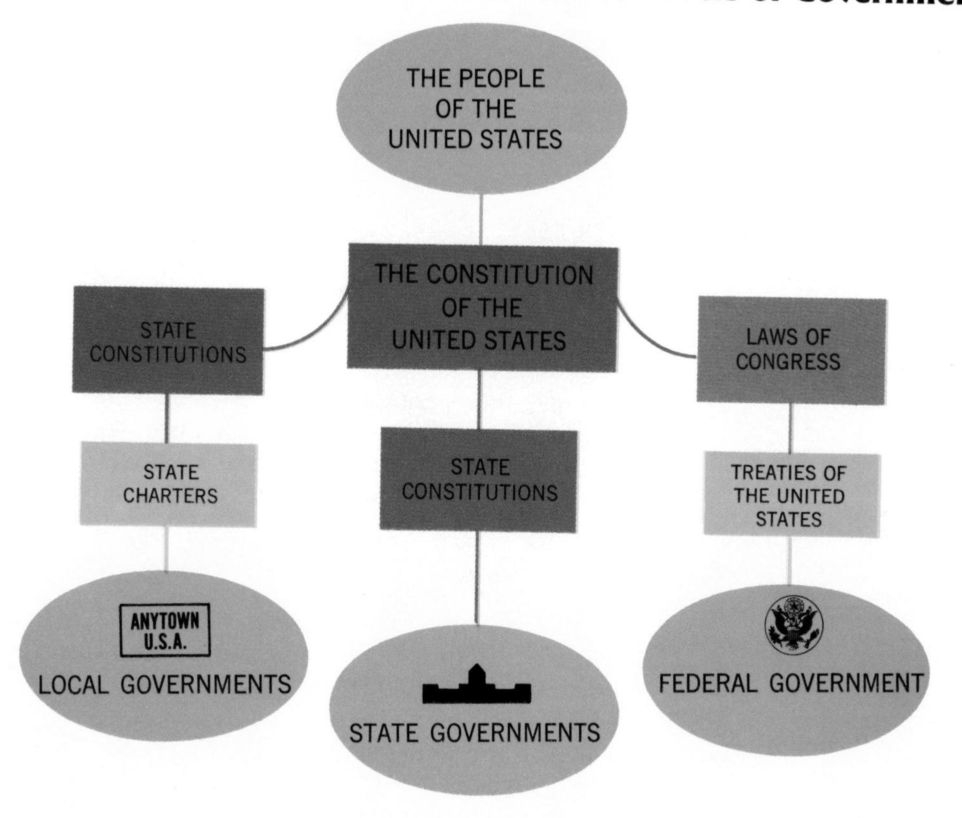

ple of any town wanted a road, they had to build it themselves. As towns spread westward, each county undertook to build connecting roads. The county called upon the local farmers and townspeople who needed the road to supply the labor or provide money to hire workers.

These early roads were often terrible. They were twisting and rutted, dusty in dry weather and muddy after rain. They were, however, cheap to build and repair. Local governments could easily handle the job of planning and paying for such roads.

As our nation grew, highways were needed to connect the East with the growing West. Therefore, Congress voted to have the federal government build some main roads to the West. The most important of these early roads was the **National Road** (or Cumberland Road). It started at Cumberland, Maryland, and went as far west as Vandalia, Illinois.

Still, for a long time, most roads were built by local governments or private companies. These roads were paid for by collecting **tolls,** or fees, from the people who used them. When the automobile was invented, it became clear that road building was no longer a local problem alone. Motorists needed highways that would stretch across their home state and connect with roads in other states.

Governments Cooperate in Road Building

Late in the 1800's, even before automobiles were in common use, New Jersey was the first state to use state funds to help its counties improve their local roads. Massachusetts

(continued on page 190)

CITIZENSHIP
IN ACTION

Saving the Covered Bridges

There once were more than 10,000 covered bridges in the United States. Today only about 1,000 of these wooden structures are still standing. A group of students in Scio (SY·oh), Oregon, decided to try to help save some of them.

Opinion Is Divided

Oregon was in the midst of a debate over which of the state's 56 covered bridges should be placed on the *National Register of Historic Places.* Bridges placed on this register are considered historical landmarks and cannot be torn down. Some people favored listing as many bridges as possible. They thought this might make it easier to get money from the federal government to preserve the bridges. Others felt that listing the bridges would cause the federal government to become too involved in local affairs.

Linn County, where the small town of Scio is located, has ten covered bridges. County officials were divided over a plan that called for placing five of the bridges on the register. In general, officials opposed the plan. They were afraid that paying for the upkeep of the bridges would cause taxes to rise.

The Scio Bridge Brigade

Since eight of the ten bridges in Linn County were near Scio, the townspeople were very interested in the county's decision. It was the students, though, who acted. Many of them passed through a covered bridge every day on their way to and from school. They had fond thoughts about the bridges. One student remembered catching his first fish from a covered bridge. Another thought of the many times she had stopped her bicycle to rest under the roof of a covered bridge. Still others knew what the bridges meant to their parents and grandparents and what they would mean to people in the future. According to one student, "We need touches of the past for our future."

At the urging of a social studies teacher, the students organized themselves into the Scio Bridge Brigade. They wrote down their thoughts about the bridges and sent them to county officials. The students didn't stop there. They went from door to door trying to win support for their cause. They spoke about the bridges at public hearings. They wrote letters to newspapers. They invited the Covered Bridge Society of Oregon to meet in Scio. From money they made from a jog-a-thon, the brigade published a pamphlet of their poems and drawings about the bridges. They carried on their campaign in as many ways as possible.

The members of the Scio Bridge Brigade were successful. As a result of their efforts, five of the county's ten covered bridges have been listed on the *National Register of Historic Places.* For its work the Scio Bridge Brigade won an award from the National Trust for Historic Preservation. The students succeeded in preserving part of our nation's heritage because they cared enough to take action.

Thinking It Over

1. What were the arguments for and against placing the covered bridges on the *National Register of Historic Places?*
2. Why do you think the students were able to convince public officials to preserve some of the bridges?
3. Do you think a special effort should be made to preserve links to America's past, such as covered bridges? Explain. What other links with our nation's past can you think of?

This well-traveled highway in Texas is part of a vast coast-to-coast highway system. It is just one example of cooperation between federal and state governments.

went a step further in 1894, when it began to build a statewide highway system. Other states soon followed the lead of New Jersey and Massachusetts and set up state highway departments to build main roads.

Today, most well-traveled roads are built and maintained by the state. Each year state governments spend billions of dollars to build and improve roads and keep them safe.

The federal government also has an important role in our states' road-building programs. It pays a large part of the cost of new state highways. It does so because good roads contribute to the welfare of all American citizens.

The **interstate highway system**, planned by the federal government, now connects all parts of the nation. It is a joint project of the federal and state governments. The states plan the routes and supervise construction of the roads. The roads must meet federal requirements.

The federal government pays 90 cents of every dollar of the cost of building and maintaining our nation's highways. This money comes from a highway trust fund to which motorists contribute when they pay taxes on gasoline. The federal government also assists state and local governments in building other highways, bridges, and tunnels.

Other Ways in Which Governments Cooperate

Our local, state, and federal governments work together in many other ways. For example, local and state police cooperate with the Federal Bureau of Investigation to capture criminals. Most states have crime laboratories, whose services also are used by local police officials. State and local police may obtain helpful information, such as fingerprints, from FBI files. Criminals arrested and convicted by local governments are often sent to prisons maintained by state governments.

Stores and businesses in your own neighborhood must obey many state laws that promote good business practices. Workers in local factories or mines are protected by state inspectors who see that safety regulations are obeyed. State bank inspectors help keep your savings safe.

State governments also serve local communities by setting up state licensing boards. These boards give examinations and issue licenses to doctors, dentists, lawyers, engineers, nurses, teachers, and accountants. This service helps ensure that communities have qualified professional workers.

Local, State, and Federal Cooperation in Education

Public education is one of the most important areas in which the various levels of government cooperate to serve the public. State governments grant funds to local communities to help them operate their schools. State boards of education provide services for local school districts and see that they obey state laws. Actual control of the schools, however, is left to local boards of education. These local boards know the needs of the students in their schools.

The federal government cooperates by helping with special funds for schools. Schools with a large number of students from poor areas receive special federal aid to enrich their educational programs. The federal government also provides school lunch programs for poor students. In addition, the federal government supports research in education.

Other Federal Aid Programs

The federal government provides local and state governments with funds to help them carry out certain important programs. Such programs include aid to the elderly and the handicapped, and medical and financial assistance to the poor. These funds are called **grants-in-aid.** They must be used for specific programs. The programs must meet the standards set by the federal government.

What about other pressing financial needs facing our local and state governments? Some of these needs are funded with help from **revenue sharing.** Under this plan, the federal government provides money to local and state governments to use, without federal controls, for programs they feel are needed.

City Governments Work Together

Our cities face many common problems. For example, city governments are concerned about how to get more money for police officers, firefighters, and teachers. They look for ways to lessen air pollution and to dispose of trash safely. The **United States Conference of Mayors** meets regularly so that the mayors of our cities may compare problems and discuss possible solutions.

As neighboring cities grow closer together, they share many problems. For example,

Through the FBI, the federal government keeps millions of sets of fingerprints on file. Local and state criminal investigators often make use of this file.

All communities face the risk of fires. Therefore, our local governments must have the funds to keep fire departments always ready for action.

many villages and townships make up Nassau County on Long Island, New York. The population of this area grew from 300,000 in 1947 to nearly a million and a half in 1970. Soon one community had merged into the next in an almost continuous line. The officials of the various local units realized that close cooperation by all Nassau County communities was becoming a necessity.

For greater efficiency and better service, the officials of the various localities got together and agreed that their communities should combine and share most of their services. Fire alarms are now answered by the fire departments of several neighboring communities. Local schools are shared, which allows students to attend schools offering special courses they need. The costs of trash collection, water, and other services are shared. Only the police departments are maintained separately by the various towns, but even here Nassau County communities cooperate closely.

Governments Also Compete

Although government cooperation is growing, governments also compete with one another. The various levels of government often compete for taxes. For example, a family may have to pay income taxes to both state and federal governments. There may be a city income tax as well. Residents may also have to pay a sizable real estate tax to their local governments.

States compete with each other to attract industry. They offer businesses lower taxes, a good supply of labor, good highways, and favorable laws to encourage industry to move to their state. Cities compete for trade and industry in similar fashion.

The federal government and federal laws sometimes seem to interfere or compete with local laws and customs. For example, the federal government may challenge the election procedures in a state or locality if such procedures conflict with federal law.

Our combined system of federal, state, and local governments is complex. It would be surprising if there were not instances of conflict. Only by working together can we make our democratic form of government work.

CHECK-UP

Vocabulary

National Road
tolls
interstate highway system
grants-in-aid
revenue sharing
United States Conference of Mayors

Review

1. Why is the federal government interested in better roads?
2. Give examples of the ways governments cooperate.
3. Give examples of the ways governments compete.

Discuss

How does your local government cooperate with other communities?

CHAPTER SUMMARY

Each of us is directly affected by local government. The governments of our cities, towns, townships, and counties take care of many of the practical needs of our lives. They provide fire and police protection, a water supply, a sewer system, trash removal, and other necessary services.

County governments serve the common needs of people over a fairly large area. In some states, more and more power has been given to the towns and cities, and the counties serve mainly as election districts.

Town meetings still serve much of New England and some parts of the Middle West. The rapid growth of population, however, has caused larger New England towns to set up representative town meetings.

Town and township governments in many areas work with the county in governing and in providing services to their communities. Special districts, especially in rural areas, provide such services as sewage systems, water supply, and local schools.

City government has had to meet many special problems in recent years. Some cities have kept the mayor-council plan of government. Others have turned to the commission plan or are using the council-manager plan of government.

Federal, state, and local governments cooperate in many ways. Sometimes, though, they compete for taxes, trade, and industry.

CIVICS SKILLS: Reading a Newspaper

- *What's on television tonight?*
- *Who won the basketball game?*
- *Where can I get a summer job?*
- *When does the school board meet?*
- *Is the President back from Europe?*

You don't have to spend hours in the library to find the answers to these questions. The work has already been done for you. All you have to do is read a copy of your daily newspaper.

Newspapers carry a wealth of information. You can quickly find out what is covered in your paper by skimming the **index.** This is the list of topics that appears on the first or second page of the paper. If your paper has more than one section, you might also look for the index on the first page of the second section.

Identifying News Stories

To find the major news of the day, you don't need the index. The news is almost always reported in articles that run on the front page of the paper. These are the **news stories,** the articles in a paper that tell you about events in the world, the nation, and your own community. The bold **headlines,** or titles, make sure you won't miss them.

If a news story breaks, or happens, outside the area in which you live, it will probably begin with a **dateline.** This line of type quickly shows you where a story was written. It might also indicate when it was written. If one of the news-gathering services prepared the story, it is identified. Today the two largest services are United Press International (UPI) and Associated Press (AP).

The sentences that follow the dateline are filled with information. Unlike other types of articles in the paper, news stories won't keep you in suspense. You get all the important facts in the first paragraph, or **lead.** Who? What? When? Why? How? These are the questions a reader wants answered right away. The rest of the details can be given in the body, or remaining paragraphs.

The one thing you should never find in a good news story is the writer's point of view. Reporters often quote other people, but they save their own comments for the editorial page. This is the part of the paper where writers can express their opinions in special articles called **editorials.** If you disagree, or have your own ideas, you can send a letter to the editor of the paper. It might be printed along with other well-written letters in a special column on the editorial page.

Practicing What You've Learned

Use the following questions to help you read the news story below.

1. What can you discover from the news story's dateline?
2. What questions are answered by the facts given in the lead?
3. Write a short editorial in support of the idea of an annual July Fourth cleanup in your community.

LAKEVILLE, Mich. (AP)—"It was the most successful celebration we've ever seen," said Lakeville officials just one day after the city's annual July Fourth cleanup.

In what has by now become a tradition, people in Lakeville once again did more than watch parades on Independence Day—they also swept sidewalks, planted flowers, and picked up litter.

The idea first caught on in 1976 when Lakeville decided to do something different for the nation's 200th birthday. Response to a city-wide cleanup was so enthusiastic, the city council decided to make it a regular event.

CHAPTER REVIEW

Vocabulary

Write a three-paragraph summary of the main ideas in this chapter. In the first paragraph use the following terms:

counties
county auditor
sheriff
county seat
county board
county manager

The second paragraph should contain the following terms:

town meeting
selectmen
moderator
special district
representative town meeting
townships

In the third paragraph use the following terms:

mayor
commission
city manager
wards
city council
city

Check-Up

1. Why do we need local governments?
2. Why have representative town meetings been used in some New England towns?
3. How has township government changed over the years?
4. Why might the problem of trash disposal lead to the formation of a special district in a state?
5. What are the three chief forms of city government? How are they alike? How do they differ?
6. Why might a small city be more likely to have a mayor than a city manager?
7. How do federal, state, and local governments cooperate in road building?
8. What are some of the other ways in which federal, state, and local governments work together?
9. Give an example of a way in which several cities might cooperate for the good of their citizens.
10. What does your state government do to encourage industry?

Civics Skills

Use a copy of your local newspaper to answer the following questions.

1. Looking at just the index, where would you expect to find the latest ball scores? a television schedule? an editorial? a movie review? the weather forecast? a letter to the editor?
2. Now select a recent news story about your local government. What facts are given in the story's lead? Was the story written by a reporter for your local newspaper or a reporter for a news service? How can you tell?

Citizenship and You

1. Prepare a report on how your local government is organized and how it operates. Name the officials, what their duties and powers are, and what services are provided by your local government.
2. Invite the mayor, a council member, or some other local official to talk to your class and explain how your community is governed.
3. Prepare a map of your community. Show the most important streets, buildings, and parks.
4. Read a book on the local history of your community. Report to the class the main facts about the founding and growth of your city or town. Also talk about the early leaders of your community.
5. Prepare a scrapbook of articles and pictures on the activities of your community. Sections of the scrapbook may be devoted to such topics as government, transportation, safety, sanitation, crime, water supply, schools, and elections.

UNIT THREE REVIEW

Reviewing the Facts

Write your answers to the items below on a separate piece of paper.

1. Which of the following is a power of *state* government? Which is a power of *local* government? Which is a power of *both* kinds of government?
   a. deciding qualifications for voting
   b. collecting a city tax
   c. running a tax-supported hospital
   d. paying costs of schools and colleges
   e. building a highway that connects two cities
2. Suppose you took your bicycle, which is worth $100, to a bicycle shop for repair. The store was robbed and your bicycle was taken. You think the store should replace your bicycle, but the store owner has refused. What court would you go to in order to sue the owner for failure to replace your property?
3. Correct the underlined part of this sentence: Most large American cities have a commission form of government.
4. Each of the following is a lawmaking body *except*
   a. a city council.
   b. a state Senate.
   c. a town meeting.
   d. a special district.
5. Complete this sentence: The ________ clause of the Constitution requires that states accept the decisions of courts in other states.
6. Complete this sentence: Some states allow citizens to take a direct part in making laws through the processes of initiative and ________.
7. The state official in charge of supervising the collection of taxes is the
   a. attorney general.
   b. state auditor.
   c. state treasurer.
   d. secretary of state.
8. All of the following powers are reserved to the states *except* the power to
   a. establish local government.
   b. regulate foreign trade.
   c. determine qualifications for voters.
   d. establish public schools.
9. Mike is a painter. He was hired by Paul to paint his new apartment for $500. Mike received $250 before beginning. But when the job was finished, Paul refused to pay what he owed. Mike asked the court to make Paul pay him $250. Is this an example of a criminal case or a civil case? Explain your answer.
10. All of the following services are provided by local governments *except*
    a. trash collection.
    b. sewer systems.
    c. a money system.
    d. police protection.

Applying What You Know

1. Write the first two paragraphs of a news story that might appear in a local newspaper the day after a session of the city council or a town meeting.
2. Suppose that a wanted criminal was thought to be hiding out in your community. How might the local, state, and federal governments work together to find the criminal?

Expanding Your Knowledge

Allen, Robert S. (ed.), *Our Fair City,* Arno. A collection of articles about different cities and their governments.

Bentley, Judith, *State Government,* Franklin Watts. History of state legislatures from colonial times to the present.

League of Women Voters Education Fund, *Know Your Community,* League of Women Voters. How you can learn about your local government.

UNIT FOUR

The Citizen in American Government

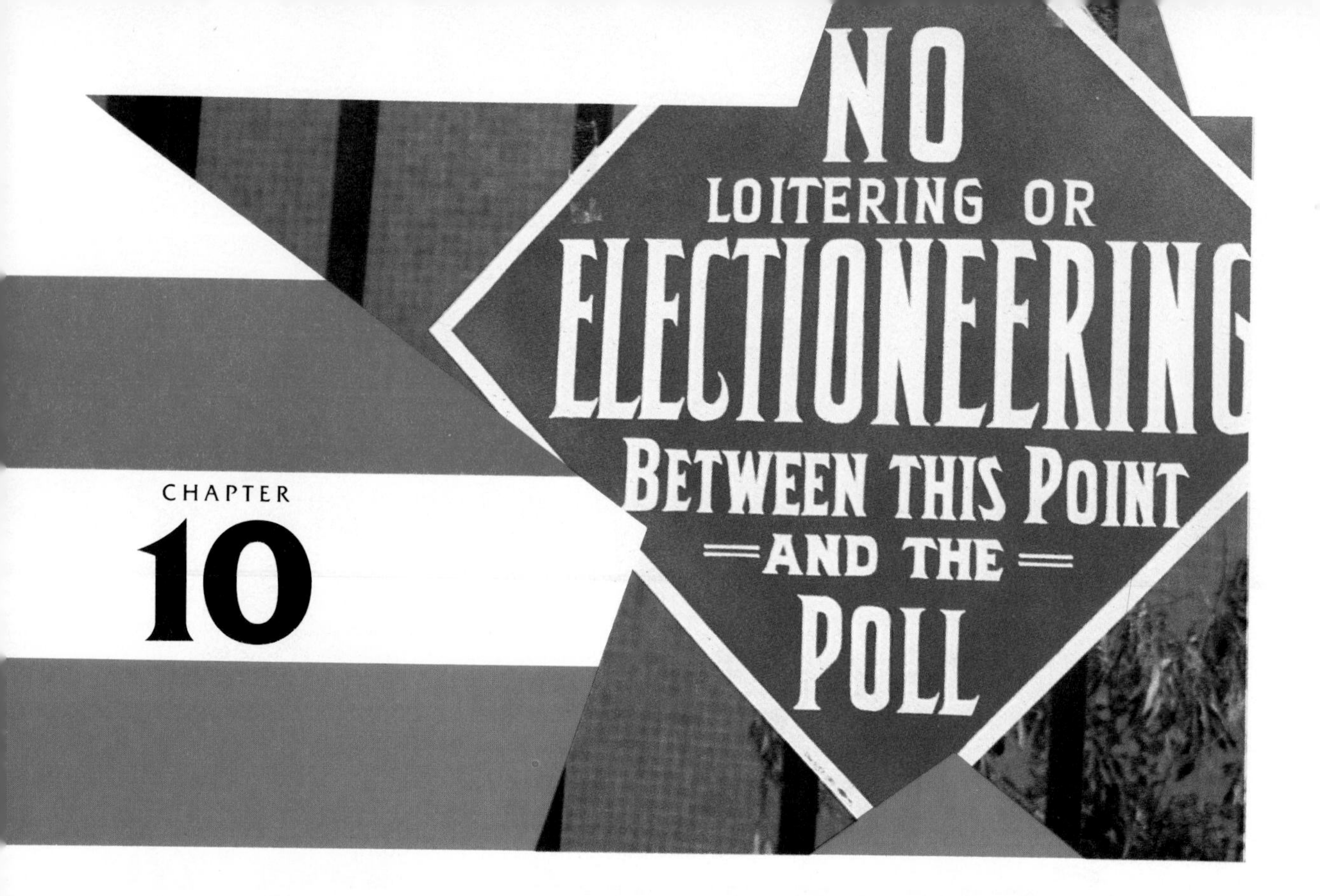

CHAPTER 10

Electing Our Leaders

Are you ready to vote? The Twenty-sixth Amendment to the Constitution of the United States gives you the right to vote when you are 18 years of age. At that time you will be faced with the decision of casting your vote intelligently for national, state, and local officials. Your vote will help choose the leaders of our nation and determine the way billions of dollars will be spent. The policies of our nation as well as of your state and local community will be determined in part by you.

Great attention is focused every four years on the Presidential election. The selection of the person who will lead our nation is important to all of us. Equally important are congressional, state, and local elections.

To make your vote count most, you should take an active part in our political system. Joining a political party and working to elect candidates you believe in is an excellent way to participate.

How do political parties work? What happens during an election campaign? These and other aspects of American elections will be examined in this chapter, as you study the following topics:

1. **Our Two-Party System of Politics**
2. **The Organization of Political Parties**
3. **The Right to Vote**
4. **Nominating and Electing Our Leaders**

1

Our Two-Party System of Politics

Nowhere in the Constitution will you find any provision for political parties. They are not an official part of the organization of our government. Anyone who has lived in our country at election time, however, knows that political parties are a very important part of our democratic way of life.

What Is a Political Party?

A **political party** is an organization made up of citizens who usually have similar ideas on public issues and who work to put their ideas into effect through government action. To achieve their purposes, political parties try to get the voters to elect to public office those whom the party favors. Parties also work hard to get laws passed that they favor.

In the United States, political parties are voluntary. All citizens are free to join the party of their choice. Or they may decide not to join any party. Americans who join a political party usually do so because they agree with most of that party's ideas. Of course, not all members of a political party agree on every issue. If members are in serious disagreement with a party on important issues, they are free to leave the party. They may then join another party or decide not to belong to any party at all.

As members of a political party, Americans can join with other citizens in trying to put their party's ideas to work in our local, state, and national governments. Political parties play a large role in helping the American people govern themselves.

Why We Have Political Parties

Why do we have political parties in the United States? The reason is simple. Political parties offer a practical way for large numbers of people with similar ideas to get things done. Political parties are concerned with practical politics. This means that the parties are concerned with what actions governments should take.

Everyone's life is affected by practical politics. When you complain about the high cost of living, you are taking a practical interest in politics. If you just complain, you are not very effective. If you join with other citizens who agree with you, however, you can make your voice heard in a way that gets better results.

Political parties also **nominate,** or select, candidates for public office. **Candidates** are the men and women who run for election to offices at various levels of our government. Most of the people who serve in public office in the United States have been elected to their offices as candidates of political parties. It is not impossible, but it is very difficult, for a person to run for office without the support of a political party.

Political parties also take positions on public issues. They try to get laws passed. During the election campaign, each party tries to convince the voters that it offers the best program.

After an election, the winning candidates become the leaders of our government—the ones who make and carry out our laws. The political party to which these leaders belong tries to make sure they do a good job. In this

How Political Parties Serve Our Nation

Select candidates who run for election to offices in our governments.

Assure that officials and lawmakers of their party do a good job so voters will reelect them.

Help to improve our governments by pointing out weaknesses and failures in other parties and their candidates.

Recommend programs and laws that determine actions taken by our governments.

Keep members informed and help keep all citizens interested in their governments.

way, it hopes to ensure that the party's candidates will win again at the next election. The party whose candidates lost will be watching for any weaknesses or mistakes the new leaders may make. This party also will be quick to inform the public if the winning party's candidates do not keep their campaign promises after they are elected.

How Our Two-Party System Started

The history of political parties dates back to the late 1700's, when our government first began to operate under the Constitution. The first political parties began during President George Washington's administration. As you read in Chapter 2, those who favored a strong federal government were called Federalists. Those who favored limiting the power of the central government were called Anti-Federalists. Later they were known as Democratic-Republicans.

Alexander Hamilton became the leader of the Federalists. He proposed policies that would make the federal government strong. Thomas Jefferson, the leader of the Democratic-Republicans, opposed Hamilton and the Federalist Party. Jefferson and the Democratic-Republicans tried to limit the power of the federal government.

As President Washington watched these two different viewpoints lead to the establishment of political parties, he became worried. He feared that the growth of parties would weaken the new nation. In his Farewell Address as President, Washington warned Americans that political parties were dangerous because they could divide the nation.

Washington's warnings, however, were soon forgotten. Political parties became a lasting part of government in the United States. Throughout most of our history, the United States has had two strong political parties.

Beginnings of the Democratic and Republican Parties

For more than 125 years, the Democratic Party and the Republican Party have been our nation's two major political parties. The present **Democratic Party** traces its roots to Jefferson's Democratic-Republican Party. In the 1820's, that party split into several different groups.

One group, led by Andrew Jackson, became the Democratic Party. Jackson believed that the federal government had fallen into the hands of the wealthy and was being run for their benefit. He was determined that the federal government should represent frontier settlers, farmers, and city laborers—the common people. Jackson was elected President in 1828, and the Democratic Party he established began its long history.

The present **Republican Party** was formed in 1854. In that year, several small groups that opposed the policies of the Democratic Party joined together. The Republican Party was started by people who were against slavery and who opposed the spread of slavery into the territories. In 1860 Abraham Lincoln became the first candidate nominated by the Republican Party to be elected President.

Advantages of a Two-Party System

Ever since then, these two political parties have had almost equal strength. Beginning with Jackson, the Democrats have elected 13 Presidents who, up to 1983, served for a total of 71 years. The Republicans, starting with Lincoln, have had 17 Presidents who, until 1983, served for a total of 74 years.

Thomas Jefferson (left) and Alexander Hamilton (right) disagreed about how government should operate. They were the leaders of our first political parties.

Theodore Roosevelt was one of our nation's most popular third-party candidates. His spirited speeches always attracted a large and enthusiastic crowd.

This **two-party system,** as we call it, has worked remarkably well. When one party fails to please a majority of voters, there is another strong party ready to take over. The newly elected party often tries different programs and policies in dealing with the nation's problems.

If we had more than two strong political parties, all of about equal strength, no one party would be able to win a majority of votes. In order to run the government, then, two or more of the political parties would have to work out a compromise and agree to work together. This agreement between two or more political parties to work together to run the government is called a **coalition.**

Coalition governments, however, have certain disadvantages. Often the political parties disagree, and the coalition breaks apart. This makes the government and the nation weak. Several European nations have this **multi-party system.** Some nations, such as Italy, have had great difficulty in governing themselves because of the many small political parties. However, in the Netherlands and other nations this system has worked well.

Third Parties in the United States

Besides the two strong political parties in the United States, there are also a number of minor political parties. In national elections, there are always several candidates who have been nominated by these minor political parties. Minor parties usually are called **third parties.** At certain times in our history, they have had great influence.

In 1912 Theodore Roosevelt was denied the Presidential nomination of the Republican Party and started a third political party called the Progressive Party. Roosevelt ran for President as the nominee of this party. He was not elected. But he took away enough votes from the Republican candidate, William Taft, to permit the Democratic candidate, Woodrow Wilson, to win.

At other times in American history, third parties have proposed new ideas that were opposed at first by the major political parties, but were later adopted. For example, in the late 1800's the Populist Party was formed by a group of Americans who favored several new ideas. One of these ideas was the election of United States senators directly by the voters. The leaders of the two major parties favored the election of senators by state legislatures as provided in the Constitution.

When Populist ideas began to find favor with the American people, some of these ideas were taken over by the major parties. In time some of these ideas, such as the direct election of senators, were put into effect. The method of electing United States senators was changed by the Seventeenth Amendment to the Constitution.

Recent Third-Party Trends

Minor political parties have been active throughout most of the nation's history. Third-party candidates continue to run for office. Usually they receive very few votes.

Sometimes, though, third-party candidates attract many voters. In 1968 George Wallace, former governor of Alabama, ran for President as the candidate of the American Independent Party. He received 9.9 million votes, or 13.5 percent of the votes. Representative John Anderson of Illinois, an Independent Presidential candidate, won 5.6 million votes, or 7 percent of the votes, in 1980.

One-Party Governments

In nations with more than one political party, the voters have a choice. They may decide which party to join and for which party to vote. In many other nations, governments have been based on a **one-party system.** That is, there is just one political party in the nation. All other political parties are forbidden by law. Such nations are sometimes called dictatorships.

In a **dictatorship,** as you have read, all power is in the hands of one person or a group of persons. In a one-party government, a single party controls the government. It dictates, or commands, and the people must obey.

Italy under Benito Mussolini and Germany under Adolf Hitler had such governments. Today the Soviet Union, the People's Republic of China, and other communist nations are dictatorships with one political party. Our nation has traditionally opposed dictatorships, because such governments do not allow freedom of thought and action to their people. Americans consider such freedoms essential because they believe government should be responsible to the people.

CHECK-UP

Vocabulary

political party
nominate
candidates
Democratic Party
Republican Party
two-party system
coalition
multi-party system
third parties
one-party system
dictatorship

Review

1. What purposes do political parties serve?
2. When and why did political parties begin in the United States?
3. What are the chief advantages of the two-party system?
4. How do third parties influence our system of government?

Discuss

Do you think there will be more third party candidates in the United States in the future? Why or why not?

2
The Organization of Political Parties

In order to work effectively, a political party must be well organized. It must have leaders, committees, and workers who are able to carry out the party's program. It must be organized at the local, state, and national levels. The party must also be able to raise money to pay for its expenses. The party must nominate its candidates for office and plan its campaign to get these candidates elected. There are hundreds of details that have to be given careful attention.

Today, our two major parties operate the way they do because their members have worked out these procedures over the years. Interestingly, both major parties are organized in much the same way.

Party Committees and Their Jobs

The planning for each political party is done through a series of committees. Each political party has a national committee, a state central committee, county committees, and city committees. Each of these party committees is headed by a chairperson. The members are usually elected by the party voters at election time. Sometimes, however, the committee members are chosen at meetings of party leaders. These meetings of party leaders are known as **caucuses.**

The National Committee. The largest party committee is the national committee. Membership on this committee carries great distinction. For many years, it consisted of one committeeman and one committeewoman from each state, each territory, and the District of Columbia. In the 1970's, each party enlarged the membership of its national committee.

Members of the national committee may be chosen in three ways. They may be elected by a state convention or by voters in a statewide election, or they may be chosen by the state central committee. The chairperson of the national committee is often chosen by the party's Presidential candidate.

The national committee selects the city in which the **national nominating convention** is to be held. At this convention, or official meeting of the party, the party's Presidential candidate is chosen. The national committee is responsible for setting the date and drawing up rules for the convention.

During an election year, the national committee publishes and distributes literature and arranges for campaign speakers. It also helps the Presidential candidate to plan and conduct the campaign. Another job of the national committee is to raise money for the party.

State Central Committees. Each political party has a state central committee to supervise the party's operation within each of the 50 states. The chairperson of the state central committee is one of the party's most prominent members in the state. He or she is often a member of the national committee.

The state central committee represents the party organization in each state. Like the national committee, it is busiest at election time. The state chairperson works with the members of the state central committee to keep up a strong state organization and to maintain party harmony. The committee works to raise money for campaigns and to help candidates win elections.

Local Committees. At the local level are county committees and city committees. Township committees are sometimes found in rural areas. Members of local committees are elected by party members. The chairperson of each committee is elected by its members. She or he is the local party leader.

The party's success or failure often depends on what the local committees and their leaders do. The county or city committee is responsible for conducting all campaigns on the local level. It raises money for the party and its candidates. Through the local chairperson it makes recommendations for political appointments and for candidates for office. A strong local chairperson may stay in office for many years and become powerful in the party.

Local Party Organization

To make voting easier for our citizens, counties, cities, and wards are divided into voting districts called **precincts.** The voters in each precinct vote at the same place, which is called a **polling place.** A rural precinct may cover large areas of countryside. A precinct in a crowded city may cover just a few blocks. The party leader in the precinct is called the **precinct captain.** The precinct captain encourages all voters to get out and vote for the party's candidates.

At election time, precinct captains are very busy. They organize volunteers to hand out the party's campaign literature. They see that pictures of the party's candidates are dis-

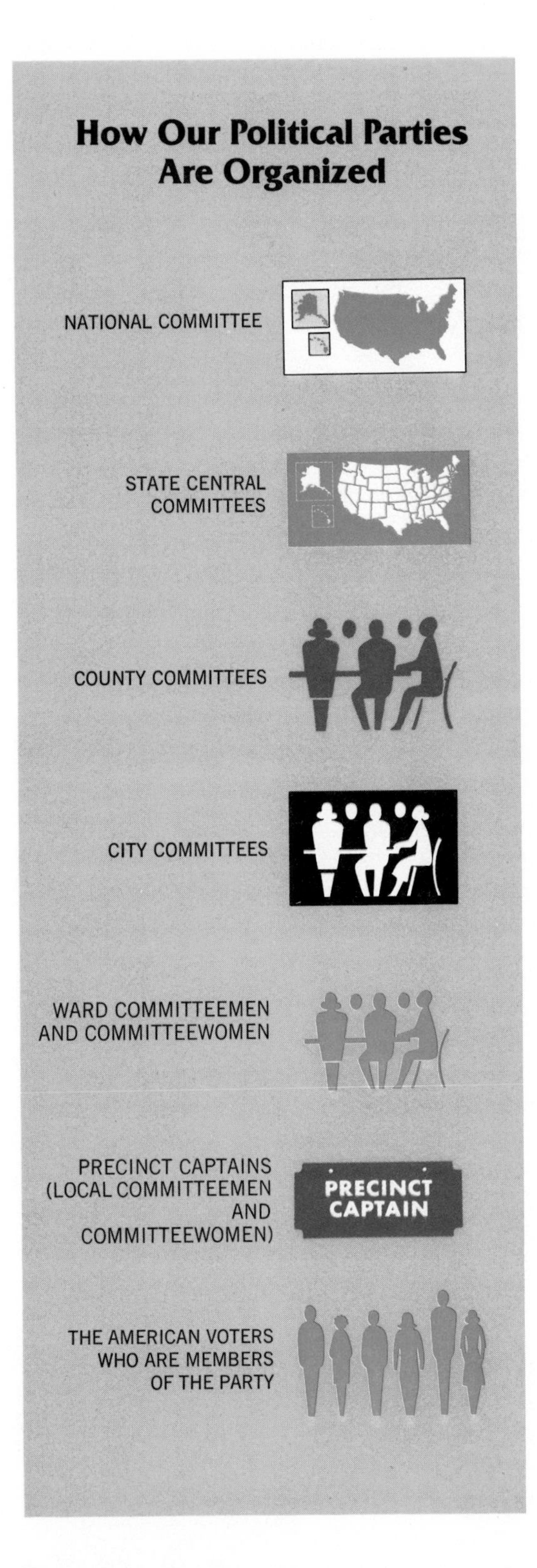

played in local shops and on neighborhood billboards. Precinct captains may arrange to have disabled voters driven to the polling place. They also see that party workers telephone voters, urging them to cast their votes for the party candidates. The precinct captains are also busy between elections getting to know the people in the neighborhood.

Political Party Finances

Running for political office is very expensive. Candidates for President, for example, need millions of dollars to run their campaigns. Their costs include office rent, secretaries, printing posters and handbills, radio and television broadcasts, and traveling expenses. From where does all this money come?

Until recently all political campaigns were paid for entirely with private contributions. Most campaigns are still paid for this way. Voters are urged to contribute to the political party of their choice. Business groups, labor unions, farm organizations, and many other kinds of groups contribute to the political party that they feel best represents their interests.

Political parties work hard to raise money. Several times a year, they hold large fund-raising dinners. The money raised at these dinners goes into the party's treasury.

Whenever large campaign contributions are made, however, people worry about corruption. Will a big contributor receive special favors in return for helping the winning candidate? To lessen the possibility of corruption, Congress passed the Federal Election Campaign Acts of 1972 and 1974.

These acts require every candidate to report the name of each person who contributes $100 or more to his or her campaign. Individuals may contribute only $1,000 to candidates before they win the nominations and $1,000 after they win the nominations. Organizations may not contribute more than $5,000 to any candidate. The provisions of

(continued on page 208)

CITIZENSHIP IN ACTION

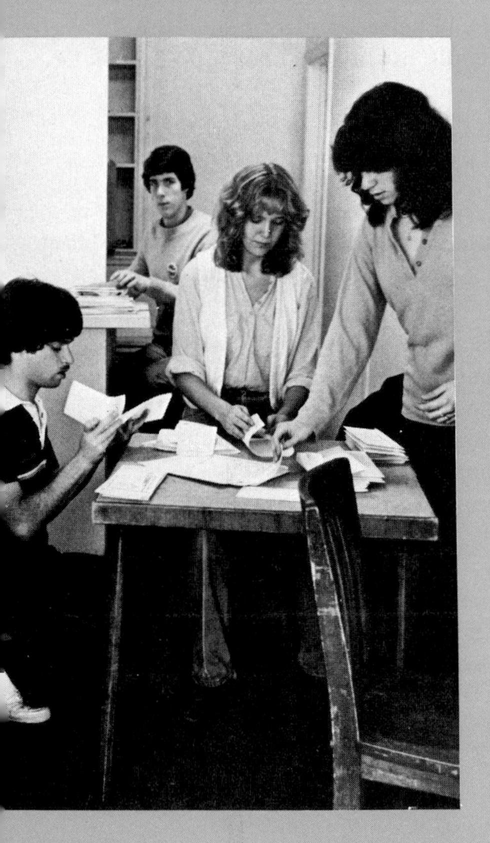

Teenagers Help Their Parties

Janet Benson and Bill Chan live far apart and have never met. She's from Minot, North Dakota, and is a Republican. He's from Phoenix, Arizona, and is a Democrat. Yet the two teenagers have something in common. They both are active in party politics and have great respect for the work carried out by their political parties.

To Janet and Bill, politics is not something that happens every four years, when a President is elected. It's an ongoing part of life. Long before they reached high school, the two students were rounding up votes for the party of their choice.

An Active Republican

Janet's interest in politics began when she was six years old. Her parents are active Republicans, who for a time advised a club of teenage Republicans. Janet began helping Republican candidates by decorating floats for election parades, putting up posters, and passing out leaflets in shopping centers. Later, in high school, she became an officer of her local TAR (Teen-Age Republican) Club. With other officers she went to Washington, D.C., for a national TAR conference.

While still in high school, Janet became convinced that politics would remain a key interest in her life. "Some people want a career in science or sports," she says. "For me, it's politics. I love it." She strongly believes that "politics doesn't end when an election is over." Members can help their political party at all times. They can, for example, hold discussions of bills being considered by the state legislature or by Congress. They also can find out what should be done to help those in need.

An Active Democrat

Like Janet, Bill Chan had an early introduction into politics. His mother held elective office and served on the Democratic national committee. To help her, Bill began stuffing campaign leaflets in doorways when he was nine years old.

As a high school junior, Bill went with his mother to a Democratic committee meeting in Washington, D.C. The purpose of the meeting was to help draw up the party platform for the national Democratic convention. Bill read over the proposals with his mother and discussed them with other Democrats. Later he went to the White House and shook hands with the President.

In high school Bill joined the Young Democrats. He enjoys "working the polls" on election day. This means taking up a post outside a polling (voting) place, talking to voters, and passing out leaflets.

Janet and Bill support different political parties. Yet both learned at an early age how important it is to take an active part in our country's political life.

Thinking It Over

1. What might be some of the advantages and disadvantages of joining a political party at a young age?
2. Do you think joining a party organization is a good way to have a say in government? Why or why not?

Fund-raising dinners are held in communities all over the country. They are used by candidates to help raise the money needed to run for political office.

these laws are enforced by the Federal Election Commission.

Public Financing

The Federal Election Campaign Act of 1974, which was amended in 1976, introduced public financing of Presidential elections. How does public financing work? The money comes from an election fund. By checking a special box on the federal income tax form, Americans can contribute one dollar of their taxes to the Presidential campaign. This neither raises nor lowers the amount of tax a person pays.

The money is distributed to the candidates by the Federal Election Commission. To be eligible to receive federal money, a candidate trying to win a party's nomination for President must first raise at least $100,000 from private contributions. Then the candidate can receive up to $5 million in matching funds. The more money a candidate raises, the more he or she receives from the federal government. However, to receive matching funds, candidates must limit their spending in nomination campaigns to $10 million.

After winning their party's nomination, candidates of the major parties cannot accept any private contributions. Their campaigns must be paid for only with the federal funds they receive. In 1980 the spending limit for each major party's Presidential candidate was $29,440,000. Candidates of minor parties receive federal funds after the election if they win at least 5 percent of the vote. The amount of money they receive is based on the number of votes they get.

CHECK-UP

Vocabulary

caucuses
national nominating convention
precincts
polling place
precinct captain

Review

1. How are political parties organized?
2. How does the precinct captain serve the party?
3. Why did Congress pass laws to regulate the amount of money individuals can contribute to political parties?
4. What are the provisions of the Federal Election Campaign Act of 1974?

Discuss

Do you think it is a good idea to have laws regulating the amount of money candidates can spend in elections? Why or why not?

3 The Right to Vote

At the age of 18, all citizens have the right to vote in national, state, and local elections. Your right to vote is one of your most important rights as an American citizen. It is the way you can most directly affect how our government is run.

State Qualifications for Voting

Each state has the right to decide qualifications for voting in state elections. However, all states must follow the provisions about voting in the Constitution of the United States. The Constitution forbids any state to deny a citizen the right to vote because of race, color, or sex. To ensure the voting rights of all citizens, Congress in 1965 passed the Voting Rights Act. An extension of this law, passed in 1970, prohibits any state from using **literacy tests,** or reading tests, as a requirement for voting.

Many states deny the right to vote to certain citizens who they believe are not eligible to vote. In many states, a person who is convicted of a serious crime loses the right to vote. Most states also deny the right to vote to mentally ill persons confined in hospitals.

Registering to Vote

When a person goes to the polls to vote, how do the officials know that she or he is a qualified voter? Most states make sure of this by requiring all voters to **register** ahead of time. This means that your name is placed on the official roll of eligible voters. When you register to vote, you give your name, address, date of birth, and other information showing that you meet the qualifications for voting.

Almost all states have permanent registration. This means you must register only once as long as you live at the same address. Some of these states, however, require a voter who does not vote in a certain number of elections to register again. A few states have periodic registration in some or all areas. This means you must register before each election or at regular intervals to remain a qualified voter.

To register, a citizen usually goes to the city hall or some place set up for this purpose. When you have registered, your name will be placed on the voters' list. You may be given a card showing that you are a registered voter.

When you register to vote, you may also be asked to register as a member of the political party of your choice. You may change your party membership at a later date by registering again. You may also choose to register as an **independent voter,** and not become a member of a political party. However, if you do not register as a member of a political party, you may not be able to vote in the primary elections.

Primary Elections

Two separate elections are held in most states. The **primary election** comes first, before the **general election.** The primary election is usually held in the spring. It gives voters a chance to choose the candidates from each party who will run for office in the general election.

There are two types of primary elections, the open primary and the closed primary. In the **closed primary,** only voters who are registered in the party can vote to choose the party's candidates. Most states use the closed primary. So in most states only registered Democrats can vote for Democratic candidates, and only registered Republicans can vote for Republican candidates. Those who have registered as independent voters cannot vote in the closed primary.

In the **open primary,** voters may vote to choose the candidates of either major party, whether or not they belong to that party. They can vote only for the candidates of one party, however.

In most states, the candidate who receives the highest number of votes is the winner of the primary election. The winning candidate does not have to get a majority, or more than 50 percent of the vote. In some states, especially in the South, the winner must get a majority of the votes. If no candidate receives a majority, there will be a **runoff election** between the two leading candidates to decide the winner. The winning candidate in the primary election then becomes the party's candidate in the general election.

To help get Americans to register to vote, registration tables may be set up on the street to make the process as easy and convenient as possible.

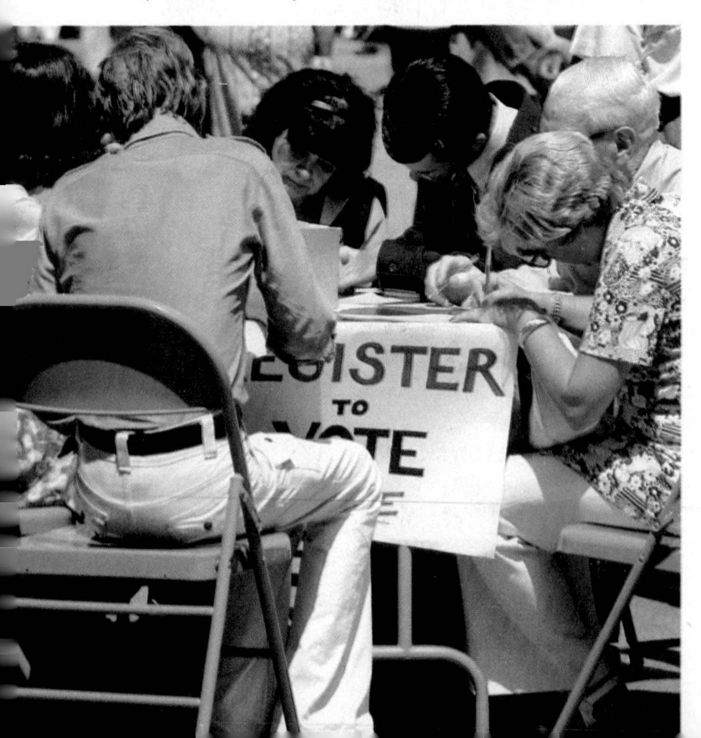

Nomination by Convention

In some states, political parties choose their candidates in a nominating convention. The people who attend and vote in the convention are elected as delegates by the various committees in the state's political organization. In a state convention, the county and city committees select the delegates. In a national convention, the state committees often select the delegates.

Independent Candidates

What about independent candidates who belong to no political party but wish to run for office? An independent candidate who can get enough supporters to sign a petition, can have his or her name printed on the ballot in the general election. Independent candidates do not get elected as often as major party candidates. But they do win some elections, mostly for local offices.

It is even possible for a person to be elected to an office when her or his name is not printed on the ballot. In some states, space is included on the ballot to "write in" the name of a person the voter prefers. It is difficult to get elected by **write-in votes,** but it does happen.

General Elections

Congress has set the date for the general elections of the President and Congress as the first Tuesday following the first Monday in November. A Presidential election takes place every four years. Congressional elections occur every two years. Most general elections for state officials are also held in November. The President and members of Congress are elected in even-numbered years. Some states elect their state officials in odd-numbered years. But elections are held at different times in different states.

On election day, the American voter faces a great responsibility and privilege of citizenship. The voter must make a choice among the candidates of the various parties. In many local elections, third parties may be strong, or write-in candidates may be well worth considering. Even in national elections, the choice is never simple.

The intelligent voter has studied hard to find the candidate whose views most closely resemble his or her own. The voter has read newspapers and magazines, listened to the candidates on radio and television, and talked about the candidates with other people.

As voters enter the polling place, they may see several neighbors at work. They are acting as inspectors, or **poll watchers.** Each party has its own poll watchers to see that the elections are conducted fairly.

★ ★ ★ ★ ★ ★ ★ ★ ★ ★ ★ ★

DID YOU KNOW THAT . . .

many terms used to describe elections were first used to describe horse races? Elections often are referred to as *races.* This is natural, since candidates *run* (often with *running mates*) to see who will *win.* A *dark horse* (or *long shot*) is a candidate who seems to have little chance to be elected. The candidate who is ahead is called the *front runner*—but the *finish* may be *neck and neck,* after all.

Voting in the Past

During the first part of the 1800's, voting in the United States was by voice vote. Voters announced aloud to the election official the name of the candidate for whom they wanted to vote.

This system of voice voting made it possible to influence the way a person voted. Suppose a person's boss was standing in line. The boss could hear how the employee voted and might fire the employee who did not vote the way the boss wanted.

In 1888 a new system of voting was adopted. A paper ballot was used. This is a paper containing the names of the candidates and a place for the voter to mark a choice. This ballot was marked in secret, so that no one knew for whom a person voted. This method of voting is called the **secret ballot.** It helped make American elections fairer and more honest.

Voting Today

More and more often, the voter today uses a **voting machine** instead of a paper ballot. The voting machine is a large, curtained booth. The voter enters the booth and pulls a lever to close the curtains. On the front of the voting machine, the voter sees several rows of small metal bars or levers with the name of a candidate under or next to each lever. A party's candidates are all on one row.

The voter may vote a **straight ticket**—that is, for all the candidates of one party. Or the voter may vote a **split ticket**—that is, for the candidates of more than one political party. When the voter has finished, she or he pulls back the lever that opens the curtains. This

Voting machines have nearly replaced paper ballots across the nation. They are easy for voters to use and make vote-counting an almost instant process.

action automatically records the vote in the machine. All the levers shift back into position, so they are ready to be pulled down by the next voter.

Voting machines keep a running count of the votes cast for each candidate. When the final vote is cast, election officials open the voting machine and read the total vote for each candidate.

On election day, the polls are usually open from early in the morning until evening. In many states, election day is a public holiday, so that there is no excuse for failing to vote. In other states, the law provides that all employers must give time off during the day to any employee who needs time to vote.

CHECK-UP

Vocabulary

literacy tests	runoff election
register	write-in votes
independent voter	poll watchers
primary election	secret ballot
general election	voting machine
closed primary	straight ticket
open primary	split ticket

Review

1. What are the qualifications for voting in most states?
2. How does a person register to vote in elections? Is the procedure the same in every state? Explain.
3. How is the states' control of elections limited by the Constitution of the United States? by Congress?
4. Explain the difference between a primary election and a general election.
5. What is the difference between voting a straight ticket and a split ticket?

Discuss

Would you be in favor of a law that required Americans to vote in all elections? Why or why not?

4

Nominating and Electing Our Leaders

Every four years, our nation is stirred with excitement as the time for the Presidential election draws near. Americans like a good, hard-fought battle. And the election of the President is one of the best. Most Americans eagerly follow the election campaign as newspapers, magazines, radio, and television report about it.

"A Hat in the Ring"

Long before election day, leading party members who want to be candidates begin to make speeches. They hope these speeches will make them better known to the public. At an appropriate time, some of these candidates announce that they intend to run for the highest office in the land—the Presidency. In the language of politics, they "throw their hats in the ring."

Choosing Convention Delegates

In each state, members of each political party choose delegates to go to their party's nominating convention. Convention delegates may either be elected in Presidential primaries or selected by party leaders.

In recent years, Presidential primaries have grown in importance. Today more than half our states and the District of Columbia hold **Presidential preference primaries.** In preference primaries, voters indicate which candidate they want the delegates to vote for at the national nominating convention.

In some states, the candidate who gets the most votes wins all the delegate votes from that state. In other states, each candidate gets some of the delegate votes based on the proportion of primary votes received. In still other states, the primaries indicate only the voters' preference. Delegates from these states may vote as they wish at the convention.

In states that do not hold primaries, the delegates are chosen by the state's party leaders in state or local party conventions. Or they are selected by state committees.

Each state sends to the national nominating convention twice as many delegates as the total number of senators and representatives that the state elects to Congress. The state of Alabama, for example, has two senators and seven representatives in Congress. Therefore, it is entitled to send 18 delegates to the national convention.

Each state may send additional delegates if the party's candidate won in that state at the last Presidential election. Both parties use complicated formulas to choose these extra delegates. States also send alternates who vote if regular delegates become ill.

The National Nominating Convention

Each party's national nominating convention is held during the summer of the Presidential election year. On the opening day of the convention, a series of exciting events begins to occur. The delegates from each state are seated throughout the great convention hall. Sometimes there are rival delegates who claim to represent the regular party organization of their state. The credentials committee of the convention must then decide which delegation to seat.

Bands play, convention delegates walk about talking to one another, the chairperson of the convention raps for order. The chairperson has been selected by the national committee beforehand from among the party's prominent members. A **keynote speaker** then delivers an inspiring opening address to both the delegates and the radio and television audience.

Then the convention gets down to business. A committee presents the **party platform.** This written statement outlines the party's views on important issues and sets forth a proposed program for our nation. This is the program the party promises to put into operation if its candidate is elected. Each part of the platform is called a **plank.** For example, the party platform may include a plank calling for an increase in defense spending or for a reduction in the federal income tax. After strong and sometimes heated debate, the platform is voted on and adopted by the convention delegates.

Choosing the Presidential Candidate

The convention now tackles its most important item of business—choosing the party's candidate for President.

Nominations. First there is a roll call of the states. As each state is called, one of its delegates may give a speech nominating, or naming, a candidate. Each nominating speech is followed by one or more seconding speeches.

Then supporters demonstrate in favor of their candidate. The band plays. Delegates who support the candidate parade around the convention floor. They wave signs and carry pictures of the candidate.

Not all state delegations, of course, nominate candidates. There may be half a dozen or more candidates nominated. Many of these nominees will have run in Presidential preference primaries. When the political party has a President in power who is eligible to run again, the convention almost always nominates this person for a second term.

Favorite Sons and Daughters. Some of the candidates named are **favorite sons or daughters.** They are party leaders who are popular in their home states. These men and women usually are governors or senators. In most cases, favorite daughters and sons have little chance of winning their party's Presidential nomination.

Why, then, do states nominate them? Sometimes the name of a favorite daughter or son is presented to honor the state's party leader. In other cases, a state names a favorite son or daughter in order to delay a decision on which of the well-known candidates it will support. These delegates vote for their favorite daughter or son on the first ballot. In later ballots, they usually switch their votes to one of the leading candidates.

Balloting. After all the candidates have been placed in nomination, the balloting begins. To win the nomination, a candidate must receive a majority of the votes of all the delegates at the convention. A roll call of the states is taken again. A delegate from each state announces how many votes the delegation is casting for each candidate.

In recent decades, one of the candidates has almost always been nominated on the first ballot. When no one candidate is strong enough to win a majority, many ballots may be needed. Supporters of the leading candidates may meet with state delegations to try to win them over. In some cases, a great deal of bargaining takes place.

When a candidate wins a majority of the delegates' votes, the huge convention hall is filled with noise and excitement. The delegates cheer and demonstrate to show their enthusiasm for the candidate who is to represent the party in the November election.

Accepting the nomination for President is an exciting moment for any candidate, as Jimmy Carter (left) and Ronald Reagan (right) showed in 1980.

Choosing the Vice Presidential Candidate

The delegates turn next to the nomination of the Vice President. Vice Presidential candidates often are chosen for their vote-getting ability. Sometimes they are from a part of the nation whose support the party needs. The Vice Presidential candidate must be well qualified to be President. This person, after all, is next in line for the Presidency if the party wins the November election.

The nominee for President has the strongest voice in deciding who the Vice Presidential candidate will be. After the Presidential candidate selects the person to run for Vice President, the choice must be approved by the delegates.

Acceptance Speeches

Finally the party's nominees for Vice President and President appear before the cheering delegates. Each gives an acceptance speech. In these speeches, the nominees set forth their position on key issues facing the nation. They urge party members to unite and work for victory in November. Then, its job done, the convention is brought to a close for another four years.

The Election Campaign

The Presidential election campaign gets under way soon after the convention ends. One of the most widely used methods of campaigning is the personal-appearance tour. Jet planes make it possible for the candidates to criss-cross our nation many times in an election campaign. In this way, candidates may make many speeches in many places in a relatively short time.

Television is another effective campaign device. Millions of Americans watch and listen as the candidates discuss their ideas and programs. Sometimes the candidates debate their views on television. As a result, Americans are able to get to know the candidates and to hear their ideas.

Millions of Americans watch the election returns on television on election night. They can learn the results of political races throughout the nation.

Election Day

The actual campaigning ends on the night before the election. Even so, election day itself is a busy one for party workers. They are busy telephoning and urging citizens to vote.

On election night, most Americans watch the election returns on television. They are able to hear complete details of all the political races across the United States. Because of the time difference, the first election returns come from the Eastern states. Gradually the election returns start coming in from the Western states. The last reports usually come in from California, Hawaii, and Alaska. Many Americans stay up late until they know who won. Sometimes the final results are not known until the next morning.

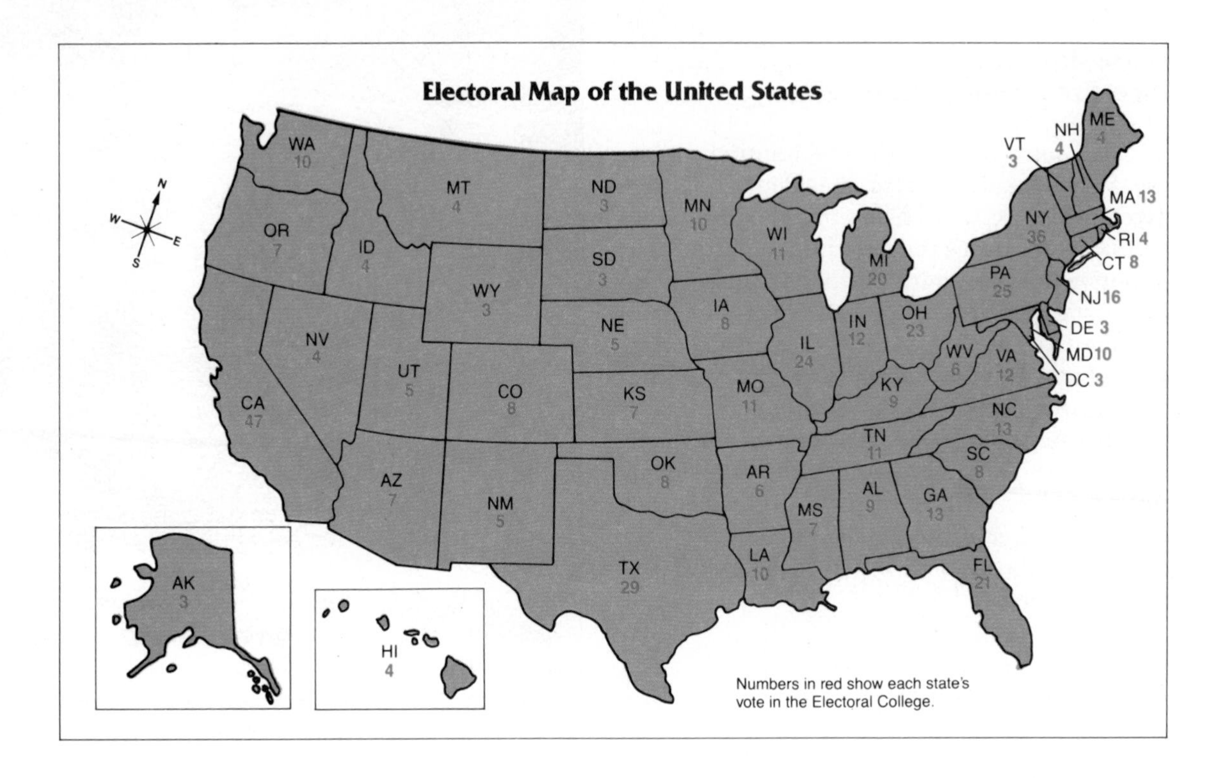

The Electoral College

In a Presidential election, American voters do not vote directly for the President. The votes they cast are known as the **popular vote.** This vote is actually for men and women called electors. These **electors** cast the official vote for the President.

The names of the electors may or may not appear on the ballot. A vote for the Democratic candidate is actually a vote for the Democratic electors. A vote for the Republican candidate is a vote for the Republican electors. Each state has as many electors as it has senators and representatives in Congress. In addition, Washington, D.C., has three electoral votes. The whole group of 538 electors is known as the **Electoral College.**

In each state, the electors gather in the state capital on the first Monday after the second Wednesday in December. The electors of the party whose candidate won a majority of the popular votes in the state in the November Presidential election cast all the state's electoral votes at this December meeting.

For example, if the Democratic Presidential candidate won a majority of the state's votes in November, it is the Democratic electors who cast the state's **electoral votes.** If the Republican candidate won, it is the Republican electors who gather at the state capital to cast the official vote. The electors are not required to vote for their party's candidate. However, only rarely are votes cast for someone else.

The votes cast by the electors are then sent to the president *pro tempore* of the Senate. On January 6, following the Presidential election, both houses of Congress gather in the House of Representatives. The votes of the electors are opened and officially counted. The candidate who receives a majority of the electoral votes is officially declared the next President of the United States.

What happens if no Presidential candidate receives a majority of the votes in the Electoral College? In that case, the President is chosen by the House of Representatives from among the three leading candidates. If no candidate receives a majority of votes for Vice

President, that official is chosen by the Senate. The choice is made from among the two candidates with the highest number of electoral votes. As you may know from your study of American history, this method has seldom been used.

The Electoral College was originally set up in the Constitution because those who planned our government were uncertain just how successful the people of the new republic would be in picking wise leaders. You will recall that they also provided for members of the Senate to be elected by state legislatures rather than directly by the people.

In recent years, many plans have been proposed for a system of direct election by popular vote to replace the Electoral College. Many Americans favor the direct election of the President and Vice President. Others favor keeping the present system.

CHECK-UP

Vocabulary

Presidential preference primaries
keynote speaker
party platform
plank
favorite sons or daughters
popular vote
electors
Electoral College
electoral votes

Review

1. How are delegates chosen to attend each party's national nominating convention?
2. How can a voter learn the views of the Presidential candidates?
3. Explain how the number of electoral votes each state has is determined.

Discuss

What qualifications do you think voters should look for in candidates?

CHAPTER SUMMARY

Elections are important and exciting events in our national life. On election day the voters choose their government leaders. Although political parties are not mentioned in the Constitution, they have become an important part of our system of government. Political parties choose the candidates who run for office and become our leaders. Political parties offer a practical way for persons to work together to put their ideas and programs into effect in our government.

Today the United States has a strong two-party system. The Republican and Democratic parties are organized at local, state, and national levels. Both parties work through a series of committees to get their candidates elected. Throughout our history, there have also been many minor political parties.

American voters may belong to a political party, or they may decide not to join a party. In any case, voters are free to vote for any person or party they wish. The Constitution provides that the states set most of the qualifications for voting, subject to the restrictions set by the Constitution and by Congress.

The Presidential election, held every four years, is a dramatic event. Americans closely follow the party nominating conventions, the election campaign, and the election results.

CIVICS SKILLS: Registering to Vote

When discussing eligible voters, what do the words "We the people" mean to you? If you answered "citizens over 18," you were right. But suppose you had been asked that question in 1800. Your answer would have been different. Women, blacks, people who didn't own property, and those under 21 years of age had not yet won the right to vote.

As you know, the restrictions that kept these groups from voting have been removed. Certain voting limitations do, however, remain in effect. All states, for example, require you to be at least 18 years old and a citizen of the United States. Some states also have a **residency requirement,** or period of time that you must have lived in the state before voting. To prove that you meet these basic qualifications, you must complete a special registration form.

Taking the First Step

The United States does not require you to register. Forms are not automatically sent to your home when you turn 18. You must start the registration process yourself.

Registration varies from state to state. In a few states you can register by mail. Several others allow you to register at or near the polling place. In most states, however, you must report to a particular location, at a certain time of year. Usually you have to appear before a **registrar,** or state voting official, no later than 30 days before the election.

Although each state issues its own registration form, most states ask similar questions about age, citizenship, and residence. They also require you to sign an **affidavit,** or statement swearing that your answers are true. In some states an entry on the registration form will give you the chance to enroll, or sign up, with a political party.

Practicing What You've Learned

The registration form below is modeled after one used in Texas. The following questions will help you interpret some of the entries.

1. Which section of the form should not be filled in? Why?
2. What do you think is the main purpose of section 5? of section 8?
3. In which section is the affidavit found?

1	**VOTER REGISTRATION APPLICATION** Please complete all of the information below. Print in ink or type.	2	OFFICIAL USE ONLY CERTIFICATE NUMBER / APPLICATION NUMBER PCT / EDR	
3	LAST NAME	FIRST NAME (NOT HUSBAND'S)	MIDDLE NAME	MAIDEN NAME
4	DATE OF BIRTH Month / Day / Year	5 PLACE OF BIRTH City or County / State or Foreign Country	6 If you are a naturalized citizen, indicate the court of naturalization or its location:	
7	PERMANENT RESIDENCE ADDRESS: STREET ADDRESS AND APARTMENT NUMBER; IF NONE, DESCRIBE LOCATION OF RESIDENCE: CITY, STATE, and ZIP:	If mail cannot be delivered to permanent residence address, provide mailing address:		
8	IF YOU ARE NOW REGISTERED IN ANOTHER TEXAS COUNTY, COMPLETE THE FOLLOWING: County of former residence:	Residence address as shown on certificate in that county:		
9	The applicant is a citizen of the United States and a resident of this county. I certify that the information provided is correct. I understand that the giving of false information to procure the registration of a voter is a felony. SIGNATURE OF APPLICANT X ______________ DATE ________			
10	FOR WITNESS: If the applicant is unable to sign his name, he shall make his mark in the presence of a witness. If the applicant is unable to make his mark, the witness shall state that fact on the application. Signature and address of witness:			

CHAPTER REVIEW

Vocabulary

Copy the following terms in your notebook. Beside each term write a sentence using the term to show its importance in our political system.

nominate
candidates
Democratic Party
Republican Party
caucuses
electoral vote
popular vote
polling places
register
primary election
general election
secret ballot
party platform
Electoral College

Check-Up

1. Why do we have political parties in the United States?
2. How is your life affected by practical politics? Give three examples.
3. What part does the local committee member play in the organization of a political party?
4. How are political parties financed? For what purposes do parties spend money?
5. What are the usual qualifications for voting in elections? What is meant by the expression "If you don't register you can't vote"? How can the right to vote be lost?
6. Why is it important to vote in the primary election as well as in the general election?
7. Describe the way in which each of our major political parties chooses its candidate for the Presidency.
8. How has television influenced Presidential election campaigns?
9. What role do you think political parties should play in elections? Do you think they have too much power or too little power? Why?
10. Do you favor keeping the present Electoral College system or changing to the direct election of the President and Vice President? Explain your reasons.

Civics Skills

Contact the election office of your town or city and request a copy of the voter registration form used in your state. After you have received this form, answer the following questions.

1. Does the voter registration form include a space for you to enroll in a political party?
2. Must a witness fill out any sections?
3. Are you required to provide all the information requested on the form? If not, what information is optional?

Citizenship and You

1. Hold a mock political campaign and election, complete with speeches, posters, and campaigning. If a local, state, or national election is going on at this time, base the mock election on the real one. It will be interesting to see how the results of the class election compare with the results of the actual election.
2. Find and bring to class newspaper or magazine articles that give various points of view on the Electoral College system. Which articles do you agree with? Explain why.
3. Attend a political rally or other meeting of voters and report to the class on what you observed.
4. Prepare an oral or written report on one of the third political parties in American history. Tell what the party's goals were, what methods it used, and how effective the party was in getting its ideas and goals adopted.
5. Committees may gather information and report to the class on such topics as "What Are the Qualifications for Voting in Our State?" "What Third Parties Are Active in Our State?" "What Were the Results of the Last Presidential Election in Our State?"

CHAPTER

11

Taking Part in Our Political System

You have been studying how our democratic government operates and how it serves you and all Americans. We turn now to one of the most important features of the American political system. That is how we, as citizens, can participate directly in our government.

Obviously, every one of us cannot actually serve as an official in the government. Instead, we elect other people to represent us. Each of us is affected by the decisions made by these public officials. Therefore, we must inform them of the actions we want them to take. We must make certain, too, that they respond to the will of the people.

Taking part in our political system is an important responsibility of citizenship. It is not something that should be left for others to do. It is essential that citizens form opinions on public issues and express them. One of the most important ways people make their opinions known is by voting.

We can also have a voice in government in many other ways. We can join or form groups working toward goals in which we believe. Working to help elect candidates of our choice is another good way to make our opinions known.

How do government officials learn what citizens want? How can citizens influence such officials to respond to their will? These and other aspects of citizenship in a free society will be examined in this chapter. You will study the following topics:

1. **Shaping Public Opinion**
2. **Interest Groups Influence Government**
3. **Taking an Active Part in Government**

1

Shaping Public Opinion

What is your opinion? You have no doubt been asked that question many times. Our **opinions,** what we believe to be true, are important to us. They can also influence what others believe or how they act.

In our American government, the opinions of the people greatly influence public affairs. For example, an elected public official who ignores the opinions of the people is likely to lose the next election. But what are the opinions of the people? When do the opinions of individuals become public opinion?

What Is Public Opinion?

We have all heard such statements as, "If elected, I pledge to follow the wishes of the people" or "Public opinion demands that something be done." The opinion a large number of people have about a particular issue is known as **public opinion.**

Of course, the opinions of individual people often differ. Everyone does not always agree about an issue. Thus the term "public opinion" is generally used to refer to the opinion held about any issue by a majority of the people. We use the term "the public" when we mean a majority of the people.

What Shapes Our Opinions?

Our opinions are shaped by influences from many sources. The first influence on our opinions is our family. It is only natural for the ideas and beliefs of our parents to become part of our own attitudes or values. Since we share so many of the same experiences with our family, we frequently have similar responses to many issues. As we grow older, other people and experiences also influence what we believe. Friends, school, and clubs play a major role in shaping our opinions.

Information is also important in shaping our opinions. Much of the information we need to make wise decisions about public issues comes from newspapers, television, radio, books, and magazines. These sources of information are called the **mass media.**

Having information, however, does not always mean that we are well informed. Sometimes the information we receive is inaccurate or one-sided. A newspaper, for example, might give more favorable coverage to the political candidate it supports. Or the facts presented on television may give only one side of a story.

Effective citizenship requires us to think critically about what we see or hear or read. It is essential to be able to recognize the difference between fact and opinion. We must therefore try to get our information from more than one source.

Propaganda and Public Opinion

Many of the ideas we get from the mass media have been directed at us for a purpose. Somebody is trying to get us to do something—to buy something, to believe some-

courtesy of Field Enterprises, Inc.

"You're wasting your time! . . My mind is totally controlled by what the mass media feeds into it!"

Think for a minute and try to identify what shapes your opinions on public issues. Are you like this man or do other factors affect your thinking?

thing, or to act in a given way. Ideas used to try to influence us are called **propaganda.**

It has been said that we live in the propaganda age. Propaganda is certainly nothing new. But it has come into its own in recent years. One reason for this development is not hard to understand. The tremendous growth of the mass media has meant that propaganda can be spread farther and faster than ever before.

There are always many people, groups, and advertisers using propaganda to try to influence public opinion. Propaganda is used by advertisers hoping to get us to buy their products. Political candidates use propaganda to try to convince us to vote for them. When a political party tries to win public support, it is using propaganda.

People often think of propaganda as a negative, or bad, thing. They speak of propaganda as something spread by the "other side," but never by them. They believe propaganda is made up of lies and distorted facts. However, most propaganda is neutral—neither good nor bad. It is simply a technique used to give only one side of an issue. Propaganda attempts to influence other people's attitudes, opinions, or behavior.

Two Forms of Propaganda

Citizens must be alert to propaganda. We must be able to recognize it and be aware of the different methods used by propagandists. When propaganda ideas are presented as facts and their sources are kept secret, they are called **concealed propaganda.** Concealed propaganda tries to fool you without letting you know it is trying to influence you.

Sometimes concealed propaganda is relatively harmless. For example, press agents may make up interesting stories about television stars to give these stars publicity. At other times, concealed propaganda may be used to create a harmful impression. A photograph may be taken in a certain way or may be retouched to make a political candidate look bad. False rumors may be spread in order to harm someone.

Revealed propaganda is much more common in the United States. In revealed propaganda, readers or listeners are aware that someone is using ideas to influence them. Almost all advertising is revealed propaganda. You know when you see most advertisements that somebody wants you to buy something or to believe as they do.

Television and radio commercials are direct appeals to the public to buy various products. During an election campaign, political parties may run commercials to get voters to support their candidates. These commercials must be clearly labeled as paid advertisements.

Your civics book also contains revealed propaganda. It is openly spreading the idea that all Americans should understand and take part in our political system.

Propaganda Techniques

Propaganda experts sometimes use cleverly designed half-truths to mislead people. Some of these propaganda methods are hard to spot. Others can easily be seen through by those who know how to recognize them. What are some of the propaganda techniques?

1. Endorsements. Political candidates and advertisers often seek endorsements from famous people. Advertising writers know, for instance, that people admire sports heroes. Therefore, they pay famous athletes to endorse, or approve, their product.

They know that if a football hero says he drives a certain automobile, many people will believe the automobile must be good. These people like the football hero, so they will trust his judgment. However, people who think for themselves know that this endorsement by a great athlete proves very little. A football player may be the greatest quarterback of all time, but this does not make him an expert on automobiles.

2. The Bandwagon. People who write propaganda know that if you say something often enough and loud enough, many people will believe it. If you can win some people over to your ideas, in time more and more people will come over to your side. This is known as the bandwagon technique of propaganda. "Everybody's doing it! Get on the bandwagon!" This method of propaganda appeals to people's desire to do what their friends and neighbors are doing.

3. Name Calling. Another propaganda technique is name calling. This is the use of an unpleasant label or description to harm a person, group, or product. Name calling is sometimes used to harm political candidates.

Propaganda Techniques

CAN YOU GUESS?

Each of the campaign slogans below was used by a successful Presidential candidate. Which President used each slogan?

Tippecanoe and Tyler Too
Return to Normalcy
A New Deal
I Like Ike

Answers are on page 562.

During an election campaign, name calling is often used by both sides. For example, you may hear that some candidate favors "reckless spending" or that another is "opposed to progress." The question to ask yourself is, What proof is given?

4. Glittering Generalities. Another method of influencing people's thinking is the glittering generality. This method uses words that sound good but have little real meaning. Many advertising slogans are glittering generalities. For example, a statement such as "It contains a miracle ingredient" has little meaning.

Candidates often use vague statements with which everyone would agree. These glittering generalities tell voters nothing about what a candidate really believes. This type of propaganda often uses such words as *home, mother, country, freedom, patriotic,* and *American.* These words are chosen because most people in our nation approve of what they stand for.

5. Plain-Folks Appeal. During election campaigns, many candidates describe themselves as plain, hard-working American citizens. They claim to understand the problems of average Americans. This plain-folks appeal is designed to get votes. Candidates work hard to show the people that, as one of them, they can best represent the interests of the average citizen.

6. Slanting Ideas. Another propaganda technique is slanting ideas. This method uses words in a certain way in order to favor a product, idea, or candidate. Newspapers, for example, may give front-page attention to the activities of the candidates they favor. The other political party and its candidates may be given smaller headlines or be reported only on the inside pages. The news is slanted to favor one party over another.

Measuring Public Opinion

The goal of our government officials is to carry out the wishes of the people. How, then, do government officials find out what the public wants? The most obvious test of public opinion is an election. Another way to measure public opinion is to conduct a **public opinion poll,** or survey.

Polls are used to find out what people think about specific issues and about politicians and their policies. A poll attempts to measure public opinion by asking the opinions of a sample of the public.

Choosing a Sample

Great care must be taken to choose a sample that is representative of the public being measured. An unrepresentative sample can cause serious errors in a poll's results. Suppose, for example, your school principal decided to conduct a poll to find out if people wanted the cafeteria to remain open during the whole school day. If only teachers and cafeteria workers were polled, the result would probably be different than if students were also included in the polling sample.

A well-known example of a sampling error occurred in 1936. A popular magazine called *Literary Digest* conducted a poll to predict the outcome of the Presidential election. President Franklin D. Roosevelt, the Democratic candidate, was opposed by the Republican candidate, Alfred M. Landon.

The *Digest* mailed out more than 10 million ballots. They were sent to names taken at random from telephone directories and automobile registration lists. More than 2 million people filled out these ballots and mailed them back to the magazine. Based on the poll results, the *Digest* predicted that Landon would be elected. The actual election results were very different. Roosevelt won by a landslide with 60 percent of the vote.

What went wrong with the poll? It failed because in 1936 only high-income people could afford telephones and automobiles. Therefore, this was an unrepresentative sample.

Once a representative sample has been chosen, care must also be taken in deciding what questions to ask. The way questions are phrased often affects the answers that will be given. For example, the neutral question "Should more firefighters be hired?" might get one answer. The question "Should taxes be raised to hire more firefighters?" might get a different answer.

Using Polls Carefully

Polls are a valuable tool for measuring public opinion. Some critics fear, however, that polls influence public opinion as well as measure it. For example, some people want to be on the winning side. Imagine that two days before the election, a poll predicts that Candidate Z will win by 15 percent. Might some voters decide in favor of Z in order to support a winner?

Polls can help us evaluate public opinion only if we do more than just look at the percentages given in the results. Other information to look for is the wording of the questions asked, the number of people responding, and the sample population chosen.

Especially important is the number of people responding as "undecided." Frequently, the number of people who are undecided is so great that no prediction is possible. In elections candidates address their strongest appeal to the group of undecided voters.

CHECK-UP

Vocabulary

opinions
public opinion
mass media
propaganda
concealed propaganda
revealed propaganda
public opinion poll

Review

1. What are some of the sources that influence our opinions?
2. Name the six propaganda techniques and give an example of each.
3. Why are some people fearful of public opinion polls?

Discuss

Today most elected leaders, including the President and members of Congress, use public opinion polls to find out what Americans think about important issues. Do you think this is a good idea? Why or why not?

2

Interest Groups Influence Government

Americans have many ways in which they can express their opinions to government officials and try to influence government policy. One of the most effective ways is through an interest group.

What Is an Interest Group?

Most people are members of one or more **interest groups.** These are organizations of people with a common interest who try to influence government decisions. An interest group is also known as a **pressure group,** or **lobby.**

Interest groups differ from political parties. Both seek to influence government.

Interest groups, however, are not primarily concerned with electing candidates to office. They often support a particular candidate. Yet their main interest is in influencing government policies.

Interest groups are not new. They have been in existence throughout our nation's history. For example, people favoring the Constitution organized to work for its approval. Before the Civil War, people opposed to slavery organized to demand that it be outlawed.

Kinds of Interest Groups

There are many different kinds of interest groups. They include business associations, labor unions, farm organizations, senior citizens' groups, veterans' organizations, teachers' associations, consumer groups, and religious groups. Each works to promote the interests of its members. The various organizations often have very different views on issues.

Many interest groups represent the economic interests of their members. These include such groups as the National Association of Manufacturers, the United Mine Workers, and the American Farm Bureau Federation. Members of these and many other economic interest groups seek to influence government policies that affect them.

For example, the American Farm Bureau Federation is an organization of farmers and ranchers. It works to get bills passed that will aid its members, and to block the passage of bills that do not favor the group's interests.

Some interest groups consist of people whose concerns are issue-oriented. That is, they focus their attention on a specific issue or cause. For example, the National Association for the Advancement of Colored People works to promote racial equality. The goal of Big Screechers, an interest group in New York City, is to reduce the city's noise level.

Groups that seek to promote the interests of the general public rather than just one part of it are sometimes called **public interest groups.** These include groups working to protect consumers and the environment.

Farmers are just one of the nation's many interest groups. Here they drive their tractors into Washington, D.C., to try to influence government policies.

How Interest Groups Work

Interest groups vary greatly in size, goals, and budgets. Most, though, use similar methods to try to influence government decisions. They often encourage members to write to the President or their senators or representatives about a specific bill. Many interest groups also hire a **lobbyist** who will represent their interests. Lobbyists work at all levels of government, although most are located in Washington, D.C.

Lobbyists get their name from the way they operated many years ago. In the past, they waited for lawmakers in the lobbies outside the legislature's meeting rooms. There they tried to talk to lawmakers and influence their decisions. The term "lobbying" has been used since the 1830's.

Today lobbyists usually are highly skilled people with a staff of research assistants. Some lobbyists were once members of the legislatures or public agencies they now seek to influence. Others are lawyers, public relations experts, journalists, or specialists in different fields.

Influencing the Government. Many of the nation's laws are the result of a struggle among interest groups. One example is the minimum wage law. This law says that workers may not be paid less than a certain amount an hour. Labor groups often seek an increase in the minimum wage. Business groups generally oppose such an increase. Lobbyists for both interest groups present their arguments to Congress. After listening to both sides and considering all the facts, Congress makes its decision.

The minimum wage law has been increased over the years. The amount of each increase, though, has been a compromise between those wanting a higher increase and those wanting a smaller one.

Lobbyists use a number of different methods to promote the action they want. They argue in support of bills they favor and against bills they oppose. Sometimes lobbyists ask members of Congress to sponsor bills favored by members of their interest group. They supply facts for the bill. They may even help write the bill. Frequently, government officials contact lobbyists to learn the position of interest groups on issues that affect them.

Lobbyists often testify at committee hearings. Frequently lobbyists from different interest groups present evidence on opposite sides of the issue. Each lobbyist comes prepared with well-developed arguments and statistics.

In fact, supplying information is one of a lobbyist's most important jobs. As you read in Chapter 5, members of Congress are faced with over 20,000 bills a year covering many different subjects. No lawmaker can be fully

Senior citizens are a steadily growing percentage of the American population. As their numbers increase, so does their power as an interest group.

informed in all these areas. Lawmakers often appreciate the help provided by lobbyists.

One way lobbyists influence government officials is by getting to know them. They meet with government officials in their offices or call them on the phone to discuss their groups' opinions. They may also invite officials to lunch or dinner for a more informal discussion.

Influencing Public Opinion. Interest groups attempt to influence not only the government but public opinion as well. For example, interest groups place advertisements in the mass media in support of their position. They often promise to help government officials in their next election campaign by supplying workers and contributions. Sometimes lobbyists urge local groups and individuals to send letters and telegrams to public officials. They hope that public support will influence the lawmakers to fulfill the wishes of their interest group.

Regulating Interest Groups

Interest groups use any legal means to influence public officials and the public itself. To keep the activities of lobbyists in the open, federal and state governments require lobbyists to register. They must indicate for whom they are working and how much money they spend in lobbying. In recent years, laws regulating lobbying have been made very strict. New laws have closed many of the loopholes, or ways of evading the laws.

The Role of Interest Groups

Lobbyists once were viewed with suspicion because many of them worked in secret. Today, however, most lobbyists work in the open. They are welcomed as sources of information and help by overworked lawmakers and government officials.

Some people are critical of interest groups and their lobbyists. They feel these groups play too great a role in the lawmaking process. Critics believe that too much attention is paid to the interest group that is best organized and has the most money. They say that important interests—such as those of the poor, the elderly, and many minorities—do not always get an equal hearing.

Nevertheless, interest groups are a crucial part of our free society. You are probably a member of a number of interest groups even though you may not be aware of it. Interest groups are the people—in our roles as students, business people, consumers, farmers, workers, or veterans. In our free society we have the right to make our opinions known to our government leaders. Interest groups are evidence of political freedom.

CHECK-UP

Vocabulary

interest group
pressure group
lobby
public interest group
lobbyist

Review

1. What is the purpose of interest groups?
2. In what ways do interest groups try to influence government decisions?
3. What methods do lobbyists use to promote the actions they want?

Discuss

Do you think interest groups have too much influence in American government? Why or why not?

3 Taking an Active Part in Government

In this chapter we have been discussing the ways Americans can influence government decisions. We have already considered the importance of public opinion and interest groups. Now we turn to the most direct way in which we, as citizens, can make government responsive to our will. This is by taking an active part in government.

There are many different ways for Americans to take part in government. We can vote in elections—local, state, and national. We can become active in a political party. Aiding our local community and speaking out on public issues are also important. As you recall, all these activities are responsibilities of citizenship. They are necessary to the workings of our democratic government.

Voting: Democracy in Action

Voting is the most important opportunity for citizens to participate in our government. Only a small percentage of citizens can actually serve in the government. Instead, we elect people to represent us. All citizens, however, can take part in selecting the people who will lead and represent us.

Elections offer every citizen the chance to be involved in governing our nation. Each voter helps to determine what actions our government will take. We are making our opinions known on public issues when we vote. When we choose candidates, we are expressing our opinion not only of their abilities but of their programs as well.

Voting is not only a right, it is an important responsibility. Yet millions of Americans do not vote. In recent Presidential elections, little more than half the voting-age population has voted. In 1980 less than 53 percent of eligible Americans voted for President. In non-Presidential elections, the percentage of voters is even smaller. This is especially the case in state and local elections.

The United States has the lowest turnout of eligible voters of any free government in the world. This low election turnout leaves the selection of our government officials to a small percentage of the people.

Why do so few people vote? Some people have not registered and thus are not eligible to vote. Some do not like any of the candidates. Some are ill and cannot get to the polling places on election day. Some are unexpectedly away from home and cannot reach the polling places at which they are registered to vote. Others have moved so recently that they do not meet residence requirements for voting.

Every Vote Counts

The most common reason for not voting, however, is a person's belief that her or his vote will not make a difference in the outcome of an election. Of course, this is not true. The vote of every individual helps determine who wins or loses an election. Only by exercising our right to vote can Americans influence the laws and policies that greatly affect our lives.

The importance of every vote can be seen by looking at the results of two close Presidential elections.

What is the cartoonist saying about elections in our nation? What do you think could be done to encourage more American citizens to vote in elections?

In 1916 Charles Evans Hughes, the Republican candidate, went to bed believing he had been elected President. Hughes would have been right if 1,983 people in California had voted for him instead of for the Democratic candidate, Woodrow Wilson. However, since Wilson received a majority of California's popular vote, he was awarded all of that state's electoral votes. California's electoral votes gave Wilson the votes he needed to win the election.

In 1976 Jimmy Carter, the Democratic candidate, defeated Gerald Ford, the Republican candidate, by nearly 1,700,000 popular votes. However, a shift of 5,599 votes in Ohio and 3,687 votes in Hawaii would have changed the electoral vote enough to give the election to Ford.

Taking Part in a Political Campaign

Another way to influence political decisions is to take part in an election campaign. Although you must be 18 years old to vote, people of any age can work as volunteers in a political campaign. **Volunteers** are people who work without pay to help others. Playing an active role as a volunteer in a political party is a good way to have a say about who represents you in government.

Political parties need the help of great numbers of people. Widespread citizen participation in campaigns is essential to a healthy democratic system. There are many jobs for volunteers during an election campaign. You can ring doorbells or make phone calls to tell voters about your candidate. You can encourage your friends to vote. People are always needed to pass out campaign literature to passersby on the street. Envelopes must be addressed and stuffed with information about the candidate.

On election day, campaign workers urge people who support their candidate to vote. They may stay with young children to enable voters to get to the polling places. All this work can make the difference in the outcome of an election.

These young people may not yet be old enough to vote, but they can still take an active part in an election campaign. How are they contributing to it?

Interest Groups and Political Campaigns

As you read earlier in this chapter, most people are members of at least one interest group. There are two major ways in which interest groups can take part in political campaigns. The first is by providing volunteer workers for candidates who are sympathetic to their program. The second is by contributing money to campaigns.

For example, many labor unions and business companies have established political action committees. These groups raise money from their members to contribute to candidates. Interest groups hope that, once elected to office, the candidates they helped will promote their interests.

Contacting Public Officials

Suppose you believe the street corner near your home needs a traffic light. Or you oppose a proposed 15-cent increase in your city's bus fare. Or the House of Representatives is voting soon on an issue important to you. How can you make your opinion known quickly?

Writing a letter to local officials or members of Congress is an excellent way to let them know what is on your mind. As you read in Chapter 5, members of Congress receive a lot of mail. They welcome these letters as a way of learning what the people they represent think about the issues.

You can also contact public officials by telephone or telegram. A personal visit to an official's office is another way to express your opinions. Many officials have regular office hours for meeting with constituents. Of course, it is always best to call first and make an appointment.

Community Action

The activities of our local government touch our lives most often and most directly. The quality of life in our town or city depends to a large extent upon how our local government serves us. It is therefore important for all Americans to take part in our local communities. Citizens can greatly influence our local governments.

Citizens often work together in community groups. For example, **block associations** have been formed in many cities by people working to improve their neighborhoods. Residents of an apartment house might form a **tenants' group** to try to improve the condition of their building. Citizens in a town might organize to raise money to buy new books for the town library or repair the school's baseball field.

Community groups are active in large and small cities, in towns, and in villages. Working together makes it easier for citizens to bring about needed improvements and changes in our communities. Citizen involvement helps make democracy work.

CHECK-UP

Vocabulary

volunteers
block associations
tenants' group

Review

1. What are some of the ways in which American citizens can take part in their government?
2. Why is it important for all eligible citizens to vote?
3. In what two ways do interest groups take part in political campaigns?

Discuss

What do you think could be done to get more Americans to take an active part in our political system?

CHAPTER SUMMARY

In our democratic republic, it is important that the government be aware of the concerns and needs of all the people. One way to measure public opinion is by using public opinion polls. If used carefully, these polls can provide helpful information to candidates and government officials.

Opinion is shaped by many different sources, beginning with our families. Information provided by the mass media also plays a major role in shaping opinions. Propaganda is often used to try to influence people. We must be able to recognize propaganda and be aware of the various propaganda techniques.

Interest groups play an important role in influencing government decisions. They also help shape public opinion. Interest groups often hire lobbyists to promote the policies they favor.

Responsible citizens take an active part in public affairs. Exercising our right to vote is an essential part of American government. By voting in elections, citizens can help select the officials who will represent us and make decisions that affect our lives. Other ways to make our opinions known include taking part in a political campaign and working with community groups.

CIVICS SKILLS: Understanding a Poll

Hello. My name is Toby and I'm calling from the Gallup Poll in Princeton, New Jersey. Is there a teenager in your home between the ages of 13 and 18 with whom I may speak?

In 1980 people from all over the United States answered yes to this question, and more than 1,000 teenagers became part of a nationwide youth survey. Each year millions of Americans are asked to participate in some kind of poll.

The people who conduct all these polls are called **pollsters.** Pollsters, as you know, work with questions. These are the tools that measure public opinion on anything from brands of soap to political candidates. For this reason, a pollster's questions have to be very precise.

Each question must mean the same thing to every person in the poll. The question also has to be neutral. If it leans, or slants, toward any one answer, it will not measure public opinion accurately. Study the question used in the poll on this page. Does it meet the standards for a good question? Explain.

Totaling the Results

Pollsters rarely ask you to think of answers of your own. They provide the answers for you. This forces everyone in the poll to choose from the same set of answers. What choices are offered in the poll on this page?

At the end of a survey, the pollster figures out the percentage of people who selected each answer. These statistics are the survey's facts. The next step is to find out what these facts say about the group that was polled. This is done by summarizing the facts in broad statements called **generalizations.**

Whenever you form a generalization, you are really tying facts together. Every generalization must be supported by the available evidence. If any of the facts don't fit, the generalization is not valid, or true. Therefore, you cannot generalize about a subject until you have collected the facts.

When you have all the facts, you need to look for patterns and relationships. In other words, you try to discover features that the facts share in common. These become the basis for your generalizations. For example, consider these two sentences: (1) "I like tacos, chili, and nachos." (2) "I like Mexican food." The first sentence lists the facts. The second one places these facts in a single category. Which is the generalization?

Practicing What You've Learned

Use the results from the poll on this page to answer the following questions.

1. What are the survey's facts?
2. "Only some Americans have a great deal of confidence in television news." Is this a valid generalization? Why or why not?

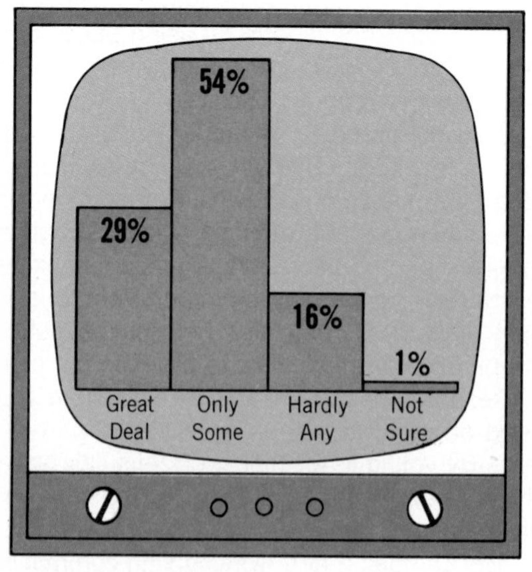

SOURCE: Louis Harris Associates.

CHAPTER REVIEW

Vocabulary

Below is a list of terms that appear in this chapter. In your notebook, use each term in a sentence that explains its meaning.

opinions
public opinion
mass media
propaganda
concealed propaganda
revealed propaganda
public opinion poll
interest group
lobbyist
volunteers

Check-Up

1. Why does effective citizenship depend upon critical thinking?
2. What is the difference between concealed propaganda and revealed propaganda? Which method do you think is more effective? Why?
3. Name some of the people and groups who use propaganda. What are their reasons for using propaganda?
4. Give examples of the ways in which television commercials use various propaganda methods.
5. Why do government officials use public opinion polls? Do you think such polls help our leaders serve the public? Explain.
6. How do interest groups carry out their work?
7. Why do you think the number of people voting in elections has decreased in recent years?
8. In what ways can citizens take part in political campaigns?
9. Do you think that the mass media, especially television, have too much influence on public opinion? Should the media be regulated in any way? Explain your answers.
10. The law requires lobbyists to register with Congress and tell who is paying them. Do you think this law is a good one? Why or why not?

Civics Skills

"Which level of government is closest to the people?" That was just one of the questions asked recently by a pollster to discover how Americans feel about their state governments. The list below shows the response to this question.

State Legislatures	77%
Congress	13%
No Difference	4%
Not Sure	6%

1. Based on the above findings, what generalizations can you make?
2. If you wanted to measure public opinion of your state government, what questions would you ask? Be sure to keep in mind the standards for good survey questions.

Citizenship and You

1. Write to the national office of an interest group that was mentioned in this chapter or to any other interest group that you know of. Ask for information on issues that concern this group. What issues is the group currently working on? What methods does this particular group use to get across its opinions?
2. Obtain several different editorials from your local newspaper on an issue that is currently important. Compare the editorials. How do they differ? How are they similar? How do they try to persuade you to agree with their point of view?
3. Collect examples of propaganda techniques from newspapers and magazines. Place your clippings in a scrapbook and identify each kind of propaganda technique used.
4. Visit a local newspaper plant. Find out how news is gathered and printed. Talk to the editor and ask about some of the problems of censorship and propaganda.

CHAPTER

12

Paying the Costs of Government

The many activities of government cost money—huge sums of money. Our federal government alone spends more than $700 billion a year. State and local governments spend many more billions of dollars. What is this money spent for? The largest share goes to help individual citizens. Large sums are needed, too, for national defense. Governments also spend money to protect our lives and property and to pay for schools, medical research, and many other programs and services.

In recent years, the costs of government have risen sharply. From where does all the needed money come? It comes from the American people. We must pay for the services our governments provide.

However, the money raised from taxpayers does not cover the enormous costs of government. As a result, the government borrows money from the people, from banks, and from other sources. This borrowing adds to the national debt, which rises each year. The interest on this debt is many billions of dollars each year. And it must be paid.

As citizens, we have a responsibility to make sure the government spends our money wisely. In this chapter, you will learn more about government spending and how the government raises the money it needs. You will study these topics:

1. **How the Government Raises Money**
2. **Many Kinds of Taxes**
3. **Managing Our Nation's Money**

1

How the Government Raises Money

Each year our federal, state, and local governments spend huge amounts of money. Our local governments provide the American people with police and firefighters. Public health programs and schools are paid for largely by local governments. They also provide paved streets, sewers, trash removal, parks, playgrounds, and many other services.

State governments provide highways and state police. They also give aid to public schools and to people who have lost their jobs. Furthermore, state governments provide money to poor people for food and housing.

The federal government provides for our nation's defense. It aids business, labor, and agriculture. It provides agencies to protect the public's health, aids in highway construction, and serves its citizens in hundreds of other ways. All these services must be paid for.

Rising Costs of Government Services

One important reason why our governments cost so much money today is that the United States has a larger population than ever before. Our federal government, for example, serves a population of nearly 230 million. Another reason is that during the past 50 years the activities of our governments have increased enormously.

The cost of government also has gone up in recent years because of the rising cost of living. Today's dollar will not buy as much as a dollar did in past years. Furthermore, the services and programs of our federal government have grown much larger and more costly.

For example, in 1913 a single two-lane highway cost a few thousand dollars a mile. Today this distance on a six-lane superhighway, with overpasses and cloverleafs, costs more than $1 million. The cost of defense, too, has risen sharply. In 1913 our nation's defense dollars were spent largely for supporting soldiers and their field supplies. Today we spend billions of dollars on missiles, nuclear-powered submarines and aircraft carriers, jet fighter planes, and electronic communication systems.

Establishing Priorities

Many Americans complain about the high costs of government. It is understandable that they should do so. All citizens have the right to expect that their government will spend their—the taxpayers'—money wisely.

In recent years, taxpayers have questioned the need for many government programs and criticized wasteful spending practices. Taxpayer revolts across the nation have forced governments to cut back on spending. In a number of states and local communities, taxpayers have voted to place limits on the amount they can be taxed.

Government officials, therefore, are faced with difficult decisions. What government programs need money most? What programs will bring the greatest benefits to the most people?

The first thing government officials do is list those activities that need money. These are listed in order of their urgency and need. This is called establishing **priorities.** Programs at the top of the list have high priority. Programs lower on the list have lower priority. Our government officials try to spend funds for those high on the list. Programs of very low priority may have to be left out. In recent years, there has been much debate over our priorities.

The Purpose of Taxes

All our American governments—federal, state, and local—raise most of the money to pay for services and programs by collecting taxes. A **tax** is a payment of money that citizens and businesses are required to make in order to help pay for the costs of government. A tax is compulsory. That is, citizens have to pay it whether they want to or not.

The chief purpose of taxes is to raise money, or **revenue.** This revenue pays for the costs of government. Another purpose of taxes is to regulate, or control, some activity.

"Only two things are certain," goes an old saying, "death and taxes." In the 1970's, though, Americans began protesting that taxes were too high.

How are taxes used to regulate activities?

Taxes on imports, for example, are sometimes fixed at a high level. Their aim is not to raise large sums of money but to discourage imports in order to encourage business activity in our own country. High taxes on cigarettes and alcoholic beverages are partly intended to discourage their use.

Some Rules of Taxation

Our governments try to follow certain rules, or principles, when they set up taxes. They follow these rules to try to make taxes as fair as possible for all our citizens. What are these principles of taxation?

1. Taxes should be based on ability to pay. Taxes should not be so high that they are difficult for many people to pay. In order to make it possible for all citizens to pay, taxes on the money people earn are lower for those citizens with low incomes and higher for those with high incomes. Other taxes, such as those on things people buy, are at a fixed rate for all citizens within a given area. These taxes are set at a reasonable level that all can pay.

2. Taxes should be applied equally to all. A local tax on property, for example, should be the same for all property worth the same amount of money. Taxes collected on the goods we buy should be the same for anyone purchasing these goods.

3. Taxes should be easy to pay. The American people want to pay their taxes quickly and easily. Therefore, a large part of some taxes is taken out of workers' paychecks before they receive their checks. These taxes are withheld by employers, who send the tax money directly to the government.

4. Taxes should be collected at convenient times. Suppose that all taxes had to be paid at the time of the Christmas holidays when many people have bills to pay. Most Americans would find paying taxes then particularly difficult. Our governments try to

Why the Costs of Our Federal Government Have Increased

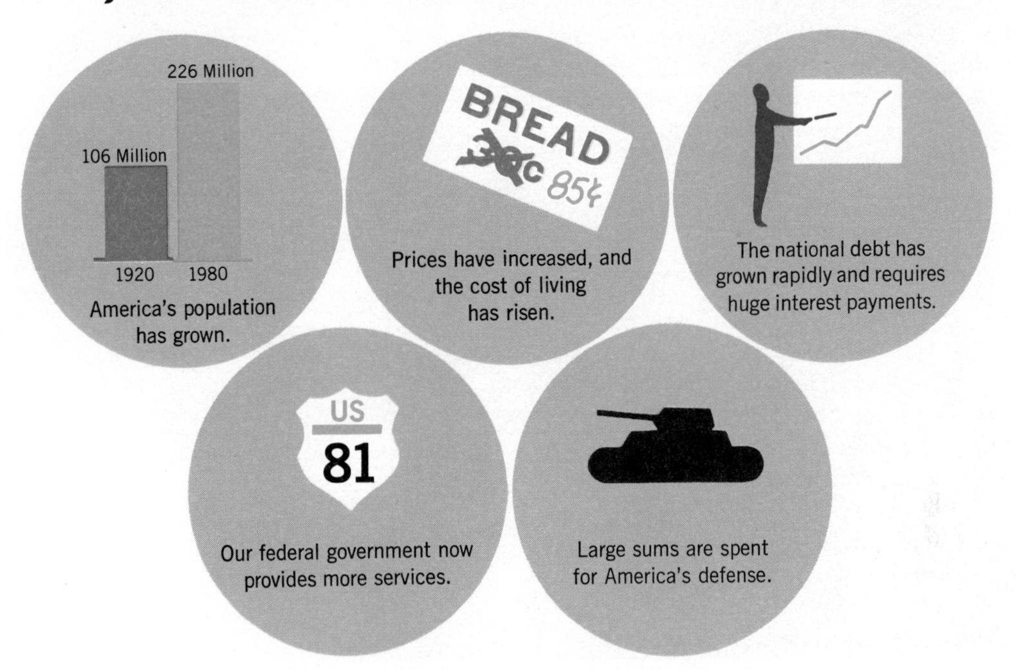

collect taxes at a time when it is easier for citizens to pay them. The United States government also tries to make it easier for citizens to pay certain taxes by collecting part of the total tax each month instead of requiring that the entire tax be paid in full all at one time.

Other Methods of Raising Revenue

Other means of raising money for governmental needs include fees, fines, and payments for special services.

Governments raise money by charging **fees,** or small payments, for various licenses—hunting licenses, dog licenses, marriage licenses, and so forth. State governments raise large sums of money from the fees they charge for drivers' licenses and automobile license plates.

Money paid by a citizen as a penalty for breaking certain laws is a **fine.** Fines add to the funds of local governments especially. Such fines are those for illegal parking, speeding, jaywalking, and violating a local building code.

Governments provide special services that are paid for directly by those who use these services. For example, the federal government sells timber from national forest reserves and electricity from certain federal dam projects. Those who receive this timber or electric power must pay for it directly. State governments collect payments from drivers who use certain toll roads and bridges. Local governments sometimes install parking meters to collect payments from those who wish to park their cars on the street.

Government Borrowing

Although our governments raise most of their funds through taxes and other forms of revenue, their needs are sometimes so great that they must borrow money. In recent years, our federal government has been trying in various ways to reduce the amount that it spends.

Not many local governments would have on hand the millions of dollars that it costs to build a school like this. So they borrow, often by issuing school bonds.

However, it still spends more money each year than it takes in. As a result, our nation is in debt for more than $1 trillion.

On state and local levels, a large project, such as a school or a bridge, costs so much to build that it usually cannot be paid for fully out of the government's income in any single year. Therefore, state and local governments must borrow the additional money they need from their citizens.

Our governments borrow money by issuing bonds. A government **bond** is a certificate stating that the government has borrowed a certain sum of money from the owner of the bond. The government promises to pay interest on this money. **Interest** is the payment made for the use of the money. Furthermore, the government promises to repay the full amount of the loan on a given date. It is generally a certain percentage of the amount borrowed. You will learn more about this form of government borrowing later in this chapter.

CHECK-UP

Vocabulary

priorities
tax
revenue
fees
fine
bond
interest

Review

1. What are some reasons for the high cost of government?
2. What are the main purposes of taxes?
3. What are the four principles that should be followed to make taxes fair for all citizens?
4. Why do governments sometimes have to borrow money?

Discuss

What services provided by the federal government do you think should have the highest priority? the lowest priority? Explain your answers.

2
Many Kinds of Taxes

When we walk on a sidewalk or drive on a paved street, we are enjoying a government service that has cost a great deal of money. When we watch telecasts of American spaceships circling the planets, we are watching the results of an important government research program that costs billions of dollars each year.

How are these and the other government services and programs paid for? Taxes are the main source of money for our federal, state, and local governments. All levels of government depend on many kinds of taxes to raise the large sums of money needed.

Personal Income Tax

The largest source of revenue for our federal government is the **personal income tax.** This is a tax on the income a person earns. It is not based on a person's total income. The personal income tax is based on the amount left over after certain amounts have been subtracted from the total income.

How Much Do We Pay? All taxpayers are allowed to deduct, or subtract, a certain amount of money for each dependent—each person they support in the family. These amounts are called **exemptions.** A working father claims exemptions for himself, his spouse, and his children. A working mother does the same when she produces all the family's income.

Taxpayers can also deduct certain expenses. These amounts are called **deductions.** For example, taxpayers can deduct money they give to charities and part of their medical bills. Other deductions include interest on money borrowed and business expenses.

The amount left over after all subtractions have been made is called **taxable income.** This is the amount on which the personal income tax is paid.

The rate at which individuals are taxed depends upon the size of their taxable income. People with higher taxable incomes pay a larger percentage of their income in taxes than those with smaller taxable incomes. For example, a person who has a taxable income of $10,000 might pay tax at a rate of 10 percent, or $1,000. A taxpayer with a taxable income of $100,000 might have a tax rate of 50 percent, or $50,000.

The amount of income taxes that people

How the Federal Government Spends Its Money

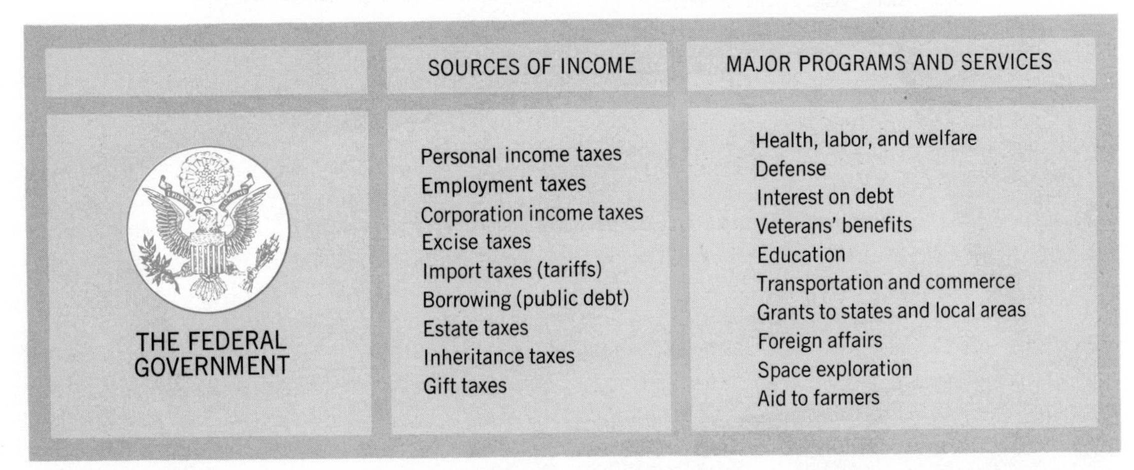

have to pay changes. Congress changes tax rates when it wants to help the economy. It also does so to encourage saving, to encourage or discourage some kinds of spending, or to improve our system of taxation.

How Do We Pay? American taxpayers must fill out and mail their tax forms on or before April 15 each year. Most taxpayers do not pay all their income tax at the time they file tax returns. Income tax payments have already been taken out of each paycheck by their employers, who forward the tax money to the government.

Filling out the tax forms shows taxpayers how much they must pay. Sometimes people learn they will get back some of the tax money withheld by their employers during the year. Sometimes they find they owe the government more money. The system of making small tax payments each payday makes it easier for most Americans to pay their personal income taxes.

State and Local Taxes. The income tax is a very successful means of raising money to support the federal government. All but a few of our state governments also collect a personal income tax. In addition, it is collected by some city governments. Each of these states and cities has its own income tax law and fixes its own income tax rate.

Some cities have also established a **payroll tax,** which is a form of income tax. For the payroll tax, the employer deducts a certain percentage of each employee's pay and sends that money to the city tax collector. This tax rate is usually the same for everyone. That is, people who earn more are not taxed at a higher rate. Payroll tax rates, as well as the state and city income tax rates, are much lower than those for the federal income tax.

Social Security Tax

Another kind of income tax that Americans pay is the **Social Security tax.** This is used mainly to pay income to retired people. All working people pay the Social Security tax at the same rate up to a certain amount, above which they are not taxed. The tax paid by each worker is matched by the employer. You will read more about how Social Security works in Chapter 18.

Corporation Income Tax

The second largest source of income for the federal government is the **corporation income tax.** It also is an important source of income

This stub from a paycheck shows the kinds of deductions that employers make from workers' paychecks for taxes. The employers then send this tax money to the government.

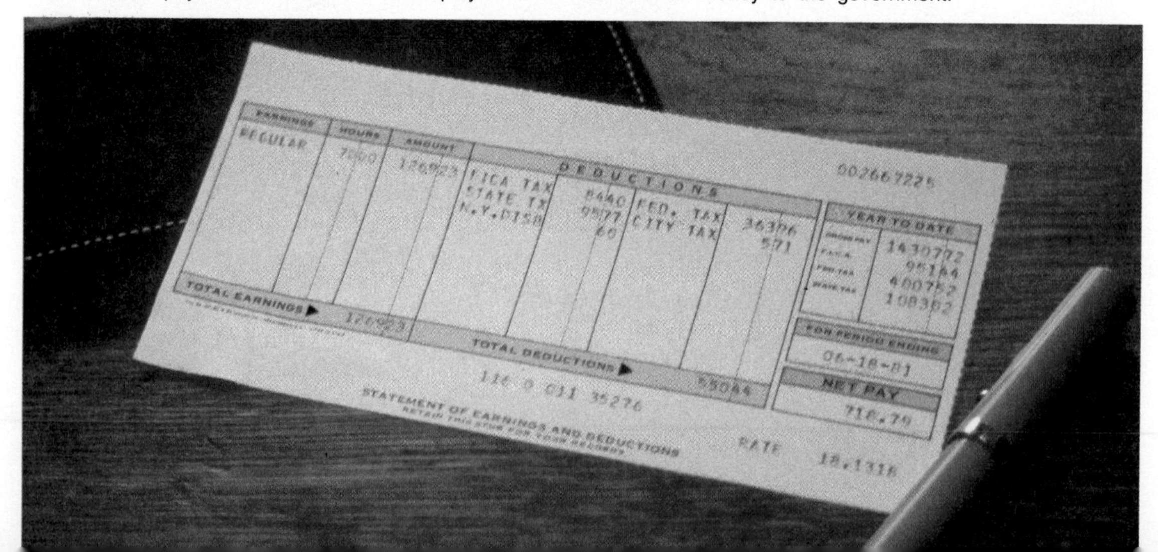

for our state governments. This tax is not based on the total income received by the corporation. It is based only on a corporation's profits. **Profit** is the income a business has left after expenses.

Like individuals, corporations may deduct certain amounts to lower their taxable income. For example, they may subtract money paid to buy new machinery or for employee salaries. Also like individuals, corporations with high taxable incomes are taxed at a higher rate.

Sales Tax

Most of our state governments and many city governments have a **sales tax.** It is collected on most products people buy. Suppose, for example, that the sales tax in your area is 5 percent. When you buy something that costs $1.00, you must pay $1.05.

The sales tax is collected by stores directly from the customer. Stores then send the sales tax money to the state treasurer or the local tax collector. Some states return part of the state sales tax to town and city governments to help them meet their expenses.

Excise Tax

Excise taxes are similar to sales taxes. The **excise tax,** though, is collected only on certain services and goods produced and sold in the United States, usually on "luxury" items. Some of the items on which excise taxes are collected are tobacco, alcoholic beverages, gasoline, automobiles, and air travel. Excise taxes are collected by the fed-

How State and Local Governments Spend Their Money

	SOURCES OF INCOME	MAJOR SERVICES
STATE GOVERNMENTS	Federal government General sales tax Personal income tax Cigarette, gasoline, and liquor taxes Corporation income tax Inheritance tax Licenses and fees	Education Public welfare Highways Health and hospitals Police Public building programs
ANYTOWN U.S.A. LOCAL GOVERNMENTS	Federal and state governments Property tax School tax Licenses and permits Fines Amusement taxes Personal property taxes	Schools Public welfare Fire and police protection Health and hospitals Utilities Streets and roads Sewage systems Parks and playgrounds Libraries

eral government and by several of our state governments.

Property Tax

The chief source of income for most local governments is the **property tax.** This is a tax on the value of the property owned by a person or a business. Property taxes are collected on two different kinds of property, real and personal.

Real property consists of land and buildings. **Personal property** includes such things as stocks, bonds, jewelry, cars, and boats. Since it is more difficult to determine the value of an individual's personal property, most governments use the property tax to cover only real property. If personal property is taxed, the rate is usually very low.

How Real Property Is Taxed. To determine the value of property for tax purposes, local governments depend upon local officials called tax assessors. These assessors visit the property and assess it, or make a judgment of its value.

When the tax assessors complete their work, the local government adds up the assessed value of all the property in the locality. The local government then figures the total amount of money it must raise by the property tax. To decide on the tax rate, it divides this amount by the total assessed value of property in the town.

To see how this works, take the example of a small town that needs revenues amounting to $100,000 from its property tax. Suppose that the total assessed value of property within the boundaries of the town is $3 million. To figure the amount that property owners will have to pay, we divide $100,000 by $3 million. This gives us a tax rate of 3 cents on each dollar, or $3 on each $100 of assessed property value. This 3 percent tax rate means that a house and land assessed at $10,000 will be taxed $300 a year.

School Taxes. In many of our states, public schools are supported by a local tax on property, sometimes called a **school tax.** The school tax is collected by the town, village, county, or school district in which the school is located. The tax money is turned over to the local school board. In most cases, public school districts also receive aid from the state government to help pay the cost of schools.

Tariff, or Import Tax

The United States government collects import taxes on many products imported from foreign countries. This import tax is called a **tariff,** or sometimes a customs duty. In the early days of our nation, the tariff was one of the largest sources of income for the federal government.

Today, however, the United States generally uses tariffs to regulate trade rather than raise money. Our government places protective tariffs on certain products. A **protective tariff** protects American industries against foreign competition.

Many foreign countries can manufacture goods at a far lower cost than they could be manufactured for in the United States. Lower manufacturing costs would allow those goods to be imported and sold here for far less than an American manufacturer would have to charge. American industry would lose business, and some American workers might lose their jobs.

A tariff on the imported product raises its price, making it as expensive as, or more expensive than, the American product. Tariffs thus protect industry. In some cases, though, tariffs hurt American consumers by raising the prices they must pay for certain products.

Estate, Inheritance, and Gift Taxes

When a person dies, the heirs may have to pay several taxes on the real estate, money, and personal property that are left behind. First there is the **estate tax.** This is a federal tax on all the wealth a person leaves. Some states also collect an estate tax. The rate at which the tax is paid by the heirs depends upon the value of the estate they receive.

Then there is a state tax on the share of the estate an individual inherits, or receives. Be sure you understand the difference between the two taxes. The estate tax is based on the value of the entire estate before it is divided. The **inheritance tax** is based on the amount an individual receives as a share of the estate.

Even a gift of money may be subject to a tax by the federal government. A **gift tax** must be paid by any person giving a gift worth more than a certain amount.

CHECK-UP

Vocabulary

personal income tax
exemptions
deductions
taxable income
payroll tax
Social Security tax
corporation income tax
profit
sales tax
excise tax
property tax
real property
personal property
school tax
tariff
protective tariff
estate tax
inheritance tax
gift tax

Review

1. How do we pay a sales tax?
2. Is anything ever taxed more than once? Give an example.
3. Which of our governments—local, state, or federal—uses the property tax to obtain most of its income?
4. How does a protective tariff work?
5. How does an estate tax differ from an inheritance tax?

Discuss

Some Americans believe that we have to pay too many different kinds of taxes. Do you think it would be better if we had to pay just one kind of tax? Why or why not?

3

Managing Our Nation's Money

One of the most important jobs of the various governments in the United States is to manage the public money wisely. As you know, our federal, state, and local governments collect and spend many billions of dollars each year. Therefore, our governments have set up separate divisions to handle public funds. In addition, each of our governments checks on the way public funds are spent.

Collecting Public Money

Each of our governments has a department that collects taxes. In the federal government, income taxes are collected by the **Internal Revenue Service (IRS).** The IRS is an agency of the Department of the Treasury, and it has branches throughout the nation. Tariffs on imports are collected by the Customs Service, another division of the Department of the Treasury. State and local governments have their own tax collection bureaus.

After tax money is collected, it is sent to the treasuries of the various governments. The tax funds of the federal government are handled by the **treasurer** of the United States. It is the treasurer's job to see that all federal tax money is kept safe and that it is paid out only as authorized by the Secretary of the Treasury. The Secretary may spend money only when authorized to do so by Congress.

In our state and local governments, the official who acts as the "watchdog of the treasury" is the **comptroller.** Comptrollers have a job similar to that of the treasurer of the United States. These state and local officials have the job of seeing that public funds are spent only as authorized by the state legislature or the city council.

★ ★ ★ ★ ★ ★ ★ ★ ★ ★ ★ ★

CAN YOU GUESS?

In early times, when money was scarce, the taxes in several Southern colonies were paid in the form of a major crop. Which crop was it? (Hint: It goes up in smoke.)

Answer is on page 562.

Planning Government Spending

All governments have budgets. A **budget** is a plan for raising and spending funds. The budget lists the amount of revenue, or money income, as well as the sources from which this revenue will be collected. It also lists the expenditures, or money to be spent, for various public purposes. A budget usually covers the government's operations for one year.

The responsibility for managing public funds is divided among the three branches of government. The chief executive of each of our governments is responsible for drawing up the budget. In a village, town, or city, the mayor, city manager, or other executive officer plans and draws up the budget. In most state governments, the governor prepares the yearly budget of the state's spending and income. The President is responsible for budget planning in the federal government.

The legislative branch must approve the budget before any public money can be spent. The head of the executive branch must see that the money is spent according to the budget's plan. The courts in the judicial branch settle disputes over the collecting and spending of the public money.

Preparing the Federal Budget

In the federal government, the President recommends how public funds may be raised and how they may be spent. The job of planning the federal budget is so complicated that the President needs the help of several government agencies.

One of the chief agencies involved in helping the President prepare the federal budget is the **Office of Management and Budget (OMB).** This important agency makes studies of our nation's economy. It then forecasts the amount of tax income the government will receive in the coming year.

Each of the executive departments makes a careful estimate of how much money it plans to spend the following year. All these estimates are submitted to the President. Then the President and the director of the OMB study the many requests. Priorities are established for the various items. Some requests may be cut in order to bring the total expenditures closer to estimated revenues.

After the budget is prepared each year, it is published in book form. This huge budget book contains hundreds of pages, listing thousands of separate items.

This scene is a common one each year as April 15 approaches. It is time to take out bills, receipts, and check stubs and fill out an income tax form.

Congress and the Budget

When the budget is in its finished form, the President sends it to Congress. Along with the budget, the President sends a message explaining the budget and urging that it be passed. Sometimes the President addresses a joint session of Congress to seek support for the budget.

Congress then makes its own study of the proposed budget. As you recall, only Congress has the power to raise funds and spend them. The House of Representatives and the Senate debate the various items in the budget and make changes. Both houses of Congress must approve the final version of the budget. The revised budget is then sent back to the President to be approved or vetoed.

This process of preparing the budget takes many months. There is a great deal of give and take before the final budget is approved. When finally completed, the budget becomes the law under which money is spent during the coming year.

Balancing the Budget

When a government has a **balanced budget,** the amount of revenue equals the amount of expenditures. That is, the amount of money received equals the amount of money spent.

Sometimes a government budget is not balanced, however. When its budget is not balanced, the government's expenses usually are greater than its income from taxes and other sources. This shortage of income is called a **deficit.** A government may, however, receive more income than it planned, so that its revenues exceed its expenditures. This excess, or extra, income is called a **surplus.**

Deficits in a government budget must be made up by borrowing. Governments obtain short-term loans by borrowing enough money from banks to tide them over for a year or less. Long-term borrowing is usually done by issuing government bonds.

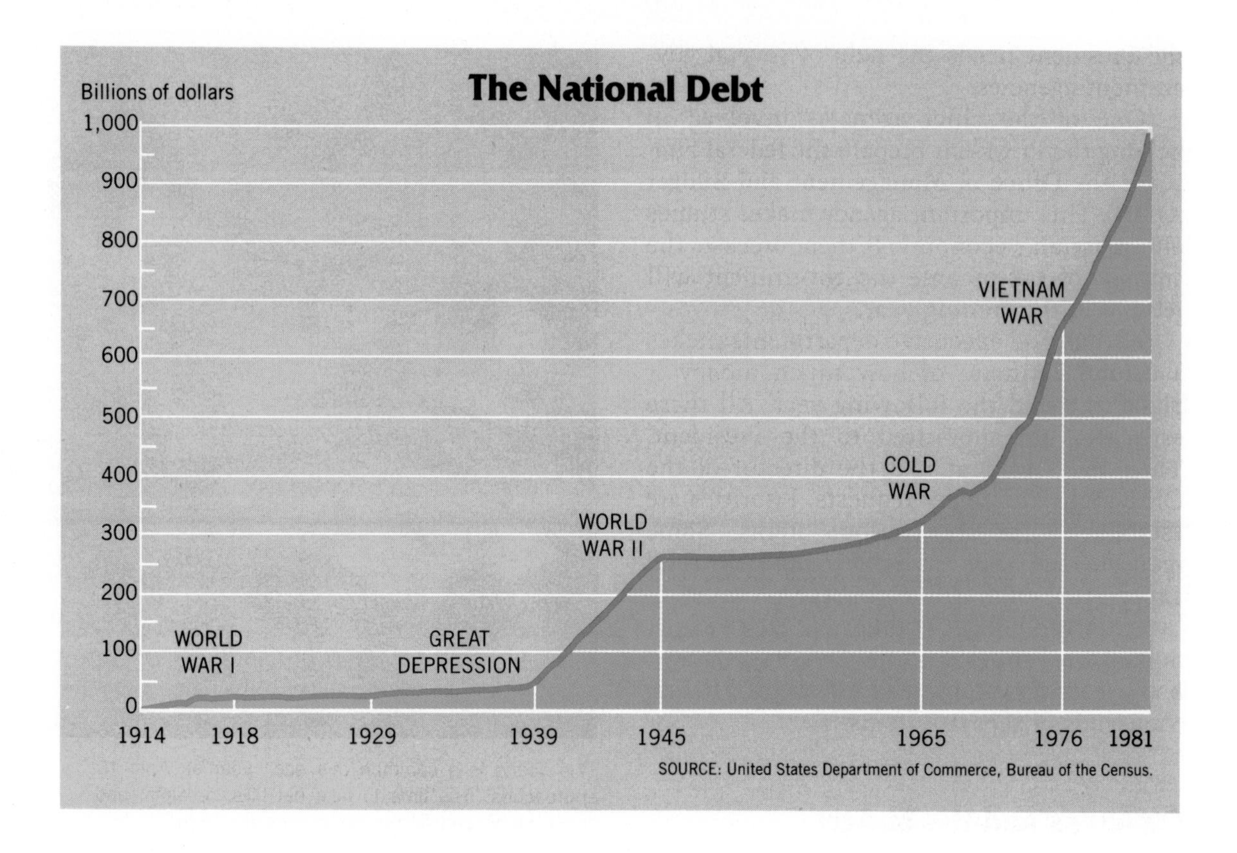

The Problem of the National Debt

The federal government has borrowed huge amounts of money in recent years to try to balance its budget. To do so, it has issued several kinds of government bonds. You may be familiar with one of these kinds of bonds—**savings bonds.**

Everyone who owns savings bonds or other federal bonds has loaned money to the government. Each year the government must pay interest on these bonds, and some of the bonds themselves must be paid off. These payments add to the cost of government and to our national debt. The chart on this page shows you how the national debt has grown.

How large a debt can our federal government owe? By law, the federal government can borrow only as much as Congress votes to permit. Congress has established a **debt limit** for the federal government. The federal government must keep its borrowing within this debt limit unless Congress votes to raise the debt limit to a higher sum.

Public Money Is a Public Trust

Handling government money is very complex. It is also of extreme importance to the nation's welfare. It is necessary to keep careful records, or accounts, of where every dollar comes from and how it is spent.

To make sure that public funds are spent according to law and can be fully accounted for, all governments provide for an audit of their accounts. An **audit** is a careful examination, or study, by a trained accountant, of every item of income and expenditure. The auditor checks to make sure every cent is accounted for and every expenditure was properly authorized.

The expenditures of local governments are usually audited by a department of the state government. Expenditures of local school districts are examined by auditors from the state Department of Education or by an independent auditing firm. In our state governments, the audit is usually made by an independent agency of the state under the direction of the comptroller. All federal expenditures are checked by the General Accounting Office, an agency of the legislative branch of the federal government.

Citizen Responsibility

The whole subject of taxes, public funds, and the national debt is a difficult one for many Americans to understand. Yet the well-being of the American nation depends on how wisely our governments handle public funds. If wise policies of raising and spending money are to be followed, the citizen must make an attempt to understand these subjects and vote for intelligent, responsible leaders.

CHECK-UP

Vocabulary

Internal Revenue Service
treasurer
comptroller
budget
Office of Management and Budget
balanced budget
deficit
surplus
savings bonds
debt limit
audit

Review

1. Describe the process of preparing the federal budget.
2. Name some of the safeguards that protect the raising and spending of public funds.
3. How do governments borrow money?
4. Why does the United States have such a large national debt?

Discuss

If you could write a budget for the nation, what would you choose as our most important national priorities? Give reasons for your choices.

CHAPTER SUMMARY

Government costs a great deal of money. This money must be provided by our citizens. Each of us shares the costs of government. Over the years, the costs of the services of government have increased greatly.

Money for our government is raised by taxes, fees, fines, special payments, and borrowing. There are many kinds of taxes. Americans pay taxes on incomes, property, purchases, imported goods, corporation profits, gasoline, and many other things. Our federal, state, and local governments all collect a share of these taxes.

There are agencies to collect this money and others to see that it is spent properly. The executive branches of our governments work closely with the legislative branches to plan government spending and money raising.

Our governments also borrow large sums to help pay their expenses. Federal borrowing has created a large national debt. The public debt is a problem that concerns all Americans. As taxpayers, we must make sure our money is used wisely.

CIVICS SKILLS: Reading a Circle Graph

Do you know that you owe more than $4,600? Impossible, you might say. However, take a few minutes to consider the national debt. Since 1940 it has soared from $43 billion to more than $1 trillion. Today that averages out to over $4,600 for every person living in the United States.

The government doesn't actually expect you to send in a check for that amount. In fact, most of the national debt is owed to American citizens—perhaps even to someone in your own family. Have you ever heard of United States savings bonds? Whenever people or businesses buy them, they are really lending money to the United States Treasury. In return the Treasury agrees to pay interest on the bonds when they mature, or reach full value.

Suppose you decide to buy some bonds. Like any careful investor, you would probably want to know how your money is going to be spent. To discover this, you could read through a copy of the federal budget. However, there is an easier way. You could look at a **circle graph** that summarizes all this information about the federal budget for you.

Interpreting a Circle Graph

Try to think of a circle graph as a pie. The circle stands for the total pie. The sections within the circle are the pie's slices, or parts. Because every circle graph equals 100 percent of something, you might want to think of it as a pie cut up into 100 slices. If, for example, you share half the pie with a friend, you each have 50 slices, or 50 percent. What percentage do you have if you give away only one fourth of the pie?

As with any graph, you begin to read a circle graph by looking at its title. The title tells you what the graph represents. Next you identify the main divisions, or categories, into which the circle has been divided. Examine the circle graph on this page. How many categories does it have? What information is shown in each one?

By comparing these various categories, you can draw some conclusions about the graph as a whole.

Practicing What You've Learned

The following questions will help you evaluate the usefulness of circle graphs.

1. Which is the largest category of government expenses? Based on this fact, what is the nation's highest priority?
2. What percentage of the national budget is devoted to interest payments? Who receives this money?
3. What are the advantages of showing information in the form of a circle graph? the disadvantages?

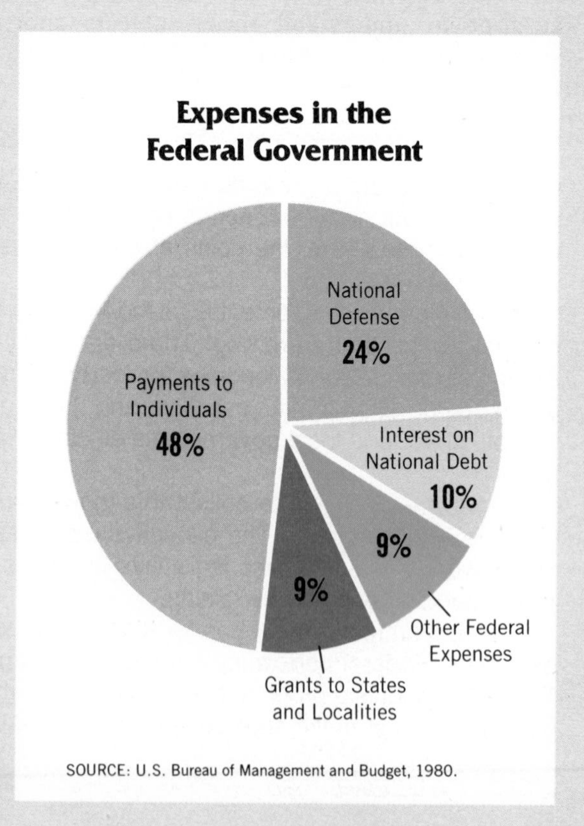

CHAPTER REVIEW

Vocabulary

Write a three-paragraph summary of the main ideas that have been presented in this chapter. In the first paragraph use the following terms:

taxes	revenue
fees	bond
fines	debt

In the second paragraph use the following terms:

property tax	Social Security tax
tariff	sales tax
income tax	excise tax

In the third paragraph use the following terms:

budget	audit
priorities	deficit
balanced budget	debt limit

Check-Up

1. Why are the costs of government increasing each year?
2. What are some of the ways in which governments raise money?
3. Do you think all taxes should be based on a person's ability to pay?
4. What is the difference between real property and personal property?
5. What is the job of a tax assessor?
6. Why do you think it is important for governments to establish priorities? How have our national priorities changed over the years?
7. What are the two purposes served by a protective tariff?
8. What is the largest source of revenue for the federal government?
9. List the steps by which the federal government's budget is prepared and approved.
10. Do you think the federal government should always have a balanced budget even if some government services have to be eliminated? Or do you think the government should be able to go into debt and continue to provide these services? Why?

Civics Skills

The figures below show the main sources of revenue for the federal government in 1980. Present this information in the form of a circle graph. Remember to label each category clearly and to place a title on the graph. Then compare the various categories and draw some conclusions about the circle graph as a whole.

Source	*Percentage*
Corporation Income Taxes	13.8
Customs and Others Taxes	4.6
Excise Taxes	5.0
Social Insurance Taxes	31.0
Personal Income Taxes	45.6

Citizenship and You

1. Participate in a class debate on this topic: *Resolved,* That the sales tax is unfair to people with small incomes.
2. With your classmates, list on the chalkboard the many kinds of taxes paid by citizens in the United States. Be sure you can explain how each tax works.
3. A photography committee may present a series of pictures showing projects and services in your community or area that are paid for with tax money.
4. Express your ideas about taxes by drawing a political cartoon. Ideas for such cartoons may be obtained by studying the ways in which similar topics are handled by cartoonists in local newspapers.

UNIT FOUR REVIEW

Reviewing the Facts

Write your answers to the items below on a separate piece of paper.

1. Complete this sentence: If a government took in $1 million in taxes and spent $1.2 million on services for the people, the result would be a budget ________.
2. Arrange the items below in the order they would occur in the election process.
   a. nominating convention
   b. primary election
   c. general election
   d. meeting of the Electoral College
3. Complete this sentence: In order to raise the money needed to pay for services the government collects ________.
4. Complete this sentence: In a ________ a representative sample of the public are asked what they think about an issue.
5. Complete this sentence: A ________ is a plan of income and expenses.
6. Labor unions, consumers, teachers' organizations, and senior citizens are all examples of
   a. political parties.
   b. interest groups.
   c. nominating conventions.
   d. priorities.
7. Our government tries to follow all these rules of taxation *except*
   a. rates of taxation should be the same for everyone.
   b. a tax should not be easy to avoid.
   c. taxes should be easy to pay.
   d. taxes should be collected at a time when it is most convenient for people to pay.
8. Political parties serve our nation in all these ways *except* by
   a. selecting candidates to run for office.
   b. recommending programs and laws.
   c. sparing citizens the need to vote.
   d. keeping the public informed about government activities.
9. Name the propaganda technique being used in each of the following examples.
   a. "Any senator who supports this bill is not a loyal American."
   b. "Most people have already decided to vote for Senator Whiz. How about you?"
   c. "Senator Whiz was born and raised right here in our community."
   d. "The mayor urges you to vote for Senator Whiz."

Applying What You Know

1. Suppose you belong to an interest group that wants to turn an unused plot of land in your neighborhood into a playground. Describe two methods you might use to sway public opinion, in the hope of getting government support for your program.
2. In recent years only about half the nation's eligible voters have actually voted in local and national elections. What might happen if fewer and fewer people bother to vote? Why might this be a problem?

Expanding Your Knowledge

Heaps, Willard, *Taxation, U.S.A.*, Houghton Mifflin. An easy-to-follow explanation of how our nation's tax system really works.

Loeb, Robert H., *Your Guide to Voting*, Franklin Watts. The best ways for you to learn about political issues and to evaluate propaganda.

Weingast, David, *We Elect a President*, Messner. Inside facts on the convention, campaign, and election.

Weiss, Ann E., *Polls and Surveys*, Franklin Watts. A close look at public opinion research.

UNIT FIVE

Citizenship: Home, School, Community

CHAPTER

13

Citizenship and the Family

In the first four units of this textbook, you have read about the ways in which different governments of the United States—national, state, and local—are organized to carry on our public business. However, much of the success of our governments depends upon the way each person carries out her or his duties and responsibilities. Where does the citizen become educated in the ways of democracy?

During the world's long history, human beings have developed many different kinds of institutions. **Institutions** are organized, customary ways of doing things. One of our most important institutions is the home, or family.

The **family** is a group of people who are united by ties of marriage, blood, or adoption. The family provides the basic needs of food, clothing, shelter, and affection for all of its members.

The family usually is the first group to which a person belongs. Infants are loved and cared for in their families. As they grow, children are taught certain skills, values, and traditions in their family. One of the traditions the individual learns about in the family is what it means to be a citizen.

In this chapter, you will learn more about the family and its influence as you study these topics:

1. **The Changing Family**
2. **Law and the Family**
3. **Your Family and You**

1

The Changing Family

The people who settled America believed in strong family ties and the importance of a good family life. Each colonial family was different from its neighbors in some ways. The families may have come from different nations or believed in different religions. Yet colonial families had much in common. Many families, for example, were large and included grandparents and other relatives in the same household.

Today most families are much smaller. Their life styles have changed. Yet despite these changes, Americans continue to believe in the importance of the family.

The Traditional Family

How different was the colonial family from the family of today? The first census of the United States, taken in 1790, showed that the average family had about four children. Many families were even larger. At that time, our country was largely rural, which means that most American people lived and worked on farms.

Each child was a welcome addition to the family, for there was plenty of work to be done on the farm. Older boys worked with their father. They learned how to plow the soil, plant seeds, and harvest the crops. They also learned to care for the animals, repair barns and fences, and do the many other chores necessary on a farm. The mother taught the daughters to sew and cook, make soap, and do the other household chores that kept the family going.

Life on the early American farm was hard. There was little time for play or schooling. Sometimes farm children attended a one-room schoolhouse. However, most learned the alphabet and numbers at home.

The early farm family was the basic work unit in the colonies. It produced most of what the family needed in order to survive. The family depended on all its members to do their part. As children grew up and were married, they did not always move away from home. Often they brought their wives or husbands with them to live on the family farm.

In these large families, everybody lived and worked together. As a man grew older, he took on lighter chores while his son or son-in-law did more of the heavier work. As a woman grew older, she too spent less time on heavy household chores. She gave more time to sewing or looking after the grandchildren.

Young or old, family members contributed what they could and received whatever care they needed. Because of this need to work together, a strong spirit of cooperation and family pride developed.

The Move to Cities

During the 1800's, American life began to change fairly rapidly. One hundred years ago, seven of every ten Americans lived on farms or in rural areas. Today only one in four Americans lives in a rural area. This change came about because of the remarkable progress in science and technology that took place during the past hundred years.

On the farms of rural America a hundred or more years ago, all members of the family had to pitch in to get the work done. Even toddlers had their jobs.

Americans soon found use for the new discoveries and inventions. These led to the building of large factories in many urban, or city, areas. The factories needed many workers. At the same time, the development of better farm machinery meant that fewer people were needed to work on the farms. Farm families began to move to urban areas to seek jobs in the factories. This movement of Americans away from the farms to the cities resulted in changes in family life.

The City Family

City families could not spend as much time together as early farm families did. The city family no longer worked together as a team the way the early farm family had. The father did not work beside his sons. He left home early in the morning to go to work, and he did not return until late at night. The younger children usually were left at home with their mother and grandparents. Children from 12 to 14 years of age were sent to work long hours in factories.

Today most city and suburban families are smaller than families of the past. Many city families have only one or two children. Children no longer work in factories. They spend much of their time at school. Fathers often travel long distances to work. Housework has become easier because of modern inventions, and many mothers work outside the home.

About half the women between 16 and 64 years old are employed outside the home. More than three out of five of these working women are married and living with their husbands. Also, many elderly people no longer live with their children. As a result of these changes, the life of the city family differs in many ways from that of the farm family of the past.

In many ways, American family life is easier and more pleasant than it was a hundred years ago. American families today generally are better educated and more prosperous. Most of us live in better homes and are better fed and clothed. We are healthier and have a great deal more free time in which to enjoy ourselves. However, the changes in American life have caused some problems for families.

The Modern American Family

The family was once the main influence in the lives of children. Many other influences also have become important for children today. Schools have taken on part of a child's education that was once thought only the job of the family. Since children spend about as much time at school as at home with their families, they are very much influenced by people their own age. Television, too, has become an important influence in the lives of the young.

Two other trends in the American way of life have been putting stress on the family. One is the increase in the divorce rate. You will read more about this later in the chapter. The other trend is the increase in the number of families in which both parents work. This brings up the problem of who is to take care of the children.

Child Care. In the past, grandparents helped to care for the young. Today, however, many families move so often that grandparents frequently do not live with or near their families. Some people think that more day care centers are the answer. However, the issue of day care and how it should be provided has been widely debated. In some areas, schools open earlier and stay open later in the afternoon for children whose parents work.

Other solutions to the problem of child care also are being tried. Among them are flexible working hours and more part-time work. Businesses and institutions that have flexible working hours permit their employees more freedom in arranging their hours of work. Employees may, for example, arrive at work earlier or later than the usual starting time or put in more hours on some days than on others.

Many mothers now take maternity leave, or several months leave of absence, after their babies are born. Some businesses also allow new fathers to take a paternity leave.

Senior Citizens. Senior citizens have also faced new problems in recent years. Not only do many older people no longer live with or near their children, they also live much longer. Today, there are more than 25 million Americans who are over 65 years of age. The number of older people in our nation's population will continue to grow because of advances in medicine. Many senior citizens in the United States live happy and healthy lives. Some, however, are in poor health, feel lonely and unwanted, and do not have enough to do.

When older people retire, their income suddenly goes down. Many find it difficult to support themselves. A number of experts think the difficulty of finding enough to live on when one is retired will continue. How to live happily and securely when one is older is a problem that affects us all. Many areas have

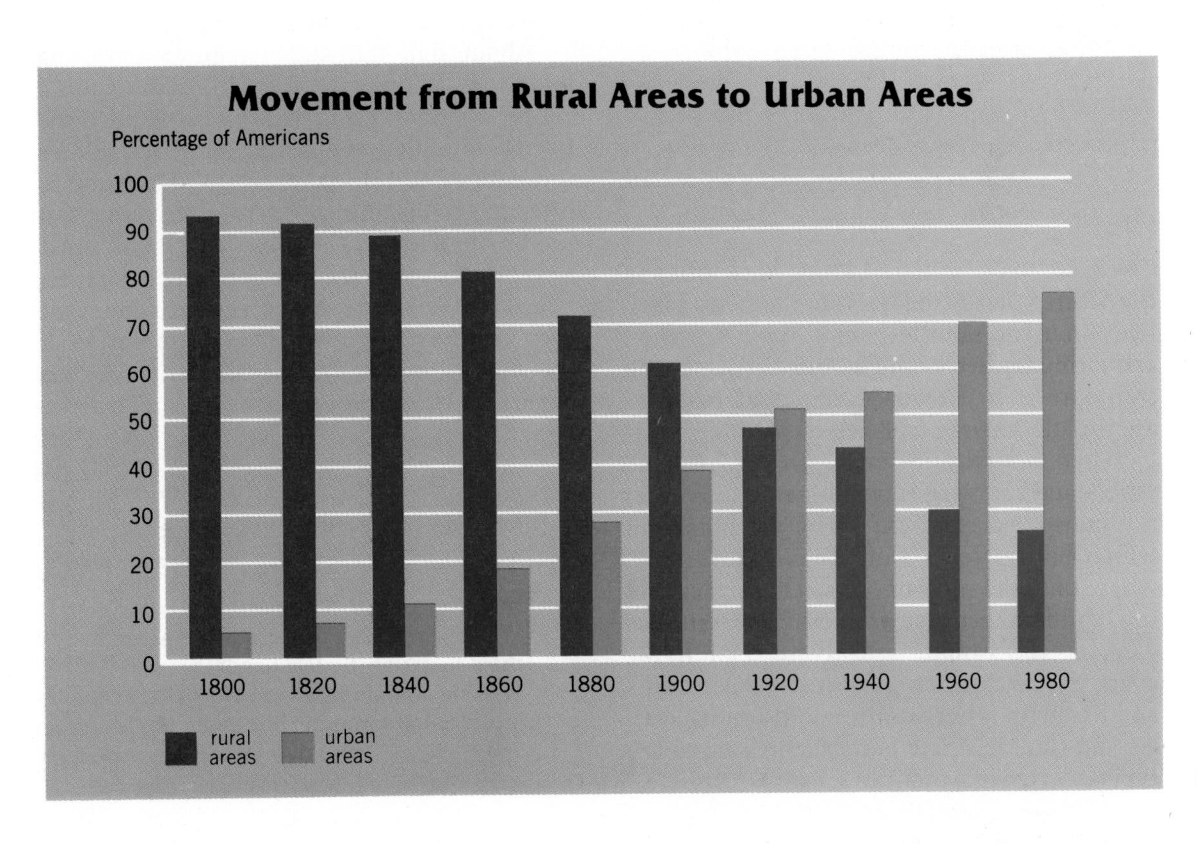

programs for the elderly, and new solutions are constantly being offered.

The American family has gone through many changes in recent years. Yet it remains the most important influence on children in our society.

CHECK-UP

Vocabulary
institutions
family

Review
1. Why did so many of the early settlers in America welcome large families?
2. In what ways has family life changed in recent years?

Discuss
Do you think that businesses should be required to provide child care centers for the children of their employees? Why or why not?

2

Law and the Family

There are many different kinds of families in the United States today. There are city families, suburban families, small town families, and farm families. Some families are rich, and some are poor. However, the great majority are middle-income families.

There are families in which the husband works and the wife stays home to look after the house and children. There are homes in which both parents work. There are homes where only the mother or father takes care of the children because the other parent has died, or the parents are divorced or living apart. Some children have lost both parents and live with other families or in orphanages. As you can see, there is no such thing as the typical, average American family.

State Laws About Marriage

Because the family is so important to our nation, many laws have been passed to protect it. These laws have been passed by state legislatures, because it is the state governments that have the power to regulate family law. **Family law** regulates marriage, divorce, and the duties of parents and children.

The more than 2 million marriages that take place each year must meet the laws of the state in which they are performed. State laws, for example, have established the earliest age at which young people may marry.

Most states require young people to be at least 18 to be married without parental consent. In many states, boys and girls may be married at 16 with the consent of their parents. In a few states, the couple also needs the consent of the court. Some states allow people to marry at younger ages. The average age at which young people married in the early 1980's was between 23 and 24 for men and between 21 and 22 for women.

About half our states require a **waiting period** of two to five days from the time a couple applies for a marriage license until the license is issued. This waiting period allows the couple to "think it over." The time is intended to discourage hasty marriages.

All but a few of the states also require that a young man and woman applying for a marriage license take a **blood test** to show that they are in good health. This examination of the blood checks for diseases that can be passed on to another person.

CAN YOU GUESS?

- **Why is a wedding ring usually worn on the third finger of the left hand?**
- **Why do wedding guests throw rice at the bride and groom after the ceremony?**

Answers are on page 562.

All states require that marriages be performed by such civil officials as a justice of the peace, judge, or mayor, or by such religious officials as a minister, priest, or rabbi. Witnesses must be present at the ceremony to testify to the fact that a legal marriage was performed.

This couple has just been married and is now considered a family unit. As husband and wife, they have certain rights that are guaranteed by state laws.

State Laws Protect Family Members

When the marriage ceremony is completed, the newly married couple is considered a family unit. Husband and wife now have certain rights guaranteed by law. If the rights of the husband or wife are neglected, the courts may be asked to step in.

Most cases of nonsupport, physical abuse, desertion, and other marital problems are tried in a domestic relations court. Usually, before a case comes to trial, the court and the lawyers will recommend that the couple consult a marriage counselor to see if they can work out their problems.

Children, too, have certain legal rights as members of the family. If a child is not given proper care by the parents, the law can step in to protect the child. Every state requires doctors and other people to report instances of **child abuse.** Children who are abused, or mistreated, mentally or physically may be taken from their parents by the state.

They may be placed in a **foster home**—the home of people who are unrelated to the child but who agree to act as his or her parents. The state pays the foster parents to care for the child. Parents who abuse their children may also have criminal charges filed against them. Sometimes parents who cannot take care of a child may ask the state to place the child in a foster home for a while.

If a child's parents die, a judge may appoint a relative or close family friend to act as a guardian to care for the child. A **guardian** is a person appointed by a state court to look after individuals who are not yet adults, or who for some reason are unable to care for themselves.

Sometimes the guardian will **adopt,** or legally establish, the child as his or her own. If no relative or friend can be found to act as a guardian, the state may put the child up for adoption.

State Laws About Separation

Marriage is a legal act recognized by law. A marriage can be officially ended only by the action of a state court. If a married couple cannot get along together, they can take their problems into a state court. The judge will hear both sides of the argument and make a decision.

In some cases, the judge may decide that a **separation** is the best answer. This means that the marriage is to continue, but the couple will separate and live apart. The husband usually must continue to support his wife and children during the period of the separation. In cases of separation, it is possible for the couple to return to living together.

State Laws About Divorce

The final, legal ending of a marriage is called **divorce.** Each state makes its own laws concerning divorce. Most states make it difficult to obtain a divorce by limiting the causes for which divorces are granted. Some grounds for divorce are desertion, nonsupport, mental and physical cruelty, frequent drunkenness, frequent use of drugs, insanity, conviction for a serious crime, and adultery.

In most states, courts in the past ruled that a divorced woman could receive a regular income from her former husband. These payments, called **alimony,** usually ended when the woman married again. Today, because more and more women can earn money on their own, alimony is much less common.

Both divorced parents usually must contribute to the support of the child or children of the marriage. Courts often decide who has the main responsibility for children, visiting rights, and other related issues.

Divorce has greatly increased in recent years. Over 1 million marriages in the United States end in divorce each year. Nearly 50 percent of all marriages in our nation end in divorce.

Some Americans believe that the best way to cut down on the number of divorces is to pass stricter marriage laws. Others believe that more preparation for marriage would result in better family life and lead to fewer divorces. Among other things, they point out that one of the best answers to the divorce problem lies in better education of all young people before they marry. Many schools have courses in marriage and family relations to help young people prepare for married life.

There are also some Americans who favor less strict divorce laws. California has made it easier to get a divorce in that state. Some Americans believe it is not healthy for children to live with two parents who are not getting along. They believe it is better for these parents to separate or divorce and work toward a new arrangement.

The stability of the family affects everyone involved. Therefore, laws are passed to protect marriage partners and their children. State agencies work to keep families together and provide funds to aid in child care and family welfare. Laws, however, cannot do the whole job. The best way to guarantee a happy family life is to encourage family members to share and work together for the good of their group. Learning to take the responsibilities of marriage and family life seriously is an important part of good citizenship.

CHECK-UP

Vocabulary

family law
waiting period
blood test
child abuse
foster home
guardian
adopt
separation
divorce
alimony

Review

1. Describe some state laws regulating marriage.
2. How does the state protect children?
3. What is the difference between separation and divorce?

Discuss

What do you think are the obligations that each family member has to the other members of the family?

3

Your Family and You

The family continues to be the most important group in American society. It is the foundation upon which our nation is built. Regardless of whether a person's family is large or small, rich or poor, it performs many important functions for its members and for the nation.

The Family Serves the Nation

There are about 60 million families in the United States. We depend on these families to teach children many of the responsibilities they will have to face as adults. What are some of the family's chief functions as it teaches us these responsibilities?

1. The family ensures the future of our nation. A country is only as strong as its people. The family helps keep the nation strong when it provides a home where children can be raised as securely and happily as possible.

2. The family educates its members. We learn many things from our families. It is in the home that children learn to walk, talk, and dress themselves. Families also teach us to get along with others and share in the work of the household.

3. The family teaches us the rules of good behavior. The child's earliest ideas of right and wrong are taught in the home. We learn how to behave from the other members of our family.

4. The family helps us manage our money. The family earns and spends money to provide food, clothing, and a place to live for its members. The family should encourage children to learn to manage money, save, and share financial responsibilities.

5. The family trains us to be good citizens. The family has the responsibility of helping children learn to respect the rights of others and understand what their responsibilities as useful citizens will be.

Good Citizenship at Home

Carrying out family functions requires work from everybody. A home is more than just four walls, a roof, floors, windows, and doors. Children soon learn that their home is a special place where the family lives together in safety, affection, and comfort. The word **home** means the familiar place that members of the same family share.

The relationship between older and younger brothers and sisters can be a learning experience for both—for learning patience, kindness, and cooperation.

The ideal home is loving and secure. However, no family can ever live up to the ideal all the time. Any group of people living together will disagree at times and need to find ways to solve their differences.

Using common sense and considering another person's viewpoint help prevent serious family trouble. Remember that each member of the family is a person worthy of respect. Each person has rights. If someone's rights are respected, that person is more likely to respect the rights of others in return.

The members of a well-adjusted family try to be sincerely interested in one another's activities. One good time to discuss everyone's daily activities is at the dinner table. Sharing problems and events of interest teaches family members to receive praise, advice, support, and criticism.

Solving Conflicts

Even family disagreements can benefit individual members. Arguments, if kept in hand, can teach you how to present your ideas effectively and help you understand the other person's point of view.

Compare this picture to the one on page 254. Obviously, it is still necessary—and often fun—for family members to work together to meet their needs.

Conflicts can occur between parents and children or among the children in a family. These disagreements require members of the family to make compromises, to give a little and take a little. One of the signs of a well-adjusted family is that members of the family are able to work together to find solutions to the irritating problems of everyday living before they grow into big, emotional crises.

By talking over ideas with members of the family, you learn to be understanding and patient. This is important in getting along with other people—friends, classmates, teachers, neighbors, and, later, workers.

The Problem of Family Funds

One problem many families have is deciding how to spend the family's money. Parents worry about earning enough money to pay for all the things the family wants. They are concerned about the best way to feed and clothe the family on their funds. The children in the family want money for school lunches, transportation, supplies for hobbies, tickets to school events or the movies, and many other things that seem important at the time.

There are just so many dollars to be divided among the different members of the family. When each person cannot have everything he or she wants, compromises must be worked out. Doing your share in handling family funds will help you to learn about spending and saving money. Learning to manage money now will be a valuable skill to you as an adult.

The Family Budget

Most families operate on some kind of a budget. The very thought of a budget scares some people. When they think of a budget, they picture a complicated bookkeeping system with column after column of figures. They also believe it usually means "pinching pennies" and denying good times to all members of the family.

A budget should not scare anyone. A budget is simply a plan for spending the family's money. In fact, if a budget is carefully planned and then put into action, it can reduce the family worries about money matters.

No one else can tell your family how to budget its money. They may make suggestions and explain a little about handling money. However, your family's own special interests and needs require that your family work out its own spending plan.

The first step is to gather facts. The next is to make a plan based on these facts and to cooperate in carrying it out. The starting point in all budgets is the total amount of money available to spend. Most families have a fixed amount of income. They must keep their spending within this income.

First on your budget would be certain **fixed expenses.** These are expenses that occur regularly and must be paid. There may be rent on an apartment or mortgage payments on a house. There is also the cost of food. This is one of the most important items in the budget. There may also be such regular payments as insurance and telephone bills. The remaining money could pay for clothing, medical expenses, amusements, and other items. You would probably want to set some money aside for savings. A plan would help you spend this money wisely.

Preparing for the Future

You can help your family follow its budget plan. One important way is to help prevent waste in your home. Try not to ask for things that upset the budget. Talk to your parents before you agree to do things that cost money. Do not insist upon doing things your family cannot afford.

If you receive a regular allowance or earn some money on your own, draw up your own budget. Decide how much you need for transportation, lunches, and other fixed expenses. Then, if you can, set aside some money for future expenses or emergencies.

Remember, too, that your home is the best place in which to learn about home management. Handling money is just one skill you will need for the future. By learning to get along with your family, you are preparing yourself for the day when you manage your own home.

CHECK-UP

Vocabulary
home
fixed expenses

Review
1. What are some of the functions the family performs?
2. Why is it important to respect the rights of other family members?
3. How can you help your family manage its finances?

Discuss
What are some ways you can try to be a good family member?

CHAPTER SUMMARY

The American family is the foundation on which our nation's future depends. It is the group in which young citizens learn valuable lessons that stay with them for the rest of their lives.

As our nation has changed, so has family life. We have changed from a nation of farm families who provided for many of their own needs to a nation of city dwellers who must buy most of the products they need. Families are smaller today. More women work outside the home, and there are many more elderly family members. In spite of these changes, many aspects of family life are the same.

To protect the family, states pass laws regulating marriage, divorce, and the rights of parents and children. The practice of family law has grown as the stress of modern life has caused family difficulties to increase. Among the problems that have arisen are divorce, nonsupport, and abuse.

Many solutions have been offered for keeping the family together. There may be no one answer. However, those who achieve a satisfactory family life work hard at it. You can help your family by cooperating, being willing to make compromises, and staying within the family budget.

CIVICS SKILLS: Using Television as a Resource

New York, 1929. *Engineers focus a camera on a statue of cartoon hero Felix the Cat. In Kansas other engineers see a face flicker on a tiny screen called a viewer. It's Felix—America's first television star.*

The Moon, 1969. *A camera outside the lunar capsule sends pictures back to earth. Over 500 million people all over the world hold their breath as U.S. astronaut Neil Armstrong steps onto the moon. It's the most exciting show in television history.*

In the 40 years between these two events, television became the nation's main source of news and entertainment. Today you can sit in the comfort of your home and watch anything from a football game to the latest American space flight. If it's news, television can bring it to you—live and in color.

Because so much of our news comes from television, you must learn to watch it with a critical eye. Luckily most news programs follow definite formats. Once you become familiar with these, it will be easier for you to interpret what you see and hear.

Watching the Evening News

The regularly scheduled news programs that are shown each evening are set up like a newspaper. The opening stories are the headline news, or the most important events of the day. In this portion of the program, you are given the hard facts, along with film clips and on-the-spot reports. Each story lasts only about 90 seconds. That means someone has carefully chosen both the pictures and the words. How might such decisions affect news coverage?

After the straight news come the **features.** These are human-interest stories, meant to amuse or entertain you. Often they appeal more to your emotions than your mind. A feature, for example, might be about a brave dog that rescued its owner. What other topics might make interesting features?

Sports and weather reports usually close a news program. In some cases, however, the last report might be a **commentary.** This is a television journalist's own interpretation of an event or issue. The commentary, like a newspaper editorial, is only one view of the facts. There could be others—including your own.

News Magazines and Documentaries

In addition to the evening news, there are many other types of news programs. The most popular are news magazines and documentaries. Both bring issues to the attention of the American people. A **news magazine** usually studies several issues in one program. Sometimes it also presents features. A **documentary** always focuses on a single issue or topic for the entire show. In each instance, journalists try to report all sides of an issue fairly. Why might such programs influence public opinion?

Practicing What You've Learned

Use the television schedule on this page to answer the following questions.

1. On which programs would you expect to find a report on the arrival of a foreign official in the United States?
2. Which programs are examples of news magazines? of documentaries?

7:00 (2,4,7) **NEWS**
(5) **P.M. MAGAZINE:** A look at the upcoming space shuttle flight.
(9) **SCIENCE WATCH:** "Life Under the Seven Seas."

8:00 (2) **60 MINUTES:** Includes segments about the volunteer army, economic growth in the Southwest, and a cross-country bicycle trip.
(4) **CHARLIE BROWN SPECIAL:** "The Great Pumpkin."
(7) **NFL FOOTBALL:** Oakland Raiders vs. Minnesota Vikings.
(9) **CIRCUIT 11 MIAMI:** Profile of circuit court judge.
(13) **AROUND THE WORLD:** An in-depth study of recent oil discoveries in Mexico.

CHAPTER REVIEW

Vocabulary

Study the following pairs of words. Tell how the words in each pair are related and how they are different.

institutions	—	family
farm family	—	city family
waiting period	—	blood test
separation	—	divorce
foster home	—	guardian

Check-Up

1. What do you think is a good definition of the word "family"?
2. Compare traditional American farm life with modern city life. How are they alike? How are they different?
3. What influences besides the family have become important for children today?
4. What problems have been placing stress on American families? What solutions are being tried?
5. What are some of the laws that protect American families?
6. Why do most states have a waiting period between the time a couple applies for a marriage license and the time the license is issued?
7. What are some of the possible solutions to the problem of divorce?
8. Name five ways in which the family serves the nation.
9. What are some of the ways in which we can practice good citizenship at home?
10. How does a budget help in the management of a family's income?
11. How can each member of the family help in managing the family budget?

Civics Skills

Prepare a written report on a television news program that is regularly broadcast each evening. The following questions will help you take notes on the show.

1. What were the program's news stories? its features?
2. How much time was devoted to sports and weather?
3. Did the program include a commentary? If so, what was the subject?
4. In your opinion, were all stories reported fairly? Explain.

Citizenship and You

1. The United States Bureau of Labor Statistics has worked out tables for family budgets. Here is the table for an urban family of four with a yearly income of about $20,000.

Food	24.6%
Housing	22.4%
Transportation	9.0%
Clothing and Personal Care	8.1%
Medical Care	5.7%
Other Family Needs	9.3%
Social Security and Taxes	20.9%

   On the class chalkboard, work out a monthly budget for this family. Show approximately how much may be spent for each item.
2. A bulletin board committee may prepare a display of photographs, drawings, and news stories called "Good Citizenship Begins at Home."
3. Reading committees can read and report on such topics as "Famous American Families," "Poems and Songs About Home," and "Family Life in Other Lands."
4. Write an essay entitled either "The Ideal Family" or "My Home in 1990."
5. Form an interview committee to talk with religious leaders, marriage counselors, judges, and police officers. Ask this question: "How Can Home Life Be Improved in Our Community?" Report on these interviews to the class.

CHAPTER

14

Citizenship in School

A senator of the United States is preparing a speech. A surgeon is about to begin an operation. An auto mechanic is preparing to repair a sports car. What do these people have in common? They are about to show the practical effects of their education.

If they have really profited from their education, the senator will make an effective speech, the surgeon may save a life, and the auto mechanic will keep the car running safely and smoothly.

The future of our nation depends, in large part, on our system of education and the way it affects citizens. America's schools and colleges must help train our citizens to meet the challenges of a complicated, rapidly changing world.

Today almost every occupation requires some special training. The progress our nation must make in science, social science, engineering, and technology depends upon a supply of well-educated persons prepared to contribute to these fields. The way to success in every occupation is through study, training, and hard work. This is true whether the job is selling, nursing, carpentry, medicine, law, or banking.

In this chapter, you will study about America's schools and the opportunities they offer you. You will also consider the best ways to make use of your school years as you study these topics:

1. **The American School System**
2. **The Best Education for You**
3. **Developing Skills in Thinking**

1
The American School System

There are about 60 million students enrolled in public and private schools and colleges in the United States. The cost of running these educational enterprises in the early 1980's was over $150 billion a year. About 3.3 million teachers are engaged in the day-by-day tasks of education. Why are the people of the United States willing to put all this money and effort into education?

The Purposes of Education

The American people are proud of the progress and achievements of their educational system. There are two main reasons for this great interest in education.

1. Schools exist to aid in the development of each individual American citizen. From the earliest days of our nation, Americans have placed great value on the individual. The first purpose of education is, therefore, to serve the individual. All citizens should be given the opportunity to study and learn in order to develop their talents and abilities.

The Declaration of Independence sets forth the American belief "that all men [and women] are created equal; that they are endowed by their Creator with certain unalienable rights; that among these are life, liberty, and the pursuit of happiness." Americans believe that all citizens should be given equal chances, through education, to make the most of their abilities.

2. Schools aid in the development of the American nation. The welfare of all Americans depends on the willingness and ability of all individuals to use their talents for the welfare of the entire nation. The aim of education is to teach Americans how to make important contributions to our society.

Education stresses the need for good citizenship. Our schools try to show how the welfare of each citizen and the welfare of the nation depend on all Americans learning to work together for the common good.

Beginnings of Our School System

The present American system of education has been growing for over 300 years. The first important step was taken in Massachusetts in 1647. A law was passed there requiring all towns except very small ones to set up schools.

The purpose of this law was to make sure all children learned to read the Bible, so that they would not fall into evil ways. This law provided for every town of 50 families or more to hire a schoolteacher, who would be paid out of town funds. By doing this, Massachusetts shifted the responsibility for schooling from the home to the community as a whole.

In many of the other colonies, however, education of the young was neglected. Children of the wealthy were sent to private schools or taught by tutors. In contrast, children of poor parents often were put to work at an early age and given little or no schooling.

It was not until the first half of the 1800's that leaders such as Horace Mann began to

Artist Winslow Homer shows us what an American country school looked like more than a hundred years ago. Students of different ages all studied in the same room.

demand free public schools for all children. The gradually developing public school system, however, did not include black Americans. Many of them were slaves, and very few received an education.

Many Americans in those days were opposed to free public schools. Some taxpayers thought it was unfair to make them pay for the education of other people's children. Owners of private schools claimed that free public schools would ruin their business. Some church-supported schools claimed that education should be under the control of the church and the home.

By the time of the Civil War, the struggle for public, or free, tax-supported schools was beginning to be won. Most Northern states and a number of Southern states had set up public school systems. However, these school systems were usually limited to elementary schools, known as common schools. There were only 55 public high schools in the whole United States in 1850. It was not until the period after the Civil War that a system of public secondary schools, or high schools, began to be set up in our states.

The Educational Ladder

Most Americans spend a large part of their lives getting an education. There are several levels in the American system of education. Our schools range from nursery schools for young children to universities for adult higher education.

Nursery Schools. Many American children attend nursery school. The nursery school is usually attended by children three and four years of age. In these schools, children learn to play and get along with other children. Most nursery schools are private. However, some American communities support nursery schools as part of their public school system. The federal government also grants funds for preschool programs in some communities.

Kindergartens. Many public school systems start with kindergarten classes for five-year-old children. The word "kindergarten" is German and means "garden for children." Kindergarten children spend a year learning how to get along with others and preparing for first grade. In some areas, they begin learning to read and write and recognize numbers.

Elementary Schools. Most children enter the first grade of elementary school at the age of five or six. In elementary school they are taught the basics of education—reading, writing, and arithmetic. The curriculum is also enriched by such subjects as history, geography, science, health, art, music, and physical education. Children attend elementary school for from five to nine years, depending upon how the school system is arranged.

Junior High Schools. Grades 7, 8, and 9 usually make up the junior high school. Some school systems have given up junior high schools in favor of middle, or intermediate, schools. **Middle schools** usually include grades 5 or 6 through 8. Some are only for grades 7 and 8.

High Schools. Students who have completed the first eight or nine grades enter high school. There are generally three kinds of high schools. Academic high schools prepare students for college. Technical and vocational high schools enable students to learn a trade or occupation. Comprehensive high schools offer college preparatory work as well as vocational courses. About 85 percent of all American girls and boys ages 14 through 17 are enrolled in public high schools.

Higher Education

The need for higher education in the United States has grown with advances in knowledge. Many jobs now require college and university training. Therefore, many high school students feel it is important that they continue their education.

Junior Colleges. The growing demand for higher education is being met in part by two-year junior colleges. These schools are sometimes called **community colleges.** They are often supported by taxpayers and offer courses free or at low tuition to local high school graduates. Courses include training for

Our Local School Districts

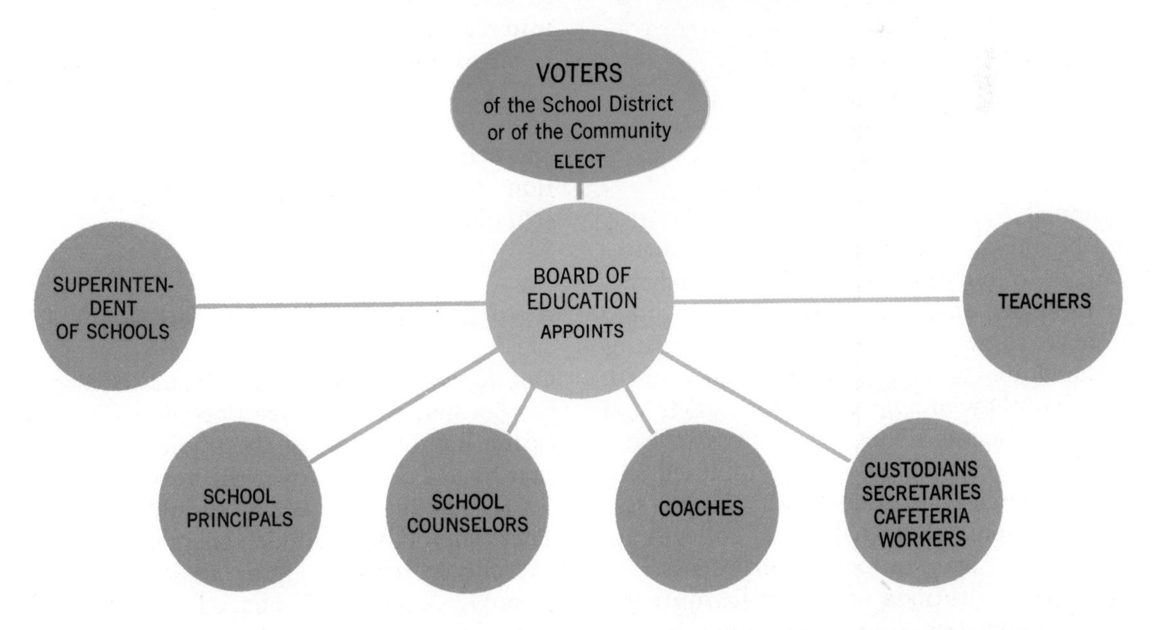

School districts are special units of local government. In some states, however, schools are dependent upon city, town, or county government. Local school boards are usually elected, but are appointed in some cities and counties.

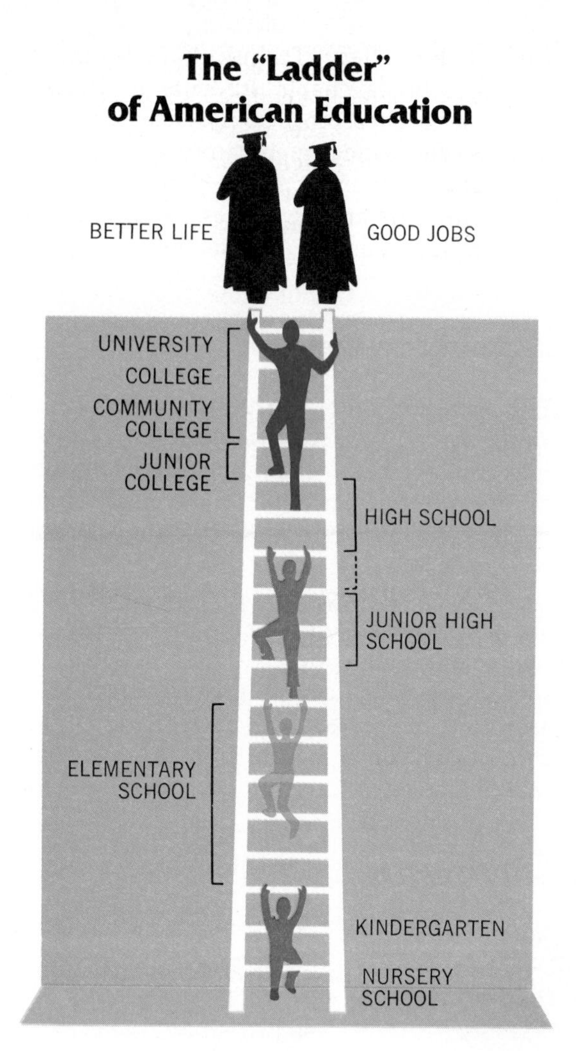

technical fields, forestry, home economics, and business. Many junior college graduates transfer to four-year colleges or universities.

Colleges and Universities. Altogether there are some 2,800 colleges and universities in the United States. Most are coeducational. That is, they are open to both men and women students. They range in size from small **colleges** with only a few hundred students to large institutions with 100,000 students or more. About half of all colleges are supported by state or local governments.

Some institutions of higher learning are called universities. A **university** includes one or more colleges as well as graduate programs in some professional field of learning, such as business, medicine, and law. A university also provides advanced studies in most subjects offered in college, including history and biology. After graduation from college, the student may go on to **graduate school** to study for an advanced degree.

Recently, many older Americans have gone back to school to earn their college or advanced degrees. Others are taking special courses at night. Among these older students are women whose children have grown up, retired people, or adults who have decided to change careers.

Special Education

Americans believe in equal opportunities for all citizens. They have therefore set up special schools and classes for the physically handicapped. In addition, there are schools for emotionally disturbed children and retarded children. Some communities also provide special educational opportunities for gifted children. In recent years, the trend has been to place children from special schools back into regular schools and classes. This practice is called **mainstreaming.**

There are also programs for adults who wish to extend their education or make up education they missed. These adult education classes are usually held at night at high schools or community colleges.

American Values in Education

Our school system has developed the way it has because the American people value education highly. Some of the traditional values that have developed over the years are:

1. Public education should be free. There should be no hidden charges to prevent any citizen from receiving a good education at public expense. Public education in the United States costs local taxpayers well over $124 billion a year. This amount includes educational expenditures by the federal government of about $13 billion.

2. Schooling should be equal and open to all. No one should be discriminated against because of race, religion, or financial status.

3. Public schools should be free of any creed or religion. The schools of the United States are open to all Americans regardless of their religious beliefs. The Supreme Court has held that no special prayer or Bible reading shall be required during the school day. However, private religious schools (sometimes called parochial schools) are permitted to exist outside the public school system.

4. Public schools should be controlled by the state and local governments within which they are located. Local school boards run the public schools under laws passed by the state legislature. State boards or departments of education assist local schools but do not give orders to district boards. Actual control of the schools rests with the local school district, where the people know what the local needs are.

5. Attendance at school should be compulsory. Each state compels school attendance by young people, usually between the ages of 7 and 16. Parents may not decide to keep their children out of school.

6. Schooling should be enriching and not limited to the basics. Schools should be places where young people can grow in mind, body, and spirit. Sports, clubs, social events, and creative arts are a part of each person's education. Schools should be lively places where individuals are encouraged to develop to their greatest potential.

Problems of Today's School System

The American school system faces certain problems today. As you recall, the Supreme Court ruled in 1954 that students do not receive equal educational opportunities when they attend public schools in which they are segregated, or separated, according to race. This ruling sometimes has led to bitter controversy. The best way to integrate our nation's school systems and provide equal

School and College Enrollment

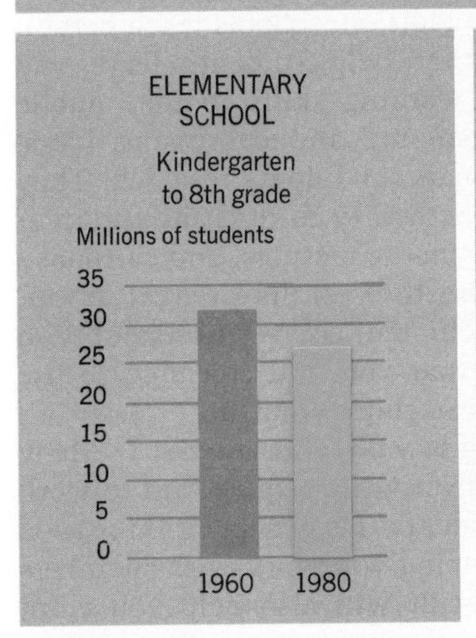

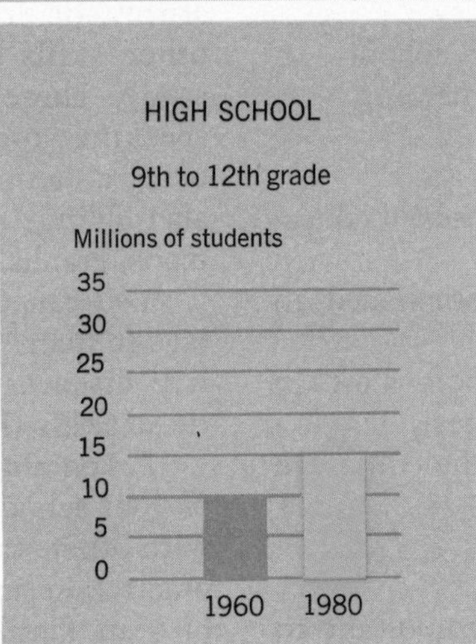

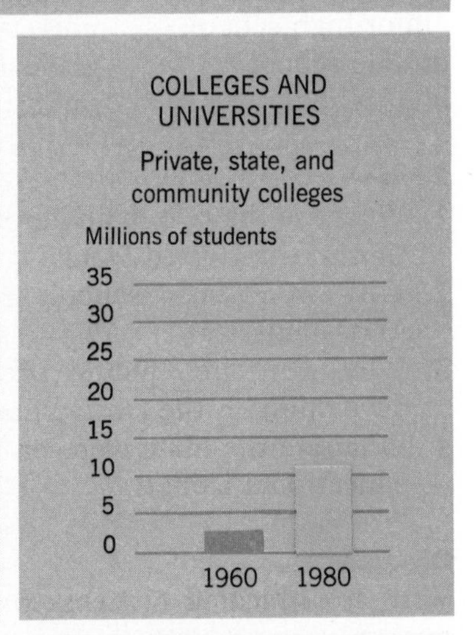

SOURCE: United States Department of Commerce, Bureau of the Census.

educational opportunities is a question that has not yet been resolved.

Busing of students to achieve integration has been tried in some areas of the country. In some places, it has worked well. In other places, parents and students prefer neighborhood schools.

There are other important problems that challenge America's schools. Many of them are caused by lack of money. Some school systems need to improve their buildings. They also need modern classroom equipment and other aids to learning. A number of schools have found it difficult to keep their buildings in good condition because of the increase in vandalism. Vandalism is the willful destruction of property. Maintaining discipline in the classroom is another problem that many school systems have faced in the 1970's and 1980's.

Such problems must be solved if our educational system is to serve Americans well in the future.

CHECK-UP

Vocabulary

nursery school	junior college
kindergarten	community college
elementary school	college
junior high school	university
middle school	graduate school
high school	mainstreaming

Review

1. What are the two main purposes of education in the United States?
2. Why were early schools established in Massachusetts?
3. Why were free public schools slow in developing in the United States?
4. What are the main steps on the American educational ladder?

Discuss

Why are educated citizens so important to our American system of government?

2

The Best Education for You

Luck has been defined as being in the right place at the right time. What we sometimes forget to add is that the lucky person is also able to see opportunities and make good use of them. This is true in school and in studying, too. You must be alert in order to take advantage of the opportunities offered in school. What are these opportunities?

What Your School Has to Offer You

Some years ago, a group of teachers and school officials listed the goals of education that American schools should try to achieve. The statement they prepared is called "The Seven Cardinal Principles of Secondary Education." As you study these goals, or principles, try to think how your school works to achieve them. Ask yourself if you are taking advantage of the opportunities offered under each heading.

1. Using basic learning skills. One of the main goals of our schools is to teach each student the skills of reading, writing, and arithmetic. In addition, schools teach certain other skills that help students learn and study. These learning skills include public speaking, organizing and expressing ideas, using a dictionary, and doing research. They also include the ability to read and interpret maps, graphs, charts, pictures, and cartoons.

You can use these skills to great advantage in many different courses in school. You will discover that you will continue to use these skills throughout your life.

2. Learning to work with others. Many of your school activities require you to work with other students. This cooperation is good practice in helping you work with members of your family. It will also help you work with other people in your community. Furthermore, your experience in working with others will be very useful when you have a job.

3. Health education. Most schools have a program in health education to teach students to develop good health habits. Health education usually also offers programs of physical activities, including sports and athletics. You will benefit from the exercise these programs provide. Moreover, the theory and practice learned in school will help you take good care of your health and keep physically fit throughout your life.

4. Training for your life's work. Your school provides the educational foundation on which special job training may be based. Your school also tries to help you prepare for job opportunities after you graduate. Employers want well-educated workers. Schools make it possible for you to become a desirable employee. By taking advantage of your education, you can prepare for a job in which you can both contribute to your nation and find satisfaction.

5. Active citizenship. To help you to become a good citizen, your school seeks to develop your interest in your community. It teaches you about the history of your nation, its institutions, and the problems it faces today. Your classes and school activities help develop in you a sense of loyalty, love of country, good judgment, and willingness to do your share.

6. Considerate behavior. Your school tries to teach students to adapt to accepted standards of behavior. It tries to develop in all students a feeling of consideration for their parents, teachers, classmates, friends, and all members of the community. It stresses, too, the importance of respecting the property of others.

7. Wise use of leisure time. Your school tries to teach you to enjoy good books, art, and music so that they may enrich your life. Your teachers encourage you to take up interesting hobbies and take part in such school activities as athletics, dramatics, glee club, or band.

By encouraging you to undertake such activities, your school is trying to help you to find a hobby or special interest to enjoy now and in the future. In this way, your school helps prepare you to make good use of your spare time throughout your lifetime.

Getting the Most Out of School

If you are to make the best use of the opportunities your school offers, you will need to remember the goals your school is trying to reach. Your years in school are very important. The success you enjoy in school and the study and learning habits you develop will help determine the kind of person you will be later in life. What kinds of study and learning habits should you try to develop?

One of the first and most important study habits all students must learn is the wise use of time. The well-organized student finds time in his or her daily schedule for study, school activities, exercise, relaxation, and the proper amount of sleep. Just as your family

(continued on page 274)

Many school courses have direct application to jobs in the working world. Here a student in a woodworking class develops skill in operating a cutting machine.

Senior Volunteers

Ruth Givens teaches French. Charles Wauneka teaches mathematics. Anna Chavez helps Spanish-speaking children learn English. These jobs aren't unusual—but the people who do them are. All three are retired people who work each week as volunteers in the public schools of Houston, Texas. No one pays them. They work for fun and because they enjoy helping others.

VIPS–SENIORS

None of these three volunteers had ever taught before joining Houston's VIPS–SENIORS progam. VIPS stands for Volunteers in Public Schools. The program is run by the Houston Independent School District. The SENIORS part of the program has drawn more than 1,000 older citizens. Its aim is to encourage retired people to share their skills with students and thereby to become more involved in their communities.

Ruth Givens is a grandmother who loves French. While raising her own children, she had studied French in her free time. Now she helps others learn to speak French. Ruth tutors seventh graders in French in a middle school.

Charles Wauneka is a retired sales executive. He works two days a week helping to teach math in an elementary school. At first Charles thought he would have difficulty explaining the importance of numbers to young students. Soon, though, he found that teaching mathematics "is more personally rewarding than anything I have ever done."

Anna Chavez retired from a job in a food-processing plant. Now, as a full-time school volunteer, she uses her ability to speak both Spanish and English fluently. Anna's goal is to encourage young people to learn. She regrets that she did not discover her love for teaching earlier. However, she says that "now I can give the students the time they need."

Time for Success

VIPS–SENIORS began in 1976 with a grant—money donated for a special project. The program was so successful that when the grant ran out, Houston businesses and foundations contributed money so that the project could continue.

Time given to individual students is the key to the VIPS–SENIORS success, says one teacher in the program. "Who but senior volunteers can give a student two hours of undivided attention each week?"

Volunteers choose the hours they want to work and the kind of work they prefer. In addition to tutoring, volunteers work in school libraries, cafeterias, and offices. If they prefer, they can serve as "living historians." These volunteers are interviewed by students three times a year—usually about life in their childhood communities or about some special period or event in their lives.

Many volunteers end up doing more than they planned. Some have given slide shows or put together cultural programs. A number of volunteers have gone back to college to become teachers. As one retired volunteer said, "After I realized how much I enjoyed teaching, I decided to become better prepared."

Thinking It Over

1. Why do you think the Houston school district wanted to use older citizens in its volunteer program?
2. What benefits might a retired person receive from being a school volunteer?
3. Why might a student want to interview a "living historian"?

Retired people also volunteer their time to help other senior citizens.

budgets its money, you will find it wise to budget your time. Work out a daily schedule for your more important activities, and form the habit of getting things done on time.

How to Study

Study your schoolwork with care and concentration. Choose a regular place to study. If possible, select a place that is quiet and has good working space and proper light. Keep the materials you need close at hand.

Take notes on your reading. You will soon find that writing down important ideas will help you understand and fix these ideas in your mind. Make sure you understand your assignment before you start. Then determine to do the best job you can.

Your textbooks are written to help you learn quickly and efficiently. Here are some useful hints to help you get the most from your textbooks.

1. Learn how to use the **study aids** in the book. Refer to the table of contents, index, glossary, maps, charts, picture captions, and any material that might be in the back of the book.

2. Note the chapter title and the section headings and other subheadings within the chapter. They give you clues to the most important ideas.

3. Read through the assignment carefully, noting topic sentences and summarizing paragraphs.

4. Reread the assignment. This time make written notes on the important ideas and facts.

5. Turn to the questions at the end of each section of the chapter, and see if you can answer each one. If you find a question you cannot answer, turn back to the page in your textbook where the subject is discussed, and find the correct answer.

6. Some people find using a card file helpful. They build up a file containing defini-

School includes the chance for a variety of extracurricular activities. Taking part in the school band is one way for students to develop their individual talents.

CAN YOU GUESS?

- **What was the first college founded in the United States?**
- **What was the nation's first coeducational college—a college accepting women on an equal basis with men?**
- **What was the first college for women founded in the United States?**

Answers are on page 562.

tions, formulas, important facts, and answers to key questions. These cards are especially good for review when preparing for a test.

Taking Part in Classwork

When you come to class, bring the material you will need in order to take an active part in the day's lesson. Pay careful attention to what is being taught in class. Think about the lesson. Do not be afraid to ask questions. Learn to form your own ideas and opinions. If you fall behind or fail to understand part of a lesson, ask for help.

If you come to class unprepared, you are hurting yourself and your classmates, who will not benefit from what you might have contributed. A class is like any group that depends on each member to function at its best. The group performs well when everyone does his or her part. The failure of one person to carry out a responsibility deprives the others of information and the satisfaction of working together for a common purpose.

How to Do Well on Tests

When the time comes for a test, go over your notes carefully. Some students find it helpful to have other members of the class ask them questions that might appear on the test. This helps them discover whether they really know the material. They want to find out what information they need to review more carefully.

When taking the test, it is a good idea to read each question carefully before attempting to answer it. Look over the entire test before beginning to see how many questions there are and how much time should be spent on each. If there is time left at the end of the test period, reread your answers. Also check carefully to see that you have answered each question.

Taking Part in School Activities

School is more than classes, homework, tests, and class projects. School clubs, choir, band, sports teams, cheerleading, dances, and social events are also part of your education. These **extracurricular activities,** in which you take part in addition to classes, can teach you a great deal. You may learn interesting skills or new ways to express yourself. You may also make new friends.

Extracurricular activities add to your fun in school. At the same time, they help you develop your own special abilities and interests. Some students are satisfied merely to "get by" in school. These students forget that they are cheating themselves.

CHECK-UP

Vocabulary

study aids
extracurricular activities

Review

1. List the seven goals of education.
2. What good study habits are suggested in this chapter?
3. What are some ways to prepare for tests?

Discuss

Which learning habits that you have developed during your school years will be most helpful to you in the future?

3

Developing Skills in Thinking

One of the main purposes of education is to help people learn how to think. The dictionary tells us that to think is to form ideas in the mind. This sounds simple enough, but how do we form these ideas? We think mainly with facts. When faced with a problem, thinking people consider all the facts they know. They then consider all possible solutions and decide which solution seems best to them. How do we obtain the facts with which we do our thinking? We learn them.

How We Learn

Almost everything we do—the way we act, think, pass along information, even the way we show emotion—is learned. People learn in many ways. However, all learning is the result of some kind of **experience,** or things that happened in the past.

The simplest kind of learning is the result of experience that involves the motor nerves—those nerves that control our muscles. For example, a person who touches a hot stove will pull back the hand because of the pain. Next time, that person will avoid hot stoves. Now suppose that while the person was reaching for the stove, someone said "Hot!" in a sharp tone. In the future, if near a hot stove, the person will draw back a hand whenever someone says "Hot!" This kind of learning is called **conditioning.**

Much of our behavior, or the way we act, is conditioned. People learn to do things because they expect to be rewarded or to gain satisfaction. Children will wash their hands before meals if they expect praise or a hug. They will continue to behave in the desired way if they are rewarded occasionally. Behavior that is repeated often usually becomes a **habit**—an action performed automatically.

People also learn by copying, or imitating, others. Young children imitate their parents and other members of the family. They try to act and think like them. They repeat their parents' opinions and habits. As adults, people often imitate their friends and others they admire.

Learning in School

Much of what we know is also learned by looking and listening. Every day of our lives we learn through our senses and take in different kinds of information. However, in our complex society, there is so much information that it has to be organized, or arranged in groups, in order to be usable. A large part of the organized information we learn is taught in school and in books.

Besides facts, schools teach students how to make the best use of information by comparing and analyzing facts, putting the facts together, and drawing conclusions. We also are taught where to find information.

Our ability to learn depends on our maturity, experience, and intelligence. It also depends on how highly motivated we are. **Motivation** is something within people that stirs them and directs their behavior.

How We Think

Thinking is a complex process. It involves our awareness, understanding, and interpretation of what we see and know. We are thinking when we solve problems by considering all the solutions we know. Every time we make a decision, we solve a problem.

Sometimes we try to find an answer to something and cannot come up with it, no matter how hard we try. Then, suddenly, the answer will spring to mind. This is called **insight.** The answer seems to come out of nowhere. Actually, it comes to mind only after we have studied the problem and ruled out several possible answers. Without realizing it, people often take what they know about something else and apply it to the subject they are studying.

Occasionally our solutions are original. The ability to find new ways of thinking and doing things is called **creativity.** Everyone can think creatively. We have other thinking abilities, too. Our abilities to reason, question, and weigh information are ways of thinking.

Critical Thinking

The kind of thinking we do in order to reach decisions and solve problems is called **critical thinking.** This type of reasoning, or clear thinking, includes a number of different steps. There is no simple way to learn the truth about an issue or solve a problem. The search for truth on many subjects is long and hard. Yet all Americans must seek answers to problems that face us and our nation every day. How can we learn to think clearly in order to make up our minds?

Defining the Problem. The first step is to make sure that the problem or question is clear in your mind. That is, you need to make certain that you fully understand it and any terms which might be involved. You may find it helpful to write down the problem to which you wish to find the answer. If it is a difficult one, you might outline the main ideas. See if you can find the relationships between the ideas. Are some ideas causes and others effects?

Distinguishing Fact from Opinion. Once the problem is clear to you, you can look for evidence that will help you understand and judge the issues involved. What are the facts? It may surprise you to discover that there are often disagreements over facts. One side may say one thing, and the other side may claim something very different. Therefore, it is important in critical thinking always to distinguish between fact and personal opinion, or judgment.

To illustrate how difficult it is to determine what is fact, let us look at the following

The successful study of science requires skill in critical thinking, including keen observation, careful analysis, and systematic reasoning.

CIVICS SKILLS: Distinguishing Fact from Opinion

- *The Dallas Cowboys are a football team.*
- *The Dallas Cowboys are the best football team in the league.*
- *The Dallas Cowboys will win this year's Super Bowl.*

If you're a Cowboys fan, you might agree with all three of the above statements. But suppose you support the Miami Dolphins or the Los Angeles Rams. Would your reaction be the same? If you're like most loyal fans, you'd probably have a lot to say about the last two statements. They are both matters of opinion, or personal judgment. Only the first statement cannot be challenged. It is a fact.

Facts, as you know, can always be proved true. They can be counted, measured, or documented in some way. Opinions are what people believe or think. Because people often use facts to back up their opinions, it is important to learn how to separate the two. You will then be better able to evaluate the information you read or hear every day.

Distinguishing the Facts

You can begin to identify facts by asking the same questions a reporter uses to write a good news story. If a statement answers the questions who, what, when, where, why, or how, it probably contains facts. Look at the campaign flier, or political advertisement, on this page. What are its facts?

Your next step is to determine how the facts are used. A single word can often change a sentence from fact to opinion. Certain phrases, such as "In our judgment . . ." or "We believe that . . .," clearly signal that an opinion is coming. Other words, however, are less obvious and may slip by you. These are loaded words, or words that carry an emotional appeal.

You come across loaded words all the time—*beautiful, boring, exciting*. The minute you spot such descriptive words, you've found an opinion. Read this statement taken from the campaign flier below. Janice Green "is a dedicated educator who has served successfully on the school board for more than 12 years." What are the sentence's loaded words? How might they affect your interpretation of the facts?

Practicing What You've Learned

1. Imagine you are a reporter for your local newspaper. What facts from the flier would you include in your news story? (Remember, reporters state facts, not opinions.)
2. Use these facts to write an editorial supporting Green.

JANICE GREEN
FOR CITY COUNCIL

Janice Green is determined to improve our city. If elected Green will:

- increase the number of buses running during rush hour. Thirty percent of public buses do not run during rush hour.
- ensure that our city taxes are reasonable. Over the past ten years, city taxes have been increased six times.
- add to and improve facilities for the elderly. At present, there are over 100 persons waiting to take part in this city's programs for the elderly.

Janice Green knows our city well. She is a dedicated educator who has served successfully on the school board for more than 12 years.

Elect ***JANICE GREEN***. She will make this a better city in which to live.

CHAPTER REVIEW

Vocabulary

Below is a list of words that appear in this chapter. Copy these words in the vocabulary section of your notebook. Beside each word write a sentence to show its meaning.

kindergarten	experience
university	conditioning
college	habit
mainstreaming	prejudices
study aids	insight

Check-Up

1. What are some of the traditional values in American education?
2. What are some of the problems facing the American school system today?
3. Why is active citizenship considered one of the major aims of the American educational system?
4. Why is it important for students to budget their time?
5. Why is it a good idea to take notes on what you read?
6. Tell why maps and charts are especially useful as study aids.
7. Why are extracurricular activities included in the school program?
8. What are some of the ways in which we learn?
9. Why are facts important when you are trying to form judgments?
10. What are some of the outside influences that affect our opinions?
11. Why are your school years important to your future?

Civics Skills

Read the paragraph below. Then answer the questions that follows.

"Americans are better educated today than ever before. According to the 1980 census, nearly 70 percent of all people over age 25 have high school diplomas. An impressive 17 percent hold college degrees. To set even higher records, I think each state should require students to attend school until they reach the age of 25."

1. Which sentences are statements of opinion? Which are statements of fact?
2. What are the loaded words in the paragraph?
3. In 1970 the census showed that 55.2 percent of Americans over age 25 had finished high school, while 11 percent had completed college. Using these two facts and the ones in the paragraph above, write a news story about education in the United States.

Citizenship and You

1. Participate in a class debate on this topic: *Resolved,* That schools should try to teach us a wise use of leisure time.
2. A small group may interview school officials, parents, and local business people to gather their opinions on the importance of education. Quotations from these persons may be put on a chart entitled "What the Public Thinks of Our Schools."
3. Read a book about American education and write a report about the ideas presented in the book.
4. Draw a cartoon to illustrate the importance of critical thinking.
5. Make a time budget, or schedule, for your day. Include in your schedule a regular time for study, recreation, meals, travel, work, household tasks, and sleep. Try to follow this schedule and see if it helps you to improve your study habits.
6. Prepare a report on the development and growth of free public education in the United States.

CHAPTER 15

Citizenship in the Community

There are very few people in the world who do not enjoy being with other people. Most people find life easier and more interesting when they can share it with others. We also need other people to provide us with goods and services that we cannot provide for ourselves.

The early settlers in America found that their lives were easier if they settled near other people. They often depended on their neighbors for help or protection. Working together was an absolute necessity. Building a barn or harvesting crops often required help from others. Moreover, social affairs were more enjoyable when neighbors got together to have fun.

Ever since America began—and indeed, ever since the beginning of human history—people have lived and worked together. Long ago, people created an institution known as the community. Like the institution of the family, which you studied in Chapter 13, the community plays a vital part in American society.

By **community,** we mean a group of people, having common interests, who live in the same area and are governed by the same laws. The people in a rural area, small town, or city neighborhood are members of a community. In this chapter, you will learn about community citizenship as you study these topics:

1. **Many Kinds of Communities**
2. **Communities Have Many Purposes**
3. **Citizens Serve Communities**

1
Many Kinds of Communities

From the beginning, American settlers tried to pick out locations that had natural advantages for their settlements. Farmers were attracted to the fertile river valleys and later to the plains. Those interested in commerce knew that a place with a good harbor would help them build a prosperous trade. A natural dam site along a river would provide power for factories. A bend in the river provided a good landing place for riverboats. Even today a warm sunny climate, beautiful sandy beaches, or snowcapped mountains may encourage the growth of a tourist center or retirement community.

Crossroads Settlements

As American settlers moved farther inland, they often settled where two main roads crossed. A **crossroads** was generally a good place to sell supplies to travelers. An enterprising settler built an inn at the crossroads. A blacksmith found business there shoeing horses and repairing wagons. Farmers came to this small settlement to trade. In time the crossroads settlement grew and became a thriving city.

Transportation Centers

Our young nation depended largely on boats for transportation. The location of America's waterways therefore helped determine the location of our cities. The largest cities in the American colonies were deep-water ports on the Atlantic coast. Boston, New York, Philadelphia, and Charleston were such cities.

Most of our large inland cities grew up at lake ports or along major rivers. St. Paul and Minneapolis, for example, are located at easy-to-reach stopping points on the upper Mississippi River. New Orleans prospered because it was at the mouth of the Mississippi River. Goods coming down the river were reloaded onto oceangoing vessels at the port of New Orleans. These cities became important **transportation centers** because of their location on major bodies of water.

The coming of the railroad also helped our cities grow. After 1840 railroad lines were built to connect various parts of our nation. They soon contributed to the further growth of our towns and cities. Railroads also created new cities. Inland cities that were not on rivers or lakes grew up as railroads provided a new and speedy method of transportation. Indianapolis, Dallas, and Denver grew prosperous because they were located along busy railroad lines.

Today Americans depend heavily on automobiles for transportation. New communities have grown up along our highways. In the open countryside, land is less expensive than in the city. For that reason, families can more easily afford to live there. On this land, new industrial plants have been built that do not have to be near railroad or water transportation. Trucks carry goods to and from them over modern highways. New communities have grown up around these plants to house the workers and provide services for them.

Resources and Climate Help Communities Grow

The United States is a nation with rich natural resources. It has a temperate climate in which vigorous activity is possible. Its broad, navigable lakes and rivers and long coastline, as you have read, furnish many good ports and harbors. Our nation also has vast stretches of fertile soil, enough rainfall, good pasture land, and abundant forests. Beneath the soil are rich deposits of metal ores, petroleum, coal, and uranium.

Climate and natural resources have aided the growth of many American communities. Duluth, Minnesota, for example, is a port on Lake Superior. It owes much of its growth to the great iron deposits located nearby in the Mesabi Range.

Our nation still has many rural communities, like this one in the Green Mountains of Vermont. In fact, some rural communities have been growing larger.

As you read in Chapter 1, communities in the South and West, called the Sunbelt, have been growing rapidly. For example, one of the fastest growing areas of the country is the Texas Gulf Coast region. Its warm climate and growing number of industries have attracted large numbers of people from other parts of the United States.

Southern California's pleasant climate also has attracted large numbers of people. Not only is the California climate pleasant, it is favorable too for growing a wide variety of crops.

Many New England communities were settled near waterfalls. The early textile mills needed water power to turn machines that spun thread and wove cloth. Many settlers in the Middle West moved there because of the rich, fertile soil—one of nature's most important resources.

America's Rural Communities

As you read in Chapter 1, a **rural area** is a region of farms and small towns. If you traveled along our nation's highways, you would see many different kinds of rural communities. One way to classify these communities is by their size. Another way is to notice the various kinds of buildings located in the community and the way in which the people make their living.

Rural Farm Communities. The people who live and work on farms make up America's smallest kind of community—the rural farm community. In most parts of the United States, you will pass farm after farm as you travel through the countryside. All parts of the United States have farms. However, farms differ from region to region because of the climate.

In Pennsylvania, for example, you will see farms on which a variety of crops are grown. These farms usually also raise some pigs, cows, and chickens and are called mixed farms. In Wisconsin you will see a large number of dairy farms, or farms that produce milk and milk products. Farther west, in Wyoming, you will see large ranches, or farms that specialize in raising cattle or sheep.

In the South, you will pass tobacco, soybean, and cotton farms. West of the Mississippi River, you will see large wheat farms. In the Imperial Valley of California, there are farms that grow fruit and vegetables for city markets. In Hawaii you will see sugar cane and pineapple plantations.

Today there are more than 2 million farms in the United States. Some farms are near others. Or they are near main highways or roads. Other farms are isolated and are a long distance from their nearest neighbors.

Small Country Towns. There is also another kind of rural community—the small country town. It has a population of less than 2,500 people and is located in a rural area, usually near open farmland. Most country towns have served as places where farmers could buy supplies and where rural people could shop, go to the movies, and attend church. They have also been marketing centers for farm crops.

During the 1930's, many of the rural areas in the United States began to lose population as farmers left to live in cities. Recently, however, some country towns have begun to grow again. This time the newcomers are not farmers. They are factory workers and business people who commute to new factories and businesses built in the countryside. This means that there are two rural Americas. One is the old rural community. The other is the rural area with farms and also businesses that have left the city.

Suburbs

As you have read, a town, village, or community located on the outskirts of a city is called a **suburb.** People who live in the suburbs often work in the city. Each morning they travel from their homes to their city offices or other places of employment.

There are several reasons why many Americans wish to live in the suburbs. Suburbs are smaller than cities, and some people prefer life in a smaller community. Others want their children to grow up in a community with more open spaces, trees, and places to play. They want a house with a backyard. Some families want to get away from city crowds, noise, and traffic.

Today nearly 100 million Americans live in suburbs. They often travel to the city to work, but prefer to live in a community with some open space.

Suburbs make it possible for such people to live away from the city even though they earn their living in the city. However, suburban towns have been growing rapidly in recent years. Many are beginning to experience some of the problems of urban areas.

Urban Areas

Suburbs and all other towns and cities of 2,500 or more people, as you may recall, are called **urban areas.** Urban communities vary greatly in size. For example, in 1980 the census listed the town of Linden, Alabama, which had a population of 2,773, as an urban

San Francisco, like many large cities, is a city of contrasts. It includes private homes, tall office buildings, theaters, hotels, and restaurants.

community. It also listed San Antonio, Texas, which had 785,410 people, and New York City, with a population of about 7 million.

More than seven of every ten Americans today live in urban communities. Those who live in the large cities are near theaters, restaurants, museums, and other cultural advantages that cities offer. They enjoy the hustle and bustle of city living. Recent studies show, however, that the suburbs are growing faster than the cities. More than half the urban population lives outside the central cities. A number of large cities actually showed a loss in population.

Metropolitan Areas

Certain American cities, such as New York, Dallas, Chicago, and Los Angeles, have become so large that each one is known as a **metropolis.** If you fly over a metropolis, you will find it hard to tell where the giant city ends and the surrounding towns and suburbs begin. In fact, there really is no dividing line. The settled area seems to have no end. For this reason, as you have read, a big city and its surrounding towns and suburbs are referred to as a **metropolitan area.** The metropolitan area of Chicago, Illinois, for example, includes several fairly large cities in neighboring Indiana, such as Gary, Hammond, and East Chicago.

There is evidence that someday soon several of our metropolitan areas, particularly those along the Atlantic coast around Boston, New York, Philadelphia, Baltimore, and Washington, will grow into a single metropolitan area. A name has been given to this type of giant urban area. It is a **megalopolis.** Three of the largest megalopolises are BosWash (Boston to Washington), ChiPitts (Chicago to Pittsburgh), and SanSan (San Francisco to San Diego).

CHECK-UP

Vocabulary

community
crossroads
transportation centers
rural area
suburb
urban area
metropolis
metropolitan area
megalopolis

Review

1. How do natural resources help determine the kind of community a settlement will become?
2. How have highways affected the settlement of the United States?
3. Why do some people prefer to live in the suburbs? Why do others prefer city life?

Discuss

Would you prefer to live in a rural or an urban community? Why?

2

Communities Have Many Purposes

At the beginning of this chapter, a community was defined as "a group of people, having common interests, who live in the same area and are governed by the same laws." What are some of their common interests? Also, how does the community serve its people?

Living and Learning in a Community

One of the most important things communities do is teach us how to live and work together. Our first lessons in living with others are learned in the home. The family, as a small community, teaches us important lessons in sharing. As we grow up, we also learn from neighbors, schoolmates, and friends.

The people of our communities teach us to talk and behave the way we do. They teach us values. The food we like, our respect for the law, the kind of person we want to be, and a hundred other things are learned by living with the people of our community.

Communication in Communities

Most of us continue to learn as long as we live. Almost every day, we share information with others about a great many things. This passing along of information, ideas, and beliefs from one person to another is known as

★ ★ ★ ★ ★ ★ ★ ★ ★ ★ ★ ★

DID YOU KNOW THAT . . .

George Washington, Benjamin Franklin, and Paul Revere all served in volunteer fire companies? In fact, it was Franklin who started the nation's first volunteer fire company. Members of the community were trained to work the equipment and were ready to rush to a fire as soon as they heard the alarm bell.

Not until the mid-1800's did large American cities begin to hire professional firefighters. Many smaller communities continued to be protected by volunteers—as they are today. Now the equipment of volunteer fire companies is modern and efficient, but the spirit of working together in the community is as old as our nation.

communication. One reason people live in communities is to be able to communicate easily. The problems people face seem to be made easier if they can talk them over with someone else. Life is also more pleasant if we can hear about the latest happenings in the neighborhood and learn new ideas from other people.

Every community has a number of important means of communication. We have already mentioned the most common one—conversation. Such modern inventions as the telephone, telegraph, radio, and television have increased our ability to learn and share information. We also communicate in writing through letters and notes.

One of the most important means of communication is the newspaper. Newspapers tell us about happenings all over the world. They also give us news of our own communities, such as what laws are passed, who is running for office at election time, and when public meetings will be held. In addition, newspapers tell us about births, marriages, and deaths in our community. Books and magazines are other important means we use to communicate ideas and facts.

Communities often provide recreation areas, like this park. Community funds and community employees maintain these areas for all to enjoy.

Communities Help Us to Enjoy Life

One important reason people form communities is to enjoy the company of others. Nearly every American city and town has movie theaters, bowling alleys, skating rinks, golf courses, and other places of recreation that are open to the public. **Recreation** is relaxation or amusement by playing or doing something different from one's usual activities. Many of our larger cities have professional baseball, football, hockey, and basketball teams whose games are eagerly followed by sports fans.

Many recreational facilities are maintained at public expense. Taxes are used to support public playgrounds, athletic fields, picnic grounds, tennis courts, and golf courses. There are also worthwhile activities sponsored by groups of citizens willing to volunteer their own time and money. The YMCA, YWCA, YMHA, Boy Scouts, Girl Scouts, Campfire Girls, Big Brothers, Big Sisters, and 4-H Clubs are examples of groups that help the members of the community enjoy playing and learning together.

Communities Help Us Use Our Free Time

Many communities have learned to take advantage of an unusually good climate or geographical location. They have promoted and developed these advantages not only for their own residents but also to attract tourists. Lake communities and seaside towns have developed boating, water skiing, and swimming as special attractions. Rural communities have made the most of the hunting and fishing opportunities in their areas. Other communities have featured skiing, horseback riding, and hiking.

Why We Live in Communities

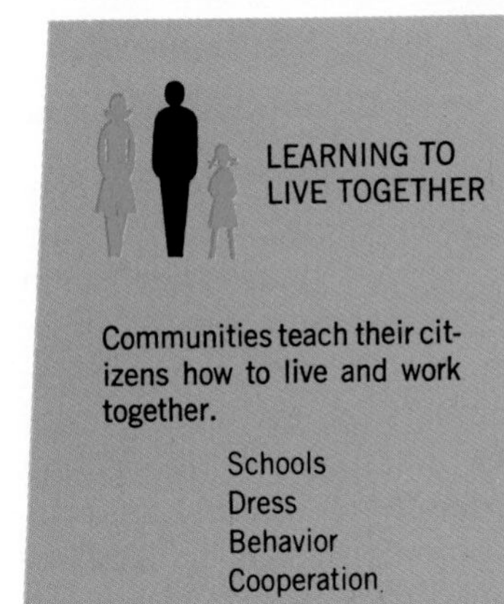

Several purposes are served by good community recreational facilities:

1. Good recreational facilities provide worthwhile ways for Americans to use their leisure time. They give people something interesting and healthful to do.

2. Good recreational facilities help members of the community keep physically fit. Well-run swimming pools, playgrounds, and recreation centers encourage good health habits and help members of the community build healthy bodies.

3. Recreation often expands our knowledge. A recreation center may help us develop new interests and hobbies. A community stamp club or coin club, for example, can teach us much about history and geography.

4. All of us benefit from recreation by relaxing and having fun in the company of others. Recreation helps us to "re-create" ourselves—to feel like new people.

Communities Provide Many Services

One of the reasons communities have been established is to provide services to their citizens. There are certain things the people of a community, working together, can do more effectively than each can do separately. A good police force helps ensure our safety. Fire protection is a worthwhile community service. Public schools are another valuable community service.

People living as neighbors also need pure water, an efficient sewer system, regular trash removal, and dependable gas and electricity. Sometimes the people of a community join together and vote to have services furnished by their local government in return for the taxes they pay. In other cases, some of the services are provided by private companies.

Communities Provide Local Government

In the United States, communities of all sizes serve their citizens by providing local government. When people live together, some kinds of laws and regulations are needed. Suppose that several neighbors get into an argument over where the boundary that separates their property is located. If there were no laws or local government, they might use force to settle their difficulties. Fortunately, though, our communities provide a local government with courts, judges, and law enforcement officers that help us maintain good order in our neighborhoods.

CHECK-UP

Vocabulary

communication
recreation

Review

1. What are some of the purposes served by communities?
2. Describe four ways in which community recreation facilities help citizens.

Discuss

What do you think are the most important services provided by your community? Explain your answer.

3

Citizens Serve Communities

Communities depend on **cooperation**—people working together for their common benefit. Communities serve their citizens. In return, their citizens should serve them. Some citizenship services are compulsory. For example, members of the community must obey the laws or pay the penalty. Young citizens must attend school. In most matters, however, communities rely on their members to respect the rights of others simply because it is the correct thing to do.

Your Communities

Each of us lives in a number of different communities. We profit from their services, and we owe certain duties in return. In many ways our family is a kind of community. The obligations of cooperation and respect for members of our family—the smallest community we live in—have already been mentioned. This cooperation should extend to people living in our immediate neighborhood. Finally, it should extend to the larger communities of our town or city, state, and nation. As citizens, we should feel responsible for all the communities in which we live.

Every community faces problems that must be solved if life in that community is to be as pleasant as it can be. These problems can be solved if every member of the community takes an interest in them.

How Americans Improve Their Communities

Groups of concerned citizens are doing something about their problems. Take the example of Las Vegas, New Mexico, a town of about 14,000 people. For years Las Vegas streets

The citizens of Boston reclaimed and restored run-down and unused warehouses to create this pleasant area of shops and restaurants, called Quincy Market.

were run-down and its sidewalks in need of repair. The town had few recreation centers. Nevertheless, the citizens of Las Vegas were proud of their community. Finally some of them decided to act to improve Las Vegas.

The mayor headed the community's improvement program. A new gymnasium was added to the high school. A community swimming pool was built. The people of the town began to feel that Las Vegas was a good place to call home. As streets and sidewalks were rebuilt, the town began to show new signs of life. Several more projects were planned to continue Las Vegas' program of improvement.

Each year other American communities face their problems and do something about them. For example, the citizens of Decatur, Illinois, undertook a program to improve their downtown areas, end slums, and reduce traffic jams. Decatur cleared and rebuilt a large part of its business district.

In similar fashion, the industrial city of Worcester, Massachusetts, established a successful new program of better schools, playgrounds, museums, and homes for the aged. Across the nation, cities such as Baltimore, Philadelphia, Houston, Denver, and St. Paul have rebuilt old areas.

The people of Pittsburgh, Pennsylvania, also took a critical look at their city. They were not pleased with what they saw. The smoke from the steel mills and factories was so thick that Pittsburgh was known as "the Smoky City." The traffic jams were awful. The central city was run-down.

The people of Pittsburgh voted to spend the money needed to improve their city. New skyscrapers were built. A successful campaign reduced the smoke in the air. More roads were built, a new water system was planned, and parks and recreation centers were added. Proud of what they had done, the citizens of Pittsburgh learned that their city must continue to plan and build and change if it is to meet their needs.

Community Volunteers

Another way citizens can improve their communities is by becoming volunteers. A volunteer, as you recall, is someone who offers to work without pay. Many Americans do not

The teenagers in this picture are members of a volunteer group that makes itself useful—and often entertaining—to the elderly and the handicapped.

realize just how much work in our society is done by volunteers. They help the sick, the poor, the handicapped, and the elderly. They collect money for charities. In some areas, volunteers put out fires and drive and assist in ambulances. Volunteers also help in schools, libraries, museums, sports groups, and many other organizations.

Communities rely on the help of volunteers because no government can know all the needs of local areas. Volunteers also help provide services a community might not otherwise be able to afford. It is up to all of us as citizens to help keep our communities healthy, clean, and safe.

Small and Large Volunteer Groups

The United States has many different kinds of volunteer groups. Some are small local groups. Others are large national organizations that depend upon local volunteers to carry out their work. A small group may be formed for specific purposes, such as cleaning up the neighborhood. After the problem is solved, the group breaks up. Some areas, however, have permanent neighborhood groups that get together regularly to discuss their community needs.

Many towns, cities, and counties have permanent volunteer groups. They include hospital volunteers, volunteer firefighters, parent-teacher associations, and various community action groups. Such groups rely on the help of citizens of all ages. Some high school students, for example, take senior citizens to their doctors' appointments. Retired people, in turn, may offer to spend a few hours each week helping out in libraries and hospitals.

Some groups require that volunteers take short courses to learn specific skills, such as carrying a stretcher or working special equipment. Those who take part in these programs have the satisfaction of performing a valuable service for their community. They also learn useful new skills.

Among the large national volunteer groups are the League of Women Voters, the American Cancer Society, the American Red Cross, the Scouts, and the Little League. These associations are supported by money from private contributors and depend on the services of volunteers. A large group such as the Red Cross has millions of volunteers working for it. Local branches of these organizations are usually started by concerned citizens. Community members can support these groups with time, ideas, and money.

Good Citizens Make Good Communities

Right now you are an active member of your local community. You attend its schools and enjoy its parks and playgrounds. You are protected by its police and fire departments. You depend on it to provide you with many other services. Tomorrow you may work in this community and raise a family there. It is important, therefore, that you be a good citizen in your community.

Each member of a community has certain duties and responsibilities. There are many things people can do besides volunteering and making donations. Take one example—that of doing one's share in keeping the community clean. Many people thoughtlessly throw garbage and rubbish on the ground or leave it lying about. **Littering,** as such carelessness is called, is a problem that costs communities millions of dollars each year. Each of us can do something about it now.

Another important way to help your community is to respect the property of others. **Vandalism,** or the willful destruction of property, harms the whole community.

Learn the facts about your community, its government, its problems, and its opportunities. Take pride in your community, and practice good citizenship wherever you are.

CHECK-UP

Vocabulary

cooperation
littering
vandalism

Review

1. What are some of the problems communities face?
2. How do volunteer groups help improve life in their communities?

Discussion

How can you and your classmates help make your community a better place in which to live?

CHAPTER SUMMARY

The United States is a nation of many communities. These communities differ greatly in size and population. However, they have many common problems wherever they are located—in rural or in urban areas.

Communities serve many important purposes. They help us enjoy living with other citizens, get a good education, and earn a good living. The prosperity of a community depends upon its location, climate, natural resources, industrial possibilities, and hard-working citizens.

Many communities are meeting their problems through a planned program of improvement. Such cities as Pittsburgh and Houston have attracted many different industries and built cleaner and more beautiful cities.

Much work remains to be done in our nation's communities. Citizens can help to improve their communities by becoming volunteers and by respecting the property of others.

CIVICS SKILLS: Working in Groups

Have you ever thought about the amount of time you spend with other people? Consider your daily schedule. You see your family in the morning and perhaps your neighbors on their way to work or school. Then there are all the hours you attend classes, talk to friends, or participate in sports. Maybe you belong to a club or have a job. In each case, you're involved in some kind of group.

Working in a group, large or small, means making decisions. To succeed as a group, members must agree upon goals and the methods of achieving them. They also have to be willing to perform different tasks, or roles. As you might guess, so many choices create a lot of opportunities for disagreement. Yet no group can survive without the cooperation of its members. As a result, it is important to learn how to resolve disputes quickly.

Settling Group Differences

Imagine the following situation. You and a friend want to go out together over the weekend, but you can't agree on what to do. You have several ways to solve the problem. You could, of course, ask a third person for his or her opinion. You could also threaten to stay home and do nothing at all. If you really want to go out, however, you probably will continue talking about your choices until you and your friend reach some kind of compromise.

A compromise, as you know, results when each side gives up part of its demands. To convince people to do this, each side needs to make sure the other gets something in return. This way all members of a group will accept a proposal, even though it might not completely satisfy everyone.

The first step in the bargaining process is to discover which interests group members share. In the boxed feature on this page, for example, both Tony and Jill want to raise money for the school chorus. A successful compromise would have to take this into account.

The next step would be to point out the benefits of a particular solution. This gives people the chance to say yes without feeling like winners or losers. If one proposal fails, try another. The important thing is to keep the discussion going until an acceptable compromise is found.

Practicing What You've Learned

Use the boxed feature below to answer the questions that follow.

1. What is the main area of disagreement in the dialogue between Tony and Jill?
2. What compromise would you propose if you belonged to this group? Why?
3. A willingness to compromise is one way to promote group cooperation. What other ways can you suggest?

TONY: How can the school chorus raise money for a new piano? The old one is almost always out of tune.

JILL: You're right. Let's hold a car wash. That's what the band did last year when they needed money for uniforms.

TONY: No—too expensive. We'd have to buy soap and sponges. Besides, shouldn't we be trying to conserve water? I think a bake sale would be a much better idea.

JILL: Well, I don't know. Everybody in this town seems to be on a diet. And we'd still have to spend money on all the ingredients. Can't we come up with something else?

CHAPTER REVIEW

Vocabulary

Write two paragraphs describing the different kinds of communities found in the United States. Include the following words and terms in your paragraphs, and underline each word or term as you use it.

crossroads	transportation center
community	rural area
metropolis	communication
suburb	megalopolis
cooperation	

Check-Up

1. What are some of the reasons people live and work in communities?
2. In what ways are ideas and information passed along in your community?
3. What are some advantages of living in the suburbs?
4. What are some advantages of living in the city?
5. How do communities help you use your free time?
6. How has the character of the small country town in the United States changed in recent years?
7. What are some of the problems that face our modern American communities? What have some communities done to solve their problems?
8. In what ways are volunteer groups essential for the success of a community? How do volunteer groups help make your community a better place to live?
9. In what ways can you help to improve your community?

Civics Skills

Suppose your civics class has raised $100 to improve one of the parks or recreational areas in your community. Some students think the money should be used to plant trees. Others want to buy picnic tables and benches. A few argue that a set of new trash cans would cut down on the litter problem. Several students believe that additional lights should be placed around the tennis courts.

Before the group can reach any decision on how to spend the money, these differences of opinion must be settled. The following questions will help you come up with possible solutions.

1. What is the main area of agreement among the members of the group? the main area of disagreement?
2. What compromises might be acceptable to the group as a whole?
3. How would each of your compromises make all group members feel that they had gained at least some of what they wanted?

Citizenship and You

1. Make a list of issues that are currently being discussed in your community.
2. You may want to visit your local chamber of commerce to learn what services it provides your community.
3. A group of students may collect posters, photographs, clippings, pamphlets, and maps about your community. These materials should be displayed on the bulletin board.
4. Several groups of students may collect information about your community. There may be committees on community history, local government, businesses and jobs, schools, recreation, natural resources, taxes and spending, traffic control, and housing. Each group should report its findings to the class.
5. Local community scrapbooks may be kept by individual students.
6. Prepare a bar graph showing facts about some feature of your community.

UNIT FIVE REVIEW

Reviewing the Facts

Write your answers to the items below on a separate piece of paper.

1. In what way does the typical modern American family differ from the typical traditional family?
   - **a.** It is smaller.
   - **b.** All its members help produce what the family needs in order to survive.
   - **c.** It is rural rather than urban.
   - **d.** The grandparents live nearby.
2. Is each of the following statements a fact or an opinion?
   - **a.** I believe that Abraham Lincoln was our greatest President.
   - **b.** Abraham Lincoln was born in Kentucky on February 12, 1809.
   - **c.** I think President Lincoln was kind.
   - **d.** The Lincoln Memorial was dedicated on May 30, 1922.
   - **e.** The Lincoln Memorial is the most beautiful sight in Washington, D.C.
3. Family law regulates all of the following *except*
   - **a.** marriage.
   - **b.** divorce.
   - **c.** family size.
   - **d.** duties of parents and children.
4. Complete this sentence: One example of community volunteer work in which high school students can participate is ________.
5. Which of the following is *not* an example of a volunteer group?
   - **a.** the American Red Cross
   - **b.** the Parent-Teacher Association
   - **c.** the Association of Bookstore Owners
   - **d.** the League of Women Voters
6. Where are you *least likely* to find a megalopolis?
   - **a.** along the Atlantic Ocean
   - **b.** along the Pacific Ocean
   - **c.** in an area joined by rivers and lakes
   - **d.** in a mountainous region
7. Below are some steps you should take to get the most out of a reading assignment. Arrange the steps in the order in which you should follow them.
   - **a.** Read the assignment, noting topic sentences and summarizing paragraphs.
   - **b.** Turn to the questions at the end of each section and try to answer them.
   - **c.** Note the titles of the chapter headings and subheadings.
   - **d.** Check the accuracy of your answers.
   - **e.** Take notes on the important facts and ideas.

Applying What You Know

1. Suppose you want to watch a special television program about the solar system. You think it will help you with your science class. Meanwhile, your sister wants to watch a television version of a play she is reading in her English class. The two programs are being televised at the same time and you have only one television set in your home. Suggest a possible compromise solution to the problem. Explain the benefits of the solution.
2. Describe three ways in which what you learn in your school experiences can make you a better family member.

Expanding Your Knowledge

Burns, Marilyn, *I Am Not a Short Adult; Getting Good at Being a Kid,* Little Brown. A thoughtful, humorous discussion of a teenager's life with family, in school, and in the community.

James, Elizabeth, and Barkin, Carol, *How to Write a Term Paper,* Lothrop, Lee & Shepard. Helpful hints and a checklist to make the project easier.

Lowe, William, *City Life,* Hayden. How life in the city is changing—major economic, political, and social trends.

UNIT SIX

The American Economy

CHAPTER

16

Our American Economic System

The United States is one of the richest nations in the world. Most Americans enjoy a high standard of living. A nation's **standard of living** is the well-being of its population based on the amount of goods and services they can afford. On the average, we have more money to spend, and more goods to buy, than the people of most other nations. Our economic system produces more goods and services than any other in the world.

What makes all this possible? There are a number of reasons for our economic success. First of all, the United States is a land of great natural resources. We have timber, minerals, energy resources, a good climate, and fertile soil in abundance. In addition, we always have had energetic and inventive people. They have taken our resources and turned them into needed and desirable products.

Furthermore, our system of government has ensured the right of private enterprise—

that is, the owning and operating of businesses by individuals rather than by the government. It has protected the right of individuals to own property and make a profit. Finally, the United States has developed an economic system in which most of its people can find work and earn financial success.

A nation's **economic system,** or **economy,** is its method of caring for the material needs of its people. It includes the production and distribution of goods and services, buying and selling, jobs, money, and savings. Our economic system has enabled the United States to become a rich and powerful nation.

We Americans are proud of what we have accomplished. In order to make our economy work even better in the future, it is important for all citizens to understand our economic system. In this chapter, we shall examine this system as we study these topics:

1. **How the American Economic System Works**
2. **How American Business Is Organized**
3. **How Business Decisions Are Made**

1

How the American Economic System Works

The American government, as you have learned, is based on certain principles of freedom. We enjoy free speech and freedom of religion. We vote in free elections. Americans can do as they choose if they do not interfere with the freedom of others. That is why the United States is called a free nation.

Our Economic Freedoms

We also enjoy important economic freedoms. It is because of these freedoms that our economic system is called a free economy. Let us examine some of these economic freedoms.

Freedom to Buy and Sell. Americans are free to buy and sell any legal product and service. Shoppers can go from store to store looking for the best quality goods and services at the lowest price. If the price seems too high, the buyer is free to go somewhere else to buy the product. Producers are free to sell goods and services at prices they think buyers will pay. If people do not buy a product or service, the producer is free to change the price or to sell something else. We use the term **free market** to refer to this exchange between buyers and sellers who are free to choose. The role of the government in our free market is limited.

Freedom to Compete. Business firms in the United States compete with one another for customers. That is, each business firm tries to get people to buy what it has to offer. Customers are free to shop where they wish. In this system of **free competition,** buyers show which goods they favor every time they make a purchase. If they do not buy a product, producers will make something else or go out of business. Therefore, producers make what they think the public will buy.

Freedom to Earn a Living. American workers are free to compete for the best jobs their training qualifies them to perform. They also may bargain with their employers for higher wages, better benefits, and better working conditions. They are free to leave their jobs and find better ones. Or they may go into business for themselves.

Freedom to Earn a Profit. Why do people start businesses? They expect to make a **profit**—to make more money than it costs to run the business. People also **invest** in, or put money into, businesses in hopes of making a profit. They invest in articles of value for the same reason. Investors use the money they have saved to make more money. This is called the **profit motive.** Without it our free economic system would not operate.

Freedom to Own Property. Americans have the right to own and use their own land, personal belongings, and other kinds of property. The free market and free competition would not work if we did not also have private ownership of property. All Americans are free to do as they like with their own money. They may spend, save, or invest it. They may buy buildings, land, tools, and machines. These forms of property may be used to produce goods and services. That is, Americans may start their own businesses and use them to earn profits. They may employ others to work for them.

Americans also have the right to profit from their ideas and inventions. They can protect this right by copyrighting what they write and by patenting their inventions. A **copyright** is the exclusive right, granted by law, to publish or sell a written, musical, or art work for a certain number of years. A **patent** gives a person the exclusive right to make and sell an invention for a certain number of years. The right to own and use property of all kinds is guaranteed in the Constitution of the United States.

The Free Economy in Action

Our American economic system, like the economy of every other nation, must deal with the problem of **scarcity.** That is, resources are limited. There are never enough to meet all our wants. We have to make decisions about what we want most.

In our nation, millions of different businesses, large and small, are at work producing all kinds of goods. Yet there is no person or group of people who decides how many automobiles, vacuum cleaners, loaves of bread, or textbooks will be produced all over the United States. Every business firm is free to make its own decisions about what and how much to produce.

About 100 million Americans are engaged in the many kinds of jobs needed to produce our goods and services. Yet there is nobody who decides how many people should be steelworkers, schoolteachers, truck drivers, or dentists. Each American is free to enter any career for which he or she is qualified.

Without anyone to supervise the process, enough goods of different kinds usually get produced. Only rarely are there shortages. Most of the time enough people, with the right training, provide needed goods and get them to market for people to buy.

Supply and Demand

One reason our free economy works so well is that it responds to the **law of supply and demand.** This important force usually determines the prices of goods. How does it work? Sometimes the supply of a product is greater than the public's demand for it at the price being charged. This means there is more of a product on the market at a price higher than the public is willing to pay. When that happens, the price of the product tends to drop. When the demand for a product is greater than the supply, the price often rises.

Let's use radios to see the law of supply and demand at work. If manufacturers make more radios than can be sold, the price may have to be lowered in order to sell them. Even at the lower price all the radios may not be sold. As a result, fewer radios will be manufactured and the supply of radios on the market will decrease.

Soon people will need to replace their old radios. Or they may want to buy newer models. For whatever reason, the demand rises. Since the supply of radios is so small, the price may be raised and all the radios still will be sold. Manufacturers also will begin to make more radios to fill the demand.

It is important to understand how supply and demand works. This principle affects everything that has a price, including labor.

What Is Capitalism?

Our American economic system is sometimes called **capitalism.** Another name for it is the capitalistic system. The money Americans invest in business is called **capital.** This

Freedom in Our American Economy

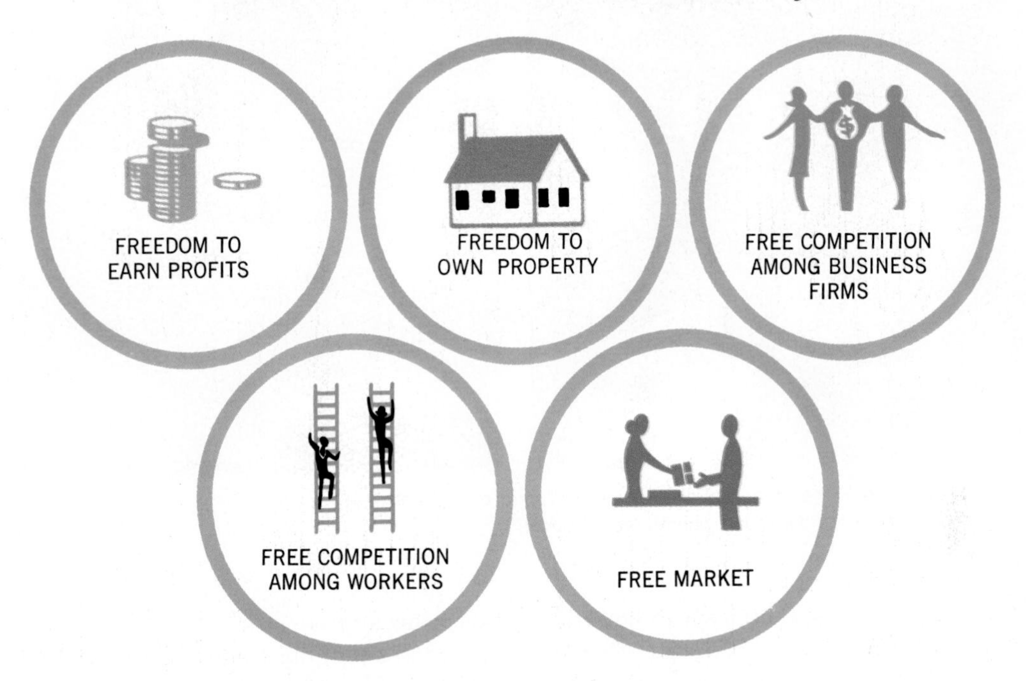

is money that Americans do not spend on living expenses but, instead, save to invest in buildings, machines, and other forms of property used to produce goods and services.

Capital is not only the money that people invest. It is also what people buy with it—tools, buildings, machines, or anything that means they own part or all of a business. Anyone who owns such things is a **capitalist.**

For example, the tools owned by a self-employed electrician are capital. The electrician had to save in order to buy them. The tools are used to produce things people want or to provide services people want. The machines that turn out automobile bodies are part of the capital of an automobile manufacturing company.

As you can see, the electrician is a capitalist on a small scale. The automobile manufacturer is a capitalist on a large scale. If you own a few shares of stock in an automobile company, you are also a capitalist. These shares of **stock** mean that you own part of the company. You had to save the money to invest in this stock. You did not spend the money to pay for living expenses or to have a good time.

People work and invest in order to get ahead financially and improve the quality of life. Because many people are doing this, our economy produces the vast number of goods we all enjoy. New and better products are constantly being offered for sale. Business people who supply Americans with the products and services they want, at a price they are willing to pay, usually make a profit. Therefore, our capitalistic system works for the benefit of the American people as a whole.

Our Free Enterprise System

American business people are basically free to run their own businesses in the way they think is best. They do not depend on some government official to tell them how to do it, as business managers do in the Soviet Union, for example. Americans depend upon their

Our free enterprise system has made available a wide range of products and services from which the American people can choose.

own enterprise—that is, their own ability and energy. For this reason, our economic system is sometimes called a **free enterprise system.** Freedom in our economy offers enterprising business people the opportunity to enjoy success and profits.

American business owners take many risks. They are free to earn profits. But they are also required to take the losses if they make mistakes. They may produce a new product and find that customers do not want it. Or they may produce their products inefficiently and have to charge more than people are willing to pay for them. If they make mistakes, they may be forced out of business. If their businesses fail, they may lose all their capital. As a rule, though, efficient businesses earn profits in our economic system.

The Rise of Big Business

From their earliest beginnings, American businesses have been privately owned, with business decisions made by their owner or owners. During the early years of our nation's history, most businesses were small. Even then, some shippers, importers, and manufacturers became wealthy. It was not until the late 1860's that big businesses began to develop in the United States.

These businesses benefited from America's new technology. For example, they used machines that were powered by steam or, later, by electricity. By placing these machines in factories, where great numbers of workers were employed, businesses were able to produce large quantities of goods at lower prices. The owners made huge profits. Some owners, however, hoping to make great fortunes and gain economic power, used business practices that would be considered unfair or illegal today.

Monopolies

Unfair business practices harm our free economy. They may interfere with the free market and affect the prices people have to pay for goods and services. Therefore, it is important to understand these practices.

One unfair method used by big business owners in the late 1800's and early 1900's was the forming of monopolies. A company has a **monopoly** if it is the only firm selling a product or providing a service. If there is no substitute for the product or service, and if it is something people really need (such as food), the monopolist controls the price. People will be forced to pay the price that is asked if they want the product or service.

The **merger** is one way of trying to form a monopoly. A merger occurs when two or more companies in the same industry combine to become one company. If all the companies in an industry merge, a monopoly will be formed. There no longer will be real competition in the industry.

Another way to create a monopoly is to form a **trust.** That is, several companies in a similar industry place their stock in the hands of a board of trustees. Even though each company remains a separate business, the trustees make sure the companies no longer compete with one another. If all the companies in an industry became part of the trust, a monopoly would be created. In this way they could charge prices that would prevent smaller companies from entering the industry.

Let's look at an example of a monopoly. Suppose that a large coffee company decides to lessen its competition by buying up all the small coffee companies or forcing them out of business. The large coffee company might do this by lowering its prices below the cost of production.

Soon all the other companies would have to lower their prices to compete and stay in business. Every coffee firm would be selling coffee at a loss. Because the big company has more capital than the small companies, it can afford to lose money longer than they can. The small companies would be forced to sell out, merge with the big company, or go out of business altogether.

The big company would now be a monopoly. It alone would produce all the coffee on the market. Moreover, it could sell this coffee at any price. Since there would be no other companies selling coffee, people would have to buy their coffee from the big company at the price charged, or drink something else.

The Importance of Big Business

It is a mistake to think that all large companies are monopolies or even have the power to act like monopolies. Today most big businesses in the United States have to face competition from other big companies and from foreign producers. Also, if their profits are high, there is always the possibility that this will encourage other companies to enter the industry. Competition would be quickly restored.

The fact that a company is big does not mean that it makes huge profits or that it abuses its power. A company should be judged by its actions, not by its size. Big businesses are essential to our economy. It would not be the same without them.

Many of the goods and services we need cannot be produced efficiently by small firms. To produce steel, electricity, automobiles, and ships, for example, large and very expensive capital equipment is needed. The term "economies of scale" is used to describe the situation where things can be produced more efficiently and cheaply by larger and larger firms.

In some industries today, a few large firms account for most of the production and sales. If these firms should get together and agree on how much to produce and what to charge for their product, they might be abusing their size and power. As you will see, there are laws to prevent this.

The Government as Referee

The referee of a basketball or football game sees that the teams observe the rules. In the same way, the federal government enforces rules to protect the American system of free enterprise.

To prevent monopolies, Congress has passed antitrust and antimonopoly laws. The Sherman Antitrust Act of 1890 was passed to help prevent monopolies. It was strengthened by the Clayton Act of 1914, which forbade practices that would lessen competition. The antitrust division of the Justice Department and the Federal Trade Commission are responsible for enforcing these laws.

In recent years, the government and the American people have been trying to decide whether to regulate business combinations known as conglomerates. A **conglomerate** is formed by the merger of businesses that produce, supply, or sell a number of unrelated goods and services. For example, a single conglomerate may control communication systems, insurance companies, hotel and restaurant chains, and others.

The government watches mergers carefully to make sure that conglomerates do not gain too much control over an industry or part of the economy. If a conglomerate gains so much power that it threatens the operation of our free economy, the government may step in as referee.

In some industries, monopolies are legal. These legal monopolies are **public utilities,** companies that provide essential services to the public. Telephone and electric companies are examples of public utilities. Their capital equipment is so expensive that it would be wasteful to have more than one company trying to provide the same service in the same area. Therefore, one company is allowed to have a monopoly. The government regulates public utilities to make sure they provide adequate services at reasonable prices.

Comparing Economic Systems

Over the past 100 years, our economic system has grown large and complicated. As a result, our national government now sometimes acts as referee and makes a number of economic decisions. Because the government makes more economic decisions than it once did, some people now describe our system as a **mixed economy.** It is still correct, however, to call it a free economy or a free enterprise economy because most economic decisions are made by individuals.

In an economy like that of the Soviet Union, the opposite is true. Most economic decisions are made by government officials who head huge planning agencies. Individuals are left with only a few decisions to make. The government decides what goods and serv-

These workers in the command economy of China work where the government assigns them to work. The wages they will be paid are also determined by the government.

ices should be provided. Workers are told what jobs they must take. Young people are told what jobs to train for. The government manages nearly everything.

For these reasons and others, we say that the Soviet Union has a **command economy.** The government completely controls, or commands, the nation's economy. The government owns almost all the capital, tools, and means of production of the Soviet Union. It tells the managers and workers in factories and on farms how much they must produce each year. If they do not produce as much as they are told to, their wages may be reduced or they may be sternly reprimanded.

CHECK-UP

Vocabulary

standard of living
economic system
economy
free market
free competition
profit
invest
profit motive
copyright
patent
scarcity
law of supply and demand
capitalism
capital
capitalist
stock
free enterprise system
monopoly
merger
trust
conglomerate
public utilities
mixed economy
command economy

Review

1. What are some of our most important economic freedoms?
2. How does the law of supply and demand work? Give an example.
3. What are the advantages of our free economic system?
4. How does the American free enterprise system differ from the command economy of the Soviet Union?

Discuss

Why is competition important in our free economy?

2
How American Business Is Organized

About 100 years ago, a young clerk in a small New York town decided to try out a new idea for increasing his store's business. He gathered several small items from the store's shelves and placed them on a table near the entrance. Then he put up a sign: "Everything on this table, 10 cents each." Customers who came into the store to buy thread or sugar began to stop at the table for a bag of clothespins, an eggbeater, or some other item that caught their eye. Business in the store began to show a good increase.

The young man then decided to open his own store and to sell only five- and ten-cent items. Unfortunately, his new store was not a success. He lost all the money he had saved and borrowed to start the business. He did not give up, however. He borrowed the money he needed to buy new goods and start over again. This time his business was a success.

The young man with the new idea was Frank W. Woolworth. With the profits from his successful business, he soon opened another store, and then another and another. When he died in 1919, Woolworth had established 1,300 five-and-ten-cent stores in the United States and Canada.

Woolworth became a wealthy man because he had a good idea and the business ability to make it succeed. Success stories like his encourage many Americans to go into business for themselves.

The Single Proprietorship

There are more than 15 million business firms in the United States today. Over 11 million are small businesses owned by one person. They include gas stations, grocery stores, beauty shops, drugstores, and other businesses that serve people who live nearby.

In the United States more than 200,000 grocery stores are single proprietorships. This owner works many hours to keep his store operating at a profit.

These small businesses, owned by one person, are called **single proprietorships.**

You probably already know some of the advantages of going into business for yourself. Single proprietors are their own bosses. They alone decide what they will sell. They decide the hours the businesses will be open and how the businesses will be run. Because they are the owners, they take all the profits.

On the other hand, there are disadvantages to being a single proprietor. Owners have to furnish all the money needed to rent or buy the buildings their businesses use and the tools and other equipment needed to run them. If they require help, they have to be able to pay the salaries of employees. Owners are hard-working people. They can hire others to help them. However, they alone are responsible for the success or the failure of their businesses.

If their businesses fail, proprietors must face the losses. Workers may lose their jobs. Proprietors, however, may have to sell everything they own to pay their business debts.

The Partnership

In the United States each year, many small businesses are started and others go out of business. Some small businesses fail because the single proprietor lacks enough capital or the business ability to earn a good profit. For such reasons, the owner of a small business sometimes seeks another person to become a partner, or part owner, of the business.

They then form a **partnership,** which gives the business firm a greater amount of capital and a better chance of success. In a partnership, there is more than one person to provide capital, share responsibility, furnish ideas, and do the work. The partners also share the risks. If the business fails, the partners share responsibility for the debts of the business.

Any two or more persons can form a business partnership. Usually they sign an agreement setting up the partnership. Unwritten partnership agreements, however, are legal and are recognized by the courts. There are a few large and wealthy American businesses that are organized as partnerships. However, most partnerships are small.

You often can recognize a partnership from the name of a business firm: Kim and Jackson, Contractors; Reilley, Cortes, and Clark, Attorneys. If the abbreviation "Inc." does not appear after the names, the business is probably a partnership. "Inc." is an abbreviation, or short form, of "incorporated." It means the business is organized as a corporation, a third form of business organization.

The Corporation

Just what is a corporation? Establishing a big business requires large sums of money—to buy land, build offices and factories, purchase tools and machinery, and employ workers. A big business can seldom be set up by an individual or even by a number of partners. Another form of business organization is needed. This form of business organization is called a **corporation.**

The corporation is the most common form of business organization for most of our nation's large companies and for many smaller ones. The corporation is a permanent organization. It is unlike proprietorships and partnerships, which end when their owners die. Corporations play a vital part in our American economy. How does a corporation work? Its most important features are these:

1. Corporations raise money by selling stocks, or shares of ownership. Each share of stock represents a part of the ownership of the corporation. The people who buy these stocks are called **stockholders.**

Suppose a new corporation is organized with a capitalization of $1 million. That means it has the legal right to accept $1 million in the form of capital from investors. It could do this, for example, by selling 10,000 shares of stock at $100 a share. Each purchaser of a single share would then own one ten-thousandth of the company.

When profits are divided each year, each owner of a single share would get one ten-thousandth of the profits. Corporation profits paid to stockholders are called **dividends.** Some stockholders own several shares. A few stockholders own many shares. Each stock-

How a Corporation Is Organized

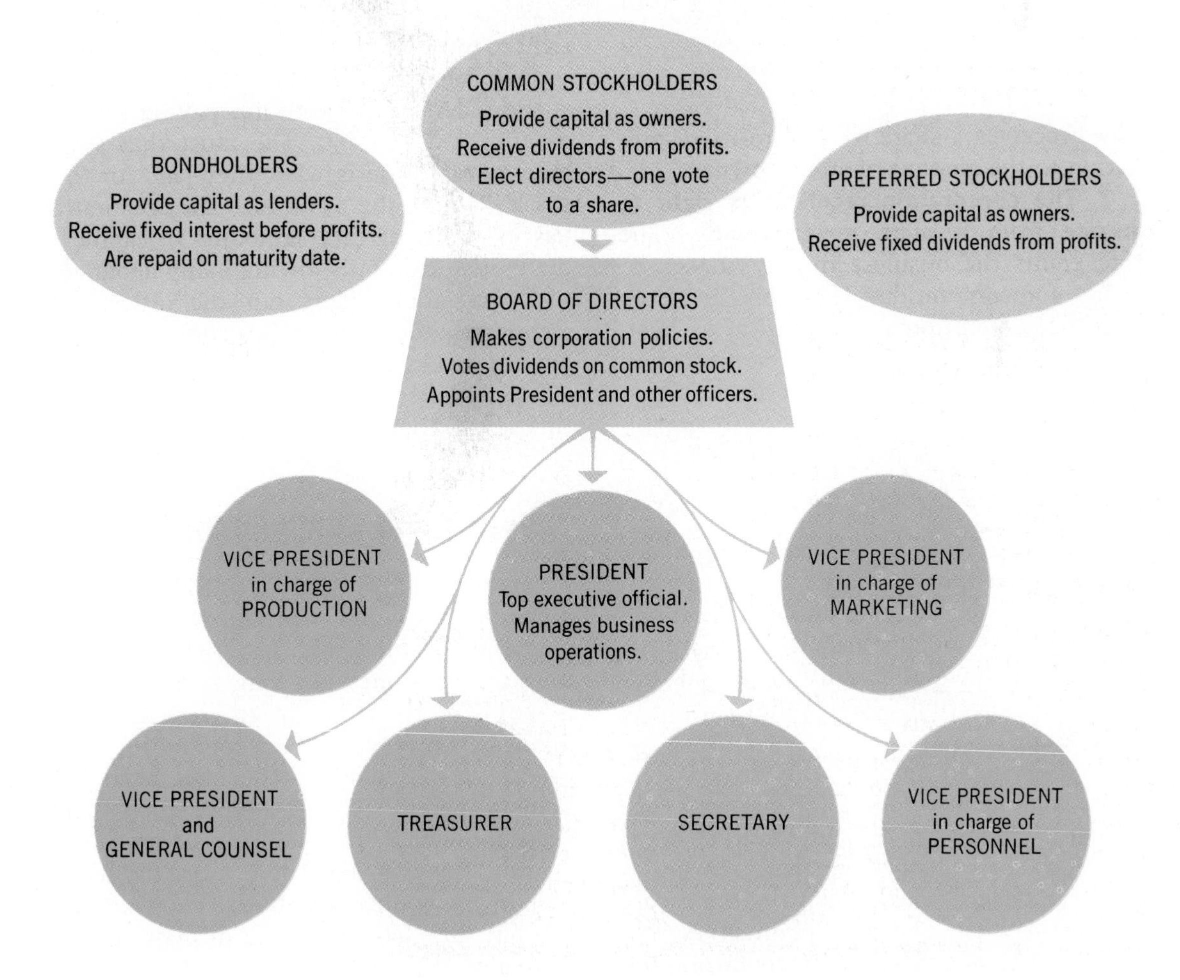

This hectic scene takes place every business day on the floor of the New York Stock Exchange, where millions of shares of stock are bought and sold.

holder receives a share of the profits in proportion to the amount of stocks owned.

2. The corporation receives its right to operate from a state government. The state grants the business firm a **charter,** or grant, of incorporation. This charter recognizes the corporation's right to carry on business, sell its stock, and receive the protection of state laws. In return, the company must obey state regulations in regard to its organization, the reports it makes public, the taxes it pays, and the way in which it sells its stock to the public.

3. The directors of the corporation are elected by the stockholders. Every corporation is required by law to hold at least one meeting of its stockholders each year. All stockholders have the right to attend and address this meeting—even if they own only one share.

At this annual meeting, the stockholders elect a board of directors. They may also vote on major changes in the corporation's business. Each share of stock entitles its owner to one vote. Major stockholders therefore cast most of the votes. The **board of directors,** representing the stockholders, meets during the year to make important decisions about the affairs of the corporation.

4. The board of directors chooses those who manage the corporation. Those who manage the affairs of the corporation are its **executives.** The top executives are elected by the board of directors. They include the president of the company, vice presidents, secretary, and treasurer. The president usually picks the other major assistants. Together, all these officials are called the **management** of the corporation.

5. Individuals are not responsible for the debts of the corporation. Corporations, as you recall, are owned by the stockholders. The money received from the sale of stock becomes the corporation's capital. The purchase of shares gives the stockholders the right to receive a part of the company's profits.

But what if the business fails? Are the stockholders responsible for paying the corporation's debts? No. The most that stockholders may lose is what they paid for their stock. This is the advantage the corporation has in gathering large amounts of capital. If the corporation fails, owing many debts, neither the stockholders nor the officers are responsible for its debts. If a corporation goes out of business, its assets (property and other valuables) are sold. The money raised from this sale is then used to pay off the debts.

Preferred and Common Stocks

A corporation may issue two kinds of stock—preferred stock and common stock. Owners of **preferred stock** take less risk when they invest their money. As long as the company makes a profit, they are guaranteed a fixed dividend every year. The corporation must pay these dividends to the preferred stockholders before paying other stockholders their dividends. Because preferred stockholders take less risk, they do not usually have a vote in the company's affairs. They are owners, but they have no voice in managing the company.

Owners of **common stock** take more risk when they invest their money. They receive dividends only if the company makes good profits. Why, then, would anyone want to risk buying common stock? There are three main advantages in owning common stock:

1. If the company's profits are high, owners of common stock may receive higher dividends than owners of preferred stock.

2. If the company's profits are high, the market price, or selling price, of the common stock usually increases. This means stockholders can sell their shares, if they wish, for more than they paid for them.

3. Common stock owners have a vote in electing the board of directors and in deciding certain company policies.

Corporation Bonds

Even with the sale of preferred and common stocks, corporations sometimes need additional large sums of money to expand operations. In such cases, one method corporations use is the issuing of **bonds.**

The issuing of bonds is a method of borrowing money. Bonds are certificates stating how much the original purchaser paid. They also declare the percentage of interest on this amount that the corporation will pay the bondholder each year. **Interest,** as you have read, is the percentage paid to individuals or banks for the use of their money. The company must pay the interest on its bonds before it pays dividends to stockholders. This interest must be paid whether or not the company earns any profits for the year.

If the company cannot repay the money borrowed from bondholders by the date stated on the bonds, the holders of the bonds may take over the business. They may close the corporation and sell its property to raise the money owed them. Or they may decide to keep the business in operation, perhaps with new management. They may do this in the hope that the corporation soon will be able to pay back the amount owed on the bonds.

CHECK-UP

Vocabulary

single proprietorship
partnership
corporation
stockholders
dividends
charter
board of directors
executives
management
preferred stock
common stock
bonds
interest

Review

1. What are the principal advantages and disadvantages of a single proprietorship? of a partnership?
2. Where does a corporation get its money?
3. Why is the corporation form of business best suited to large industries?

Discuss

Would you rather work for someone else or own your own business? Why?

3

How Business Decisions Are Made

You now know that Americans can run a business as individual proprietors, members of a partnership, or managers of a corporation. No matter how a business is organized, its success depends mainly upon decisions about the use of four things: land, capital, labor, and management. These are called the **factors of production.**

Production Requires Land

Suppose that Maria Morano decides to start a bakery business. She will need a place to conduct her business. That is, she needs land. Every business enterprise requires land.

(continued on page 314)

CITIZENSHIP IN ACTION

Students Run a Business

Running a business isn't easy. It takes thought, hard work, and patience. It also requires the ability to enjoy a challenge. That's what Rosa Furvo and Jonathan Banks think, and they should know. In their sophomore year in high school, Rosa and Jonathan learned the responsibilities of running a business. Rosa worked as president of a company, factory worker, and door-to-door salesperson. Jonathan was company treasurer, package handler, and salesperson.

A Junior Achievement Company

Rosa and Jonathan did all those jobs in a Junior Achievement Company. With other students they formed a manufacturing company and ran it from beginning to end. Their company was one of hundreds around the United States that are formed each year as part of Junior Achievement (J.A.).

Junior Achievement is a national organization whose goal is to teach high school students about the free enterprise system. Every year some 200,000 students learn how to organize, run, and liquidate (shut down) a business. J.A. businesses usually

ONE SHARE • NON-TRANSFERABLE • NON-LEGAL REDEEMABLE WITHIN ONE YEAR AFTER DATE OF ISSUE

STOCK CERTIFICATE R0544297

JA

JUNIOR ACHIEVEMENT

______________________ *a Junior Achievement Company*

in ______________ CITY *Certifies that* ______________ NAME

is the owner of one share, par value one dollar of the Capital stock subject to information on the Certificate.

PAR VALUE ONE DOLLAR $1.00 LIMIT ONE SHARE PER PERSON

______________ REPRESENTATIVE ______________ DATE

THE STOCKHOLDER BY SIGNATURE APPOINTS THE REPRESENTATIVE PROXY TO VOTE FOR ELECTION OF BOARD OF DIRECTORS.

© JUNIOR ACHIEVEMENT INC. 1975

Students in a Junior Achievement company work together to organize their business.

follow the school calendar. Students meet once a week for two hours on their own time for 30 weeks.

Rosa and Jonathan's company was named Double-M—for Double the Money! It made and sold desk lamps and decorated T-shirts. In order to raise money to buy materials and run the business, the students sold stock in their company. They sold 130 shares, mostly to family and friends, at $1 a share.

After the stocks were sold, the students elected company officers and divided up the jobs. They also chose the products they wanted to sell and settled on prices. Help came from two sources. One source was a national Junior Achievement booklet that explains how to decide on a price. The booklet points out typical manufacturing and sales costs that must be taken into account. The most common costs include raw materials and supplies, salaries and sales commissions, office or factory rentals, and bank charges. The booklet also discusses how much the students should add to the selling price in order to keep the price competitive yet enable their company to make a profit.

The second source of help was an adult adviser who sat in on the company meetings. J.A. advisers are local businesspeople who volunteer their time. Usually it is such advisers who start Junior Achievement programs in the community and keep them going. They ask local industries to donate funds to pay for a space where the student companies can meet and work. In Rosa and Jonathan's home town, three companies worked side by side in a former bakery that the advisers rented.

Most J.A. companies sell a product. Some, however, choose to provide a service. A company in Youngstown, Ohio, for example, bought a house, made repairs, and repainted it. Then they sold it at a profit.

Meeting the Challenge

Most people who start their own businesses don't have to learn how to do several jobs in a few weeks. What was it like for students who had to learn all those new jobs so quickly?

As president of Double-M, Rosa had a lot of work to do. She learned that "the president really has to get out and work. She or he can't just sit back and watch."

As treasurer, Jonathan had to learn to give financial details his constant attention. "It's so easy to forget to write down a few cents here and a few cents there. But it makes a difference in the long run."

All the members of the company cooperated in decorating the T-shirts and making the desk lamps. Rosa had the extra duty of seeing that things ran smoothly. She set up an assembly line to make the products. "Organization is the key to working on an assembly line," she discovered. "Jobs have to be done in the correct order to keep things rolling. We also have to know how to stay out of each other's way."

When the products were ready, all company members became salespeople. They found door-to-door selling the most effective way of making sales. By May most of the products were sold, except for a half dozen desk lamps. The students worked extra hard and thought up new ways of trying to sell the lamps quickly, so that they could close down the company by the end of the school year.

Company members make all the products that will be sold by their business.

Liquidating the Company

The students ended their business by publishing an annual report and closing their record books. They were able to declare a profit—as most J.A. companies do. This meant that they not only returned the $1 that each stockholder had invested but also paid a dividend. A dividend is the share of the profit each stockholder receives in return for having taken a risk.

Members of J.A. companies from all over the country are congratulated for their achievements at an annual conference.

How did Rosa and Jonathan feel about having spent so much time on their J. A. company in addition to their regular school work? Both agreed that the experience had more than repaid all their effort. "We learned a lot and are ready to go again," they said.

Thinking about what they learned with Double-M, Jonathan and Rosa think the company might have done better with less expensive products. "We should have chosen something cheaper to sell. Our material costs were high. Spending $5 just for the desk lamp ran up our price."

Thinking It Over

1. What are the advantages and disadvantages of learning to do several jobs in the same company?
2. Why is it necessary to keep track of all the money that is made and spent in a company?
3. What are some of the things you might take into account in deciding what is the right product to sell?
4. Do you think running a Junior Achievement company is a good way to learn about the free enterprise system? Why or why not? How else might a person learn how our economic system works?

The word **land** includes more than a place to locate a store, factory, or office. It also includes all the natural resources that come from the land. The wheat used to make flour for Maria Morano's bakery comes from the land. The wood for her bread racks comes from trees grown on the land. All the raw materials needed to produce goods of all kinds come from the mines, fields, and forests that are a part of the land.

Our nation's total supply of actual land is limited. In some places land is so scarce that there are many businesses in every city block. People who wish to start new businesses must make decisions about their location.

Maria Morano, for example, must decide whether or not to own the property on which her business will be located. She can buy either a piece of land with a building on it or land on which she can build. Or she can pay rent for a building. **Rent** is what a person pays to use land or other property belonging to someone else.

Rents and land prices are higher in crowded business areas where land is scarce than in less densely populated areas. Maria Morano must decide which location will give her the most profit. If she pays a high rent or price for land, she will be nearer customers. If she goes to the edge of town where land or rent is cheaper, customers will have to travel farther to get to her bakery. Maria must also make decisions about the quality and costs of the flour and other raw materials she will use.

Production Requires Capital

Maria Morano will also need such equipment as mixers and ovens. She may rent her equipment. Or, if she has enough money, she may buy it. As you can see, Maria cannot go into business without money. Her decision to rent or buy equipment will depend on how much capital she has available and how she wants to use it. Capital, you recall, is money used to pay for tools and other capital goods such as trucks, machines, office equipment, and factory buildings.

How will Maria obtain the capital she needs? Perhaps she will decide to go ahead alone and set up her business as a single proprietorship. To do so, she must have saved some money as capital. If she does not have enough, she may ask the bank for a loan.

If the bank officials decide that Maria is a good risk, they will give her a loan. They will think she is a good risk if she can prove that

The Four Factors of Production

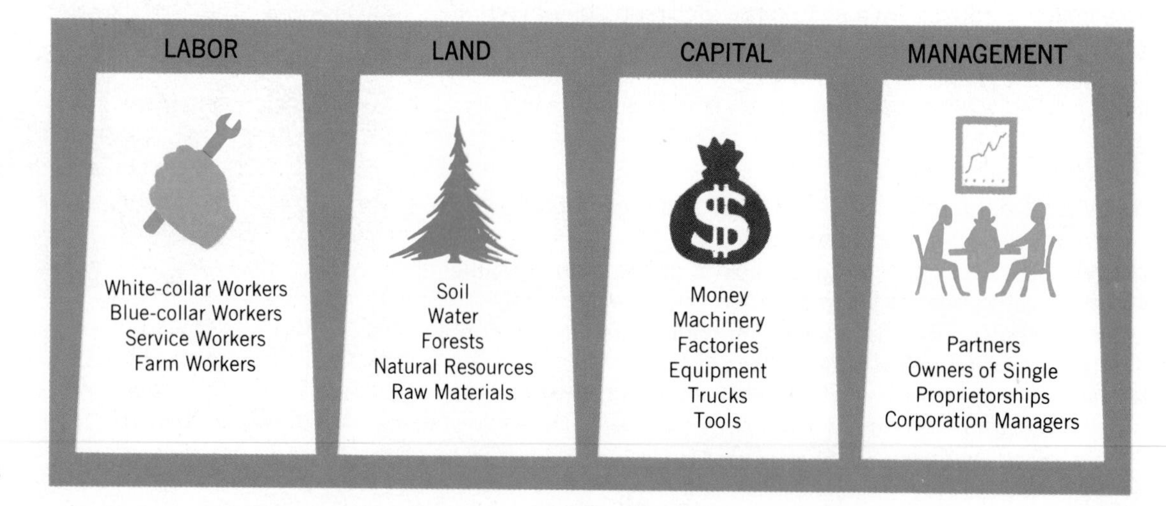

she has good ideas for a business and is likely to pay back the loan. If Maria takes out a loan, she will have to pay the bank interest.

Perhaps Maria will decide instead to seek one or more partners who are willing to invest in the bakery business. Or she may decide to set up her business as a corporation and sell stock to raise capital. She would do this if she decided to go into the bakery business on a large scale.

Production Requires Labor

All human effort used to produce goods or services is called **labor.** However, the word "labor" often is used to mean workers as opposed to owners and the people who manage companies. The workers in businesses, industries, and on farms usually earn wages. **Wages** are the money earned by workers each hour. They are paid on either a daily or a weekly basis. Those who manage companies generally are paid salaries. **Salaries** are fixed incomes paid twice a month or monthly.

If Maria Morano does her own work, the amount of bread and rolls she can produce in her bakery will be limited. If she hires more labor, her production will be greater. She will then have more goods to sell.

The money Maria gets for the additional bread and rolls should be at least enough to pay the wages of the new workers. If it is more than enough, she will increase her profits. If it is not enough to pay the workers' wages, she will have to discharge them, lower their pay, or find some way of increasing their productivity. **Productivity** is the amount a worker produces in an hour.

Production Requires Good Management

These kinds of decisions must be made by all business owners, or **entrepreneurs** (ahn·truh·pruh·NURS). Then, after the business is started, they must make decisions about

Three of the four factors of production can be seen in this pencil factory. Can you tell which three factors they are? What is the fourth factor of production?

how to distribute the product, how much to charge, whether to hire more people, and many others.

Those who operate businesses are called **managers.** The group of managers of a single business, you will recall, is called its management. Their decisions determine whether the business will succeed. If management makes the wrong decisions, the business may fail. If management makes wise decisions, the business will usually prosper.

When managers make decisions, they take risks. If business people did not take risks, the average standard of living in the United States would not be so high. Because Thomas Edison and other business people took risks, for example, Americans were among the first people to enjoy the benefits of electricity. Because Henry Ford and others took risks, Americans had the first low-priced, mass-produced cars. Because David Sarnoff and hundreds of others took risks, Americans enjoy radio and television.

These people were successful. Their decisions turned out well. Many other people, however, were not successful. Why, then, are Americans willing to take business risks?

DID YOU KNOW THAT . . .

the first permanent settlement in the 13 American colonies was sponsored by a corporation? A group of English investors formed a corporation called the London Company to send settlers to America. The profits made by the settlers were to be distributed as dividends. In 1607 the settlers sent by the London Company founded Jamestown, Virginia.

Jamestown made history, but unfortunately it did not make much money for the corporation. At first all the land was owned by the London Company. Only when the individual settlers were allowed to own land themselves did the colony begin to succeed.

Management and Profits

Management takes risks because it hopes to produce profits. What are profits, and how are they determined?

The money a firm receives from the sale of its goods or services is called **gross income.** Out of gross income, the firm must pay the costs of making and distributing its product.

The cost of materials and supplies used in the business must be paid. Rent must be paid. If the business owns its own land and buildings, property taxes must be paid. Machines wear out. So money must be put aside to repair machinery or replace it. If the business has borrowed money, interest must be paid. Workers and those who manage the business must be paid. Even if single proprietors do all the work themselves, the salary they pay themselves is a business cost.

If the business firm has been well managed, and if other conditions are right, money will be left over after all the costs have been paid. The amount left over is called **net income.** What happens to this net income? Part of it will go to pay income taxes. Some may be set aside in a bank to meet future business needs. The rest is profit. As you may recall, profit is money remaining after all the firm's obligations have been met. In a corporation, profits are distributed among the stockholders as dividends.

Government's Role in Business

As you have read, government has a role in our free enterprise system. Our government does not tell business people what they must do. However, it does influence business in many ways. For example, government acts as a referee to make sure that big corporations do not destroy the competition of small businesses. Our Constitution protects the rights of private property. Federal laws protect our right to buy and sell in a free market. Other laws protect the right of business people to take risks to make profits.

Many agencies of the federal government help businesses. One agency, the Small Business Administration, helps small businesses as they compete in our economy.

In some ways the federal government acts as an overseer of our economy. There are laws that ensure that women and members of minority groups are not unfairly kept from getting jobs. Laws protect the health and safety of workers and prevent pollution of the environment. Laws protect consumers from dishonest practices and harmful products.

The government plays many other roles in business. It tries to help business by providing information that managers can use in planning their production levels, sales, and costs. It sometimes provides loans and other types of aid to businesses. The government also tries to keep the economy running smoothly.

Some people say government has gone too far in doing its job as overseer. For example, in the early 1980's nearly 100,000 pages were required to print all the regulations issued by the federal government. This was three times as many pages as in 1971. Some regulations are considered necessary. Some, however, may add to the costs of doing business without providing much benefit to the people. Businesses usually must raise their prices in order to cover the costs of meeting government regulations.

Achieving the right balance of government activity is not easy. The question of how much government regulation is necessary is much debated.

CHECK-UP

Vocabulary

factors of production
land
rent
labor
wages
salaries
productivity
entrepreneurs
managers
gross income
net income

Review

1. Why are the four factors of production important?
2. What is the relationship between good management and profits?
3. What are some ways in which the federal government plays a role in our economy?

Discuss

If you were starting a new business, what are some things you would have to decide about your use of the four factors of production?

CHAPTER SUMMARY

The American economy, or economic system, is based on ideas of personal freedom. As Americans, we are free to choose our own jobs, work for others, or go into business for ourselves. We are free to buy and sell the goods and services we wish.

The American economic system is known as capitalism, or as a free enterprise economy. This means that it is based on a free market, free competition, private ownership of property, and the right to make a profit on business activities. Government does not tell business what to do. It acts as a referee in our economic system. The free American economy based on capitalism is clearly different from a system like that of the Soviet Union, which is based on a command economy.

American business firms may be organized as single proprietorships, partnerships, or corporations. A corporation usually is owned by many people. These people own shares of stock in the corporation. The money they pay to buy the stock is the capital that the corporation uses to engage in business.

Business owners must make decisions about their use of the four factors of production—land (which includes raw materials), capital, labor, and management. In the American economy, most of these decisions are freely made by business people as they seek to earn profits.

CIVICS SKILLS: Understanding a Warranty

- *A young woman in Chicago, Illinois, bought a sports car from a used-car dealer. One month later, she noticed a crack in the steering wheel.*
- *A family in Las Vegas, Nevada, picked up their new color television set from the store. That night a wire shorted out and the set started smoking.*

Whenever you buy a product, you naturally expect it to work properly. The same is true when you pay for a service. You want the job to be done well. What would you do if you found yourself in a situation such as those described above? You could, of course, just accept the fact that you've lost money. Or you could take the case to court. The best approach, however, is to make sure that you deal with a business that backs up its product or service with a written promise called a **warranty.**

A warranty, or guarantee, tells you what happens if something goes wrong. Not all companies issue warranties. Those that do usually make different kinds of promises. As a result, you should always ask to see a warranty before making any purchase. A careful reading of this document will save you a lot of trouble if something you buy does not work properly.

Studying a Warranty

According to federal law, all warranties have to meet certain guidelines. A warranty, for example, must be easy to read. It should also outline the obligations of both buyer and seller. Finally, a warranty should carry one of two labels—"full" or "limited."

The difference between these two types of warranties is important. A full warranty promises that a company will pay the total cost of a repair. A limited warranty covers only part of the expense. If a warranty is limited, you should find out what the limitations are. You may want to shop around to find the company with the best guarantees.

Practicing What You've Learned

1. Is the warranty shown below a full or a limited warranty?
2. Who pays for labor after 90 days?
3. What must the owner do to get service under the warranty?
4. Does this warranty meet federal guidelines? Why or why not?

LIMITED WARRANTY TO ORIGINAL PURCHASER
CAR RADIO/CAR STEREO

- This Hi-Tech product is warranted against manufacturing defects for the following period:

PARTS	LABOR
1 YEAR	90 DAYS

- Hi-Tech will repair or replace at no charge, any part(s) found to be defective during the warranty period.
- This warranty period starts on the date of purchase by the original owner.
- The warranty repairs must be performed at a Hi-Tech authorized service station. A list of Hi-Tech authorized service centers can be obtained at any Hi-Tech dealer.

OBLIGATIONS OF THE ORIGINAL OWNER

- The dealer's original bill of sale must be kept as proof of purchase and must be presented to the Hi-Tech authorized service station.
- Transportation to and from the service center is the responsibility of the customer.

EXCLUSIONS OF THE WARRANTY

- This warranty does not cover accident, misuse, or damage caused by improper installation.
- This warranty is valid only on products purchased and used in the United States.

CHAPTER REVIEW

Vocabulary

List each of the following terms in your notebook. Then write three paragraphs using each term to explain how our free economy works.

economy	command economy
standard of living	corporation
free market	stockholder
free competition	bonds
capitalist	single proprietorship
profit	board of directors
free enterprise	land
monopoly	rent
partnership	interest
dividends	net income
factors of production	manager

Check-Up

1. Describe several characteristics of a free economy.
2. What role does incentive play in our free enterprise system?
3. How does the law of supply and demand help our economy work well?
4. Describe two ways in which a monopoly is formed.
5. Do you think public utilities should be owned by the government or by private companies? Explain.
6. What was the secret of Frank W. Woolworth's success?
7. If you wanted to establish a corporation, what steps would you take?
8. Would you rather own bonds, common stock, or preferred stock? Why?
9. How can an individual obtain the capital needed to start a business?
10. How does our government aid and protect business?
11. Do you think there is too much government interference in business? Why or why not?

Civics Skills

What products would you most want to see covered by a warranty? Pick one of these products, and write a warranty that would protect both you and the manufacturer. Be sure your warranty meets the federal guidelines noted on page 318 of the textbook. Write your warranty so that it answers the following questions often asked by a careful buyer.

1. Is this a full or limited warranty?
2. Who is giving the warranty—the manufacturer or the store selling the product?
3. On what date does the warranty begin? When does it expire?
4. What are the terms of the warranty if something goes wrong with the product?
5. If the product cannot be repaired, is the purchase price refunded? If so, how is this money collected?

Citizenship and You

1. Invite a local business owner to tell the class how she or he established a business. Ask the owner about labor relations, taxes, government regulations, efficiency and productivity, and other problems faced by management.
2. Prepare a bulletin board exhibit on "The American Way of Business."
3. Imagine that you want to set up your own business. Keeping in mind the four factors of production, write a report explaining the steps you would take to set up the business.
4. Prepare a chart showing several advantages and disadvantages of the single proprietorship, the partnership, and the corporation.
5. On a chalkboard, compare the ways in which decisions are made in the economic systems of the United States and the Soviet Union.

CHAPTER

17

How Our Goods Are Produced and Marketed

One of the outstanding features of the American economic system is its ability to produce. Just about any product you might want to buy is made in our nation. In recent years, the United States has produced over $2 trillion worth of goods and services a year! This is more than any other nation in the world.

The dollar value of what we produce is called the **Gross National Product (GNP).** It is figured by adding up the dollar value of all goods and services produced in the United States during the year.

Economists—the people who study the economy—use the GNP as one measure of how well our economy is performing. If the GNP rises year after year, the nation's economy is doing well generally. If the GNP for any one year falls, the economy probably slowed down during that year. This means that people did not have as much money to spend, save, or invest.

There are also other ways of judging the health of an economy. The number of unemployed people, the number of business failures, and the amount of tax income produced by the nation all help tell us how healthy the economy is.

In this chapter, you will look at the system of production that makes it possible for the United States to have such a high Gross National Product. You will also learn how our goods and services get to the people who want and need them. You will learn about some of the laws that protect consumers and get some tips on intelligent buying. These are the topics you will study in this chapter:

1. **The American System of Mass Production**
2. **Marketing America's Goods**
3. **You, the Consumer**

1

The American System of Mass Production

During one recent year, the United States produced nearly 12 million automobiles, trucks, and buses. In a single year we produced over 775 million tons (698 million metric tons) of coal, over 136 million tons (122 million metric tons) of steel, and more than 7 billion bushels (246 billion liters) of corn. Millions of other goods are produced every year in our nation. What makes this huge production possible?

Mass Production

There are many factors that make the United States capable of such an enormous output. One is mass production. **Mass production** means huge amounts of goods being made rapidly by machines to supply the needs and wants of the nation's large population. Mass production requires many big machines and vast amounts of power. American inventors have developed machines that can make, or help make, almost any product that you can imagine.

One of the first inventors to make mass production possible was Eli Whitney. (You may remember him as the inventor of the cotton gin.) In 1800 Whitney signed a contract to make muskets, or guns, for the United States Army. He promised to manufacture 10,000 guns in two years' time. The promise seemed impossible to keep. This was because up to that time guns had been made by hand, one by one. To prove that he could keep his promise, Whitney agreed to show some government officials how he planned to make the guns.

From a box, he took ten gun barrels, ten triggers, ten stocks, and ten locks for exploding the powder. He asked the officials to choose one of each of these parts. Whitney then took the four parts and quickly put together a finished musket. To show that the parts were all alike, he continued to put together muskets until all ten were completed. He had made ten identical guns from a box containing identical parts. Moreover, he was able to do this very rapidly.

Eli Whitney's methods have become the basis of all mass production, from radios and sewing machines to automobiles and tractors. What are these methods?

1. Use of Machine Tools. Whitney developed **machine tools,** or machinery carefully built to turn out parts that were exactly the same. Instead of boring each gun barrel by hand, for example, he made a machine that did nothing but bore gun barrels, all in the same way.

2. Use of Standard Parts. Each of Whitney's machine tools made parts that were exactly alike, called **standard parts.** That is, any Whitney gun barrel would fit any gun made by Whitney. Other parts were all alike and would fit any of the guns. This was a great advantage. If a part wore out, it could easily be replaced by a new standard part.

3. Use of Division of Labor. Barrels, triggers, stocks, and locks for Whitney's guns were made by different groups of workers, each operating a separate machine. No one worker made a complete gun. The whole job was divided among the various workers. In this **division of labor,** each worker was a specialist at part of the job.

The use of machine tools, standard parts, and division of labor helped increase production. Yet the early machines used by Whitney and others were small and inefficient. Many machines used in factories today are enormous and highly efficient.

Large Machines Require Great Power

For many years, Americans used the force of falling water, or water power, as the source of energy to operate their machines. Early factories were therefore located near streams. Dams were built to hold back water so that it could be released when necessary to turn water wheels. As these big wheels turned, their power was used to turn machines within the factory.

Then a great change took place. James Watt, a Scottish engineer, invented a practical steam engine. This invention became more and more popular in the United States. Soon steam power began to replace water power.

Steam power continued to be the leading source of industrial power during the 1800's. In the 1900's several new sources of power were developed. For instance, the internal combustion engine used the power released by exploding gasoline. It was often used to run small machines. The main use of the internal combustion engine, however, was in the automobile.

The source of power that really made modern mass production possible was electricity. In the late 1800's the work of Thomas Edison made practical the widespread use of electricity. At first it was used mainly for lighting. As time went on, it was used in many other ways. American families now use electricity to run their toasters, fans, refrigerators, air conditioners, washers, dryers, vacuum cleaners, radios, and television sets. Today nearly every American factory uses electricity as its source of power. In addition, scientists are constantly searching for even better sources of power.

★ ★ ★ ★ ★ ★ ★ ★ ★ ★ ★ ★

CAN YOU GUESS?

- **One of our Presidents was also an inventor. Who was he?**
- **An 1893 invention that helps us get into and out of our clothes was first marketed as a "clasp locker or unlocker for shoes." What is it?**
- **Chewing gum, first manufactured for sale in 1872, has a long history. Who were the first people to use it?**

Answers are on page 562.

Mass Production in an Automobile Factory

One of the best ways to understand modern mass production is to visit an automobile manufacturing plant. Suppose you were to go to Detroit, Michigan, to make such a visit. What would you see?

After you enter the factory, it may take a few minutes to get used to all the activity and noise. As you look about, you begin to see how Eli Whitney's methods of manufacturing are still used by American industry.

As an engine block moves by, a team of workers goes to work on it. First a huge machine tool bores 87 holes into the block, all in one operation. As the block moves along, workers fit pistons, valves, and bolts into the holes. The block has become an internal combustion engine. Other teams of workers fasten carburetors, ignitions, and

Foundations of Modern Mass Production

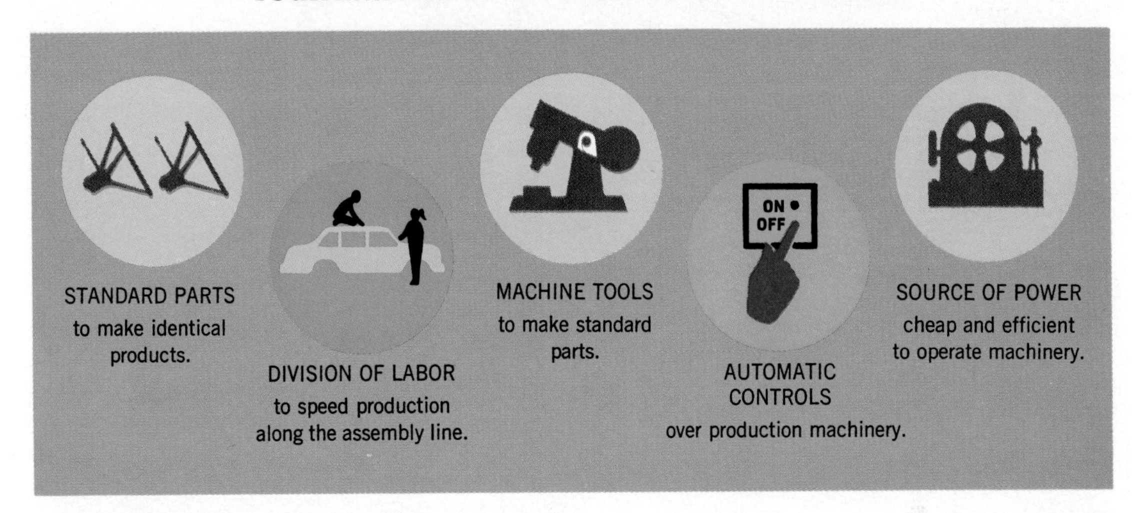

other parts to the engine. One automobile engine after another is made in this way, each exactly alike.

How does modern mass production use Whitney's methods? Think about what you have just seen in the automobile plant. You saw a machine tool used to produce identical parts—in this case, bored engine blocks for cars. You saw many examples of the division of labor. Each worker does a special job and has become highly skilled. You saw many standard parts, such as valves, being used. Each valve fits exactly into a hole in the engine block. Each wire fits into a part where it belongs. Eli Whitney's ideas for making guns really started something important!

The Assembly Line

One feature of modern mass production is different from Whitney's day. That feature is the **assembly line.** How does the assembly line work?

Let's watch it again in our visit to the automobile plant. Starting with just the frame, the car moves along on a very large **conveyor belt.** The belt slowly moves many car frames at a time through the factory.

As the car frame moves slowly along the assembly line, the four wheels are added to the frame. Then the engine, transmission, windshield, steering wheel, and gears are added. Seats, door panels, and lights are put on next. The car moves on to the paint shop. There it is spray-painted and dried. It is finally driven off the assembly line and tested. The car is now ready to be shipped to an automobile dealer's showroom. There customers may look at it, test drive it, and buy it.

How do the various parts arrive at the assembly line just in time to become parts of the finished automobile? At the beginning of your tour, you recall, you saw an engine being made. This engine was not then on the main assembly line. It was on a side line, or **feeder line.** The engine's movement along the feeder line was timed so that the engine was completed just as the feeder line met the main assembly line.

The engine was then lowered into place in the car from its overhead conveyor belt. In this way, feeder lines are used to assemble many parts of the car and bring them to the main assembly line exactly when and where they are needed.

Your imaginary visit to an automobile plant should have helped you understand the

This American automobile plant includes many features of modern mass production. Here automobiles are shown moving along a robot welding assembly line.

mass production methods that are used in nearly all of our large industries. The automobile industry, while important, is just one of our nation's many large industries.

Bread from a bakery is made in a similar way. Flour and other ingredients are dumped into mixers from overhead bins. Conveyor belts running from the storage rooms supply the bins. After the loaf is shaped, it is carried on a conveyor belt through a block-long oven. By the time it reaches the other end of the oven, the bread is baked.

The finished loaf travels through another machine that slices and wraps it. Still another machine packs loaves in boxes. A conveyor then transports the boxes to trucks for delivery to stores.

Mass Production in the World

Mass production was first developed in the United States, but it has spread to other nations. European nations have made use of it for years. Japan has adopted and perfected methods of mass production.

The Soviet Union also uses mass production methods. But it has not been as successful as other nations. One reason may be that in the Soviet Union, as you recall, the government controls the economy. Property is not privately owned. People are not free to start their own businesses as they wish. They cannot decide what prices to charge or the amount of goods and services to produce. This kind of economy—a command economy—does not have the same incentives, or motives, that a free economy has. The lack of incentive discourages people from working hard or producing more.

A free economy stimulates business people to take risks. When there is no incentive to make a profit by taking a risk, people may be less inclined to take risks. What, for example, was Eli Whitney's incentive? He invented a new method of production because he hoped to profit from it. So did all the other business people who adopted and perfected our system of mass production.

Business people must be quick to grasp new ideas. To continue competing, they must be ready to change from old ways to new ways. They must do this even if it means rebuilding factories and buying costly new machinery.

CHECK-UP

Vocabulary

Gross National Product	standard parts
economists	division of labor
mass production	assembly line
machine tools	conveyor belt
	feeder line

Review

1. What did Eli Whitney contribute to the American economic system?
2. Why were early factories built near streams? What source of power is used by nearly every American factory today?
3. Describe the methods of mass production that are used in the American automobile industry today.
4. How does the incentive to make a profit affect the American economy?

Discuss

From the worker's point of view, what might be some of the advantages and disadvantages of mass production methods?

2
Marketing America's Goods

American industry and business produce goods and services that supply our needs. Yet production is only one part of supplying our needs. The other is **distribution.** After goods are produced, they must be distributed to the people who want them.

Distribution has two sides: transportation and marketing. **Transportation** is essential for bringing goods from the places where they are made to the places where people can buy or use them. Getting people to buy the goods is called **marketing.**

Transporting America's Goods

In such a vast land as the United States, transportation has always been important. Early in our history, the American people learned that a good system of transportation was necessary to bring together, or unify, the nation. As a result, young America went through a long period of road, canal, and railroad building. This made it possible for American businesses and industries to transport their goods to all parts of the nation.

American industry was greatly aided by the growth of railroads. Railroads that fanned out all over the nation helped create a single huge market for products. Long freight trains rolled from coast to coast carrying raw materials, machine tools, standard parts, and countless other products. The railroads brought up-to-date products to every American city, to most towns, and within reach of all farms. They brought business people a means of rapid travel and communication.

Railroad Transportation Today

Railroads were the nation's chief method of transporting passengers and freight for nearly a century. In the mid-1900's, however, railroads found it difficult to compete with other means of transportation—trucks, buses, automobiles, and airplanes. In the 1960's and 1970's, many railroads went out of business. Railroads carried a smaller percentage of passengers and freight.

Some experts think our railroads cannot become profitable unless they modernize. The tracks and equipment of many railroad lines in the United States are in poor condition. Also, our trains are not as speedy as more modern trains in some nations. For example, the Amtrak Metroliner travels between New York and Washington, D.C., at speeds of up to 90 miles (144 kilometers) an hour. But the newest train in France travel at speeds of 230 miles (370 kilometers) an hour.

Railroads, though, are an important part of our transportation system. They are needed to carry bulk cargo, such as coal and grain. They carry passengers. They give people jobs. Trying to save the railroads, Congress created a new national rail passenger system called Amtrak in 1971. Organized with funds from the federal government, Amtrak is working hard to improve the nation's railroads.

Air Transportation

Today railroads must compete with other forms of transportation. In passenger transportation, the airlines have grown rapidly. In 1950 railroads carried over 6 percent of the passengers traveling between cities. Airlines carried less than 2 percent. By the early 1980's, the airlines had over 10 percent of passenger traffic. The railroads had less than 1 percent. Modern research, equipment, and management methods have made airlines in the United States among the best and safest in the world.

Airlines now carry all first-class mail between American cities over a certain distance apart. They are also important in transporting freight. Airlines can carry all kinds of freight—from small packages to large industrial machinery, and autos—with great speed.

Our Highway System

The automobile is the leading means of transportation in the United States. Private automobiles carry over 86 percent of passengers—more than all other kinds of transportation combined. More than 120 million cars are registered in the United States. That is about one vehicle for every two persons.

Rapid highway transportation depends on good roads. To speed motor traffic, our nation has built a great highway system. We now have more than 3.8 million miles (6.1 million kilometers) of roads.

Some of our highways are toll roads. Drivers must pay a toll, or fee, to use these roads. Other roads are freeways, which are free of

Railroads helped make possible the tremendous growth of American industry. Today railroads remain an important part of our nation's transportation system.

charge. More and more of the recently built roads are limited-access superhighways. Limited access means that cars can enter the highways only at certain points. Superhighways have several lanes and higher speed limits. The interstate highway system provides a network of highways that reaches every part of the nation.

Buses, cars, and trucks can be seen on our highways at all hours. Cars create the heaviest traffic. Large trucks carry 60 percent of the nation's freight. Heavy traffic on highways and roads has caused a number of problems. Among them are traffic jams, accidents, air pollution, and heavy use of oil—a nonrenewable resource. Among the steps being taken to solve these problems are lower speed limits, nonpolluting cars, smaller cars, and better public transportation.

It may seem hard to believe today, but the term "supermarket" did not even exist 40 years ago. Now supermarkets are a necessary part of everyday life.

Mass Marketing

Selling goods in large quantities is called **mass marketing.** This kind of large-scale selling is well illustrated by the modern supermarket. The **supermarket** is a huge store that sells hundreds of different kinds of products of nearly every brand. At first the supermarket was mainly a food store. Now it also often sells drugs, auto supplies, phonograph records, clothes, hardware, and many other products.

The customer pushes a cart up and down the aisles, selecting articles from well-stocked shelves. When the customer has finished shopping, she or he rolls the cart to the checkout counter. There a cashier rings up the purchases on a cash register.

Another example of mass marketing is the **department store.** This is a large store that has many separate sections for selling different kinds of goods.

The type of marketing that is used in supermarkets and department stores is called **self-service.** It is an efficient and inexpensive way to sell goods because it is labor-saving. Self-service is a modern method of marketing. Fifty years ago, storekeepers hired clerks to sell their goods. Each clerk waited on only one customer at a time. In today's self-service stores, many customers can shop at the same time, and one clerk can help many more people.

Standard packaging also adds to the efficiency of the self-service system of marketing. Goods come from the factory already wrapped. Crackers, for instance, are sealed in double wrappers and sold in boxes. Sugar comes in boxes or bags of different weights. Steaks, chops, and other meats are cut in convenient sizes and wrapped in plastic. Years ago crackers came in a barrel. They were weighed out for each customer. Sugar also was scooped out of a barrel. It was poured into a paper bag and weighed for each customer. Today few items have to be weighed or measured in the store.

(continued on page 330)

CITIZENSHIP IN ACTION

Foxfire—A Class Project Becomes a Big Business

Eliot Wigginton (right) and his students publish *Foxfire* four times a year.

Can a group of teenagers in a rural high school start a successful magazine? They can, and they did. Students in Rabun County High School in northeastern Georgia publish a magazine that is read throughout the country.

Creating a Magazine

The idea for the magazine started with Eliot Wigginton during his first year as an English teacher in Rabun County High School. He wanted to find a way to help his students learn language arts skills. He also wanted to help them understand their own backgrounds and the community in which they live. Only by knowing how their community actually works, he believed, could they become committed to its future and help plan appropriate methods for improving the community.

A magazine put out by the students seemed to be an ideal way to fulfill these goals. Moreover, publishing a magazine would give students the opportunity to create and run a business. From the start the plan was for students to do all the work—everything from raising money to writing articles and preparing material for the printer.

The contents of the magazine were drawn from the students' own community, which is in the Appalachian Mountains—an area with a rich culture and heritage. The articles included stories about the people of the community. Older citizens told students about their experiences and what they had learned from them. Relatives and neighbors also demonstrated, step by step, many traditional skills such as woodcarving, weaving, and building a log cabin.

The class named their magazine *Foxfire,* after a lichen, or mosslike plant, that glows in the dark. The students went from door to door asking for contributions to help them pay the printer for the first issue. They collected $440, enough for 600 copies of the magazine. When they sold those copies, they had enough money to print the next issue. In a short time the magazine paid for itself.

The Magazine Is a Success

The students published *Foxfire* four times a year, and readers kept asking for it year after year. Soon the magazine was known throughout the country. Articles from the magazine were collected in *The Foxfire Book,* which sold more than 3 million copies. Many other *Foxfire* books have followed. A classroom project had turned into a huge success!

Many years have passed since *Foxfire* was started in 1966. New groups of students have taken over, and the magazine has branched into new fields. Income from the magazine and books pays for college scholarships and enables *Foxfire* to hire students to work during the summer. Today more than half the staff members are former students who returned after graduating from college. These staff members also work at the high school. They help students continue to publish the magazine and books, and help them produce daily shows about the community for the local cable television station. Students also produce and market a series of record albums and conduct environmental studies in the region. When the operation needed more space, the students were able to buy land and move and reconstruct 24 traditional log buildings.

The magazine continues to be popular. One reason for its success is that it is filled with useful information. It explains, for example, how to use common items to make quilts, toys, and baskets. Readers have learned about blacksmithing and well digging.

The students who worked on the magazine discovered that the people of their community possessed a vast amount of information that was appreciated by millions of other Americans. The success of *Foxfire* encouraged students in other communities to start similar projects. Similar magazines are now being published in high schools all across the country.

Many older citizens demonstrate their traditional handicrafts for *Foxfire.*

Thinking It Over

1. How does *Foxfire* make use of the special human resources of the Appalachian region?
2. What do you think students might learn about business by putting out magazines such as *Foxfire?*

DID YOU KNOW THAT . . .

advertising was used to settle the United States? In the late 1800's the Great Plains had few settlers. Railroad companies, extending their tracks into the region, had land they wanted to sell. They also hoped to profit from farmers who would ship freight on their lines. So the railroads started a huge advertising campaign to encourage men and women to settle in the West.

The railroads ran ads in newspapers and put up hundreds of posters. Sometimes they even offered immigrants free transportation to visit their native lands if they agreed to persuade others to return to the United States with them. Thousands of people responded, and many new communities grew up almost overnight.

Another feature of mass marketing is the **one-price system.** This means that the selling price is stamped on every item. The one-price system was first used by Wanamaker's department store in Philadelphia more than 100 years ago. Now it is standard everywhere. Before the one-price system, customers often bargained with salespeople to try to get the price down a little. Imagine how much time a shopper would spend in buying the week's groceries if he or she had to bargain for every item instead of paying the price marked on the product!

Shopping Malls and Centers

An outgrowth of the supermarket has been the **shopping mall,** or **shopping center.** This is a large cluster of different kinds of stores, partly or completely surrounded by a big parking area. The center of the mall or shopping center is usually a food supermarket or a large department store. There may also be a drugstore, shoe store, hardware store, restaurant, and a dozen or more stores and shops of other kinds.

The mall or shopping center is an example of highly efficient marketing. Customers can drive in, park their cars, and buy almost everything they need. Many stores can afford to sell goods at lower prices because so many goods are being sold so rapidly in the shopping center.

Chain Stores and Specialty Shops

Many of the stores in a shopping mall or center are chain stores. A **chain store** is owned and operated by a company that has many of the same kind of stores. The company may purchase its goods directly from the factory or farm. Or it may own its own factory or farm. The chain store can get its products at lower cost because it buys or produces goods in large quantities.

Many stores are independent. That is, they do not belong to a chain of stores. Many such stores are **specialty shops.** They sell only certain kinds of goods or offer a particular kind of service. They may sell only women's or men's clothing, books, or toys and games.

These small, independent stores often offer special services not provided by larger stores. For instance, smaller stores often handle special products for which there is not a great demand. These locally owned stores are important to most communities. The business people who own and operate them make an important contribution to the prosperity of any community.

Wholesalers and Retailers

Products may pass through several hands from the time they leave the factory to the time they reach the customer. A factory often sells goods in large quantities to a **wholesaler.** This business person owns a large warehouse where goods can be stored. The wholesaler sells to **retailers.** A **retail store** is one that sells directly to the public.

Wholesalers are often called distributors. They perform a service in linking the factory and the retailer. In the end, of course, the customer must pay for this service. Chain stores, large department stores, and supermarkets often have their own warehouses. They have no need for distributors. Therefore, sometimes they can offer goods to the public at lower prices.

The distribution and marketing of goods, whatever methods are used, cost a great deal of money. Sometimes it costs as much to market a product as it did to make it. Inefficient marketing may add to the price you pay for a product. Just as in mass production, efficiency in mass distribution reduces the prices of the things you buy.

Advertising

Mass marketing of goods would not be possible without advertising. **Advertising** tells people about new products and tries to persuade some of them to buy these products. It speeds up the movement of goods from factories to the public.

In the competition between producers of similar products, advertising often makes the difference between the success of one product and the failure of another. Some people say this is bad. They say it would be better and less wasteful not to have so many products. Others say that competition among mass producers, marketers, and advertisers helps to keep quality high and prices low.

National advertising makes it possible for producers to sell their products all over the country. They do this by getting people to recognize their products by their brand name. A **brand name** product is usually widely advertised and distributed over a large area. When customers shop, they may choose a product with a brand name they have heard about most favorably or most often. By using national advertising, small producers may be able to grow into large national producers. Then they can mass produce for a larger market at lower costs.

Shoppers are sometimes confused by advertising, especially when several producers claim that their product is best or most effective. Yet advertising is a useful way for a producer to inform shoppers about a new product. In the next section, you will learn how you can get good value for your money in the American system of mass production and mass marketing.

CHECK-UP

Vocabulary

distribution
transportation
marketing
mass marketing
supermarket
department store
self-service
standard packaging
one-price system
shopping mall
shopping center
chain store
specialty shop
wholesaler
retailer
retail store
advertising
brand name

Review

1. Why is a good system of transportation important to the American economy?
2. How did the growth of railroads affect business?
3. How does mass marketing affect the way you shop?
4. What is the role of advertising in American business?

Discuss

Are you more likely to buy a product that has been advertised? Explain.

3

You, the Consumer

Each one of us is a consumer, or customer. A **consumer** is one who buys or uses products and services. As consumers we play an extremely important part in the American free economic system.

Each year business firms spend billions of dollars to get us to buy their products. They run advertisements in newspapers and magazines, on billboards and posters, over radio and television. They think up clever slogans they hope we will remember. They know that some of us will buy the product whose slogan appeals to us. Often the slogan has nothing to do with the quality or the usefulness of the product.

Some shoppers are **impulse buyers.** They buy just because they see something they think they want. They like the slogan or the advertising skit on television. So they buy the product. They buy without thinking about the price or about the real usefulness of the product. Other people buy intelligently. Anyone can learn to buy intelligently.

Learning Where and When to Buy

There are a number of ways in which consumers can get the most for their shopping dollars. For example, wise food shoppers study the food advertisements in the local paper. They find out which stores are having special sales. At certain times of the year, chicken may be priced very low. At other times, certain fruits and vegetables may be bargains.

By watching for sales, you can often buy suits, dresses, coats, shirts, blouses, neckties, and other articles at reduced prices. Some people never pay the full price for an article. They stock up when the price is low.

A low price on an item, however, does not always mean the item is a bargain. Furniture, automobiles, television sets, and even houses are often advertised as bargains. Yet a bargain is not a bargain if it is something you cannot really use or if it is poorly made. It is not a bargain if the one you already have is just as good as a new one.

How to Judge Price and Quality

Wise shoppers must be able to judge the quality of a product. They also must know how they plan to use it. Of the many goods and services available, shoppers must make sure that they choose those that are best suited to their own needs. Many consumers solve the problem by shopping only at well-known stores that guarantee the quality of anything they sell. Others learn how to shop at various stores and look for real bargains.

Many people buy articles by brand name. They trust certain business firms. They believe that all products bearing the brand names of these firms must be of good quality. This may or may not be true. Large nationwide firms, as you have read, sell their products under brand names. They spend billions of dollars making consumers aware of these names. One way to be sure of the quality of a product is to study its label carefully.

How to Study Labels

Labels are placed on foods, clothing, and other articles in order to protect you, the consumer. Our governments require that certain kinds of information be included on these labels to help consumers judge the quality of the products.

There are a number of federal laws on labeling. For example, the Food, Drug, and Cosmetic Act provides that all packages of food, as well as drugs and some cosmetics, must state all the things these products contain. The Wool Products Act requires that the label on clothing state how much wool it contains.

Watching for sales is an excellent way to buy something you need at a reduced price. But remember, the wise consumer is always a careful shopper.

Manufacturers must also state the name of the fabric in every garment, whether wool, cotton, or artificial fiber. They must also tell how to clean it. The Fur Products Labeling Act orders the maker of a fur garment to state from what animal the fur was taken and from what country the fur came.

Some of our state and local governments require that every package of meat carry information about its contents. If it is hamburger, for example, the package must name the part of the animal from which the ground meat comes. It also must state whether anything besides meat has been added.

Many products, such as bread, milk, and cheese, must be stamped with a date. This is the date by which the product must be sold. Dating a product ensures that it will be fresh when purchased.

Some laws require **unit pricing.** That is, the price tag must show how much money is being asked a unit—for an ounce or a gram, for example. A 10-ounce (283-gram) can of peaches would be a better buy than a can at the same price with only 8 ounces (227 grams). Also, a can with fewer peaches and more syrup would not be as good a buy as one with less syrup and more peaches, even if the weight marked on the can was the same.

Unless people are able to read labels intelligently, the labels will be of no help to them. Beware of a term such as "highest quality." These words sound good. Yet they often have no real meaning. A label stating that a piece of clothing is "pre-shrunk" means little. The label does not tell you how much the piece of clothing is likely to shrink when it is washed. If the label says "Sanforized," however, you know the clothing will not shrink more than 1 percent. The word "Sanforized" is a standardized term that has this meaning in the clothing industry.

Organizations that Aid Consumers

Sometimes people find that a product has been falsely labeled or advertised. If you believe you have been misled by an unfair business practice, you should first try to seek satisfaction from the business that sold you the product or service. If you are still not satisfied, you should get in touch with the local **Better Business Bureau.** There is one in or near most communities. This organization gives advice and assistance to people who feel they have been cheated or treated unfairly by a business firm.

The federal government also protects the consumer in a number of ways. The Federal Trade Commission, for instance, has the power to bring to court any business firm that uses false or misleading advertising or false labeling. The National Bureau of Standards tests and grades many products. The Department of Agriculture inspects and grades meat, poultry, and certain other foods sold in interstate commerce. The United States Postal Service sees that business firms do not use the mails to cheat the public. The Consumer Product Safety Commission checks products to be sure they will not cause injuries.

The variety of products available in the United States means that consumers have a chance to compare quality and price before making a purchase.

A number of cities also have commissioners or departments of consumer affairs. They publish consumer advice and warn business firms if they violate consumer laws. The firms are brought to court if they persist in cheating consumers.

There are a number of private organizations that help consumers. These include Consumers' Research and Consumers Union. These organizations test and rate nearly every product the public buys. They publish the results of their tests in magazines and special reports. A visit to the library to examine their publications may help you compare various brands of the same product. In this way you can learn which is best for your own needs and which is the best buy.

Problems Caused by Consumers

Consumers often accuse businesses of misleading advertising, poor service, and inferior products. Sometimes, however, consumers cause problems for businesses.

Shoplifting, for example, costs billions of dollars each year. Some people damage the store owner's property or demand refunds for merchandise they have already used or abused. Items in motels, hotels, and restaurants are frequently stolen or damaged. Sometimes people fail to pay for purchases obtained on credit.

These people are not professional criminals. They seem to think their actions are unimportant. They often feel that the business—especially if it is a big business—can afford the loss. However, they may be hurting other consumers because these dishonest acts add to the costs of doing business. The prices of products and services may have to be increased to help cover the losses.

Pay Now or Later?

When you buy something, you may pay cash. You also may charge it. Or you may buy it on the installment plan. Just what are the advantages and disadvantages of buying merchandise in these three ways?

The person who pays cash is likely to be a careful buyer. Since the buyer must pay the full amount at the time of purchase, he or she is likely to think carefully before handing the money to the sales clerk. In addition, a person with cash is sometimes able to buy a product for a lower price than someone who has to rely on credit. She or he may be able to shop in a store that sells products at a reduced price for cash only.

On the other hand, suppose you find a real bargain on something you need. However, you do not have the cash to pay for it. At such times, a charge account can be of help. A **charge account** is an easy form of credit that stores grant to many of their customers. A charge account can usually be obtained by people who have a steady job and a record of paying their bills on time. A charge account permits customers to buy now and pay later. That is, they can make their purchases during the month but not pay for them until the end of the month, or whenever they get the bill from the store.

If customers fail to pay their bills when they are due, the store may close their charge accounts. Such customers become bad credit risks. As a result, they may find it difficult to obtain a charge account somewhere else. Stores compare information about customers. This enables them to find out whether a person is a good credit risk.

Shopping Tips for Consumers

- Shop around. Prices do vary. Comparison-shop at stores in your area. Keep an eye on the ads.
- Watch for genuine sales and specials. Not everything advertised is at a better price today than it will be tomorrow. Hunt out the real bargains. There always are some around. Watch and learn which stores put what things on sale and when.
- Be careful about impulse buying. Supermarket shoppers often buy more than they put down on their shopping lists. Don't permit impulse to trick you into buying things you don't need or even want.
- Buy what's right for you. In clothing, for example, classic styles may be more suited to you than the latest fashion craze. Let your own experience guide you.
- Investigate the store brands in food, clothing, and appliance lines. They may be priced lower than national brands. Test the quality. Learn which store labels or brands you prefer.
- Read the label information. Clothing labels, for example, will tell you important facts about size, the materials used, and proper cleaning methods.
- Look for low maintenance. Many product improvements in recent years have focused on easy care. One example is machine-washable sweaters. In some cases these products may cost more, however. Don't pay more for convenience than it is worth to you.
- Consider service and "returns." Deal with retailers and manufacturers who stand behind what they sell and who will service or replace a product. If they go out of their way to serve you, they want your business. And they may deserve it.

Pros and Cons of Charge Accounts

There are advantages to using charge accounts. What are some of them?

A charge account makes it easy for you to keep track of what you have bought and what you paid for various articles. You do not have to carry large amounts of cash with you when you go shopping. If you have a charge account, it is easier for you to return purchases you decide you do not want. Charge account customers often receive notices of sales before the sales are advertised in the local newspapers.

Most important, when you have charge

Advertising plays a major role in informing consumers about products being sold. Why is it important to pay careful attention to all advertisements?

accounts and pay your bills regularly, you establish a good credit rating for yourself. A **credit rating** tells how well customers pay their bills. A good credit rating is valuable when you want to open other charge accounts, take out a bank loan, or buy a house.

There are also disadvantages in having a charge account. What are some of them?

Charge account customers often pick up the phone and order what they want without shopping around for the best values. They may buy things on impulse that they do not need. They may find themselves paying more for what they buy. Stores that sell for cash often sell items for less because they do not have to hire clerks or pay for computers to keep charge account records.

Stores that allow charge accounts often charge interest on unpaid balances. If the bill is not paid by the due date (usually 10 to 30 days after the customer receives the bill), most stores add a percent of the unpaid balance to the bill. The interest is often over 19 percent a year. The federal Truth in Lending Law now requires stores to print this kind of information on their bills.

Buying on the Installment Plan

There is another way for consumers to buy goods without paying the full amount in cash when they make their purchases. They can use the **installment plan.** In this system of buying, the buyer uses cash to pay part of the purchase price. This is called the **down payment.** The rest of what the buyer owes is called the **balance.** This is paid in small equal payments, or **installments,** over a period of weeks or months. The installment plan allows a buyer to have the use of a product while paying for it.

Automobiles, refrigerators, furniture, and other large items are often bought on the installment plan. The purchaser signs a written contract with the seller. The contract states how much the installment payments must be and how often they must be paid. It also states that the article still belongs to the seller.

If the customer does not complete the necessary number of installment payments, the seller can **repossess,** or take back, the article. When this happens, the purchaser loses the article. He or she also loses the amount of money that has already been paid.

Buying an article on the installment plan

increases its cost. In addition to the regular price, a **carrying charge** as well as interest on the unpaid balance is included in the installment payments.

If you should ever think of buying something on the installment plan, you may find it cheaper to borrow the money from a bank. You can then pay cash for the article and pay the bank back in installments. This is called **installment credit.** Banks usually charge only interest, and not an additional carrying charge, for installment loans. The interest paid to the bank may be less than the combined carrying charge and interest under an installment plan contract.

Whether you buy an article under an installment plan or installment credit, it is wise to make as large a down payment as possible. Also it is wise to pay off the balance as quickly as possible.

CHECK-UP

Vocabulary

consumer
impulse buyers
unit pricing
Better Business Bureau
charge account
credit rating
installment plan
down payment
balance
installments
repossess
carrying charge
installment credit

Review

1. What can the label on a product tell you?
2. What organizations help consumers get a fair deal?
3. What are the advantages and disadvantages of installment buying?

Discuss

If you were going to buy a radio, how would you make sure you were getting a good buy?

CHAPTER SUMMARY

The American system of mass production makes possible the wide variety of goods and services Americans can buy. The easy availability of all these products enables the American people to enjoy a high standard of living.

Mass production is made possible by machine tools, standard parts, and division of labor. It requires great sources of power to run the machines. These elements of mass production are organized in an assembly line on which the products move as they are manufactured.

Once products are manufactured, there must be a good system of distribution—transportation and marketing. Railroads, trucks, ships, and planes transport goods from factories, farms, and warehouses. They take them to places where consumers can buy them. Our mass marketing system includes many kinds of stores and service organizations. It also requires the labor of many workers.

As consumers, or customers, each of us has an important role to play in our economy. In knowing how to judge price and quality and in buying wisely, we help manufacturers and retailers know how they can serve us best. By making use of the consumer organizations that serve us and by learning the best ways to pay for goods, whether with cash or on credit, we get good value for our money.

CIVICS SKILLS: Reading a Label

Imagine that you've been sent to the supermarket to buy a can of sliced peaches. That might seem easy at first. However, as you walk down the canned-fruit aisle, you see at least a dozen different kinds of peaches, with as many different prices. Should you reach for the cheapest brand? Or would the most expensive one be the best choice? How do you decide which brand would be both nutritious and a good buy? One way is by carefully reading the **label,** or product description, attached to each can.

Labels, as you learned in this chapter, are placed on a product to protect you, the consumer. They tell you what a product contains. In the case of a food item, this means the ingredients that were used to make it. By law, a label must list ingredients in the order of their amounts. The main ingredient appears first, and the ingredient used in the smallest amount appears last. Examine the ingredients on the label below. Which ingredient was used in the greatest quantity? the smallest?

Identifying the Nutritional Content

A list of ingredients gives you a lot of information about a product. However, you can't always learn a food's nutritional value from this list alone. To determine if a certain food would be a healthy part of your diet, you need to study two other sets of facts found on a food label.

Like most information printed on labels, nutritional information has to meet guidelines established by the federal government. In the section entitled "Nutrition Information Per Serving," for example, you must be told how many servings are in the container. You must also be informed of the serving size, as well as the amount of calories, proteins, carbohydrates, and fat per serving. Some of these facts will be given in grams, others will be in ounces.

To find out about a product's vitamin and mineral content, you need to read another section of the label, entitled "Percent of U.S. Recommended Daily Allowance (RDA)." Here you will learn how much of your daily vitamin and mineral needs—your RDA—are filled by one serving of a particular food. According to federal law, the percentages for at least seven essential vitamins and minerals must be reported. Why might these figures influence your decision to choose one brand over another?

Practicing What You've Learned

Use the label on this page to answer the following questions.

1. How many grams (g) of protein are in each serving of peaches? How many grams of protein are in the whole can?
2. What percentage of your daily requirement of vitamin A is supplied by one serving of peaches? of calcium?
3. Why do you think the number of calories in a serving would interest some people?

Sliced Peaches

NUTRITION INFORMATION PER SERVING

SERVING SIZE	4 OZ.	PROTEIN	1g
SERVINGS PER CONTAINER	2	CARBOHYDRATE	12g
CALORIES	50	FAT	0

PERCENT OF U.S. RECOMMENDED DAILY ALLOWANCE (U.S. RDA)

VITAMIN A	10	NIACIN	4
VITAMIN C	6	CALCIUM	*
THIAMINE (B_1)	*	IRON	*
RIBOFLAVIN (B_2)	*		

*CONTAINS LESS THAN 2 PERCENT OF U.S. RDA OF THESE NUTRIENTS.

INGREDIENTS: PEACHES, WATER, CONCENTRATED PEAR JUICE, CONCENTRATED APPLE JUICE, AND CONCENTRATED GRAPE JUICE.

STERLING FRUIT COMPANY
LA GRANGE, IL. 60525 U.S.A.

CHAPTER REVIEW

Vocabulary

Get to know the following terms by using them in sentences. Use each term to explain how our system of production and distribution works.

unit pricing	machine tools
Gross National Product	standard parts
mass production	assembly line
retail store	wholesaler
distribution	consumer
installment plan	credit rating
	charge account

Check-Up

1. How did Eli Whitney help make mass production possible?
2. How has our national system of transportation changed in recent years?
3. Name three features of mass marketing.
4. Why can chain stores sell articles for less than small local stores can? How do some small stores stay in business?
5. How does the wholesaler serve our national economy?
6. How does advertising help make mass marketing possible?
7. What is the danger of being an impulse buyer?
8. Give some rules for wise buying.
9. In what ways does the federal government protect consumers?
10. How do some consumers cause problems for businesses and other consumers?

Civics Skills

In a supermarket, find two brands of the same food product such as chicken soup, green beans, or tomato juice. Compare the information given on each label, and answer the following questions.

1. How many servings are in each can or package? What is the serving size?
2. What are the differences between the ingredients and vitamins in each?
3. If you had to choose one of these brands, which would it be? Why?

Citizenship and You

1. Imagine that you are trying to sell a new product. Write an advertisement that would make people want to buy this product.
2. Divide the class into committees to visit local industries, wholesale markets, retail stores, trucking firms, and the chamber of commerce. The committees should investigate and report on local methods of production and distribution. Some features that can be investigated are mass production, transportation and marketing, self-service stores, standard packaging, the use of credit, and installment buying. The reports may be made either in writing or by panel discussions.
3. Draw sketches or collect photographs for a bulletin board display on the history of transportation in America.
4. Prepare a report on the contribution of one of the following to American economic growth: Henry Ford, Andrew Carnegie, Elizabeth Lucas Pinckney, John D. Rockefeller, George Washington Carver, Thomas Edison, J. P. Morgan, Eli Whitney, Cyrus McCormick, or Jan Matzeliger.
5. A display of local products may be arranged. Each person contributing to the exhibit should be prepared to tell how his or her local product is manufactured. The source of the material used to make it, and the marketing methods used to get the product to customers should also be explained.
6. Invite a member of your local Better Business Bureau to address the class. Have the speaker inform you about its activities, and about some things consumers should be aware of when shopping.

CHAPTER

18

How Americans Manage Their Money

In this chapter, you will read about a subject that interests everyone—money! Money is one of the most useful devices ever invented. Without it the whole process of mass production, marketing, and consumption (what we buy) would grind to a halt. Without money we would have to depend on barter. **Barter** is the swapping of one product for another. Barter was used in early societies before money became the basis of trade.

Barter was often difficult. Suppose you are a shoemaker living in the days when barter was the chief method of trade. You have more shoes than you can use, but how can you obtain other things you need? You will have to swap shoes for them.

You take several pairs of shoes and set out for the marketplace. You may need flour, chickens, a shirt, a dress, and a broom. When you get to the market, you meet a miller with flour to sell. But the flour is packed in huge sacks, and all you want is a small sack of flour. The miller is willing to trade a large sack of flour for all your shoes. After thinking it over, you agree to the trade.

You now try to trade flour for the things you want. You trade some of the flour for a broom. You meet a butcher who has chickens but who doesn't want any flour. The butcher would like to trade several chickens for some pottery. So you hurry around the marketplace to find someone who has pottery and needs flour. Then you return to the butcher and exchange the pottery for the chickens you need.

By this time, it is late evening. You are too tired to do anything about finding a dress or a shirt. As you return home, tired and discouraged, you think there must be a better way of doing business. In this chapter, you will learn how money, banking, investment, and insurance contribute to better ways of handling financial affairs. You will study these topics:

1. **Money and Credit**
2. **Banks and Banking**
3. **Saving and Investing**
4. **Insurance Against Hardship**

1

Money and Credit

At various times and in various places, people have used many different things for money. Cows, pigs, guns, playing cards, furs, salt, olive oil, big stones, knives, tobacco, copper, iron, wampum beads, shells, rings, silver, and diamonds have all been used for money.

During World War II, American soldiers in Europe used chocolate bars for money. They used chocolate because in several nations the official paper money was worthless. Chocolate bars were valuable because people wanted chocolate and would accept it in payment for goods and services.

What Is Money?

The use of chocolate bars for money helps you understand what money really is. **Money** is something sellers will take in exchange for whatever they have to sell. Buyers can exchange it for whatever they want to buy. Money is a medium, or means, of exchange.

To a banker, the term "money" may include checks, bank accounts, and other kinds of writing on pieces of paper. You will read later about some of these kinds of money. For now, think about the "jingling money" and "folding money" that people carry in their pockets or purses. Another name used for these kinds of money is **currency.**

Paper bills and coins do not get their value as means of exchange just because the government prints them or stamps them out of metal. Money in these forms has value only because it will buy something. For a nation's currency to be worth something, the nation's economy must produce something for its people to buy. One reason the United States can produce so much is that American citizens are able to buy what is produced. American currency is also valuable in the world's markets because our nation produces so much.

Every Nation Has Its Currency

Every nation has its own supply of currency. In all nations, currency is alike in four important ways. What are the four common features of currency?

1. Currency must be easy to carry and must take up little space. People must be able to carry it with them for everyday use.

2. Currency must be based on a system of units that are easy to multiply and divide. That is, it should not take too long to figure out the number of coins and bills needed to exchange for any article.

3. Currency must be durable, or last a long time. It should not wear out too quickly or fall apart. People must be able to keep currency until they are ready to spend it.

4. Currency must be made in a standard form and be guaranteed by the nation's government. In this way, all people can be certain that their coins and bills will be accepted by everyone else in exchange for goods and services.

The currency used by Americans is issued, or made, by the federal government. All United States paper money and coins are considered **legal tender.** That is, the law requires that every American accept this money as payment in exchange for all goods and services.

United States Coins and Paper Money

You may recall that one of the weaknesses of the nation under the Articles of Confederation was the lack of a standard currency. The Constitution solved this weakness by granting to Congress the sole right "to coin money, regulating the value thereof . . . ." In 1792 a **mint,** or special plant where coins are made, was established in Philadelphia. There are now two other mints, one in Denver and one in San Francisco.

Coins are sometimes called "hard money" because they are usually made of hard metal. In the United States, five principal coins are used: pennies, nickels, dimes, quarters, and half dollars. These coins are parts of one dollar. A quarter, for example, is one fourth of a dollar. A one dollar coin is also made.

For many years, the value of a coin was decided by the amount of metal it contained. A silver dollar, for example, yielded about a dollar's worth of silver when melted down. In the past, many Americans would accept only hard money. They thought it was more valuable and reliable than paper money.

Today only about 1 percent of our total money supply is in coins. Coins are used mainly for small purchases or for making change. There is no gold or silver in today's coins. All coins are now made of an alloy, or mixture, of 75 percent copper and 25 percent nickel.

Why do Americans accept coins that are not made of gold or silver? They accept them because they have faith in the United States government. They know that the coins will be accepted as legal tender when they are presented at stores, banks, or elsewhere. They also know that the government has a supply of gold and silver bullion, or bars. This bullion is kept in a depository at Fort Knox, Kentucky. It could be used to pay our debts with foreign nations. It also helps to strengthen our nation's financial position.

Most of the money issued by the government today is paper money. It is printed in Washington, D.C., at the Bureau of Engraving and Printing of the Treasury Department. Bills are printed in denominations of $1, $2, $5, $10, $20, $50, and $100. Bills in denominations of $500, $1,000, and $5,000 are no longer issued, although some of them are still around.

Checkbook Money

Very little of what is bought and sold in the United States is paid for in either coins or paper money, the currency you have been reading about. Many Americans make greater use of another kind of money. This is the money represented by checks. A **check** is a written and signed order to a bank to pay a sum of money from a checking account to the person or firm named on the check.

Most of our total money supply is in the form of bank deposits. Bank deposits are the figures in a checking account or savings account. These figures represent the amount

★ ★ ★ ★ ★ ★ ★ ★ ★ ★ ★ ★

CAN YOU GUESS?

Whose face appears on a $1 bill, a $5 bill, a $10 dollar bill, and a $20 bill?

Answers are on page 562.

of credit in a person's or business firm's account. **Credit** is what the bank owes the person or the firm. The person or business firm spends money out of this account by writing a check.

The check is just a piece of paper. It is not legal tender because it is not guaranteed by the federal government. Most sellers, however, will accept a check that has been written by a responsible person or firm. The person or firm who writes the check has built up the account by depositing cash or checks—such as paychecks—from other persons or firms.

Many people never see most of their money because of the wide use of this kind of credit. What they mainly see is a column of figures the bank sends them on their monthly statement. This **statement** tells them how much credit they have in their bank account.

These coins have just been made at a government mint. This machine counts them and places them in bags for shipment throughout the nation.

Charge Accounts and Credit Cards

As you read in Chapter 17, a charge account is a method by which a store extends credit to its customers. Customers can walk into the store and buy an item. They do not pay for it at that time. The store adds the price of the item to their charge account. At the end of a month, the store sends them a bill. The bill is a list of figures telling them how much they owe for what they bought.

The customer writes a check, payable to the store, for this amount. The store deposits the check in its own bank, which sends the check to the customer's bank. The customer's bank subtracts the amount from the customer's bank account. It then sends its own check to the store's bank. No one has seen any currency. (Banks do not collect from one another check by check. They use large collection agencies that handle many checks.)

Credit cards are a substitute for money. Credit cards are issued by banks and other business firms that specialize in this kind of service. People get credit cards by applying for them in much the same way they obtain charge accounts. But in this case, thousands of stores and other businesses throughout the country will accept the credit card in place of currency or checks.

The customer shows the credit card when making a purchase. The store then charges the credit card company. The credit card company pays the store and charges the customer. The customer pays all the credit card charges with one check at the end of a month. Again, no currency has changed hands.

Credit in Business

Credit is used instead of currency in most sales involving large amounts of goods. Wholesale grocers may order half a truckload of canned goods, for example. They promise to pay for this order at the end of the month or, sometimes, within 90 days. Because they

Are we becoming a "cashless society"? This woman uses a credit card to pay for a purchase. When the bill arrives, she probably will pay it by check.

have good credit, the wholesalers can get the canned goods right away.

If they can sell the canned goods before their debt is due, the wholesalers will have the money they need to repay their debt. Credit gives wholesalers a chance to do a larger amount of business than they could do if they had to pay for the goods immediately.

Credit, however, is sometimes used unwisely. Suppose business people use credit more often than they should. When the time comes for them to pay their bills, they find themselves in trouble. They cannot pay the bills they piled up by using credit. Then their **creditors**—those they owe money to—may force them to sell their businesses to pay their debts.

Credit in the Family

Credit can also be an advantage to the average American family if used wisely. Emergencies occur in most families. Sometimes a product or service is needed immediately. The family washing machine, for example, may break down. A new one may be needed. If the family does not have enough money in the bank to pay for it, a new washing machine can usually be obtained on credit.

If the family plans to pay for the machine within a few weeks, it needs only **short-term credit.** On the other hand, the family may need several months to pay. If so, it will plan to pay a certain amount each month until the total has been paid. This **long-term credit,** as you recall, is also called installment credit. Most American families use this kind of credit to make large purchases, such as homes, automobiles, or furniture.

Like some business people, families may use credit unwisely. Suppose a family buys so many things on credit that it cannot afford to meet the payments. What will happen? The stores will take back their products. The family will lose all the money it has already paid for the products. It is easy to see why a family must plan ahead when it uses credit.

Credit in the Overall Economy

Credit, as you have seen, plays several important roles in the buying and selling of goods and services that goes on all the time in our free market. It also plays an important role in the successful operation of the American economy as a whole.

In a healthy economic system, the supply of money must increase or decrease in relation to the general condition of the economy. When production picks up and business is brisk, there must be plenty of money available to consumers. Otherwise, goods that are produced cannot be sold. In that case, production would have to slow down again. Free-flowing money in the form of credit makes it possible for customers to buy whenever there are goods to be sold.

If too much money is available when production slacks off, prices may go too high. That would happen because there would be more money to spend than there were goods to buy. Customers would try to outbid each other to get the limited supply of goods. But with our credit system, when production drops, banks may extend less credit to customers. Therefore, buying slows down.

Our American society is made up, for the most part, of honest people. As a result, the widespread use of credit has become possible as a means of exchange. If buyers and sellers could not trust each other, credit would not be possible.

CHECK-UP

Vocabulary

barter	credit
money	statement
currency	credit cards
legal tender	creditors
mint	short-term credit
check	long-term credit

Review

1. What are four common features of every nation's currency?
2. What is checkbook money?
3. Explain how our system of credit works.

Discuss

How can a family use credit to its best advantage? Give some examples.

2 Banks and Banking

A thousand years ago, money was a problem just as it is for many people today. In fact, money was almost as much of a problem for the rich as for the poor. People with a lot of money had a difficult time finding a safe place to keep it. If they carried a large amount of money with them, thieves might steal it. Even if they put the money in a secret hiding place in their homes, the money still might not be safe.

How Banking Began

In most communities, however, there were people who kept their wealth heavily guarded. These people were goldsmiths, who made articles out of gold. Because gold was very valuable, most goldsmiths had strong safes. It became common for the goldsmiths to do their neighbors a favor by allowing them to keep money in their safes. Soon other people in the towns began to bring their money to the goldsmiths for safekeeping. Before long, local goldsmiths found themselves in the money-keeping business. They began to charge a small fee for performing this needed service.

It was a natural next step for the local goldsmith to become a moneylender. Townspeople who needed money began to come to the goldsmith for loans. In return for the loans, they signed a paper promising to repay the money within a certain time. They also promised to pay an added sum called interest for the use of the money.

People who borrowed money had to give some guarantee that they would repay the loan. Borrowers who owned property had to promise to give it to the moneylender if they could not pay their loan when it was due. Property used to guarantee that a loan will be repaid is called **collateral.**

Bank machines like this one make it possible to deposit money, withdraw it, or transfer money from one account to another, even when the bank is closed.

These practices started by the early moneylenders, as well as many other later business practices, developed into the banking system we know today.

What Is a Bank?

Banks are among the most familiar buildings in every American town and city. But they are more than buildings. A **bank** is a business firm that deals in money and credit. A bank takes the deposits of some of its customers, usually in the form of checks and other kinds of credit. It makes loans to other customers, usually in the form of checks or credits to their checking accounts.

By law a bank always has to keep a certain percentage of its deposits on reserve. The rest can be loaned out or used to buy government bonds or other investments.

If a bank is chartered to do business under state laws, it is a **state bank.** If it is chartered under federal laws, it is a **national bank.** In order to get a charter, a bank must have enough capital to do business. It also must operate in accordance with either state or federal laws. Like other business firms, a bank has a board of directors, officers, and stockholders.

Kinds of Banks

There are two main kinds of banks in the United States, savings banks and commercial banks. In the past, savings banks sought small, interest-paying accounts. Commercial banks stressed checking accounts. Today, however, the difference between these banks is not as great.

The **savings bank** puts the deposits of most of its customers into savings accounts. In the 1970's, many savings banks also began to offer checking services to their customers. Savings banks make loans to individuals, primarily to people buying houses.

The **commercial bank** puts the deposits of most of its customers into checking accounts. Most commercial banks also have savings departments. Many have trust departments that help customers manage property and invest money. Commercial banks make loans to businesses and individuals.

The money depositors put in a checking account is called a **demand deposit.** That is, the account is payable on demand. This means that the bank must give depositors their money back any time the depositors request it by writing a check.

The money depositors put in a savings account is called a **time deposit.** Depositors may be required to give the bank advance notice when they wish to withdraw their money. Most banks do not require advance notice of withdrawals from regular savings accounts. However, on certain types of time deposits, which pay higher interest rates, money may be withdrawn only at the end of a 90-day period. In some cases it must stay in the account from two to six years.

From long experience, banks have found that only a certain number of depositors will want their money at any one time. This is why the law requires that only a small percentage (such as 16 percent) of the deposits must be kept on reserve. The banks can earn interest by lending the rest.

George McClain Gets a Bank Loan

What really happens when a person borrows money from a bank? Consider the example of George McClain, a young man who owns and operates a gas station. George needs $5,000 to purchase some new equipment. He goes to a commercial bank and asks to speak to one of the bank's officers. The bank official listens to George and tells him that the bank will probably make the loan. George must show that he is a good credit risk.

George then brings in his business records. They show that his gas station is a profitable business. He also points out that he owns his home, a car, and a boat and that he has no large business debts. All this convinces the bank that George McClain will be able to repay the loan when it is due. The bank then agrees to make the loan and to consider George's house as the collateral, or guarantee, for the loan.

Many loans made by commercial banks are short-term loans. They are to be paid back in 30, 60, or 90 days. George McClain receives a short-term loan of $5,000, due in 90 days. However, he does not receive any currency or even a check. What he gets is a credit in his checking account.

George does not get the full $5,000 credit. The bank takes out, say, $100 in advance as the interest it is charging for the loan. George receives a credit of $4,900 in his checking account. Taking out, or deducting, the interest on a loan in advance is referred to as **discounting.**

After he receives his loan, George McClain buys his new equipment. He pays for it by check. George begins to take in more money because his gas station can now offer better service.

The equipment company, richer now by George's borrowed credit, uses the money to expand its business. In fact, with George's check and the checks of other customers coming in, the equipment company may borrow money from a commercial bank for its own expansion. In this way, credit circulates, or moves around, and grows throughout the American economy. Each transaction makes possible other transactions.

George McClain Renews His Loan

What happens when the loan is due at the end of the 90-day period? If George McClain's business has done well enough, he can now repay the loan. But suppose the new equipment was late in arriving, or business did not increase quite as fast as expected. George

Bank loans to small businesses, like this pet shop, enable business owners to buy new products and equipment so they can attract more customers.

may have to go to the bank and ask that his loan be renewed, or continued. Then he will not have to repay the loan for another 90 days.

Usually a bank will renew a loan to a person like George McClain, whose credit is good. George, of course, will have to pay interest again on the loan renewal.

Suppose, however, that bank officials think George has not done a good job managing his business with the new equipment. They may decide he is no longer a good risk and may refuse to renew the loan. George must then find some way to repay the loan at once. In order to save his house, which is the collateral for his loan, he may have to sell his car and boat. He may even have to sell his business. As you can see, a loan involves a risk both for the bank and for the person who borrows the money.

This couple is applying for a loan to expand their business. Their business records convince the bank they will be able to repay the loan when it is due.

Government Regulation of the Banking System

There was a time when banks were allowed to do business just about as they wished. They sometimes loaned money without enough collateral. They sometimes did not keep enough money in reserve. Under these conditions, rumors might spread that the bank was shaky. Depositors would start "a run on the bank"—that is, go to the bank and demand all their money. Sometimes so many depositors withdrew their money that the bank had no funds left. As a result, other depositors lost their money.

Bank failures happened so often in our nation's history that the federal government finally stepped in with a plan to regulate banking. In 1913 Congress established the **Federal Reserve System.** All national banks were required to belong to this system. State banks might join if they wished, and many did.

For many years, the Federal Reserve had direct control only over its member banks. For example, only the member banks had to keep part of their deposits on reserve with the "Fed," as the system is called. Then in 1980 a law was passed stating that all banks had to meet the Fed's reserve requirements.

The Federal Reserve System

This is how the Federal Reserve System is set up. The United States is divided into 12 Federal Districts. There is a large Federal Reserve Bank in each district. The Federal Reserve Banks do not usually do business with individuals or business firms. Instead, they act as the bankers for the federal government and for other banks.

The Federal Reserve Banks serve two main purposes. First, the federal government uses the Federal Reserve Banks to handle its own banking needs. The Secretary of the Treasury deposits the funds of the United States government in these banks. Then the

CAN YOU GUESS?

- **How long does an average dollar bill last before it wears out?**
- **If a piece is missing from paper money, is the bill still worth anything?**
- **What is done with paper money when it wears out?**

Answers are on page 562.

Secretary writes checks on the federal government's account, just as an individual does who has a checking account. The Federal Reserve Banks also handle the sale of bonds issued by the government. Most United States currency, both paper money and coins, is put into circulation through the Federal Reserve System.

Second, the Federal Reserve Banks also provide services to the state and national banks and help control our banking system. Even banks sometimes have to borrow money. A member bank can go to the Federal Reserve Bank in its district and borrow money in order to increase its own reserve. The member bank then is able to make more loans or investments. The bank must pay interest on these loans. The rate of interest charged by the Federal Reserve is called the **discount rate.**

The Federal Reserve at Work

The Federal Reserve System is managed by a seven-member **board of governors.** Each member is appointed by the President, with the consent of the Senate, for a single 14-year term. The board of governors makes most of the major decisions for the Federal Reserve System.

A healthy economy must have enough money and credit in circulation, but not too much. Through its influence over the banking system, the Federal Reserve tries to keep the right amount of money in circulation. When our nation's economy is growing, we need more money in circulation. Remember, money is simply a useful tool that helps us exchange goods and services more efficiently. If more goods and services are being produced, more money is needed.

If the supply of money grows faster than the supply of goods, prices will rise. To prevent this, the Federal Reserve may try to slow down the growth of the money supply or even take money out of circulation.

If the Federal Reserve wants to speed up our economic growth, it will put more money into circulation. It will usually do this by purchasing government bonds from banks or others holding these bonds. Then these banks or people have more money to spend or lend, and the money goes into our economy. To take money out of circulation, the Federal Reserve does the opposite. It sells government bonds back to banks or people. After buying these bonds, individuals or banks have less money to spend or lend.

CHECK-UP

Vocabulary

collateral
bank
state bank
national bank
savings bank
commercial bank
demand deposit
time deposit
discounting
Federal Reserve System
discount rate
board of governors

Review

1. What are the two main kinds of banks? What services does each offer?
2. Why did Congress establish the Federal Reserve System?
3. What are the responsibilities of the Federal Reserve System?

Discuss

How do banks stimulate business?

3

Saving and Investing

Most of us want money in order to spend it. But we do not have to spend it right away. One of the features of money is that it can be kept and spent at some future time. Most people try to keep some money in case they have unexpected expenses. Keeping money by setting it aside is called **saving.**

Why People Save

Almost everyone saves, or tries to save. Families try to put aside money for their children's education or to buy a house. They try to save money to meet emergencies, such as medical and hospital bills, loss of a job, or other unexpected difficulties. People try to save money for their retirement years. Saving is a part of knowing how to manage money wisely.

There are several ways to save money. Some kinds of saving make it possible for people to get together enough money to pay for expensive items, such as vacations, clothing, and household appliances. True, the American credit system allows us to obtain expensive goods and services without paying cash for them. Yet even in our credit system, the customer often must make a fairly large down payment.

The largest purchases most persons ever make are houses and cars. To buy a house, you must first pay a sizable part of the total cost as a down payment. Builders may advertise, "Only 10 percent down—pay the rest as rent." But 10 percent of the cost of a $65,000 house is $6,500. The average family has to save a long time to accumulate $6,500.

Used-car dealers may advertise, "No money down, drive it home today!" But without a down payment, the monthly payments on a car may be higher than the buyer can afford. The smaller the down payment, the greater the amount of interest and the larger the monthly payments. The extra interest will also make the total cost of the car greater. Learning to save and practicing saving throughout life can be useful for everyone.

This bank wants to increase the money it has to invest. It offers potential depositors a wide variety of free gifts if they will place their savings there.

How People Save

There are various ways to save money, of course. You can hide your money under a mattress, put it in a cookie jar, or keep it in a piggy bank. Most Americans find that there are better ways to save money.

1. Many Americans save by putting money in the bank. They put aside a regular amount each week in a savings account at a bank. Or whenever they make extra money, they put it in their savings account instead of spending it. The bank pays interest on money deposited in a savings account. By saving in

Different Ways of Saving

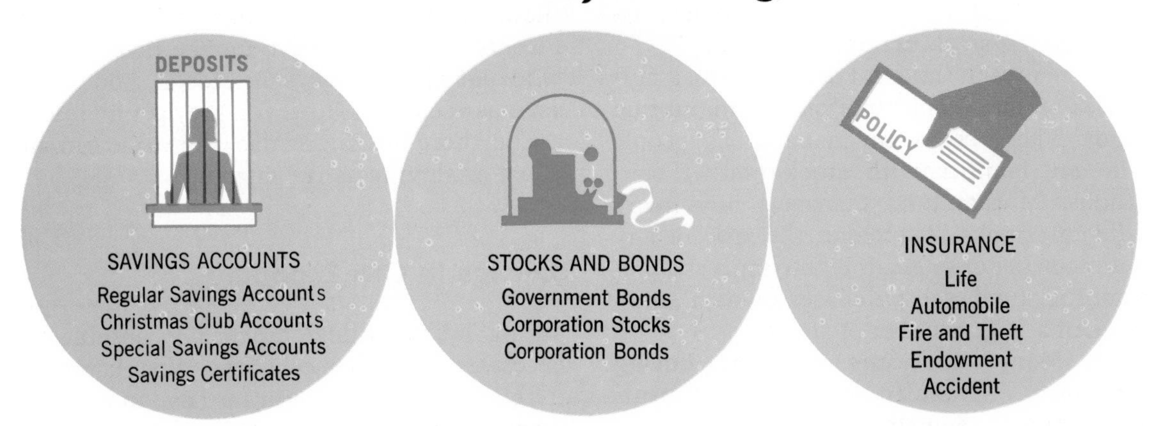

this way, a person's money earns more money for him or her. The money is always there to be withdrawn when it is needed.

Similar to a savings bank is a **savings and loan association.** This institution pays interest on money that savers deposit. It lends money mostly to people who are buying houses. Another way to save is in a **credit association.** Many business firms have credit associations. There, employees can save regularly and, when necessary, borrow money at a low rate of interest.

2. Many Americans save by buying bonds. You probably remember that when you buy a bond, you are lending money to the business or government that issues the bond. When the bond reaches maturity, you get the money back. In the meantime, your money is earning interest. Agencies that issue bonds include the United States government, many state and local governments, and large corporations.

United States government bonds, as well as the bonds of most states, localities, and corporations, are a safe form of savings. In most cases, bondholders receive regular interest payments.

One form of bond, the United States savings bond, does not pay interest until it is cashed in. For example, a savings bond bought for $100 earns $100 in interest after a certain period of years. The purchaser who paid $100 for a bond gets back $200. Meantime, the buyer's money is safe because the United States government will always repay its debt. However, the interest rate for savings bonds is not as high as it is for many other kinds of investments.

3. Many Americans save by buying stocks. You read about common stocks and preferred stocks in Chapter 16. There are regular organizations that buy and sell stocks for their customers. These organizations are called **brokerage houses.** The officials they employ are called **brokers.** Each brokerage house is a member of a **stock exchange.** Millions of shares of stock are bought and sold every working day at the stock exchange.

Anyone can buy stocks by getting in touch with a brokerage house. However, people need a great deal of knowledge about the stock market before they buy stocks. There are both safe stocks and risky stocks.

People who buy common stocks are taking a chance. They hope their investment will earn more money—perhaps much more—than it would earn in a savings account or a bond purchase. Annual stock dividends may be higher than interest payments would be. Also, if the value of a stock rises in the stock exchange, the customer may sell that stock, take a profit, and buy a new stock. However, the stock may pay small dividends or none at all. Moreover, its value on the stock market may fall.

To reduce the amount of risk in stock purchases, some people buy shares in **mutual funds.** These funds are managed by people who are familiar with stock market conditions. Mutual fund managers buy many different stocks. Therefore, the risk in any one stock is not so great. By buying a share in a mutual fund, the purchaser owns a small piece of a large number of stocks.

4. Many Americans save by buying insurance. There are many kinds of insurance. Some of them are, in part, forms of saving. A private life insurance policy, for example, may be "surrendered" for its cash value after a certain number of years. You will read more about insurance later in this chapter.

5. Other ways of saving. In recent years, Americans have been able to save in other ways too. They have been investing in savings certificates and money market funds. These often pay higher rates of interest than regular savings deposits and bonds.

Savings certificates are issued by banks. Savers are required to invest at least a minimum amount of money for a specific length of time. Interest rates are guaranteed, and the money is insured by the government. However, there is a penalty for early withdrawal. For example, $10,000 may be the minimum required to buy a six-month savings certificate paying 13 percent interest. That rate of interest will be guaranteed for the full six months. If you have to take out your money before the six-month period ends, you will lose a percentage of the interest.

Money market funds, like mutual funds, buy types of investments that most individuals could not purchase alone. Savers can withdraw their money at any time. However, money market funds do not guarantee a specified amount of interest. The rate of interest can either rise or fall. Moreover, this form of saving is not insured by the government.

People also have been buying gold, silver, jewels, paintings, and other precious items as a form of saving. They hope the value of these things will rise sharply. If they do, the owners may make more money than people who put their savings in stocks, bonds, or savings accounts. However, they get no interest on these holdings. Also, the value can go down as sharply as it can go up.

Savings in Our Economy

Saving by individual citizens is absolutely necessary in our free economy. What happens to the money that Americans have in savings accounts, bonds, stocks, and other forms of saving? That money is used to help expand our nation's economy. You have read that continued growth of production is important to a nation's economy. How is continued growth of production made possible?

Continued growth is possible only if factories and other means of production are continually expanded. How does this happen? The means of production expand only when there is capital available to pay for new factories, machine tools, and other capital goods. You read about capital as one of the factors of production in Chapter 16.

Where does capital come from? It comes from savings. Suppose you have $10. You spend $5 of it and put the other $5 in a bank. The $5 you spend represents goods that you consume. That is, you spend the money for something you want. But you do not consume the $5 you put in the bank. It is money that can be used for another purpose. It can be invested. The bank can use this money to make loans to business people who need funds.

Using Savings to Invest

Saving and investing are not the same thing. Money in a piggy bank is saved, but is not invested. Money you deposit in a savings account in a bank is both saved and invested. It is saved by you. It is invested by the bank.

When you buy stocks or bonds, you are both saving and investing.

When you invest, you turn money into capital. What the money buys is not consumed. It is used to produce goods and services. Thus, investing money results in the production of goods and services. This production, in turn, results in the making of more money, or profits.

The ability of the American people to save large amounts of money, and the ability of our economic system to invest this money, help keep our nation prosperous. The ability of our free economy to raise large amounts of capital has made it possible for American business firms to build huge factories that turn out vast amounts of goods.

Business firms also save in order to raise part of their own capital. The managers of most corporations put aside a certain part of their companies' profits before they pay dividends to stockholders. This money is then put back into their business in the form of new capital.

The new capital helps businesses invest in new machines or expand their factories. It also helps businesses establish new branches or add new lines of products to what they already produce. This new capital for expansion is in addition to the money set aside to

Saving Keeps Our Nation Prosperous

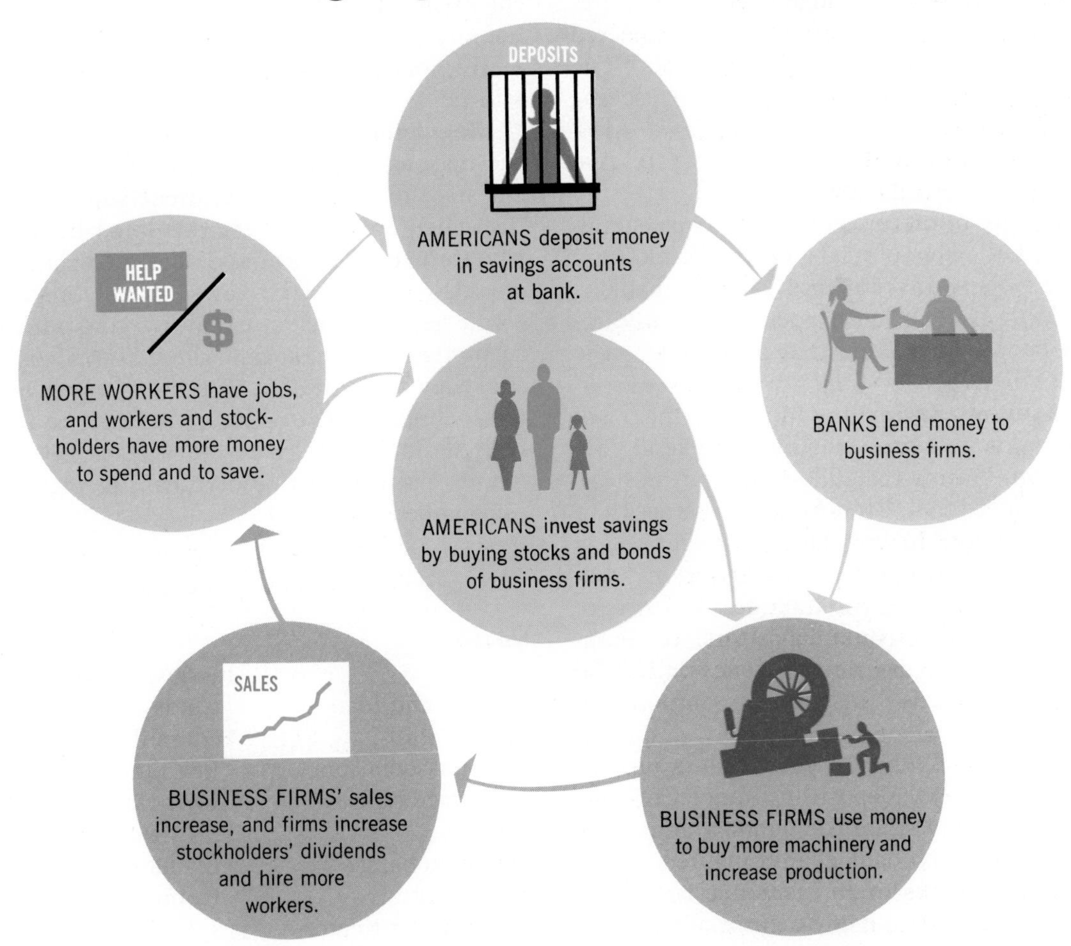

replace older buildings and equipment when they wear out.

Making Saving Safe

When people put their money into a bank, they want to know their money will be safe. They want to know they will be able to get it back when they ask for it. Also, when people buy stocks or bonds, they want to feel they are not taking unnecessary risks.

For these reasons, our federal and state governments have passed laws to regulate the activities of those institutions that handle the savings of others. All banks must receive a state or federal charter to operate. Our governments charter only banks that are properly organized and have enough capital.

After a bank is chartered, it is inspected regularly by state or federal officials. The bank's directors are responsible for seeing that their bank obeys all banking laws. Also, you may recall, all banks must keep reserve funds in Federal Reserve Banks.

In spite of these regulations, banks sometimes fail. The officials of the bank may make unwise investments, and the bank is forced to close. What happens to the savings that people have deposited in a bank if the bank fails?

Insuring Savings. Most savings accounts are now protected by the federal government. During the 1930's, many American banks closed their doors because business and industry were having difficult times. As a result, many depositors lost all or most of their savings. Congress then decided to take steps to protect bank depositors. It established a federal government agency called the **Federal Deposit Insurance Corporation (FDIC).**

You can tell whether your bank is a member of the Federal Deposit Insurance Corporation. It will say so on the window and in its advertising. Each bank that is insured by the FDIC contributes to an insurance fund held by the government. If any member bank fails, all depositors will be paid the amount of their deposits in the bank up to $100,000.

Regulating Stock Exchanges. Also in the 1930's, Congress established the **Securities and Exchange Commission (SEC)** to ensure that all offerings of stocks and bonds on the nation's stock exchanges would be honest. In the past, people sometimes sold "watered-down" stock. This was stock that did not fully represent the value claimed for it. There were many other stock "dodges," or tricks, by which dishonest people cheated the public.

The regulations of the Securities and Exchange Commission have put a stop to such practices. The SEC constantly examines the practices of the nation's stock exchanges and of the brokers who buy and sell stock for the public. This does not mean that all stocks are safe investments. A company can be perfectly honest, meet all the SEC's rules, and still fail.

Regulating Savings Organizations. All the nation's savings organizations come under state or federal government supervision. Insurance companies are regulated by state governments. Savings and loan associations are also regulated by laws. Even company credit associations must allow government accountants to examine their books to be sure they are being run properly. Since saving is so important to the prosperity of the United States, it is in the interest of the whole nation that individual savings be safeguarded.

CHECK-UP

Vocabulary

saving
savings and loan association
credit association
brokerage houses
brokers
stock exchange
mutual funds
savings certificates
money market funds
Federal Deposit Insurance Corporation
Securities and Exchange Commission

Review

1. What are some of the reasons people save money?
2. Name five ways in which people can save.
3. How do savings help business?
4. How does the federal government protect bank depositors?

Discuss

How does saving your money help to protect your future and the future of the American economy?

4 Insurance Against Hardship

Life is full of risks and uncertainties. There is the chance of illness or accident. There is the possibility of losing one's job. A person's house could burn down or be destroyed by earthquake or flood. A motorist could be involved in an accident and be sued for thousands of dollars by someone injured in the accident. A father might die, leaving his widow with young children to support. There is the uncertainty of old age, when a person may not be able to work and earn a living.

Our economic system includes arrangements that protect people, at least in part, against such risks and uncertainties. These protections are called **insurance.**

What Is Insurance?

Suppose you thought you might suffer a loss of $100,000 from some cause. Would you be willing to pay a small sum—say $75 each year—just to make sure you did not run this risk? That is what insurance is. It is a system of paying a small amount to avoid the risk of a large loss.

The small amount a person pays for this protection is called the **premium.** Premiums may be paid yearly, or at regular times throughout the year. The large loss against which a person is insured is the **principal sum.** The contract that gives this kind of protection is an **insurance policy.**

Private insurance is voluntary. That is, individuals and companies choose to pay for it. **Social insurance** is required by state and federal laws. Individuals and companies must pay for social insurance programs.

Private Insurance

There are many different kinds of private insurance companies. Altogether, they write insurance policies covering almost every possible kind of risk. Each company usually specializes in one or a few kinds of insurance.

How can insurance companies do what they do? How can they take small amounts of money from people, yet pay them a large sum if hardship occurs to them? The reason is

Without a health and accident insurance policy, this girl's family would have had to pay all the medical expenses for her broken leg themselves.

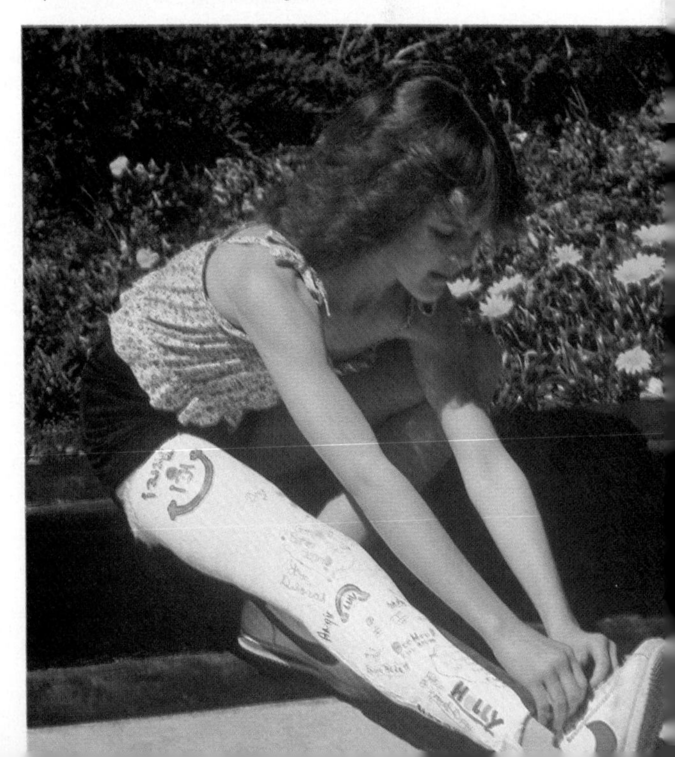

simple. Not everybody has a hardship. You may pay premiums on accident insurance all your life. Yet you may never collect a cent because you never have an accident. You cannot, however, be sure you will never have an accident. Most people consider it wise to buy insurance against such a risk.

A large insurance company has millions of policyholders who pay their small premiums regularly. Part of this money goes into a reserve fund. State laws specify how much of a reserve fund a company must maintain. The amount depends on the kind of insurance the company issues and the number of policyholders it has.

When someone has a hardship of the type specified in the company's policies, payment of the principal sum is made from the reserve fund. Even with millions of policyholders, there may be only a few thousand payments out of the reserve fund each year.

Except for money held in reserve funds, insurance companies invest the premiums they collect. They buy stocks and bonds and make other forms of investment. The dividends, interest, and other income from the investments pay the expenses of these companies and earn profits for their shareholders. Their investments help provide the capital needed in our economy.

Life Insurance. One of the most valuable forms of insurance for a person to have is **life insurance.** The main purpose of life insurance is to provide money in case the insured person dies. In this way, the family is protected from financial hardship. The person named in the policy to receive the money in case of the policyholder's death is called the **beneficiary.**

Insurance companies offer many different kinds of life insurance. **Annuities,** for instance, provide retirement income for policyholders if they do not die before reaching a certain age. Individuals also can purchase **endowment policies** that pay the principal sum after a certain number of years. They can plan to receive the principal sum when their children are ready for college, for example.

Accident and Health Insurance. There are many forms of insurance that make regular payments to policyholders if they are injured in an accident or become too ill to work. **Accident insurance** may cover total disability or partial disability or both. Some

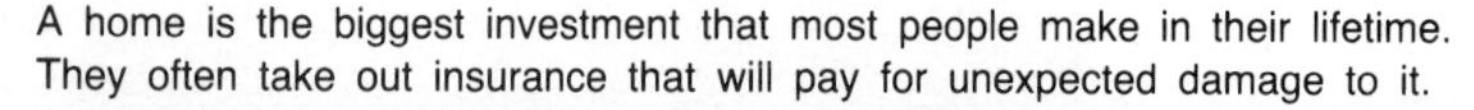
A home is the biggest investment that most people make in their lifetime. They often take out insurance that will pay for unexpected damage to it.

policies cover all kinds of accidents—even breaking a leg by slipping on the soap in the bathtub. Other kinds of policies cover only accidents on common carriers—that is, on airplanes, trains, buses, and other means of public transportation. In case of death, the beneficiary receives the principal sum.

Health insurance makes regular payments to policyholders when they cannot work because of illness not caused by an accident. Health insurance premiums are higher than accident insurance premiums because people are sick more often than they are injured.

Hospitalization insurance pays part of a policyholder's hospital expenses. Other insurance plans pay doctors' bills, dentists' bills, and other medical expenses. The premiums for these kinds of insurance are often paid in part by the policyholders and in part by their employers.

Property Insurance. For people who own a home, property insurance is probably the greatest single investment. If the home should burn down, they might be financially ruined. For this reason, most homeowners carry some form of property insurance. **Fire insurance** is the most common form. Americans buy fire insurance on their factories, stores, offices, and other places of business as well as on their homes.

In addition, many people take out **homeowners' insurance.** This covers a person's home not only for fire but also for many other kinds of risks—windstorm, hail, flood, theft, burglary, and legal liability.

Liability Insurance. Suppose someone comes to your door on an icy day and falls coming up the steps. The person breaks a leg and has to go to the hospital. You are legally liable, or responsible, because the accident happened on your property—even if you did not invite the person or put the ice there. You might even have posted a sign by your door saying "Warning—Ice—Slippery." It makes no difference.

You are legally liable for the injury to that person. He or she can sue you in court and collect payment, called damages. **Liability insurance** can protect property owners from high costs in cases of this kind.

Sometimes doctors are sued by patients who claim they have been neglected or incorrectly treated. Doctors performing extremely risky operations are most often involved in such cases. To protect themselves, doctors purchase **malpractice insurance,** or professional liability insurance.

Automobile Insurance. The most common form of liability insurance is the kind that automobile owners buy to protect themselves. **Automobile liability insurance** covers automobile owners in case their cars kill or injure other people or damage property. Some states, such as New York, require all automobile owners to have liability insurance before they are able to register a car. Most automobile insurance policies also protect the owner from loss by fire and theft.

Insurance Against Dishonesty. Among the many kinds of private insurance are some that protect people against losses caused by burglars, embezzlers, and swindlers. Business firms, stores, banks, and homeowners carry burglary insurance. Banks and other businesses that deal in valuable documents carry forgery insurance. Forgery is the crime of falsely making or changing a check or other document.

Companies that handle money pay to have their employees **bonded.** This means the company is repaid if an employee disappears with the company's money. Such policies also cover embezzling, which occurs when an employee steals from the company by making false entries in the company's records.

Social Insurance

The business failures of the 1930's caused much hardship and suffering among the American people. Many business firms and factories closed down. Millions of men and women lost their jobs. Banks failed, and thousands of persons lost their life savings. Money they had counted on for old age was gone.

To meet the problems of this troubled period, called the Great Depression, President Franklin D. Roosevelt recommended many new laws. Congress passed most of them. Together these laws were called the New Deal. Some of the new laws brought immediate assistance to needy people. Other laws, looking to the future, offered protection to individual Americans against severe economic risks and hardships.

Government programs that are meant to protect individuals from future hardship are called social insurance. They make certain forms of insurance compulsory, or required, for nearly all the nation's people. In this way, almost everyone can receive its benefits.

An important program of social insurance was adopted by Congress and President Roosevelt in the Social Security Act of 1935. The act set up an insurance system called **Social Security.** It has two major parts: old-age and survivors insurance and unemployment insurance.

Old-Age and Survivors Insurance. The basic idea of old-age and survivors insurance is simple. People pay a percentage of their salary each month while they work in order to get back cash benefits when they most need them. During the years when workers earn money, they and their employers make contributions to a fund. This fund is called the Social Security Trust Fund. When workers retire, or if they become disabled and their earnings stop, they receive payments from the fund as long as they live.

If workers die before reaching retirement age, their families receive payments from the Social Security Trust Fund. A payment is made for each child in the family under 18 years of age and for the widow or widower. Payments for children stop when they reach the age of 18.

Paying for Social Security. Monthly contributions under the Social Security Act are paid equally by workers and by their employers. The contributions are actually a tax, because they are compulsory. The program was made compulsory because Congress wanted as many Americans as possible to be spared some of the money problems they had faced during the Great Depression.

Since 1935 the program has been expanded from time to time. Coverage has been extended to workers in almost every industry, business, or profession. Self-employed people must also participate in the Social Security program. They pay the whole contribution themselves.

Receiving Social Security. The benefits paid by Social Security have gradually increased since 1935. So has the amount of the contribution. The amount workers and their employers pay depends on how much the workers earn a year. The amount workers receive when they retire is based on their average earnings over a long period of time.

Upon retirement the workers are paid a certain amount each month. A male worker also gets an additional amount for his wife if she is at retirement age and does not claim separate benefits. If the male worker dies, his wife continues to receive payments as long as she lives. A wife who has worked and paid Social Security taxes is entitled to her own benefits. She may draw either her own benefits or part of her husband's, whichever is greater.

Benefits under old age and survivors insurance provide a cushion against the worst hardships caused by the disability, death, or retirement of the wage earner. But the benefits are not large. Many people supplement their social insurance by buying private insurance of various kinds.

Unemployment Insurance. The problem of unemployment, or lack of jobs, was extremely serious when the Social Security Act was passed in 1935. At that time, between 12 and 15 million Americans were unemployed. Most of these people had lost their jobs because of the depression in the American economy. Most of them wanted to work but could not find jobs. The Social Security Act contained a plan for future assistance in difficulties of that kind—the unemployment insurance program.

How the Social Security Law Works

THE FEDERAL GOVERNMENT

administers

Retirement and Old-Age Insurance Program and Health Insurance Program

Contributions by

Employer

Workers

Self-employed workers

used for

Disability and Survivors' Payments

Retirement Payments

Hospital Care*

*A voluntary medical insurance plan also covers doctors' costs.

FEDERAL GOVERNMENT sets standards and makes contributions to

STATE GOVERNMENTS

administer and pay part of cost

Unemployment Insurance Program

Contributions by

Employer

used for

Unemployment Insurance Benefits

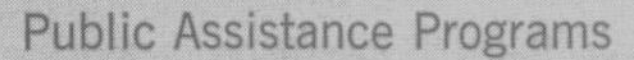

Public Assistance Programs

Maternal and Child Health

Crippled Children

Child Welfare

Aid to the Aged

Aid to Dependent Children

Aid to the Blind

Aid to the Handicapped

Medical Assistance to the Aged

People pay Social Security insurance during the years they are working. They hope that it will help them afford an enjoyable life when they retire.

Unemployment insurance operates in the following manner. When individuals lose their jobs, they register at a nearby state employment office. They report periodically to the office to see if it can find them jobs. Businesses in the area call the state employment office when they have openings.

If they do not find a job right away, unemployed workers begin to receive unemployment benefits based on their average earnings over the past year. The amount they receive weekly varies from state to state. Jobless workers receive payments until they find a job, or for 26 to 30 weeks at most. In areas of high unemployment, the payments are sometimes extended to 39 or more weeks. These benefits are not large. However, they help people support themselves and their families while they are looking for work.

How is the unemployment insurance program paid for? Federal law requires all business firms that employ at least one worker to pay a special tax to the federal government. This tax is a small percentage of a firm's payroll. The state governments pay unemployment benefits out of the sums collected by the federal government.

Medicare and Medicaid. The federal government has also set up programs to help elderly and poor Americans pay their medical expenses. In 1965 Congress passed the health insurance program known as **Medicare.** This program helps people 65 years of age and older to pay for hospital care and for some nursing home care. The program also includes a voluntary medical insurance plan to help older citizens pay their doctor's bills.

The **Medicaid** health insurance program was also passed by Congress in 1965. Under this program, the federal government provides money to help the states pay the medical costs of poor people.

CHECK-UP

Vocabulary

insurance
premium
principal sum
insurance policy
private insurance
social insurance
life insurance
beneficiary
annuities
endowment policies
accident insurance
health insurance
hospitalization insurance
fire insurance
homeowners' insurance
liability insurance
malpractice insurance
automobile liability insurance
bonded
Social Security
unemployment insurance
Medicare
Medicaid

Review

1. What is the principle upon which all insurance is based?
2. Why is insurance important to the financial security of the individual?
3. How can insurance companies cover a large risk for a small premium?
4. In what major ways is social insurance different from private insurance?
5. Name some of the principal kinds of private insurance and the purposes they serve.

Discuss

What kinds of insurance does the average American carry? Why?

CHAPTER SUMMARY

Money is a medium of exchange. We give it in return for goods and services. Most modern money has no value in itself. We value it because the government guarantees it. We also value it because sellers will accept it in exchange for the things we want to buy.

Very little of what is bought and sold is paid for with coins or paper money. Checks are written to pay for most of our trade. Banks play a key role in the process of paying by check. Banks are safe places in which to keep money. They also provide the checking service that transfers balances from one account to another when checks are written to pay for goods and services. Banks also aid business firms and individuals by making loans.

The Federal Reserve System helps regulate banking in our nation. Federal Reserve Banks are the banks in which the federal government keeps its funds. They also are the banks for other banks. They help regulate the use of credit in our economy. The Federal Reserve System tries to keep our money supply at the right level.

When money is saved, it may be invested. That is, it may earn more money for the investor. The money we put in savings banks, for instance, is usually invested by the bank.

Our federal and state governments help protect our savings and investments by regulating banks, insurance companies, and the sale of stocks and bonds. Insurance companies, as well as the federal government, issue policies that may help protect us from most of the financial hazards of life.

CIVICS SKILLS: Writing a Check

Over the years, people have hidden it in many different places. Some have stuffed it into their pockets and carried it around with them. Others have stored it in coffee cans or under mattresses. A few have even buried it in the ground. Can you guess what "it" is?

If you said money, you were right. Today, as you know, you don't have to worry about finding a safe place for your money. You can put it into a bank where it can't be removed without your written permission. One way to give this permission is by completing a special order form called a **check.**

Filling Out a Check

Before opening a checking account, you should decide which type of account will be best for you. If you think you'll be writing a lot of checks, you might consider a **regular checking account.** Such an account doesn't charge any fees as long as you keep a minimum balance, or certain amount of money, in the bank. However, if you plan on writing only a few checks, you might look into a **special checking account.** Although this kind of account usually charges a small fee for every check you write, you won't have to keep a minimum balance.

After you have selected an account, you must complete an identification card showing your name, address, and signature. You will then receive a book of checks. Your account number will appear in the lower left-hand corner of each check. Study the sample check on this page. What other information is printed on it?

Whenever you need to use money in your account, simply fill out the blanks on a check. If you examine the handwritten parts of the check below, you will notice that the amount of the check is given twice—once in figures and once in words. This makes sure that the bank will know exactly how much money to withdraw. You will also see that both numbers are written so they start at the far left of each line. This prevents anyone from changing the total amount.

Equally important information is provided on the remaining lines. On the line that reads PAY TO THE ORDER OF, you tell the bank whom you want to pay. On the line in the lower right-hand corner, you sign your name. This authorizes the bank to carry out your instructions. Remember, however, no one can receive payment until they endorse the check, or sign their name, on the back.

Practicing What You've Learned

1. What information is recorded on the memo line of the check below? Why might this be useful?
2. Why do you think a check must be endorsed?

PAUL W. ROGERS

NO. 257

September 9, 1983 4-0/210

PAY TO THE ORDER OF Bill's Sport Shop $32 80/100

Thirty-two and 80/100 DOLLARS

Urban National Bank
524 PACIFIC AVENUE
PORTLAND, OREGON 97204

MEMO tennis racket Paul W. Rogers

⑆0280010B1⑆ 07910 2064⑈ 0171

CHAPTER REVIEW

Vocabulary

Write a three-paragraph summary of the main ideas presented in this chapter. In the first paragraph, use the following words:

barter	checks
money	credit
legal tender	credit cards

In the second paragraph, sentences should contain these words:

interest	bank
collateral	Federal Reserve Bank

These words should appear in the third paragraph:

insurance	savings certificate
savings bank	mutual funds
stock exchange	money market funds

Check-Up

1. Describe four different forms that money can take.
2. What is the chief advantage of checkbook money over other forms of money? What is the chief disadvantage?
3. What gives our paper money its value?
4. How does credit help our American economic system?
5. How is a bank chartered? What services do commercial banks and savings banks provide their customers?
6. What are the two main purposes of the Federal Reserve Banks?
7. How does saving help to keep our economy prosperous?
8. How does the federal government help make your bank savings safe?
9. How does insurance serve the individual? What are some important kinds of private insurance?
10. What is social insurance? What are the main kinds of social insurance?

Civics Skills

Draw a personal check, using the same basic design as the one on page 362 of your textbook. Be sure to print your full name at the top and the name and address of a local bank at the bottom.

After you have finished drawing your check, show how you would fill it out if you were buying an $8.50 tape recording at the Discomat Record Store. Remember to write all figures to the far left of the appropriate lines. Don't forget to sign your check.

Citizenship and You

1. A group may prepare a picture chart showing currency of the United States and several other nations. How do they differ?
2. Prepare a map of the United States showing the 12 Federal Reserve Districts. Explain how the Federal Reserve Banks serve their member banks.
3. Prepare a report on the work of the Federal Deposit Insurance Corporation.
4. Using statistics in the *World Almanac* or a similar reference book, draw a bar graph that compares the different ways in which people save.
5. In the financial pages of the newspaper, check the prices of the stocks of a few well-known corporations for one month. Note whether the stock market price goes up or down. Then see if you can find any news articles to explain the rise or fall.
6. Hold a quiz show in which your class is divided into two equal teams. The teacher asks questions about money and banking of each team. If a team member cannot answer a question, then the next person on the other team may try to answer. Count one point for each correct answer. The quiz show ends after each team member has had a turn.

CHAPTER

19

Our Economy Faces Challenges

The United States is a very rich nation. Yet our economic system continues to face some serious challenges. The average American is earning more money than ever before, but the money buys fewer goods and services. The reason is that prices have been going up faster than wages. Therefore, it is sometimes hard to plan for the future. Many people worry that their money may buy fewer goods next year than this year.

Our economy has grown tremendously since our nation was founded, but its growth has not been steady. Throughout most of our history, business has been good. At these times more goods and services have been produced than ever before. Then things have slowed down. Some businesses have failed, and fewer goods and services have been produced. These ups and downs in our economy have caused problems for businesses, consumers, workers, and the government.

In order to produce goods and services, businesses need labor. That is, they need workers. Workers, in turn, need jobs. Management does the hiring. As you can see, workers and managers need each other. Yet labor and management sometimes disagree. Our entire economy can be hurt when production stops because labor and management cannot settle their differences.

In this chapter, we shall examine these challenges facing our economic system. You will learn how you are affected by them, what causes them, and what might be done to solve them. You will consider these topics:

1. **Dealing with Inflation**
2. **Boom or Bust**
3. **Labor and Management**

1

Dealing with Inflation

One of the main challenges facing the American economic system is inflation. Many different explanations for inflation have been given. We will look at some of them in this section. Briefly, **inflation** means a rise in the prices of most goods and services. If your income is not rising as fast as prices, you will be able to buy fewer things.

For example, suppose you work during the summer to buy a new bicycle that you saw in a store window. The price was $180. After earning the $180, you find that the price is now $200. You are the victim of inflation. Your money will buy less than before.

Inflation Affects Everyone

People often talk about rising prices. Perhaps they had to change their plans to take a vacation or buy a television set because the price rose too high. Inflation causes problems for many people. Inflation is especially serious for old people living on fixed incomes. Their incomes stay the same while prices go up.

Let's look at the case of Sara Golden, an elderly woman who retired in 1967. Sara worked hard all her life. When she retired, she received a pension from the company for which she had worked. She also received some money from the government's Social Security plan. In all she received $100 a week. At the time, this was enough to meet her needs.

However, since 1967 prices have increased greatly. Now Sara can barely pay her rent, buy food, and meet her other needs. In fact, it would take over $275 today to buy the same goods and services her $100 bought in 1967.

Consider another example of how inflation hurts people. Ten years ago, the Harvin family built a new house. It cost them $40,000. They took out a fire insurance policy for $40,000. They thought that if their house ever burned down they would be able to build a new one with the money from the insurance.

This year their house was destroyed by fire. The Harvins collected $40,000 from the insurance company, but this was not enough to build a new house. To build a similar house now would cost $80,000. The price of lumber, electric wiring, plumbing, labor, and everything else that it takes to build a house has doubled.

Inflation and Savings

Inflation also hurts savers. Many people put their savings into savings accounts or invest in government savings bonds. In this way they earn interest on their savings. They hope that in the future they will be able to use the money they have saved to send their children to college, buy a new car, or travel. Some people may be hoping to use their savings to start their own business.

Even though they are getting interest on

In periods of inflation, food prices rise along with all other prices. Here a group of consumers show their anger over food prices by staging a protest march.

their savings, however, savers may be losing money. For instance, suppose the Garcia family put $1,000 in a savings account ten years ago. Today they have about $1,700 in their account because the $1,000 has been earning interest. That is, their money has been increasing by about 5¼ percent a year. Prices, however, have been increasing much faster.

Suppose the Garcias had planned to use the money to pay for their daughter Gloria's first year in college. Ten years ago, this would have cost $1,000 at the college Gloria wants to attend. Now it costs over $2,000 a year to attend that college. The money the Garcias saved is not enough, even though it has been earning interest.

Some Causes of Inflation

Economists often give different reasons for rising prices. One major cause of inflation that they cite is "too much money, too few goods." If people have increasing amounts of money to spend but the supply of goods is not increasing as fast, prices will rise. This is because shoppers will be competing with each other for the scarce supply of goods.

It is almost like an auction. People at an auction offer to pay higher and higher prices for the object being sold. The supply of an item being auctioned is limited. Therefore, the price keeps going up as more people try to buy it.

Let's look more closely at some of the possible causes of inflation.

Too Much Money. In Chapter 18 you learned how the Federal Reserve tries to control the amount of money and credit in our economy. Some economists believe the major cause of inflation is the circulation of too much money. They think the Federal Reserve has put too much money into our economy. As people spend this additional money, they cause prices to rise.

Too Much Bank Credit. Some economists blame the banks for making too many loans. This has the same effect as putting more money into the economy. People and business firms borrow from the banks and spend what they have borrowed. Up go the prices.

Government Spending. As you know, the government spends many billions of dollars each year. It spends for roads, dams, education, aid to farmers, army bases, pollution control, and many other things. Soldiers, members of Congress, federal judges, postal workers, and many others who are employed by the government must be paid. Much of the money spent by the government comes from taxes paid by individuals and business firms. The government also borrows some of the money it spends.

Many people believe the government is borrowing and spending too much. Government borrowing, like bank loans to individuals, puts more money into our economy and helps raise prices. Government spending puts money into the economy but does not add to the supply of goods available for sale to the public.

Consumer Spending. Perhaps we, as consumers, share some of the blame for inflation. Many people borrow money to buy things they cannot afford and do not really need. On the average, Americans save a very small part of their income. Too little saving and too much spending by consumers may help cause inflation.

Low Productivity. Productivity, as you recall, means the amount a worker produces in an hour. For example, suppose you work in a factory making pens. You produce ten pens in an hour. Your boss sells the pens for $1 each, or a total of $10. Your productivity is ten pens, or $10. The most your boss can afford to pay you is $10 an hour.

Suppose, however, you demand $11 an hour. To meet this demand your boss must raise the price of the pens. Your boss has to pay you 10 percent more. Yet you are not producing 10 percent more pens. Many economists believe the most important reason for inflation is that wages have been rising faster than workers' productivity.

Other Possible Causes. The price of energy sources, such as oil and gas, has gone up sharply in recent years. This has caused the price of nearly everything else to go up because we use energy to produce all goods and services. For instance, the cost of attending college has risen partly because of higher energy prices. It takes a great deal of fuel to heat college buildings. (You will learn more about the energy problem in Chapter 25.)

Sometimes nature creates inflation problems. Storms, droughts, or floods may destroy crops. This causes shortages of farm crops and raises the price of food.

In Chapter 16 you learned about monopolies. If one firm gets a monopoly of a product or service, it might be able to raise the price. Suppose several companies in an industry get together and decide to set one price for that industry's product. The price of the product will probably rise.

Controlling Inflation

It is not easy to control inflation. One reason is that the steps necessary to control it can be unpleasant for many people. Let's go back over each possible cause of inflation and examine some possible ways of stopping it.

Control Money and Credit. The Federal Reserve could try to keep the money supply from growing too quickly. It has to be careful, however. If the Federal Reserve cuts our money supply too sharply, business may decline. People will have less to spend, and business

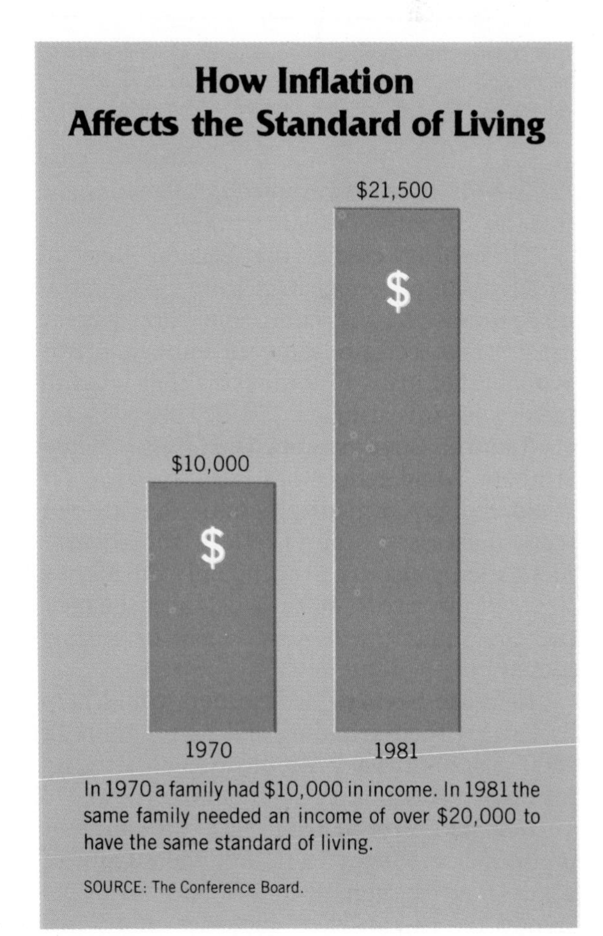

In 1970 a family had $10,000 in income. In 1981 the same family needed an income of over $20,000 to have the same standard of living.

SOURCE: The Conference Board.

The speaker here seems to have given up hope that he can do anything to control inflation. What is his solution for dealing with the problem of inflation?

firms will have lower profits. They might then lay off some of their workers.

To control credit, the Federal Reserve could try to prevent banks from making too many loans. At the same time, however, it must make certain there is enough credit available for loans to businesses that want to make wise investments.

Reduce Government Spending. Government could reduce wasteful spending. It could end government programs that are not really necessary. Many believe the government should also try to spend only the money it gets from taxes. With a balanced budget, the government would not have to borrow money.

Increase Saving. Consumers could help by cutting their spending and saving more of their incomes. They should use credit only for buying things they really need.

Increase Productivity. If the amount produced each hour is raised, the supply of goods will be increased. Business managers should try to run their factories more efficiently. Workers should learn to do their jobs better and make fewer mistakes. If workers' productivity increases, they can get higher pay without helping to cause inflation. Some economists suggest that wages should not increase faster than productivity increases.

Other Steps. Many economists believe we need to conserve fuel and other energy sources. They suggest that people drive less or that they share rides in order to save gasoline. Oil and electricity can also be saved by keeping houses cooler in winter and warmer in summer. By using less of these energy sources, we can help hold down their prices. Many economists also believe we should try to conserve such valuable resources as farmland, timber, and minerals.

CHECK-UP

Vocabulary
inflation

Review
1. How does inflation cause problems for people?
2. What are some of the causes of inflation?
3. What are some possible ways to control inflation?

Discuss
In what ways have you and people you know been affected by inflation?

2

Boom or Bust

Although Americans enjoy a high standard of living, our economy does not always behave the way we want it to. Sometimes we have a period of prosperity, called a boom. During a boom, business is good. Jobs are plentiful, and profits are high. Then business slows down. Some companies begin to lose money, and many workers find themselves without jobs. The nation enters a period of hard times, known as a bust. This tendency—to go from good times to bad, then back to good times again, and so on—is called the **business cycle.** Let's look more closely at the ups and downs of the business cycle.

Prosperity and Inflation

One of the problems that often come with a boom is inflation. As the prices of goods and services increase, your money buys less than before. Why does inflation accompany a boom?

There are many reasons. During a period of prosperity, most people have jobs and good incomes. As you recall, when people spend money they raise the demand for goods and services. If businesses are already turning out goods as fast as they can, they will be unable to increase the supply. Prices will rise as customers compete with one another to buy scarce goods.

The costs of doing business will also increase. Businesses will have to pay more for raw materials and transportation. Because jobs are plentiful at such times, business owners may have to increase wages to keep their workers and attract new ones. Wages, payments for raw materials, transportation, rent, and interest on money borrowed are **costs of production.** When these costs rise, business firms may have to raise the prices of their products in order to pay the costs and still make a profit.

These are just a few of the reasons prices usually rise during a boom period.

Depressions and Recessions

Economists speak of a period of hard times as a **depression.** During a depression, the number of people without jobs is high. People who are out of work cannot buy many goods and services. As a result, many business firms must close down because they cannot make enough money to cover their costs.

The whole economy slows down during a depression. That is, the nation produces fewer goods and services. Jobs become scarce. Teen-age workers and people with few skills and little education are particularly hard hit. In a bad depression, even workers with a great deal of training and experience may not be able to find jobs.

The worst depression in our nation's history took place during the 1930's. This period, as you have read, is known as the **Great Depression.** The first sign of trouble came in October 1929, when the prices of stocks fell sharply. People who had paid hundreds of dollars for stocks found that they could sell them for only a few cents. Or they could find no buyers at all. Many banks failed. Depositors lost their life savings.

By 1932 business was producing only half as much as it had produced in 1929. Thousands of firms were closed down. Farm prices

DID YOU KNOW THAT . . .

since 1900 the cost of many items has increased about 2,000 percent? This means that today many things cost about 20 times what they cost in 1900! In that year, $8.95 would buy a deluxe new bicycle. Today, because of inflation, you would have to spend nearly $200.

were lower than ever before. By 1933 about 13 million people—nearly one fourth of American workers—had lost their jobs. Most of these people had families to support. Unable to repay their mortgages, many homeowners lost their houses. Many farmers had to leave their land. Jobless people stood in line for hours to get free soup. Children in school sometimes fainted from hunger. These are only a few of the severe hardships people suffered during the Great Depression.

Sometimes the economy begins to slow down or stays in a decline for several months. Businesses fail, the number of people out of work rises, and profits decline. Yet things do not get so bad that we call it a depression. Economists call this period a **recession.** Our nation has experienced several recessions.

During the Great Depression millions of Americans were unemployed, and tried to make a living any way they could. This was a common sight on streets then.

Old Theories of the Business Cycle

Before the Great Depression of the 1930's, most economists believed the business cycle should be left alone. They thought the government should not step in and try to stimulate the economy, control inflation, or end unemployment.

Most economists believed the problems that came with the business cycle would cure themselves. If prices rose too high, people would stop buying goods and services until the prices came down again. Also, high prices and attractive profits would convince some people to go into business. The supply of goods and services would therefore increase. This would prevent prices from rising.

Many economists also thought that recessions could not last very long. Workers who lost their jobs would soon be willing to accept lower wages. Businesses would then be able to hire people for lower pay. Other costs of production also would be low. This would encourage businesses to produce more. As businesses expanded and increased their spending, they would help other businesses. Soon new businesses would be started. The economy would improve. Salaries would be raised and more people would be hired. People would buy more, and so on. Then came the Great Depression. The old theories did not seem to work.

Government Efforts to Aid the Economy

Wages were very low during the Great Depression. Millions of unemployed people were willing to accept any pay, no matter how low, rather than be without work. Yet businesses did not hire them. Moreover, businesses did not expand because there was no point in producing more goods when few people had enough money to buy them. To the surprise of the economists, the Great Depression did not end in a fairly short time. It went on year after year.

Does this look like a desert sandstorm? It is really farmland that was turned into a "Dust Bowl" by drought. During the 1930's many farmers lost their land.

Finally, many people were willing to have the government step in and do something to try to improve the economy. As you recall, President Franklin D. Roosevelt established a program known as the **New Deal.** Under this program, unemployed workers were hired by the government to do useful work, such as creating parks and building schools. Young people could join the Civilian Conservation Corps. They worked on projects to restore our forests and other natural resources. Homeowners and farmers could get loans to help pay their mortgages.

You may remember from Chapter 18 that the Federal Deposit Insurance Corporation was set up to insure bank deposits. The Social Security System was established to give regular payments to elderly citizens and help others in need. Unemployment insurance was created to provide workers with some money when they lost their jobs.

Many of the measures established during the Great Depression have remained in effect. However, they have not put an end to the business cycle. We still have periods when business is slow. The number of unemployed people has remained high during both good and bad periods. Furthermore, inflation continues to cause prices to rise, so that it costs us more to live each year. Economists once believed that prices always fell during a recession. During the 1970's, however, we continued to have inflation, even during serious recessions.

Government and the Business Cycle

There are several remedies the federal government has tried in an effort to control the business cycle. For one, it has changed its **fiscal policy,** or program for taxing and spending. If the economy is going into a recession, for instance, the government may reduce taxes. Lower taxes give people more money to spend. Increased spending encourages businesses to produce more, which leads to the creation of more jobs.

During recessions the government may step up its own spending. It buys more goods

Government efforts to put people back to work in the 1930's were portrayed by the American artist William Gropper in this painting called "Building a Dam."

and hires more people to work for the government. In the past, it has built public projects, such as bridges, dams, and hospitals. The government also may give larger payments to the unemployed, the poor, and the elderly.

The government has also tried to control the business cycle by changing its **monetary policy,** or money policy. This policy is handled by the Federal Reserve System. As you may recall from Chapter 18, Federal Reserve Banks serve as banks for other banks. They try to control the amount of money in the economy. If we are entering a recession, the Federal Reserve may increase the money supply by making it easier for banks to lend money to businesses at lower rates. It is hoped that this will encourage businesses to expand, thus creating more jobs and income.

If we are in a boom period, these actions may be reversed. When inflation becomes too high, the federal government may raise taxes and reduce its spending. The Federal Reserve may make it harder for banks to lend money to businesses. This decreases the amount of money in the economy.

At times the government has used direct controls over the economy. In 1971, for example, a **wage-price freeze** was attempted. Most prices and wages could not be raised for several months, and then only a little. However, the freeze was soon lifted because it did not work very well.

We have not yet learned how to control the economy. Some economists believe it does not have to be controlled. They think the government should keep out of the economy. They also believe programs begun under the New Deal have contributed to inflation. Other economists believe the government can help the economy. They say that without government actions, inflation would have been worse. They claim that government efforts have helped to prevent another Great Depression.

The debate will no doubt continue as economists, government leaders, and the

American people try to deal with inflation and keep our economy healthy.

CHECK-UP

Vocabulary

business cycle
costs of production
depression
Great Depression
recession
New Deal
fiscal policy
monetary policy
wage-price freeze

Review

1. Why do prices usually rise during a boom period?
2. What effect did the Great Depression have on jobs?
3. What are some ways in which the federal government tries to control the business cycle in the American economy?

Discuss

Is our country now in a period of inflation, depression, or recession? Explain.

3 Labor and Management

One day you will join the working population of our nation. You may be part of the labor force—perhaps a worker in the steel or automobile industry. Or you may be part of management—one of the owners or managers of a business. Therefore, it is important to understand the relationship between labor and management.

Working Conditions in the Past

In the early days of our nation, many Americans were self-employed. They worked for themselves on small farms or in their own workshops or stores. They then sold the goods they produced to neighbors and friends. Most businesses were small. They employed only a few workers, or wage earners. Wage earners usually worked side by side with the owner of a business. They knew the owner personally.

If workers were not satisfied, they could speak to the owner and ask for better wages or improved working conditions. If the owner refused, they could quit their jobs. They could work elsewhere because industry was growing and the nation was expanding westward. There was little labor-saving machinery. Most of the time, there were more jobs than workers. Therefore, employers often considered it important to treat their employees fairly.

Between 1800 and 1850, working conditions for many wage earners changed greatly. Large factories were built, using machines to make products. Many of these factories employed hundreds of workers, including young children.

In these new factories, relations between employers and workers were different. Factory managers and owners had little or no contact with workers. The working day was long—12 or even 16 hours. Wages usually were low. Working conditions were often poor, but workers could do little to improve them. When the western lands began to be filled in by settlers, it became more difficult for dissatisfied workers to leave their jobs and start on their own.

The Rise of Labor Unions

As American businesses continued to expand between 1850 and 1900, the number of workers also increased. American workers began to organize in groups, hoping to improve wages and working conditions. These organizations of workers became known as **labor unions.** Several small labor unions had been established on a local basis earlier. However, local unions were not always successful in dealing with employers. Workers came to

There is always plenty of work to do on a farm. On this apple orchard, for example, many farm workers are needed to help out at harvest time.

farm worker. Experts predict that the need for farm workers will continue to decline. By 1990 only about one worker in every 47 will be a farm worker.

CHECK-UP

Vocabulary

white-collar workers
professions
technicians
managers
executives
clerical workers
sales workers
blue-collar workers
craft workers
apprenticeship
operatives
laborers
service workers
service industries
farm workers

Review

1. Why must those who enter the professions spend many years training for their careers?
2. What training must a worker have to become a master craft worker?
3. Why has the demand for laborers decreased over the years?
4. Name some kinds of service workers.

Discuss

Would you rather be self-employed or work for a large corporation? Why?

3 Opportunities Unlimited

Whether a person is a professional, technician, craft worker, service worker, or laborer, there are opportunities for advancement. Young women and men who complete a high school commercial course might start their careers as stenographers, filing clerks, or bookkeepers. By attending special night school classes, they may later qualify for better paid positions.

They might study accounting, for example, and learn how to keep business financial records. Skilled accountants are needed by management as part of the business team. If young men and women are prepared, they will be ready when the right opportunity presents itself.

Government Jobs

Our nation's largest employer is the United States government. About 3 million Americans work for the federal government, not counting those who serve in the armed forces. Federal employees perform a wide range of jobs.

Some deliver the mail, care for war veterans, or protect us against counterfeiting. Others run the national parks, forecast the weather, or inspect food and drugs to make sure they are pure. Many thousands of clerks, typists, and secretaries are also required to carry out the everyday business of the United States government.

Applicants must take a test to qualify for most federal jobs. The tests are called **civil service examinations.** They are announced when government job openings occur. The jobs go to those who have received the highest test scores.

State and local governments also employ many different kinds of workers. Like federal employees, state and local workers usually are chosen on the basis of civil service examinations. Notices of job openings in federal, state, and local governments are sent to school counselors. You also may see these notices on post office bulletin boards or in local newspapers.

Opportunities in the Armed Forces

With the recent emphasis upon a volunteer army, careers in the military are being made more attractive. Salaries have been raised, and there is a greater choice of occupation.

A high school diploma is helpful in qualifying for most good jobs in the armed forces. High school graduates may receive technical training in the armed forces for such jobs as electronic technician, radar operator and technician, medical equipment technician, and motor mechanic. They may also be trained as surveyors, printers, medical technicians, photographers, and for many other jobs.

As you have read, our nation has four officer training schools. To qualify for the Army, Navy, Air Force, or Coast Guard academies, you must be a high school graduate. Applicants must be recommended by their United States senator or representative. They must also pass scholastic and physical tests.

(continued on page 396)

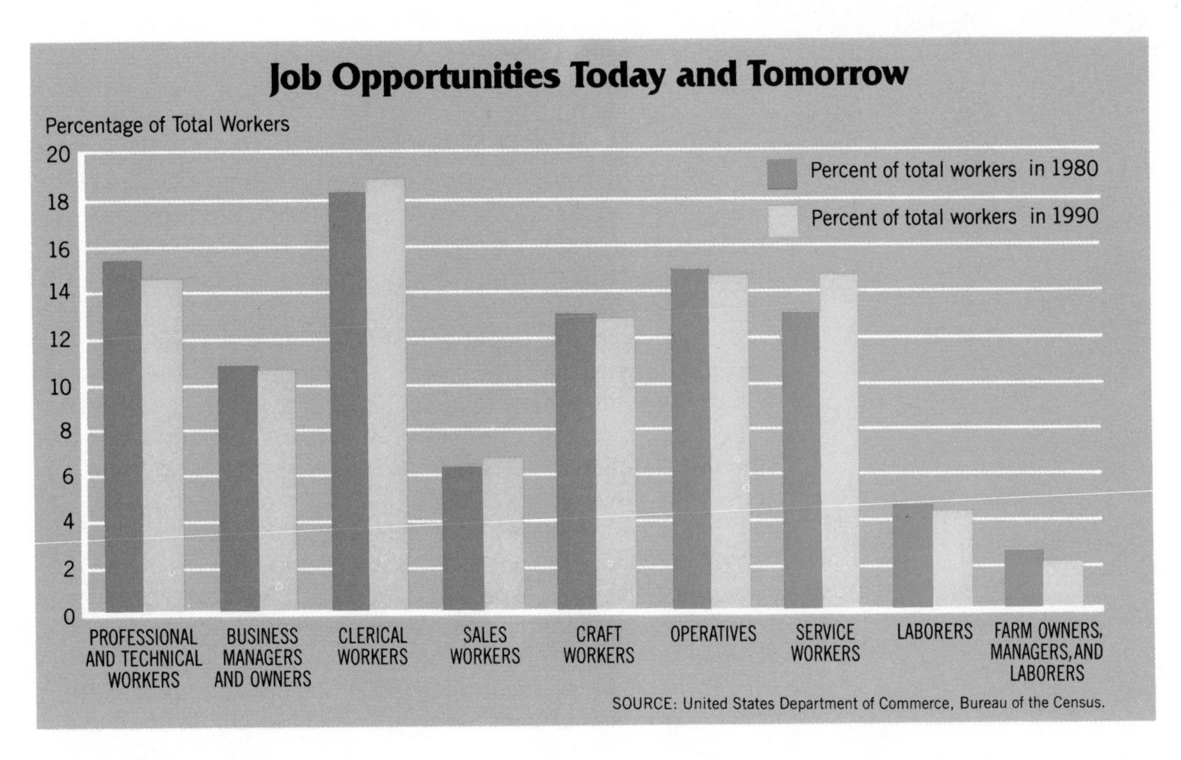

Getting a Jump on Careers

Would you know how to get a monkey to take its medicine? Or how to interest a six-year-old in the alphabet? Could you run a television news show? Each of these tasks requires a special talent—one that could help you choose a career someday.

Janice Buhl, Cassandra Cole, and Mark Shichtman began their career search even before finishing high school. Janice worked in a zoo. Cassandra started a school on the back porch of her home. Mark started his own news show on cable television. Each of them learned the skills mentioned above—and much more!

"Housekeeping" at the Zoo

The high school in Honolulu, Hawaii, that Janice attended offered a special class in zoo work. Since Janice had always been interested in animals, she signed up for the course. It required one zoo class a week at the high school and two mornings a week at the city zoo.

Each year about 25 juniors and seniors take the zoo course. Students are asked to keep a daily journal of their zoo-related work. They do many different tasks at the zoo. For example, they might help clean elephant teeth for a display. One group helped massage the limbs of a gorilla that had been paralyzed by an accident.

Janice was amazed at the variety of jobs in a zoo. One of her jobs was to take tour groups through the zoo. Her work taught her about many different kinds of animals—birds, reptiles, and mammals. She had to learn enough information to tell the groups about the animals and to be able to answer the questions they might ask her.

After she graduated from high school, Janice took a part-time job at the zoo. Her work as an aide to the animal keeper was much like housekeeping. She helped feed the animals and clean their pens and cages. When an animal became sick, she helped treat it.

At first, one of Janice's biggest problems was figuring out how to give medicine to a sick animal. Then she learned that one of the best ways is to "make use of the animal's eating habits." She found that many animals keep their appetites unless they are very sick. One favorite monkey, she remembers, "always ate as if it were starving. When it became sick, I put a pill in a banana, and the monkey—Jake, we called him—was in such a hurry to eat that it never noticed the medicine."

Janice learned a lot about zoos and animals. She learned, too, that she wants to make working with animals her career. "It will be wonderful," she says, "to be paid for doing something I enjoy so much."

Reporting the News on Television

Appearing on television is routine for Mark Shichtman. His news show—*Kids News*—appears every Thursday afternoon. It can be seen in thousands of homes in New York City.

Mark became a TV news reporter when he was in the fifth grade. He approached a cable television company with the idea for a news program by and for young people. The company agreed, and before long Mark and several friends were television stars. By the time they reached eighth grade, their classmates were teasing them about their "fame."

Kids News reports on a wide range of events. Mark and the other members of the news team get most of their stories from newspapers or from other television news shows. Each reporter is responsible for a special area. They cover local, national, and international news. Other features include a weather forecast and a sports report. A special feature of the show is "Citiline," which explores what's happening for kids in New York.

Mark would like to make his show more like a regular news program. Camera equipment would make it possible for the team to go out and cover stories directly—that is, film it as it happens. If Mark decides to make a career on television, he will certainly have a jump on most people his age.

A School of Her Own

Cassandra Cole took a different approach to her career search. She knew at the age of 12 that she wanted to teach. She decided then and there to open her own summer school in her home in Chicago, Illinois.

Cassandra's parents agreed to let her use the porch and yard for the summer, provided she kept them clean. Cassandra

then gathered materials to use in the school, signed up some students, and went to work. The school was such a success that Cassandra kept it going summer after summer.

The school is free, but each student must have his or her parents' permission to attend. Cassandra's goal is to help younger children do well during the regular school year. There are usually 15 students. To make sure they get the attention they need, Cassandra's teenage cousin helps with the teaching.

The classes are held from 12:30 to 3:00 on weekday afternoons. A typical day begins with the class reciting the Pledge of Allegiance. The first subject is reading, followed by spelling. After a break for juice, the students study mathematics. The afternoon ends with a game like Bingo, in which the winner gets a prize or a star. After the homework assignments are passed out, students are asked to help clean up.

Cassandra expects the students to do all their homework. The teacher does homework too. On Saturday afternoons Cassandra goes to the library to choose books and records for the students to use during the week.

Cassandra's own teachers have praised her initiative and leadership skills. Her summer school has been written about in newspapers and magazines, and the class has appeared on a local television program. What does Cassandra think about her success? She says that someday "I might like to have my own nursery school."

Thinking It Over

1. Name some of the talents a person might need to work in a zoo.
2. Why do you think Cassandra's teachers admire her?
3. Might Mark sometimes need adult help in preparing his weekly news show? Why or why not?
4. Do you have any special interests that might lead to a possible career for yourself? Explain.

Workers in High Demand

The United States Department of Labor constantly studies job opportunities in our nation. Each year it reports where women and men are working and what jobs they are doing. This department also studies the job needs of our nation. What skills are needed right now? What will be needed ten years from now?

In a study made in 1980, the Department of Labor estimated that through the 1980's the demand would be high for the following workers:

Accountants
Bank clerks
Bookkeepers
Building custodians
Carpenters
Cashiers
Computer operators and programmers
Construction workers
Cooks and chefs
Cosmetologists
Engineering and science technicians
Household workers
Industrial machine repairers
Kindergarten and elementary school teachers
Lawyers
Machinists
Practical nurses
Receptionists
Registered nurses
Sales workers
Secretaries
Social workers
Stenographers
Truck drivers
Typists

A career in teaching offers many rewards. A teacher has the chance to continue to enjoy a favorite subject and introduce it to many different students.

Keep in mind that the need for a particular type of worker may be greater in some parts of the nation than in others. This study is for the nation as a whole. Local needs often reflect a demand for certain kinds of workers.

Other kinds of workers, too, are almost always in demand. For example, law enforcement officers and members of the armed forces are usually needed. Also, remember that in all jobs there is a constant turnover because of promotions, job changes, or retirements. These events almost always create a job opening. The well-prepared person will be ready to seize this type of job opportunity when it occurs.

Equal Employment Opportunity

In your study of career opportunities, you may have noticed in newspaper classified advertisements the phrase "An Equal Opportunity Employer." This means that the employer does not discriminate against job applicants because of their sex, age, skin color, or ethnic background.

Congress passed the Civil Rights Acts of 1964 and 1968 to help end discrimination in hiring and in wage rates. These acts have opened up new job opportunities for women and minority groups. An **Equal Employment Opportunity Commission,** appointed by the

President, upholds fair employment standards. Several states have similar laws and commissions to enforce them.

Women are gaining the right to be considered for any job. Today women are members of Congress, generals, judges, jockeys, scientists, airline pilots, cab drivers—indeed, few fields are not open to women now. In industry, distinctions between women's and men's jobs are breaking down.

American business firms are urging young women to study for scientific and technical jobs that once were open only to men. The Women's Bureau of the Department of Labor has predicted that our nation's future needs for technical and scientific workers cannot be met unless more women enter these fields.

The profession of nursing is a field in which men as well as women are urgently needed. Many nursing positions are now open, and more will be open in the future. Nurses are needed for hospitals, public health agencies, nursing homes, industry, schools, doctors' offices, and the armed forces.

In the early days of computers, the people who ran them were mostly men. Today women are entering the computer field in growing numbers.

Periods of Unemployment

As you read in Chapter 19, there are times when our economic system goes through a recession or depression. At such times many people are out of work. Others are working but cannot find jobs in their chosen fields.

The young person studying careers should remember that there have always been periods of unemployment. It is wise to have more than one interest and if possible to develop skills in more than one area of work. You might want to consider job possibilities from the viewpoint of security before you make a final decision.

CHECK-UP

Vocabulary

civil service examinations
Equal Employment Opportunity Commission

Review

1. In what jobs will opportunities be especially good through the 1980's?
2. What qualifications must one have for a career as an army officer?
3. What does the phrase "An Equal Opportunity Employer" mean?
4. Why should a person studying different careers consider the importance of employment security?

Discuss

Why might a good salary and job satisfaction both be important?

4

Learning More About Careers

You are probably discovering that you know a great deal more about careers and jobs than you thought you did. For one thing, in your earlier studies you often have read about the careers of famous men and women. However, no single book, even one on careers, can give you all the information you need about various jobs. You may have to spend a lot of time hunting in different places to get the facts you need in order to discover the job that is best for you.

Reading About Careers

One of the best ways to learn about jobs is to read the many available books, magazines, and pamphlets on the subject. Explore your library, the newsstands, and any literature you may have at home. Your local state employment office has a number of booklets about careers in your community. Usually, these booklets may be obtained free of charge. Since large business firms are always on the lookout for good employees, many of them put out interesting brochures that contain useful job information.

Another source of information about jobs is the United States Department of Labor. It publishes a news bulletin called "Occupations in Demand for Young Jobseekers."

Reading about career opportunities in order to find a job field that interests you is like doing detective work. One clue leads to another as the job picture becomes clearer. You may find a clue in a novel or biography. Then you may find another bit of evidence in a newspaper column or magazine article. You are acting as a detective in solving the problem of your own career.

As you read about jobs, of course, you must remember your own interests, needs, and abilities. You should also try to keep an open mind. You may discover a career you never thought about before.

Watching Others at Work

Reading about jobs will help you gather many facts about them. But why not take a closer look by investigating job opportunities in your community? Through school-sponsored trips, you can find out a great deal about jobs available in factories, offices, and stores in your locality. Someone in your family may be able to arrange for you to visit his or her place of employment. You can also learn about jobs as you go about your daily affairs. Observe the work of bus drivers, police officers, teachers, salespeople, office workers, and others you meet each day.

You will gain more from watching people at work if you go about it in a careful way. Take notes on what you learn. Ask questions. Interview people who are working at jobs that interest you. Ask them what they like best and what they like least about their work. Talk about jobs with your parents, friends, and counselors. Discussing your thoughts with others will help make many ideas clearer in your own mind.

Learning by Working at a Job

One good way to discover more about careers is to get a job. For many students, responsibilities at home make a job impossible. Some students, though, work at part-time or summer jobs. You can learn something from any job.

Baby-sitting, for example, may lead you to think about a future job in a day care center. If not, it will at least give you a chance to learn more about people. Baby-sitting can also teach you why being prompt and dependable is important in any job. Being a newspaper carrier, supermarket clerk, gasoline station attendant, or movie usher are other ways you can get to know what working is like.

Here are just four of the hundreds of jobs you might choose. What kinds of work does each involve? What kinds of skills does each job require?

Don't overlook hobbies as a means of finding out what you like to do and can do well. Many people have turned their hobbies into their life's work. Hobbies may help you determine whether you have special talents. You can then begin to think about jobs that require similar abilities.

Another good way to explore your abilities is to take an active interest in school life. Try writing for the school newspaper. Manage a team. Serve on a class committee. Help decorate for school dances. Sell tickets for local affairs. These and other activities will give you a chance to see whether you enjoy writing, managing, selling, decorating, or some other skill that you may be able to use later in a job.

Job Questions to Ask Yourself

As you consider your future career, you can avoid guesswork if you ask yourself the seven important questions listed on the next page. Your answers should indicate whether you are making a wise choice.

1. What kind of work will I do in this job? Will I be working alone or with other people? Will I be working mostly with my hands or with my brain? What skills will I need to develop in order to do the job well? Does the job involve study and careful planning, or does it involve repeating the same task?

2. What personal qualifications does the job require? How important in this job are neatness, promptness, dependability, and pleasant personality? Must I be able to follow directions? Will I be expected to give directions and to lead others? Does the job call for strong muscles?

3. How much education and training does the job require? Must I be a high school graduate? Is a college education necessary? Is any specialized training required? Is a period of apprenticeship needed for the job? If so, how long does it last?

4. Are job opportunities in this field good? Are there many openings now? Is this a growing field of work? Will there be more openings when I am ready to look for a job? Is this the kind of career in which I can develop my abilities and move ahead?

5. What salary does the job pay? Is the starting salary only the first step toward a higher income? What training must I have to receive salary increases? Will I be satisfied with the **salary range** (beginning salary, possible raises, and highest salary) that the work offers? What other benefits, such as insurance, sick pay, on-the-job training, and pleasant working conditions, are available?

6. How do I feel about this job? Do I believe this is a job worth doing? Will I be making a contribution to the community? Will I be happy with the kinds of people who may be working with me?

7. Where will I have to live and work for this kind of job? Will I have to move to another part of the country? Does the job require that I travel a lot? Will I have to live in a large city? Are most work-

Working on a school newspaper is just a hobby for these students now. But if they like the work and are good at it, they may choose careers in the news field.

ers in this field employed in factories, on farms, in offices, or in their own homes?

A Sample Job Quiz

Why is it so important to ask yourself these questions—and to find the answers to them? You probably have guessed the reason. It is one of the best ways to find out whether the job you are considering is the right job for you.

Suppose that Janet Smith, a ninth grade student, is interested in a job as a medical technician. The following seven questions should help Janet decide whether she wants that kind of career.

Question 1: What kind of work will I do in this job?

Answer: Medical technicians usually work with doctors in the laboratories of hospitals and clinics. Medical technicians perform tests that help doctors decide how to treat diseases. They take blood tests, for example, and report the results of these tests. They help prepare various tests that doctors give patients to check for many diseases.

Question 2: What personal qualifications are required?

Answer: The medical technician must be a dependable, accurate person who is interested in science. She or he must be intelligent, careful, and able to follow directions. She or he must also have good eyesight and skillful hands.

Question 3: How much education and training does the job require?

Answer: At least three years of college are required, plus a year of special training in a hospital to learn laboratory procedures.

Question 4: Are job opportunities in this field good?

Answer: There is a shortage of medical technicians. Well-trained workers will have no trouble getting jobs. The work can lead to a job in medical research, to ownership of an independent laboratory, or to a job as a laboratory supervisor.

Question 5: What salary does the job pay?

Answer: The starting salary of a college-trained medical technician is about $15,000. It can be more or less than this, depending on the exact nature of the job. Also, salaries vary in different parts of the country. Salaries increase with experience.

Question 6: How do I feel about this job?

Answer: Medical technicians do interesting and important work. They help the sick get well again.

Question 7: Where will I have to live and work for this kind of job?

Answer: The medical technician works in the hospitals, medical centers, private laboratories, clinics, and doctors' offices that are located in most communities. The worker can live anywhere within commuting distance of the job.

This job quiz should help the person who is deciding whether or not to become a medical technician. It should also give you and the rest of your class a good idea of the work done by a medical technician.

Using the seven questions listed above, you and your classmates can work out quizzes for any occupations that interest you.

CHECK-UP

Vocabulary

salary range

Review

1. Where can you get information about careers?
2. How can a part-time job help you in choosing a career?
3. How are hobbies useful in deciding what kind of work you might like to do?
4. What are seven important questions to keep in mind when considering a job?

Discuss

Why is it important to have a plan to reach your career goal?

5 Learning More About Yourself

Some jobs may interest you because they seem exciting and glamorous. Many young people think about becoming singers, actors, or professional athletes. But many of them discover that succeeding in these jobs is too difficult. Or they learn that they are more interested in some other job.

Of course, if you decide that you have what it takes to be a success in one of these fields, you should work as hard as you can to get into it. However, if you study your interests and abilities and discover you are more likely to succeed in some other occupation, you would be wiser to choose that career.

To learn about yourself is not easy. It is difficult for most of us to look at ourselves honestly and to judge our own qualifications. It is worth the effort, though, if we finally are able to get a true picture of ourselves. We must also learn how we appear to other people. Often other people can help us see ourselves better and discover the kind of person we are. What are some ways in which we can learn to know ourselves?

Preparing to Apply for a Job

When the time comes to look for your first job, you will probably have to fill out a **job application.** This is a printed form on which you are asked to supply important information about yourself. Your job application helps the employer decide if you are the right person for the job.

Large business firms have **personnel workers** whose job it is to hire or recommend new employees. Personnel workers examine job applications and interview people to determine the best-qualified applicant for the available job.

You will probably find it helpful to practice filling out a job application. Then, when you apply for a job later on, you will know what type of information you will be asked to give.

You can practice writing out job applications in several ways. Perhaps you can fill out a real application used by a local business firm. Or you can prepare an outline of important facts about yourself. Many students prefer to write short autobiographies, including the chief facts about their lives. No matter which you choose, you will find it useful in filling out a job application.

What Employers Want to Know

To prepare your own job application, you should know the information employers need when they are seeking a new employee. In general, they will want to know the following facts about you.

1. Your School History. Your school record tells the employer a lot about you. List the subjects you have taken in the last two years and the grades you received. Then look at the reasons for these grades. What do grades mean? Perhaps you have high marks in English because you enjoy expressing yourself through writing. This may show that you should consider an occupation in which you can use your writing talent. On the other hand, you may have poor grades in mathematics. Does this mean you should not even consider a job that requires mathematical ability? Not necessarily!

Grades do not always tell the whole story. Some students with low marks in mathematics may be late in discovering their ability in this subject. Perhaps they had trouble understanding number concepts in their earlier math courses. After special effort, they may be catching up in their studies. They may now be on their way to mastering math and getting higher grades. As you see, low grades in any subject are not necessarily a sign that the student cannot learn. Low marks frequently indicate lack of effort rather than lack of ability.

Perhaps in listing your subjects and grades you should include a third column entitled "Reasons for the Grades." This column will help you judge your own abilities and interests. It will also tell you how well you have used them up to now.

2. Your Health Record. Good health is an important qualification for any job. Some occupations even require that workers have special physical qualifications. Sometimes good eyesight is essential. A medical technician, surgeon, or jeweler, for instance, needs good eyesight. You will want to examine your health record and review your program for keeping fit.

There are many job opportunities, however, for persons with physical handicaps. The history of American business and industry contains countless stories of people who succeeded in spite of their handicaps. As just one example, Thomas Edison, the great inventor, was deaf. Yet his life was filled with outstanding accomplishments. A person may not be able to eliminate certain physical disabilities. Yet he or she can choose a job in which such handicaps are no drawback.

3. Your Outside Activities. Make a list of your hobbies, the school offices you have held, sports in which you take part, school organizations you belong to, and your part-time and summer jobs. After you have completed this list, take another look at it. Does it show many different activities? What part of each did you like best? This review can tell you and an employer a great deal about your potential job skills.

4. Your Special Interests. The things that interest you now may also point the way to the future. List all your interests that you think might help you make a career choice. Check back on the subjects you have liked best in school. Try to see if your interests have helped you do well in these subjects. Finally, review your hobbies and your part-time work activities to see which interests they emphasize.

A future employer will know and understand you better if he or she is aware of your special interests. They will show the employer whether you prefer indoor or outdoor work, whether you would rather work alone or with others, or whether you want to be a leader or a follower.

Study Your Test Record

Tests are another means of helping you understand yourself and your abilities. Every test you take in school measures certain skills. You have probably already taken tests that show how well you study, how accurately you remember what you read, and how well you express yourself. Go back over your test scores and consider the reasons for these grades. They should reveal your ability to do certain things. Here are some of the strengths such tests seek to measure.

Motor Skills. Certain tests are used to determine how well people can use their

The young people shown here are developing their motor skills. The skills required to repair a bicycle could lead to profitable careers in the future.

These students are rehearsing a school play. They have a chance to pursue their interest in theater and to determine if they have any special talents for it.

hands—their motor skills. They measure how fast individuals can do things with their hands. They also check how accurately they do things. Certain other tests determine how well people can handle and arrange small objects. You can understand why good motor skills are useful to a watchmaker or a worker assembling small electronic equipment.

Number Skills. One of the most common tests measures a person's ability to work with numbers quickly and accurately. Such number skills are essential to bookkeepers, carpenters, and accountants. Many scientists also need to be skilled in using numbers.

Perceptual Skills. How well can you picture things—that is, see them in your mind? In order to read a blueprint, for example, you must be able to picture in your mind the way a building will look when finished. You must be able to see depth and width in a flat drawing. The ability to think in this way is a part of perceptual skills.

Language Skills. A teacher explaining an idea to students, a salesperson talking to a customer, and a parent describing to a child how to draw all have skills in using language. An editor, an advertising specialist, and an executive in a business firm must be skilled in using written language. Many kinds of tests check these abilities, called language skills, or linguistic ability.

Special Talents. Some tests include sections that try to discover whether a person has artistic and creative talent. Sometimes there is also a section that measures the ability to organize and present facts. People can use these special talents in many different kinds of jobs. Publishing companies and advertising agencies, for example, need designers and writers.

Personal Relationships. There are tests to check how well you handle personal relationships—how well you get along with others. This is important in many jobs. Teachers should rank high in this skill. So should salespeople, receptionists, and other workers who deal with many people.

Interests and Aptitudes. There are certain other tests you take in school that can help you to know yourself better. These are called interest tests, or **aptitude tests.** They are easy to take and reveal interesting things about you. Your teacher or counselor will help explain the results of these tests and the meaning they have for you.

Such tests probably will not tell you the exact job you should look for. No test can map out the future for you. What these tests are supposed to do is help you discover your abilities and interests. Then it is up to you to match what you have discovered about yourself with what you learn about various job opportunities.

By now you probably have made a good start in getting to know yourself better. As you study jobs that interest you, compare your opportunities with your abilities. Your present aim should be to choose a general field of work—a type of work rather than a specific job. Leave the way open so that you can change to another kind of work if you need to do so. Remember, a person's first job choice may not be the final one.

CHECK-UP

Vocabulary

job application
personnel workers
motor skills
number skills
perceptual skills
language skills
aptitude tests

Review

1. Why is it a good idea to practice filling out job applications?
2. Why is your school history important to an employer?
3. Why would an employer want to know about a job applicant's health?
4. What can your special interests indicate to a future employer?
5. What does an aptitude test reveal about a person?

Discuss

If you were interviewing applicants for a variety of jobs, what questions would you ask them? What qualities would you look for?

CHAPTER SUMMARY

All young Americans must plan for their future careers. There are many job opportunities for young people. But these opportunities keep changing. You must get up-to-date information on jobs if you are to make a wise career choice.

In considering job possibilities, you should know about the work done by people in the professions and by managers, technicians, service workers, craft workers, operatives, and farm workers. The choice of your career must be made by you alone. However, there are certain general guides that you may find helpful. You can read widely about jobs, explore jobs in your community, interview workers, and work at a part-time job.

An important step in deciding upon a career is to learn more about yourself. Your school and health records, your special interests, your outside activities, and your work experience will be of interest to prospective employers.

You can prepare yourself now so that you will know what employers look for when hiring new workers. Learn about jobs that are available, not only in your community but throughout the country as well. Use your school years wisely. The skills and knowledge you acquire in school will help you for the rest of your life.

CIVICS SKILLS: Reading a Help Wanted Ad

Fourteen-year-old Sean Riley likes to draw cartoons. His older sister, Ellen, spends much of her spare time tinkering with gadgets and machines. Their cousin, Alice Miller, lands a role in just about every school play. What kinds of jobs might interest each of these people?

Do you have some special hobby or skill? Perhaps you have a favorite subject in school. Maybe you prefer outdoor activities to those done indoors. Matching your personal interests with an occupation, or career, is important. As an adult, you'll work at a job, on the average, 40 hours a week, 50 weeks a year. You will, therefore, want to find a job that you would enjoy doing day after day, on a year-round basis.

Looking for a Job

A good place to start a job search is with the "Classified" section of your local newspaper. This is where the **help wanted ads,** or job offers, are located.

As a rule, most help wanted ads follow the same general organization. For example, they appear roughly in alphabetical order according to type of business or job title. This information usually runs across the top of each ad to help you spot job possibilities quickly. What job is advertised in the ad on this page? Is it listed by business or by job title?

Whenever you see an interesting ad, you naturally look at it more closely. If you don't have the right training or experience, you might think about how you can get it. In addition, carefully study any promises made in the ad. Is the salary listed? What about such benefits as vacation, on-the-job training, or health insurance? The answers to these and other questions will help you decide whether or not you might want to apply for a particular job.

One final word of advice. Help wanted ads aren't written by the newspaper staff. The newspaper sells space to advertisers who, in turn, supply the words. Pay special attention to ads placed by employment agencies, or businesses that charge money to fill a position. The company that actually has the job opening often pays the agency fee—but not always. Sometimes it is the successful job applicant who must pay the agency's fee.

Practicing What You've Learned

1. What qualifications are needed for the job in the ad below?
2. Who is advertising the position? Is there any fee involved?
3. What features of the job are used to attract applicants?
4. If you wanted to apply for the job, how would you go about it?
5. Besides the information supplied in the ad, what else would you want to know about the job before accepting this position?

RECEPTIONIST
ART GALLERY

$225/fee paid

Bright energetic H.S. grad. to handle front desk and busy phones. Typing 55 w.p.m.

Neat appearance and punctuality a must. Knowledge of modern art would be useful. Excellent vacations and fringe benefits. Immediate hire.

Winston Agency 724-3791

An Equal Opportunity Employer

CHAPTER REVIEW

Vocabulary

In the sentences below, the words in italics are used incorrectly. They make each of the sentences false. Correct the sentences by supplying the words that make each statement true.

1. The *professions* are jobs that require little or no training.
2. The men and women who manage large business firms or corporations are known as *apprentices*.
3. Most *operatives* have special trades or occupations that require long periods of training.
4. Large business firms have *craft workers* to interview job applicants.
5. The widespread use of computers in business calls for skilled *executives* to repair them.
6. Tailors, barbers, and beauticians are examples of *clerical workers*.
7. *Technicians* usually acquire their skills in a short time on the job.

Check-up

1. What is meant by freedom of job choice in America?
2. What are some of the qualities employers look for in their workers?
3. How does a person prepare for a career in a profession?
4. What is the difference between a craft worker and an operative?
5. Do you think women now have equal opportunities in employment with men? Explain your answer.
6. What are the most important questions to ask yourself when considering a new career?
7. Why are employers interested in knowing how you did in school?
8. What are motor skills? number skills? language skills? perceptual skills?

Civics Skills

Which jobs interest you the most? Select one of these, and write a "Help Wanted" ad for that position. Be sure to investigate the training and experience needed for this kind of work. Try to learn what salary and other benefits might be offered.

Next, read through the classified section of your local newspaper to find an ad for the kind of job you have chosen. Clip it out and mount it on a separate piece of paper. How does this ad compare with the one that you have written?

Citizenship and You

1. Construct a chart showing different kinds of jobs that may be listed under the following headings: White-Collar Workers, Blue-Collar Workers, Service Workers, and Farm Workers.
2. Write a report called "My Future Career." Gather facts about a possible career for yourself. Then organize them into a presentation that describes the kind of work you would do, the training needed, the skills required, the salary and benefits, and ways in which the job would help others.
3. In the "Help Wanted" section of your local newspaper, look for a job that interests you. Write a letter of application for that job.
4. Invite people from your community who hold various jobs to talk to your class about the work they do. The class should prepare a list of questions to ask each person.
5. Make a list of five things you most enjoy doing. Then make a list of five things you dislike doing. What jobs can you think of that would enable you to do most of the things you enjoy but few of the things you dislike?

UNIT SIX REVIEW

Reviewing the Facts

Write your answers to the items below on a separate piece of paper.

1. The goal of an economic system is to
   a. keep prices low.
   b. enable people to use credit.
   c. raise productivity.
   d. provide for people's material needs.
2. The free enterprise system encourages all of the following *except*
   a. the profit motive.
   b. private investment.
   c. government control.
   d. economic competition.
3. Complete the last sentence: A new game suddenly becomes very popular. People want to buy more games than the manufacturer can produce. The price of the game will probably increase. This will happen to the price because of the economic law of ________.
4. Hill and Chen, Attorneys-at-Law, is probably an example of
   a. a single proprietorship.
   b. a partnership.
   c. a corporation.
   d. none of the above.
5. Complete this sentence: When labor union and management representatives discuss the features of a new contract for the workers, the process is known as ________.
6. All of the following contributed to the growth of mass production *except*
   a. hand tools.
   b. standard parts.
   c. the division of labor.
   d. machine tools.
7. Which of the following makes it possible to buy now and pay later?
   a. a charge account
   b. a checking account
   c. a savings account
   d. all of the above
8. Complete this sentence: If a corporation sold stocks that were actually worthless, it would probably be investigated by the ________.
9. If inflation is very high, the Federal Reserve might
   a. try to take money out of circulation.
   b. open new banks.
   c. print more money.
   d. tell people to stop buying stocks.
10. If you interview for a job, the employer would probably want to know about all of the following *except*
    a. your skills and interests.
    b. your education.
    c. your father's occupation.
    d. your ability to follow directions.

Applying What You Know

1. Describe three ways in which you take part in the American economic system.
2. Describe how each of the following people probably would feel about high inflation:
   a. a person living on a fixed income
   b. a person who owes money
   c. a person whose savings are in a savings account paying 5½ percent interest.

Expanding Your Knowledge

Allentuck, Andrew, and Bivens, Gordon, *Consumer Choice: The Economics of Personal Living,* Harcourt Brace Jovanovich. How to earn money, budget, save, invest, and make wise consumer choices.

Antell, Gerson, and Harris, Walter, *Economics for Everybody,* Amsco. Case studies explain how our economic system works.

Cooke, David C., *How Money Is Made,* Dodd, Mead. Money—where it comes from and how it is distributed.

Halacy, D. S., Jr., *Survival in the World of Work,* Scribner's. The variety of jobs and how to prepare for them.

UNIT SEVEN

America in Today's World

CHAPTER

21

Establishing Our Foreign Policy

On the desk of the President of the United States is a bright red telephone. It connects the President directly with Soviet leaders in Moscow, the capital city of the Soviet Union. This "hot line" is not for regular communication between the two nations. It is to be used only in the gravest emergency. Suppose, for example, that through some accident one nation launched a nuclear missile toward the territory of the other. The phone would be used to warn the other side of the danger and to deny warlike intentions.

The fact that a hot line is needed indicates the perils of international affairs in today's world. Hydrogen bombs with massive destructive power are stockpiled in a number of nations. A nuclear war would mean the end of civilization. It is little wonder that the world's leaders are seeking new ways to keep peace and improve relations with their neighbors, near and far.

Much of the time and attention of officials of the American government are devoted to keeping the peace and improving international relations. The President meets often with the heads of other nations to reach needed agreements. The Secretary of State may appear before the United Nations to appeal for a desired course of action.

At the same time, Congress may be considering legislation that will affect our foreign relations. Working behind the scenes are hundreds of other officials gathering information, preparing agreements, seeking allies, and working toward better relations.

It is important that each citizen understand how our government deals with other nations, for our lives and welfare may depend on it. In this chapter, we shall consider the following topics:

1. **Conducting Our Foreign Relations**
2. **Working for Peace**
3. **The United Nations**

1

Conducting Our Foreign Relations

The plan that our nation works out for dealing with other nations is called our **foreign policy.** The purpose of this policy is to maintain peace, trade, and friendship throughout the world. The way in which this policy is carried out and its success or failure affects our **foreign relations.** That means it affects the way we get along with the governments of other nations.

In carrying out its foreign policy, the United States depends on a number of people. Government officials make contact with the leaders of other nations. Business firms carry on foreign trade, which affects our foreign relations. Even United States tourists traveling in other nations may influence the attitude of other people toward our nation. How does the United States government establish our foreign policy?

The President and Foreign Relations

President Harry S. Truman once said, "I make American foreign policy." By this he meant that the President is responsible for the conduct of our nation's foreign policy. Although aided by officials of the Department of State and other advisers, the President is responsible for the major decisions. Article II, Section 2, of the Constitution of the United States gives the President the following powers over foreign relations:

1. Military Powers. As Commander in Chief of the armed forces of the United States, the President makes recommendations to Congress concerning the size of the military and the kinds of weapons to have. Only Congress can declare war. But the President, as head of the armed forces, can order troops, planes, and warships into the world's trouble spots. The troops sent abroad must be recalled within 60 days unless Congress approves the action.

2. Treaty-Making Powers. Written agreements, or treaties, with other nations are an important part of our foreign relations. With the advice and consent of the Senate, the President has the power to make three kinds of treaties.

Peace treaties are agreements to end wars. Peace treaties spell out the terms for ending the fighting. They must be consented to by all sides in the conflict. **Alliance treaties** are agreements in which nations promise to help defend each other in case of attack. The United States has established alliances with many nations of the world. **Commercial treaties,** or **trade treaties,** are agreements by two or more nations to trade with each other on favorable terms.

Treaties must be approved by a two-thirds vote of the Senate. However, our nation sometimes reaches agreements with other nations without signing treaties. The Presi-

The President meets often with other world leaders. Here President Reagan meets with Prime Minister Margaret Thatcher of Great Britain.

dent of the United States and the leader of a foreign government may meet and come to a mutual understanding. This is known as an **executive agreement.** It is then announced in a joint statement to the people of the two nations. Or the leaders may exchange official letters or notes in which they spell out details of their agreement. For the most important negotiations on policy, however, a treaty must be signed.

3. Diplomatic Powers. The President, again with the approval of the Senate, appoints **ambassadors** to represent the United States in foreign nations. The President also receives ambassadors from other nations to the United States.

The right of the President to receive ambassadors from foreign nations includes the power of **diplomatic recognition.** That is, the President may decide whether to deal formally with the government of a foreign nation. To recognize a foreign government means to establish official relations with that government. Sending an American ambassador there and receiving that nation's ambassador means that official recognition has taken place.

The President may refuse to recognize a government whose foreign policies are considered unfriendly or dangerous to the United States. For many years, the United States refused to recognize the communist government of China. Recognition was granted in the 1970's. Ambassadors were then exchanged.

Sometimes it is necessary to break off relations with a foreign nation. Breaking off relations means ending all official dealings with that nation. In breaking off relations, the United States recalls our ambassador, and the other nation's ambassador returns home. The United States broke off relations with Iran in 1980 when American diplomats were held hostage there. Breaking off relations is a very serious move. It occurs only when two nations are unable to settle a serious dispute.

In deciding on and carrying out the foreign policy of the United States, the President may call upon any department of the government for assistance. The President also hires foreign policy experts to assist in this important responsibility. These policy-making experts are part of the Executive Office of the President.

The Department of State

The President decides on foreign policy. The Department of State is the principal organization for carrying out that policy. It also acts as "the eyes and ears of the President" in obtaining information upon which our foreign relations are based.

The Department of State is headed by the

Secretary of State, who is appointed by the President with the approval of the Senate. The Secretary of State reports directly to the President and is assisted by a deputy secretary, undersecretaries, and many assistant secretaries.

The Secretary of State advises the President and supervises the activities of American ambassadors. The ambassadors are our nation's major representatives in other nations. They are stationed in the capital cities of most foreign nations.

In a few smaller nations, American representatives are known as **ministers.** In many foreign cities, American representatives who are known as **consuls** help American business people and travelers. Ambassadors, ministers, and consuls, with their assistants, are members of our **diplomatic corps.**

Members of the diplomatic corps work for friendly relations with the nations in which they are stationed. They report to the Secretary of State on any events of importance that are happening there. Their reports are sent in secret code. Or they may be carried by special messengers called **couriers.** Sometimes ambassadors or ministers will hurry to Washington to meet with the Secretary of State or the President on some special problem.

Information obtained in this way helps the President and advisers to decide on our policy and actions toward other countries. American consuls also send regular reports on business and trade conditions. These reports help American business firms plan their operations in foreign countries.

The Department of Defense

An important source of military information for the President is the Department of Defense. The Secretary of Defense advises the President on troop movements, placement of military bases at home and abroad, and development of weapons.

The Secretary of Defense and the President receive advice on military matters from the Joint Chiefs of Staff. The Joint Chiefs include a chairman and the highest-ranking military officer of the Army, Navy, Air Force, and Marines. All these officials are appointed by the President.

Agencies Aid the President

Every other department of the executive branch of our government also becomes involved in foreign policy at various times. The Secretary of Agriculture, for example, keeps the President advised of available surplus foods that may be sent to a needy nation. The Secretary of the Treasury handles the financial transactions relating to aid to other countries. The Secretary of Health and Human Services supplies information essential to medical aid for foreign lands. Other executive departments assist in their fields of specialization.

In addition to the help provided by the regular departments, Congress has established a number of specialized agencies to help decide on and carry out our foreign policy. You are already familiar with some of these agencies from your study of Chapter 6. The **Central Intelligence Agency (CIA),** you may recall, is responsible for gathering secret information essential to our national defense. The CIA also helps keep the President informed about political trends in various nations.

★ ★ ★ ★ ★ ★ ★ ★ ★ ★ ★ ★

CAN YOU GUESS?

- **Who was the first American President to win a Nobel peace prize?**
- **Who was the first American President to travel to Europe while in office? (Hint: He was also the second President to win a Nobel peace prize.)**

Answers are on page 562.

This fact-finding meeting, attended by members of the Department of State, will provide some of the information necessary for the making of foreign policy.

The **National Security Council (NSC)** is part of the Executive Office of the President. Its members are the President, the Vice President, and the Secretaries of State and Defense. The head of the Joint Chiefs of Staff and the director of the Central Intelligence Agency attend all NSC meetings. The NSC was created to help coordinate American military and foreign policy.

The **United States Information Agency (USIA)** helps keep the world informed about the American way of life and about American points of view on world problems. It does this through information centers set up in 125 countries around the world. The USIA also publishes booklets, distributes films, and sponsors "Voice of America" radio programs. It was formerly called the International Communications Agency.

The **Arms Control and Disarmament Agency** seeks to prevent dangerous weapons-building races. It does so by negotiating with other nations and seeking to reach agreements on arms limitations.

Another group established to influence foreign relations is the **Agency for International Development (AID).** It provides technical and financial assistance to developing nations. AID has provided billions of dollars' worth of modern machinery, raw materials, food, fuel, medical supplies, and loans to help the world's peoples. AID also provides money and technical assistance during emergencies resulting from floods, epidemics, earthquakes, and other disasters.

Congress and Foreign Relations

The President leads our nation in dealing with world affairs. Congress also plays a major role. It is essential that the President work closely with leaders in both houses of Congress when deciding on foreign policies.

It is the responsibility of the Senate Foreign Relations Committee and the House Committee on Foreign Affairs to make important recommendations to Congress and the President on questions of foreign relations.

1. Approval Powers. The Senate, as you know, must approve all treaties between the United States and other nations by a two-thirds vote. What happens if the Senate refuses to approve a treaty?

After World War I, President Woodrow Wilson wanted the United States to join the League of Nations. A provision for joining this peace-keeping organization was included as a part of the Treaty of Versailles that ended World War I. However, a powerful group of senators opposed membership of the United States in the League of Nations. These senators wanted the United States to stay out of European affairs and to concentrate on solving its own problems. They eventually succeeded in preventing a two-thirds majority vote in the Senate in favor of the treaty. As a result, the United States did not approve the Treaty of Versailles or join the League of Nations.

The Senate also must approve the appointment of all ambassadors by majority vote. The President's nominations are almost always approved.

2. War-Making Powers. Under the Constitution, as you recall, only Congress can declare war. Over the years, however, Presidents have sent troops to fight in foreign countries without a declaration of war. In 1973 Congress passed the War Powers Act. This act limits the President's power to commit troops abroad without the approval of Congress.

3. Money Powers. As you have read, both houses of Congress must approve all expenditures of public funds. This too gives Congress power in foreign affairs. All spending for national defense, for example, must be approved by Congress. The President may recommend that a new weapon be built or that our armed forces be expanded. Unless Congress votes the necessary money, however, these policies cannot be carried out.

CHECK-UP

Vocabulary

foreign policy
foreign relations
peace treaties
alliance treaties
commercial treaties
trade treaties
executive agreement
ambassadors
diplomatic recognition
ministers
consuls
diplomatic corps
couriers
Central Intelligence Agency
National Security Council
United States Information Agency
Arms Control and Disarmament Agency
Agency for International Development

Review

1. What is the purpose of American foreign policy?
2. What are the President's powers over foreign policy?
3. What are some of the government agencies that help the President carry out foreign policy?
4. How can Congress check the President's activities in international affairs?

Discuss

Why do you think the Constitution gave the President the major responsibility for foreign policy?

2

Working for Peace

The fact that so many departments and agencies of our government devote so much time to foreign affairs indicates its importance to us. The chief goal of our foreign policy is to maintain peace in the world. Government officials work to achieve this goal in a number of ways.

Diplomacy

The process of conducting relations between nations, as you recall, is called **diplomacy.** It is used to prevent war, negotiate an end to conflicts, solve problems, and establish communication between nations. As you know, the President is our nation's chief diplomat.

To carry out this role, Presidents make frequent use of **personal diplomacy.** That is, they travel to other countries to meet with foreign leaders. They also confer with foreign leaders and ambassadors in the United States. One example of personal diplomacy is the **summit conference.** This is a meeting with the heads of other nations, or heads of state, as they are sometimes called. Summit conferences first became popular during World War II, when Allied leaders met to discuss wartime strategy.

Diplomacy is also carried out by other government officials. For example, State Department officials often represent the President in trying to settle conflicts between other nations. In recent years, American diplomats have flown back and forth between different nations so often that this kind of peace-seeking has become known as **shuttle diplomacy.**

Our Many Alliances

The United States has alliances with many individual nations, such as Japan, South Korea, and the Philippines. It has also established alliances with several large groups of nations.

The **North Atlantic Treaty Organization (NATO)** includes these 15 nations: the United States, Belgium, Canada, Denmark, France, Great Britain, Greece, Iceland, Italy, Luxembourg, the Netherlands, Norway, Portugal, Turkey, and West Germany. It was created in 1949 to establish a united front against the threat of aggression by the Soviet Union in Europe and the Middle East. The members of NATO have agreed that "armed attack against one will be considered an attack on all."

A current President may ask former Presidents to go on special diplomatic missions.
Here President Reagan thanks Jimmy Carter, Richard Nixon, and Gerald Ford for their help.

A joint NATO military command, called the Supreme Headquarters Allied Powers Europe (SHAPE), plans military strategy for the NATO powers. France is not a member of this military arm of NATO.

Australia, New Zealand, and the United States are joined in an alliance called **ANZUS,** established in 1951. Its purpose is to protect the mutual interests of the member nations.

In the Western Hemisphere, the United States and most of the nations of Latin America formed the **Organization of American States (OAS)** in 1948. The goal of the OAS is to defend the member nations and work for peace.

Members of the OAS meet often to work out ways to be "good neighbors"—to help one another improve standards of living in all the member nations.

Foreign Aid

Our nation also uses foreign aid to help achieve its foreign policy goals. **Foreign aid** is a government program that provides economic and military assistance to other nations. Our foreign aid policy began shortly after the end of World War II. The war-torn nations of Europe needed help. People were badly in need of food, clothing, homes, and jobs.

In 1947 the United States Secretary of State, George Marshall, proposed a plan to help the nations of Europe rebuild their factories, farms, homes, and transportation systems. Congress agreed that these nations needed American help. It granted $12.5 billion for aid under the **Marshall Plan.** By 1951 the economies of Western Europe had recovered to a remarkable degree. Marshall Plan aid, having done its job, was ended.

Since World War II, the United States has given or loaned over $190 billion in aid to nations around the world. Some of this aid has been in the form of grants, or gifts. In recent years, it has more often been in the form of low-interest loans. A large part of American foreign aid is managed through the Agency for International Development.

In the past few years, about one percent of our federal budget has been spent on foreign aid. More than 50 nations have received military aid to help them maintain their independence. Economic assistance has been given to help new nations in Africa and Asia become self-supporting. Foodstuffs, such as wheat, corn, and rice, have been sent from the United States to help feed the hungry people of the world.

Another kind of foreign aid has been provided by individual Americans. The **Peace Corps** was established in the early 1960's to send volunteers into countries that requested help. Peace Corps volunteers in such fields as teaching, farming, medicine, and industry have worked in countries throughout the world.

American foreign aid sometimes takes the form of food for the victims of famine. Here food has been sent to starving people in Africa's Sahara desert.

Questions About Foreign Aid

Should the United States continue to spend one percent of its federal budget on foreign aid? Should it spend more? Should it spend less? Foreign aid has always been a controversial subject. There are many arguments for and against foreign aid.

Those who favor foreign aid point to the necessity of assisting developing nations. If we do not help, they say, these nations may turn for aid to the communist governments of the Soviet Union or China. Supporters of foreign aid argue, too, that our wealthy nation should not watch people starve without offering assistance. The foreign aid we have given in the past, they say, has helped build stronger nations and has contributed to world peace. They point out that most of the foreign aid money is spent by foreign nations to buy American goods and services.

Those opposing foreign aid claim it is wasteful and takes money out of our nation. They also say we should not bear so many of the world's burdens. Some critics believe that too much aid is in the form of military assistance. They question whether this kind of aid helps peace. Critics also oppose giving foreign aid to countries that are dictatorships or that violate human rights.

Foreign Trade

Trade is another important part of American foreign policy. Early in American history, our nation began to collect taxes on certain imported goods. These taxes, or tariffs, were intended to protect American industries from foreign competition. As you read in Chapter 12, such taxes are called **protective tariffs.**

Tariff rates were set high enough so that the prices stores had to charge for imported goods were equal to, or higher than, the prices of similar goods made in the United States. A protective tariff helps American manufacturers. Yet it also means American consumers must pay more for what they buy.

Many nations have used protective tariffs. This sometimes causes difficulties in relations between nations. When an importing nation raises its tariffs, an exporting nation loses business. Sometimes when one nation raises its tariffs, other nations do the same. These "tariff wars" harm international trade.

To improve world trade, the United States and many other nations have joined in a General Agreement on Tariffs and Trade (GATT). This agreement helps encourage **free trade,** or trade not restricted by tariffs and other trade barriers. We have also made **reciprocal trade agreements** with other countries. Under these agreements, both sides consent to lower certain tariffs.

Congress has given the President power to raise or lower tariffs when it is believed the change will be in the national interest. This power makes it possible for the President to take prompt action in lowering tariffs when certain materials or products are in short supply and imports need to be encouraged. Tariffs may also be raised to discourage certain imports. The President may raise all tariffs and then work out lower reciprocal rates with individual nations.

Balance of Payments

Foreign trade, of course, involves both what our country sells to other countries and what we buy from them. The difference in value between the nation's exports and imports is called the **balance of trade.** In recent years, the United States has suffered serious deficits in its balance of trade. This means more dollars are going out of the country to buy for-

Trade is an important part of our nation's foreign policy. Each year we export American-made products and import goods from around the world.

eign goods than are coming into the country from those who buy American goods. The deficit creates problems for our economy.

Much of the deficit is caused by the increase in the price of oil, or petroleum. The price of most oil imported by the United States is set by members of the **Organization of Petroleum-Exporting Countries (OPEC).** It consists of the major oil-exporting countries. The cost of a barrel of oil rose from $2.50 in 1970 to about $36.00 in 1980.

The United States has acted to reduce its dependence on foreign oil in several ways. Americans are conserving energy, drilling for new oil in this country, and making use of other sources of energy, such as coal and the sun. By using less foreign oil, the United States can improve its balance of trade.

CHECK-UP

Vocabulary

diplomacy
personal diplomacy
summit conference
shuttle diplomacy
North Atlantic Treaty Organization
ANZUS
Organization of American States
foreign aid
Marshall Plan
Peace Corps
protective tariffs
free trade
reciprocal trade agreements
balance of trade
Organization of Petroleum-Exporting Countries

Review

1. In what ways does the President carry out the role of the nation's chief diplomat?
2. What are the main purposes of our alliances with other nations?
3. What have been the goals of our foreign aid program from the period of the Marshall Plan to recent years?

Discuss

What do you think our foreign aid policy should be in the future?

3
The United Nations

In 1941 President Franklin D. Roosevelt met with Winston Churchill, the prime minister of Great Britain, to discuss the aims of the Allies in World War II. The meeting was held on a ship in the Atlantic Ocean off the coast of Newfoundland. The agreement reached by these two leaders was known as the **Atlantic Charter.** This document stated the following principles:

1. No nation should try to gain territory as a result of the war.

2. All peoples should have the right to choose the kind of government they want.

3. All nations should have the right to trade and secure raw materials.

4. The peoples of the world should be able to live free from fear or want.

5. Nations in the future should not use military force to try to settle their international disputes.

The principles set forth in the Atlantic Charter have continued to guide the nations of the world in their search for peace.

Establishing the United Nations

In 1945 representatives from 50 nations met in San Francisco to establish an organization that would stress peaceful coexistence and cooperation among all the nations of the world. This organization is called the **United Nations (UN).** In its constitution, or charter, the nations pledged to save the people of the future from war. They also agreed to support basic human rights, including the equal rights of men and women and of large and small nations. They promised, as well, to live together in peace as good neighbors.

Today the United Nations is an international organization with more than 150 permanent members. Its headquarters is located in New York City.

How the United Nations Is Organized

The United Nations is organized into six main divisions. You can see the organization of the United Nations in the chart on page 422. The six divisions are described briefly below.

1. General Assembly. The body that discusses, debates, and recommends solutions for problems that come before the United Nations is called the General Assembly. Each member nation has one vote in the General Assembly. All important issues, such as decisions on matters concerning world peace, adding new members, or passing the budget, must be agreed upon by a two-thirds majority in the Assembly. Other issues are decided by a simple majority vote.

The Assembly meets annually. Its sessions begin on the third Tuesday in September. If necessary, it may be called into emergency session at any time. The Assembly elects its own president and makes its own rules of procedure.

2. Security Council. The body mainly responsible for keeping the peace is the Security Council. It is composed of 15 members. There are five permanent members: the United States, the Soviet Union, Great Britain, France, and China. Ten temporary members are chosen by the General Assembly for two-year terms. The 15 countries are each represented by one delegate.

All measures that come before the Security Council must receive the vote of 9 of the 15 members in order to pass. However, if one of the permanent members of the Council votes against it, the measure is automatically defeated, or vetoed.

To help prevent war, the Security Council may call upon quarreling nations to work out a peaceful settlement. If any nation refuses to negotiate or refuses the Council's offer to help settle the dispute, the Council may take action. It may call upon all members of the United Nations to break off relations and end all trade with the offending nation.

The United Nations was founded by 50 nations in 1945. Today the flags of most nations of the world fly outside UN headquarters in New York City.

If all else fails, the Security Council may recommend that United Nations members use military force against an aggressor nation or nations. When North Korea invaded South Korea in 1950, the Council asked members of the United Nations to send troops to help South Korea. The United States and 15 other nations responded.

3. International Court of Justice. Member nations may take disputes about international law to the United Nations law court—the International Court of Justice. They do not have to do so, but many disputing nations have voluntarily agreed to come before the Court. It is also known as the **World Court.**

The Court consists of 15 judges from various nations who are elected for nine-year terms by the General Assembly and the Security Council. The Court's decisions are made by majority vote. The Court meets at The Hague, in the Netherlands. It may be called upon by United Nations members to decide such matters as boundary disputes, debt payments, and interpretations of the United Nations Charter.

4. Economic and Social Council. The General Assembly elects representatives from 54 nations to serve as members of the Economic and Social Council. This group conducts studies on such important topics as the use of narcotic drugs, human rights, and international trade. It may then make recommendations to the General Assembly.

5. Trusteeship Council. Certain islands and areas of the world that were once colonies are supervised by the Trusteeship Council. It assists these areas to prepare for self-government. The United States and other nations act as trustees and are responsible for the progress of the trustee areas. Trustees make an official report to the Trusteeship Council each year. The council also sends committees to trustee areas to inspect conditions there.

6. Secretariat. The day-to-day activities of the United Nations are carried out by the Secretariat. This division has a staff of more than 9,000 clerks, typists, guides, translators, research experts, technicians, and administrators.

The Secretariat is headed by the **Secretary**

Organization of the United Nations

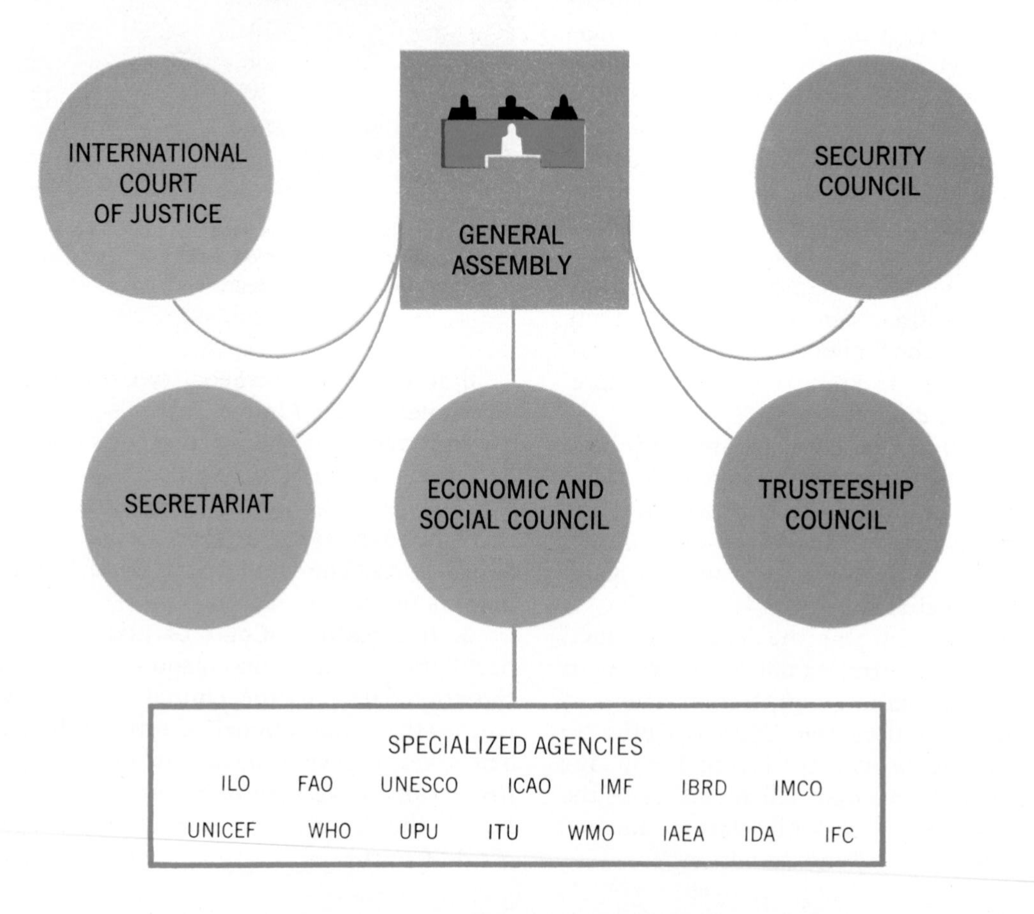

General, who is elected by the General Assembly for a five-year term. The Secretary General is the chief executive of the United Nations. The Secretary General prepares the agenda, or list of items to be discussed, for the meetings of the General Assembly, Security Council, Trusteeship Council, and Economic and Social Council. The Secretary General is also responsible for carrying out the decisions of these bodies. The Secretary General may bring before the United Nations any problems that threaten world peace.

The United Nations Depends Upon Cooperation

The United Nations has no armed forces of its own. Without the cooperation of its members, it cannot keep the peace. At certain times it has obtained soldiers from its members to carry on a "police action." Usually it relies upon moral persuasion, or a sense of obligation on the part of its member nations, in settling disputes.

In other words, the United Nations is not a supergovernment that can force its will upon its members. The United Nations has become a kind of "town meeting" of the world. There all nations have an opportunity to express their viewpoints about conditions that threaten the peace.

Specialized Agencies

Specialized agencies of the United Nations have worked to improve the lives of people in many parts of the world. What are some of these agencies, and what do they do?

UNICEF. The hearts of all people go out to a sick or hungry child. At its first meeting, the United Nations decided to do something for the children of the world. The United Nations International Children's Emergency Fund was set up to help feed and care for sick and hungry children anywhere in the world. Today the organization is called the United Nations Children's Fund, or UNICEF.

UNICEF is funded by contributions from people and governments. Perhaps your school has helped to raise money for UNICEF. It provides milk, medicine, clothing, blankets, and other necessities to needy children. Children in more than 100 countries receive help from UNICEF.

WHO. The World Health Organization (WHO) is fighting a worldwide battle against disease. The weapons in this battle are medicine, insect sprays, vaccines, sanitation programs, water purification, and health education. WHO has a great victory to its credit. A worldwide vaccination program conducted by WHO succeeded in eliminating smallpox from the world.

FAO. The Food and Agriculture Organization (FAO) helps nations grow more and better food for their people. FAO has helped develop a special kind of disease-resistant rice in India. It has introduced steel plows in developing nations. FAO experts are helping many nations with forest planting, soil conservation, irrigation, and improvement of farming methods.

UNESCO. The United Nations Educational, Scientific, and Cultural Organization (UNESCO) was established to extend educational opportunities everywhere in the world. People who cannot read or write are often unable to learn new and better ways of doing things. UNESCO has sponsored programs to set up schools in developing nations. This agency also promotes the exchange of students and teachers among countries. In addition, it encourages people to protect and develop their traditional arts and cultures.

In recent years, UNESCO has been the center of controversy. One problem is the attempt by some nations to use the agency for political purposes.

IBRD. The International Bank for Reconstruction and Development (IBRD), sometimes called the World Bank, makes loans and gives technical advice to help nations improve their economies. It is assisted by two other agencies, the International Development Association (IDA) and the International

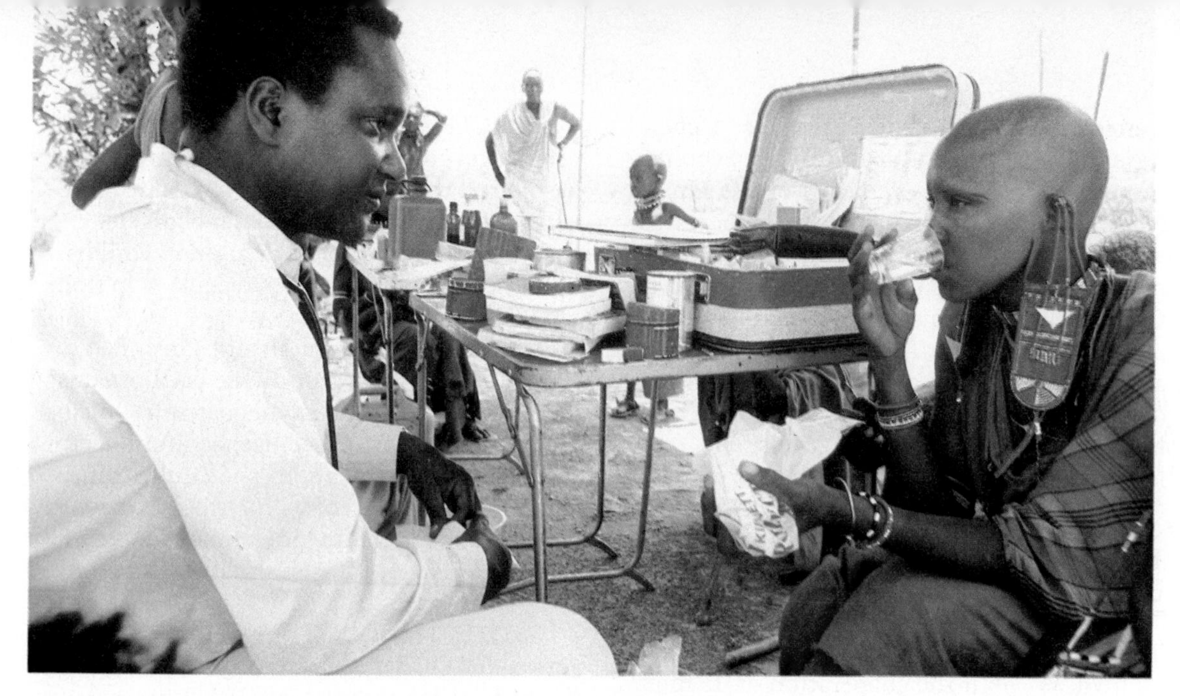

The World Health Organization brings medical care to people in remote areas of the world. It has helped improve the health of millions of people.

Finance Corporation (IFC). The IBRD has loaned more than $7 billion a year to developing nations.

IAEA. The International Atomic Energy Agency (IAEA) was set up to promote the use of atomic energy for peaceful purposes. When nations reach agreements about control of atomic weapons, IAEA has the responsibility of making sure that all signers of the treaty live up to its terms.

Other Specialized Agencies. If you study the chart of the United Nations organization, you will see that there are many other specialized agencies. They include the International Labor Organization (ILO), which attempts to improve the welfare of the world's workers. The World Meteorological Organization (WMO) keeps a world weather watch to obtain data for long-range weather forecasting. The International Civil Aviation Organization (ICAO) promotes safety in air transportation. The International Monetary Fund (IMF) promotes world trade.

Other agencies are the International Telecommunications Union (ITU), the Universal Postal Union (UPU), the World Intellectual Property Organization (WIPO), and the Intergovernmental Maritime Consultative Organization (IMCO).

Arguments For and Against the United Nations

Some Americans are critical of the United Nations. They become impatient when the Soviet Union too often uses its veto to keep the Security Council from acting. They point out that the many small nations can outvote the large nations in the General Assembly. They argue that the organization has failed to create a permanent police force to prevent military attacks and stop trouble when it first breaks out.

On the other hand, some Americans believe the United Nations is the world's best hope for peace. They note that it has frequently succeeded in leading quarreling nations to the conference table. They do not believe the lack of a United Nations police force is a problem. They argue that such a force, over which we would have no control, would be unacceptable to our nation or any world power. Those in favor of the United Nations claim that creating a forum where all nations can be heard is a good way to encourage world peace.

CHECK-UP

Vocabulary

Atlantic Charter
United Nations
General Assembly
Security Council
International Court of Justice
World Court
Economic and Social Council
Trusteeship Council
Secretariat
Secretary General

Review

1. Why did the United States and other nations establish the United Nations in 1945?
2. How does the Secretary General serve the United Nations?
3. Give several examples of the specialized agencies of the United Nations and describe the work they do.
4. What are some of the major arguments Americans use for and against the United Nations?

Discuss

Do you think the United Nations is doing a good job? Why or why not?

CHAPTER SUMMARY

The plan our nation follows in dealing with other nations is called our foreign policy. The goals of American foreign policy are peace, prosperity, and friendship. To keep the peace and advance American interests, we send ambassadors, ministers, and consuls to represent us in other nations. We in turn receive representatives from other nations.

The President is responsible for conducting our foreign relations. The President is aided by personal advisers, the Department of State, and other departments and agencies of the executive branch.

Congress, too, is concerned with foreign affairs. It votes the money needed to carry out the nation's policies. The Senate must approve all treaties and the appointments of representatives to foreign lands.

The United States plays a large role in the world today. The President and officials of the State Department engage in personal diplomacy with world leaders. Alliances with other nations serve mutual defense and security needs. Foreign aid helps developing nations grow and protect themselves. The United States carries on trade with other nations and seeks to aid the flow of world goods.

The United Nations provides an organization in which nations may discuss serious problems and work out reasonable solutions. The specialized agencies of the United Nations work to serve the needs of the people of the world. The future of this world organization depends upon the willingness and ability of nations to work together in peace.

CIVICS SKILLS: Reading a Table

- *A teenager in San Antonio, Texas, bites into a juicy red apple from New York.*
- *A contractor in Mobile, Alabama, orders a shipment of steel from Pennsylvania.*
- *A family in San Diego, California, drives one of the newest compact cars made in Detroit, Michigan.*

If you look around your home, you'll probably find lots of evidence of trade among the states. You might have Florida orange juice in your refrigerator. Maybe there are Idaho or Maine potatoes in your kitchen. Perhaps you own a jacket made of cloth woven in a North Carolina mill. And what about electricity? Your power company may be burning coal from the mines of West Virginia.

Just as different states or regions in the United States have their own specialties, so do other parts of the world. Each year the United States does billions of dollars worth of business with nations all around the globe. Our nation exports many things, including cotton, wheat, and machinery. We also import many items, such as diamonds, radios, and chocolate.

Keeping track of all this trade can be very complicated. Interpreting the final totals, however, doesn't have to be. A table, such as the one on this page, can give you a quick overview of our trade with the rest of the world.

Comparing Facts

Tables are handy tools for organizing and presenting facts. As with graphs, you can learn a lot about a table by studying its title and labels. In the case of a table, the most important labels are the headings at the top of each vertical column and at the start of each horizontal row. These identify the main categories of information on the table. What categories are listed on the table below?

To locate specific facts on a table, you simply look down a column or across a row. For example, skim down the *Imports* column on the table below until you reach the *1980* row. What was the total amount of money spent on imports during that year? What totals are listed in the rest of the column?

Once you have examined the facts on a table, you are ready to compare them. This means spotting significant similarities and differences. You can do this row by row, or column by column. If you compare the first two figures in the *1980* row, you'll see that imports outnumbered exports. Now compare these two sets of figures for the other years on the table. On the basis of these comparisons, what general conclusions can you draw about United States trade from 1975 to 1980?

Practicing What You've Learned

1. Study the last five numbers in the *Balance* column of the table below. The minus signs point to one important similarity. What is it?
2. How do these numbers differ from the first figure in the *Balance* column?
3. Using the latest copy of the *Statistical Abstract,* update the table on this page. What conclusions might you draw on the basis of these new facts?

Balance of Trade: 1975-1980
(in billions of dollars)

YEAR	EXPORTS	IMPORTS	BALANCE
1975	107.1	98.0	+ 9.1
1976	114.7	124.0	− 9.3
1977	120.8	151.7	−30.9
1978	142.0	175.8	−33.8
1979	182.1	206.3	−24.2
1980	220.7	240.1	−19.4

CHAPTER REVIEW

Vocabulary

Write a sentence using each of the following terms correctly.

alliance treaties
foreign policy
diplomatic recognition
foreign relations
summit conference
ambassador
diplomacy
reciprocal trade agreements
Security Council
balance of trade

Check-Up

1. What powers over foreign policy are given to the President by the Constitution?
2. What are the chief kinds of treaties that the United States makes with foreign nations?
3. What role do the Department of State and the Department of Defense play in American foreign policy?
4. What powers over foreign policy does Congress have?
5. What was the purpose of the Marshall Plan?
6. What are the main arguments for and against foreign aid?
7. What are the main divisions of the United Nations? How does each work to keep the peace?
8. How can the United Nations enforce its decisions?
9. Which specialized agency of the United Nations do you think is the most important? Explain your answer.
10. List and explain what you think should be the goals of American foreign policy in the future.
11. How much economic and military aid do you think the United States should provide to other nations? Explain.
12. Do you think the United States should establish agreements with nations that disregard human rights? Explain your answer.

Civics Skills

The figures below are part of a 1981 United Nations study of world population. Organize this information into a table entitled "World Population Growth: 1981–2000." On the basis of your table, what conclusions can you draw about population changes during the closing years of the 20th century?

1981: Africa—486 million; Latin America—366 million; Asia—2,608 million; Oceania—23 million; North America—254 million; Europe—486 million.

2000: Africa—833 million; Latin America—562 million; Asia—3,564 million; Oceania—30 million; North America—286 million; Europe—511 million.

Citizenship and You

1. Conduct a public opinion poll to find out what people think about the United Nations. Report your findings to the class.
2. A class committee may prepare a chart showing how the United States government is organized to conduct its foreign relations.
3. A bulletin board committee may prepare a display called "Conducting Our Foreign Relations" by gathering pictures and news items showing the President meeting with foreign leaders. The clippings may be displayed around a world map, with colored strings from the clippings to the places on the map with which they deal.
4. Prepare an oral report on one of the following people and his or her role at the United Nations: Dag Hammarskjold, U Thant, Ralph Bunche, Eleanor Roosevelt, Vijaya L. Pandit, Kurt Waldheim, Javier Perez de Cuellar.
5. Prepare a report on the work of the Peace Corps.

CHAPTER

22

Changing Foreign Policies for Changing Times

Approximately 200 years ago, Thomas Jefferson headed the State Department with a staff of about half a dozen people and a budget of about $6,000. Today more than 22,000 people work in the State Department. Their budget exceeds $1.5 billion a year.

Less than 50 years ago, the United States had diplomatic relations with 60 nations. It was tied by trade treaties to only a few nations, and just a few hundred American troops were stationed in other nations. Today the United States has relations with more than 140 nations. It is tied to many nations by mutual defense and security treaties as well as by trade treaties. In addition, hundreds of thousands of American troops are stationed overseas.

The United States has come a long way since its beginning in the late 1700's, when it was a small and weak nation. In those days many European nations wondered if the young American nation would even survive. What has enabled the United States not only to survive but to become a world leader? What has brought the American nation so deeply into world affairs in recent decades? In this chapter, you will study how foreign policy has changed to keep up with changing times. The topics around which this study will center are:

1. **The Development of American Foreign Policy**
2. **The Cold War and Containment**
3. **New Trends in American Foreign Policy**

I

The Development of American Foreign Policy

Our foreign policy has helped the nation grow. For many years the policy that worked best for our nation was to avoid involvement in the affairs of other nations. This policy of staying out of foreign affairs worked as long as the United States was somewhat isolated from the rest of the world.

Gradually steamships, telegraph and telephone systems, and airplanes made nations across the seas our neighbors. Then the United States could not avoid being interested and involved in international affairs. As you will see, events in the 1900's caused our nation to become a world power.

Isolationism

When our nation began, it was deeply in debt and struggling to build its industries. It was also looking for solutions to many domestic problems. Most of the leaders of the new government thought the United States should concentrate on its own development and stay out of European affairs. This belief that the United States should avoid becoming involved in foreign concerns is known as **isolationism.**

At no time in our history has the policy of isolationism been an easy one to follow. Even in the late 1700's, President Washington found it difficult to practice this policy. To the north of the United States was the British-owned colony of Canada and a troubled border situation. To the south and west lay Spanish territory. It blocked American expansion westward and threatened American commerce on the Mississippi River. When American ships ventured out to sea, as they had to do to keep trade alive, they were stopped and seized by ships of the British or French navy.

The War of 1812

Finally, in 1812, it seemed that war with Great Britain could not be avoided. Americans claimed that Great Britain was stirring up the Indians on our western frontier, occupying forts on United States soil, and taking American sailors off our ships. This was the time, they said, to take Canada and make it a part of the United States.

The War of 1812 with Great Britain ended in a stalemate. That is, neither side won a clear-cut victory. However, the peace treaty that ended the war led in time to greatly improved relations with Great Britain. Most important, the War of 1812 won a new respect for the United States among the nations of Europe. For nearly 100 years following the war, the United States was able to stay out of European conflicts and build up the nation at home.

The United States and Canada

The War of 1812 also marked a turning point in our relations with Canada. American attempts to invade Canada during the war had proved unsuccessful. After the war, Canada and the United States began to build forts

Here President James Monroe (center) meets with his Cabinet to develop an American policy forbidding any further European interference in Latin America.

along their border and station fleets of warships on the Great Lakes. This was the kind of situation that could lead to border incidents and perhaps to war.

The leaders of both nations wisely decided to act to ensure the peace. In 1817 they met to talk over their differences and sign a treaty of friendship. The result was the **Rush-Bagot Agreement.** This treaty provided that the United States and Canada would settle their disputes with each other by peaceful means. As proof of their desire for peace, the two nations agreed that the boundary between the United States and Canada should no longer be fortified.

The friendly spirit of the Rush-Bagot Agreement has shaped our relations with Canada ever since. When difficulties arise, the leaders of the two countries talk over their problems until they reach a workable agreement.

The Monroe Doctrine

Most of the nations of Latin America, the region south of the United States, won their independence from Spain in the early 1800's. Yet Spain and its European allies were determined that Spain should win back its American colonies. For a while it looked as if Europe was about to interfere in the affairs of the new nations of Latin America. The United States government decided that our nation had to take a strong stand to prevent the new nations of Latin America from being conquered again by Spain or any other European nation.

President James Monroe used his annual message to Congress in 1823 to let the world know what the United States thought about this matter. He declared that any attempt by European nations to interfere in the affairs of any nation in the Western Hemisphere would be considered an unfriendly act by the United States. He promised we would not interfere in European concerns or those of European colonies already established in the Americas. But he also declared that the Americas were no longer open to colonization by European nations.

This policy came to be known as the **Monroe Doctrine.** A foreign policy doctrine sets forth a new policy of action with respect to other nations. It is a statement of United States policy and is not necessarily an agreement with any other nation. The Monroe Doctrine set the course of our relations with Latin America as well as with Europe for many years.

The United States and Latin America

At first the nations of Latin America welcomed the support of the United States. As "watchdog of the Western world," the United States helped settle boundary disputes between Latin American countries. When certain European countries threatened to use force to collect debts owed by Latin American countries, the United States acted to prevent such interference. When Cuba rebelled against Spain in 1898, the United States declared war on Spain and easily defeated the Spanish fleet.

President Theodore Roosevelt strengthened the Monroe Doctrine in 1904. He declared that in the future the United States would take on the role of police officer of the Western Hemisphere. If Latin American countries could not manage their own affairs, the United States would step in. This policy became known as the **Roosevelt Corollary** to the Monroe Doctrine. A corollary is something that follows as a normal result.

Americans in growing numbers then began to invest money in Latin American companies. When these investments were threatened by internal disorders, the United States sometimes sent troops to keep the peace. Our policy in Latin America became known as **dollar diplomacy.**

The Good Neighbor Policy

In some ways, the actions of the United States in Central and South America helped the nations there. However, these actions also stirred up bad feelings because they insulted the national pride of Latin American nations. Latin American leaders declared that the United States had turned from protector to oppressor. As a result, the United States took steps to improve its dealings with Latin America.

Under the Good Neighbor Policy of President Franklin D. Roosevelt, the United States and Latin America agreed to improve relations and work together.

courtesy of The Cleveland Plain Dealer

In the 1920's the United States stated that the Monroe Doctrine would no longer be used to justify United States intervention in the internal affairs of any neighbor. In the 1930's President Franklin D. Roosevelt announced the **Good Neighbor Policy.** This policy opposed armed intervention by the United States in Latin American affairs. Also, it emphasized friendly agreements.

In 1948, as you read in Chapter 21, the nations of the Western Hemisphere joined together in the Organization of American States (OAS).

The End of Isolationism

In 1914, when World War I broke out in Europe, the United States attempted to stay out of the conflict. President Woodrow Wilson announced a policy of **neutrality**. That is, the United States would neither aid nor favor either side. This policy was difficult to maintain. It became impossible when German submarines began to sink American merchant ships without warning and without regard for the safety of the passengers. In response to a war message by President Wilson, Congress declared war on Germany in 1917.

President Wilson stated that our aim in fighting World War I was to help "make the world safe for democracy." The victory of the Allies brought hope for a new era of peace. Wilson centered his hopes in a new international organization called the **League of Nations.** The members of the League promised to solve their differences in a friendly fashion and go to war only as a last resort.

As you may recall, provision for joining the League of Nations was submitted to the Senate as a part of the treaty ending World War I. Many Americans, however, including some powerful senators, opposed United States membership in the League. They feared that if the United States joined the League, our nation would be drawn into future European conflicts. The spirit of isolationism was still strong. It helped keep the United States out of the League of Nations.

President Woodrow Wilson (center, in top hat) hoped to keep the United States out of World War I. He finally concluded that neutrality was impossible.

The beginning of World War II found the United States again in a neutral position. Congress passed Neutrality Acts in the mid-1930's forbidding the sale of arms, or weapons, to warring nations. In 1939 the United States did agree to sell arms, but only on a "cash and carry" basis. The arms had to be carried in foreign ships. Soon the United States became the "arsenal of democracy," supplying arms needed by the Allies.

Once again our neutrality and the isolationist views of some Americans did not keep us out of war. The bombing of Pearl Harbor by the Japanese on December 7, 1941, shocked the American people. They realized that isolationism in a worldwide conflict was not possible. The United States declared war on Japan and, soon afterward, on Germany and Italy.

While World War II was still being fought, plans were underway for a postwar organization of nations to keep the peace. In 1945, as you have read, Americans joined the people of three fourths of the world in forming the United Nations.

CHECK-UP

Vocabulary

isolationism	dollar diplomacy
Rush-Bagot Agreement	Good Neighbor Policy
Monroe Doctrine	neutrality
Roosevelt Corollary	League of Nations

Review

1. Why did the United States follow a policy of isolationism in its early history? Why was it difficult to maintain this policy?
2. How did the Monroe Doctrine please and displease countries in Latin America?
3. Why was the United States unable to continue its policy of neutrality in World War I and World War II?

Discuss

Why is the policy of isolationism difficult to maintain in today's world?

2
The Cold War and Containment

During World War II, the United States and the Soviet Union were allied in fighting Nazi Germany. Soon after the war ended, however, relations between the two nations changed and they came into conflict. What caused this change? The roots of the conflict are in the two nations' very different economic systems and forms of government. The United States is a representative democracy, or republic, while the Soviet Union is a communist nation.

What Is Communism?

The ideas behind modern communism come mainly from a German writer named Karl Marx. He believed that factory owners, or capitalists, throughout the world were getting rich by treating workers unfairly. With another writer, Friedrich Engels, Marx wrote a book called the *Communist Manifesto.*

In this book, Marx and Engels proposed a new economic system called **communism.** They argued that in the future the workers, called the **proletariat** (pro·la·TER·ee·at), would take over factories and business firms. Under communism, said Marx, the proletariat in all nations would own or control all the means of production—the land, capital, and labor. Private individuals—capitalists, that is—would not be permitted to own or control these things in order to make profits. Later Marx expanded these ideas in another book called *Das Kapital* (from the German word for capital).

According to Marx, the proletariat would run the government. Everything from raw materials to finished products would be owned by the government in the name of the workers. In the process of this change, capitalism would be overthrown, by force and violence if necessary. The workers would establish a "dictatorship of the proletariat" throughout the world. Communism thus would be both an economic and a political system.

Communism in the Soviet Union

In 1917 Russia became the first nation to adopt communism. Russia's ruler, the tsar, was overthrown and a communist government was established under V. I. Lenin. Russia now became known as the Union of Soviet Socialist Republics (U.S.S.R.), or the Soviet Union. Lenin was succeeded by Joseph Stalin, and a new, harsh period began. Stalin established a communist dictatorship that completely controlled the Soviet Union.

Today the Communist Party of the Soviet Union is all-powerful. No other party exists. It makes all decisions in the nation. The government of the Soviet Union owns and operates all of the nation's industries. It regulates not only the economy but many other aspects of the lives of the people as well.

In the Soviet Union, the government controls the press. The people get their news only from the government news agency, Tass.

Elections in the Soviet Union are very different from those in the United States. In the Soviet Union, all candidates are members of the Communist Party. The people must vote either yes or no for the candidates. Very few people dare to vote no. Top party leaders have absolute control. The Secretary of the Communist Party is the most powerful person in the Soviet Union.

Compare this system with the democratic system in the United States. American voters can choose the candidates who run for office. If the voters do not like what one party does in government, they can vote for candidates of another party at election time. In our nation, political power reflects the will of all the people, not the will of a few at the top.

The people of the Soviet Union have suffered many hardships under communism. Nevertheless, the Soviet Union has become a modern industrial nation. In 1912 Russia ranked fifth among the industrial nations of the world. By 1950 the Soviet Union was in second place, surpassed only by the United States. Compared with the United States, however, Soviet living standards are low. Moreover, the people of the Soviet Union lack the economic and political freedoms enjoyed by Americans.

The Spread of Communism

After World War II, hopes were high that the Soviet Union and the United States, allies in the war, would remain friends. It was hoped that the Soviet Union would share the ideals expressed in the Atlantic Charter and the Charter of the United Nations. Everywhere, people of all nations hoped that the world might now find a way to live in peace.

These hopes were soon shattered. During World War II, the Soviet Union occupied large parts of Poland and Rumania. After the war, in country after country in Eastern Europe, leaders of political parties opposed to communism were jailed, forced to flee, or assassinated. Within a few years, communist governments were set up in Poland, Rumania, Bulgaria, Hungary, Czechoslovakia, Albania, and East Germany. In this way, the Soviet Union turned the nations along its borders into **satellite nations**—nations that take orders from Moscow.

Soviet leaders maintained that they were taking these actions so that the Soviet Union would never again be attacked by Germany or any other nation or nations of Western Europe. Leaders in the United States and Western Europe thought Soviet leaders had more in mind than defense of their own country. They believed the Soviet Union, with its great new military strength, would try to impose Soviet-dominated forms of government wherever it could.

Only the fear of American atomic bombs, some believed, prevented Soviet forces from trying to overrun all Western Europe and Great Britain. At that time, only the United States had atomic weapons.

CAN YOU GUESS?

- **"GI" is a common name for members of the United States armed forces. What do the initials "GI" stand for?**
- **The term "Rosie the Riveter" referred to certain women in World War II. Who were these women?**

Answers are on page 562.

The Cold War Begins

With the satellite nations of Eastern Europe under its control, the Soviet Union tried to increase Soviet power in the eastern Mediterranean Sea and the Middle East. The Soviet Union wanted an ice-free route for Soviet ships into the oceans of the world. It also wanted influence in the oil-rich lands of the Middle East.

Troops from the Soviet Union had occupied part of Iran, with its rich oil fields, during World War II. Instead of being withdrawn after the war, these troops were strengthened. A Communist Party was encouraged in Greece. Turkey was faced with a demand for a Soviet naval base within its territory. The United States and other noncommunist nations saw these southward thrusts of Soviet power as severe threats to their security and to world peace.

Thus, soon after World War II, much of the world was caught up in what was called the **Cold War.** On one side was the Soviet Union and its satellite nations. On the other side was the United States and other noncommunist nations. Both sides used propaganda, spying, alliances, foreign aid, and all other methods of conflict short of actually starting an all-out war that might destroy the world.

Waging the Cold War while also trying to end it were the major problems of American foreign policy in the 25 or 30 years after World War II, as you will see.

The Policy of Containment

The President of the United States in the immediate postwar period was Harry S. Truman. He warned the Soviet Union that it must get out of Iran. He was successful. Stalin removed Soviet troops. President Truman then asked Congress to provide military equipment and economic aid to Greece and Turkey to help them resist Soviet influence. Because of this aid, Greece and Turkey did not become satellites of the Soviet Union.

The success of American aid to Greece and Turkey encouraged our government to give similar aid to other European nations. This policy of helping free nations resist aggression became known as the **Truman Doctrine.**

The idea behind this policy came to be known as **containment.** The purpose of containment was to prevent Soviet communism from spreading. The forces of the Soviet

Berlin is still a divided city. No one can cross between East and West Berlin without being checked through stations like this one in West Berlin.

Union were to be "contained" within the area in which they had been successful up to 1948.

The Berlin Blockade

The next showdown between the United States and the Soviet Union came in 1948 in Berlin. At the end of World War II, Germany was divided into two separate nations. East Germany became a communist nation. West Germany became a republic. The city of Berlin, although located in East Germany, was not part of that nation.

Berlin was occupied by troops of four nations—France, Great Britain, the United States, and the Soviet Union. Each nation controlled a part of the city. Even though Berlin was within the area of Germany controlled by the Soviet Union, the noncommunist nations had free access to the city over special land routes through East Germany. In June 1948 the Soviet Union closed these routes. That is, it started a **blockade** of Berlin.

Soviet strategy in closing the East German routes into Berlin was to force the noncommunist occupation forces to leave and then to make the city a communist center. The German people living in the British, French, and American sections of the city, called West Berlin, were cut off from food, coal, and other necessities. They faced cold and starvation.

The United States and Great Britain took prompt action. They began a massive airlift of fuel, food, clothing, and other vital items. Airplanes were loaded with supplies and flown into the city. Day after day, in all kinds of weather, American and British planes landed in West Berlin. More than 250,000 flights brought huge amounts of needed goods into West Berlin. The Soviet strategy failed. The Soviet Union agreed to reopen the land routes.

Communism Wins in China

After World War II, a full-scale civil war broke out in China. In 1949 the government led by Chiang Kai-shek (JEEANG ky·shek) was defeated by Chinese communists. Chiang's forces fled to the island of Formosa (now called Taiwan), off the mainland of southern China. There they set up a government in exile, called Nationalist China.

The communists held the mainland, which became known as the People's Republic of China, or Communist China. The first head of Communist China was Mao Zedong (MOU DZUH·DOONG).

The United States refused to recognize Communist China. Instead, our nation provided economic and military aid to Nationalist China. With the support of the United States and other noncommunist nations, Nationalist China was allowed to remain a member of the United Nations, with a permanent seat in the Security Council. Membership was denied to Communist China.

The Cuban Missile Crisis

The Cold War between the Soviet Union and the United States took a dangerous turn after 1949 when the Soviet Union began testing and developing atomic weapons. Each side increased its ability to destroy the other along with most of the rest of the world. Foreign policy in Washington and Moscow moved toward a "balance of terror." The United States faced a severe crisis in the Cold War in October 1962.

The event took place on the island of Cuba, 90 miles (145 kilometers) from the American mainland. There, in 1959, Fidel Castro had set up a communist government.

In October 1962 President John F. Kennedy was informed that the Soviet Union was building secret missile bases in Cuba. These missile bases, if finished, would have been a threat to the United States and to other parts of the Western Hemisphere.

President Kennedy demanded that the Soviet Union remove its missiles from Cuba immediately. To force the Soviet Union to agree, President Kennedy declared that our nation was prepared to take whatever steps might be required, including military force.

As a first step, the American government announced that it would not allow the delivery of more offensive weapons—weapons of attack—to Cuba. The Navy sent destroyers to stop and search foreign ships bound for Cuba. The Air Force flew over the Atlantic Ocean to locate and photograph ships on their way to Cuba. Army troops, stationed in Florida, were put on the alert.

As a result of this show of American military strength and determination, the Soviet Union backed down. It agreed to remove Soviet long-range missiles from Cuba and to take down the missile launching sites.

From that time on, Soviet and American leaders understood the "balance of terror." They continued to pursue their own interests and probe for each other's weaknesses. However, they drew back several times from situations that threatened to develop into a third world war, which was certain to destroy much of the world.

The Korean Conflict

This did not mean that the United States did not ever get involved in war. The wars, though, were limited ones. A **limited war** is fought without using a nation's full power, especially nuclear weapons.

The two wars our country has fought since World War II took place in Asia. They both occurred in countries that had been divided into communist and noncommunist halves. The first of these wars was fought in Korea.

As a result of an agreement reached after World War II, the nation of Korea, which juts out of eastern Asia into the Pacific Ocean, was divided into communist North Korea and noncommunist South Korea. In June 1950 the army of North Korea invaded South Korea in a surprise attack. Its goal was to reunite both parts of Korea as a communist nation. North Korea was equipped with Soviet weapons and aided by Chinese communists.

In late 1951 the two sides in the Korean conflict drew a line across a map of Korea and agreed to stop firing across it. Nevertheless, the war dragged on.

The United States government called upon the United Nations to halt the invasion. The Security Council of the United Nations, with the Soviet Union absent, held a special session. It voted to send aid to the South Koreans.

Led by troops from the United States, combat forces sent by 15 other members of the United Nations helped defend South Korea. The Korean conflict lasted three years. By July 1953 the conflict had reached a point where neither side could win a clear-cut victory. The two sides agreed that Korea would remain divided into communist North Korea and noncommunist South Korea. Since then tensions between the two Korean nations have continued.

Involvement in Vietnam

Under agreements passed in 1954, several French colonies in Southeast Asia—Vietnam, Laos, and Cambodia—became independent. Vietnam, like Korea, was divided into a communist northern half and a noncommunist southern half. The agreements called for elections to be held throughout Vietnam in 1956 to reunite the country.

When the elections did not take place, war broke out in South Vietnam in the late 1950's. Communist forces in the south were supported by troops, supplies, guidance, and other aid from North Vietnam. The North Vietnamese received military supplies from the Soviet Union and Communist China.

American officials feared that if South Vietnam fell to the communists, other nations of Southeast Asia—Laos, Cambodia, and Thailand—might also fall. But how should these new forces of communism be contained? The United States began to send economic aid and military advisers to South Vietnam.

Gradually the United States became more deeply involved. In 1964, at the request of President Lyndon B. Johnson, Congress passed the Gulf of Tonkin Resolution. It gave the President the power to take all necessary actions in Vietnam. It was not, however, a declaration of war. American combat troops soon were sent into action in South Vietnam. By 1969 over 500,000 Americans were fighting there.

Perhaps no other conflict in American history brought more heated debate than our involvement in Vietnam. Those in favor of stronger military action argued that America's honor and position of world leadership were at stake. Opponents of the war maintained that its cost in lives and money was not justified.

Finally, in January 1973, a peace agreement was announced. After more than eight years of war, with almost 50,000 Americans killed and more than 300,000 wounded, and at a cost of over $111 billion, the war came to an end for the United States. Despite the agreement, however, fighting continued in Vietnam. In 1975 the communists launched a new offensive and South Vietnam fell. The communists now ruled all of Vietnam.

CHECK-UP

Vocabulary

proletariat
communism
satellite nations
Cold War
Truman Doctrine
containment
blockade
limited war

Review

1. What were some of the ideas of Karl Marx?
2. How did the spread of communism to other nations after World War II lead to the Cold War?
3. How did the United States break the Berlin blockade?
4. How did the United States deal with the Cuban missile crisis?

Discuss

Do you think that the United States is still involved in the Cold War? Give evidence to support your opinion.

3

New Trends in American Foreign Policy

In recent years, the American people and their leaders have been rethinking foreign policy. The problem has been to work out new policies for a rapidly changing world. New policies were especially needed to meet developments among the communist nations and the newer developing nations.

The Split in the Communist World

For a number of years after World War II, communism seemed to be a single political and economic movement that threatened to take over the rest of the world. The Soviet Union controlled the countries of Eastern Europe and some of central Europe.

In Asia, as you have read, the Soviet Union and Communist China assisted North Korea in its aggression against South Korea. They also supported North Vietnam in its attempt to seize control of South Vietnam. The Soviet Union backed Fidel Castro in Cuba and his attempts to spread communism in Latin America. Some African nations also came under the influence of the Soviet Union.

As the years passed, however, it became evident that communism was not a single worldwide movement. In central Europe, Yugoslavia was a communist nation. However, it refused to become a Soviet satellite. In the 1960's the Soviet Union withdrew its support of Communist China when the two nations disagreed over policies for China's development. They then became enemies in a dis-

The cartoonist depended on symbols to make his point in this drawing. What symbols has he used? What situation does his cartoon portray?

BEARBAITING

pute over their borders. In Europe, Albania sided with China against the Soviet Union.

Détente with the Soviet Union

These and similar events suggested to American leaders that there were possibilities for working out peaceful relations between communist and noncommunist nations. In a speech in 1963, President John F. Kennedy said, "History teaches us that bad feeling between nations does not last forever." He went on to suggest that our country should reexamine its attitude toward the Soviet Union.

The pursuit of peaceful relations with the Soviet Union came to be known as **détente** (day·TANT). (The word is from the French word for easing, in this case the easing of tensions.) President Richard M. Nixon dramatized détente in 1972 when he flew to Peking and Moscow to talk with the leaders of Communist China and the Soviet Union.

Out of these talks came new trade agreements and a freer exchange of journalists, scholars, and tourists. Détente also led to other opportunities to develop better relations. However, neither side gave up its opposition to the political and economic system of the other.

Limiting Nuclear Arms

One of the most important results of détente was progress in controlling the nuclear arms race. Earlier, in 1963, the United States and the Soviet Union had agreed in the Nuclear Test Ban Treaty to protect the earth's environment by testing nuclear weapons only underground. In 1968 they and 60 other nations signed the Nuclear Nonproliferation Treaty. It forbade the spread of nuclear weapons to nations that did not already have them.

Strategic Arms Limitation Talks—known as SALT—began in the early 1970's. The first SALT agreement limiting the number of offensive weapons was reached in 1972. It limited certain weapons to those already in existence or then being manufactured. Negotiations for more arms limitations have continued since then.

Changing Relations with the Soviet Union

The policy of détente was seriously affected when the Soviet Union invaded the Asian nation of Afghanistan late in 1979. Two years later events in Poland led to increased tensions between the United States and the Soviet Union.

In late 1981, following a movement by the Polish people for greater freedom, their communist government imposed martial law. Under **martial law,** the army takes power and the rights of the people are restricted. The United States and its NATO allies condemned the Soviet Union for pressuring the Polish government to put down by force the movement for political and economic freedom.

Relations with the Third World

Since the 1960's, American foreign policy has devoted increasing attention to a group of nations aligned on neither the communist nor the noncommunist side. These nations, located in Latin America, Asia, and Africa, are known as the **Third World.** Most of them formerly were colonies of Great Britain, France, Spain, Portugal, or the Netherlands. They won their independence in the years after World War II. Many of these nations still need help in developing their economies. For this reason, they are sometimes referred to as **developing nations.**

Third World nations have a large part of the world's population. They also make up the largest group in the United Nations. Some of these nations have important natural resources. A major goal of American foreign policy is to maintain friendly relations with Third World nations and to prevent the Soviet Union from gaining too much influence over them.

Relations with the Middle East

The United States has attempted to be friendly with all the nations in the Middle East—Egypt and Israel and the other nations of southwestern Asia. At the same time, however, the United States has been the chief supporter of Israel. Israel is surrounded by Arab nations. It has fought four wars with these nations since its creation as a nation in 1948.

After the fourth Arab-Israeli war in 1973, oil-rich Arab nations tried to punish the United States and its European allies for supporting Israel. They did so by putting an **embargo** on oil to those nations. That is, the Arab nations refused to sell them oil. The result was a shortage of fuel and gasoline in some nations.

The Arab nations ended the embargo in a few months. However, the embargo made Americans realize how dependent the United States can be on other nations for raw materials. It also showed how important our relations are with nations in the Middle East. The United States has a clear interest in peace between Israel and the Arab nations. Therefore, our nation has worked hard to encourage negotiations between Israel and the Arab nations to bring peace to the Middle East.

Iran has been another trouble spot in the Middle East. In January 1979 Iran's ruler, the shah, was overthrown. The new government was controlled by Islamic religious leaders. Their goal was to eliminate all Western influences from the country. They were critical of the United States for having supported the shah. In November 1979 Iranians seized control of the United States embassy in Tehran, the capital of Iran. They took 52 Americans as hostages. Finally, after 444 days in captivity, the hostages were released and returned to the United States.

Representatives from oil-rich Arab nations meet often to set oil prices. Their policy of raising prices has led to strained relations with oil-buying nations.

Relations with Africa

Another problem area is Africa. Most nations there have been independent only since the 1960's or later. These nations, most of whose people are black, have often resented their former white colonial rulers in Europe. The United States has worked to persuade these nations of its good will toward them.

The United States has been concerned that several African nations, such as Angola, Mozambique, and Ethiopia, have a communist type of government. Some of them have become friendly with the Soviet Union.

In South Africa most of the people are black, but they are ruled by a white minority.

(continued on page 444)

CITIZENSHIP IN ACTION

Felicia's Year in the United States

Felicia de Rosado stood up and raised her baton. As the band played the national anthem of Colombia, South America, she felt great pride in her homeland. However, her pride was mixed with a little homesickness.

Promoting International Understanding

Felicia was directing a high school band in Maplewood, New Jersey—a long way from home. She had left Colombia to spend her junior year as an exchange student in the United States. The student exchange program is sponsored by American volunteers as a step toward forming a better understanding among nations.

The spring concert at which Felicia directed the band was one of the high points of her year in the United States. During her stay she took part in many American activities. She even

played soccer. At home in Colombia, she said, "Girls play basketball and volleyball, but soccer? Never!" However, Felicia had to give up soccer because the band took up so much time. And the band was her first love.

Two Different Cultures

At first Felicia found it difficult to get used to American ways. "Everything was so different, although English was my biggest frustration." She had studied English in high school in Colombia. "However, I suddenly had to think quickly in English and find the correct words to make myself understood. It wasn't easy."

She found the customs different too. One of the practices she had trouble adjusting to was dating. In Colombia, "we don't go out with just one person at such a young age. We go many more places with groups of friends."

The Block family, with whom Felicia lived in Maplewood, also had to get used to her ways. "Felicia was always cooperative, but we could tell when things upset her. She wasn't used to doing jobs like drying dishes and cleaning her room," said Viola Block. "In Colombia her family has servants." The Block family also was struck by Felicia's amazement at the many "ordinary" household appliances that Americans own—vacuum cleaners, washing machines, freezers, and calculators. Very few people own these items in Colombia.

Felicia and the Block family think their year together helped each better understand the other's country. For Felicia, the year in the United States was "a wonderful experience, something I'll never forget. No one who visits here just for a few weeks could learn so much." She also made many friends with whom she hopes to keep in touch. Through their friendship, they feel they have formed a bond of understanding between two very different countries.

Thinking It Over

1. What do you think Felicia's friends in the United States learned about Colombia from getting to know Felicia?
2. Do you think foreign exchange programs for students can help form a better understanding among nations? Explain.

Student foreign exchange programs are one way to improve understanding between Americans and the people of other nations.

As blacks struggle to obtain equal rights, the danger of conflict involving neighboring nations becomes greater.

Relations with Communist China

China is the largest nation in the world and has about one fifth of the total world population. In recent years, it has become increasingly important in world affairs.

For many years, the United States did not recognize the communist government of China. Gradually, however, our nation began to change its policy.

In 1971 the United Nations voted to expel Nationalist China and to give its membership to Communist China. A year later, President Richard M. Nixon became the first American President to visit Communist China. In 1979 the United States gave full diplomatic recognition to Communist China, and the two nations exchanged ambassadors.

Relations with Latin America

The United States has been concerned about the spread of communism to some Latin American countries. The communist government of Fidel Castro has remained firmly in control in Cuba. Moreover, the Cubans have tried to spread communism to other Latin American countries.

Another issue that caused tension was the Panama Canal. The United States built the canal early in the 1900's and purchased from the new government of Panama the right to control the canal forever. However, the people of Panama wanted it under their control. In 1978 Congress passed two treaties that would turn the canal over to Panama in the year 2000. Many Latin Americans viewed the return of the canal as a sign of the good will of the United States toward its Latin American neighbors.

Your Role in Foreign Policy

The United States government listens to the opinions of its citizens on foreign policy. You are living during a time in which young Americans are becoming more interested than ever before in politics, social conditions, and international affairs. They are finding effective ways to express their interests and concerns about the issues of the day. Therefore, it is important that you be as informed as possible.

In many schools in the United States, students write letters to students in other lands. Many American schools also send funds to help support a child in a foreign land. Some American schools exchange a student from their school with a student from abroad. The foreign students who come here live with American families. They attend our schools and take part in our social life. These students learn about American democracy first hand.

CHECK-UP

Vocabulary

détente
martial law
Third World
developing nations
embargo

Review

1. How have relations between the United States and the Soviet Union changed since the late 1940's?
2. What policy has the United States followed in the conflict between Israel and the Arab nations?
3. What is the chief concern of the United States in Latin America?
4. What are some ways in which Americans can show friendship toward people in other lands?

Discuss

What do you think are the most important foreign policy concerns of the United States today? Why?

CHAPTER SUMMARY

Through the years, the United States has moved from a policy of isolationism to deep involvement in world affairs. In the present century, our nation has fought in two world wars.

After the end of World War II, the world was dominated by two opposing groups of nations. The communist nations were determined to spread their ideas and their form of government throughout the world. Noncommunist nations, led by the United States, opposed the spread of communism. The worldwide struggle between communist and noncommunist nations, using every means short of all-out war, became known as the Cold War.

The United States began a policy of containment. Its aim was to resist the spread of communism. The United States fought limited wars with communist forces in Korea and Vietnam.

Since the 1960's, divisions within the communist world have become evident. For a time the United States and the Soviet Union sought ways to achieve better understanding and reduce the danger of war. These explorations resulted in new trade agreements and treaties limiting the use of nuclear weapons. Détente, however, has suffered as a result of aggressive actions by the Soviet Union.

In recent years, Third World nations have gained importance. Yet political differences among some of them have caused wars and other conflicts. The United States has encouraged peace efforts in many areas, especially in the Middle East. American citizens must study foreign policy carefully and use their influence for the peaceful solution of international problems.

CIVICS SKILLS: Using Primary Sources

Did you ever wonder what it might have been like to live during some other period in our nation's history? Can you imagine, for instance, how it felt to vote for the first President of the United States? Or how it felt to be the first President? To find out, you can read the documents, articles, and eyewitness accounts of the people who actually lived at that time. These materials are the period's **primary sources.**

Primary sources are different from secondary sources of information. **Secondary sources** are usually written after an event has taken place, often by someone who did not see or participate in that event. Your textbook and most reference books are secondary sources.

Both primary and secondary sources provide important facts about the past. Only a primary source, however, allows you to see an event through the eyes of a person who experienced it. It not only provides information about the event, but it also gives you a glimpse of the attitudes and feelings of the people living then.

Look around you. What types of information might serve as primary sources about the 1980's?

Interpreting a Primary Source

It is important to remember that a primary source is not necessarily more objective or more accurate than a secondary source. The author, for example, may have intentionally left out important information. As a result, you must examine carefully such things as what kind of person the author is and the conditions under which the source was written. These facts will help you decide if the source is reliable.

After you have examined the background of a primary source, you are ready to interpret its contents. As you read through the source, be sure to identify all facts, or statements that can be proven true. Also note any statements that give you an insight into the opinions of the author or the period in general. Based on this evidence, you will then be able to draw certain conclusions about the topic or event described in the source.

The primary source on this page is part of a speech delivered by President George Washington in 1796 as he was about to leave office. In it, he discusses American foreign policy. Why might this be a good source of information on foreign policy in the 1790's?

Practicing What You've Learned

Use the primary source below to answer the following questions.

1. Which statements in the speech prove that President Washington favored a policy of strict isolationism?
2. Based on secondary information in your textbook, why might President Washington have supported this policy?

The great rule of conduct for us is to extend our commercial relations with foreign nations, but to have as little political connection with foreign nations as possible. Let us fulfill our previous commitments. Here let us stop.

Europe's interests have little relation to ours. It is engaged in frequent controversies that are not important to us. Thus it is unwise for us to let artificial ties involve us in Europe's politics.

Our distance from Europe permits us to pursue a different course. Why give up the advantages of our special situation? Why entangle our peace and prosperity in the web of European ambition, rivalry, interest, and whim?

It is our true policy to steer clear of permanent alliances with any foreign nation.

(Adapted from George Washington's *Farewell Address*, September 17, 1796.)

CHAPTER REVIEW

Vocabulary

List each of the following terms in your notebook. Then write a sentence using each term correctly.

isolationism
Monroe Doctrine
dollar diplomacy
neutrality
proletariat
communism
Cold War
containment
détente
Third World
limited war

Check-Up

1. Why is the War of 1812 called a turning point in our foreign policy?
2. What were the main terms of the Rush-Bagot Agreement?
3. What was the purpose of the Monroe Doctrine? Why was it replaced by the Good Neighbor Policy?
4. Why can the form of government in the Soviet Union be considered a dictatorship?
5. How did the Cold War start? Who were the principal opponents?
6. What was the main purpose of the Truman Doctrine?
7. What is the policy of containment?
8. Why did the presence of Soviet missile bases in Cuba create a crisis in the Cold War?
9. Why did the United States participate in the Korean conflict?
10. Why did the United States become involved in the war in Vietnam? What was the result of that conflict?
11. What is the policy of détente? What changes did it bring about in American relations with Communist China and the Soviet Union?
12. How did actions of the Soviet Union affect détente?
13. How was the oil embargo related to our foreign policy in the Middle East?
14. Do you think the United States should limit the number of its nuclear weapons? Explain your answer.

Civics Skills

Study the following passage taken from President Harry S. Truman's address to Congress on March 1947. Compare the remarks in this primary source with those made by President George Washington in his *Farewell Address* (see page 446). How had the nation's foreign policy changed since Washington's time? What statements in Truman's speech help explain possible reasons for this change?

> Our victory in World War II was won over countries that sought to impose their will and their way of life upon other nations. The peoples of a number of countries have recently had totalitarian regimes [governments of total control] forced upon them against their will.
>
> I believe that it must be the policy of the United States to support the peoples who are resisting control by armed minorities or by outside pressures. We must assist free peoples to work out their own destinies in their own way.

Citizenship and You

1. Participate in a debate on the topic, "Can We Live in Peace with the Soviet Union and the People's Republic of China?"
2. Hold a class discussion on the meaning of communism and compare life in the communist nations with life in the United States.
3. Draw a political cartoon on a current problem in our nation's foreign relations.
4. Make a list of trouble spots in the world today. Locate these places on a world map and find out about the background of the current problem in each place.

UNIT SEVEN REVIEW

Reviewing the Facts

Write your answers to the items below on a separate piece of paper.

1. Foreign relations involve all of the following *except*
   a. making treaties with other nations.
   b. deciding where military posts should be located in the United States.
   c. drawing up international trade agreements.
   d. granting diplomatic recognition.
2. Which of the following might be part of foreign aid?
   a. food for a nation whose people are starving
   b. weapons for a friendly nation
   c. loans of money at low interest to a developing nation
   d. all of the above
3. Complete this sentence: Two ways in which Congress can affect foreign policy are ________ and ________.
4. All of the following are goals of American foreign policy *except*
   a. maintaining peace in the world.
   b. encouraging immigration to the United States.
   c. defending our nation.
   d. encouraging trade.
5. All of the following help the President in carrying out foreign policy *except*
   a. the Department of Defense.
   b. the Central Intelligence Agency.
   c. UNICEF.
   d. the Department of State.
6. Correct the underlined part of this sentence: All members of the United Nations vote in the <u>Security Council</u>.
7. The Truman Doctrine grew out of the American policy of
   a. neutrality.
   b. limited war.
   c. containment.
   d. balance of trade.
8. Complete this sentence: At various times in its history, the American government followed a policy of ________ in the hope of avoiding involvement in the affairs of other nations.
9. The following are all examples of policies designed to pursue détente *except*
   a. exchanging journalists.
   b. opening up tourism.
   c. exchanging military troops.
   d. drawing up new trade agreements.
10. Complete this sentence: A country that spends more on imports than it earns from exports has a trade ________.
11. Complete this sentence: Soon after World War II, much of the world was caught up in a struggle known as the ________.

Applying What You Know

1. Write a paragraph explaining three differences between a democratic country and a communist country.
2. What do you think is the most difficult problem the United States faces in foreign relations today? Explain the reasons for your answer.

Expanding Your Knowledge

Archer, Jules, *China in the 20th Century,* Macmillan. Explains developments in China and American involvement with that nation.

Helitzer, Morrie, *The Cold War,* Franklin Watts. An exploration of relations between the United States and the Soviet Union.

Vincent, Jack, *A Handbook of International Relations,* Barron's. Contains hundreds of items about foreign affairs, alphabetically arranged for quick reference.

UNIT 

Meeting the Challenges of the Future

CHAPTER

23

Improving Life for All Americans

The American people have always worked to improve life for themselves and their children. Today Americans continue to seek more opportunities—better jobs and education, better pay, and a chance to develop their own interests.

Throughout most of our nation's history, Americans have tried to improve their standard of living by moving to the cities, which offered more and different kinds of jobs. Gradually, however, this population movement has begun to shift. The 1980 census showed that, for the first time in more than 100 years, the rural areas of our nation were growing faster than the urban areas. What could account for this change?

Many of our cities have serious problems. Overcrowding, crime, poor transportation and housing, inadequate health facilities, and loss of jobs have led many people to leave the cities. They have moved mainly to the suburbs, which then began to face many of the same problems. Today our communities are working hard to improve conditions for their people.

Our nation was founded on the ideal of equal rights and opportunities for all. Yet many Americans have been denied these precious rights and freedoms during much of our history. Black Americans, Hispanic Americans, American Indians, women, the elderly, the handicapped, and other groups of citizens have struggled to improve their lives. They have made important gains. However, more needs to be done if all Americans are to enjoy equal rights.

How can we improve the quality of life for all Americans in our communities? In this chapter, you will read about some of the problems and possible solutions as you study these topics:

1. **Aiding Our Communities**
2. **Ensuring Rights for All**
3. **Protecting Our Health and Safety**

1

Aiding Our Communities

The United States, as you have read, has many different kinds of communities. They vary from small rural towns and villages to huge sprawling cities. Today most Americans live in or around large cities. Many of these urban areas face serious problems. They include poor housing, run-down transportation systems, and crime. Such problems exist not only in our cities but also in suburbs and rural areas. They are found in communities throughout the world as well.

The problems of our communities affect all of us. Finding solutions to these problems and making our communities more pleasant places in which to live is important to all Americans.

The Growth of American Cities

America began as a rural country with small, scattered settlements. At the time of the first census in 1790, the largest cities in the United States were New York City, with about 33,000 people, and Philadelphia, with 28,000. These places had grown as port cities specializing in trade.

The 1800's saw rapid growth in the size and number of cities in the United States. By 1900 New York City had grown to a population of 3.4 million. Chicago was the second largest city in the United States, with nearly 1.7 million people. Philadelphia also had over a million people.

Today New York City has a population of about 7 million. Chicago has about 3 million. Los Angeles, which was a small town of about 6,000 people in 1870, has a population of about 3 million.

Large cities also have grown up in other areas of the nation. For example, Houston has over 1.5 million people and Atlanta has about 500,000 people. Today the cities of the South and West are increasing in population while the older cities of the North and East are losing population. Many of the older large cities have developed problems that have caused residents to seek new places to live. Can the newer cities avoid the same problems?

Patterns of Growth

All American cities and towns were once small communities. Those that grew into large cities usually spread over the surrounding countryside in a typical pattern. Most American cities have spread outward, away from the original settlement. If you were to draw a diagram showing how the typical city grew, it would look like a target. As you can see on the chart on page 452, the old downtown area would be in the center. It would be surrounded by several circles, each larger and larger as you go outward from the center.

The old central part of the city usually is the downtown business center. Here you find stores, office buildings, factories, and warehouses. Sometimes modern hotels and luxury apartment houses also are located in the downtown section. Yet areas in and around it may be run-down.

The next circle outward from the downtown area is occupied by apartment buildings, small private homes, and neighborhood shops and stores. These buildings are often built side by side with little or no space between them.

The next circle is sometimes called the **greenbelt.** Houses with yards and lawns, trees, and shrubbery are often found in this section. The greenbelt usually lies only partly within the city boundaries. It also extends beyond city lines, where it is called the suburbs. Suburbs, as you recall, are the small, independent communities that surround a city.

On the edge of the greenbelt is the **rural-urban fringe.** This is where the city meets the countryside. There are often farms and small towns in this area. The rural-urban fringe may stretch as far away as 50 to 100 miles (80 to 160 kilometers) from the city's downtown center.

In recent years, many factories, businesses, and stores have moved from the cities into the rural areas. These industries and firms left the cities because country areas often offer cheaper land, lower taxes, better housing, and less crowded traffic and parking conditions.

How Many American Communities Grew

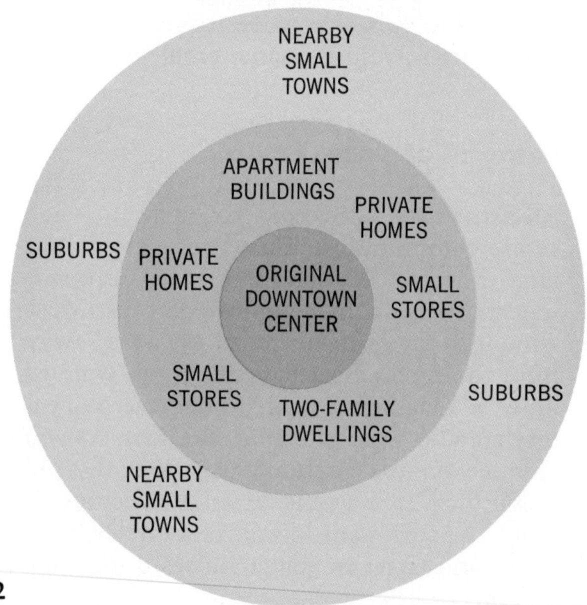

From Metropolis to Megalopolis

As you may remember, a large city with its surrounding area of suburbs and small towns is known as a metropolitan area. The Census Bureau lists any city of 50,000 or over, with its surrounding urban and suburban areas, as a **Standard Metropolitan Statistical Area.** In 1981 there were about 288 metropolitan areas in the United States, an increase of 45 since 1970.

As metropolitan areas expand and grow outward, the rural areas between them are also built up. Small towns become larger and larger. In some cases, whole new cities are born. As you have read, a growing area of overlapping cities like this has been given the name megalopolis.

In the United States there are three such heavily populated areas in which urban development is almost continuous. As you read in Chapter 15, they are BosWash (Boston to Washington), ChiPitts (Chicago to Pittsburgh), and SanSan (San Francisco to San Diego). A large percentage of the nation's population lives in these megalopolises.

The Move of Middle-Income Families

Although the number of metropolitan areas has been growing, the centers of our cities have been losing population. More people have moved out of the central cities than have moved in. By 1970 more people were living in the towns and suburbs of metropolitan areas than were living within city limits.

Why are people leaving the cities? There are, of course, many reasons. Some people seek fresh air, sunshine, and neighborhoods with yards and trees. The number of crimes in some cities is so high that many people are afraid to live there.

Some Americans have left the cities to avoid paying high rents and city taxes. Others seek better schools for their children and an escape from urban noise and bustle. People also move to be near the new jobs that are opening up in the suburbs as businesses move there.

This shift of people to the suburbs has had serious effects on American cities. For the most part, those who move are middle-class or upper-middle-class families. Many of these people still work in the city and use its services. Those who travel from suburban homes to city places of business are called **commuters.** Commuters often pay little or no tax to the city government.

Furthermore, since the federal government's aid to cities is based on urban population figures, the cities lose federal aid when people leave. As residents move out, urban areas lose federal funds for housing, schools, transportation, welfare, and other services. Cities also lose voters when people move to the suburbs. This means a loss of representatives in state government and in Congress.

Large metropolitan areas have grown up throughout the nation. Many people living in suburbs commute from their homes to their jobs in the cities.

The Problem of Slums

As people shifted to the suburbs, the older areas of many cities became slums. A **slum** is a run-down section of the city where the buildings are neglected and families live crowded together. The run-down apartment buildings are called **tenements.**

Life is often difficult for people living in slums. In these crowded areas, the rates of disease and death are high. Compared with other sections of the city, slums have higher proportions of school dropouts, unemployed people, and criminals. Worst of all is the feeling of hopelessness. Slum dwellers often have no jobs and little hope for the future.

Slums create problems for everyone, not just for those who live in them. For instance, slums cost everyone money. The number of fires is greater in slum areas. More police officers are also needed to protect these areas because they have more crime than other neighborhoods. More of the city's money must be spent on health needs, welfare, child care, and other services in slum areas than in any other part of the city. Thus all the people in the city help pay the cost of allowing slums to exist.

Planning to End Slums

American cities have tried several plans to end slums. Some communities have been replacing slum dwellings with **public housing projects.** These are apartment houses built with public funds. The rents in these projects are low, and the apartments are open primarily to low-income families. The main problem with this plan is that sometimes the housing projects have also turned into slums.

Another plan to end slums calls for redeveloping, or completely rebuilding, the center of the city. Sometimes large new public buildings are constructed on the site of the torn-down buildings to form a civic center. Facilities are provided for business conferences, concerts, sporting events, and public exhibits. Private corporations are often encouraged to take part in the redevelopment or even to plan it. Usually better housing for those whose homes are torn down is provided nearby.

A third kind of community plan to end slums is to restore and maintain the buildings in the area. Buildings that can be saved are repaired by their owners. Sometimes owners get financial help from the city. Buildings that cannot be repaired are torn down. They are replaced with new dwellings or with parks and playgrounds.

Programs such as the ones you have just read about are called **redevelopment programs.** Usually they are planned and carried out by local agencies, such as city or community planning commissions.

Redevelopment programs have had considerable success in such cities as Baltimore, Philadelphia, New York, St. Louis, and San Francisco. The city of Baltimore, for example, has restored its run-down waterfront to its former beauty. An area of business, cultural, and residential buildings, and gardens now attracts both city residents and visitors.

These redevelopment programs are costly. Sometimes land and old buildings must be purchased from their owners. Tearing down unwanted buildings is expensive. Construction of new ones requires a great deal of money. Therefore, Congress has provided money to help many cities rebuild run-down areas.

What "irregularity" do you suppose the "zoning commission" has found? Do you believe communities should have zoning laws? Why or why not?

courtesy of The Chicago Tribune—New York News Syndicate, Inc.

"THE ZONING COMMISSION WOULD LIKE TO POINT OUT AN IRREGULARITY!"

Zoning Laws

American communities have acted not just to solve old housing problems but also to prevent new problems. Many local governments, for example, have passed **zoning laws.** Such laws regulate the kinds of buildings that may be put up in a zone, or particular area. Only certain types of buildings or businesses are allowed in each zone.

Towns and cities also pass laws that builders must follow in making new structures safe and attractive. To keep track of these new buildings, local governments require builders to obtain permits before they start working. Other laws require owners to keep their buildings comfortable and in good repair. As a result, buildings that are being worked on as well as all apartment houses, office buildings, and other buildings open to the public are inspected regularly to make sure local regulations are followed. Such laws are part of an area's **building code.**

Suburban Problems

Suburbs and other small communities also have problems to solve. If you go for a drive in the country, notice some of the things you pass. You will probably see new communities with attractive homes. You may also pass old, run-down homes or poorly built stores. Other common sights may be gas stations, signs and billboards, junkyards, and drive-in snack stands—all of which were built without a well-thought-out plan. Such conditions are often called suburban blight.

As suburbs and other communities have grown in size and population, some of them have had problems of water supply, trash removal, sewage disposal, increasing crime, and high taxes. Like the large cities, these communities have established programs to redevelop their run-down areas. They too have tried to prevent problems through zoning laws and community action.

The Transportation Tangle

"Dirty, inefficient, debt-ridden!" These are the words increasingly used to describe mass transit. **Mass transit** includes various forms of public transportation, such as subways, buses, and commuter railroads. All are plagued with problems. Fewer passengers. Poorer service. Increased fares. What is causing the crisis in mass transit? Is there a remedy?

The movement of large numbers of city workers to the suburbs is one cause of the decline of mass transportation. Many suburban commuters prefer to drive their cars, even though highways leading into the city are choked with traffic. The loss of riders has caused mass transit systems to lose money.

Rising payroll and maintenance costs on mass transit lines are another problem. Higher operating costs mean higher fares. Higher fares mean a further drop in the number of passengers. As service becomes worse, still other passengers take to the highways or, if possible, walk or bicycle to work.

Another transportation difficulty has been caused by dependence on the automobile. In many communities, residents prefer to use automobiles rather than mass transit. Because of poor planning, some of these places suffer from enormous traffic jams, lack of parking spaces, and air pollution. Also, superhighways and large parking garages take up space that could be used for buildings.

These problems plus the increasing cost of gasoline have caused some cities to make plans for building or modernizing their mass transit systems. For example, BART (Bay Area Rapid Transit), which began running in 1972, links San Francisco with nearby communities. A new subway system was also built in Washington, D.C.

Various solutions have been suggested for transportation troubles. Most of these solutions involve some degree of tax support and help from the federal government.

Despite their many problems, mass transit systems are essential to every large city. They are as vital as the highways and airlines that connect the city with the rest of the nation and the world. They must be made to succeed if cities and their surrounding communities are to flourish.

Planning for the Future

So many people have moved out of the inner, or central, city to the suburbs and rural areas that a number of problems have been created in the entire metropolitan area. How, for

Have you ever been caught in a scene like this? What steps do you think communities can take to avoid such traffic jams?

example, can essential services, such as water supply, trash removal, electric power, and mass transportation, be provided for such great numbers of people living throughout the metropolitan area?

Many counties, cities, and towns have community planning commissions that work to improve conditions. Some large groups of cities also have regional planning groups, which study the problems of the entire area. These regional groups sometimes are made up entirely of private citizens.

All planning groups employ experts to help them. Among the specialists they consult are traffic engineers, population specialists, economists, and health experts. Landscape architects and scientists are also asked to study the land and its uses.

One kind of problem that often requires regional planning is transportation. The streets of the city and the roads of the suburbs are a part of one system. Therefore, many cities and suburbs have formed **metropolitan transit authorities.** Representatives from the city and suburban communities are included in the transit authority. These groups study the traffic problems in their areas and work to solve them.

Before a new expressway is built, for example, experts study the proposed route carefully. Forecasts are made of traffic flow and of what the new highway will do to traffic patterns.

Similar groups are developing plans to cooperate in solving other problems, such as air pollution and waste disposal. Groups are also working to develop joint health services, parks, and recreational areas.

Solutions to the problems of our communities are not always easy to find or carry out. Many solutions would require a lot of money. Yet money alone is not the answer. Our communities also need imaginative planning. Above all, they need citizens who are willing to do their part to make our communities better places in which to live.

CHECK-UP

Vocabulary

greenbelt
rural-urban fringe
Standard Metropolitan Statistical Area
commuters
slum
tenements
public housing projects
redevelopment programs
zoning laws
building code
mass transit
metropolitan transit authorities

Review

1. Explain the pattern by which most American cities have grown.
2. How does the movement of people away from the city affect city finances?
3. What are some of the problems that have plagued our system of mass transit?
4. What are some of the problems that local and regional planning commissions try to solve?

Discuss

Do you think that more tax money alone would solve the problems of our large and small communities? Why or why not?

2 Ensuring Rights for All

The quality of life in our communities depends not just on beautiful buildings, parks, and efficient services. It requires, too, that all Americans have equal rights and opportunities. These rights, of course, are guaranteed to all citizens in the Constitution of the United States. Yet, in spite of this guarantee, Americans have not always shared these rights equally. Many groups of Americans have had to work hard to win their rights as citizens.

Our Rich Cultural Heritage

As you read in Chapter 1, people from all over the world have settled in our country and contributed to its heritage. As group after group came to America, they brought with them different languages, ideas, and customs. For instance, almost every language in the world is spoken somewhere in the United States. Also, the special holidays of many different groups add a richness to the lives of all Americans.

Our country's many different groups are proud of their varied backgrounds. Sometimes, however, because of their different customs and beliefs, they have misunderstood each other. This has happened not only in our country but in every land throughout history.

Minority Groups

People whose ways are different from others are often referred to as **minority groups.** The word "minority" in this case does not necessarily mean that the group is outnumbered. Rather, it means that it is not the group in power. It also means that the group is set apart from other people in the society because of race, nationality, language, customs, or religion.

Minority groups often have met with prejudice and discrimination. **Prejudice** is an unfair opinion, not based on the facts, of members of a particular group. **Discrimination** refers to unfair actions taken against people because they belong to a particular group. Prejudice and discrimination have been present throughout human history. In the United States, too, some Americans have looked upon others who were "different" from them with fear and distrust.

These feelings, as well as acts of discrimination, were not uncommon in the early years of our nation. For example, the Indians were often treated badly by the settlers from Europe. Some English settlers did not welcome the early Scotch-Irish and Germans. In later years, some Americans were unfriendly to newly arriving Catholics from Ireland and Germany. Still later, these people looked with distrust on the new immigrants from southern and eastern Europe.

Throughout our nation's history, black Americans have suffered greatly as a result of prejudice and discrimination. Also, Mexican Americans and other Spanish-speaking Americans as well as Asian Americans often have faced resentment and hostility.

All of the minority groups you have been reading about are ethnic groups. An **ethnic group** is a group of people of the same race, nationality, or religion who share a common and distinctive culture and heritage.

In recent years women, older Americans, and people with physical and mental handicaps also have been regarded as minority groups. These groups have not been set apart by language, race, or religion. Yet many of these people believe that they, too, have not been given their full equal rights.

The Struggle for Equal Rights

As you may recall, the rights of citizenship that all Americans are entitled to are called **civil rights.** They include the right to vote and to equal treatment under the law. Civil rights also include the right to be considered for any job for which one is qualified. Civil rights mean, too, the right to use and enjoy public places and facilities.

The struggle for equal rights is an old one. For more than 200 years, black Americans were forced to live in slavery. Although slavery was ended after the Civil War, most blacks were denied their rights as free Americans. Laws in many states caused blacks to be treated as second-class citizens.

Some of the southern states passed laws to prevent black Americans from voting. These states also passed **segregation laws.** As you have read, these laws segregated, or separated, black Americans. There were separate schools for blacks, separate parks, separate drinking fountains, and other separate facilities. Black Americans could not buy homes in certain sections of a community. They were not allowed to work at certain jobs.

Black Americans in the North were also denied full civil rights. The northern states did not actually pass laws that took away the civil rights of black citizens. However, black Americans in the North also had trouble finding jobs. They were forced to live in areas where only blacks lived and where schools were inferior.

Black Americans have worked to achieve equal rights for many years. One of the earliest groups formed to aid in this struggle was the National Association for the Advancement of Colored People (NAACP), which was founded in 1909.

An important step toward obtaining equal rights for all Americans was made in 1954. In that year, as you read in Chapter 7, the Supreme Court gave its landmark decision in the case of *Brown v. Board of Education of Topeka.* The Court ruled that segregation in public schools was a denial of equal rights to black citizens.

The Civil Rights Movement

After the *Brown* decision, the struggle for equal rights grew even stronger. It has come to be known as the **civil rights movement.** Americans who supported the civil rights movement were opposed to laws that denied black Americans equal rights.

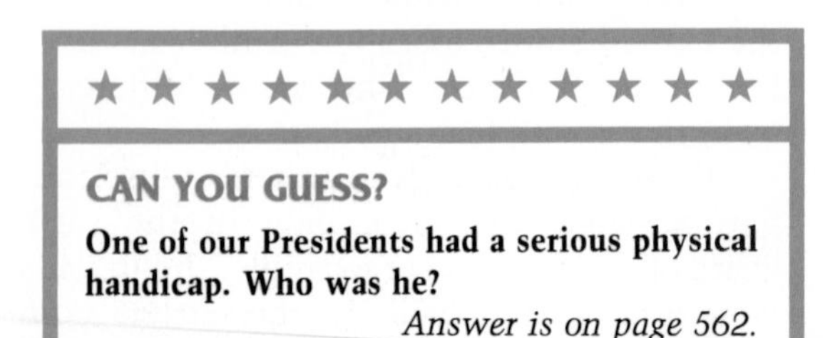

In 1963 more than 200,000 Americans staged a "March on Washington." They came from all over the nation to urge the passage of civil rights laws.

Under our American form of government, citizens can express their **dissent**—their disagreement with a law—in many ways. People involved in the civil rights movement used many different methods of dissent. For example, they wrote letters, made phone calls, and sent telegrams to their elected lawmakers. They wrote articles and letters to the editors of newspapers and magazines. They wrote books and made speeches. Supporters of the civil rights movement also organized demonstrations. During a **demonstration,** dissenters march in public carrying signs, singing songs, and making speeches.

The right of all Americans to express their dissent against laws in these and many other ways is protected by our state and federal constitutions. However, people do not have the right to break the laws while expressing their dissent.

Sometimes, though, citizens have used some or all of these forms of dissent, but without results. Is there anything more they can do to change a law that they think is wrong?

During the civil rights movement, and at other times in the past, some Americans have shown their dissent by disobeying laws they believed to be wrong. As you know, people who disobey a law must face the consequences. Supporters of the civil rights movement who disobeyed a law they objected to knew they could be arrested. They hoped their willingness to lose their freedom would make other people look more closely at the opposed law. Perhaps others would help get the law changed.

Progress in Civil Rights

Large numbers of Americans have taken part in the civil rights movement. It has had a great impact on our nation. In response to demands for equal rights, Congress passed

(continued on page 462)

CITIZENSHIP IN ACTION

Rosa Parks was fingerprinted after her arrest for not giving up her seat.

Rosa Parks—The Woman Who Kept Her Seat

Should a person who has a seat on a bus be forced to give up the seat to someone else? On December 1, 1955, Rosa Parks of Montgomery, Alabama, stayed seated after being told to move to the back of the bus. She was arrested.

A Policy of Segregation

By not giving up her seat on the bus, Rosa Parks was breaking the law. At that time many parts of the South had laws that called for segregation, or separation, of blacks and whites in public places. Black Americans and white Americans had to use separate restaurants, schools, and even water fountains. They rode the same buses and trains, but they were not allowed to sit together. Under the policy of Montgomery's bus company, the first four rows of the bus were reserved for whites. If the white section filled up, blacks had to give up their seats.

On the evening that Rosa Parks refused to move to the back of the bus, all the seats in the white section were taken. When more white passengers boarded the bus, the driver ordered Rosa Parks and three other black riders to move. Rosa was tired after sewing hems on dresses in a department store all day. She stayed seated. The bus driver called a police officer, and Rosa was taken to jail.

After the end of the Montgomery bus boycott, a policy of "first come, first seated" became the law.

This wasn't the first time a black person had been arrested for keeping a seat on a Montgomery bus. Less than a year before, a 15-year-old girl had refused to move and was led away in handcuffs. The incident caused only a brief stir.

In 1955, however, the attitudes of many Americans were beginning to change. The year before, the United States Supreme Court had ruled that segregation in public schools was unconstitutional. As a result of that decision, black Americans became more determined to fight for their rights.

The Montgomery Bus Boycott

Rosa Parks was a respected member of her community, a college graduate, and an active member of her church. Immediately after her arrest, the black community of Montgomery went into action. "This is no time to talk," black leaders decided. "It is time to act." They asked all black people in the city to boycott the buses—that is, to stop riding them—until the bus company started a "first come, first seated" policy. The boycott won wide support. Black citizens of Montgomery walked or shared rides. As empty and near-empty buses rolled through the streets of the city, the nation watched to see what would happen.

Rosa Parks decided not to pay the fine the court had set for her. Her lawyer appealed, and the case reached the United States Supreme Court. In 1956 the Court ruled that segregation on buses was unconstitutional. The bus boycott ended, although the struggle for equal rights continued. Martin Luther King, Jr., the 27-year-old black minister who led the boycott, went on to become one of the best-known leaders of the national civil rights movement.

Years later Rosa Parks was asked about that day when she refused to give up her seat. She remembered feeling that she just couldn't stand being denied equal rights. "There was no way I would ever stop being mistreated," she said, "if I allowed myself to be mistreated."

The bus boycott, led by Rosa Parks and Martin Luther King, Jr., was an early victory for the civil rights movement.

Thinking It Over

1. Why do you think the black leaders of Montgomery decided to boycott buses as a way to win equal rights?
2. Explain why you think Rosa Parks did not pay her fine.
3. In your opinion, was Rosa Parks right to act as she did? Why or why not?

"Disabled doesn't mean unable" is the slogan used by groups working for equal rights for the handicapped. How does this picture show the truth of that slogan?

several civil rights laws. These laws established the following six principles to guarantee the rights of black Americans and other minority groups.

1. The right to vote cannot be denied because of race or color.

2. Discrimination in public schools must be ended.

3. The right to work or belong to a union shall not be denied because of race or color.

4. Any business open to the public, such as restaurants and theaters, shall be open equally to all people.

5. Public places of amusement, such as parks and swimming pools, shall be open to all people.

6. Discrimination in the rental or sale of houses is forbidden.

The voting rights of minorities were further strengthened by voting rights acts and by the Twenty-fourth Amendment to the Constitution. This amendment, passed in 1964, prohibits the use of poll taxes or other taxes as a requirement for voting in federal elections. (See page 74.)

Extending Equal Rights to Other Minority Groups

In recent years the progress made by black Americans has encouraged other minority groups. As a result they, too, have worked to end discrimination.

Hispanic Americans. Hispanic Americans, for example, are the fastest growing ethnic minority in the United States. This Spanish-speaking group includes Mexican Americans, Puerto Ricans, Cubans, and people from Central and South America. Spanish-speaking Americans, like black Americans, have suffered discrimination in employment, education, and housing.

Hispanic Americans have become increasingly united in their efforts to gain better working and living conditions. In addition, many parents have also urged that public schools teach in Spanish as well as in English. A number of laws have guaranteed educational, voting, and other rights to Spanish-speaking citizens.

American Indians. The American Indians make up what is perhaps the country's smallest ethnic minority. For most of our nation's history, the federal government considered the Indians to be a conquered people with their own governments. As a result, they were long denied many of the civil rights guaranteed to all Americans. For example, Indians could not vote until 1924, when they were granted American citizenship. Since the 1960's protests, court cases, and lobbying efforts have brought about many changes and improvements in the treatment of American Indians.

Women. Many women as well have joined together to work for equal rights. From the earliest period in our nation's history, women have not had the same rights as men. For many years women could not own property. Most women could not vote until the Nineteenth Amendment to the Constitution was passed in 1920. They also did not enjoy the same educational and career opportunities as men.

In recent years our federal and state governments have passed laws guaranteeing women equal rights. Many businesses have hired women in jobs formerly reserved for men. However, some professions and unions still admit very few women. Also, women do not always get the same pay as men doing the same jobs. As a result, the movement for equal rights for women continues strong today.

Senior Citizens and the Handicapped. Other minority groups also have organized to influence the government to respond to their needs. Senior citizens and the handicapped, for instance, have pointed out that they, too, are minority groups. They often have been discriminated against in housing, employment, the securing of credit, and in many other areas.

A group called the Gray Panthers has been especially active on behalf of older Americans. The demands of handicapped people also have gained attention. Laws have been passed guaranteeing them equal opportunities. Their needs have been stressed in many ways. For example, 1981 was observed as the "International Year of Disabled Persons."

Working Together for Equal Rights

Much has been accomplished in moving toward the goal of equal rights for all American citizens. However, many groups are still working toward fuller civil rights and opportunities in their communities and throughout the nation.

Our nation was founded and made free and strong through the efforts and contributions of the many different groups that settled here. Over the years, many of these groups have struggled to secure their lawful rights. It is up to all of us as responsible citizens to uphold the laws that guarantee these rights for all Americans.

Compare this recent picture with the 1912 picture on page 82. What progress have women made toward equal rights? What progress do they still want to make?

CHECK-UP

Vocabulary

minority groups
prejudice
discrimination
ethnic group
civil rights
segregation laws
civil rights movement
dissent
demonstration

Review

1. What problems have some minority groups faced in the United States?
2. How did the 1954 Supreme Court decision affect the civil rights movement?
3. Name the six principles of civil rights established by Congress.
4. In what ways did the civil rights movement help other minority groups besides black Americans?

Discuss

Do you think new laws are needed to ensure equal rights for all Americans? Explain.

3

Protecting Our Health and Safety

The welfare of each of our communities depends upon the good health of our citizens. Every individual is responsible for forming his or her own good health and safety habits. However, the poor health of individuals can affect the entire community.

For example, the drug addict who turns to crime endangers others. The ill and elderly poor become the responsibilities of their families and local health resources. Persons with communicable diseases may endanger those around them. Unsafe working and living conditions, poor roadways, and reckless behavior can harm us all. For these and other reasons, the nation's health and safety are of concern to all Americans.

The Federal Government and Health

The Department of Health and Human Services has one of the largest budgets in the federal government. It spends many billions of dollars a year on health programs alone. The department also advises state and local governments and distributes federal funds to local health programs.

One of the most important agencies of the department is the United States **Public Health Service.** It carries on medical research in such fields as cancer and heart disease. The Public Health Service makes sure our nation's water supplies are pure. In addition, it works with foreign governments to prevent the spread of disease and maintains the largest medical library in the world.

Three important agencies are under the direction of the Public Health Service. They are the Food and Drug Administration, the Health Services and Mental Health Administration, and the National Institutes of Health. These three agencies serve the public in numerous ways.

State Public Health Departments

Each state has a department of public health. Its function is to see that health laws are carried out in every part of the state. This department has broad powers covering every city, town, village, and rural community.

State public health departments assist local boards of health in several ways. They work with local boards when cases of communicable diseases, such as measles or flu, are especially numerous. They provide laboratory services for doctors and local health authorities who need help in diagnosing disease. State health departments regularly publish bulletins and pamphlets containing useful information for the general public. They also provide drugs and vaccines for the prevention of various diseases.

State public health departments have other duties as well. They must examine all plans for public buildings. They inspect all public buildings and factories and other workplaces to make sure they are safe and have satisfactory air and sanitary conditions. Also under the supervision of these departments are state water systems and the disposal of garbage and sewage.

The Community Guards Our Health

Nearly every American city and town has a local health department to enforce rules of sanitation and cleanliness. It also offers aid in the prevention and cure of disease. This department keeps records of cases of disease and acts to stop disease from spreading.

The health departments in most cities have laboratories that test foods to make sure they are pure. They inspect all restaurants and other places that serve food to the public or perform services that could affect someone's health.

Most communities have local hospitals that are supported in part by local funds. Some communities also have public clinics where medical care is offered free or at a small cost.

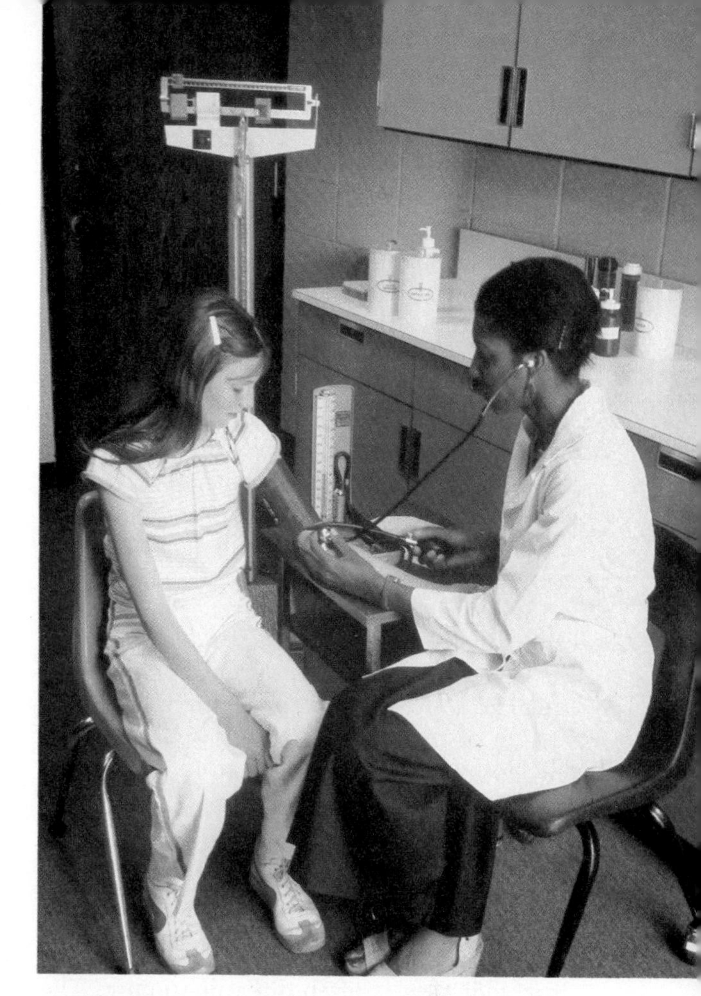

Federal, state, and local levels of government all offer public health services. What public health services are available in your community?

The Drug Problem

Widespread use of drugs has become a serious problem for people concerned with health and safety in American communities. We live in a society where drugs are a part of everyday life for many people. The medicine chest in the average American home usually contains many different kinds of drugs. Depending on their use, they may be helpful or harmful.

Drugs are prescribed by physicians in the treatment of disease. When taken as directed, they benefit people. Drugs also are used in self-medication. If used correctly, they may be helpful. However, some people take drugs for the wrong reason. They take drugs to seek a new thrill, to forget, or for "kicks." This use of drugs is called **drug abuse.**

Drug Abuse

Most of the drugs used by drug abusers are habit-forming. Drug abuse can cause serious health problems and have other side effects. For example, a drug abuser will show poor judgment when driving. Continued use of drugs causes the users to become **addicts,** or slaves to the habit. Addicts must have the drug or they suffer headaches and pains in the stomach, muscles, and bones. As their dependence grows, they require stronger and stronger doses of most drugs in order to get the effect they desire.

The quality of drugs sold illegally by

"pushers" is not regulated. Therefore, the drugs may be too strong or mixed with something harmful. When this happens, individuals may take too strong a dose, or overdose (OD), and "freak out." That is, they may imagine terrible things are happening to them and have to be hospitalized. An overdose may also lead to death.

Much of the increase in crime in the United States is related to the illegal sale, possession, and purchase of drugs. Needing from $25 to $100 or more a day to buy illegal drugs, the addict often turns to crime. A large proportion of the crimes of mugging, shoplifting, and burglary are committed by habitual drug users in search of money.

Selling drugs without a license is a serious crime. In 1970 Congress passed a law making the illegal sale of drugs punishable by as much as a life sentence. The purchase or possession of illegal drugs is also a crime, punishable by imprisonment of from five to ten years.

Drug addiction alone is not a crime but an illness. Both public and private hospitals have programs for treating and curing addicts. Private groups also run special centers where addicts may live while being cured. However, drug addiction is often difficult to cure. The best way to treat drug abuse and addiction is to prevent it. Therefore, public health officials run many programs to educate students, school officials, and parents.

The Problem of Alcohol

Many people do not think of alcohol as a problem. Yet too much alcohol can be harmful to health. It too may be habit-forming. Nearly 8 million Americans are problem drinkers. These problem drinkers are called alcoholics. They suffer from a disease called **alcoholism.**

Alcohol affects people differently. Under its influence, the user may stagger or become talkative or quarrelsome, sick to the stomach, or merely sleepy. Alcohol also affects judgment. Those who drink too much cause many accidents to themselves and others. Recent studies have shown that drunken drivers cause almost 70 percent of the injuries and deaths from automobiles.

There are other costs of alcoholism also. The families of problem drinkers may suffer from anxiety or have financial difficulties. Alcoholics are often absent from work and therefore have difficulty keeping a job. Alcoholics may cause accidents on the job and their absenteeism slows down the production schedule.

In recent years more young people have become alcoholics. A White House Conference on Youth reported that one of the most harmful problems of modern youth is the use and abuse of alcohol. All states have laws prohibiting the sale of alcoholic beverages to persons under a certain age, usually 18 or 21 years of age. These laws are intended to protect young people from the unwise use of alcohol.

The Problem of Smoking

Since the early 1950's, scientists have studied the lives and health of people who smoke, especially those who smoke cigarettes. They have reported that smokers run great risks of lung cancer, respiratory ailments, and heart disease. So powerful was their evidence that Congress in 1970 passed a law banning cigarette advertisements from television.

A federal law also provides that every pack of cigarettes and every cigarette advertisement shall carry a printed message. It says: "Warning: The Surgeon General Has Determined That Cigarette Smoking Is Dangerous to Your Health." As Americans have become more aware of its dangers, smoking increasingly has been banned or limited in theaters, planes, and other public places.

Smoking, too, is habit-forming. Once a person starts, it is difficult to stop. The best way to prevent the smoking habit is not to begin.

Promoting Public Safety

Every community wants to be a safe place for its citizens to live, work, and play in. Yet each year more than 70 million Americans are hurt in accidents. About 11 million of these people must remain in bed for at least a day. Over 100,000 die, and more than 400,000 are permanently disabled. A large percentage of the accidents that cause death or permanent disability take place at work or at home. The rest occur on highways, in schools, on playgrounds, and in other public places.

Over 300 million accidents will take place in American homes during the 1980's. Falls are the main cause of serious injuries in the home. Other causes of injury are fires, faulty household equipment, or the careless handling of equipment.

Nearly one third of all school accidents take place in school gymnasiums. They usually result from careless play, not organized sports and games. All Americans need to learn safety at play.

Each year thousands of Americans are killed and injured while they are having fun. During good weather, when more people are jogging, playing baseball, swimming, roller skating, boating, and so on, the number of accidents increases. Serious sunburn, broken arms and legs, and cuts are only some of the injuries suffered by people taking part in sports. Think of the tragedies that might be avoided if common-sense rules of safety were observed.

Safety on the Highway

Most of the nation's serious accidents occur on streets and highways. Each year over 50,000 people are killed in accidents involving automobiles, bicycles, and public transportation. The accident rate would be higher if it were not for safety belts, well-designed highways, police patrols, a lower speed limit, and the fact that most Americans are careful drivers.

Traffic accidents can be reduced. One way is to require that all beginners take driver training courses before they are allowed to operate a car, as many states do. Another way is for all drivers to observe speed and traffic laws. The main cause of accidents is speeding. Speeders are a danger to the lives of those who drive with care. For this reason, many states have introduced a **point system.** Any driver caught speeding is fined a certain number of points. After a specific number of points, a driver's license is taken away.

Wearing safety equipment while taking part in any kind of athletic activity is a good way to protect yourself while having fun.

Industrial Safety

Many accidents, as you have read, occur on the job. Machinery, chemicals, minerals, and gases can be harmful if they are not handled properly. Therefore, our governments regularly check factories, plants, and laboratories. Businesses also inspect their workplaces. They make sure that places of employment contain no safety hazards.

Industry is required to place safety devices on dangerous machines, to ventilate buildings properly, and to provide enough fire escapes and fire exits. Workers also must be instructed in how to handle machinery. Many factories are required to provide their workers with special clothing, gloves, masks, goggles, or ear mufflers.

Conditions in most workplaces are safe. Yet in some jobs workers continue to run a high risk of disease. Therefore, research on health and safety in the workplace is carried out by many businesses as well as by the National Institute of Occupational Health. The Institute also gathers information and distributes it to state and local governments.

Fight Against Fire

Every year over 3 million fires occur in the United States. This year, unless conditions change, about 6,000 people will die in fires. The property loss will be over $4 billion.

What causes all these fires? In most instances, the problem is either carelessness or defective equipment. About 12 percent of building fires can be traced to the careless use of matches and to careless smoking. More than 11 percent of all fires are caused by defective electrical equipment and bad wiring in homes and other buildings. Many fires are the result of faulty heating equipment and chimneys, sparks from fires, improper use of cleaning fluids, and faulty stoves.

Most communities have local fire departments with trained firefighters. However, some small towns have too few fires to need paid firefighters. They rely on volunteer firefighters. These people give their time freely because they have a sense of responsibility to their families and neighbors.

The best way to fight fire, of course, is to prevent it. Communities do several things to reduce the chances of fire. Most cities and towns hire inspectors to enforce local fire laws and inspect buildings in search of fire hazards. These inspectors do not ordinarily go into private homes.

Avoiding fire hazards in the home is the responsibility of each family. Fortunately, there is a safety device that can detect smoke in the air. Once installed in a home, a **smoke detector** sounds an alarm if a fire breaks out. This early warning can enable everyone in the family to escape safely. Many communities now require smoke detectors in all houses and apartments.

Everyone should practice fire prevention. To remind citizens that fire safety pays, many communities have special fire prevention campaigns. Each year the President of the United States sets aside a week in October as Fire Prevention Week. The success of such campaigns, of course, depends on all citizens doing their part to prevent fires.

★ ★ ★ ★ ★ ★ ★ ★ ★ ★ ★ ★

CAN YOU GUESS?

Fire trucks are equipped with many different tools and supplies. How many of these things can you name?

Answer is on page 562.

Acting in an Emergency

Education is important in knowing how to act if an emergency occurs. The Red Cross gives first aid and lifesaving courses that help many people each year. Many businesses offer their employees courses in artificial respiration and aid to those who are choking. Schools and businesses have fire drills.

Safety is serious business. Many communities train volunteer ambulance corps and firefighters. If there is an emergency, call the telephone operator or consult your local telephone book. It will have a listing of emergency numbers for hospitals, fire stations, police, poison control centers, and so on.

Some emergencies can be prevented. Sometimes people fall over a toy or object that has not been put away. Fire and safety hazards, such as oily rags, frayed electric cords, sliding rugs, and poorly lighted stairways are not always taken care of properly. Dangerous chemicals and drugs may not have been placed out of the reach of children. Remember, safety starts at home, where "the life you save may be your own."

CHECK-UP

Vocabulary

Public Health Service
drug abuse
addicts
alcoholism
point system
smoke detector

Review

1. How does the federal government help guard the health of the American people?
2. Why do alcoholism and drug abuse concern us all?
3. Where do many of the accidents in the United States occur? Why?

Discuss

Do you think smoking should be banned in all public places except in areas set aside for it? Why or why not?

CHAPTER SUMMARY

Americans have always tried to improve their way of life. Early in our nation's history, for example, men and women began moving to the cities to find new and more interesting jobs. There they hoped to make a better life for themselves and their children.

As time passed, however, and our population continued to grow, Americans began leaving the large cities. They moved out into smaller towns and suburbs. For the most part, the problems of our nation's cities are responsible for this movement of the American people.

The centers of many of our cities have deteriorated. Many areas have become slums. Mass transportation has declined. As the population of many small towns and suburbs has grown, these areas have developed similar problems. Many communities across the country are working hard to improve conditions.

Our communities are made up of many different minority groups. These groups have contributed much to the richness of our society. Unfortunately, many groups have been victims of prejudice and discrimination. They have had to struggle to achieve their full civil rights.

The good health of people in our communities is very important. There are many things that each person can do to safeguard his or her health and safety. For example, you can learn about the causes of alcoholism and drug abuse, help prevent accidents, and know what to do in an emergency.

CIVICS SKILLS: Reading a Map

Many Americans today are on the move. They are heading out of the "Snowbelt" states of the North and into the "Sunbelt" states of the South and West. They are also leaving crowded cities in search of places with fewer people, such as the forests of Vermont, the mountains of Colorado, or the rocky coasts of Oregon and Maine.

If you have any trouble picturing these trends, just glance at a map such as the one on this page. **Maps,** like graphs and charts, summarize in one drawing what might otherwise take pages of words to explain. Reading maps is easy, especially if you keep in mind several basic tips.

Using a Map

Mapmakers, or **cartographers,** use a variety of symbols, colors, and lines to communicate information about geography, climate, population, and much more. These techniques are part of a map's special language. To translate this language correctly, you need to study the **legend,** or key, that usually appears with a map. Look at the map legend on this page. What does each of the colors and symbols represent?

In addition to the legend, a map also includes other handy tools. The **scale,** for instance, shows the relationship between distances on the map and the actual distances on earth. Many scales, such as the one below, measure distances in both miles and kilometers. How would you measure the number of miles between Chicago and Houston? the number of kilometers?

The **compass rose,** or direction indicator, is another useful tool found on many maps. This is a set of arrows, or sometimes lines, pointing to the four main directions on the map: North, South, East, and West. The compass rose on this page also shows four halfway, or intermediate, directions. One of these is Southwest. Can you guess what the others might be?

Practicing What You've Learned

1. Using the colors in the map below, what generalizations can you make about population movement in the United States?
2. On the basis of evidence in the map, what conclusions can you draw about growth in the nation's largest cities?
3. What does the map tell you about population shifts during the 1970's in your state?

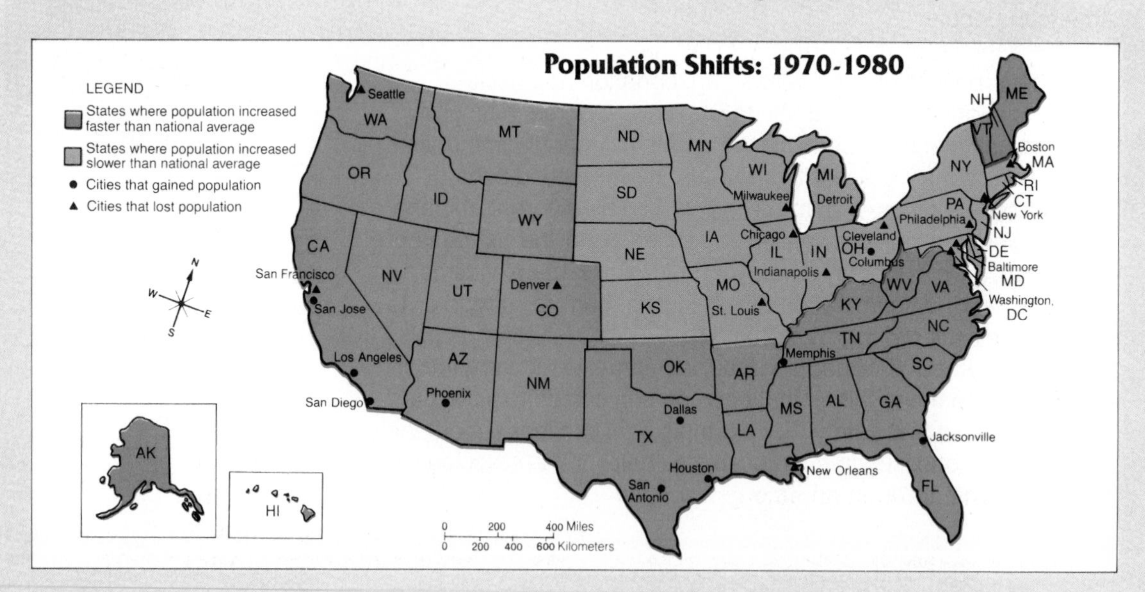

CHAPTER REVIEW

Vocabulary

On a separate piece of paper or in your notebook, write the terms listed below. Then read the definitions that follow and write the number of the definition that fits next to each term.

slum	civil rights
zoning laws	dissent
prejudice	quarantine
discrimination	drug abuse

1. Regulations that specify the types of buildings that can go up in each area of a city.
2. Taking drugs to seek a new thrill, to forget, or for "kicks."
3. A run-down city area where houses and apartments are overcrowded and need repair.
4. An unfair opinion, not based on the facts, of members of a particular group.
5. The rights of citizenship belonging to all Americans.
6. Taking unfair actions against people because they belong to a particular group.
7. Keeping a person who has an infectious disease at home.
8. Expressing one's disagreement with a law or an action taken by the government.

Check-Up

1. What are some of the problems that American cities face?
2. Describe the ways in which many American communities have grown from their downtown centers to their suburbs.
3. How did certain areas in our nation become slums?
4. What is the purpose of a regional planning group?
5. What were some of the important steps in the struggle to achieve equal rights for black Americans?
6. What are some legal means that citizens can use to protest against unjust laws?
7. How is the illegal sale, purchase, and use of drugs related to crime?
8. How can each citizen help prevent fires from occurring in the home and in the community?
9. In what ways are the use of drugs, tobacco, and alcohol personal questions and in what ways are they public problems?
10. What do you think are possible solutions to the problems of slums in our cities?

Civics Skills

Turn to the map of the United States on pages 516–517 of your textbook, and use it to answer the following questions.

1. What three symbols are identified in the map's legend? What other symbols has the mapmaker used?
2. Which states lie north, south, east, and west of Kansas?
3. In what direction would you travel if you wanted to fly from Sacramento, California, to Austin, Texas? from Sante Fe, New Mexico, to Richmond, Virginia?
4. About how many miles is it from your state capital to Washington, D.C.? about how many kilometers?
5. Why do you think Hawaii and Alaska have separate scales?

Citizenship and You

1. Read about and prepare a report on the history and growth of your community.
2. Using a local newspaper, clip out headlines and articles discussing local community problems. Display these clippings in class.
3. A committee might visit and interview a local fire official. Report to the class on what you learn, especially about the problem of false alarms.

CHAPTER

24

You and the Law

One of our most important duties as citizens, as you know, is to obey our nation's laws. Unfortunately, every period of history has had its own special kinds of crime to fight. Long ago Americans worried about horse theft and cattle rustling. Today we are trying to find ways to deal with computer crime and terrorism.

Yet new types of criminal activity are only a small part of the total problem facing Americans and people throughout the world. Offenses in almost all categories are increasing at an alarming rate. The need to find solutions is urgent.

Americans are worried about the increase in crime. They are concerned too about protecting the civil rights of those suspected of committing a crime. Americans have debated the proper role of the police, the justice of court and prison systems, and the treatment of juvenile delinquents.

In this chapter, you will examine some of the ways Americans and their officials try to deal with these and other problems. You will read about the following topics:

1. **Crime in the United States**
2. **The Criminal Justice System**
3. **Treating Juvenile Crime**

1 Crime in the United States

According to the Federal Bureau of Investigation (FBI), major crimes in the United States have more than tripled since 1960. Over 12 million serious crimes were committed each year during the early 1980's. Americans have become increasingly alarmed, not only by the number of crimes but also by the new types of crime that continue to appear.

What is considered a crime? A **crime** is any act that breaks the law and for which a punishment has been established. Crimes range from murder and robbery to speeding on highways, littering on the streets, and camping overnight on public beaches.

The FBI divides crimes into two general categories—crimes against persons and crimes against property.

Crimes Against Persons

Crimes against persons are acts that harm or end a person's life or threaten to do so. The worst such crime is, of course, murder. More than 20,000 murders are committed in the United States each year.

Most states define a **first-degree murder** as one that is planned and carried out deliberately. It may be punished by life imprisonment. A number of states have laws that permit some first-degree murderers to be executed.

A murder that is carried out on the spur of the moment, often in a fit of rage, is called a **second-degree murder.** This type of murder is sometimes called **manslaughter.** Punishment may be many years in prison.

The most common crime against persons is called **aggravated assault.** It is any kind of physical injury that is done intentionally to another person. Such assault often is committed during the act of robbing someone. In the early 1980's, there were more than 500,000 cases of aggravated assault each year.

Crimes Against Property

Most crimes committed in the United States are crimes against property. This type of crime includes actions that involve stealing or destroying someone else's property. The forcible or illegal entry into someone's home or other property with the intention to steal is called **burglary.** Over 3 million burglaries a year were reported in the early 1980's. This is more than one fourth of the crimes listed by the FBI.

Larceny is the theft of property without forcible or illegal entry. Examples of larceny are theft of an outboard motor, stealing from a cash drawer, and shoplifting. If the property is worth over a certain amount of money (which varies from state to state), the theft is called **grand larceny.** A theft of goods valued under this amount is called **petty larceny.**

The theft of automobiles is the most common form of larceny. It is a serious national problem. Almost one million cars are reported stolen each year. Some are taken by organized gangs, who resell them or strip them and sell the tires, batteries, and other parts. However, most stolen cars are taken by young people who drive them for a while, risking arrest, and then abandon them.

Robbery is a crime against both property and persons. It may be defined as taking something from a person by threatening the person with injury. The robber may demand "your money or your life" and back up the threat with a weapon. About half a million

Each year about 19,000 persons are arrested in the United States for the crime of arson. The effects of arson are felt by the whole community.

robberies take place in our country each year. Most of them are done with firearms. A murder committed during a robbery, even if unplanned, is first-degree murder.

Another kind of crime against property is **vandalism,** or the willful destruction of property. **Arson** is the destruction of property by setting fire to it. The damaging of schools and other public buildings and property by vandalism and arson has been increasing greatly. These forms of crime hurt all the citizens in a community.

Victimless Crimes

Some crimes, such as gambling and the use of illegal drugs, are known as **victimless crimes.** In such crimes there is no victim whose rights are invaded by another. These crimes mainly harm the lawbreakers themselves. Nevertheless, victimless crimes are harmful to society. The sale and possession of illegal drugs increases the death rate and often leads to other types of crime. Gamblers who lose their money may turn to stealing and other crimes.

White-Collar Crimes

Crimes committed by white-collar workers on the job are called **white-collar crimes.** They range from stealing paper clips to embezzlement and fraud. **Embezzlement** is taking for one's own use money that has been entrusted to one's care. **Fraud** is taking someone else's money or property through dishonesty. A person may commit fraud by charging for services that were not done, for example.

As the number of white-collar workers has increased, so has the number of crimes they commit. Theft by employees and businesses costs far more than street crime. The United States Chamber of Commerce estimates that white-collar criminals steal more than $40 billion a year. One insurance company found that at least 30 percent of all business failures each year are the result of employee dishonesty.

Many of the most recent types of white-collar crime involve the use of computers. Today nearly all large businesses and government offices in the United States use computers. They often use them to keep track of bills and records, payroll, inventory, and other financial matters. Some people have used computers to commit electronic theft, fraud, and embezzlement.

Terrorism

Terrorism is not a new type of crime. However, it has taken new forms in recent years. **Terrorism** is committing acts to force someone else, usually the government or a powerful group, to give in to one's demands. It usually involves violent crime.

Political terrorism was once regarded by Americans as a crime that happened only in other nations. Since the 1960's and 1970's, though, the number of terrorist acts in the United States has increased. Terrorism is a widespread international problem and may break out anywhere. Bombings, airplane hijackings, and the taking of hostages by individuals and political groups have become a part of the crime picture today.

The Rising Crime Rate

National statistics of criminal offenses are collected from local police officers by the FBI. The findings are published each year as a part of *Crime in the United States—Uniform Crime Reports*. These reports show that every year the number of almost every type of crime increases.

We do not know how many crimes are actually committed each year. Police statistics do not include all crimes. One reason is that citizens often do not report crimes to the police. We can be sure that the crime rate is even higher than the statistics show.

The Causes of Crime

No one really knows why people commit crimes. There have been many theories. The causes usually given for crime and its increase are poverty, unemployment, and certain trends in society.

Poverty. The most common explanation for crime is probably poverty. Many poor people live in slums, where there is overcrowding, poor education, and unstable family life. Under these conditions, many people do not get the training they need for better jobs. In such an environment people often feel helpless and angry. Some people break the law in an attempt to "get even" with society for the kind of life they have.

Unemployment. Unemployment is another probable cause of crime. When economic conditions are unfavorable and people lose their jobs, some of them may turn to robbery or commit other crimes against people or property.

Permissive Society. Some experts think a permissive society contributes to the increase of crime. They say many parents spoil their children and permit them to do anything they want. These children sometimes find it difficult to control their behavior when they are older and do not get what they want. They have not learned to act responsibly in their own lives and toward others.

Other people believe our courts are too permissive. They say judges often are too lenient with convicted criminals.

Population Shifts. Some experts point to two other reasons for the increase in crime—the large percentage of young people now in the population and urbanization.

There are many kinds of crime, such as automobile theft, that are committed mainly by young people. Today over 42 percent of the population is made up of people between the ages of 15 and 24. Also, more offenses have always been committed in cities than in rural areas. Since the United States has become a nation of cities, it is not surprising that the number of crimes has gone up.

One of the costs of crime is fear. As a result of the increase in crime, many people have taken precautions to protect their lives and property.

The Costs of Crime

Whatever its causes, crime is a problem that must be solved if people are to live in safety and without fear. Crime harms everyone. The cost to society is over $24 billion a year. More than $13 billion is spent on public law enforcement alone. Not included in these figures are private sums that are spent for insurance and for crime prevention services and equipment.

There are psychological costs as well. Among the highest costs are the pain and suffering of its victims. The constant worry by those who live and work in high-crime areas also must be taken into account.

Can we end crime? We can start by trying to lower the number of illegal acts committed. This can be done if all citizens take precautions to ensure their safety and protect their property. Also, each citizen should support those who are trying to prevent crime and bring criminals to justice.

CHECK-UP

Vocabulary

crime
first-degree murder
second-degree murder
manslaughter
aggravated assault
burglary
larceny
grand larceny
petty larceny
robbery
vandalism
arson
victimless crimes
white-collar crimes
embezzlement
fraud
terrorism

Review

1. What are crimes against persons? against property? Give two examples of each type of crime.
2. Why is white-collar crime increasing?
3. What are some of the most common causes of crime, according to experts?

Discuss

Many people complain that white-collar criminals receive too little punishment for their crimes. Should they receive the same treatment as other kinds of criminals? Why or why not?

2 The Criminal Justice System

Our society depends on responsible citizens. It needs people who obey the law and go about their daily tasks in a peaceful and orderly fashion. To help achieve this goal of "domestic tranquillity," police forces have been established at local, state, and national levels.

Keeping the peace requires more than hiring efficient police officers. Once arrested, criminals must be tried and, if found guilty, imprisoned. The entire system of police, courts, and prisons needed to bring criminals to justice is known as the **criminal justice system.**

The Role of the Police

The police have a number of duties. These are to protect life and property, prevent crime, seek out and arrest those who violate the law, protect the rights of the individual, maintain peace and order, and control the flow of traffic on streets and highways.

It is not a police officer's job to punish lawbreakers or decide who is guilty or not guilty. Deciding questions about guilt and punishment is the function of courts of law. Good police officers try to use their trained judgment about whom to arrest and on what grounds. They try to avoid the use of undue force and to be patient in the face of insults and threats of personal injury. They try to act as peacemakers, advisers, protectors, and friends, as well as law enforcers.

The job of police officers is not an easy one. It can also be a discouraging one because of overcrowding and other problems in the American court system.

The Training of Police Officers

Modern police officers are carefully selected and trained. Before they are hired, they are fully checked and investigated. They must pass aptitude and intelligence tests, as well as civil service examinations or similar written tests. In addition, they must pass rigid physical and psychological examinations. Most cities require police officers to be high school graduates. In recent years some cities have been seeking college graduates.

New police officers attend special police academies. They learn about law, dealing with people, evidence, arrest procedures, and recordkeeping. They also receive on-the-job training that includes the use of weapons and other physical skills. They are taught how to deal calmly with the public, how to handle emergencies, and how to give first aid. When trouble occurs, they must be ready to arrest suspects, prepare reports for the courts, and appear in the courts as witnesses.

Police Patrols Help Prevent Crime

New police officers may begin their careers by "walking a beat," or patrolling an assigned area. Many experts believe that such foot patrols are an effective way to prevent crime, especially at night. Officers on foot patrol can cover a territory carefully. They also can get to know the people who live and work in the neighborhood.

Most communities cannot afford all the foot patrol officers they need. They add to the strength and mobility of their force by using patrol cars. Radio-equipped police cars can be sent to any part of the city when trouble is

★ ★ ★ ★ ★ ★ ★ ★ ★ ★ ★ ★

DID YOU KNOW THAT . . .

for a long time American cities had no paid police officers? Some cities, however, were served by volunteer patrols called "watch and ward" societies. Their members walked the streets on the lookout for criminals and fires. New York City organized the first paid police force in 1844. Other cities and towns soon followed.

The police had many different nicknames. The most common, *cop* (from *copper*), may have come from the Latin word *capere*, "to catch." Or it may have started with the copper buttons worn by early police officers. The name *fuzz* goes back to the 1930's, and probably comes from the word "fussy."

Police officers walking a beat are often an effective way to prevent crime. They get to know the people in the neighborhood and are welcomed by them.

reported or suspected. Cruising patrol cars often catch lawbreakers in action.

The main job of the police officer is to prevent crime. The well-trained officer knows the danger signs that invite crime—burned-out street lights, open doors, broken windows. By preventing crime, police officers save lives, money, and property. They also make the community a better and safer place in which to live.

When a crime is committed, the police officer's job is to round up suspects, collect evidence, and recover property whenever possible. The officer must also take care to protect the rights of suspects and witnesses.

From Arrest to Sentencing

A police officer must have **probable cause** to arrest a suspect. This means that a crime must have been committed and that the officer must have seen it or gathered enough evidence to make an arrest. If the suspect has not been seen committing the crime, an arrest warrant may be necessary. An **arrest warrant** is an authorization by the court to make the arrest.

All suspects are entitled to due process. As you have read, this means they must receive all protections guaranteed by law. Suspects who are arrested must be informed of their rights immediately. They must be told that they have the right to remain silent and to be represented by a lawyer during all questioning. If a suspect is not given this information when arrested, any statement she or he makes cannot be used as evidence in court.

After an arrest, the suspect is taken to the police station for **booking.** That is, a record of the arrest will be made. An officer will write down the name of the suspect, the time of the arrest, and the charges involved. The suspect will be fingerprinted and photographed.

Preliminary Hearing. Within the next few days, a preliminary hearing will be held. During this procedure a judge must decide if there is enough evidence to send the case to trial. If there is not, the judge can dismiss, or drop, the charges against the suspect. If the charges are not dropped, the judge must decide whether or not to set bail.

Bail, as you recall, is money the suspect posts as a guarantee that he or she will return for trial. The amount of bail is determined by the seriousness of the offense.

If the offense is minor, the judge may agree to release the suspect on his or her **own recognizance,** that is, without bail. This usually is done if the suspect lives in the community and has a good reputation. It is assumed from this that the suspect will appear in court for the trial.

Indictment. Next a formal charge must be made. In some states, a grand jury hears the evidence in order to decide whether to send the case to trial. If the grand jury does find probable cause, the suspect is indicted, or charged formally with the crime.

Arraignment. The accused person then goes before a judge to be arraigned. That means the accused enters a plea of guilty or innocent of the charge. If the person pleads guilty, no trial is necessary.

Trial. If the accused person pleads innocent, the case goes to trial. The **defense** is the accused person's side of the case. The government's side of the case is the **prosecution.** The defense and prosecution lawyers choose the jurors from a large group of people. Both lawyers have the right to question prospective jurors, and to reject those they believe to be prejudiced against their case.

After the jury has been selected, the prosecutor and the defense lawyer make opening statements to the jury. Each outlines the facts he or she will try to prove.

Then the prosecutor presents the case against the **defendant,** or accused person. Witnesses are sworn in, questioned by the prosecutor, and cross-examined—that is, questioned by the defense attorney. Next the defense presents its case. The defendant may choose whether or not to testify. Under the Constitution, no defendant can be forced to testify against himself or herself.

After all the evidence has been presented by each side, both lawyers make a **closing statement** that summarizes their arguments. Before the jury leaves the courtroom to reach a **verdict,** or decision, the judge tells them what they can and cannot consider in reaching their verdict.

The defendant is always presumed to be innocent. It is the job of the prosecution to prove that the accused person is guilty beyond a reasonable doubt. If there is any reasonable doubt of guilt, the jury must find the defendant not guilty. Usually the jury must reach a unanimous verdict. As you have read, if the defendant believes that an error was made in the conduct of the trial, he or she may appeal the verdict.

Sentencing. If the defendant is found guilty, the judge must decide the **sentence,** or punishment. Usually the law sets a minimum (least) and maximum (most) penalty for the type of crime that has been committed. In some cases the judge may suspend the sentence. This means the defendant will not have to go to prison at all. The past record and reputation of the defendant will greatly influence the judge's sentence.

Plea Bargaining

Many cases never go to trial. They are taken care of quickly by **plea bargaining.** This means that the accused person is allowed to plead guilty to a lesser offense than the original charge. The penalty is therefore lighter than it would be if the accused were tried before a jury and found guilty of the more serious crime.

Under the Constitution, all persons accused of a crime are entitled to due process. When arrested they must be informed of their rights immediately.

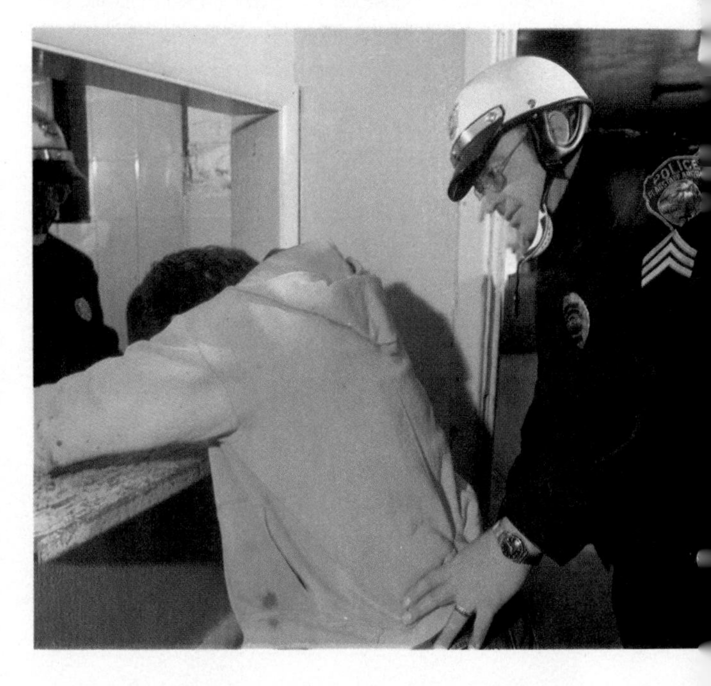

Many people support the use of plea bargaining. They say the practice keeps the courts from becoming overloaded with cases. Without it, they say, the number of judges and courts would have to be greatly increased. Critics argue that plea bargaining allows criminals to avoid adequate punishment. Opponents of plea bargaining also say it encourages accused persons to give up their constitutional right to a trial.

Punishing Lawbreakers

In the past, some Americans believed that harsh punishment would prevent crime. Public whippings, chain gangs, and even public hangings were used. It was hoped that such punishment would discourage others from committing crimes.

The whippings, prisons, and executions of the past did not prevent crimes. In fact, old-style prisons frequently made criminals worse. Today there is debate about the way lawbreakers should be punished.

The problem of reforming criminals still exists, especially in many prisons that are overcrowded. When first offenders are put in cells with habitual criminals, prisons all too often become schools for crime.

The treatment of prisoners generally has improved in recent years. Modern prisons have workshops to teach prisoners useful trades. Some prisons offer a variety of educational programs and counseling help. Other efforts have been made to help the lawbreaker learn how to live lawfully with others after leaving prison.

Another change in the treatment of prisoners is the use of the **indeterminate sentence.** When people are sentenced to prison, the exact length of time they must serve is not stated. They are told the minimum period and the maximum period they may have to serve. They may be sentenced, for example, to serve a prison term of from six to ten years. If they behave well in prison, they will be released after the minimum of six years.

After serving only a part of their sentence, prisoners may be eligible for **parole,** or

Cameras are forbidden in most courtrooms. Therefore the mass media often hire artists to show the jury and other courtroom scenes.

Prison sentences punish criminals and remove them from society for a time. Some prisons offer training programs to help people get jobs after their release.

release, on condition that they obey certain rules and keep out of trouble. A parole board studies each application for parole and decides on it.

When prisoners are paroled, they must report regularly to parole officers. Their parole usually lasts until the end of the maximum part of their sentences.

Capital Punishment. The harshest punishment is capital punishment—putting the criminal to death for serious crimes. Some people oppose capital punishment, or the death penalty. They believe it violates the Eighth Amendment's prohibition against "cruel and unusual punishments." Other people say the death penalty is a just punishment, especially for a person who has committed a murder. In 1976 the United States Supreme Court ruled that capital punishment as a penalty for murder is constitutional. Each state passes its own laws about capital punishment.

CHECK-UP

Vocabulary

criminal justice system
probable cause
arrest warrant
booking
preliminary hearing
own recognizance
indictment
arraignment
defense
prosecution
defendant
closing statement
verdict
sentence
plea bargaining
indeterminate sentence
parole
capital punishment

Review

1. What are some of the functions of a police department?
2. What are the main steps a suspect must go through before being sentenced or set free?
3. How does the parole system work?

Discuss

Some people want to make plea bargaining illegal. Do you agree or disagree? Why?

3 Treating Juvenile Crime

Young people are responsible for a large number of our nation's crimes. They commit many of the serious crimes against property, such as burglary, larceny, vandalism, arson, and automobile theft. The rate of crime among those between the ages of 15 and 24 has jumped considerably since the early 1970's.

Juvenile Delinquency

Every state has special laws for dealing with young offenders. The ages to which these laws apply vary from state to state. Most states define **juveniles** as people under 18.

Programs like the Police Athletic League work to bring police officers and young people into close contact. Why might police departments want such programs?

Some set the age as low as 16 and others as high as 21. Juveniles become **delinquents** when they are found guilty of breaking a law.

Statistics show that young people often commit serious crimes. However, most commit minor offenses that bring them into conflict with society. Juveniles who stay out late at night, constantly disobey their parents, or repeatedly run away from home may be termed delinquent. A youth whose behavior is impossible for parents and teachers to control is said to be **incorrigible.** After repeated instances of incorrigible behavior, a young person may be turned over to the juvenile authorities.

Causes of Juvenile Delinquency

Why are some young people lawbreakers and incorrigibles, while most live law-abiding and useful lives? According to experts who have studied the problem, there is no single answer. All individuals are complicated. Their behavior, whether it be good or bad, may have many causes. Following are some of the more important causes of delinquency. Some of these are the same as for crime in general.

1. Poor Home Conditions. Many juvenile delinquents come from homes in which parents take little responsibility for their children. Often one parent has permanently left and the other is rarely at home. Youngsters whose parents are alcoholics or drug addicts may spend a lot of time on the streets, where they get into trouble.

2. Slums. The slum areas in our cities frequently have a higher rate of crime than other areas. People who live crowded together under unpleasant conditions often are tense and angry. Many young people in these areas get into trouble while seeking outlets for their frustration or unhappiness. Sometimes their actions are a search for thrills and adventure.

3. Membership in Gangs. Some young people who get into trouble are members of neighborhood gangs. It is natural for a young person to want to be with a group and take part in group activities. If the group turns against the community and breaks the law, it becomes a bad influence.

4. School Dropouts and Unemployment. When young people have nothing to do, no place to go, and no money to spend, they may be headed for trouble. A person who drops out of school is not necessarily headed for a life of crime. Nevertheless, facts show that unemployed youths with little skill and training often become delinquents.

5. Alcohol and Drugs. Laws forbid the sale of alcoholic beverages to anyone under a certain age. They also ban the sale of habit-forming drugs to anyone who does not have a prescription from a doctor. Yet many young people manage to get hold of these substances. Under the influence of alcohol or drugs, they frequently do things they would not do under normal circumstances. People addicted to drugs, who need money to pay for their habit, often turn to crime—sometimes violent crime.

6. Problems of Mental Health. Some young people get into trouble because of mental and emotional problems. They need help. Delinquents are often unhappy people. Deep down inside, they may be afraid of the world or feel that society is against them.

Treatment of Juvenile Delinquents

Before the late 1800's, juveniles at least 14 years old were held responsible for the crimes they committed. They were put on trial in criminal courts and sentenced to prison and even death. However, during the 1870's reformers began working to change the way young offenders were treated. They said very young people were not really responsible for their actions. Instead of being punished as adults, juveniles needed to be given special understanding.

As a result, many communities set up a juvenile court system. Its purpose was not to punish but to save children from the harmful environment in which they lived. The reformers also hoped to reeducate delinquents by giving them care, treatment, discipline, and responsible supervision.

Instead of trials, juvenile courts hold hearings, which may be attended only by parents and people directly involved in the case. The reason for the hearings is to determine the guilt or innocence of juveniles. The meetings are informal, and the records of them are kept secret. The purpose of a separate court system for juveniles is to do what is best for the young people involved. For many years it was believed that their parents and court officials would protect their rights.

(continued on page 488)

One way to stay out of trouble is to take part in sports. These young people have found a way to play basketball on the street where they live.

Teenagers in the Jury Box

Every Wednesday afternoon a group of teenagers head for juvenile court in Duluth, Minnesota. Are they in trouble? No. They are high school students who serve on a teen jury. They serve on the Youth Court once a week for three weeks.

How the Jury Works

Although the teenagers, like adult jurors, sit in a jury box, they do not act as a regular jury. First, there is no judge in the room. An officer from Duluth's juvenile probation program is present. The officer's job is to keep the case running smoothly and point out legal facts. Usually the parents of the person "on trial" are also present.

Second, the jury does not decide guilt. It deals only with first-time teenage offenders who have already admitted their guilt. The crimes the teenagers have committed must be minor ones—that is, misdemeanors.

At the beginning of the hearing, the probation officer tells the jury the facts in the case. The jurors don't just sit quietly

Members of the Youth Court are told the facts in a case by a probation officer. They then question teenage offenders about their involvement.

After getting the information they need, the jurors discuss the case among themselves and then vote on the sentence.

and listen. They ask questions. They may ask the teenager why he or she committed the crime or became involved in it. They also may ask a parent to describe the offender's home life.

A Typical Case

Many of the cases presented are similar. Here is a typical case that the teenage jurors might hear:

A 17-year-old boy and some friends were out riding around town after midnight. The car they were in ran out of gas. After a short argument, the group decided that the easiest thing to do was to steal some gas from a stranger's car parked nearby. The 17-year-old was caught. He pleaded guilty to stealing gas.

"Why didn't you get out and walk?" asks one juror.

"Why didn't you call home?" asks another.

Sometimes the jury asks the parents to leave the room. "We usually find it easier to talk to the offender without the mother and father in the room," says one former juror. "Many offenders find it easier to open up to us that way."

Setting the Sentence

When the jurors think they have enough information, they discuss the case among themselves. The teenagers may question whether they should give a punishment or whether the offender seems to need more supervision or some special kind of help. They often discuss what might be the best way to make the offender see the seriousness of the crime that was committed. Then they vote on a sentence.

In the case of the 17-year-old who stole gas, the sentence had two parts. The youth was told to work 30 hours at a hospital. He also was put on probation for 60 days. That meant he had to report regularly to a court officer.

The teen juries are limited in the sentences they can set. They cannot send an offender to jail. They cannot remove a teenager from home. The teen juries also cannot ask an offender to pay more than $100 to a victim.

How the Program Started

The idea for the teen juries came from the Duluth Youth Council. In the late 1970's the council asked the mayor to try the program. A number of people were opposed to such a program. Some school officials and parents were afraid that the teenage jurors might be in danger from offenders who resented their sentences. So far, though, the Youth Court program has been a success.

One reason may be the attitude of the jurors. "I look at it as a discussion," says one juror. "The offender has already admitted guilt," she adds, "so we are working together on a problem. Everyone has good feelings about it afterward." She thinks it is important for both the members of the jury and the offenders to see that they are all "just ordinary people."

One of the supervisors of the probation office that runs the teen jury program agrees. In his opinion the juries have not prevented juvenile crime, but they have had a good effect on teenagers in Duluth. The jury members learn a lot about young people who commit crimes. Teen juries also teach responsibility to the young jurors. They have to think about the possible consequences of the sentences they give. Equally important, says the supervisor, the students get to see those "who got caught doing something they themselves might have done."

High school students in Duluth seem eager to be jurors. Since the program started, hundreds of students have volunteered. Some jurors have liked the job so much that they have signed up for more jury terms. The large number of applicants

The punishments imposed by the teen juries usually include some form of community service, such as turning a vacant lot into a garden (below) or cleaning city streets (opposite).

for Youth Court has made it clear that the teenagers welcome the opportunity to do something responsible for themselves and for their community.

Thinking It Over

1. How are teen juries similar to adult juries? In what ways are they different?
2. Do you think working in a hospital is a good punishment for a teenager guilty of stealing gas? Why or why not?
3. Why do you think the Youth Council wanted to start a teenage jury program?
4. What might students on a teen jury learn that will help them become more effective citizens?

Probation officers stay in close touch with the juvenile offenders assigned to report to them. These officers work to keep young offenders out of further trouble.

In 1967 a Supreme Court decision brought major changes to the juvenile justice system. The Court ruled that juveniles have the same rights of due process as adults. That is, they have the right to be informed of the charges against them, be represented by a lawyer, confront and question all witnesses, and refuse to testify against themselves. However, the Supreme Court also ruled that juveniles do not have the right to a jury trial or bail. Nevertheless, 16 states allow young people to be tried before juries.

Punishing Juvenile Delinquents

After hearing all of the evidence, the judge must decide the guilt or innocence of the juvenile. If the juvenile is found guilty as charged, the judge may send the delinquent to a foster home; commit him or her to a training school, or **reformatory;** or place the delinquent on probation.

Probation is a period during which a person guilty of an offense is given an opportunity to show that she or he can reform. The judge sets the conditions of the probation.

For example, the judge may say to a delinquent, "I am placing you on probation. You will report to your probation officer, and I will expect a good report about you. You will obey your parents and be home every night by eleven o'clock. You will make restitution for the damage you did. By **restitution** I mean that you will pay the costs as directed by your probation officer. If you do not behave yourself during your probation, or if you appear before me in the future on any other charge, I will have to consider sending you to a House of Correction."

In deciding the proper punishment, the judge considers the offense and the home and background of the juvenile offender. The judge takes into account the facts of the case as well as the recommendations of social workers, teachers, religious leaders, and former employers.

Serious Crimes by Juveniles

In recent years, there has been an increase in the number of serious crimes committed by young people. Therefore, many Americans are demanding that juvenile offenders be tried as adults. Under the traditional juvenile justice system, a young person who commits a brutal murder may be on the street again after only a few years in a reformatory. In spite of the good intentions of correction officers, that juvenile may not be reformed. He or she may commit another murder soon after being set free.

In response to the public demand for protection, some states have begun to punish juveniles accused of serious crimes as they would punish adults. Some people want to get rid of juvenile courts completely.

Juvenile Decency

Most of our nation's young people are good citizens who stay out of serious trouble. They obey the law and the rules of society. Criminologists—scientists who study crime and the behavior of criminals—give the following suggestions to young people who want to avoid trouble with the law.

1. Do not get started on drugs. Those who try drugs often end up in criminal courts and reformatories or jails.

2. Get the best education possible. It will keep you busy and increase your chances for a good job.

3. Avoid acts of vandalism and arson. These are not the proper ways to express discontent or hostility.

4. Have the courage to say no when friends suggest illegal acts.

5. Live a full life, with plenty of physical activity and interesting hobbies. The person who is busy doing challenging things does not get bored and turn to criminal activities as an outlet.

CHECK-UP

Vocabulary

juveniles	reformatory
delinquents	probation
incorrigible	restitution

Review

1. What are some of the causes of juvenile delinquency?
2. Why are juveniles usually tried in special courts?
3. Describe what happens when juveniles are charged with breaking the law.

Discuss

Do you think that young people who commit serious crimes should be tried as adults? Why or why not?

CHAPTER SUMMARY

Americans want and need to be protected from crime. Such protection is one of the services governments provide for their citizens. However, crime has become an increasingly serious problem in our nation. Many more offenses are committed, and several new types of crimes have appeared. The financial and psychological costs of crime are alarmingly high.

The American criminal justice system operates to protect everyone, even those who are accused of criminal actions. Police officers are trained to deal with the public, handle emergencies, and control situations that may lead to crime. They must also tell suspects what their rights are. From the moment of arrest, Americans are entitled to the due process of law.

Although most of the nation's young people are law-abiding citizens, juvenile delinquency has become an increasingly pressing problem. A large percentage of certain offenses are committed by young people. Juveniles who commit crimes tend to continue a life of crime. Therefore, special courts have been set up to deal with the problems of juvenile delinquents.

CIVICS SKILLS: Doing Library Research

How far is it from the earth to the moon? Who holds the Olympic record in speed skating? Where did the Vice President of the United States attend college?

You can find the answers to these and many more questions in the reference section of your library. This is where you'll discover a wide collection of fact-filled books especially designed for easy research. You might already be familiar with one of these—the encyclopedia.

An **encyclopedia** has articles on a wide range of subjects. Most encyclopedias consist of several volumes in which topics are arranged alphabetically. Some, however, such as an encyclopedia of American history, have all their information in only one or two volumes.

If you're like a lot of students, you probably start your research with an encyclopedia. But suppose you can't find a particular fact. Where do you look next? All reference books contain facts, but the type of facts varies with the reference. Choosing the right reference book saves you a lot of time. In some cases, the encyclopedia may not be the best place to begin.

Selecting a Reference

A handy source of both historical and up-to-date facts is an **almanac.** Here you will find statistics on anything from baseball to elections. To find this information, simply turn to the index. However, don't expect to see this list at the back of the book. The index in an almanac often appears at the front so that you can quickly skim for specific facts.

If you're looking for information on well-known people, you might go to a **biographical dictionary.** This will summarize the key events and dates in a person's life. For important figures in American history, check the *Dictionary of American Biography.* For famous people in the present, consult dictionaries such as *Who's Who in America* or *Current Biography.*

To locate maps and statistics on the United States or other parts of the world, try an atlas. An **atlas** is a book of maps. It also may provide many interesting facts and figures, including information on geography, population, or climate. If you need similar data about places during the past, study a **historical atlas.** This will show you how boundaries of nations, for example, have changed over time.

Whenever you want current information on a topic, refer to the *Reader's Guide to Periodical Literature.* This useful book records all the articles that have appeared in many popular magazines. To find stories on a particular subject, turn to that subject heading in the Guide. If an article has been published, it will be listed along with the name, date, and page of the magazine in which it appeared. Should you have trouble understanding abbreviations, or shortened words, turn to the key at the front of the book.

Practicing What You've Learned

Read the boxed information below and answer the following questions.

1. Which reference might be more useful to Kim and Andy: an encyclopedia or the *Reader's Guide to Periodical Literature?* Explain.
2. Why might they check an almanac?
3. Look through the reference section of your library. What additional sources could Kim and Andy have used?

KIM'S SITUATION: Kim's civics class has just finished a unit on crime in America. Instead of a unit test, the teacher has assigned each student a research project. Kim's topic is white-collar crime. Her friend, Andy, must investigate the training given at police academies. Along with a written report, both Kim and Andy have to turn in at least one table or graph summarizing their findings. Together they walk to the library wondering where they should begin their research.

CHAPTER REVIEW

Vocabulary

Copy the following words or terms in the vocabulary section of your notebook. Then write a sentence for each.

crime
burglary
larceny
arson
white-collar crimes
indeterminate sentence
terrorism
criminal justice system
verdict
arraigned
plea bargaining
probation

Check-Up

1. What is the difference between first- and second-degree murder?
2. Why are some criminal acts called victimless crimes?
3. What are some of the forms terrorism has taken in recent years?
4. What are some of the responsibilities of a police officer?
5. What is plea bargaining? What arguments are used for and against the use of plea bargaining?
6. What are some of the changes in recent years in the treatment of prisoners?
7. How have attitudes toward juvenile offenders changed in recent years?
8. What may a judge do if he or she finds a juvenile guilty of a crime?
9. What should young people do in order to avoid getting in trouble with the law?
10. What do you think could be done to help lower the increasing crime rate?

Civics Skills

Make a list of the library references discussed on page 490 of your textbook. Then decide which of these you would use to find the answers to each of the following questions. See if you were right by actually looking up the answers in the reference section of your school or local library.

1. What was the crime rate in your state last year?
2. In what state did Supreme Court Justice Sandra Day O'Connor first practice law?
3. When was the Federal Bureau of Investigation (FBI) founded?
4. What kinds of problems do police officers face today?
5. When was William Howard Taft Chief Justice of the Supreme Court?

Citizenship and You

1. Participate in a class discussion on the different causes of juvenile delinquency and what might be done to remove these causes?
2. A small committee might visit a local courtroom to observe an actual trial. Note the ways in which the rights of the accused person are protected. Report your observations to the class.
3. Write an editorial setting forth your ideas about the way criminals are treated in the United States. Do research to support your ideas.
4. Invite a local police officer to talk about law enforcement in your community. Class members should ask the officer to suggest ways in which you, as young citizens, can help make law enforcement more effective.
5. A committee could make a study of the local police force. How many people are on the force? How many of them are women? What special divisions does the force have? What qualifications and training must officers have?
6. Arrange a bulletin board display of articles and pictures from local newspapers on the activities of the local police force.

Saving the Earth

It was Christmas Eve. American astronaut James Lovell, halfway to the moon, looked out the window of his spacecraft. There among the stars he saw a round ball, a planet. One side of it was in shadow. The other side was streaked with color—blue, brown, green, and white. It was beautiful. It looked, he said, "like a grand oasis in the vastness of space."

Lovell, with a grin, asked if this planet might be inhabited. The other astronauts laughed. Of course it was inhabited. It was the planet earth. For the first time in history, humans could view the entire world from a great distance. The earth could be seen as a "spacecraft" among the stars. We are all riding on it, passengers together, dependent upon it for all the necessities of life.

The earth has been good to us. It has provided us with air to breathe, water to drink, food to eat, and materials to make our lives easier. Over the years, these natural resources have been taken for granted, as though they could never be used up. However, now we know that the natural resources of the earth are not limitless. They need protection, especially from humans.

In order not to use up what nature has provided, we must begin to take better care of our earth and its natural resources. We must understand what the dangers are. What is happening to our land? What can we do to make sure that "Spaceship Earth" will continue to carry its passengers safely now and in the future? These are the questions to think about as you read and study these topics:

1. **Ecology—the Vital Key**
2. **The Problem of Pollution**
3. **Energy for Today and Tomorrow**
4. **Protecting Our Future**

1

Ecology—the Vital Key

The world around us is our **environment.** It is made up of a layer of air, water covering three fourths of the surface of the globe, and soil upon which we depend for food, clothing, and shelter. Every part of this environment is important to us.

What happens, however, when our environment changes? Everyday buildings go up. Highways are built. Jet planes streak through the skies. These changes can be helpful. They can also create serious problems.

What Is Ecology?

All living things depend on each other. The study of the relationship of living things to each other and their environment is called **ecology.**

Human beings and animals, for example, depend on green plants for the oxygen they breathe. Plants take carbon dioxide out of the air. They then break it down into carbon and oxygen. The plants use the carbon to make their own food. The pure oxygen, which they cannot use, is released back into the atmosphere. Animals breathe in this oxygen, which they need to live. They breathe out carbon dioxide, and the cycle begins again. Without green plants and the oxygen they supply, no animal or human being could live.

There are many other ways in which living things depend upon each other. Bacteria feed on fallen leaves, causing them to decay. This decaying matter enriches the soil, so that more plants and trees can grow. They in turn supply food for many animals, such as rabbits, squirrels, deer, and many kinds of birds. Some birds eat insects that feed on the plants. Tiny marine animals called plankton live in marshes and wetlands and provide food for shrimp, oysters, and minnows. These in turn become food for larger fish and make possible the great schools of herring, tuna, salmon, and other seafood so important to humans.

In such ways, all living things, including humans, are like links in a chain. Take away one link of the chain and all living things depending on that link will suffer. Reduce the amount of forests and fields in the world, and the number of wild birds also will be reduced. Without enough birds to eat them, insects will multiply too quickly. Drain or pollute the wetlands, and there will be fewer fish.

Reduce the wild areas of the country, and eagles, hawks, coyotes, mountain lions, and other animals who live in them will no longer have a home. Without these natural enemies, other animals, such as mice and deer, will increase too quickly. With too many plant-eating animals, not enough plants will decay to enrich the soil and hold moisture. Later there will be fewer plants, and the plant eaters too will suffer.

These are only a few simple examples. Perhaps you can think of others. The way in which all living things, including humans, relate to one another is called the **balance of nature.** The study of this complex subject, ecology, is of great importance to us. People sometimes upset the balance of nature without realizing the harmful side effects of their activities.

America's Early Environment

Long before any European settlers came here, the North American continent was a land of great natural wealth and beauty. This part of the world had moderate climates, with plenty of sunshine and a good supply of rain in most places. Trees grew thick and tall in the forests. The plains were covered with wild grasses. The river valleys were fertile and green. Many kinds of wild animals lived in balance with each other.

America's abundance was the result of natural forces that had been at work for thousands of years. The sun, wind, and rain had worn away huge rocks and reduced them to soil. Melting snow had formed streams that carried soil down from the mountains into the valleys. Huge rivers were formed. These rivers dug out great channels and canyons and left more soil in their paths.

Plants grew in this soil, and when they decayed their leaves and roots enriched the soil. As the soil was built up, trees were able to grow. Some of these grew in rocky places. Their roots helped break up the rocks and make more soil. Their leaves decayed and built up the soil even more. Then other trees took root and huge forests were born.

These great forests provided protection and food for many kinds of animals. Other animals, such as the great herds of American bison (buffalo), grazed on the open plains. Different species of birds, insects, and animals kept each other in balance. Each plant or animal took what it needed from the environment. In turn it contributed to the needs of others.

At this time, humans also were part of the balance of nature. The Indians hunted ani-

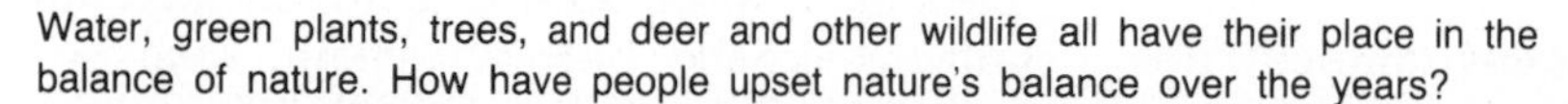
Water, green plants, trees, and deer and other wildlife all have their place in the balance of nature. How have people upset nature's balance over the years?

mals for food and used the hides for clothing and shelter. Hunting with spears or bows and arrows, they rarely killed more than they needed to feed themselves. The Indians had great respect for the earth and for the other creatures with whom they shared it.

Upsetting America's Ecology

The early European settlers were amazed by the natural wealth of America. In Europe most of the land was divided up and had been farmed for hundreds of years. There were few forests and little wild game left. No wonder the fertile land, the forests, and the wildlife of America seemed unlimited to early European settlers.

America's forests were so thick that settlers in the East first had to clear away the trees in order to grow crops. They used some of the wood to build their houses and furniture. They burned what they did not need. Then they started sending lumber back to Europe. The tallest and straightest trees were used to make the masts of great sailing ships.

As the number of settlers increased and the demand for wood grew, more and more forests were cut down. No new trees were planted in their place. If people wanted more wood, there were many more forests to the west.

However, forests were not only for people. As the trees disappeared, so did much of the wildlife that depended on them for food and shelter. Many other wild animals were killed, not only for food but also for their furs or for sport.

Beavers were trapped by the millions because beaver hats were popular in Europe. Whole herds of buffalo were shot for hides or for sport, while their meat was left to rot. Other animals and birds of prey, including foxes, bears, mountain lions, owls, hawks, and eagles, were shot as pests because they sometimes attacked chickens, cattle, or other livestock.

The cutting down of vast timberlands in the past greatly changed American ecology. Today more care is taken to replant forests as trees are cut.

Destroying these animals upset the balance of nature. These creatures fed mostly on other wild animals, including mice and snakes. Soon mice and other small animals began to grow unchecked. Another result of the thoughtless killing of so many animals was that some species, including the American eagle, were almost destroyed. They must now be protected by special laws.

Farming the Land

The land cleared for farming was at first very fertile. This rich soil produced wonderful crops of vegetables, wheat, oats, corn, cotton, and tobacco. However, when the farmer

Technology has helped make American farmland the most productive on earth. Continued high production has been aided by such methods as contour farming.

planted a crop and harvested it, nothing was left to decay and rebuild the soil. As the land was farmed year after year, the supply of plant food in the soil was used up and nothing was put back.

In the West, cattle raisers and sheepherders took the land for granted too. Their huge herds ate all the plants on the prairies they roamed. Without plants to hold water, the land dried out. Much good grassland was ruined in this way. New land was always available, most people thought.

By the early 1900's, our vast continent was filling up with people. There was no longer an endless supply of untouched farmland. Farmers were plowing up more and more of the flat grasslands on the Great Plains. Then in the 1930's, the plains went through a long dry period. With no grass growing, vast amounts of rich soil were blown away by the wind. A few years later, all that was left was a barren "dust bowl."

In the 1930's, President Franklin D. Roosevelt urged Congress to pass a program to conserve the nation's farmlands. Under this program, called the **soil bank,** landowners were rewarded if they did not farm some of their land. The government paid them to grow trees or grass on it instead. This ensured that a supply of good land would be left for the future.

Modern Agriculture

The population of the United States was increasing. New farmland was scarce. Old farmland was wearing out. Some of the land was no longer farmed at all. How were all the new people to be fed?

The answer came from modern science and technology. Farmers learned how to keep the soil from being worn out. They could prevent topsoil from washing or blowing away by many different techniques. Some farmers tried a method called **contour farming.** By plowing across slopes instead of up and down, they prevented the soil from being worn away.

Many built drainage channels, small dams, and terraces—flat, level spaces on the slopes. Others planted **cover crops,** such as clover, soybeans, and hay, because they hold the soil better than other crops. They also practiced **crop rotation,** planting different crops on the land each year. This helps restore nitrogen to the soil and increases crop yields.

Fertilizers and Pesticides

With the help of science, farmers can now grow more food on less land. This miracle was made possible by the use of chemical fertilizers and pesticides.

Fertilizers are special plant foods that make crops grow faster and bigger. The most important fertilizers are nitrates, which contain nitrogen. Nitrates can be mixed with water and pumped into the ground, or they can be spread as powder to soak in with the next rain. When a field is fertilized with nitrates, plants grow so quickly that much more food can be harvested. Nitrates are now used by almost all farmers. They are used as well by home gardeners on their lawns and flower beds.

Pesticides are special chemicals that kill insect pests. Many kinds of insects attack different food plants, and they can ruin a farmer's whole crop. A pesticide called DDT, introduced in the 1940's, seemed to be the answer. Farmers mixed DDT with their fertilizer to control corn borers, boll weevils, cabbage moths, and hundreds of other insect pests. People sprayed it on their lawns to get rid of mosquitoes and on their windows to get rid of flies. Forests were sprayed with DDT from airplanes to kill gypsy moths and other insects that attacked trees.

Science has solved many problems with fertilizers and pesticides. American farmers have been able to produce more and more food. Unfortunately, we are learning now that some of these chemicals are causing problems that may be worse than those they solve. Nitrates and DDT, for example, have had unexpected and dangerous effects on our environment.

Overpopulation—A Threat to Our Resources

Our farmers have proved that they can produce enough food to feed the present population of the United States, with some left over for export. Will they still be able to do so in the future, as more and more land is covered with cities, dams, highways, and other kinds of development?

Consider too the increasing problems of living space, water supply, and disposal of trash and waste, as more and more people crowd the earth. How many people can the United States and the rest of the world hold and still provide a decent standard of living for all?

The increase in the world's population has been called a population explosion. It took more than a million years for the human population to reach one billion by the year 1850. However, it took only 80 years to arrive at the second billion, in 1930. Today the world's population is over 4 billion. If it keeps increasing at the same rate, the world's population will reach 6.2 billion by the year 2000.

This rapid growth greatly concerns the United States. At present, food must be sent to many nations because they cannot feed all their people. Even with this aid, about half a billion people in the world suffer from starvation each year.

The population of the United States is growing but not rapidly. It is increasing at less than 1 percent a year. In the early 1980's, there were more than 3 million births and fewer than 2 million deaths a year. Thus the natural increase in our population was a little above a million a year. In addition, about 600,000 immigrants came to live and work in the United States every year during this same period.

Even if our nation continues at this low rate of growth, we will have more than 260 million people by the year 2000. The people we have now are already using up our resources at an alarming rate. Where will the United States be able find the resources to provide a high standard of living for so many more? This is a challenge Americans face for the future.

CHECK-UP

Vocabulary

environment
ecology
balance of nature
soil bank
contour farming
cover crops
crop rotation
fertilizers
pesticides

Review

1. How do plants and animals depend on each other?
2. What are some ways in which humans upset the balance of nature?
3. Why is overpopulation a threat to our resources?

Discuss

What is the place of humans in the balance of nature?

2 The Problem of Pollution

Our natural resources are precious. Unfortunately, however, many people have taken the air, land, and water around us for granted. They have polluted our environment.

Pollution occurs when we cause any part of our environment to become dirty or contaminated—made unfit for use. Pollution can destroy plants and animals and can upset the balance of nature. Among the countless living creatures that pollution harms are the ones who cause it—human beings.

Why Do We Have Pollution?

Pollution may occur when we get rid of something we do not want. Harmful unburned gases from our automobile engines are added to the air. Unwanted smoke and gases from factories, power plants, and home furnaces go up millions of smokestacks and chimneys. Ashes, soot, and gases are carried far and wide by the wind and make the air unhealthy to breathe. People throw away tires, bottles, cans, and even old automobiles along the highways and in streams. Chemical plants and steel mills pour their wastes into rivers, lakes, and oceans.

Why do people pollute their environment? They do it because they started doing it long ago when the damage caused by dumping was less evident. For example, an early town bought a piece of swampland to serve as its dump. There was plenty of other land, so hardly anyone was aware of this small-scale damage of the environment.

An early factory was built beside a river. It dumped its waste into the river. The river did not belong to anyone in particular, and few people complained. When there were fewer towns and factories scattered throughout our vast land, not many people worried about these methods of getting rid of unwanted refuse.

Causes of Pollution

Since the early history of our nation, however, three things have happened that have made these practices unsuitable. First, our population has grown enormously. Every person produces garbage, sewage, and other kinds of waste. The more people we have, the more garbage we produce. As long as our population continues to grow, so will the problem of disposing of our waste.

Second, our economy has developed such enormous capacity that we manufacture and use more and more goods every year. Americans use more than 149 million automobiles, trucks, and buses to move people and goods from place to place. Billions of metal cans and nonreturnable bottles are used every year and then thrown away.

Third, new inventions have led to products that complicate our trash disposal problem. Plastics and some chemicals do not decay and, if burned, may pollute the air. Detergents may upset the natural balance in streams and lakes.

These are only a few of the new and old products that cause trouble in our environment. Because our economy gives us so much, we must dispose of mountains of trash. We must also control tons and tons of waste that may pollute the air and water.

Air Pollution

The air we breathe is a unique mixture of nitrogen, oxygen, carbon dioxide, and small amounts of other gases. It is a **renewable resource.** That is, it can be replaced. Under good conditions, nature can clean the air of germs that are breathed into it by people, or of dirt and harmful gases put into it by furnaces, factories, and automobiles. In recent years, however, the pollution in the air sometimes has become so great that nature cannot get rid of it.

As a result, the air over many of our cities sometimes is filled with **smog**—a combination of smoke, gases, and fog. Smog burns the eyes, causes coughing, and is dangerous for anyone with a breathing ailment.

Automobiles in America pour more than 100 million tons of pollutants into the air each year. However, automobiles are by no means solely responsible for our bad air. Nearly 50 million tons of pollutants are spewed into the atmosphere by the fuel we burn to heat our homes and to power the generators for electricity.

Furthermore, each year almost 36 million tons of pollutants come from factories. In some parts of the country, factories are the worst polluters of all. In addition, almost 5 million tons of ashes and gases enter the atmosphere each year from the burning dumps and incinerators near almost all our cities and towns.

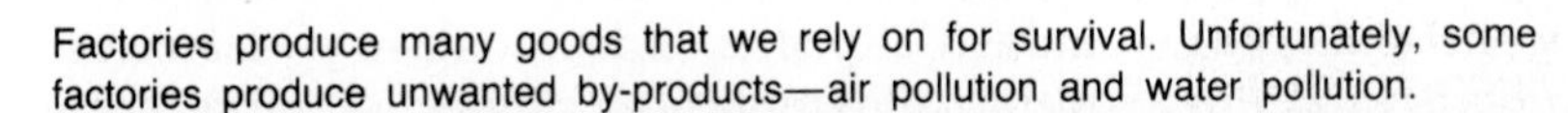

Factories produce many goods that we rely on for survival. Unfortunately, some factories produce unwanted by-products—air pollution and water pollution.

Effects of Air Pollution

Every year it costs government and business about $17 billion to try to control and reduce air pollution. The pollutants eat away metal, damage crops, and waste our resources.

Furthermore, changes in the makeup of the air, some scientists say, are affecting the earth's climate. Harmful gases and tiny particles of foreign matter are increasing in the upper atmosphere. When the sun's rays strike these particles, the rays are scattered back into space. It will not take long, these scientists say, for this process to cut down the amount of sunlight that reaches the earth.

The effect of this will be to reduce plant life and eventually to threaten all life on earth. Smog already has been seen over the oceans and even at the North Pole. Airplanes flying at high speeds in the upper atmosphere may increase the danger.

Our Water Supply

While we have plenty of air to breathe, even if it is polluted, we do not have plenty of fresh water. Ninety-seven percent of all the water in the world is salt water. Of the remaining 3 percent, all but a tiny fraction is frozen in the polar icecaps. Thus our supply of usable water is strictly limited. Nevertheless, Americans use water as though it were plentiful.

All fresh water comes from the clouds—as rain, snow, or other precipitation. It sinks into the earth, follows underground routes, and forms underground pools. Excess water runs into rivers, lakes, and oceans. Eventually it evaporates into the atmosphere, to fall again upon the land. This process is called the **water cycle.**

Underground water reserves are one of the keys to life on the land. Underground water nourishes plants. Bubbling out in wells and springs, it helps supply the water needs of humans and animals. A good supply of underground water is assured when trees, plants, and grasses cover the earth's soil. The roots of trees and other plants help keep the soil moist. They slow the flow of water. Trees and plants give off moisture into the atmosphere to help keep the water cycle working.

When trees and other plants are removed from great areas of land, the rain tends to rush down slopes instead of sinking slowly into the ground. That has happened in many parts of the United States. The level of water under the ground, the **water table,** is slowly sinking. As a result, our supply of usable water is decreasing.

Yet we are using more water than ever before. Some scientists say that every day we take twice as much from ground water reserves as flows in. This situation is made worse because we are rapidly polluting much of our surface water—the water of rivers, lakes, and reservoirs.

What Are the Water Pollutants?

Anything in the water that makes it less useful or less healthful is a pollutant. Water pollution can be classified into five types: chemical, sewage, thermal, silt, and crud.

Chemical pollutants come mainly from industrial plants. In fact, industry—factories, mills, and mines—accounts for more than half of all water pollution. Insect sprays and artificial fertilizers used in agriculture are also responsible for the chemical pollution of water. There are other forms of chemical pollution. For instance, many detergents we use contain substances called phosphates. These phosphates make detergents act more quickly. However, they also pollute the waters in much the same way fertilizers do.

Sewage comes mainly from cities and other communities that dump waste, including that of humans, into lakes and streams. Water pollution also comes from sewage treatment plants and septic tanks.

Thermal pollution occurs when industries use cold water from a stream or lake to cool their products, then pump the warmer water back into the body of water. Steel plants, nuclear power plants, and others pump warmed water into streams. The temperature of the water, raised in this manner, may kill fish and other marine life. It also upsets the balance of nature that helps renew the purity of fresh water. Algae, or tiny water plants, may grow in the warmer water and begin to smell.

Silt is soil, sand, or mud that has washed into streams. It comes mainly from sloping land that does not have enough trees or other plants to hold the soil. Silt pollution often is caused by improper mining and agricultural practices, road building, and earth moving.

Crud, usually a slang word, can also refer to trash, such as old tires, bottles, and other used items. Such things become crud when they are thrown by thoughtless people into streams and lakes, as well as onto the land.

Cleaning Our Water

The cure for water pollution is to rid water of all impurities before it is returned to the ground, streams, and lakes. Purification is costly. It requires the building of more and better sewage treatment plants. Industrial plants need to install more purifying equipment or find better ways to get rid of their waste.

Americans use about 360 billion gallons (1,366 billion liters) of water a day—for drinking, bathing, industry, and all other purposes. About 70 percent of this water becomes sewage. All this sewage would have to be treated if we really wanted our water to be pure.

Noise Pollution

Loud, harsh, irritating sounds have become a part of our modern civilization. The roar of jet planes, the blare of automobile horns and transistor radios, the rumble of trucks, the penetrating sounds of jackhammers and riveting guns—all of these and more cause noise pollution. Listening to disturbing noise for a long period of time may lead to heart disease, high blood pressure, stomach ulcers, nervous disorders, and deafness.

One common source of noise pollution is the roar of jet planes taking off and landing. The problem is most severe in neighborhoods that are near airports.

To understand the problem of noise pollution, we need to know something about the nature of sound. The loudness of sound is measured in decibels. We can barely hear a difference of one decibel. We usually speak in tones of about 50 to 60 decibels.

When sound reaches about 100 decibels, it becomes uncomfortable. At 140 decibels, it is painful. The sound of a jet plane taking off, at 150 decibels, is harmful to human eardrums. Some workers at airports wear protective devices over their ears. Citizens who daily endure a traffic noise level of 80 decibels, or a subway roar of 100 decibels, also suffer.

People have begun to do something about noise pollution. The federal government is spending millions of dollars to lessen the noise of jet planes. Federal, state, and local governments have passed laws to control noise levels. More effective mufflers are now manufactured for trucks and buses. Quieter machines are being made by industry. Fans of rock music are urged to lower the music's volume from its loud range of 100 to 160 decibels, which can cause ear troubles. Concerned citizens are also working to make the public aware of the many problems of noise pollution.

An International Problem

Pollution does not respect political boundaries. A polluted stream may flow from one state to the next. Polluted air from one city's factories drifts over another city or even into other countries. Polluted water from one state fouls the shoreline of other states. Ships dump or spill oil into the oceans of the world. Atomic fallout affects every section of the globe. Some people in Japan wear masks to help protect them against smog. Sonic booms from fast-flying planes echo over Africa. The problem of pollution calls for international cooperation.

In 1972 the United Nations held the first global Conference on the Human Environment in Stockholm, Sweden. There were delegates from 114 nations. Together they launched a worldwide fight against pollution. The conference set up 110 stations throughout the world to obtain data on the extent and nature of each area's pollution.

The nations of the world are all affected by what happens to the air and the oceans. The future of the earth as a home for human beings may depend on how well all of us can work together to control pollution.

CHECK-UP

Vocabulary

pollution
renewable resource
smog
water cycle
water table

Review

1. What three factors have increased pollution in modern times?
2. How does air pollution affect people?
3. Name five water pollutants and give an example of each.
4. What can be done about noise pollution?

Discuss

What are some of the causes of pollution in your locality? What can be done about them?

3

Energy for Today and Tomorrow

Today most Americans are aware of the problems of pollution and the need to protect our natural resources. Until recently, however, many Americans believed our country's resources would last forever. Ever since the European settlers arrived in America, people have been using up the land and its resources faster and faster. Besides cutting down the forests, Americans have covered the land with cement and asphalt. They have also stripped mountains bare for coal, copper, silver, gold, and other minerals.

The United States has about five percent of the world's population. However, it uses much of the world's natural resources. This places a heavy burden on the earth's limited supplies.

America's Share of the World's Resources

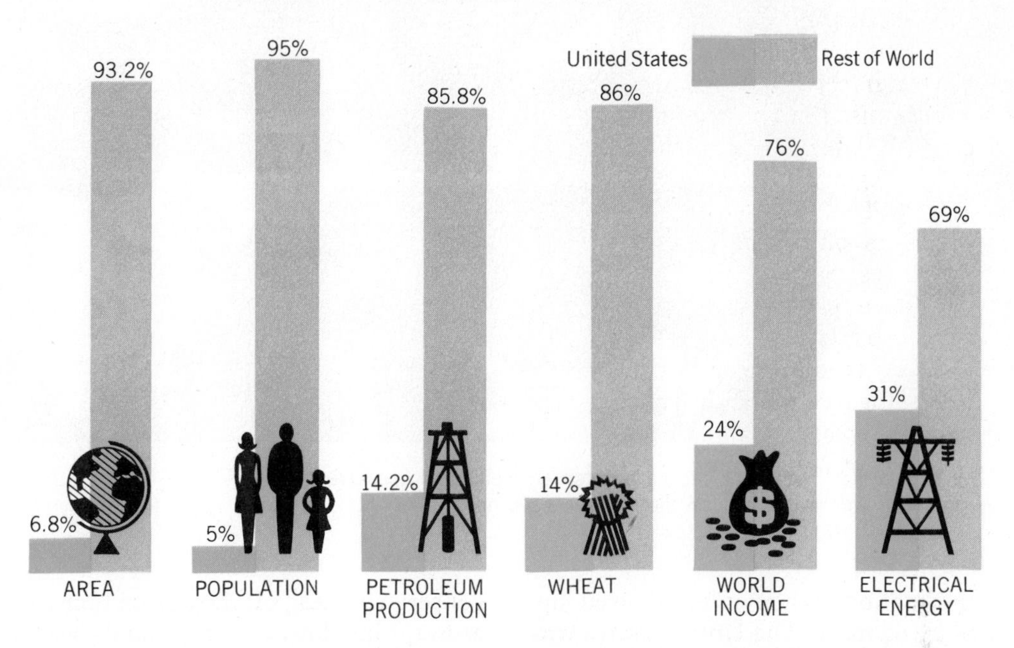

SOURCE: United Nations and United States Department of Commerce, Bureau of the Census. Figures are for 1980.

Our Energy Resources

Among the natural wealth we are using up quickly are our **energy resources.** These resources—coal, petroleum, and natural gas—furnish the power for doing the nation's work. Between 1950 and 1970, we doubled the amount of energy used in running our machines. That means we used up a large amount of our energy resources. Some of these fuels were also imported. The United States is not the only industrial nation to use up energy at a fast rate. Moreover, developing nations around the world are now demanding a greater share of the world's energy resources.

Unless we take steps now, we will soon be without valuable energy resources. These fuels are limited. They also are nonrenewable. That is, they can be used only once. Without them our way of life would be in danger. Our factories would stop running. Our homes would be dark and cold. Our transportation systems would come to a halt. Our national defense would be in danger. To understand better why this would happen, let us examine the energy situation.

Oil for Industry

The energy source we depend on most is petroleum, or oil, as it is commonly called. It lies deep within the earth in great pools. These pools were formed from microscopic plants and animals that lived millions of years ago. They were covered with mud, rocks, and water. After centuries of decay and pressure from the earth, petroleum, an energy source of great value, was formed.

Pumped to the surface and refined, petroleum furnishes the energy to heat our homes, the gasoline to run our cars and trucks, and the lubricating oil to grease the wheels of industry. It also is the basis of a great variety of by-products, such as plastics, fertilizers, dyes, and many different chemicals.

However, only a certain amount of oil is

For the first time in their history, Americans are actively working to conserve oil. What steps can you take to help in the effort to save energy?

left in the ground. When it is all used up, there will be no more. The United States was for many years the leading oil-producing nation in the world. Yet by the early 1980's, we were behind the Soviet Union and Saudi Arabia in oil production. Moreover, we had to import about 40 percent of our oil.

Some experts think the world's existing oil supply will run out by the year 2000. Of course, discovery of new oil deposits will give us an additional supply. To aid in the search for more oil, the federal government has leased drilling sites off our coastlines to oil companies. These companies seek oil beneath the ocean floor.

Conserving Oil

Another way for Americans to stretch our available oil resources is through conservation. **Conservation** is the safeguarding of our natural resources by using them wisely. The lowering of speed limits on highways to 55 miles (88 kilometers) an hour has saved gasoline. It has saved lives as well. The auto industry is cooperating by making smaller cars that use less gasoline.

Homeowners must also do their part to conserve heating oil. Lowering home temperatures, insulating attics and walls, and putting in storm windows and doors are some ways to save oil. It would also help if certain industries would stop using oil and substitute coal and other fuels. In the meantime, our nation must find new resources to take the place of oil.

A Shortage of Natural Gas

The second most widely used fuel in the United States is natural gas. It is usually found with petroleum. At one time, natural gas was burned off as it came out of the oil well. However, this clean-burning fuel found favor with homeowners and industry. It began to be used in even larger amounts. Over half the homes in our nation are now heated with gas. Industry relies on gas for about 30 percent of its energy needs.

During the 1960's, energy experts began warning that our natural gas supplies were running low. Production began to fall around 1974, creating a shortage of natural gas. Some producers blamed the gas shortage on the low price of natural gas. They claimed producers were unwilling to spend money to find new sources because the price was too low to make a profit.

The federal government had been keeping the price of natural gas lower than the world price. The availability of cheap fuel and the belief that the nation's resources would last forever led people to become wasteful. Now Americans no longer can afford to use fuel so carelessly.

To encourage Americans to save energy resources, the government decided to gradually lift price controls on gas. Still, even if prices rise and new sources of natural gas are found, American needs can be met for only a while. We must continue to use what we have now wisely and without waste.

Coal for the Future

The United States is fortunate in having a large supply of coal. We are thought to have enough coal to last for hundreds of years. The problem is that much of this coal lies deep in the earth where it was formed millions of years ago. Getting this coal out of the ground is difficult and dangerous, even with improved methods and machines. Coal is also expensive to transport.

Other deposits of coal lie near the surface and can be reached by stripping off the soil on top. The coal is then scooped up by machines. This **strip mining** has been severely criticized for its effects on the environment. It often leaves ugly scars on the land. Without trees or plants to hold it together, the soil washes down the hills and into streams. It muddies the water and sometimes clogs waterways.

To solve this problem, Congress passed a strip mining act in 1977. It requires mining companies to re-cover the area with soil, plants, and trees after they have removed the coal. This policy has been opposed by some people. They say it is too costly and raises the cost of coal.

Coal is looked upon by many as the best energy source for the near future—until other sources have been discovered or developed. To use coal, many industries will have to convert from oil and natural gas. However, it is difficult to burn coal without polluting the air. Researchers are looking for ways to prevent this from happening. They are trying to change coal into gas and oil so it will burn cleaner and more efficiently. In the meantime, many industries have installed expensive "scrubbing" equipment to prevent polluting materials from reaching our air.

Using Nuclear Energy

Nuclear plants were in operation in all regions of the United States by the early 1980's. Nuclear reactors run on a small amount of fuel. They produce large amounts of energy very efficiently. It was estimated that during the energy crisis of 1973, half a million jobs were saved because of nuclear energy.

Many people object to the building of more nuclear power plants. They are concerned about radioactivity and thermal pollution. **Radioactivity** is the giving off of rays that are dangerous to health. Nuclear plants may upset the balance of nature.

Public confidence in nuclear energy was shaken severely in 1979 by an accident at the nuclear-powered electric plant at Three Mile Island in Middletown, Pennsylvania. Because of a series of human and mechanical errors, the radioactive core of the reactor started to overheat. This caused some radioactive gas to escape into the air.

It was days before the danger of an explosion at Three Mile Island ended. The accident caused some Americans to question the wisdom of building more nuclear power plants. It also led them to question our ways of disposing of nuclear wastes. The wastes from nuclear plants remain radioactive and hazardous for thousands of years. We must find ways to store or treat these waste materials so that they will not be dangerous to the earth in the future. We also need to find ways to make nuclear plants less expensive to build.

Energy from the Sun

One of the most promising new sources of energy for the future is energy from the sun—**solar energy.** The sun gives off an enormous amount of energy, which cannot be used up anytime soon. Research on this type of energy is still in the beginning stages. Solar energy is already proving to be a possible way to heat and cool specially constructed homes and offices.

To encourage the study and use of solar energy, the federal government is giving grants to people who put solar heaters in their homes. This clean and plentiful source of power holds great promise for the future.

In the 1970's Americans suddenly found that gasoline supplies had become limited. What does this cartoon say about the possible causes of the shortage?

"Who Was Navigating, Anyhow?"

from *Herblock On All Fronts* (New American Library, 1980)

Other Sources of Energy

The continuing energy shortage has convinced many Americans that action is needed to avoid serious problems. We can no longer assume that our nation has an endless supply of energy. Therefore, private industry, government agencies, and university research centers have all been engaged in the search for new and practical sources of energy.

One possible source being investigated is **geothermal energy.** Scientists are trying to use the heat from deep within the earth to produce energy. They are also studying ways to expand our use of **hydroelectric power**—energy from water, including the movement of ocean tides and waves.

Some companies have started to produce **synfuels,** or synthetic fuels, although they are expensive to make. Most synfuel is made from oil shale, tar sands, and coal. Oil shale is a hard, light, gray rock that can be burned to produce oil and gas. Tar sands are sands that contain a gooey, tarlike oil. Synfuel can be made from coal by turning it into a liquid. This requires a lot of coal and huge, expensive plants.

A small but growing number of people use gasohol as fuel for their cars. **Gasohol** is made from gasoline and ethanol, an alcoholic product. Other possible sources of energy being investigated are more efficient windmills and the conversion of manure into methane gas. Some communities are burning biomass and changing it into energy. **Biomass** is the leftover or unused parts of plants and animals. It includes garbage and plants, shells, bushes, stems, and so on. These and other ideas must be studied if Americans are to have enough energy for the future.

Energy and the Environment

Americans must be careful about how our new energy resources are developed. Each time we develop an area, we may upset its ecological balance. Development, of course, continues to be necessary for the well-being of our nation. Today, however, Americans are determined that in the future our development will not harm the environment, as it often did in the past.

Even though our nation needs new sources of energy, many Americans do not want new nuclear plants, mines, or dams to be built near areas where they live. Nor do they want oil drilling sites off their coastal shores. Too many oil spills from tankers and barges have ruined our beaches. Over a million tons of oil a year have leaked into the oceans from tankers, barges, oil rigs, and coastal installations.

Because of the harm that has been done to the environment, the federal government and some states and local communities have passed laws to control new development. They require developers of some new plants, mines, and installations to study the effects their developments will have on the environment. Before any work can begin, they must prove they will meet the standards that have been set.

Development Versus Conservation

Some Americans are worried about the high costs of keeping our environment clean. They say the new safeguards and equipment make it too costly to build new plants or carry out new development. In order to have the energy and raw materials we need, some people think we must continue to use the land and its resources as we have been doing. They believe it may even be necessary to relax some of the standards we have set for a cleaner environment.

Conservationists say that continuing to pollute the environment or upset the balance of nature is dangerous. Their study of ecology has convinced them that what affects our land and its wildlife will eventually affect us. They also remind us that conservation is not a miserly saving of resources for some future time. It is "wise use" now.

CHECK-UP

Vocabulary

energy resources
conservation
strip mining
radioactivity
solar energy
geothermal energy
hydroelectric power
synfuels
gasohol
biomass

Review

1. What are some of the ways in which oil resources may be conserved?
2. What is the chief advantage of using natural gas instead of oil or coal?
3. What are the main arguments for and against continuing to use resources as we have in the past?

Discuss

Should we relax some of the standards that have been set for a cleaner environment? Why or why not?

4

Protecting Our Future

Over 100 years ago, in 1872, our government set aside a portion of northwestern Wyoming as a national park. Its forests, rivers, waterfalls, geysers, hot springs, and wildlife became the property of all Americans. The land was to remain in its natural state, to be enjoyed as a place of beauty and an area for outdoor recreation. The region was named Yellowstone National Park. Since then 38 other national parks have been reserved for recreational use.

Early Conservation Efforts

The National Park Service of the United States is only one of many agencies that help to preserve the natural resources of our country. Early in the 1900's, President Theodore

Roosevelt called a conference of the governors of the states to consider how best to conserve our land and resources.

The National Forest Service was established to supervise vast areas of our forest land to help conserve its timber. Later, laws were passed to limit the amount of oil and minerals that could be taken from the ground each year. Laws governing grazing practices helped stop the destruction of grasslands. The United States Department of Agriculture and state governments encouraged and helped farmers use soil conservation methods.

Under President Franklin D. Roosevelt, as you have read, a program of soil banks was established. Land was set aside to be improved and renewed. Dams were built to irrigate farmlands and control floods. The dams also provide electricity and furnish recreation areas.

These efforts, however, did not stop waste and pollution. By the 1950's, concerned citizens began to point out that an environmental crisis was at hand because of our misuse of resources. Today we know that firm conservation measures are needed.

Oil spilled from tankers or offshore wells can wash up on nearby beaches, ruining them for wildlife and for people. Here, volunteers clean up after an oil spill.

The Federal Government and Conservation

Congress has passed a number of laws to reduce pollution and restore the environment. The following were the most significant of these acts.

The National Environmental Policy Act. This 1969 act is sometimes called the Environmental Bill of Rights. It set up the Council on Environmental Quality to advise the President and oversee the nation's pollution controls. As a result of advice from this body, stricter laws were passed regulating pesticides, oil spills, and ocean dumping.

The 1969 act also provides that every federal agency must make and publish an environmental impact statement. This document must describe the expected effects on the environment of any project to be undertaken with federal aid.

Clean Air Acts. The first clean air act was passed in 1955 and was amended and strengthened several times. The clean air acts provide funds for research and set standards to be met by all industries and buildings. They also make it possible for the government to stop certain forms of air pollution. The automobile industry, for example, was told it must develop engines that give off reduced amounts of exhaust pollution.

Water Pollution Control Acts. As early as 1899, Congress passed a law making it a crime to dump refuse into any navigable waterway. This law was not strictly enforced until recent times. It has been strengthened by the Water Quality Act of 1965. This law sets standards of water quality for the interstate and coastal waters of the United States.

Again in 1966 and 1969, clean water acts were passed by Congress. Under these acts, the federal government has helped local communities build sewage treatment plants. In

1972 a law was passed to stop the discharge of wastes into our waters in the future.

Other Acts of Congress. Americans have become very aware of the problems of using and disposing of chemicals. These substances pollute our land, water, and air in ever-increasing amounts. Some chemicals are toxic, or poisonous. To protect our health, Congress passed the Resource Recovery and Conservation Act in 1976. It enables the government to check the use of chemicals by industry in all stages of production.

Americans in favor of a better environment have also brought pressure on Congress to preserve the beauty of the land and conserve its wildlife. The National Wild Rivers Act and the Wilderness Act set aside areas to be kept in their natural state for the pleasure of people.

Hundreds of plants and animals in the United States alone are threatened with extinction. Endangered species acts have listed wildlife, such as the whooping crane and the Utah prairie dog, that should be protected. Laws have been passed to keep them from dying out and to help them multiply.

The United States is also concerned with saving wildlife in other parts of the world. Our federal laws forbid the importation of the feathers and skins of many animals for use in clothing and in other unnecessary ways.

DID YOU KNOW THAT . . .

early conservation efforts saved the buffalo from dying out? The buffalo, or American bison, once roamed freely throughout the American West. According to one estimate, there were at least 100 million buffalo on the Great Plains as late as 1866. But then came thousands of hunters and the railroads. Mass killing of the herds followed. In 1889 a buffalo census revealed a shocking fact—there were only about 500 buffalo left.

A special society was formed in 1913-1914 to protect the animals. As a result, the buffalo population steadily increased. By 1933 there were 4,000 buffalo. Today about 15,000 buffalo live on lands set aside for them by the United States government.

The Environmental Protection Agency

Many federal bureaus that deal with pollution and other ecological problems have been organized under an independent agency. Called the **Environmental Protection Agency (EPA),** it reports directly to the President of the United States.

The EPA includes several offices responsible for controlling water and air pollution. It also oversees the management of solid wastes and radiation. In addition, the EPA deals with pesticide problems and carries out studies of ecological systems.

State and Local Activities

Every state government and most local governments have laws that help provide better environments for their citizens. These laws range from provisions for the preservation of the state's natural resources and scenic beauty to local laws governing trash disposal.

Some states have taken giant steps forward by studying large areas and starting programs to preserve or restore their ecological balance. Oregon, for example, has made its entire Pacific shoreline public property. It also has a program to preserve its natural

Why is it important to conserve natural areas like this one? What can you do to help safeguard our nation's remaining wilderness areas?

beauty. The state of New York has set up the Department of Environmental Conservation, with powers to set standards for purer air and water. It enforces these standards with heavy fines.

Some states have passed laws regulating the disposal of soda bottles. These laws require that soft drinks and some other liquids be sold in returnable bottles. Customers who return their bottles will receive back their deposit for them.

In our local communities, we can often see how well or how poorly the environment is being protected. Smoke, for example, is a sign of air pollution. Many communities have laws against open-air burning of leaves, grass, and trash. They also have laws against unnecessary smoke coming from chimneys and smokestacks.

One sign of water pollution that may be seen locally is an oil slick along our beaches. Another is dead fish in rivers, lakes, and bays, caused by chemical or thermal pollution. Local citizens may also be aware of unpleasant odors in the air, smog, and many other signs of air pollution. Litter often can be seen along roads and in streams. These conditions can be improved if citizens are willing to take action in their own communities.

Conservation and the Individual Citizen

Federal, state, and local laws cannot guarantee that our environment will be saved. Even huge amounts of money will not do the job. The future of our nation and our earth depends upon the cooperation of every inhabitant of this small planet. The task begins with you, the individual citizen. As more and more individuals become actively involved, hope for the future increases.

Here are some steps you can take now to help conserve America's resources:

1. Prevent waste of all kinds in your home and school. Don't waste food, water, electricity, or anything else.

2. Take part with your class in a conservation project, such as tree planting, cleaning up streams, or soil conservation.

3. Take an interest in the natural resources you find all around you in your community. Study ways in which they might be used more wisely.

4. Participate in recycling projects. Newspapers, cans, bottles, and other materials can be reused in new products. Find out about companies in your area that accept such materials, and join in collection projects.

5. Be careful of fires when in a forest or wooded area. Put out your campfire with water. Then shovel dirt on it to make sure it is out.

6. Do not destroy wildlife or damage forests or other public places. Vandalism is a serious crime against the environment.

7. Obey laws against open burning, littering, pollution, and other crimes against the environment.

8. Keep informed on ecological problems in your area. Make your opinion known by writing to your governmental representatives. Attend meetings and support petitions for a better environment.

9. Be aware of the sources of noise pollution, and join the fight for a quieter land.

10. Start thinking about what you can do to help keep the world a fit place for people, including you!

CHECK-UP

Vocabulary

Environmental Protection Agency

Review

1. Describe the various steps taken by the federal government to reduce pollution and restore the environment.
2. Why is the National Environmental Policy Act sometimes called the Environmental Bill of Rights?
3. How can the average citizen help conserve our natural resources?

Discuss

Do you think the government should have the power to order companies to install equipment that would lessen pollution? Why or why not?

CHAPTER SUMMARY

The United States is rich in natural resources. Yet many of our practices have upset nature's balance. Air and water pollution are among our greatest problems. We have also become aware of the dangers of noise and chemical pollution. Getting rid of pollution will be costly, but the cost must be met.

To understand the effects of pollution, we must understand ecology—the study of nature's balance and the relationship between all parts of the environment. Damage to any part of nature may result in damage to all of it, including humans.

Unwise development of land and the misuse of natural resources have resulted in the destruction of some wildlife and scenic areas. They also have upset the balance of nature. Problems have been caused by oil spills, careless mining and land use, nitrates, and the use of DDT and other pesticides. In addition, we face shortages of natural resources, especially of energy sources such as oil and natural gas. Besides conserving these resources, Americans are turning to other energy sources, such as nuclear power, solar power, and geothermal energy.

To protect our nation's future, federal, state, and local laws have been passed to ensure the wise use of natural resources. However, it is up to individual citizens to do their share and to work toward a better environment, now and for the future.

CIVICS SKILLS: Comparing Points of View

We travel together, passengers on a small spaceship. We are dependent on its easily damaged supplies of air and soil. We are kept alive only by the care, the work, and I will say the love, we give to our fragile craft—planet earth.

These thoughts were expressed in 1965 by an American ambassador to the United Nations. Less than 10 years later, Americans had to wait in long lines for one of earth's important sources of energy—gasoline.

To help relieve the gasoline shortage, Congress passed the Emergency Highway Energy Conservation Act in 1974. According to this law, all states had to adopt a 55 mile-per-hour (m.p.h.) speed limit. Since automobiles tend to run more efficiently and more safely at 55 m.p.h. than at higher speeds, Congress hoped this law would save both gas and lives.

Response to the 55 m.p.h. law has been mixed. For example, some Americans want the law repealed, or canceled. Others want it enforced more strictly. Whenever people disagree over an issue, they are said to have conflicting points of view. Before you can decide whether to support or oppose the 55 m.p.h. law, you will need to determine what each side is saying and why.

Studying the Arguments

The first step in comparing points of view is to identify the arguments offered in defense of the various positions. You might find it helpful to list each set of arguments in a separate column on a piece of paper. This will make it easier for you to compare all sides of an issue.

Comparing points of view means looking for areas of agreement and areas of disagreement. Areas of disagreement highlight the real basis for debate over an issue. Areas of agreement suggest possibilities for compromise. For instance, if you read the boxed material below, you'll discover that Charlie and Gail share one opinion in common. They both want to conserve earth's natural resources. However, they don't agree about one conservation measure—the national speed limit.

Practicing What You've Learned

1. What arguments does Charlie offer in support of the national speed limit? What arguments does Gail offer to oppose it?
2. What are their main areas of disagreement?

CHARLIE'S POINT OF VIEW: I support the idea of a 55 m.p.h. speed limit. By driving slower, Americans are saving about 3.5 billion gallons (13 billion liters) of gasoline a year. Even more important, the lower speed limit saves thousands of lives. We're not only cutting back on our oil imports, we're also driving more safely. Furthermore, we're doing our part to conserve a valuable source of energy.

The oil shortages of the 1970's taught us an important lesson: We live in a world of limited natural resources. By passing the 55 m.p.h. law, Congress acted in the best interests of our entire nation.

GAIL'S POINT OF VIEW: Sure I want to protect the earth's natural resources. Who doesn't? I just don't think a national speed limit is the best way to do it. First, we're saving less than one percent of the total fuel used in the United States each year. Second, we're placing a hardship on those Americans who live in states with long stretches of open highway.

In my opinion, the millions of dollars that it takes to enforce this law could be spent on other, more effective conservation measures. This is a matter in which the states are better able to decide which speed limits are not only safe, but fair.

CHAPTER REVIEW

Vocabulary

On a separate piece of paper, write the terms that are listed below. Choose the definition that best fits each term, and write the correct definition beside the term it matches.

environment	pollution
renewable resource	water cycle
ecology	balance of nature
soil bank	conservation
geothermal energy	radioactivity

1. Causing any part of our environment to become dirty, impure, or unfit for use.
2. The way in which all living things relate to one another.
3. A source of energy produced by using heat from deep within the earth.
4. Natural resource that can be purified and reused or replaced.
5. Fields that are set aside and not farmed so they will be renewed and improved.
6. The process of water falling to the earth, being absorbed into the earth and streams, evaporating, returning to the atmosphere, condensing, and falling to earth again.
7. The world around us.
8. The wise use of natural resources.
9. The study of how all living things relate to each other and their environment.
10. Giving off rays that are dangerous to health.

Check-Up

1. What is ecology and why is it important?
2. Give an example of how the balance of nature works.
3. What is the purpose of crop rotation and contour farming?
4. How have fertilizers and pesticides caused problems for the environment?
5. What are the causes of air pollution? How could air pollution change the earth's climate?
6. Why has water supply become a problem in the United States?
7. What are some of the remedies for water, air, and noise pollution?
8. What are some of the possible new sources of energy that are currently being investigated?
9. Why has the federal government set up national parks and seashores?

Civics Skills

Read the letters to the editor that appear on the editorial page of your local newspaper or at the front of a popular newsmagazine. Clip out two letters that express different points of view on some aspect of environmental protection. Use these letters to answer the following questions.

1. What is the main issue in both letters?
2. What arguments are used to defend each position?
3. Based on a comparison of these arguments, why does there seem to be disagreement over this issue?
4. With which letter do you most agree? Or do you have a different point of view? Explain your answer.

Citizenship and You

1. Conduct a panel discussion on the topic, "Ecological Problems and Practices in Our State."
2. A committee can prepare posters, charts, graphs, and maps for a bulletin board display on the problems of pollution. The committee might also cut out political cartoons on pollution from your local newspaper.
3. Groups within your class may take part in local conservation projects. Some groups have improved their school grounds, gathered papers and cans for recycling, or planted trees.

UNIT EIGHT REVIEW

Reviewing the Facts

Write your answers to the items below on a separate piece of paper.

1. Complete this sentence: The rights of citizenship that all Americans are entitled to are called ________.
2. All of the following have helped to cause problems for American cities *except*
   a. the decrease in the city's tax base.
   b. rising employment in the city.
   c. the departure of middle-class families from the city.
   d. the decline of mass transit systems.
3. Which *two* of the following might be examples of minority groups working for equal rights?
   a. a senior citizens' association
   b. a lawyers' organization
   c. the American Medical Association
   d. an organization for the handicapped
4. Correct the underlined part of this sentence: During a trial, the government's side of the case is the defense.
5. Drug abuse is a problem that
   a. harms only the person who actually uses the drugs.
   b. refers only to the use of illegal drugs.
   c. has contributed to the rising crime rate.
   d. none of the above.
6. The taking of hostages by a political group is an example of
   a. quarantine.
   b. terrorism.
   c. arson.
   d. vandalism.
7. When the police suspect a person of a crime, several steps must occur before that person can be convicted. Some are listed below. In what order would the following steps occur?
   a. indictment d. preliminary hearing
   b. arrest e. booking
   c. trial f. arraignment
8. The way in which all living things relate to one another is called
   a. conservation.
   b. ecology.
   c. the balance of nature.
   d. the environment.
9. Complete this sentence: The types of buildings that can be constructed in a neighborhood are regulated by local ________.
10. Complete this sentence: Commuter trains and buses are two examples of ________.
11. Complete this sentence: Smog and high noise levels are examples of ________.

Applying What You Know

1. As the crime rate has gone up, the issue of capital punishment has been much debated. Write a paragraph presenting arguments in favor of capital punishment. Then write a paragraph presenting the arguments against it.
2. The earth has often been compared to a spaceship. Describe three ways in which the earth is like a spaceship.

Expanding Your Knowledge

Colby, C., *Police: Skill and Science Combat Crime,* Coward-McCann. A well-illustrated book on modern police methods.

Leinwand, Gerald, *Civil Rights and Liberties,* Pocket Books. Interesting readings on the struggle for freedom of expression, equality, and justice.

Swiger, Elinor Porter, *The Law in Your Everyday Life,* Prentice-Hall. Laws—how they are enforced and relate to young people.

Watson, Jane Werner, *Alternate Energy Sources,* Franklin Watts. A discussion of solar, wind, geothermal, and other new forms of energy.

Reference Section

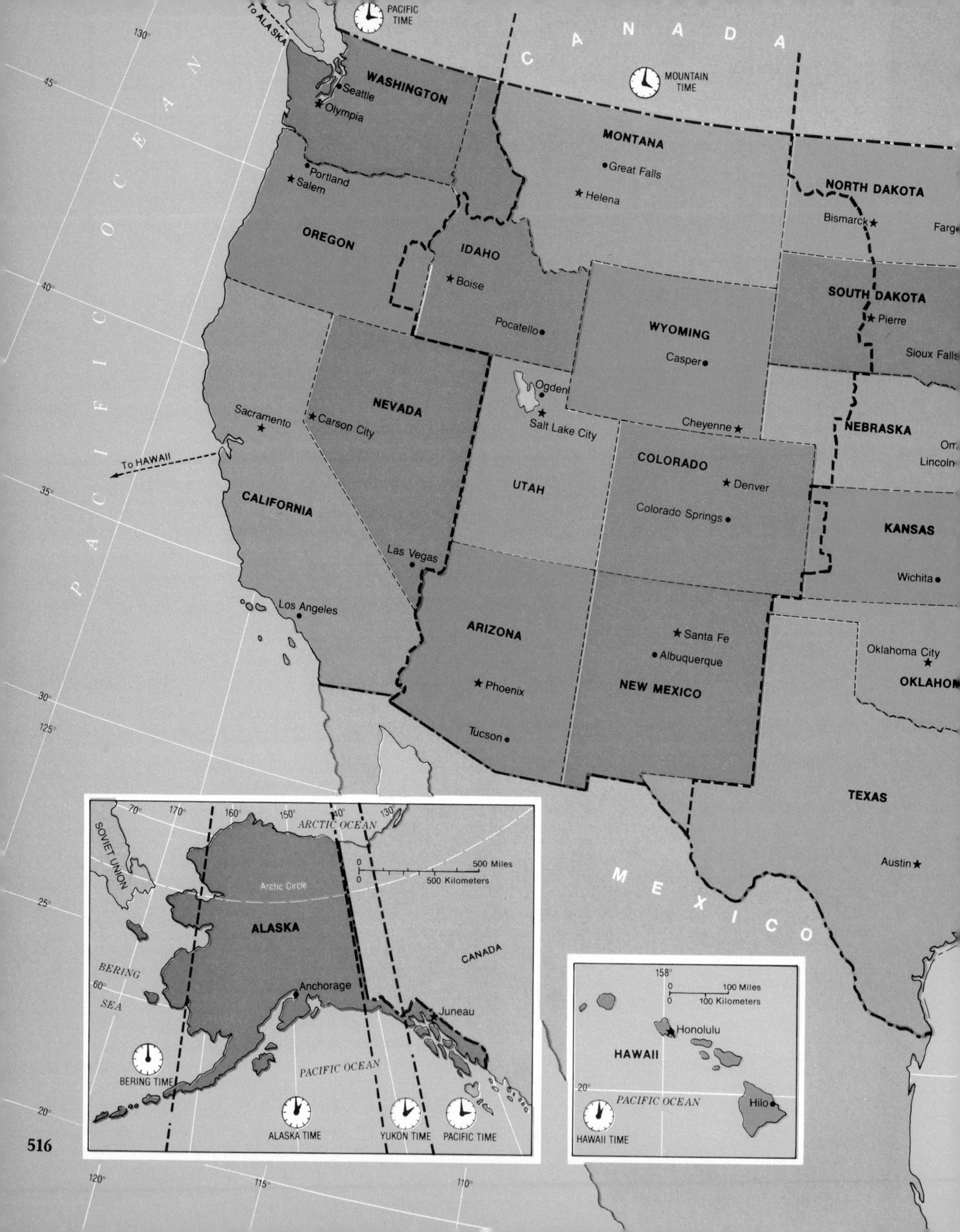

PACIFIC TIME
MOUNTAIN TIME
To ALASKA
CANADA
PACIFIC OCEAN
WASHINGTON
Seattle
Olympia
MONTANA
Great Falls
Helena
NORTH DAKOTA
Bismarck
Farg
Portland
Salem
OREGON
IDAHO
Boise
Pocatello
WYOMING
Casper
SOUTH DAKOTA
Pierre
Sioux Falls
NEVADA
Carson City
Ogden
Salt Lake City
Cheyenne
NEBRASKA
Lincoln
Sacramento
To HAWAII
CALIFORNIA
UTAH
COLORADO
Denver
Colorado Springs
KANSAS
Wichita
Las Vegas
Los Angeles
ARIZONA
Phoenix
Tucson
NEW MEXICO
Santa Fe
Albuquerque
Oklahoma City
OKLAHOM
TEXAS
Austin
MEXICO
130°
45°
40°
35°
30°
125°
25°
20°
120°
115°
110°
SOVIET UNION
ARCTIC OCEAN
Arctic Circle
500 Miles
500 Kilometers
ALASKA
CANADA
BERING SEA
Anchorage
Juneau
PACIFIC OCEAN
BERING TIME
ALASKA TIME
YUKON TIME
PACIFIC TIME
170°
160°
150°
140°
130°
60°
158°
100 Miles
100 Kilometers
HAWAII
Honolulu
Hilo
PACIFIC OCEAN
HAWAII TIME

The United States
CENTRAL TIME
EASTERN TIME
CANADA
Lake Superior
Lake Michigan
Lake Huron
Lake Ontario
Lake Erie
MICHIGAN
MINNESOTA
St. Paul
Minneapolis
WISCONSIN
Madison
Milwaukee
Lansing
Detroit
IOWA
Cedar Rapids
Des Moines
Chicago
ILLINOIS
Springfield
Ft. Wayne
Indianapolis
INDIANA
OHIO
Columbus
Cleveland
PENNSYLVANIA
Harrisburg
Philadelphia
Wilmington
Baltimore
Washington, D.C.
Annapolis
MD
DE
Dover
NJ
Trenton
Newark
New York
NEW YORK
Albany
Bridgeport
Hartford
CT
RI
Providence
MA
Boston
NH
Concord
Manchester
VT
Montpelier
Burlington
MAINE
Augusta
Portland
WV
Charleston
Huntington
VIRGINIA
Richmond
Norfolk
KENTUCKY
Frankfort
Louisville
Topeka
Jefferson City
St. Louis
MISSOURI
Tulsa
Fort Smith
Little Rock
ARKANSAS
TENNESSEE
Nashville
Memphis
NORTH CAROLINA
Raleigh
Charlotte
SOUTH CAROLINA
Columbia
Charleston
GEORGIA
Atlanta
Columbus
ALABAMA
Birmingham
Montgomery
MISSISSIPPI
Jackson
Meridian
LOUISIANA
Baton Rouge
New Orleans
Houston
FLORIDA
Tallahassee
Jacksonville
GULF OF MEXICO
ATLANTIC OCEAN
CUBA
N
E
S
W
National capital
State capital
Major city other than capital
United States standard time zones are indicated by clocks (When it is 12:00 noon in western Alaska, it is 6:00 PM along the eastern coast of the United States.)
Boundaries of time zones
West longitude
North latitude
0 500 Miles
0 800 Kilometers
95°
90°
85°
80°
75°
70°
60°
45°
40°
35°
30°
25°
20°
65°

ARCTIC OCEAN
SOVIET UNION
ALASKA
CANADA
BERING SEA
ALEUTIAN ISLANDS
NORTH
ASIA
KOREA
JAPAN
CHINA
UNITED
PACIFIC
TIBET
INDIA
MIDWAY IS.
MEXICO
Tropic of Cancer
BURMA
WAKE I.
HAWAII
MARIANA IS.
VIETNAM
PHILIPPINES
JOHNSTON I.
GUAM
MARSHALL IS.
YAP IS.
OCEAN
MAYLAYSIA
KINGMAN REEF
PALMYRA I.
PALAU IS.
CAROLINE IS.
HOWLAND I.
BAKER I.
JARVIS I.
Equator
INDONESIA
AMERICAN SAMOA
INDIAN OCEAN
Tropic of Capricorn
AUSTRALIA
NEW ZEALAND
0
2000 Miles
0
3200 Kilometers

The United States and the World
GREENLAND
ICELAND
Arctic Circle
NORWAY
SWEDEN
FINLAND
ASIA
GREAT BRITAIN
IRELAND
GER.
POLAND
SOVIET UNION
CANADA
AMERICA
EUROPE
FRANCE
STATES
PORTUGAL
SPAIN
ITALY
GREECE
TURKEY
ATLANTIC
TUNISIA
MOROCCO
ISRAEL
SYRIA
IRAQ
IRAN
AFGHANISTAN
PAKISTAN
ALGERIA
LIBYA
EGYPT
SAUDI ARABIA
INDIA
CUBA
PUERTO RICO
VIRGIN IS.
MAURITANIA
MALI
NIGER
CHAD
AFRICA
SUDAN
CENTRAL AMERICA
OCEAN
GHANA
NIGERIA
ETHIOPIA
VENEZUELA
LIBERIA
PANAMA CANAL
COLOMBIA
SOMALIA
INDIAN
KENYA
ECUADOR
ZAIRE
OCEAN
TANZANIA
SOUTH
AMERICA
PERU
ANGOLA
BOLIVIA
BRAZIL
MADAGASCAR
PARAGUAY
CHILE
REPUBLIC OF SOUTH AFRICA
URUGUAY
ARGENTINA
N
W
E
S
United States
VIRGIN IS.
U.S. possessions and other areas associated with the U.S. (underlined)
UN trusteeship area administrated by the U.S.
International Date Line

AMERICAN PRESIDENTS

1
George Washington
1732–1799
Elected from: Virginia
In office: 1789–1797

2
John Adams
1735–1826
Elected from: Massachusetts
Federalist
In office: 1797–1801

3
Thomas Jefferson
1743–1826
Elected from: Virginia
Democratic-Republican
In office: 1801–1809

4
James Madison
1751–1836
Elected from: Virginia
Democratic-Republican
In office: 1809–1817

5
James Monroe
1758–1831
Elected from: Virginia
Democratic-Republican
In office: 1817–1825

6
John Quincy Adams
1767–1848
Elected from: Massachusetts
National-Republican
In office: 1825–1829

7
Andrew Jackson
1767–1845
Elected from: Tennessee
Democrat
In office: 1829–1837

8
Martin Van Buren
1782–1862
Elected from: New York
Democrat
In office: 1837–1841

9
William Henry Harrison
1773–1841
Elected from: Ohio
Whig
In office: 1841

10
John Tyler
1790–1862
Elected from: Virginia
Whig
In office: 1841–1845

11
James K. Polk
1795–1849
Elected from: Tennessee
Democrat
In office: 1845–1849

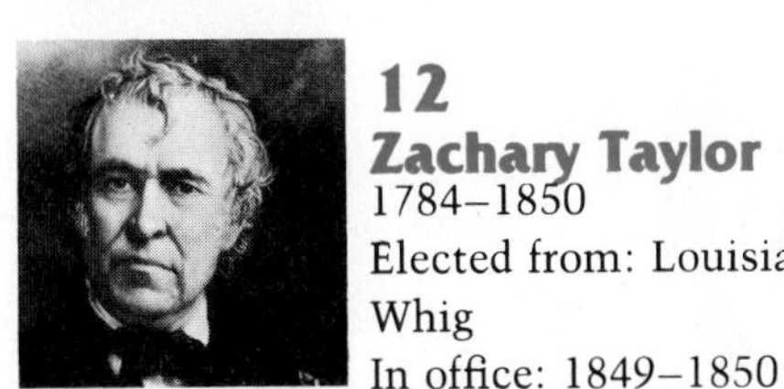

12
Zachary Taylor
1784–1850
Elected from: Louisiana
Whig
In office: 1849–1850

13
Millard Fillmore
1800–1874
Elected from: New York
Whig
In office: 1850–1853

14
Franklin Pierce
1804–1869
Elected from: New Hampshire
Democrat
In office: 1853–1857

15
James Buchanan
1791–1868
Elected from: Pennsylvania
Democrat
In office: 1857–1861

16
Abraham Lincoln
1809–1865
Elected from: Illinois
Republican
In office: 1861–1865

17
Andrew Johnson
1808–1875
Elected from: Tennessee
Republican
In office: 1865–1869

18
Ulysses S. Grant
1822–1885
Elected from: Illinois
Republican
In office: 1869–1877

19
Rutherford B. Hayes
1822–1893
Elected from: Ohio
Republican
In office: 1877–1881

20
James A. Garfield
1831–1881
Elected from: Ohio
Republican
In office: 1881

21
Chester A. Arthur
1830–1886
Elected from: New York
Republican
In office: 1881–1885

22
Grover Cleveland
1837–1908
Elected from: New York
Democrat
In office: 1885–1889

23
Benjamin Harrison
1833–1901
Elected from: Indiana
Republican
In office: 1889–1893

24
Grover Cleveland
1837–1908
Elected from: New York
Democrat
In office: 1893–1897

25
William McKinley
1843–1901
Elected from: Ohio
Republican
In office: 1897–1901

26
Theodore Roosevelt
1858–1919
Elected from: New York
Republican
In office: 1901–1909

27
William H. Taft
1857–1930
Elected from: Ohio
Republican
In office: 1909–1913

28
Woodrow Wilson
1856–1924
Elected from: New Jersey
Democrat
In office: 1913–1921

29
Warren G. Harding
1865–1923
Elected from: Ohio
Republican
In office: 1921–1923

30
Calvin Coolidge
1872–1933
Elected from: Massachusetts
Republican
In office: 1923–1929

31
Herbert C. Hoover
1874–1964
Elected from: California
Republican
In office: 1929–1933

32
Franklin D. Roosevelt
1882–1945
Elected from: New York
Democrat
In office: 1933–1945

33
Harry S. Truman
1884–1972
Elected from: Missouri
Democrat
In office: 1945–1953

34
Dwight D. Eisenhower
1890–1969
Elected from: Pennsylvania
Republican
In office: 1953–1961

35
John F. Kennedy
1917–1963
Elected from: Massachusetts
Democrat
In office: 1961–1963

36
Lyndon B. Johnson
1908–1973
Elected from: Texas
Democrat
In office: 1963–1969

37
Richard M. Nixon
1913–
Elected from: New York
Republican
In office: 1969–1974

38
Gerald R. Ford
1913–
Elected from: Michigan
Republican
In office: 1974–1977

39
Jimmy Carter
1924–
Elected from: Georgia
Democrat
In office: 1977–1981

40
Ronald W. Reagan
1911–
Elected from: California
Republican
In office: 1981–

OUR 50 STATES

The number in parentheses is the order in which each state was admitted to the Union. For the original 13 states, this is the order in which each state approved the Constitution. Population figures are based on the 1980 census. The nickname of each state is in *italics.*

Alabama (22)
Admitted to Union: 1819
Capital: Montgomery
Population: 3,890,061
Yellowhammer State

Alaska (49)
Admitted to Union: 1959
Capital: Juneau
Population: 400,481
The Last Frontier

Arizona (48)
Admitted to Union: 1912
Capital: Phoenix
Population: 2,717,866
Grand Canyon State

Arkansas (25)
Admitted to Union: 1836
Capital: Little Rock
Population: 2,285,513
Land of Opportunity

California (31)
Admitted to Union: 1850
Capital: Sacramento
Population: 23,668,562
Golden State

Colorado (38)
Admitted to Union: 1876
Capital: Denver
Population: 2,888,834
Centennial State

Connecticut (5)
Admitted to Union: 1788
Capital: Hartford
Population: 3,107,576
Nutmeg State

Delaware (1)
Admitted to Union: 1787
Capital: Dover
Population: 595,225
First State

Florida (27)
Admitted to Union: 1845
Capital: Tallahassee
Population: 9,739,992
Sunshine State

Georgia (4)
Admitted to Union: 1788
Capital: Atlanta
Population: 5,464,265
Peach State

Hawaii (50)
Admitted to Union: 1959
Capital: Honolulu
Population: 965,000
Aloha State

Idaho (43)
Admitted to Union: 1890
Capital: Boise
Population: 943,935
Gem State

Illinois (21)
Admitted to Union: 1818
Capital: Springfield
Population: 11,418,461
Prairie State

Indiana (19)
Admitted to Union: 1816
Capital: Indianapolis
Population: 5,490,179
Hoosier State

Iowa (29)
Admitted to Union: 1846
Capital: Des Moines
Population: 2,913,387
Hawkeye State

Kansas (34)
Admitted to Union: 1861
Capital: Topeka
Population: 2,363,208
Sunflower State

Kentucky (15)
Admitted to Union: 1792
Capital: Frankfort
Population: 3,661,433
Bluegrass State

Louisiana (18)
Admitted to Union: 1812
Capital: Baton Rouge
Population: 4,203,972
Pelican State

Maine (23)
Admitted to Union: 1820
Capital: Augusta
Population: 1,124,660
Pine Tree State

Maryland (7)
Admitted to Union: 1788
Capital: Annapolis
Population: 4,216,446
Free State

Massachusetts (6)
Admitted to Union: 1788
Capital: Boston
Population: 5,737,037
Bay State

Michigan (26)
Admitted to Union: 1837
Capital: Lansing
Population: 9,258,344
Wolverine State

Minnesota (32)
Admitted to Union: 1858
Capital: St. Paul
Population: 4,077,148
North Star State

Mississippi (20)
Admitted to Union: 1817
Capital: Jackson
Population: 2,520,638
Magnolia State

Missouri (24)
Admitted to Union: 1821
Capital: Jefferson City
Population: 4,917,444
Show Me State

Montana (41)
Admitted to Union: 1889
Capital: Helena
Population: 786,690
Treasure State

Nebraska (37)
Admitted to Union: 1867
Capital: Lincoln
Population: 1,570,006
Cornhusker State

Nevada (36)
Admitted to Union: 1864
Capital: Carson City
Population: 799,184
Sagebrush State

New Hampshire (9)
Admitted to Union: 1788
Capital: Concord
Population: 920,610
Granite State

New Jersey (3)
Admitted to Union: 1787
Capital: Trenton
Population: 7,364,158
Garden State

New Mexico (47)
Admitted to Union: 1912
Capital: Santa Fe
Population: 1,299,968
Land of Enchantment

New York (11)
Admitted to Union: 1788
Capital: Albany
Population: 17,557,288
Empire State

North Carolina (12)
Admitted to Union: 1789
Capital: Raleigh
Population: 5,874,429
Tar Heel State

North Dakota (39)
Admitted to Union: 1889
Capital: Bismarck
Population: 652,695
Sioux State

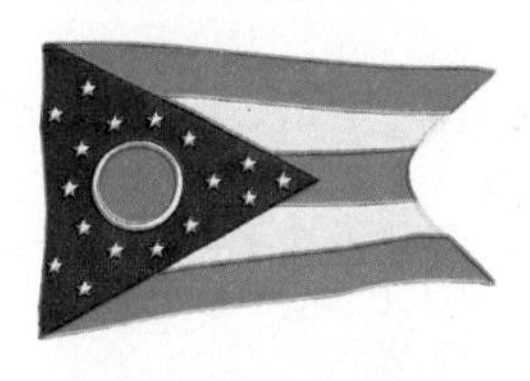

Ohio (17)
Admitted to Union: 1803
Capital: Columbus
Population: 10,797,419
Buckeye State

Oklahoma (46)
Admitted to Union: 1907
Capital: Oklahoma City
Population: 3,025,266
Sooner State

Oregon (33)
Admitted to Union: 1859
Capital: Salem
Population: 2,632,663
Beaver State

Pennsylvania (2)
Admitted to Union: 1787
Capital: Harrisburg
Population: 11,866,728
Keystone State

Rhode Island (13)
Admitted to Union: 1790
Capital: Providence
Population: 947,154
Ocean State

South Carolina (8)
Admitted to Union: 1788
Capital: Columbia
Population: 3,119,208
Palmetto State

South Dakota (40)
Admitted to Union: 1889
Capital: Pierre
Population: 690,178
Coyote State

Tennessee (16)
Admitted to Union: 1796
Capital: Nashville
Population: 4,590,750
Volunteer State

Texas (28)
Admitted to Union: 1845
Capital: Austin
Population: 14,228,383
Lone Star State

Utah (45)
Admitted to Union: 1896
Capital: Salt Lake City
Population: 1,461,037
Beehive State

Vermont (14)
Admitted to Union: 1791
Capital: Montpelier
Population: 511,456
Green Mountain State

Virginia (10)
Admitted to Union: 1788
Capital: Richmond
Population: 5,346,279
Old Dominion

Washington (42)
Admitted to Union: 1889
Capital: Olympia
Population: 4,130,163
Evergreen State

West Virginia (35)
Admitted to Union: 1863
Capital: Charleston
Population: 1,949,644
Mountain State

Wisconsin (30)
Admitted to Union: 1848
Capital: Madison
Population: 4,705,335
Badger State

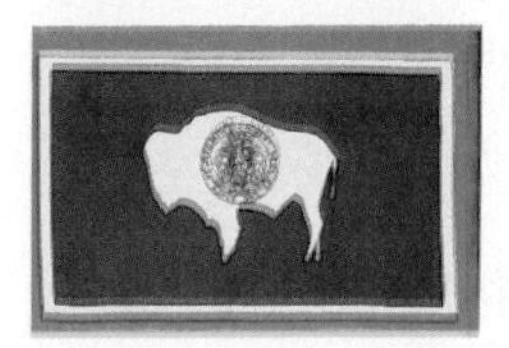

Wyoming (44)
Admitted to Union: 1890
Capital: Cheyenne
Population: 470,816
Equality State

THE AMERICAN FLAG

The American flag is a symbol of our country. It is recognized instantly, whether it is a big banner waving in the wind or a tiny emblem worn in a lapel. The flag is so important that it is a major theme of our national anthem, "The Star-Spangled Banner." One of the most popular names for our flag is the "Stars and Stripes." It is also known as "Old Glory."

The Meaning of the Flag

The American flag has 13 stripes—7 red and 6 white. In the upper left corner is the union—50 white stars against a blue background.

The 13 stripes stand for the original 13 states, and the 50 stars represent the states of the nation today. According to the United States Department of State, the colors of the flag are symbolic, too:

Red stands for courage.
White symbolizes purity.
Blue is the color of vigilance,
perseverance, and justice.

Early American Flags

Before the United States declared its independence in 1776, the colonies used many different flags. A favorite colonial design of the southern colonies was a flag with a rattlesnake and the motto, "Don't Tread on Me." Another colonial symbol was the pine tree, which symbolized the strength and courage of New England. The first flag to represent all the colonies was called the "Continental Colors." It had 13 alternating red and white stripes and the British flag at the upper left (showing that the colonies belonged to Great Britain).

Adopting the Stars and Stripes

After the Declaration of Independence was adopted, the Continental Congress no longer wanted the British flag to be part of the American flag. On June 14, 1777, the Congress decided that the flag of the United States should have 13 red and white stripes and 13 stars "representing a new constellation." According to legend, a Philadelphia seamstress named Betsy Ross helped design this flag and made the first one. The story is probably not true, although she did make other flags.

After Vermont and Kentucky joined the Union, in the 1790's, two additional stars and stripes were added to the flag. As you can

imagine, adding a stripe for every new state would have created problems. So in 1818 Congress ruled that the number of stripes should remain at 13, with a star added for each new state.

Saluting the Flag

The United States, like other countries, has a flag code, or rules for displaying and honoring the flag. For example, all those present should stand at attention facing the flag and saluting when it is being raised or lowered or when it is carried past them in a parade. A man wearing a hat should take if off and hold it with his right hand over his heart. All women and hatless men should stand with their right hands over their hearts.

Displaying the Flag

Our flag should not be displayed in bad weather. It should be displayed outdoors only from sunrise to sunset, except on certain occasions. In a few special places, however, it is always allowed to be flown day and night. When flown at night, the flag must be spotlighted.

Near a speaker's platform, the flag should occupy the place of honor at the speaker's right. When carried in a parade with other flags, the American flag should be on the marching right or in front at the center. When flying with state flags, the national flag must be at the center and the highest point. In a group of national flags, all should be of equal size and be flown from staffs of equal height.

The flag should never touch the ground, the floor, or water. It should not be marked with any insignia, pictures, or words. Nor should it be used in any disrespectful way—as an advertising decoration, for instance. The flag should never be dipped to honor any person or thing.

Special Occasions

When the flag is flown upside down, with the stars at the bottom, it is a signal of distress. Flown at half-staff, it is a symbol of mourning. It may be draped over the casket of a person who has served in the United States armed forces. After the funeral, this flag is folded and given to a family member.

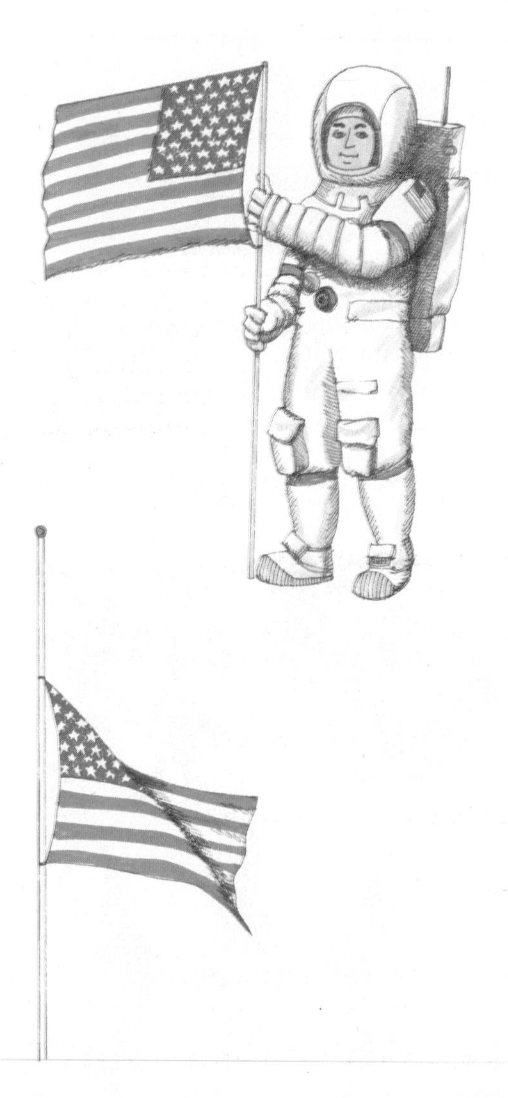

One of the best-known occasions for displaying the American flag was the first landing of Americans on the moon in July 1969. The astronauts placed a metal flag there because the moon has no atmosphere, and thus no wind. As far as we know, the flag is still there.

The Pledge of Allegiance

The Pledge of Allegiance was written by a Massachusetts magazine editor named Francis Bellamy in 1892. (The words "under God" were added in 1954.) These are the words:

> I pledge allegiance to the Flag of the United States of America and to the Republic for which it stands, one Nation under God, indivisible, with liberty and justice for all.

Civilians should say the Pledge with their right hands on their hearts. People in the armed forces give the military salute. By saying the Pledge of Allegiance, we promise loyalty ("pledge allegiance") to our nation and its ideals.

The "Star-Spangled Banner"

The "Star-Spangled Banner" is the national anthem of the United States. It was written by Francis Scott Key during the War of 1812. While being held aboard a British ship on September 13, 1814, Key watched the bombardment of the American Fort McHenry at Baltimore. The attack lasted for 25 hours. The smoke was so thick that Key could not tell who had won. Then the air cleared, and Key saw the American flag still flying over the fort. To express his joy, he wrote most of the words of the song in a few minutes on the back of an envelope. "The Star-Spangled Banner" is sung to music written by John Stafford Smith.

Star-Spangled Banner

I

Oh, say can you see by the dawn's early light

What so proudly we hailed at the twilight's last gleaming?

Whose bright stripes and bright stars through the perilous fight,

O'er the ramparts we watched were so gallantly streaming?

And the rocket's red glare, the bombs bursting in air,

Gave proof through the night that our flag was still there.

Oh, says does that star-spangled banner yet wave

O'er the land of the free and the home of the brave?

II

On the shore, dimly seen through the mists of the deep,

Where the foe's haughty host in dread silence reposes,

What is that which the breeze, o'er the towering steep,

As it fitfully blows, half conceals, half discloses?

Now it catches the gleam of the morning's first beam,

In full glory reflected now shines in the stream:

'Tis the star-spangled banner! Oh, long may it wave

O'er the land of the free and the home of the brave!

III

And where is that band who so vauntingly swore

That the havoc of war and the battle's confusion,

A home and a country should leave us no more!

Their blood has washed out their foul footstep's pollution.

No refuge could save the hireling and slave

From terror of flight, or the gloom of the grave:

And the star-spangled banner in triumph doth wave

O'er the land of the free and the home of the brave!

IV

Oh! thus be it ever, when freemen shall stand

Between their loved home and the war's desolation!

Blest with victory and peace, may the heaven rescued land

Praise the Power that hath made and preserved us a nation.

Then conquer we must, when our cause it is just,

And this be our motto: "In God is our trust."

And the star-spangled banner in triumph shall wave

O'er the land of the free and the home of the brave!

AMERICAN HOLIDAYS

Holidays are special occasions usually marked by celebrations and vacations from school and work. Religious holidays are celebrated by people of various faiths. For example, Christians celebrate Christmas (marking the birth of Christ) and Jews celebrate Rosh Hashanah (marking the beginning of the Jewish New Year). On legal holidays, banks, schools, and most government and business offices are closed.

National holidays usually commemorate, or remind people of, a special event in a nation's past. Strictly speaking, the United States has no official national holidays. It is up to the states, not the federal government, to determine which days will be celebrated. But the federal government influences these by designating the days to be observed in Washington, D.C., and by all federal employees. Along with New Year's Day (January 1) and Christmas (December 25), the following five legal holidays are observed throughout the United States.

Washington's Birthday
(third Monday in February)

February 22 is the day we think of as George Washington's birthday. However, he was actually born on February 11 according to the calendar in use in 1732, the year of his birth. In the 1970's the celebration of his birthday was changed to the third Monday in February. Some states observe this day as President's Day.

Cherries and hatchets are traditionally associated with the celebration of Washington's birthday. This is because of a legend made popular by an early biographer of Washington. As a young boy, according to tradition, George cut down his father's cherry tree. When questioned George confessed, saying, "Father, I cannot tell a lie."

Independence Day
(July 4)

Fireworks, parades, and picnics mark this holiday, regarded as the birthday of our country. It commemorates the day in 1776 when the Continental Congress adopted the Declaration of Independence. Even then John Adams, one of the leaders in the struggle for American independence, said of the day: "I am apt to believe that it will be celebrated by succeeding generations as the great anniversary festival." Time has proved him to be right.

Labor Day
(first Monday in September)

A union leader, Peter J. McGuire, first suggested a holiday to honor working people. Various states observed the day in the 1880's. It has been celebrated by the whole nation since 1894. Labor Day is marked with parades or speeches honoring workers. It also has come to mean the end of summer and is celebrated with a last day at the beach, a cookout, or community festivities.

Veterans Day
(November 11)

This holiday is unusual because it is also a special day in many European nations. Formerly called Armistice Day, it originally marked the armistice, or truce, that ended World War I on November 11, 1918. In 1954 the United States changed the observance to honor all the men and women who have served in the armed forces. Military parades are common on Veterans Day. Special services are also held at the Tomb of the Unknown Soldier in Arlington National Cemetery, near the nation's capital.

Thanksgiving Day
(fourth Thursday in November)

For hundreds of years, people have held autumn festivals to give thanks for a good harvest. The American celebration of Thanksgiving began with the Pilgrims in Plymouth Colony. They observed the first Thanksgiving in 1621 to mark the end of their first difficult year in America and the gathering of the harvest. Their celebration lasted three days. During that time the Pilgrims and their Indian guests feasted on wild turkey and venison.

Thereafter, many communities observed a day of Thanksgiving at various times in the fall. Finally, in 1863, President Abraham Lincoln declared that the day should be celebrated nationally. Thanksgiving Day is, above all, a time for families. They meet for a festive dinner to give thanks for what they have.

AMERICAN SYMBOLS

The Statue of Liberty

At the entrance to New York Harbor, on Liberty Island, stands one of the best-known symbols of the United States—the Statue of Liberty. The full name of this colossal figure is *Liberty Enlightening the World.* Slightly over 150 feet (45 meters) tall, it is the largest statue ever made.

The statue was a gift from the people of France to the United States. It was presented as a symbol of friendship and in honor of the 100th anniversary of American independence. It was designed by Frédéric Bartholdi and constructed by Alexandre Eiffel.

The Statue of Liberty was built in Paris, taken apart, and then shipped to the United States in 214 crates. It was placed on a pedestal built with money raised by the American people. President Grover Cleveland dedicated it in 1886.

The statue represents a woman dressed in long flowing robes and wearing a crown with seven spikes. At her feet are the broken chains of tyranny. Her right arm holds a torch high in the air. In her left hand is a law book with the date of the Declaration of Independence, July 4, 1776. An elevator in the pedestal brings visitors to the foot of the statue. From there they may climb a narrow, spiral staircase to the statue's crown, which provides a beautiful view of the harbor.

The Statue of Liberty has long been a symbol of freedom for millions of immigrants to the United States. "The New Colossus," a poem by Emma Lazarus to welcome immigrants, was inscribed on a tablet in the pedestal in 1903. It ends with these lines:

Give me your tired, your poor,
Your huddled masses yearning to breathe free,
The wretched refuse of your teeming shore.
Send these, the homeless, tempest-tost to me,
I lift my lamp beside the golden door!

The Liberty Bell

The Liberty Bell has been a symbol of American freedom ever since it rang on July 8, 1776, to announce the adoption of the Declaration of Independence. This giant bronze bell was made in England in 1752 for the State House (now Independence Hall) in Philadelphia. The bell's inscription—"Proclaim Liberty throughout all the land unto all the inhabitants thereof"—is from the Bible.

The Liberty Bell cracked soon after its arrival in Philadelphia and had to be recast. It rang at every anniversary of the Declaration of Independence until 1835. In that year it cracked again while tolling after the death of John Marshall, Chief Justice of the Supreme

Court. Finally, while ringing in honor of George Washington's birthday in 1846, the bell was damaged so badly that it could not be tolled again.

It was on view in Independence Hall until 1976. Then, in celebration of the nation's 200th anniversary, the Liberty Bell was moved to its own glass building. There it is viewed by many thousands of visitors each year.

The Great Seal of the United States

For more than 1,000 years, officials have used seals, or engraved stamps, as guarantees that documents are authentic. At one time kings even wore signet, or seal, rings. The Great Seal of the United States was adopted by the new nation in 1782. Today it is kept in the Department of State and is used only on certain important kinds of documents, such as treaties. Only the face of the seal is used to seal official documents. However, both sides of the seal appear on the back of the $1 bill.

The Face

The face of the seal shows an American bald eagle with raised wings. On its breast is a shield with 13 alternate red and white stripes representing the original states. In the eagle's right claw is an olive branch with 13 leaves and 13 olives. In its left claw are 13 arrows. These symbols indicate our nation's wish to live in peace, but also its ability to wage war. In the eagle's beak is a ribbon with the words *E Pluribus Unum*. This Latin phrase means "from many [states], one [nation]." Above the eagle's head are 13 stars surrounded by rays of light breaking through a cloud.

The Reverse

The reverse side of the Great Seal shows a pyramid made up of 13 layers of stone, representing the new nation. The base of the pyramid has a date in Roman numerals—MDCCLXXVI (1776)—the year of the signing of the Declaration of Independence. The pyramid is guarded by an eye surrounded by rays of light. Above are the Latin words *Annuit Coeptis*, meaning "He [God] has favored our undertaking." Below is the phrase *Novus Ordo Seclorum*, which means "a new order of the ages."

The Bald Eagle

The bald eagle, which appears on the Great Seal, is the official emblem of the United States. This bird is not actually bald, but sometimes appears to be so because its head and neck are pure white. The eagle has symbolized official power since the days of ancient Egypt.

The bald eagle was chosen as the national bird of the United States in 1872. The choice was not unanimous though. Benjamin Franklin would have preferred a native bird, the turkey, but he was overruled.

Uncle Sam

The figure of Uncle Sam is an American symbol as widely recognized as our flag. He has symbolized the United States since the War of 1812.

During that war, a storeyard in Troy, New York, stamped the initials "U.S." on barrels of salted meat for American soldiers. The "U.S." stood for United States. Workers, though, jokingly claimed that the initials really stood for "Uncle Sam" (Samuel) Wilson, who managed the storeyard. The idea of equating Uncle Sam with the United States spread rapidly. After all Great Britain, our opponent in the war, already had a personal symbol of its own—the figure of an English farmer, John Bull.

Uncle Sam as we know him today was first drawn in the 1860's by the American cartoonist Thomas Nast. The symbol of Uncle Sam usually has long hair and a white beard. His pants have red and white stripes, his stovepipe hat is decorated with stars, and he wears a cutaway coat.

The Donkey and the Elephant

Two well-known symbols—the donkey and the elephant—represent our nation's major political parties. They were first used as symbols of the Democratic Party and the Republican Party by the cartoonist Thomas Nast.

The donkey was used for the first time as a political symbol by Andrew Jackson after his opponents in the 1828 Presidential election called him a "jackass." Later, Nast used the donkey in his cartoons to stand for the Democratic Party. The donkey soon became recognized as the symbol of the Democratic Party.

The elephant as a symbol of the Republican Party first appeared in a cartoon by Nast in *Harper's Weekly* in 1874. He used the elephant first to represent the Republican vote and then drew it often as a Republican symbol. It soon came to stand for the Republican Party.

Glossary of Civics Terms

This glossary is a handy civics dictionary. It contains many of the words you need to understand in your study of civics. After each word there is a brief definition, or explanation, of the meaning of the word or term as it is usually used in civics. Note that the meanings given in this glossary also show the way in which these words and terms are used in your textbook. The numbers in parentheses refer to the page on which each term is introduced in the textbook.

The brief definitions in this civics glossary do not always provide you with all the information that you may need about many of these civics terms. In most cases, however, your textbook provides a more complete discussion. Therefore, you will find it useful to turn to the page listed in parentheses to read more about any of the terms. Remember, this glossary is included to help you. Develop the habit of making use of it as you continue your study of civics.

Absolute monarch: an all-powerful king or queen. (21)

Act (see **Law**).

Addict: a person who is physically dependent, or "hooked," on a habit-forming drug. (465)

Administrative law: law made by government agencies. (136)

Adopt: to legally establish a child as one's own. (257)

Advertising: the use of the mass media by businesses to inform people about products and to persuade people to buy them. (331)

Affidavit: a written statement that a person signs to affirm that answers given to questions on a voter registration application (or other document) are true. (218)

Agency shop: a place of employment in which workers must pay dues to the union but are not required to become union members. (375)

Alcoholism: addiction to alcohol (liquor). (466)

Alien: a person who lives in a nation but who is not a citizen of that nation. (9)

Alimony: regular payments sometimes made to one spouse—wife or husband—by the other after a divorce. (258)

Alliance treaty: an agreement between nations, usually for purposes of defense. (411)

Ambassador: the highest-ranking official representing his or her government in a foreign country. (124)

Amendment: a written change or addition made in the Constitution. (50)

Anti-Federalist: an opponent of the Constitution, who urged its rejection in 1787. (31)

Appeal: the right of a convicted person to ask a higher court to review his or her case. (138)

Appellate jurisdiction: the authority given to some courts to review cases that already have been tried in a lower court. (139)

Apprenticeship: a period of salaried, on-the-job training by new members of a craft, or skilled trade, such as plumbers. (388)

Appropriation bills (or **money bills**): bills that call for the spending of public money; must be introduced in the House of Representatives. (106)

Arbitration: a method of settling differences between labor unions and employers in which a third party's decision must be accepted by both sides. (378)

Arraignment: an accused person's appearance before a judge at which time he or she pleads either guilty or innocent. (479)

Arson: the deliberate destruction of property by setting a fire. (474)

Articles of Confederation: our nation's first written plan of government, in effect from 1781 to 1789. (25)

Assembly line: a system in which individual workers do specialized jobs in making a product that is passed along on a slowly moving belt. (323)

Attorney general: the chief legal officer of the nation or a state; in the federal government, the head of the Department of Justice. (124)

Audit: a careful examination, or study, by an accountant of government or business expenditures. (246)

Bail: money or property deposited with a court as a guarantee that an accused person will be in court at the time of trial. (81)

Balanced budget: a budget in which the amount of income equals the amount of expenses. (245)

Balance of nature: the relationship of all living things to one another. (494)

Balance of trade: the difference in value between a nation's imports and exports. (419)

Bank: a business firm that deals in money and credit. (346)

Barter: the swapping of one product for another. (340)

Beneficiary: the person named in an insurance policy to receive the money in case of the policyholder's death. (356)

Better Business Bureau: a local organization that aids people who feel they have been treated unfairly by a business firm. (334)

Bicameral legislature: a lawmaking body consisting of two houses. (28)

Bill: a proposed law being considered by a lawmaking body. (99)

Bill of attainder: a law sentencing a person to jail without granting him or her a fair public trial. (104)

Bill of Rights: the first ten amendments to the Constitution, which set forth the basic rights, or freedoms, guaranteed to all Americans. (77)

Birth rate: the number of births per 1,000 persons during one year. (11)

Blockade: the closing of routes to a certain area in order to restrict access. (436)

Block association: an organization of residents who work together to improve their neighborhood. (231)

Blue-collar workers: people who provide labor for industry. (388)

Board of directors: the people who direct the affairs of a corporation. (308)

Board of Education (or **local school board):** a group of individuals who are responsible for managing the public schools in a community. (181)

Bonds: certificates of debt issued by governments or corporations to persons from whom they have borrowed money. (309)

Boroughs: in Pennsylvania, a unit of local government similar to a town. (179)

Brand name: the widely advertised name of a product that is usually distributed over a large area. (331)

Brokerage houses: organizations that buy and sell stocks for their clients. (351)

Budget: a plan of spending; a yearly plan of income and expenses of the federal and local governments. (165)

Building code: the local laws that regulate the construction and repair of buildings in a community. (455)

Bureaucracy: the government agencies and departments at the federal, state, and local levels. (131)

Burglary: illegal entry into someone's home with the intent to steal. (473)

Business cycle: an economy's tendency to go back and forth between periods of prosperity and periods of depression. (369)

Cabinet: the heads of executive departments in the federal government, who also act as advisers to the President. (52)

Candidates: the people who run for election to government offices. (199)

Capital: the money that people invest in business; also, the property and equipment used to produce goods or services. (300)

Capitalism (or **capitalistic system**): an economic system based on private ownership of the means of production. (300)

Capitalist: a person who owns any part of a business, or capital. (301)

Capital punishment: putting a criminal to death for his or her crime. (481)

Caucus: meeting of party leaders to determine the party's policy on proposed laws or to choose the party's candidates for public office. (98)

Census: an official count of the number of people in the United States taken every ten years. (11)

Central Intelligence Agency (CIA): a federal agency that gathers and studies information about foreign nations. (123)

Chain store: a store that is owned and operated by a company that has many of the same kinds of stores. (330)

Charge account: a form of credit that allows a store's customers to receive goods now and pay for them later. (335)

Charter: a plan of government granted by a state legislature to a local government. Also, a document permitting a business firm to form a corporation. (175, 308)

Check: a written order to a bank to pay a certain sum of money to the person or organization that is named on the check. (342)

Checks and balances: the way in which the powers of government are balanced, or divided, among three branches so that each branch may check, or limit, the other branches. (44)

Chief Executive: the President of the United States. (118)

Chief of State: the President's role as the symbol of the United States and its people. (121)

Child abuse: the mental or physical mistreatment of a child. (257)

Circuit: one of the twelve judicial districts covered by a court of appeals. (141)

City: a unit of local government, usually having a population of at least 2,500. (182)

City council: the lawmaking body of a city or town. (183)

City manager: head of a city government hired by the city council to enforce city laws and to help govern the city. (186)

Civics: the study of what it means to be an American citizen. (3)

Civil cases: cases involving disputes over money or property between two or more individuals or businesses. (169)

Civil rights: the political, social, and economic rights guaranteed to all American citizens. (82)

Civil rights movement: the struggle for equal rights for all American citizens. (458)

Civil service examination: a test that must be taken by applicants for most federal, state, and local government jobs. (391)

Closed primary: a primary election in which only voters who are members of the party may vote for that party's candidates. (210)

Closed shop: a place of employment in which a worker may not be hired unless he or she is already a member of a union; made illegal in some states by right-to-work laws. (375)

Cloture: a vote to end debate on a bill in the Senate; a vote of three fifths of the full Senate is needed. (110)

Coalition: an agreement between two or more political parties to work together to run the government. (202)

Cold War: the worldwide political struggle that developed between the United States and the Soviet Union and their allies after World War II. (435)

Collateral: property used to guarantee that a loan will be paid back. (345)

Collective bargaining: a process in which representatives of a labor union and an employer work to reach an agreement about wages and working conditions. (374)

Command economy: an economic system in which the government completely controls, or commands, the nation's economy. (305)

Commander in Chief: the President's role as head of the armed forces. (119)

Commercial bank: a bank whose major purpose is to handle checking accounts and make loans to individuals and businesses. (346)

Commercial treaty (or **trade treaty**): an agreement between two or more nations to trade on favorable terms. (411)

Commission: a local government body that has both legislative and executive powers. (185)

Commission plan: a system of local government in which the voters elect commissioners who head city departments and make and carry out the laws. (185)

Committee of the Whole: the Senate or House of Representatives acting as one committee to discuss a bill. (110)

Committee on committees: the group within each party, in the Senate and the House of Representatives, that assigns party members to the various standing committees. (100)

Committees: small groups into which each house of Congress is divided in order to consider bills. (99)

Common law: customary law that develops from judges' decisions. These laws are followed in situations that are not covered by statutory laws. (136)

Common stock: corporation stock on which dividends are paid and which give the owner the right to have a vote in corporate affairs. (309)

Communism: an economic system based on the theories of Marx and Engels in which the means of production are owned by the government; the government decides what will be produced and where people will work. It is the basis of the governments of many countries, including the Soviet Union and the People's Republic of China. (433)

Community: a group of people who have common interests, live in the same area, and are governed by the same laws. (283)

Commutation: a shortening of the sentence of a convicted person. (121)

Commuters: people who travel from their homes in the suburbs to work in a city. (453)

Competition (see **Free competition**).

Compromise: an agreement in which each side gives up part of its demands. (29)

Concealed propaganda: information or ideas that are used to try to influence people without their being aware of it. (222)

Concurring opinion: a statement written by a Supreme Court Justice who agrees with the majority decision but for different reasons. (147)

Confederation: a loose association of states. (25)

Conference committee: a temporary committee made up of members of both houses of Congress that is formed to reach a compromise on a bill passed in different forms by each house. (100)

Conglomerate: a large company that controls many different kinds of smaller companies. (304)

Congress: the lawmaking body of the federal government. (93)

Congressional districts: divisions of a state in each of which the voters elect one member of the House of Representatives. (94)

Conservation: using natural resources wisely in order to ensure an adequate supply of these resources in the future. (504)

Constituents: people of a district who are represented by the members of a lawmaking body. (105)

Constitution: a written plan of government describing how a government is organized, listing its purpose, some of the basic laws, and the rights of the people. (22)

Constitutional: within the limits and safeguards of the Constitution. (38)

Constitutional Convention: the meeting in Philadelphia in 1787 at which the Constitution of the United States was written. (27)

Constitutional law: law that is based on the Constitution and has higher authority than all other laws. (136)

Constitution of the United States: the plan of government approved in 1789 to be the supreme law of the land. (27)

Consul: an official in a foreign country who works to promote American trade and who aids American citizens who do business there. (124)

Consumer: one who buys or uses products and services. (332)

Containment: American policy of preventing the spread of communism. (435)

Copyright: the legal right given to an individual or group to publish or sell a written, musical, or art work for a certain number of years. (300)

Corporation: a business chartered by a state government and given power to issue stocks, own property, make contracts, and sue and be sued in court. (306)

Corporation income tax: a tax on the profits of a corporation. (240)

Council-manager plan: a system of local government in which the voters elect a city council to make the laws and the council hires a city manager as the chief executive. (185)

Council member-at-large: a member of a local council who is elected by all the voters of the community. (183)

County: a subdivision of state government established to carry out state laws, collect taxes, and supervise elections. (176)

County executive: an official hired by the county board or elected by the voters to carry on the work of the county government. (178)

County seat: the town or city in which the county government is located. (176)

Court-martial: a trial of a person in the armed services accused of breaking a military law. (142)

Court of claims: a federal court that hears property claims against the federal government. (142)

Courts of appeals: federal (or state) courts to which a convicted person may take his or her case for review. (141)

Craft union (or **trade union**): an organization made up of all members of a craft, or skilled trade. (375)

Credit: the amount of money a person or business firm has in a checking account. (343)

Credit card: a card issued by banks and businesses, used in place of money. The user of the card is billed and pays for his or her purchase at a later time. (343)

Credit rating: a record of how well a customer pays his or her bills. (336)

Crime: any act that breaks the law or fails to fulfill some requirement of the law. (473)

Criminal cases: court cases in which a person is accused by the state of breaking a law. (168)

Criminal justice system: the system of police, courts, and prisons used to bring criminals to justice. (476)

Currency: the coins and paper bills that are used as money. (341)

Customs court: the federal court that hears cases involving import taxes. (142)

Death rate: the number of deaths per 1,000 persons during one year. (11)

Debt limit: a limit on the amount of money that a government may borrow. (246)

Declaration of Independence: a key document of American freedom, adopted on July 4, 1776, declaring the 13 American colonies to be free and independent of Great Britain. (24)

Deductions: expenses that taxpayers are allowed to subtract in figuring their taxable income. (239)

Defendant: a person accused of a crime in a court case. (479)

Defense: an accused person's side in a court case. (479)

Deficit: the amount of money by which a government's expenses exceed its income. (245)

Delegates: representatives who were chosen to attend the Constitutional Convention. Also, the representatives who attend the convention of a political party. (27)

Delinquents: young people who break the law. (482)

Democracy: a form of government in which the people rule themselves either directly or through elected representatives. (21)

Democratic Party: one of the two major political parties in the United States. (201)

Depression: a sharp decline in a nation's business activity, during which large numbers of workers lose their jobs and many businesses close down. (369)

Détente: a term used to refer to the effort to improve relations between the United States and the Soviet Union. (440)

Developing nations: nations that are still in the process of developing their economies. (440)

Dictatorship: a form of government in which all power is in the hands of one person or a group of persons. (21)

Diplomacy: the process of conducting relations with foreign governments. (120)

Diplomatic corps: a nation's ambassadors and other representatives in foreign countries. (413)

Direct democracy: a form of government in which all the people meet together in one place to make laws and decide what actions the government should take. (21)

Discount rate: the interest rate charged by the Federal Reserve Banks on loans to member banks. (349)

Discrimination: unfair actions taken against someone because he or she belongs to a particular group. (457)

Dissent: to disagree, to hold or express a different opinion; the expression of such opinions. (459)

Distribution: the method of getting products to the people who want and need them. (325)

District courts: federal courts in each of the 50 states that have original jurisdiction in most cases involving federal laws. (139)

Dividends: profits paid to stockholders of a corporation. (307)

Division of labor: a system in which each worker does a portion of a total job. (322)

Divorce: the legal ending of a marriage. (258)

Down payment: the initial cash paid on the price of an item bought on the installment plan. (336)

Draft: the requiring of men to serve in the military. (85)

Drug abuse: the taking of drugs that may cause addiction or be harmful to one's health. (465)

Due process of law: the right of all Americans to a fair trial. (80)

Ecology: the relation of all living things to their environment. (493)

Economist: a specialist who studies economics. (320)

Economy (or **economic system**): a nation's system of producing, distributing, and consuming goods and services. (299)

Editorial: an article in a newspaper or magazine that gives the writer's opinion of an issue. (194)

Elastic clause: Article 1, Section 8, of the Constitution, or the "necessary and proper" clause; allows Congress to extend its powers listed in the Constitution to cover other areas. (102)

Electoral College: the group of people who cast the official votes that elect the President and Vice President. (216)

Electoral votes: the votes cast by the Electoral College, which determine the winner of a Presidential election. (216)

Electors: the people elected by the voters in a Presidential election as members of the Electoral College. (216)

Embargo: a decision made by a government to stop selling a product to a particular country. (441)

Embassy: the official residence of an ambassador in a foreign country. (124)

Eminent domain: the power of the government to take private property for public use. (80)

Entrepreneur: a business owner. (315)

Environment: our natural surroundings, such as rivers and lakes, trees, oceans, soil, and air. (493)

Estate tax: a tax on the money, property, and other valuables left by a person who has died. (243)

Ethnic group: a group of people of the same race, nationality, or religion who share a common culture and heritage. (458)

Excise tax: a federal tax collected on certain luxury articles produced and sold in the United States. (241)

Executive agreement: an agreement between the President of the United States and the leader of a foreign government. This type of agreement does not require Senate approval. (412)

Executive branch: the branch of our federal, state, or local government that carries out the laws. (43)

Executive departments: the major departments in the executive branch of the federal government, the heads of which form the President's Cabinet. (123)

Exemption: a certain amount of money that a taxpayer can subtract from his or her taxable income. (239)

Exports: goods and services that are sold to other countries. (419)

***Ex post facto* law:** a law that is passed making illegal an action that occurred in the past. (104)

Extracurricular activities: school activities, such as school clubs, sports teams, bands, and social events. (275)

Extradition: the return of escaped prisoners or accused persons from one state to the state where the crime was committed. (160)

Factors of production: the four means of production—land, capital, labor, and management. (309)

Family: a group of people united by

marriage, blood, or adoption. (252)

Family law: the legal regulation of marriage, divorce, and the duties of parents and children. (256)

Farm workers: people who own, manage, or work on a farm. (389)

Favorite sons or daughters: popular men or women in a state party, usually governors or senators, who are nominated for President by that state's delegates on the first ballot at the national nominating convention. (214)

Federal Deposit Insurance Corporation (FDIC): the agency of the federal government that insures the deposits of its member banks up to $100,000 for each depositor. (354)

Federal government: the national government of our nation. (40)

Federalist: a supporter of the Constitution, who urged its adoption in 1787. (30)

Federal Reserve System: the banking system in the United States that handles the banking needs of the federal government and regulates the supply of money. (348)

Federal system: the American system of government in which the powers of government are divided between the national government, which governs the whole American nation, and the state governments, which govern the people of each state. (29)

Fees: money payments charged by state and local governments for licenses. (237)

Felonies: serious crimes, such as burglary, kidnapping, and murder. (168)

Filibuster: a method in the Senate of delaying or preventing a vote on a bill by making long speeches. (110)

Fines: money paid to local governments as a penalty by citizens who break certain laws. (237)

Fiscal policy: a government's program of taxation and spending. (371)

Fixed expenses: expenses that must be paid and that occur on a regular basis. (260)

Floor leaders: party leaders in both houses of Congress who work for the passage of bills. (98)

Foreign aid: a government program that provides economic and military assistance to other nations. (417)

Foreign policy: a nation's plan for dealing with the other nations of the world. (411)

Foreign relations: the way a government carries out its foreign policy and how it gets along with the governments of other nations. (411)

Foster home: the home of people who are unrelated to a child but agree to act as his or her parents. (257)

Free competition: the right of business firms to produce goods and services and to compete with one another for customers. (299)

Freedom of assembly: the right to meet with other people in public meetings. (78)

Freedom of petition: the right to ask the government to take or not take certain actions. (78)

Freedom of the press: the right to express any idea in writing. (78)

Freedom of speech: the right to express ideas and opinions as well as listen to the thoughts and opinions of others. (77)

Free enterprise system: economic system in which people are free to run their businesses as they see fit. (302)

Free market: the right to buy and sell any product or service we choose. (299)

Free trade: the exchange of goods between countries without tariffs or any other kinds of trade barriers. (419)

General Assembly: a division of the United Nations in which every member nation has a vote. (421)

General election: an election in which the voters elect the leaders of our government. (209)

Gift tax: a tax collected on items received as gifts that are worth more than a certain amount. (243)

Government: the authority, or power, that rules on behalf of a group of people. (3)

Governor: the head of the executive branch in our state governments. (165)

Grand jury: the group of persons that hears the evidence in a criminal case and decides whether there is reason enough to bring the accused person to trial. (137)

Grants-in-aid: funds provided by the federal government to state governments to assist in the carrying out of specific programs. (191)

Great Compromise: the agreement reached by the Constitutional Convention that all the states should have equal representation in the Senate and be represented according to the size of their populations in the House of Representatives. (29)

Gross income: the money a company receives from the sale of its goods or services. (316)

Gross National Product (GNP): the total value of the goods and services produced in a nation each year. (320)

Guardian: a person appointed by a state court to look after individuals who are not yet adults or who are unable to care for themselves. (257)

Hearings: special meetings called by congressional committees to consider a bill. (107)

House of Representatives (or the **House**): the lower house of Congress in which states are represented according to their population. (93)

Ideals: basic beliefs or standards of conduct that people attempt to live up to. (3)

Immigrant: a person who comes to a nation to settle as a permanent resident. (7)

Impeachment: formal charge, or indictment, brought against a government official. In the federal government, the House of Representatives has the power to impeach the President and other high officials; an impeached official is tried by the Senate. (103)

Implied powers: authority not specifically granted to Congress by the Constitution but which is implied, or suggested, to be necessary in order to carry out the specific powers. (102)

Imports: goods and services that are purchased from other countries. (419)

Independent agencies: agencies in the executive branch of the federal government established by Congress to help the government enforce laws and regulations not covered by the executive departments. (129)

Independent voter: a citizen who registers to vote without becoming a member of a political party. (209)

Indeterminate sentence: a prison sentence that sets a minimum and maximum number of years that must be served. (480)

Indictment: a formal charge against an accused person. (79)

Industrial union: an organization of workers that includes all workers (skilled and unskilled) in an industry. (376)

Inflation: a rise in the prices of most goods and services. (365)

Inheritance tax: a tax on money and property received from an estate. (243)

Initiative: the process by which citizens of a state may propose a law by collecting a certain number of signatures on a petition. (164)

Installment plan: a system of buying in which the buyer makes a cash down payment and then pays the balance over a period of time. (336)

Insurance: a planned method of saving by which an individual makes regular payments for protection against emergencies, such as fire, theft, or loss of life. (355)

Interest: payment for the use of loaned money. (238)

Interest groups (also known as **lobbies** or **pressure groups**): organizations of people with a common interest who try to influence government policies. (225)

Internal Revenue Service (IRS): the federal agency that collects income taxes. (244)

Invest: to use money to buy buildings, machinery, other means of production, or other articles of value with the hope of making a profit. (299)

Isolationism: the policy of avoiding all involvement in foreign affairs. (429)

Item veto: the power of a governor to veto, or reject, one part of a bill and approve the rest of it. (164)

Joint Chiefs of Staff: the group made up of the highest-ranking military officers from the Army, Navy, and Air Force that advises the President on military affairs. The head of the Marine Corps attends all meetings. (125)

Joint committee: a committee made up of members of both houses of Congress that meets to discuss matters of interest to both houses. (99)

Judicial branch: the branch of the federal, state, or local government that decides if laws have been broken and that punishes lawbreakers. (44)

Judicial review: the power of the Supreme Court to decide whether an action of the President or a law passed by Congress or by state or local governments violates any provision of the Constitution. (146)

Jurisdiction: the authority to judge and administer the laws. Also, the extent or range of that authority. (139)

Jurisdictional strike: a strike to determine which labor union will represent workers in a particular industry. (376)

Jurors: members of the trial jury who judge the evidence and determine the verdict in a court case. (137)

Jury duty: the duty of citizens to serve on a jury when called. (137)

Justice: a member of the Supreme Court. (143)

Justice of the peace: the judge who presides over a state justice court, trying misdemeanors and some civil cases. (169)

Juveniles: young persons, usually under 18 years of age, who are not legally adults. (481)

Keynote speaker: person who gives the opening speech at a national nominating convention. (213)

Labor: any kind of work that helps to produce goods or to provide services. Also, the total work force. (389)

Labor contract: a written agreement between a labor union and an employer that spells out workers' wages and working conditions. (374)

Labor unions: organizations of workers established to bargain for higher wages and for improved working conditions and to protect workers' rights. (373)

Lame duck: an elected official who continues to hold office during the period between defeat for reelection and the inauguration of a successor. (560)

Land: the soil and all of the natural resources and raw materials used to produce goods. (314)

Larceny: a legal term for the theft of property without forcible or illegal entry. (473)

Law of supply and demand: in economics, a general rule which states that the price of an item is determined by the relationship between its availability and the demand for it at any particular time. (300)

Laws: all the rules of conduct of a nation that are enforced by government. (22)

Legal tender: paper money and coins that all Americans must accept as payment in exchange for goods and services. (342)

Legislative branch: the branch of our federal, state, or local government that makes the laws. (43)

Legislature: a lawmaking body of the local, state, or federal government. (29)

Lieutenant governor: the elected official who succeeds the governor if the governor dies or resigns. (167)

Limited war: a war fought without using a nation's full military power, especially nuclear weapons. (437)

Literacy test: a test, now illegal, that required voters to prove they could read and write English before being allowed to vote. (209)

Lobbyist: a person who is paid to represent an interest group's point of view at congressional committee hearings and who tries to influence the votes of members of Congress. (227)

Local school board (see **Board of Education).**

Magistrate: the official in a district court who hears evidence in a case and decides whether the case should be presented to a grand jury. (140)

Magna Carta: an English document signed in 1215 guaranteeing the rights of English citizens, on which many of the ideals expressed in the American Constitution are based. (28)

Mainstreaming: the practice of placing handicapped students in regular classes. (268)

Majority party: the political party that has the most members in Congress or in a state legislature. (98)

Majority rule: the system in which

the decision of more than half the people is accepted by all; under our American government, the majority must always respect the rights of the minority. (40)

Managers: the people who run a business firm and decide how it should operate. (315)

Manslaughter: a legal term for the unplanned killing of a person. In some states it is known as second-degree murder. (473)

Marketing: the method of trying to get people to buy goods and services. (325)

Marshal: the official in each federal district court who makes arrests, issues subpoenas, and carries out the orders of the court. (140)

Martial law: the limitation of people's rights and freedoms under military authority. (440)

Mass marketing: transporting and selling large amounts of goods to millions of customers. Also, the method of selling goods and services to millions of people. (327)

Mass media: the sources of information—such as newspapers, magazines, books, radio, and television—by which large numbers of people are reached. (221)

Mass production: producing huge amounts of goods rapidly by machine to supply the needs and wants of large numbers of people. (321)

Mass transit: public transportation, including buses, subways, and railroads. (455)

Mayor: the chief executive of a city government. (183)

Mayor-council plan: a system of local government in which voters elect a city council to make the laws and a mayor to carry out the laws. (183)

Mediation: a method of settling disputes between labor unions and employers through the use of a third party who offers a solution. (378)

Medicaid: the federal program that helps poor people pay for hospital and medical expenses. (360)

Medicare: the federal program of health insurance for people aged 65 and over. (360)

Megalopolis: a continuous urban area that includes many cities and extends over a vast area. (286)

Metropolitan area: a large city and its nearby suburbs and small towns. (14)

Migration: the movement by people to different parts of the nation. (15)

Minority group: a group that is not in power and is set apart from other people in the same society because of race, nationality, language, customs, or religion. (457)

Minority party: the political party that has fewer members in Congress or a state legislature. (98)

Misdemeanors: less serious crimes, such as traffic violations and disorderly conduct. (168)

Mixed economy: a system in which both business and government make decisions that affect the economic situation of the country. (304)

Monetary policy: the government's program for controlling the amount of money in the economy. (372)

Money: the paper and coins that are a nation's standard means of exchange used to purchase goods and services. (341)

Monopoly: a company that produces and markets all or most of the total supply of a product or service. (302)

National nominating convention: a meeting held by the major political parties every four years to draw up the party platform and to choose the party candidates for President and Vice President. (204)

National Security Council: the group of top advisers to the President of the United States on matters concerning defense and foreign policy. (123)

Native-born citizens: Americans who are born as citizens of the United States. (8)

Naturalization: the legal process by which aliens become American citizens. (9)

Net income: the money that a company has left after all of its costs have been paid. (316)

Neutrality: a policy of not favoring one side or the other in a conflict. (432)

News story: an article in a newspaper giving the facts about an event. (194)

Nominate: to select candidates who will run for public office. (199)

North Atlantic Treaty Organization (NATO): a mutual defense alliance made up of the United States and 14 European nations. (416)

Northwest Ordinance: a law passed in 1787 that set up a plan for governing territories and forming them into states. (159)

Office of Management and Budget (OMB): the government agency that helps prepare the federal budget. (123)

Open primary: a primary election in which the voters may vote for the candidates of any party. (210)

Open shop: a place of employment where workers may be hired whether or not they belong to a union. (375)

Opinion: what people believe or think. Also, the Supreme Court's written explanation of why it came to a particular decision about a case. (147, 221)

Ordinances: laws and regulations passed by local lawmaking bodies. (176)

Organization of American States (OAS): a mutual defense alliance made up of the United States and most of the nations of Latin America. (417)

Organization of Petroleum-Exporting Countries (OPEC): a group consisting of the world's major oil-exporting countries, which sets the price of oil sold by the member countries. (420)

Original jurisdiction: the authority of some courts to hold trials first in certain kinds of cases. (139)

Pardon: an official act by the President or by a governor forgiving a person of a crime. (121)

Parish: in Louisiana, a subdivision of state government similar to a county. (176)

Parliament: the lawmaking body of Great Britain. (28)

Parole: the release of a convicted person from prison (on certain conditions) before the completion of the sentence. (480)

Partnership: a business organization in which two or more persons share the ownership, profits, and losses of the business. (306)

Party caucus (see **Caucus**).

Party platform: a written statement that outlines a political party's views on important issues and describes the program it proposes. (213)

Party whip: an assistant to the floor leader in each house of Congress who tries to persuade members of the party to vote for all the bills the party supports. (98)

Passport: a document issued by the State Department that permits American citizens to travel abroad. (124)

Patent: the right given to one person to make and sell an invention for a certain number of years. (300)

Peace Corps: an American volunteer agency founded in 1961 that sends Americans to foreign nations to help people learn needed skills. (417)

Personal income tax: a federal, state, or local tax on the income a person earns. (239)

Personal property: possessions such as money, stocks, bonds, jewelry, cars, and boats on which local property taxes may be collected. (242)

Plank: each part of a political party's platform. (213)

Plea bargaining: an agreement between the prosecutor and defense in which the accused person agrees to plead guilty to a reduced charge. (479)

Pocket veto: a means the President has of rejecting a bill passed by Congress. Any bill presented to the President within ten days before the end of the session is "pocket vetoed" if not signed before Congress adjourns. (111)

Political party: an organization of citizens who have similar views on public issues and who work for the election of party members to public office and for the passage of bills in order to put these ideas into effect. (199)

Polling place: the place where citizens go to vote. (204)

Poll tax: a special tax, now illegal, that a person had to pay in some states in order to be able to vote. (84)

Pollsters: the people who conduct public opinion polls. (232)

Pollution: the contaminating of our earth, air, or water. (498)

Popular vote: the total votes cast by individual voters in a Presidential election. (216)

Preamble: the beginning of the Constitution, which describes its purposes. Also, the beginning of a state constitution. (39)

Precinct captain: the political party leader in a local voting district. (204)

Precincts: the local voting districts in counties, cities, and wards. (204)

Preferred stock: corporation stock on which fixed dividends are paid but which gives the owner no vote in corporate affairs. (308)

Prejudice: an unfair opinion, not based on facts, about members of a particular group. (279)

Preliminary hearing: a procedure in a criminal case in which a judge decides if the accused person should be held for trial. (478)

Premiums: the payments made for insurance protection. (355)

President: the Chief Executive, or head, of the executive branch of the federal government. (115)

Presidential preference primary: a primary election in which voters in a state select the Presidential candidate they wish their delegates to support at the party's national nominating convention. (213)

Presidential succession: the order in which the office of President is to be filled when it becomes vacant. (117)

President *pro tempore:* the official who presides over the Senate when the Vice President is absent. (98)

Press secretary: a Presidential assistant who represents the President to the mass media and the public. (123)

Primary election: an election in which the voters of various parties choose their candidates to run for office in the general election. (209)

Primary sources: original documents, articles, and eyewitness accounts of an event written by people who took part in what they are writing about. (446)

Priorities: the order of importance of national needs. (235)

Probation: a kind of sentence in which a person convicted of a crime does not go to prison but must follow certain rules and report to a person named by the court. (488)

Productivity: the amount a worker produces in an hour. (315)

Profession: a job that involves mostly mental work and requires many years of education and training. (386)

Profit: income that a business has left after expenses. (241)

Propaganda: ideas or beliefs that are spread by individuals or groups in order to influence people's opinions or behavior. (222)

Property tax: a local or state tax collected on real property or personal property. (242)

Prosecution: the government's side in a criminal case. (479)

Protective tariff: a high tax on imported goods intended to protect American industries against foreign competition. (243)

Public opinion: the opinion a large number of people have about a particular issue. (221)

Public opinion poll: a method of measuring the public's views on specific issues by asking for the opinions of a sample of the population. (224)

Public utilities: legal monopolies that provide services, such as gas, electricity, water, and transportation, required by people of the community. (304)

Quorum: the minimum number of members who must be present before a legislative body can do business. (110)

Quota: a limit on the number of immigrants who may come to the United States each year. (7)

Ratification: approval, such as of the Constitution in 1787 or of a constitutional amendment. (30)

Real property: land and buildings on which local property taxes are usually collected. (242)

Recession: a period when a nation's business activity declines. (370)

Reciprocal trade agreement: agreement by which nations lower tariffs on certain goods imported from each other. (419)

Referendum: the method of referring certain kinds of bills to the voters for approval before they can become law. (164)

Refugees: people who flee their homeland and seek refuge in another nation. (8)

Register: to place one's name in the official record of eligible voters in order to be able to vote. (209)

Regulatory agencies: independent agencies created by Congress that have power to make rules concerning certain activities and to bring violators into court. (129)

Renewable resources: natural resources that are not expected to run out or that can be replaced, such as air and forests. (499)

Rent: the payment for the use of property belonging to someone else, such as land and buildings. (314)

Representative democracy (also known as a **republic**): a system of government in which the people elect representatives to carry on the work of government for them. (21)

Representative town meeting (or **limited town meeting**): town government in which the people elect representatives to attend the town meeting and to make decisions for them. (180)

Representatives: members of the House of Representatives. (93)

Reprieve: a postponement in the carrying out of a prison sentence. (121)

Republic: a system of government in which the people elect representatives to carry on the work of government for them. (21)

Republican Party: one of the two major political parties in the United States. (201)

Reserved powers: powers set aside for the state governments or the people by the Constitution. (41)

Retail stores: businesses that buy goods from wholesalers and then sell them to the public. (331)

Revealed propaganda: propaganda, such as advertising, that openly tries to influence people. (222)

Revenue: income collected by the government to pay its costs. (236)

Revenue sharing: a plan in which the federal government provides money to state and local governments to use as they see fit for needed programs. (191)

Right-to-work laws: state laws that make it illegal to require a person to join a union in order to get or keep a job; such laws prohibit closed shops and union shops. (375)

Roll-call vote: a vote in Congress in which a record is made of how each member votes. (110)

Runoff election: an election in which voters choose between the two leading candidates in a primary to determine the party's candidate in the general election. (210)

Rural areas: regions of farms and small towns (14)

Salary: regular, fixed income paid weekly or once or twice a month. (315)

Sales tax: a state or city tax on items or services that are sold to the public. (241)

SALT (Strategic Arms Limitation Talks): negotiations between the United States and the Soviet Union to limit the number of nuclear weapons. (440)

Satellite nations: term used to describe the communist nations of Eastern Europe controlled by the Soviet Union. (435)

Saving: keeping money by setting it aside. (350)

Savings bank: a bank whose major purpose is to handle savings accounts and lend money to individuals. (346)

Scarcity: the economic problem of limited resources and unlimited wants. (300)

School tax: a tax on property collected to support local public schools. (243)

Search warrant: a legal paper granted by a judge that permits the police to enter and search a place where there is good reason to believe evidence of a crime will be found. (79)

Secondary sources: anything written by people who did not take part in what they are writing about. (446)

Secretary: the official who heads an executive department in the federal government, such as the Secretary of State. (124)

Secretary general: the chief executive of the United Nations. (422)

Securities and Exchange Commission (SEC): the federal agency that monitors the practices of the stock exchanges to protect the interests of investors. (130)

Security Council: the division of the United Nations that has the main responsibility of maintaining the peace; consists of five permanent member-nations and ten nations elected for two-year terms. (421)

Segregation laws: laws, now illegal, that forced black Americans to go to separate schools and to use separate public facilities. (458)

Select committee: a temporary House or Senate committee that is formed to deal with an area not handled by a standing committee. (99)

Selectmen: the men or women who manage a town's affairs during the period between regular town meetings. (179)

Senate: the upper house of Congress in which each state is represented by two senators. (94)

Senators: members of the United States Senate. (94)

Seniority system: the custom of giving the post of committee chairperson to the member of the majority party with the most years of service on that committee. (100)

Senior senator: the senator from each state who was elected first. (95)

Sentence: the punishment given to a person convicted of a crime. (479)

Separation of powers: the three-way division of power among the branches of the federal government. (43)

Service workers: people who perform services for the public, such as hair cutters and repairers. (389)

Sheriff: the chief law-enforcement official in some county governments. (177)

Single proprietorship: a business owned by one person. (306)

Slum: a run-down city area where apartments and houses need repairs and where families live crowded together. (453)

Small claims courts: state courts that hear civil cases involving small amounts of money; lawyers usually are not needed. (170)

Social Security: the federal system that provides aid to unemployed, disabled, and retired workers, paid for by a special tax on workers and their employers. (358)

Solar energy: power that is obtained by using the heat produced by the sun. (506)

Speaker: the presiding officer of the House of Representatives. (98)

Special district: a unit of local government set up to provide a specific service. School districts are the most numerous special districts. (181)

Special session: a special meeting of Congress called by the President. (97)

Split ticket: a ballot on which a person has voted for the candidates of more than one political party. (211)

Standard Metropolitan Statistical Area (SMSA): any city of 50,000 or more people, and its surrounding urban and suburban areas. (452)

Standard of living: the level of well-being of a nation's population based on the amount of goods and services they can afford. (298)

Standard parts: identical parts of a manufactured product that are mass produced and interchangeable. (321)

Standing committee: a permanent House or Senate committee that considers bills in a certain field of government. (99)

State auditor: the state official who ensures that no public funds are paid out of the state treasury without legal authorization. (167)

State legislature: the general term for a state lawmaking body. (162)

State of the Union Message: the yearly report of the President to Congress, as required by the Constitution, in which the nation's condition is described and programs and policies are recommended. (118)

State treasurer: the state official responsible for the handling of all state funds, including the collection of taxes and payment of bills. (167)

Statutory laws: laws passed by Congress and by lawmaking bodies of state and local governments. (135)

Stock: a share of ownership in a corporation. (301)

Stock exchange: an organized market for the buying and selling of stocks. (351)

Stockholders: people who own stock in a corporation. (307)

Straight ticket: a ballot on which a person votes for all the candidates of the same political party. (211)

Strike: a work stoppage by members of a labor union to try to get employers to agree to their demands for better wages and working conditions. (374)

Strong-mayor plan: a form of city government in which the mayor has strong executive powers that are not limited by the city council. (183)

Subcommittee: a division of a standing congressional committee that deals with specific issues in the area handled by the committee as a whole. (99)

Subpoenas: official court documents that require persons to appear in court. (140)

Suburb: a residential community located near a large city. (14)

Suffrage: the right to vote. (83)

Summit conference: meeting between the President of the United States and the leaders of other nations. (416)

Sunbelt: the region made up of states in the South and West. (15)

Superintendent of schools: an official appointed by a local Board of Education to manage the schools. (181)

Supreme Court: the highest court in the United States. Also, the name given to the highest court in many of our states. (141)

Surplus: the amount by which income exceeds expenditures. (245)

Tariff (or **customs duty**): a tax on products imported from other countries. (243)

Tax: a payment of money that citizens and businesses are required to make to help pay the costs of government. (236)

Taxable income: the amount of income, less deductions, on which an individual and a business must pay taxes. (239)

Tax court: the independent agency that hears appeals cases involving federal taxes. (142)

Tenement: a run-down apartment building. (453)

Territory: an area, governed by the United States, that is eligible to become a state. (159)

Terrorism: committing illegal acts to force someone, usually a government or a powerful group, to give in to demands. (475)

Third parties: political organizations in the United States other than the Democratic and Republican parties, usually set up to work for special causes. (202)

Third World: (also known as **developing nations**): nations of Asia, Africa, and Latin America usually not aligned with the communist or anti-communist side. (440)

Totalitarian government: a government that has total power over the lives of the people. (21)

Town: a unit of local government, usually larger than a village and smaller than a city. (178)

Town meeting: a form of government in which all citizens of the town meet together to discuss the town's problems and to decide how to handle them. (179)

Townships: local government units in the Middle Atlantic states that maintain local roads and rural schools within counties. (180)

Treaty: a written agreement between nations. (119)

Trial jury: the people who hear the evidence and decide the verdict in a court case. Between six and twelve people may serve on a jury. (137)

Two-party system: a political system in which two major political parties have almost equal strength; when one party fails to satisfy the voters, the other is ready to take its place; in the United States the Democratic and Republican parties. (202)

Unconstitutional: going against the Constitution, or beyond the powers granted by the Constitution. (146)

Unemployment insurance: money paid to jobless workers under the Social Security program. (358)

Unicameral legislature: a lawmaking body consisting of one house. (161)

Unions (see **Labor unions**).

Union shop: a place of employment in which workers are required to join the union after they are hired; made illegal in some states by right-to-work laws. (375)

United Nations: an international organization to which most nations belong; works to promote world peace and progress. (420)

United States attorney: a district court official who is a lawyer for the federal government. (141)

Unit pricing: a method of pricing under which a price tag must show how much money a product costs per ounce, gram, or other unit of measure. (333)

Unwritten Constitution: the traditional ways of doing things in our federal government that are seldom written down or made into laws. (52)

Urban areas: cities and towns with a population of 2,500 or more people. (14)

Vandalism: the deliberate destruction of property. (293)

Verdict: the decision of a jury. (479)

Veto: the refusal of the President or a governor to sign a bill, which is then sent back to Congress or the state legislature with a message giving the reasons for its rejection. (45)

Vice President: the second-highest official of the United States government; succeeds to the Presidency if the President dies or resigns. (116)

Victimless crimes: crimes, such as gambling, in which no one is directly harmed by another person. (474)

Village: a small settlement consisting of homes and other buildings. (179)

Voice vote: a vote in which individuals announce aloud how they are voting. (179)

Volunteers: people who work without pay to help others. (230)

Voting machine: a machine, usually in a large curtained booth, in which voters record their votes by pulling down levers to indicate the candidates they favor. (211)

Wages: money earned by a worker each hour and paid daily or weekly. (315)

Wards: election districts within cities or counties. (183)

Warrant: an order to pay out government funds, or an announcement of a town meeting. Also, a written order for someone's arrest. (167, 179, 478)

Weak-mayor plan: a form of city government in which most of the power is held by the city council and not by the mayor. (183)

White-collar crimes: crimes committed by white-collar workers while on the job. (474)

White-collar workers: people who do professional, technical, clerical, managerial, or sales work. (386)

White House: the official residence of the President of the United States; located in Washington, D.C. (116)

White House Office: the group of people that includes the President's closest personal and political advisers. (123)

Wholesaler: a person who owns a warehouse where goods are stored and who sells these goods to a retailer. (331)

Write-in votes: votes cast for a candidate whose name does not appear on the ballot and that must be written in by the voter. (210)

Writ of *habeas corpus*: an order requiring that a person accused of a crime be brought to court without unreasonable delay to determine if there is enough evidence to hold him or her for a trial. (104)

Zoning laws: local government regulations on the kinds of buildings that may be constructed in a certain area. (454)

Index

Italicized page numbers preceded by *c, m,* or *p* refer to a chart *(c)*, map *(m)*, or picture *(p)* on the page. **Boldface** page numbers refer to definitions of important terms. For a list of Civics Skills features see page xi. For a list of Charts and Maps see pages xii–xiii. For a list of Citizenship in Action features see page xiv.

Acknowledgments

KEY: (*t*) top; (*c*) center; (*b*) bottom; (*l*) left; (*r*) right.

CHARTS: Cliff Line and Donald Crews.
ORIGINAL ART: Murray Fleminger and Manny Haller.
COVER: SUVA/DPI.
TITLE PAGE PHOTOGRAPHS: page ii, (*tl*) James H. Karales/Peter Arnold, (*tr*) Dennis Stock/Magnum, (*cl*) courtesy, Junior Achievement, (*bl*) Wil Blanche/DPI, (*br*) Bettmann Archive.

UNIT ONE: page 1, Guy Gillette/Photo Researchers; 2, HBJ Photo; 4, HBJ Photo; 5, Mike L. Wannemacher/Taurus; 6, L. L. T. Rhodes/Taurus; 8, (*tl*) HBJ Photo, (*tr*) HBJ Photo, (*bl*) Elaine Wicks/Taurus, (*bc*) HBJ Photo, (*br*) HBJ Photo; 9, Mimi Forsyth/Monkmeyer; 12, (*t*) Jeffrey Jay Foxx/Woodfin Camp, (*b*) *Southern Living*/Photo Researchers; 13, Bettmann Archive; 15, Bill Weems/Woodfin Camp; 16, Paul Conklin/Monkmeyer; 20, Russell Thompson/Taurus; 23, (*tl*) courtesy, HBJ Library, (*tr*) Tom Myers/Photo Researchers; 24, Bettmann Archive; 26, William S. Nawrocki; 29, (*tl*) Bettmann Archive, (*tr*) Granger Collection; 31, Bettmann Archive; 33, Bettmann Archive; 38, Granger Collection; 41, Dick Hanley/Photo Researchers; 46, UPI; 47, UPI; 48, (*all*) UPI; 49, Dennis Brack/Black Star; 51, Brown Brothers; 76, Bob Witt/DPI; 78, Dick Hanley/Photo Researchers; 79, Sybil Shackman/Monkmeyer; 82, Bettmann Archive; 84, Bruce Roberts/Photo Researchers; 85, HBJ Photo.

UNIT TWO: page 91, Vance Henry/Taurus; 92, Dennis Stock/Magnum; 98, Paul Conklin/Monkmeyer; 99, U. S. Capitol Historical Society; 104, Bob Fitch/Black Star; 108, Don Carl Steffen/Photo Researchers; 114, Roddey E. Mims/Sygma; 116, UPI; 117, Wide World; 119, Wally McNamee/Woodfin Camp; 121, Larry Downing/Woodfin Camp; 124, (*l*) Granger Collection, (*r*) Bill Fitzpatrick/The White House; 125, Bruce Wolfe/Uniphoto; 129, *Sentinel Star*/Sygma; 130, Historical Picture Service; 134, Tommy Noonan/Uniphoto; 137, HBJ Photo; 141, Larry Mulvehill/Photo Researchers; 142, Chris Sorensen/DPI; 144, UPI; 146, Bettmann Archive; 147, White House Photo/Black Star; 149, (*l*) Bettmann Archive, (*r*) Bruce Roberts.

UNIT THREE: page 155, Craig Aurness/Woodfin Camp; 156, J. Alex Langley/DPI; 159, Mimi Forsyth/Monkmeyer; 164, Wide World Photos; 169, Marty Heitner/Taurus; 174, Freda Leinwand/Monkmeyer; 179, Dick Hanley/Photo Researchers; 181, HBJ Photo; 185, Girard Mouton/Uniphoto; 188, Porterfield-Chickering/Photo Researchers; 189, (*b*) courtesy of Mark Woolley; 190, Marvin Ickow/Uniphoto; 191, John Running/Stock, Boston; 192, Wil Blanche/DPI.

UNIT FOUR: page 197, Ted Demas/DPI; 198, Monkmeyer; 201, (*both*) Granger Collection; 202, Granger Collection; 206, Sybil Shelton/Peter Arnold; 207, (*tr*) photo Mark Milligan, *Potomac News*, courtesy National TAR Headquarters, (*bl*) D. Porges/Peter Arnold; 208, Ken Hawkins/Sygma; 210, Wil Blanche/DPI; 212, Mimi Forsyth/Monkmeyer; 214, (*l*) Lester Sloan/Woodfin Camp, (*r*) Wally McNamee/Woodfin Camp; 215, Robert McElroy/Woodfin Camp; 220, Philip Jon Bailey/Taurus; 226, Ken Hawkins/Sygma; 227, Bert Miller/Black Star; 230, Mimi Forsyth/Monkmeyer; 234, Charles Anderson/Monkmeyer; 236, Syd Greenberg/Photo Researchers; 238, Bruce Roberts/Rapho-Guillumette-Photo Researchers; 240, OMNI Photo-Communications; 245, HBJ Photo.

UNIT FIVE: page 251, John Lei/OMNI Photo-Communications; 252, Joan Menschenfreund; 254, Bettmann Archive; 257, Ginger Chih/Peter Arnold; 259, John Lei/Stock, Boston; 260, George Roos/Peter Arnold; 264, HBJ Photo; 266, St. Louis Art Museum; 271, Jean-Claude Lejeune/Stock, Boston; 272, Sybil Shackman/Monkmeyer; 273, (*t*) VIPS-Seniors, Houston Independent School District, (*b*) Paul Conklin/Monkmeyer; 274, Hugh Rogers/Monkmeyer; 277, Mimi Forsyth/Monkmeyer; 278, Arthur Sirdofsky; 282, Ann Hagen Griffiths/DPI; 284, Peter Miller/Photo Researchers; 285, Frank Siteman/Stock, Boston; 286, Richard Choy/Peter Arnold; 288, Peter Vadnai/Editorial Photocolor Archives; 291, Peter Vadnai/Editorial Photocolor Archives; 292, James H. Karales/Peter Arnold.

UNIT SIX: page 297, Scott Ransom/Taurus; 298, Paul Fusco/Magnum; 302, (*l*) Jay Dorin/OMNI Photo-Communications, (*r*) HBJ, courtesy "Furniture-in-the-Raw"; 304, Herbert Lanks/Monkmeyer; 306, Ellis Herwig/Stock, Boston; 308, Robert McElroy/Woodfin Camp; 311, 312, 313 (*both*), courtesy, Junior Achievement; 315, Guy Gillette/Photo Researchers; 320, Ginger Chih/Peter Arnold; 324, Dick Durrance II/Woodfin Camp; 326, courtesy, HBJ Library; 327, Mimi Forsyth/Monkmeyer; 328 (*both*) The Foxfire Fund, Inc.; 329, (*t*) Lowell Georgia/Photo Researchers, (*b*) Michal Heron/Woodfin Camp; 333, James H. Karales/Peter Arnold; 334, Peter Vadnai/Editorial Photocolor Archives; 340, Pam Sauer/DPI; 343, Jim Amos/Photo Researchers; 344, Larry Mulvehill/Photo Researchers; 346, Dennis Brack/Black Star; 347, HBJ Photo; 348, HBJ Photo; 350, Owen Franken/Stock, Boston; 355, L.L.T. Rhodes/Taurus; 356, Fredrik D. Bodin/Stock, Boston; 360, Richard Weiss/Peter Arnold; 364, Andrew Sacks/Black Star; 366, Daniel Brody/Editorial Photocolor Archives; 370, 371, Bettman Archive; 372, Department of the Interior; 375, Archives of Labor and Urban Affairs, Wayne State University and Nashville Tennessean; 382, James Fesler/Shostal; 384, Freda Leinwand/Monkmeyer; 385, Jean-Claude Lejeune/Stock, Boston; 387, Szkodzinsky/Editorial Photocolor Archives; 388, Dick Durrance II/Woodfin Camp; 390, Doug Wilson/Black Star; 392, Ira Block/Woodfin Camp; 393, (*tr*) Nathan Benn/Woodfin Camp, (*bl*) Steven Borns; 394, (*tl*) Steven Borns, (*br*) courtesy, Cassandra Cole; 395, courtesy, Cassandra Cole; 396, HBJ Photo; 397, Ken Biggs/DPI; 399, (*tl*) Freda Leinwand/Monkmeyer, (*tr*) Michal Heron/Woodfin Camp, (*bl*) Owen Franken/Stock, Boston, (*br*) Yoram Kahana/Peter Arnold; 400, Wil Blanche/DPI; 403, Clyde H. Smith/Peter Arnold; 404, Owen Franken/Stock, Boston.

UNIT SEVEN: page 409, Monkmeyer; 410, The White House; 412, UPI; 414, Elie Mann/Sygma; 416, UPI; 417, Organization of American States; 418, Agency for International Development; 419, James R. Holland/Stock, Boston; 421, Richard Choy/Peter Arnold; 424, Yoram Kahana/Peter Arnold; 428, The White House; 430, Bettmann Archive; 432, Bettmann Archive; 434, Paolo Koch/Photo Researchers; 436, Herman J. Kokojan/Black Star; 437, UPI; 441, T. Schmitt/Sygma; 442, (*l*) Jeffrey Jay Foxx/Woodfin Camp, (*c*) Cary Wolinsky/Stock, Boston, (*r*) DPI; 443, (*t*) Cary Wolinsky/Stock, Boston, (*b*) Jeffrey Jay Foxx/Woodfin Camp; 444, HBJ Photo.

UNIT EIGHT: page 449, George Hall/Woodfin Camp; 450, Sam C. Pierson, Jr./Photo Researchers; 453, Steve Proehl/Photo Researchers; 456, Peter Vadnai/Editorial Photocolor Archives; 459, Fred Ward/Black Star; 460, (*both*) Wide World; 461, UPI; 462, UPI; 463, Martin A. Levick/Black Star; 465, Peter Vadnai/Editorial Photocolor Archives; 467, Warren Boister/Focus on Sports; 472, Lincoln Russell/Stock, Boston; 474, Bruce Anspach/Editorial Photocolor Archives; 476, Mike Mazzaschi/Stock, Boston; 478, Menschenfreund/Taurus; 479, John Running/Stock, Boston; 480, Marilyn Church; 481, Charles Gatewood; 482, Erik Anderson/Stock, Boston; 483, Joel Gordon/DPI; 484, 485, Thomas S. England, *People* Weekly © 1980 Time, Inc.; 486, Erik Anderson/Stock, Boston; 487, Richard Choy/Peter Arnold; 488, Tony O'Brien, Criminal Justice Publications; 492, NASA; 494, W. J. Schoonmaker/National Audubon Society-Photo Researchers; 495, Porterfield-Chickering/Photo Researchers; 496, U. S. Department of Agriculture, courtesy, HBJ Library; 499, Kim Steele/Black Star; 501, Michael Philip Manheim/Photo Researchers; 504, Hugh Rogers/Monkmeyer; 508, C. Springmann/Black Star; 510, Bill Weems/Woodfin Camp.

PRESIDENTS: page 520, (*1*) detail, painting by Gilbert Stuart, Metropolitan Museum of Art, (*5*) Metropolitan Museum of Art, bequest of Seth Low, (*all others*) Library of Congress; 521, (*12*) Charles Phelps Cushing, (*16*) Bettmann Archive, (*all others*) Library of Congress; 522, (*29*) Ewing Galloway, (*31*) Fabian Bachrach, (*32*) Franklin D. Roosevelt Library, Hyde Park, N.Y., (*33*) Charles Phelps Cushing, (*34*) Chase News Photo, (*all others*) Library of Congress; 523, (*35*) Henry Grossman, (*36*) Fabian Bachrach, (*37*) Official White House Photograph, (*38*) courtesy of Gerald Ford's Office in Congress, (*39*) The White House, (*40*) UPI.

Answers to "Can You Guess?"

Page 52: Nearly one million people visit the exhibition hall of the National Archives Building each year to see the Declaration of Independence and the Constitution.

Page 95: A lame duck is a defeated candidate who holds office after his or her replacement has been chosen. This person, like a lame duck, is rather helpless—that is, has little influence.

Page 115: John F. Kennedy was the youngest person ever elected President. He was 43 years old when elected in 1960.

Ronald W. Reagan was the oldest person ever elected President. He was 69 years old when elected in 1980.

Page 163: The state capitals with their states are:

Jefferson City, Missouri
Madison, Wisconsin
Jackson, Mississippi
Lincoln, Nebraska

Page 168: Hawaii is the only state that contains a former royal palace. The Iolani Palace, near Honolulu, was the residence of Queen Liliuokalani, Hawaii's last royal ruler.

Texas is the only state that was an independent republic before joining the Union. After winning its independence from Mexico in 1836, Texas was a republic until it became part of the United States in 1845.

Page 183: St. Augustine, Florida, is the oldest city in the United States. It was founded by the Spanish in 1565, on the site of an ancient Indian village.

Chicago, Illinois, has the tallest building in the United States. It is the Sears Tower, which is 1,454 feet (443 meters) high and has 110 stories.

New York City, with a population of 7,135,000 (1980 census), has more people than any other city in the United States.

Houston, Texas, is the location of the NASA Space Center.

Page 224: "Tippecanoe and Tyler Too" was the slogan used by William Henry Harrison and John Tyler in 1840. "Tippecanoe" referred to a victorious battle General Harrison had fought against Indians at Tippecanoe Creek, Indiana, in 1811.

"Return to Normalcy" was the slogan used by Warren G. Harding in 1920. By "normalcy," Harding referred to the way Americans had lived before World War I.

"A New Deal" was the slogan used by Franklin D. Roosevelt in 1932.

"I Like Ike" was the slogan used by Dwight D. Eisenhower in 1952. "Ike" was Eisenhower's nickname.

Page 244: In early times, taxes in several Southern colonies were paid in the form of tobacco. It was legal tender in Virginia, Maryland, and North Carolina.

Page 256: The wedding ring is usually worn on the third finger of the left hand because people used to believe that a vein or nerve ran directly from this finger to the heart.

Rice is a symbol of earth's bounty. Wedding guests originally threw rice at the bride and groom after the ceremony as a way of wishing that the married couple would have children.

Page 275: The first college established in the United States was Harvard College (now part of Harvard University) in Cambridge, Massachusetts. Harvard College was founded in 1636.

The nation's first coeducational college was Oberlin College in Ohio—founded in 1833.

The first college for women in the United States was Mount Holyoke Female Seminary (now Mount Holyoke College)—founded in 1837.

Page 322: President Thomas Jefferson was also an inventor. His inventions included the revolving chair, the revolving desk, and the seven-day clock.

The 1893 invention that helps us get into and out of our clothes is the zipper. It was invented by Whitcomb L. Judson to replace the buttons on high-button shoes.

The first people to use chewing gum were the American Indians, who collected chicle—the sap from certain trees. When making long journeys, they tucked pieces of chicle inside their cheeks to keep their mouths moist.

Page 342: President George Washington's portrait appears on a $1 bill.

President Abraham Lincoln's portrait appears on a $5 bill.

Alexander Hamilton's portrait appears on a $10 bill.

President Andrew Jackson's portrait appears on a $20 bill.

Page 349: An average 1 dollar bill lasts 18 months before it wears out.

If a piece is missing from paper money, the bill may still be worth something, depending on how much of the bill is left. If three fifths remains, the bill is worth its full value. If between two fifths and three fifths is left, the bill is worth half its full value. But if less than two fifths is left, the bill is worthless.

When paper money wears out, it is collected by the Federal Reserve Banks. There, the bills are cut in two lengthwise. The halves are shipped (in separate batches) to the Treasury Department in Washington, D.C., where they are then burned.

Page 386: Several Presidents began their careers in areas outside politics:

Andrew Johnson—Tailor
Warren Harding—Journalist
Woodrow Wilson—College Professor
Herbert Hoover—Engineer
Ronald Reagan—Actor

Page 413: The first American President to win a Nobel peace prize was Theodore Roosevelt, in 1906. He helped bring an end to the Russo-Japanese War of 1904–1905.

Woodrow Wilson was the first American President to travel to Europe while in office. He went to France after World War I to meet with America's allies and draft a peace treaty. He was awarded the Nobel peace prize in 1919 for his part in ending the war.

Page 435: "G.I." is an abbreviation for "general issue" or "government issue." The term referred to equipment distributed, or issued, to members of the armed forces. "G.I." was first used to refer to a member of the American armed forces in World War II.

During World War II, over 2 million women worked in American defense industries. The term "Rosie the Riveter" was used to refer to these women. The name probably was first used to describe a woman working in an industry such as shipbuilding. There, "Rosie" sometimes used machines that drilled bolts, or rivets, into thick metal plates.

Page 458: President Franklin D. Roosevelt had a serious physical handicap. In 1921 he came down with polio, which left his legs paralyzed. Roosevelt helped found a national organization whose research led to the development of a successful antipolio vaccine.

Page 468: Some of the things that fire trucks carry are pike poles, axes, ropes, sledges, hoses, hammers, crow bars, power saws, and bolt cutters. These tools are used to break into buildings and rooms. Fire trucks also carry first-aid kits, oxygen tanks and masks, chemical fire extinguishers, and devices that remove smoke.

C 4
D 5
E 6
F 7
G 8
H 9
I 0
J 1